# Congress Reconsidered

**Fourth Edition**

**Edited by**

**Lawrence C. Dodd**
*University of Colorado*

**Bruce I. Oppenheimer**
*University of Houston*

**CQ PRESS**

A Division of Congressional Quarterly Inc.
1414 22nd Street N.W., Washington, D.C. 20037

Library of Congress Cataloging-in-Publication Data

Congress reconsidered.

    Bibliography: p.
    Includes index.
    1. United States. Congress. I. Dodd, Lawrence C.,
1946-  . II. Oppenheimer, Bruce Ian.
JK1061.C587   1989        328.73         88-37618
ISBN 0-87187-490-3

# Congress Reconsidered

## Fourth Edition

# CONTENTS

# TABLES AND FIGURES

## TABLES

# FIGURES

# PREFACE

*Congress Reconsidered,* 4th edition, documents a dramatic shift in the modern Congress. Throughout the 1970s and early 1980s Congress was becoming a fragmented, decentralized institution, dominated by subcommittee government. The mid- and late 1980s have witnessed a very different pattern. With the coming of President Ronald Reagan's tax cuts and fiscal austerity, there has been little discretionary money for new programs and thus for policy innovation by the authorizing subcommittees in Congress. Power has shifted toward the party leadership and a few elite committees that deal with essential annual legislation.

This shift forces scholars to reconsider the nature of congressional politics and its implications for American politics. The present volume offers nineteen original essays written specifically to aid this reassessment. Most of these essays are new, and the others have been substantially revised and brought up to date since the third edition. All address issues that help us better understand the new era of centralized leadership and the responses of committees and subcommittees.

Like the first three editions, this one examines the contemporary Congress in a way that appeals to a broad audience, maintains the highest quality of research scholarship, and is as current as possible. The prologue analyzes the 1988 presidential election, evaluates House and Senate outcomes, and explains the impact of these contests on parties, leaders, and policy making in Congress.

Following the prologue, the book is divided into six parts. The first, "Patterns and Dynamics of Congressional Change," contains an overview of the Senate, a new essay on the House of Representatives, and an essay on career patterns in Congress. Part II, "Elections and Constituencies," includes new articles providing historical perspectives on incumbency and home style, a major update of an essay on voters and elections, and the most current look at parties and PACs in congressional elections. The third section, "Committee and Subcommittee Politics," includes two new essays, one analyzing general patterns of committee politics and the other, the use of multiple referrals of legislation. In addition, an updated essay examines changes in revenue policy and the roles of the Ways and Means and Finance committees.

The essays in Part IV, "Congressional Leadership and Party Politics," examine House and Senate leadership both historically and in their present state, including a behind-the-scenes look at the leadership style of Speaker of the House Jim Wright. In addition, a new essay discusses leadership strategy for managing House and Senate floor activity. A fourth essay explores congressional caucuses. Although policy implications are discussed throughout the book, Part V, "Congress, the Executive and Public Policy," focuses entirely on analyses of congressional activity in domestic and foreign policy. In particular, the essays deal with telecommunications policy and the executive-legislative conflict resulting from the Iran-contra affair.

In the final section of the book, "Congress at Work," we are especially pleased to have an essay by Representative David Price, D-N.C. As a political scientist teaching at Duke University, Price was a contributor to the second and third editions of the book. Now, as a member of the House, he combines his academic and political experience to offer insights about running for office and serving as a freshman member. Our final essay aims to add perspective to the others and addresses the changes that have characterized the institution over the past sixteen years or so.

In preparing this book we have been fortunate, as we were in the previous three editions, to have the thoughts, assistance, and encouragement of others. Once again, our contributors have been critical to the success of this project. Their first-rate essays have made our task as editors more manageable. Our departmental colleagues at the University of Colorado at Boulder and the University of Houston have created a stimulating professional environment that has aided us directly and indirectly in the preparation of this volume.

The success of *Congress Reconsidered* is due in large part to the numerous scholars who contributed such excellent work to the first three editions. Our effort to explore new issues and to maintain up-to-date coverage has required us to replace essays and contributors from edition to edition. But we consider all past contributors and essays a part of the ongoing effort to chart and assess the development and performance of the contemporary Congress. Therefore, we express our deep appreciation to all the contributors whose talent and hard work helped make the present volume possible.

Much of the credit for the quality of this book rests with the fine staff of CQ Press. Once again we enjoyed the chance to work with CQ

Press director Joanne Daniels. She provided us with an excellent mix of toughness and empathy. We appreciate Carolyn Goldinger's serious attention to the quality of writing in this collection. We are also indebted to Kerry Kern for her fine work on production and to Kathryn Suárez's professionalism in marketing. In addition, we owe a continuing debt to Jean Woy, who persuaded us to work with CQ Press nearly a decade ago. It was a good decision.

Fourteen years now have passed since we were APSA Congressional Fellows, yet we continue to accrue benefits from participation in the program. It not only gave us the chance to collaborate on *Congress Reconsidered* but also served as a crucial stimulus to our research and professional careers.

Finally, we again acknowledge the professional and personal debt of each to the other during the past fourteen years.

# PERSPECTIVES ON THE 1988
# CONGRESSIONAL ELECTIONS

*Lawrence C. Dodd and Bruce I. Oppenheimer*

---

The 1988 election demonstrated the further decoupling of presidential and congressional voting. George Bush won the presidency with nearly 54 percent of the popular vote and 426 electoral college votes, but the Republican party suffered small net losses in both the House and the Senate. Preliminary evidence suggests that split-ticket voting was particularly high in this election. Perhaps the best that can be said for congressional Republicans is that the Bush candidacy kept Republican losses from being even greater.

Unlike Ronald Reagan in 1980, Bush did not bring with him a Republican majority in the Senate or make gains in the House. This failure undercuts his ability to put together majorities for legislative programs of his own making, a consequence reinforced by his failure to seek a policy mandate in the election campaign. Moreover, it adds to the importance of independent congressional leadership in the development of public policy. Not only will the opposition Democrats control Congress, but also they will do so with a relatively secure majority.

## Senate Elections

The Senate elections remind us that Senate incumbents, even in good economic times, may not be as safe as House incumbents. In 1988, four of the twenty-seven incumbents who sought reelection were defeated, and in three other races incumbents were held to less than 55 percent of the vote. Although this number is lower than in 1986 when seven incumbent senators of the twenty-eight seeking reelection were defeated, it nevertheless demonstrates that, despite the widespread scholarly and media attention to the power of incumbency in electoral politics, Senate incumbents are not necessarily safe.

The 1988 election gave Democrats a net gain of one seat, producing a 55-45 Democratic advantage in the Senate. Moreover, because of the distribution of Senate races, the Democrats should maintain control at least until 1992. In returning to majority status in

Table 1   The Partisan Distribution of Senate Seats, 1981-1989, and Contested Seats, 1990

| Congress | East | Midwest | South | West | Total |
|---|---|---|---|---|---|
| 97th (all seats) | | | | | |
| Democrats | 13 | 10 | 15 | 9 | 47 |
| Republicans | 11 | 14 | 11 | 17 | 53 |
| 99th (all seats) | | | | | |
| Democrats | 13 | 12 | 14 | 8 | 47 |
| Republicans | 11 | 12 | 12 | 18 | 53 |
| 101st (all seats) | | | | | |
| Democrats | 15 | 13 | 17 | 10 | 55 |
| Republicans | 9 | 11 | 9 | 16 | 45 |
| 102d | | | | | |
| Democrats | 5 | 4 | 6 | 1 | 16 |
| Republicans | 2 | 3 | 6 | 6 | 1 |

NOTE: *East:* Conn., Del., Maine, Md., Mass., N.H., N.J., N.Y., Pa., R.I., Vt., W.Va. *Midwest:* Ill., Ind., Iowa, Kan., Mich., Minn., Mo., Neb., N.D., Ohio, S.D., Wis. *South:* Ala., Ark., Fla., Ga., Ky., La., Miss., N.C., Okla., S.C., Tenn., Texas, Va. *West:* Alaska, Ariz., Calif., Colo., Hawaii, Idaho, Mont., Nev., N.M., Ore., Utah, Wash., Wyo.

1986 and reinforcing their control in 1988, the Democrats made gains in all regions—East, Midwest, South, and West—as Table 1 shows. Democrats now hold a majority of Senate seats in all regions except the West, where the Republicans have a sixteen-to-ten advantage.

Why is it that some senators enjoy electoral safety and others are vulnerable? Senate incumbents have the same advantages as House incumbents—visibility, the perquisites of office, staff, and the capacity to attract campaign financing—and to a greater degree than their House counterparts. One of the reasons that senators are more vulnerable is that they may attract better challengers than House incumbents do. States, after all, generally are larger and more heterogeneous and have better partisan balance than individual congressional districts. These differences mean that the available field of challengers is larger and that a challenger may be able to establish a minimal base of support. In addition, potential Senate challengers and potential investors in campaigns may be willing to risk more when the prize is a six-year term in a body of 100 members than a two-year term in a body of 435. Ironically, this same reasoning might lead one to conclude that the most vulnerable Senate incumbents are those from the large, heterogeneous, competitive states, but senators from very large states have had a high rate of reelection in recent years. The most vulnerable Senate incumbents appear to be those from small and middle-sized states. In 1988 the Senate incumbents who were defeated came from Connecticut, Montana, Nebraska, and Nevada. Another incumbent from a low-population state, Republican Malcolm Wallop of Wyoming, barely won reelection.

It may be that low-population states do not have many potentially strong challengers, but these states are precisely the places where modest financial investments can create real contests. That situation may be the reason we saw sizable Senate turnovers in 1980 and 1986; senators on that election schedule most heavily represent low-population states.

Looking ahead to the 1990 elections, we see that it may be difficult for the Republicans to successfully challenge for control of the Senate. First, the sixteen Democratic senators who will be up for reelection in 1990 were strong enough in 1984 to survive the coattail effect of the Reagan landslide. Second, with seventeen Republicans, this cohort is almost equally split between the parties, thereby giving the Republicans only a limited number of targets with which to overcome the Democrats' seat advantage. Third, as Table 1 shows, the Senate seats are distributed geographically in a manner designed to limit the possibility of Republican gains, with only one Democratic seat to be available in 1990 in the West, the area of greatest Democratic vulnerability. In the South, the other vulnerable area, the Democratic seats are held by David Boren (Oklahoma), Albert Gore (Tennessee), Howell Heflin (Alabama), J. Bennett Johnston (Louisiana), Sam Nunn (Georgia), and David Pryor (Arkansas). These senators are strong incumbents, unlikely to be ready to retire in 1990.

Nevertheless, we should expect the Republican party to remain far more competitive in its attempt to win back control of the Senate than in its effort to establish a majority in the House. First, the Republican prospects for winning Senate control increase in 1992; twenty of the thirty-four seats up for election then are currently held by Democrats. Second, as we noted, a disproportionate number of seats open in 1992 are in low-population states. Third, the Republicans are strong in the low-population states, especially those in the western mountains, so that small-state vulnerability may fall particularly on the Democrats.

The return of Democratic control in the 1986 elections made the Senate a less conservative body, but it is harder to evaluate the ideological consequences of the 1988 elections. In some cases a party switch may not have made much difference. For example, in Mississippi, Republican Trent Lott replaced John Stennis, one of the most conservative Democrats in the Senate, thereby maintaining a conservative cast to that seat. Likewise, Joseph Lieberman, a freshman

Democrat, replaced Lowell Weicker, a liberal Republican, keeping the Connecticut seat moderate to liberal. In other cases the ideological predisposition of the newly elected senator is difficult to predict. Aside from Lott, only one of the other nine new senators, Connie Mack, can be clearly labeled a strong conservative. On the other hand, several of the Democrats—Robert Kerry of Nebraska, Richard Bryan of Nevada, and Chuck Robb of Virginia—were considered moderates when they served as state governors. Overall, we can say that the Senate will be more liberal than it was in the early 1980s, when it was in Republican hands, and probably at least as liberal as in the last years of the Reagan administration, when it had returned to Democratic control, although how liberal is difficult to estimate.

## House Elections

The 1988 elections continued the Democratic party's dominance of the House of Representatives that began in 1930. Despite the overwhelming victory of George Bush in the presidential contest, the Democrats made a net gain of 3 seats in the House. Holding 260 seats to 175 for the Republicans, the Democrats entered the 101st Congress 6 seats above their average for the past fifty years. Republican presidential landslides in the 1980s have not placed the establishment of a Republican majority in the House even within arms reach.

The 1988 House elections are remarkable for the low turnover of members. Of the 435 members of the House in the 101st Congress, 402 were members of the 100th Congress, making the turnover rate the lowest in the history of the House of Representatives. With twenty-three retirements and three vacancies due to death or resignation, 409 incumbents sought reelection. Only seven incumbents, one in a primary and six in the general election, were defeated. A record 98.3 percent of incumbents seeking reelection were successful, exceeding the previous high of 98.0 percent set in 1986.

We have grown accustomed to high rates of reelection success among House incumbents since 1950. Only four times has the rate dropped below 90 percent, and then just slightly. For explanations of incumbency advantage in the House, analyses focus on the decline of party attachments of voters, the lack of quality challengers, the campaign funding advantages of incumbents, and their use of office resources such as casework, staffing, and the franking privilege. All of these explanations have their adherents. But why is it that the reelection rate of House incumbents continues to rise? It exceeded 95 percent in each of the last three elections, and the few incumbents defeated were those involved in political or personal scandal.

We suggest some explanations for the growth in incumbency

success in recent House elections. First, since 1982 the parties have been close to their equilibrium seat level in the House of Representatives. With the Democrats holding 253, 258, and 260 seats, respectively, in the 99th, 100th, and 101st Congresses, they have been very close to the 254-seat average for the party since 1938. At seat divisions near this equilibrium level, the parties are likely to hold few seats that they would not ordinarily hold, and the number of highly vulnerable incumbents is small. By contrast, when the Democrats held 292 seats, as they did after the 1976 election, they had won many seats that were not ordinarily in Democratic hands and, therefore, had many vulnerable incumbents. Lacking strong short-term election forces to disrupt an equilibrium seat split, the extraordinarily high rate of incumbent reelection success should not be surprising.

Second, incumbency is even more of a self-fulfilling prophecy than in the past. As everyone learns that incumbents are hard to beat, it becomes increasingly more difficult to find or create strong challengers. The tendency increases for potential challengers to pass up a race against a House incumbent and run for another office or wait for an open House seat. Even when the parties are able to find potentially good challengers and provide them with party resources, many choose not to run. Thus, in the 1988 general elections, eighty House candidates were elected without major party opposition.

Today, those who fund political campaigns are more reluctant than ever to invest in a challenger. While organizations such as NCPAC (National Conservative Political Action Committee) had great success in 1980 financing Republican challengers, that initial success was not repeated even where sizable investments of party and PAC money were made. Increasingly, PACs find it in their interest to invest money in likely winners who will then provide PACS with some line of access on Capitol Hill, even if they differ on policy issues. A PAC may see little advantage in investing in challengers, even when those challengers are attuned to PAC interests, because challengers so seldom win.

With 98 percent of incumbents reelected in 1986, the search for good challengers in 1988 was especially difficult. Of 435 House races, the winning candidate received less than 55 percent of the vote in only 36. Of these, the Democrats won 21 and the Republicans 15. Even a shift of 5 percent of the vote either way would have produced a remarkably small shift in seats. In 1984 we were surprised that only 48 seats fell within this framework. This and other evidence suggest that there are few good challengers, and many of them do not have the resources with which to operate effective campaigns. For the cost of investing in a challenger's House campaign, a party or PACs might

Table 2  The Partisan Distribution of House Seats, 1981-1989

| Congress | East | Midwest | South | West | Total |
|---|---|---|---|---|---|
| 97th | | | | | |
| Democrats | 68 | 58 | 78 | 39 | 243 |
| Republicans | 49 | 63 | 43 | 37 | 192 |
| 99th | | | | | |
| Democrats | 65 | 62 | 82 | 44 | 253 |
| Republicans | 43 | 51 | 47 | 41 | 182 |
| 101st | | | | | |
| Democrats | 66 | 64 | 85 | 45 | 260 |
| Republicans | 42 | 49 | 44 | 40 | 175 |

NOTE: The regional categories are the same as in Table 1.

invest more fruitfully in Senate campaigns in low-population states. Without good challengers and without a threshold level of resources for challengers, the high levels of incumbent reelection success should be expected.

As Table 2 shows, in the House the Democrats hold the majority of seats in all four regions. Unlike the Senate, in which the low-population states of the West give the Republicans an advantage, Democratic success in California more than offsets Republican success in the mountain states. Interestingly, the Democrats' largest majority in House seats is still in the South, where they hold a nearly two-to-one edge. Of the Republican's forty-four House seats in the South, twenty-two of them, half of their total southern contingent, come from Virginia, Florida, and Texas. Republicans have made only small inroads into the deep South.

One suggested explanation of the failure of Republicans to make gains in the House is linked to incumbency. The claim is that incumbency serves as an insulation for the House Democratic majority. If this were the case, however, then we would still expect Republicans to make gains in open seat contests. In 1988 there were twenty-seven open seat contests. Of these, Democrats held twelve in the 100th Congress, and the Republicans held fifteen. After the election, Democrats held thirteen, a net gain of one seat. While one might expect the Republicans to make gains in open seats, owing to the absence of an incumbency factor, in fact they did slightly worse than in seats held by incumbents. And this result is not atypical. Over the last decade the Republicans have fared only slightly better in open seat contests than they have when challenging incumbents.

Clearly, the Democratic majority in the House rests on factors other than the incumbency advantage, particularly the existence of many more House districts that correspond to a natural Democratic base. This pattern is totally in keeping with the apportionment basis of the House. If the House were apportioned on the basis of voters rather than population, the Republicans would no doubt fare better. The reverse is true of the Republican advantage in Senate contests, in which Republicans tend to benefit from turnout that is higher in Republican House districts than in Democratic districts.

## Governing in the 101st Congress

Perhaps the greatest unknown in the immediate aftermath of the 1988 election is the character of the new Senate leaders. As an institution, the Senate is strongly shaped by the personality and skillfulness of its leaders. Consider the contrast between the leadership styles of Lyndon Johnson (Texas) and Mike Mansfield (Montana) or that of Robert Dole (Kansas) and Robert Byrd (West Virginia). With Byrd's decision to relinquish the Senate majority leadership position and become the Appropriations Committee chair, the Senate chooses its fourth majority leader of the 1980s, an unusually high turnover for the Senate. The selection of the new leader offers the Democrats the chance to choose someone who can provide high-visibility leadership to the party and who can rival Speaker of the House Jim Wright as the party's chief national spokesman.

The new Senate majority leader will head a Senate Democratic party that appears likely to be in firm control of the chamber. This control provides the leader with a period of stability at least until the 1992 elections. The party is strengthened by the return of Lloyd Bentsen of Texas to the Senate as chair of the Finance Committee; Bentsen's popularity as the party's 1988 vice presidential nominee should allow him to play a more visible role as Finance chair, thereby aiding the Senate in fiscal leadership of the nation. Likewise, Byrd's move to the Appropriations Committee chair places a seasoned and nationally visible legislator in that position, which further bolsters the national leadership role of the Senate.

The House remains a solidly Democratic institution. It enjoys the prospects of a very stable leadership. Short of a shocking scandal concerning Wright, the party leadership team—Speaker of the House Wright, Majority Leader Tom Foley, and Majority Whip Tony Coelho—should remain in place through 1992. Experienced as a result of service together in the 100th Congress, the leadership team should prove adept at the political game. President Bush, therefore, faces in Wright a savvy partisan competitor.

Moreover, the House should prove to be a relatively cohesive body, less prone to the fragmentation of the mid- and late 1970s. All evidence points to the likelihood that a committee oligarchy will remain in control of the House because there is little likelihood that sufficient financial resources will exist to resuscitate the various authorization committees and subcommittees. In reviewing the Senate and the House, it is evident that the majority Democrats in both institutions are in relatively strong positions to assert leadership. Given Bush's lack of a strong policy mandate in the 1988 election, Congress could be in a position to exercise control over the policy direction of the nation. However, congressional initiative is unlikely to come in taxes and revenue, the area perhaps the most in need of leadership, because of the political sensitivity of the topic. But in domestic policy and in certain foreign policy issues, the Democrats can be expected to play a strong role.

## Conclusion

Seldom has the election of a new president and Congress changed so little as did the 1988 elections. The Republicans maintain control of the presidency, with Bush replacing Reagan but maintaining Reagan's appeal to the same conservative national constituency. The Democrats keep control of the Senate and the House, slightly increasing margins in both chambers and thereby continuing the presence of a strong commitment to liberal social programs within the national government.

The period of divided party control of Congress and the presidency, which began in 1980 with the election of Ronald Reagan, now enters its ninth year, the longest such period in modern times. The nation appears to be locked in a period of continued party drift, with no overarching vision or policy direction. The presidency, dominated by the Republican party, is dedicated to low taxes and military spending. Congress, controlled by Democrats, continues to protect social programs and, while willing in principle to consider higher taxes, appears to be unwilling to pay the political price involved in battling a recalcitrant president on this issue. The nation's deficit continues to mount, provoking dire predictions by economists and political commentators. The 1988 election produced no obvious political outcome that would break this policy stalemate and address the problems of the national budget. Short of major national crisis and a dramatic election upheaval, there is little reason to expect this stalemate to be ended soon.

The power of incumbency is so strong that it is virtually inconceivable that the House of Representatives would fall into Republican hands in 1990. Thus, even if the Senate were to become Republican in 1990, also unlikely, divided government of some sort appears virtually certain to remain in effect until 1992. If the

Republicans are able to maintain their lock on the electoral college and the presidency during the 1990s, the nation could be in for a long siege of divided government and policy stalemate, a prospect that must worry anyone concerned with national government. The inability to address core problems such as the deficit undoubtedly will have serious long-term repercussions. One can only hope that the president and Congress, although lacking a partisan or policy consensus, find common ground on which to meet.

*Part I*

PATTERNS AND DYNAMICS
OF CONGRESSIONAL CHANGE

# 1. CHANGE IN THE SENATE: TOWARD THE 1990s

*Norman J. Ornstein, Robert L. Peabody, and David W. Rohde*

Few political institutions have captured the attention of the American public as the U.S. Senate has. From televised hearings on crime, communism, Watergate, and the Iran-contra affair, from media coverage of Senate-based presidential contenders, and from classic movies like *Mr. Smith Goes to Washington* and *Advise and Consent,* the public is much more aware of the Senate than it is of "the other body," the House of Representatives. Curiously, however, the public's awareness of the Senate is not always matched by a comprehensive or systematic analysis of how the Senate operates and how senators behave. We know a good deal about the Senate of the 1950s, thanks primarily to the efforts of two outstanding political scientists, Ralph K. Huitt and Donald R. Matthews.[1] And we have some good work tracking change in the Senate in the 1960s.[2] But, like the rest of the American political system, the Senate has changed considerably since the 1960s and continues to change—in the nature of its membership, in its formal and informal leadership, in its internal processes and structures, and in its policy directions. Many of the changes are ongoing trends over nearly three decades, but others are part of cycles, moving the Senate back toward earlier patterns of behavior. This essay attempts to sort out the changes, showing how the Senate is different, how it has stabilized, and why.

## The Membership

The membership of the Senate has changed a great deal since Huitt and Matthews wrote about it. Sometimes the changes have come gradually, and other times they have occurred in large jolts—like the elections of 1980 and 1986. The aggregate effect of these changes has been substantial. When the 100th Congress convened in January 1987, only 4 senators who had served before John Kennedy became president remained in the Senate, and 60 of the 100 members were new to the chamber since Jimmy Carter's election in 1976. Membership change is more than just a matter of substituting one senator for another. With respect to a variety of attributes, different kinds of senators have replaced those who served earlier, and this turnover has had a substantial impact on the operation of the Senate and the policies it has produced. We will consider three particular attributes related to these changes: partisan division, ideology, and sectional party affiliation.

The most obvious change has been in the party affiliation of the membership. From the end of World War II through most of the 1950s, the partisan division of the Senate was very close; neither party ever controlled the body by more than a few votes. In the election of 1958, however, the Democratic membership of the Senate jumped from forty-nine to sixty-four seats. Through the 1970s, the number of Democrats was usually higher than sixty. But 1981 brought a stunning reversal: Democrats saw their two decades of dominance transformed into a narrow Republican majority that remained in control of the Senate through 1986. After nearly two decades of being in the majority, Senate Democrats suddenly were thrust into the foreign condition of minority status, while Senate Republicans, long accustomed to being in the minority, gained the power—and responsibilities—of the majority. The election of 1986 reversed fortunes again, restoring a narrow Democratic majority. It appears likely that Senate control will remain "up for grabs" for the near future.

A second aspect of change is the regional character of the two parties. Through the 1950s, Democratic membership was concentrated in the South and West, while Republicans came primarily from the East and Midwest. In 1957, for example, the Democrats held every Senate seat from the South and thirteen of the twenty-two seats from the West, but only five of the twenty eastern seats and three of the twenty-two midwestern seats. By the 1970s, however, these regional patterns had changed. In 1979 the Democrats held majorities in every region except the West (where Republicans held fourteen of twenty-six seats), including thirteen of twenty-two in the Midwest. These dramatic gains by Democrats were offset somewhat by losses in the South. In the early 1980s the Republicans built their majority on significant gains in the South and Midwest, but 1986 restored the distribution of seats to a pattern very similar to 1979. Again, the only region where Republicans held a majority was the West.

The partisan and regional changes in the Senate contributed to changes in the ideological character of the membership. Table 1-1 shows the proportions of liberals, moderates, and conservatives among various groups of senators in the 85th Congress (1957-1958), and in the first sessions of the 94th (1975), 96th (1979), 98th (1983), and 100th (1987) Congresses.[3]

Table 1-1    Ideological Divisions in the Senate, 85th Congress and the First Sessions of the 94th Congress, 96th Congress, 98th Congress, and 100th Congress (in percentages)

| | Northern Democrats | Southern Democrats | All Democrats | Repub-licans | All members |
|---|---|---|---|---|---|
| **85th Congress** | | | | | |
| (1957-1958) | (27) | (22) | (49) | (47) | (96) |
| Liberals | 67 | 9 | 41 | 2 | 22 |
| Moderates | 19 | 27 | 22 | 26 | 24 |
| Conservatives | 15 | 64 | 37 | 72 | 54 |
| **94th Congress (1975)** | (46) | (16) | (62) | (38) | (100) |
| Liberals | 85 | — | 63 | 16 | 45 |
| Moderates | 15 | 19 | 16 | 26 | 20 |
| Conservatives | — | 81 | 21 | 58 | 35 |
| **96th Congress (1979)** | (43) | (16) | (59) | (41) | (100) |
| Liberals | 58 | — | 42 | 7 | 28 |
| Moderates | 37 | 31 | 36 | 32 | 34 |
| Conservatives | 5 | 69 | 22 | 61 | 38 |
| **98th Congress (1983)** | (35) | (11) | (46) | (54) | (100) |
| Liberals | 47 | — | 39 | — | 20 |
| Moderates | 47 | 55 | 39 | 30 | 34 |
| Conservatives | 6 | 45 | 22 | 70 | 46 |
| **100th Congress (1987)** | (38) | (16) | (54) | (46) | (100) |
| Liberals | 53 | — | 37 | — | 20 |
| Moderates | 39 | 50 | 43 | 24 | 34 |
| Conservatives | 8 | 50 | 20 | 76 | 46 |

SOURCES: The scores for 1957-1958 were calculated from the appropriate roll calls listed in the *Congressional Quarterly Almanac* for those years. The scores for 1975 were taken from the *Congressional Quarterly Weekly Report,* Jan. 24, 1976, 174; and the 1979 scores from *Congressional Quarterly Weekly Report,* Jan. 26, 1980, 198. The 1983 scores are from *Vital Statistics on Congress,* 1984-1985, ed. Norman J. Ornstein et al. (Washington, D.C.: American Enterprise Institute, 1984). The 1987 scores are taken from *Congressional Quarterly Weekly Report,* Jan. 16, 1988, 107.

NOTE: The classification is based on a variation of the conservative coalition support score published annually by Congressional Quarterly. The support score of a member was divided by the sum of his or her support and opposition scores, which removes the effect of absences. Members whose scores were 0-30 were classified as liberals, 31-70 as moderates, and 71-100 as conservatives. The number of persons used to compute each percentage is shown in parentheses.

Democrats in the 85th Congress were divided almost evenly between liberals and conservatives, whereas the Republicans were overwhelmingly conservative. This ideological makeup produced a conservative majority in the Senate in 1957-1958. The subsequent sharp increase in the number of Democrats and almost matching decline in the number of Republicans produced a liberal plurality by 1975.

Not all of the ideological change was due to these numerical shifts, however. The makeup of various subgroups in the Senate also was different, as Table 1-1 indicates. In the 85th Congress, for example, northern Democrats and southern Democrats had distinct ideological characters, but there was also heterogeneity within each group. By the 94th Congress this mixture no longer existed; there were no northern conservatives and no southern liberals, and the proportion of moderates in each group also had declined. On the other hand, over the same period the Republicans in the Senate became considerably more heterogeneous.

In the 96th Congress these trends began to reverse. In the late 1970s and 1980s, the Republicans became more homogeneous and the Democrats more diverse. As the years passed, moderates represented a larger share of the Democratic coalition in the Senate. For all the partisan change that occurred, there has been relatively little change in the overall ideological makeup of the Senate in the last decade.

Yet this analysis tells only part of the story, for it applies only to aspects of liberalism-conservatism that are captured by the conservative coalition support scores employed in Table 1-1. This measure has its origins in the 1950s, when southern Democrats and Republicans shared conservative attitudes on a wide range of issues. The conservative coalition was defined to exist on any vote on which a majority of northern Democrats voted in opposition to a majority of southern Democrats and a majority of Republicans. This coalition used to form quite often. In most years from the mid-1960s through the early 1980s, it existed on between 20 percent and 30 percent of the roll call votes in the Senate. This is, however, no longer true.

One of the most consequential changes in the character of the Senate's membership in the 1980s was the election of a large contingent of southern Democrats who respond to a wide range of issues in ways similar to their northern colleagues. This change has had a dual effect. First, the conservative coalition is much less likely to form because there have been fewer issues on which southern Democrats were inclined to agree with the Republicans. In 1987 the coalition appeared on only 7.6 percent of the Senate votes, an all-time low. Second, on votes that divided the parties from one another, southern Democrats were substantially more loyal to their party than in the past. In the mid-1970s the average support among Senate southern Democrats for the Democratic position on votes on which a majority of Democrats voted in opposition to a majority of Republicans was less than 50 percent.[4] In

1987 this percentage had jumped to 80 percent, only eight points less than the average among northerners. Indeed, only four of the sixteen southern Democrats supported their party position less than 80 percent of the time.

These changes have meant Democratic solidarity across regional lines on many issues that would have almost certainly produced conservative coalitions in the past. In 1987, for example, majorities of both northern and southern Democrats supported the party's fiscal 1988 budget resolution, limits on testing of a space-based antiballistic missile system, and a prohibition on exceeding the missile limits of the SALT II treaty, and opposed Robert Bork's nomination to the Supreme Court. If this new orientation among southern Democrats persists, the pattern of policy making in the Senate will be radically different from the pattern of the postwar period.

## Norms and Rules

The Senate is a decision-making institution, and as such it has a set of formal rules that regulate its operations. It is also a group of individuals, and "just as any other group of human beings, it has its unwritten rules of the same, its norms of conduct, its approved manner of behavior." [5] The Senate, therefore, has both formal and informal rules, and, while there has been a great deal of continuity in both categories for more than three decades, there have also been some significant changes.

The unwritten rules or norms of the Senate are patterns of behavior senators think they and other senators should follow. Most members share similar expectations about how a senator ought or ought not to behave. In his study of the Senate in the mid-1950s, Matthews cited six norms or "folkways": legislative work, specialization, courtesy, reciprocity, institutional patriotism, and apprenticeship.

The first norm required that senators devote a major portion of their time to their legislative duties in committee and on the floor and not seek personal publicity at the expense of these legislative obligations. Second, a senator was expected to concentrate on matters pertaining to committee business or directly affecting constituents. The third norm, courtesy, required that the political conflicts within the Senate should not become personal conflicts. References to colleagues in legislative situations should be formal and indirect, and personal attacks were deemed unacceptable. Reciprocity, the fourth folkway, meant that senators were expected to help colleagues whenever possible and to avoid pressing their formal powers too far (for example, by systematically objecting to unanimous consent agreements). A senator was to understand and appreciate the problems of colleagues and to keep bargains once they were struck. The fifth norm of institutional patriotism required that a member protect the Senate as an institution, avoiding behavior that would bring it or its members into disrepute. Finally, new senators were expected to serve a period of apprenticeship. A freshman senator, it was felt, should wait a substantial amount of time before participating fully in the work of the Senate. During this time freshmen were expected to learn about the Senate and seek the advice of senior members.

Many of these folkways provide substantial benefits to the collective membership, and it is not surprising that most of them are still recognized in the Senate today. But, as patterns of power and ambition inside and outside the Senate have changed, the sanctions available for violation of the norms have diminished, and violations are much more frequent. The norms of legislative work and specialization are two that clearly persist as expectations. The Senate, like the House, is characterized by division of labor through the committee system. This system allocates legislative responsibilities to members, and these responsibilities have grown substantially since the 1950s. The Senate's ability to make policy and to function effectively depends in large measure upon each member living up to his or her individual responsibilities. The norms of legislative work and specialization express the expectations of members that each of them ought to do so.

The way to have influence in the Senate, according to one senator, was "just year after year of patience—willingness to carry at least your fair share of the work." Another said on the same point, "I believe the principle could be stated very simply—that is, keep up with your work." When asked about specialization, a third senator commented:

> I believe that senators do specialize in their activities as far as their committee . . . that doesn't mean that they can't learn a lot about other things . . . but you are expected to know in greater detail and greater accuracy about the things that your committee has jurisdiction over. That is an obligation.[6]

If legislative work and specialization still exist as norms—as expectations—why are they observed much less frequently in the late 1980s than they were in the 1950s? One answer is that the Senate has become a veritable breeding ground for presidential candidates. Many members are absent from the Senate for extended periods of time to explore or promote presidential campaigns. Even if senators are not actively seeking the White House, the chance to become a national celebrity, through appearances on the "CBS Evening News" or through profiles in *Newsweek,* is tempting. Legislative drudgery or committee detail in the back halls of Congress are not the route to extensive public and media attention.[7] Therefore, more senators get involved in a wide spectrum of policy areas extending beyond their committee assignments and often well beyond their Senate work.

Like legislative work and specialization, the folkways of courtesy, reciprocity, and institutional patriotism continue in the Senate but are violated more than in the past. Courtesy permits political conflict to remain depersonalized, allowing yesterday's opponent to be tomorrow's ally. (As one Republican senator said, "It's the catalyst that maintains a semblance of order.") The ideological divisions in the contemporary Senate, however, frequently have pitted one or more of the staunch liberals (such as Democrat Howard Metzenbaum of Ohio) or, more often, the extreme conservatives (such as Republican Jesse Helms of North Carolina) against colleagues in public and often bitter exchanges. Late in 1982, for example, a mainstream conservative Republican, Alan Simpson of Wyoming, said on the Senate floor of the uncollegial behavior of Senator Helms, "Seldom have I seen a more obnoxious and obdurate performance." In another example from the Foreign Relations Committee in 1987, Chairman Claiborne Pell, D-R.I., tried to bring the committee to a vote despite ongoing objections from Jesse Helms. Helms responded, "You can't take the floor away from me. If you railroad me, Mr. Chairman, you'll regret it." [8] Despite the lapses, the norm of reciprocity, particularly its aspect of individual integrity, continues to be important in an institution that operates informally and in which virtually all agreements are oral.

Institutional patriotism tends to be reinforced by the increase in competition between Congress and the executive branch for control over foreign policy and the budget. But the partisan divisions between House and Senate, and the public disapproval of Congress as an institution, have made it easier for senators to criticize the Senate with impunity.

As has been shown, five of the folkways that were operative in the Senate still describe "expected" (although, less often actual) behavior within the present institution. Even this is not true, however, of the sixth norm, apprenticeship. Unlike the other folkways, it is difficult to discern what benefits apprenticeship provided to the Senate as an institution or to its members individually. As Matthews noted, apprenticeship had its roots very early in the Senate's history.[9] Nevertheless, by the 1950s the only groups that could be seen to benefit from the observance of this norm were the senior conservatives in both parties who dominated the Senate's positions of power. Beginning with the 1958 election, more and more liberal northern Democrats entered the Senate, and the conservative dominance began to break down.[10] Consequently, junior members had less incentive to observe the norm.

Gradually, as these junior senators of the early 1960s became senior members, the expectations regarding the norm became less widely shared.

As the Senate returned to conservatism in the late 1970s and early 1980s, the continuing influx of junior members who made the ideological reversion possible had no interest whatsoever in restoring the norm that their earlier liberal brethren had helped abolish. Today, junior members across the board neither want nor feel the need to serve an apprenticeship; furthermore, no senior members expect them to do so, as these statements from senators indicate:

> All the communications suggest "get involved, offer amendments, make speeches. The Senate has changed, we're all equals, you should act accordingly." [A junior Democrat]
>
> Well, that [apprenticeship] doesn't exist at all in the Senate. The senior senators have made that very clear, both Democrats and Republicans. [A junior Republican]
>
> We now hope and expect and encourage the younger guys to dive right into the middle of it. [A senior conservative Republican]

Thus, the Senate of the 1980s is a more egalitarian institution when considered along seniority lines than it used to be. Junior members now play important roles, and this change in the informal rule structure of the body has contributed to several changes in the formal rules.[11]

In 1970, for example, a rule was adopted that limited members to service on only one of the Senate's four most prestigious committees: Appropriations, Armed Services, Finance, and Foreign Relations. This rule prevented senior members from monopolizing these important committee posts and facilitated the appointment of relatively junior senators much earlier in their careers than had previously been possible. In addition, both parties adopted rules limiting the role of seniority in the selection of committee chairmen.

As junior members became more active, they began to feel more intensely the disparity of resources between themselves and senior senators, particularly with regard to staff. Therefore, the junior members sponsored and aggressively pushed a resolution that permitted them to hire additional legislative staff members to assist in their committee duties. The Senate adopted the resolution in 1975.

A number of the other reforms adopted by the Senate in the 1970s were not a direct consequence of the expanded role of newer senators vis-à-vis their more senior colleagues. Certainly the most publicized of these was the 1975 change in the Senate's rule for cutting off debate. Since the late 1950s, liberals had been seeking to alter the rule that required the vote of two-thirds of the members present and voting to end a filibuster. The new provision required the affirmative vote of only three-fifths of the entire Senate membership. Since the adoption of the rules change, cloture has proved somewhat easier to achieve, but filibusters continue to be significant events in the Senate—including the "filibuster by amendment" ploy used in the late 1970s by conservative James Allen, D-Ala., and by liberals Metzenbaum and Lowell Weicker, R-Conn. They have underscored the power of individual senators to stymie the legislative process.

With the GOP takeover in 1981, there was no move to dismantle the changes wrought by junior members in earlier Senates or to return to a pattern of apprenticeship. It would not have been easy, if attempted; the Republican freshman class of 1980 was sixteen strong or a full 30 percent of the Republican party, and half the majority was in its first term. In another example of assertiveness by freshman senators, the Democrats first elected in 1986 have begun pressing for new institutional reforms that would make the Senate more efficient. Their effort is due partly to their common experiences: eight of the freshmen previously served in the House where the process is more structured. Indeed, some of them favor the creation of a Senate rules committee that would structure debate like its House counterpart. As Thomas Daschle, D-S.D., said, "Simply to come here and work in a museum is not my idea of a modern legislative process."

In sum, junior members have come to play an increasingly important role in Senate activity, and the expectations of senior members have gradually adapted to these changes. Partially as a consequence of this, the Senate has altered a number of its formal procedures. The overall effect of changes in the informal norms of conduct and written rules is that the Senate of the 1980s—for both parties—is a much more egalitarian and open institution in which the ability to affect policy is less dependent on a senator's formal position or seniority.

## Leadership

Viewing Senate party leadership from the vantage point of the 1950s, Donald Matthews observed:

> Democratic party leadership is highly personalized, informal, centralized in the hands of the floor leader. . . . Even when compared to a Democratic party under a relatively weak leader, the Republican leadership is more formalized, institutionalized, and decentralized.[12]

Both parties elect a floor leader, an assistant floor leader or whip, and a conference secretary. But the Democratic floor leader also presides over meetings of Democratic senators in caucuses and directs the formulation of party strategy and the scheduling of legislation as chairman of the Democratic Policy Committee. In addition, the floor leader oversees committee assignments as the chairman of the party's Steering Committee or Committee on Committees. In contrast, the Senate Republicans divide these responsibilities among four different senators. In terms of structural advantages, therefore, the potential for strong, concentrated leadership remains much higher for Senate Democrats than for Senate Republicans. Still, appearances can be deceptive. Assertive GOP leaders such as Robert Taft or Everett Dirksen could transform the obligations of these lesser officers into mainly supportive roles.[13]

From the early 1950s through 1988, only three men—Lyndon Johnson (Texas), Mike Mansfield (Montana), and Robert Byrd (West Virginia)—served as Democratic floor leaders in the Senate. The Republicans were led by six senators: Robert Taft (Ohio, 1953), William Knowland (California, 1953-1958), Everett Dirksen (Illinois, 1959-1969), Hugh Scott (Pennsylvania, 1970-1976), Howard Baker (Tennessee, 1977-1984), and Robert Dole (Kansas, 1985-1987).

Dole won the Senate majority leadership when Baker decided to resign from the Senate after serving three terms. Senate Republicans chose Dole, the chairman of the Senate Finance Committee, over Ted Stevens of Alaska, the assistant majority leader, 28-25. On earlier secret-ballot votes, three other candidates, first James McClure of Idaho, then Pete Domenici of New Mexico, and finally, Richard Lugar of Indiana, had been eliminated on a "low-man out" principle.

As is the case with all party leadership contests, Dole won for a variety of reasons, including his national prominence. Clearly, in narrowing the contest to Dole and Stevens, Senate Republicans were looking for a more assertive and independent leadership style than Baker had provided.

Further observations will be offered about the contrasting styles of these two Republican leaders, as well as prospects for further Senate leadership change. But first, it will be useful to provide a brief overview of past leadership performances.

### Historical Trends

The mid-1950s are remembered as an era of strong leaders in the Senate—Johnson on the majority side and Knowland and Dirksen for the minority. As Huitt, Matthews, and others have noted, their leadership both contributed to the tight hierarchical structure of the institution and reinforced it.[14] But with the election of 1958, the ability of a leader to "strong-arm" the Senate declined dramatically. Johnson's last two years as majority leader, 1959 to 1960, were much more difficult for him than his earlier tenure because of the larger number of independent freshman Democrats.[15]

Mansfield, Johnson's successor, was very different from Johnson. Easygoing and unwilling to accumulate personal power to exert leverage over his colleagues, Mansfield fit the changing institution he inherited—and he acted deliberately to accelerate the change. Mansfield served an unprecedented sixteen years as majority leader, from 1961 to his retirement in 1976. When he left, the Senate was once again in the process of change—in some ways, as has been shown, back in the direction of an earlier era—and Byrd, his successor, fit the pattern of his time. Byrd, like Mansfield, moved to the top leadership position after a stint as the number two leader, majority whip. Byrd had shifted over the years from a conservative to a moderate stance on most issues, thus becoming more like his colleagues in the late 1970s. And, although Byrd was no Lyndon Johnson, his leadership style was somewhat more assertive than Mansfield's, especially in parliamentary management and strategy, and it satisfied most senators who were nevertheless uneasy with the burgeoning workload and unpredictable schedule of the Senate from the 1970s on.

While Byrd was ascending to the majority leader's post in January 1977, the minority Republicans had their own leadership change. On the opening day of the contest for the slot, Robert Griffin (Michigan), the minority whip since 1959, was edged out by Baker by a slim 19-18 margin. Baker had challenged his predecessor, Scott, twice previously but failed to win the position of Republican floor leader. Baker beat Griffin in 1977, not as a result of ideological differences but because a majority of the incoming Republican freshmen were convinced that he would make a stronger external spokesman and internal leader. Four years later Baker became majority leader (he was unopposed after potential rivals such as Paul Laxalt of Nevada declined to run), and he showed even greater strength working with a narrow majority and his own party's president.[16]

## Lyndon Johnson and Mike Mansfield

From 1955 through 1976, men with starkly contrasting personalities and leadership styles led the Democrats.[17] Johnson sought to centralize control over organizational and policy decisions in himself. Mansfield's objective, on the other hand, was to serve the Senate, to create and maintain a body that "permitted individual, coequal senators the opportunity to conduct their affairs in whatever ways they deemed appropriate." [18] One Democrat who served with both men summarized their differences this way:

Johnson was aggressive and Mansfield is more the organizer, manager. I think he senses his primary duty is to insure the Senate moves in the conduct of its business in the most orderly fashion that we can. The result of our actions, while I'm sure he feels strongly on a lot of issues, he leaves up to each individual. Lyndon Johnson wanted to influence the outcome of every decision—not just to insure that we acted, but acted in a certain way.[19]

What can be concluded about the relative success of these two majority leaders? In his study of the last two Congresses under Johnson's direction and the first two under Mansfield's, John Stewart concluded:

Despite the dispersal of many tasks of party leadership and the generally permissive if not at times passive attitude displayed by the majority leader [Mansfield] in managing the legislative program, the senatorial party in the Eighty-seventh and Eighty-eighth Congresses [1961-1964] functioned effectively, and its performance compared favorably with and often surpassed the record compiled by the Eighty-fifth and Eighty-sixth Congresses [1957-1960] under the driving and centralized leadership of Lyndon Johnson.[20]

Although greater historical perspective is needed to evaluate fully the relative effectiveness of these two leaders, they clearly exemplify the wide range of styles, given different environmental settings, allowable in effective Senate leadership. Mansfield's relaxed manner and his conscious attempts to bring junior members into Senate decision making contributed to the diffusion of power and the opening of procedures that characterized the Senate in the 1970s. Byrd in the 95th Congress appeared to borrow techniques and strategies that seemed to work for his predecessors and to fuse them with his own personality and sense of the Senate. But with his party's abrupt shift to minority status in 1981, Byrd exercised a less dynamic personal leadership. When Senate Democrats regained control of the Senate in 1987, however, Byrd as majority leader took a more active role in scheduling and influencing legislation.

## Robert Byrd

Byrd was first elected to Congress in 1952 as a member of the House of Representatives and then in 1958 as a senator from West Virginia. He therefore gained firsthand knowledge of Johnson's leadership style and techniques. Byrd also served under Mansfield's leadership for ten years, first as secretary to the party conference and later as party whip. Given the enhanced independence of members and the breakdown of the apprenticeship norm, Byrd was well aware that he could not revert to a 1950s style of centralized command. Nor did he care to emulate many of Mansfield's more laissez-faire tactics. The result was a gradual consolidation of control over party instrumentalities such as the Policy Committee, which discusses issues and helps set the legislative agenda, and the Steering Committee, which makes committee assignments.

Byrd's relationships with the Carter White House were initially rather strained and testy. By the second session of the 95th Congress, however, the new majority leader had developed a reasonable working relationship with the Democratic administration, especially on important legislative items such as the ratification of the Panama Canal treaties, the Revenue Act, and the energy programs. Byrd's dogged devotion to detail, his mastery of Senate rules, his willingness to confront but also to compromise with pivotal senators such as Russell Long, D-La., Edmund Muskie, D-Maine, Republican leader Baker, and even his old antagonist, Edward Kennedy, D-Mass., contributed to his reputation as an effective majority leader.

As minority leader in the 1980s, however, Byrd was not viewed quite so positively by his colleagues. He retained his impressive work habits and parliamentary skill but lost some of his zest for legislative combat and strategic legerdemain. One of his colleagues noted midway through 1981:

> Byrd doesn't have his heart in it. He views the minority leadership
> as a demotion, and he's kind of withdrawn from any strong
> leadership role.

Byrd rebounded somewhat in election years as the opportunities to regain control of the Senate mounted. By the 98th and 99th Congresses, Democrats had begun to coalesce more as a minority party. As the critical 1986 election year approached, the year in which the vulnerable Republican class of 1980 would be up for reelection, Byrd's willingness to share the legislative load and his spokesmanship role resulted in more positive collegial assessments.

## Howard Baker and Robert Dole

Just after Baker defeated Griffin in January 1977 for the post of minority leader, he was asked what his relationship with incoming Democratic president Carter would be. Baker replied that he "intended to hear him out" and act in the best interests of the country. "There is no longer a minority President, only a minority in Congress," he said. Following the presidencies of Richard Nixon and Gerald R. Ford, the Republican leaders in the Senate—Baker, newly elected whip Stevens, and holdover Policy Committee chairman John Tower of Texas—had to shift their roles. No longer did they endeavor to win passage of a Republican president's programs or uphold his vetoes. Instead they became responsible for voicing GOP alternatives in cooperation with the Republican House leadership and the Republican National Committee.

Everett Dirksen, Baker's father-in-law, had been especially adept at maximizing the role of the minority party in the Senate. Depending on the issues, he either thwarted or cooperated with Democratic presidents. Baker followed in Dirksen's footsteps. Despite opposition from many GOP constituents, Baker supplied crucial support in favor of ratification of the Panama Canal treaties. He also played a critical role in support of Carter's sale of military jet planes to Saudi Arabia and Egypt, as well as to Israel.

Sidestepping a possible challenge from the right after the 1980 Republican surge, Baker and Stevens were reelected to their Senate posts without opposition. The unprecedented influx of sixteen freshman Republican senators, nearly all staunch conservatives, immediately confronted Baker with the problem of leading a large bloc of members who had no personal ties to him and often were not ideologically in tune with his views. The freshman group also split GOP ranks along generational lines because more senior Republicans—for example, Weicker, Charles McC. Mathias (Maryland), Mark Hatfield (Oregon), and Robert Stafford (Vermont)—tended to be more moderate or even liberal.

Baker worked closely with GOP committee chairmen Domenici of Budget and Dole of Finance in 1981, however, to pass Ronald Reagan's economic package virtually intact, winning the kudos of the president and his conservative Senate colleagues. Throughout the 97th and 98th Congresses, Baker balanced loyal support for President Reagan with equally loyal attention to his Senate charges. He also balanced his attempt to accomplish policy goals on the Senate agenda with a sensitivity to the personal and policy demands, however impetuous, of his individual colleagues, from both left and right.

In the contemporary Senate, Baker was unable to twist arms or employ sanctions as had his late father-in-law, but his leadership by patience, savvy, and good humor was universally respected and admired. One colleague said, "Baker's the best leader we've had in the Senate in a half-century." Baker also recognized that he could not rely for long on Republican party discipline, so he tailored his majority leadership to appeal to Democrats as well. For four years as minority leader, Baker had enjoyed a positive relationship with his majority counterpart, Robert Byrd; in 1981 he took steps to cement that relationship. For example, the new majority leader diplomatically declined to take over the plush suite of offices occupied by Byrd, opting instead to stay in his old minority leader quarters and thus forestalling for Byrd the humiliation of a move.

Still, for all of Baker's skill, the leadership post proved increasingly frustrating. By 1983 the Senate schedule had become more uncontrollable, and Baker found himself buffeted between the demands of ultraconservatives such as Helms and John East (North Carolina) and the filibusters of liberals such as Weicker and Metzenbaum. In 1984 Baker announced that he would leave the Senate at the end of the year with the objective of seeking the presidency in 1988 or later.

In the 1984 elections Senate Republicans suffered a net loss of two seats. The same November 1984 conference that chose Robert Dole as majority leader selected an entirely new slate of leaders headed by Dole and Alan Simpson as the new assistant majority leader. In early December Minority Leader Byrd withstood a late challenge from Florida's Lawton Chiles and retained his position by a 36-11 vote.

Throughout the 99th Congress Dole faced the delicate task of demonstrating his assertiveness without excessively aberrating the White House or plunging Senate Republicans into further disarray. For example, he won a dramatic late-night, one-vote victory on the budget in May 1985 by having GOP senator Pete Wilson of California brought from the hospital and wheeled onto the floor, intravenous hook-up and all, to gain a tie vote. Wilson's presence gave Vice President George Bush the opportunity to cast the winning vote for the Republican plan. Picking his issues carefully, usually siding with the president, but sometimes opposing his programs or seeking modifications, Dole won a series of legislative battles. Despite taking every opportunity to put Republican freshmen forward, Dole's intensive campaign efforts on behalf of his colleagues fell short of the mark in the 1986 elections. Democratic challengers picked up nine of the twenty-two contested seats previously held by Republicans and lost only one of their own—Missouri. After six uneasy years in the minority, Democrats again controlled the Senate, this time by a 55-45 margin.[21]

Marked by intense partisanship and increasing legislative stalemate, the 100th Congress was also characterized by enhanced speculation about its future Senate leaders. Minority Leader Dole gave little indication that he would resign from his leadership position in the Senate, even as his bid for the GOP presidential nomination entered into its most intensive and critical phases in early 1988. When his presidential bid foundered, Dole returned to his Senate leadership post.

Meanwhile, Byrd, who had served as Democratic floor leader since 1977, was giving veiled signals that he would seek reelection to ' the Senate in 1988, but might relinquish his leadership position to accept other powerful and prestigious posts—chairman of the Senate Appropriations Committee and president pro tempore of the Senate, providing the Senate remains in Democratic hands. Finally, in April 1988, Byrd announced just that—leaving the Democratic post open to a contest among Daniel Inouye (Hawaii), J. Bennett Johnston (Louisiana), and George Mitchell (Maine). Decisions about these and other Senate leadership positions awaited the outcome of the 1988 elections and the organization of the 101st Congress (1989-1990).

## Committees

From its earliest days, the U.S. Senate, like the House of Representatives, has used a division of labor in a committee system to organize its work. The committee system is the single most important feature affecting legislative outcomes in the Senate; not surprisingly, it has changed as other aspects of the Senate—workload, membership, power—have changed.

### Committee Assignments

Shortly after being sworn in every senator is given committee assignments. When vacancies occur on a more attractive committee, senators can and do switch assignments. The assignment process and the selection of committee and subcommittee chairmen are crucial to the Senate, because they can determine the policy orientation and activity of the committees. The Democratic and Republican parties handle their members' assignments differently. Democrats use a twenty-two-member Steering Committee chaired by the Democratic leader, while Republicans have a nine-member Committee on Committees with an elected leader (Paul Trible of Virginia in the 100th Congress). In the 1940s and early 1950s, committee assignments reflected the norm of apprenticeship; freshmen were assigned only to minor committees, and senior members dominated prestigious committees such as Foreign Relations, Appropriations, Finance, and Armed Services. When Lyndon Johnson became majority leader in 1955, he changed these procedures by instituting the "Johnson Rule," which guaranteed every Democrat, no matter how junior, a major committee assignment. However, as has been shown, Johnson ran the Steering Committee as a one-man show, and he handed out truly choice assignments very selectively. Senior, more conservative members continued to dominate the most prestigious panels.

After Johnson, the process became more democratic, especially under Mansfield. Assignments to all committees became more open to junior and liberal Democrats, in part because there were more of them. But, because of the importance members attach to committee slots, the process frequently has generated controversy. Soon after Byrd's election as majority leader in 1977, junior liberal Democrats, led by Iowa's John Culver, forced an acrimonious debate in the Democratic Caucus to protest Byrd's choices to fill Steering Committee vacancies, fearing that the committee assignment selection power would be handled by an unrepresentative group not sensitive to their needs. They won an agreement, still in effect, that future Steering Committee choices would be submitted in advance to the party membership.

Moreover, controversy has come to light about the party leader having the additional clout of chairing this committee. After Byrd announced in April 1988 that he would step down as Democratic leader before the 101st Congress, the contenders for the post began to discuss the option of separating the party leader position from the chairmanships of the Steering and Policy committees, as the Republicans do. The Republicans also employ a different assignment process, relying on a more automatic process based on seniority. Still, in the 1970s and 1980s, as important committees were enlarged, limits were imposed on the ability of senior members to "stockpile" all the good assignments, and junior Republicans, increased in number, changed the GOP makeup of many important committees. Junior Republicans were a particularly striking force after the 1980 election, with their huge freshman class (sixteen in number) that rivaled the 1958 Democratic group; but the change in party ratios on committees after the Democrats lost the Senate did not allow for many vacancies on the blue-chip committees like Finance and Armed Services.

These changes combined to swing the Senate committees in a more junior and liberal direction in the mid- to late-1970s, but then back in a more conservative direction after 1980. The Democratic recapture of the Senate majority in 1986 changed the committee system makeup once again. The entry of eleven freshman Democrats, replacing in many instances conservative Republicans, moved many committees in a more liberal direction. Two of the freshman Democrats won seats on Appropriations, three on Budget, two on Armed Services, two on Foreign Relations, and one on Finance. This record of success would not have satisfied many of the more aggressive freshmen of the mid-1970s, but it was perfectly acceptable to the class of '86.

## Chairmanships

For many decades, Senate committee chairmanships and ranking minority memberships have been selected through the process of seniority, even though there are no formal requirements to do so. The process is not entirely clean and consistent, however. Because some senators with longevity become senior on more than one committee, they can choose which one to chair, creating an occasional pattern of musical chairs. In the 100th Congress, for example, Ted Kennedy chose the Labor and Human Resources Committee chairmanship over that of the Judiciary Committee, which he had chaired in the late 1970s. Kennedy's move enabled Joseph Biden, D-Del., to take over Judiciary—but blocked Howard Metzenbaum from chairing Labor. Kennedy did not make his choice to help Biden or hinder Metzenbaum, but he did end up shaping the agendas and directions of the two committees. In 1981 conservative Republicans persuaded Strom Thurmond, R-S.C., to choose the chairmanship of Judiciary over Armed Services, where he was also senior, specifically to keep liberal Charles Mathias from assuming the Judiciary reins.

The seniority process became controversial for Republicans after the 1986 election. Ultraconservative Jesse Helms, the senior Republican on both Agriculture and Foreign Relations, had chosen for constituency reasons to chair Agriculture in the 99th Congress, leaving Foreign Relations to the more junior and more moderate Richard Lugar of Indiana. But after the Republicans lost the Senate in 1986, Helms decided to assert his seniority rights and make the switch to become ranking Republican on Foreign Relations. Lugar, who had been an effective and well-respected chairman, vigorously contested Helms. Despite the sharp ideological differences between the two, the issue became the sanctity of the seniority system. Liberal Republican Lowell Weicker, afraid of what breaking the seniority precedent would do to his own future chances of chairing the Appropriations Committee, came out publicly for his archfoe Helms, as did several other senior Republicans, both moderates and liberals. Helms won, solidifying the seniority principle in the GOP.

Weicker and many of his colleagues voted for Helms to preserve a seniority process that has dampened the overall trends in ideology and region that have affected the Senate as a whole and the committee rosters in particular. The preference for seniority over ideology held for Democrats in the 1970s, for Republicans during their majority status in the Senate from 1981 through 1986, and for the Democrats again in the 100th Congress. Thanks to the seniority process, the decline in the 1970s in the number of southern Democrats in the Senate was reflected only partially in committee chairmanships. In 1975 southerners accounted for only 26 percent of Senate Democrats, but they held 39 percent of chairmanships, heading powerful panels such as Appropriations, Armed Services, Finance, Foreign Relations, and Judiciary.

Seniority also limited the impact of the conservative trend in American politics and the Senate in the late 1970s and early 1980s. The senior majority members in the Republican Senate in 1981 were more moderate than their colleagues. The top quartile in 1981 had an average conservative coalition score of seventy-two, compared with an average of eighty-eight for the more junior three-fourths of Republicans. As a result, nearly half of the major committee chairmen in the Republican Senate were more liberal than their committee colleagues, including the chairmen of Appropriations and Foreign Relations.

By the time the Democrats regained control of the chamber in 1987, a number of post-1958 northern liberals had departed, through defeat or retirement, while several post-1970 vintage southerners had moved steadily up the seniority ladder, joining a few of their senior, die-hard colleagues. Therefore, in the 100th Congress, southern Democrats once again had a disproportionate share of the chairmanships, holding seven of sixteen standing committees, or 44 percent, while having only 29 percent of the party membership. And included among the seven chairmanships were some of the most significant committees: Appropriations, Finance, Armed Services, Commerce, and Budget.

## Workload

With a small membership, the Senate is profoundly affected by its workload. The 1960s and 1970s saw that workload burgeon, leading to calls for reform, some of them successful. While the workload stabilized and, in some ways, even declined in the 1980s, senators' level of satisfaction with their output and lifestyle deteriorated—leading to more calls for reform. Work activity took particularly sharp increases in the early 1970s. There were five times as many roll call votes on the Senate floor in the 95th Congress as there were in the 84th (1,151 to 224); the huge number of votes was accompanied by increases in the number of bills introduced and hearings held.

In response to the increasing number and complexity of decisions senators had to make, the Senate expanded the committee system. In 1957 there were 15 standing committees with 118 subcommittees; by 1975 there were 18 standing committees with 140 subcommittees. If special, select, and joint committees were included in the tally, it would reach 31 committees and 174 subcommittees.

More important, perhaps, the sizes of the panels also increased. Because the Senate had increased by only four members since the mid-1950s (with the admission of Alaska and Hawaii in 1959), this meant more assignments per member. In 1957 each senator averaged 2.8 committees and 6.3 subcommittees. But by 1976 senators on the average served on 4 committees and 14 subcommittees. Junior members in particular objected to the fragmentation and frenetic scheduling that flowed from this process. At their urging, the Senate early in 1976 created a twelve-member, bipartisan committee chaired by Adlai E.

Stevenson III, D-Ill., to revamp the committee system. Called the Temporary Select Committee to Study the Senate Committee System, the panel recommended substantial reductions in the number of committees and subcommittees and even greater reductions in the number of assignments allowed senators.

S. Res. 4, which passed the Senate early in 1977, eliminated 3 standing and 5 select and joint committees, rearranged several others, and resulted in a dramatic drop in the number of subcommittees (from an overall total of 174 to 110) and in the number of assignments (from an average of 4 committees and 14 subcommittees to 3 committees and 7.5 subcommittees). In a trend typical for an individualized, democratized institution, however, the assignments immediately began to escalate again, well beyond the limits set by S. Res. 4. By the 98th Congress, the average number of assignments was up nearly to twelve, and forty senators violated, in one way or another, the chamber rules on assignment limitations. In frustration, the Senate created yet another Select Committee to Study the Committee System, chaired by Republican Dan Quayle of Indiana. The Quayle committee essentially recommended that the Senate simply enforce the assignment limitations already in the rules, but to little avail. In the 100th Congress the average number of assignments was eleven, and forty-nine senators continued to violate the assignment rules. The system is more compact than it was in the mid-1970s, but member satisfaction is, if anything, lower. Multiple assignments and fragmented responsibilities, added to frustration over erratic and unpredictable Senate scheduling that made normal family life impossible, led to increased grumbling among senators. In 1987 junior and mid-seniority senators, led by Democrat David Pryor of Arkansas, began to meet as an informal task force to recommend change. Partly due to their efforts, the Senate altered its schedule, moving to a three-weeks-on, one-week-off pattern, to regularize the schedule. The premature voluntary retirements in 1988 of Chiles, Trible, and Dan Evans, R-Wash., raised further concerns about the Senate and senators. Additional changes, including perhaps another go at the committee system, seemed likely.

To cope with the workload, the Senate enlarged professional staffs, both committee and personal. Committee staff grew from roughly 300 in the 85th Congress to well over 1,200 (including permanent and investigative staff) by the 95th. The numbers stabilized and even declined thereafter, settling at just under 1,100 in the 100th Congress. The larger staffs in the modern Senate have had several effects. Senators have been able to cope better with their heavier workload and responsibilities—but entrepreneurial, active, and ambitious staff also have created more work by promoting ideas, writing amendments, and drafting bills and speeches. Larger staffs also have contributed to the democratization and decentralization of the Senate. In recent years, staffs have been allocated increasingly through sub-committees rather than through full committees, which has accentuated the spread of power to junior senators and has correspondingly reduced the power of committee chairmen.

Along with expanding subcommittee chairmanships and expanding staffs, committee deliberations have become more open. Together, these factors have loosened the control that committee leaders once maintained over their committee rank-and-file. Junior senators now have subcommittee bases from which to challenge the policy recommendations of committee chairmen. Moreover, senators who do not serve on a particular committee have enough access to information to enable them to offer successful amendments on the floor to the committee's bills. Thus, committees have become less cohesive internally, and their bills have become more vulnerable to challenge on the Senate floor. To combat these trends, some savvy chairmen have begun to use closed meetings and sessions, along with attempts at restricted debate via unanimous consent, to get more control over the Senate's legislative process; the 1982 tax bill and tax reform in 1986 are good examples. But these efforts are few and far between.

During the 1970s the legislative struggle shifted from the committee rooms to the Senate floor, while the functions of agenda setting and legislative oversight moved from the committees to the subcommittees. During the 1980s legislative activity declined somewhat; the Senate considered fewer bills, took fewer roll call votes, and passed fewer laws than it had in the preceding several years, in both Democratic- and Republican-controlled Senates. Nevertheless, the patterns of legislative initiation and the relative importance of Senate institutions remain the same. Committees continue to be highly important; all legislation is referred to them, as are all executive and judicial nominations, and they retain the authority either to kill or to report out the bills and nominations. But the present-day Senate is a more open, fluid, and decentralized body than that of the 1950s. Power, resources, and decision-making authority have become more diffuse. The combined impact of changes in membership, norms, leadership, workload, committees, and, as we shall see, television coverage have produced a markedly different Senate in the 1980s, with more changes ahead for the 1990s.

## The Senate and the Presidency

The Senate does not operate in a vacuum; it has been and is affected by trends in society and in the broader political system, and it has, in turn, an impact on American politics. Nowhere is this impact felt more strongly than in presidential nominations. The Senate has been a major breeding ground for presidential candidates for many decades, but in the period from 1960 to 1972, it was dominant. Since then, the Senate has lost some luster, but it continues to be an institution that turns out many presidential contenders and that attracts many who also aspire to the Oval Office.

During the "golden" era of 1960 to 1972, the two parties nominated either senators (John Kennedy, Barry Goldwater, and George McGovern) or former senators who became vice presidents (Richard Nixon, Lyndon Johnson, and Hubert Humphrey). Why this importance for the Senate? The near revolutionary growth in media influence over politics, particularly through television, focused public attention on Washington, and especially the Senate. Television contributed to, and was affected by, the increasing nationalization of party politics. A national attentiveness to foreign affairs heightened the importance of the Senate, with its well-defined constitutional role in foreign policy.

Many of these trends and conditions remained, of course, beyond 1972. But after the Watergate scandal, a turn in public attitudes about Washington enabled Jimmy Carter, a young ex-governor with no Washington experience, to capture the Democratic nomination in 1976 and to run successfully for president by campaigning against Washington politics. Despite the continuing role of senators and ex-senators as candidates in 1980 (Howard Baker, Bob Dole, and Edward Kennedy) and in 1984 (Gary Hart, John Glenn, Alan Cranston, and Ernest Hollings), another former governor, Ronald Reagan, won the GOP nod in 1980, while former vice president (and senator) Walter Mondale beat out the more contemporary Senate contingent for the Democratic nomination in 1984.

There are several reasons for the decline in presidential competitiveness of senators: the emergence of a number of attractive governors from important states and the increased national attention paid to the House after 1979, when it began to televise its floor sessions over cable television's C-SPAN. In 1986, frustrated over their comparative decline in national attention, senators finally brought gavel-to-gavel television coverage to their own proceedings.

In 1988 several more senators entered the presidential sweepstakes, including Bob Dole, who, as floor leader, could benefit from the television coverage, and Democrats Paul Simon of Illinois and Albert Gore, Jr., of Tennessee. Dole showed early success from his leadership vantage point, winning a large victory in the Iowa caucuses, and Gore managed to stay in the race after several others had faltered; but the party nominations once again went to nonsenators—Vice President George Bush and Governor Michael Dukakis of Massachusetts.

Despite the recent lack of presidential successes, the Senate remains an institution that receives national and international attention and produces numerous serious presidential contenders. Many senators consider themselves presidential possibilities, or they are mentioned as such on television networks and in the polls. Senators tailor their behavior accordingly, spreading out their legislative interests, increasing their activity and media visibility. The preoccupation with presidential aspirations has contributed to violations of the norms of specialization and legislative work. It has also increased the pressure within the Senate to distribute resources and power to junior members.

## Conclusions

The Senate has changed in a variety of ways since the 1950s. The nature of its membership, its internal norms and rules, its leadership styles and effects, its committees, and its role as a breeding ground for presidential candidates have all evolved to make the Senate of the 1980s an institution quite different from its postwar incarnation—and to make the Senate of the late 1980s different from that of the early part of the decade.

The Senate has gone from a close partisan balance during the Truman and Eisenhower presidencies in the 1950s to a dominant Democratic party control in the 1960s and 1970s to a narrow Republican majority in the early and mid-1980s, and back to narrow Democratic control after 1986. A powerful southern Democratic wing maintained great power through the seniority system and a coalition with like-minded Republicans, then diminished in size and influence, and made a comeback of sorts by the time the Democrats recaptured the Senate. At the same time, another group of Democrats, elected in the 1970s and mostly in their forties, began to move into positions of influence—senators like Joe Biden, chairman of the Judiciary Committee, Sam Nunn of Georgia, chairman of the Armed Services Committee, Bennett Johnston, chairman of the Energy Committee, and Donald Riegle of Michigan, scheduled to chair the Banking Committee on William Proxmire's retirement.

With these and other movements of blocs of power, the Senate, overall, has become a more open, more fluid, more decentralized, and more democratized chamber. Individual senators, from the most senior down to the most junior, have benefited—but have also become increasingly frustrated with the institutional consequences of these trends. While the overall work burden has decreased in the past few years, declining roughly to the levels of the mid-1970s, the Senate has become more preoccupied for extended periods of time with a small number of issues, especially the budget, which seem never to get resolved in any satisfactory way. Filibusters, once rare and reserved for the weightiest of issues, are now employed routinely on even trivial matters, tying up the institution even more.

The lack of movement on many issues and the preoccupation with talk over action have not resulted in a return to the leisurely, "clublike" atmosphere of the past or greatly increased the role, level, or quality of debate. While televised sessions have improved floor attendance and show promise for the quality of floor speeches, the evidence is spotty at best. In today's Senate there is no clear institutional direction or identity. Neither a great deliberative body nor an efficient processor of laws, the Senate, after years of dramatic change, is an institution in search of an identity. That search will produce even more change into the 1990s.

## Notes

1. See the collection of articles by Huitt in *Congress: Two Decades of Analysis,* Ralph K. Huitt and Robert L. Peabody (New York: Harper & Row, 1969); and Donald R. Matthews, *U.S. Senators and Their World* (New York: Vintage Books, 1960).
2. See, for example, Michael Foley, *The New Senate* (New Haven, Conn.: Yale University Press, 1980); Elizabeth Drew, *Senators* (New York: Simon & Schuster, 1979); Ross G. Baker, *Friend and Foe in the U.S. Senate* (New York: Free Press, 1980); Bernard Asbell, *The Senate Nobody Knows* (Baltimore: Johns Hopkins University Press, 1978).
3. The number of Democrats in Table 1-1 is 54 rather than 55 because of the death of Senator Edward Zorinsky, D-Neb., in 1987, and his replacement by Republican senator David Karnes.
4. These figures are taken from *Vital Statistics on Congress, 1984-1985,* ed. Norman J. Ornstein et al. (Washington, D.C.: American Enterprise Institute, 1984), 182-183. For an analysis of changing party loyalty among southern Democrats in the House, see David W. Rohde, " 'Something's Happening Here: What It Is Ain't Exactly Clear': Southern Democrats in the House of Representatives" (Paper delivered at a conference in honor of Richard F. Fenno, Jr., Washington, D.C., Aug. 27, 1986).
5. Matthews, *U.S. Senators and Their World,* 92.
6. These quotations and others used below are taken from semistructured, taped interviews with more than sixty sitting or former senators conducted between 1973 and 1979. The interviews are part of a broader study of the Senate conducted by the authors with the help of a grant from the Russell Sage Foundation.

7. For more on the Senate's move from a closed system to an open one, see Norman J. Ornstein, "The Open Congress Meets the President," in *Both Ends of the Avenue,* ed. Anthony King (Washington, D.C.: American Enterprise Institute, 1983), 185-211.
8. Quoted in the *Washington Post,* Oct. 22, 1987, A21.
9. Matthews, *U.S. Senators and Their World,* 116-117.
10. For a discussion of the changes during the 1960s, see Randall B. Ripley, *Power in the Senate* (New York: St. Martin's Press, 1969).
11. For a more extensive treatment of the changes in Senate norms, see David W. Rohde, Norman J. Ornstein, and Robert L. Peabody, "Political Change and Legislative Norms in the U.S. Senate, 1957-1974," in *Studies of Congress,* ed. Glenn R. Parker (Washington, D.C.: CQ Press, 1985), 147-188.
12. Matthews, *U.S. Senators and Their World,* 123-124.
13. Robert L. Peabody, *Leadership in Congress* (Boston: Little, Brown, 1976), 332-333; Robert L. Peabody, "Senate Party Leadership: From the 1950s to the 1980s," in *Understanding Congressional Leadership,* ed. Frank H. Mackaman (Washington, D.C.: CQ Press, 1981), 56.
14. See also Rowland Evans and Robert Novak, *Lyndon B. Johnson: The Exercise of Power* (New York: New American Library, 1966); Randall B. Ripley, *Majority Party Leadership in Congress* (Boston: Little, Brown, 1969); and John G. Stewart, "Two Strategies of Leadership: Johnson and Mansfield," in *Congressional Behavior,* ed. Nelson W. Polsby (New York: Random House, 1971), 61-92. Also see Neil MacNeil, *Dirksen: Portrait of a Public Man* (New York: World Publications, 1970); Jean Torcom Cronin, "Minority Leadership in the United States Senate: The Role and Style of Everett Dirksen" (Ph.D. diss., Johns Hopkins University, 1979); and Charles O. Jones, *The Minority Party in Congress* (Boston: Little, Brown, 1970).
15. Evans and Novak, *Lyndon B. Johnson,* 195-224.
16. Robert L. Peabody, "The Selection of a Senate Majority Leader, 1985," unpublished manuscript, 1986.
17. Stewart, "Two Strategies of Leadership"; and Peabody, *Leadership in Congress,* 333-345.
18. Stewart, "Two Strategies of Leadership," 87.
19. Rohde, Ornstein, and Peabody, "Political Change and Legislative Norms in the U.S. Senate," 163.
20. Stewart, "Two Strategies of Leadership," 87.
21. Norman J. Ornstein, Robert L. Peabody, and David W. Rohde, "Party Leadership and the Institutional Context: The Senate from Baker to Dole" (Revised version of a paper delivered at the annual meeting of the American Political Science Association, Washington, D.C., Aug. 28-31, 1986).

## 2. CONSOLIDATING POWER IN THE HOUSE: THE RISE OF A NEW OLIGARCHY

*Lawrence C. Dodd and Bruce I. Oppenheimer*

The 1980s confronted the House of Representatives with a dilemma. With the landslide victories of Ronald Reagan in 1980 and 1984, the Democratic House majority faced a president of the opposite party and a Republican Senate for six of Reagan's eight years in office. The House was the center of "loyal opposition" to the government and the institution most likely to provide visible leadership to opposition forces. But the members of the House had spent the previous decade instituting a highly dispersed system of subcommittee power, a system designed to provide specialized decision making rather than strong policy leadership. Thus, the dilemma: how could the House Democratic majority play a strong role in national governance despite Reagan and the subcommittee system.

The response to this dilemma, we argue, has been the consolidation of institutional power in a new House oligarchy composed of the majority party leadership and members of a few elite committees. This solution emerged partly through accident and partly through conscious efforts of party members. This essay describes and assesses the development of the new power structure, starting with a discussion of membership change and rules reforms over the past twenty years.

### Membership Change

From 1971 to 1981 the House experienced significant membership turnover. The percentage of House "careerists," members serving in their tenth or greater term, declined from a record high of 20 percent at the start of the 92d Congress to 11 percent at the start of the 97th.[1] Naturally, there was a corresponding increase in junior members, those with three or fewer terms (Figure 2-1). Their numbers grew from 150 in the 92d Congress to a high of 214 in the 96th.[2] That trend has been reversed. At the start of the 100th Congress, careerists numbered 69 (16 percent of the membership) and junior members were down to 159 (37 percent of the membership).

Figure 2-1   House Service: New Members (Three or Fewer Terms)
and Careerists (Ten or More Terms), 1911-1987

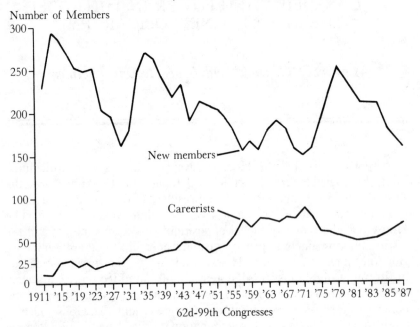

Number of Members

62d-99th Congresses

## Why Has the Trend Reversed?

The obvious reason for the change in the seniority trend in the House can be seen in the number of first-term members entering the House. The 1984 and 1986 elections, respectively, produced only thirty-nine and forty-eight new House members. By comparison, the previous five elections had resulted in an average of seventy-six freshmen. The two factors contributing to this low number of first-term members were few retirements and high rates of incumbent reelection. After six elections in which an average of more than forty-two members voluntarily retired from the House, the average from 1984 and 1986 dropped to thirty, about the same level the House experienced from 1946 to 1970. Although many of the conditions used to explain the high retirement levels in the late 1970s are still present, fewer members are choosing to leave.[3] In 1988 only twenty-three members of the 100th House are retiring.

Many of those who leave the House seek another office, and with some success. Of the eighty-three House members who retired in 1984, 1986, and 1988, forty-seven did so to run for another office, usually the U.S. Senate. At the start of the 100th Congress, eighteen of the thirty-six senators first elected since November 1980 had come directly from serving in the House. By comparison, only eighteen of the sixty-four senators first elected before November 1980 came directly from the House.

The high rate of incumbent reelection has had an even more dramatic effect than the low number of retirements on the House turnover rate. In the 1984 and 1986 elections combined, only twenty-seven incumbents were defeated in a primary or general election. Of those incumbents seeking reelection in 1986, a record high 98 percent were successful.[4] With neither a high number of retirements as in the late 1970s nor a sizable number of incumbents defeated as in the early 1980s, House membership appears to be entering a new phase of careerism.

## Democratic Party Control Continues

It is not surprising that low membership turnover means the continuation of a Democratic party majority in the House. Even with the Reagan landslide victories and with six years of holding a Senate majority, the Republicans did not come close to capturing the House. At the start of the 100th Congress the Democrats held 258 seats, slightly more than the mean number of seats they have held since the era of Democratic House control stabilized in the 1930s.[5]

The prospects for Republicans in House elections are not encouraging. One may be tempted to see the success rate of incumbents in the House as a major obstacle to Republican inroads, but Republicans have fared nearly as badly in open seat House contests as in races involving incumbents. In the five elections from 1976 through 1984, when Republicans made gains and then took the Senate, they won only 41.3 percent of victories in races with no incumbents running.[6]

It is easy to understand why Republican House members may become discouraged. The decision of Trent Lott, R-Miss., to give up his safe House seat and run in a competitive U.S. Senate race in 1988 illustrates the frustration. At the time of his departure from the House, Lott was the House minority whip and a member of the Rules Committee. With eight terms in the House and still in his forties, Lott was in a competitive position to succeed Bob Michel as Republican floor leader or, at worst, to become the ranking Republican on the Rules Committee. But the prospect of remaining as a leader within the minority party was obviously not sufficient incentive to stay in the House.

## Ideological Change and Membership Diversity

In the past an analysis of ideological change in the House would have focused on a comparison over time of conservative coalition support scores of northern Democrats, southern Democrats, and Republicans.[7] In general, one could expect the House to be more liberal as the number of northern Democrats grew and more conservative as the number of Republicans grew, with the number of southern Democrats remaining relatively unchanged historically.

Several occurrences make this analysis less useful than it once was. First, since the full implementation of the Voting Rights Act, southern Democratic House members have become more ideologically diverse; they are not all conservatives. Second, when Republicans make House gains, they may come at the expense of southern, not just northern, Democrats. Third, and most important, the conservative coalition appears less often. Conservative coalition votes—those in which a majority of northern Democrats are opposed by a majority of Republicans and a majority of southern Democrats—comprised a fifth to a quarter of the roll call votes in Congress until the 1980s. Since then there has been a steady but continuous decline. In the 99th Congress the conservative coalition came together on only 12 percent of the House roll calls. In 1987 the number dropped to 8.8 percent.[8]

As the conservative coalition declined, interparty conflict grew. Party votes—those on which a majority of Democrats opposed a majority of Republicans—comprised 59 percent of all House roll call votes in the 99th Congress, the highest level in the post-World War II era; in 1987 party votes reached 64 percent. The growth in partisan conflict has been accompanied by an increase in intraparty cohesion. The average party-unity score for House members has risen to record levels, with House Democrats averaging 81 percent in 1987.[9]

With the decline in turnover, the trend toward a younger, more diverse House membership has been reversed. At the start of the 98th Congress, the average age of a House member was 45.5 years, a post-World War II low. By the start of the 100th Congress, the average age had risen to 50.7 years. Growth in the number of women and blacks in the House has slowed. The number of women House members in the 100th Congress, twenty-three, is only one more than the total for the 98th and 99th Congresses; and the number of black members in the 100th Congress—twenty-two—is only two more than the 98th and 99th. Without membership turnover, the opportunity for further diversification of the House is limited.

## Rules and Procedures

Because the House is a much larger institution than the Senate, it must rely more heavily on formal rules and explicit procedures than on norms. Norms such as reciprocity, courtesy, hard work, expertise, and the most hallowed of all, seniority, exist in the House.[10] But the rules of party caucuses, of committees, and the rules of the House itself are the primary guides to member behavior and the centers of contention in power struggles. In the early to mid-1970s, the period of increased turnover, the rules were subjected to their most extensive restructuring in sixty years, altering the formal power structure of the House in dramatic ways.

## House Reforms

The reform movement of the 1970s really began in the late 1950s with the creation of the Democratic Study Group (DSG), an organization committed to liberal legislation and liberal control of the House.[11] Throughout the 1960s the group pushed for changes in House procedures and party practice. Liberals' efforts in the 1960s to bring about formal changes in House rules resulted in the 1970 Legislative Reorganization Act. That measure, passed by a coalition of House Republicans and liberal Democrats, liberalized and formalized parliamentary procedure in committees and on the floor of the House.

During the late 1960s, just when these formal rules changes were approaching ratification, liberal Democrats developed a new strategy. They shifted their attention to reform of the House Democratic party. In January 1969 the Democratic Caucus, which had been dormant for most of the century, was revitalized by the passage of a rule stating that a caucus meeting could be held each month if fifty members demanded the meeting in writing. Using the party caucus, liberals throughout the early 1970s pushed for the creation of committees to study the House and propose reforms of its structure and procedures.

Three reform committees were formed as a result of Democratic Caucus activity.[12] All were chaired by Julia Butler Hansen, D-Wash., and their proposals became known collectively as the Hansen Committee Reforms. The proposals of Hansen I were debated and passed in January 1971, Hansen II in January 1973, and Hansen III in 1974. Another reform effort initiated by Speaker Carl Albert, D-Okla., was the creation of a Select Committee on Committees headed by Richard Bolling, D-Mo. The Bolling Committee introduced its proposals in 1974, but they were defeated by the House, which chose instead to implement the proposals of Hansen III.[13]

These reform efforts had five particularly important consequences. First, they established a clear procedure for the Democratic Caucus to select committee chairs by secret ballot. This change in the traditional voting procedure provided a way to defeat renominations of incumbent committee chairs and bypass the norm of committee seniority. Second, the reforms increased the number and strength of subcommittees. Third, the House moved to open to the public virtually all committee and subcommittee meetings. Fourth, the reforms increased the power of the Speaker by giving the post considerable control over the referral of legislation. A fifth change, which was not actually part of these caucus reforms but stemmed from the overall reform movement, was the creation in 1974 of a new congressional budget process and a House Budget Committee. But, the defeat of the Bolling Committee provisions restructuring committee jurisdictions left the maze of overlapping committee and subcommittee jurisdictions relatively untouched.

Other reforms of the post-1973 period also were adopted. In the 94th Congress, House Democrats refined the procedure for nominating committee chairs and voted down several incumbents. The caucus also adopted a rule requiring nominees for Appropriations subcommittee chairs to be approved by similar procedures. This rule, which seemed in order because Appropriations subcommittees are in many cases more powerful than other standing committees, was employed in the 95th Congress to deny a subcommittee position to Robert Sikes, D-Fla., who had been reprimanded for financial misconduct.

### The Ethics Issue

The Sikes case, as well as the sex and public payroll scandals involving Wayne Hays, D-Ohio, and the probe of South Korean influence-peddling on Capitol Hill, focused attention on the inadequacy of House ethics provisions. During the 95th Congress the House, following the recommendations of the bipartisan Commission on Administrative Review chaired by David Obey, D-Wis., adopted a new code of ethics. The code required annual financial disclosure by House members, officers, and professional staff; prohibited gifts totaling $100 or more from a lobbyist or a foreign national; prohibited unofficial office accounts; placed new restrictions on the use of the franking privilege; and limited the amount of outside earned income members could receive.

The ethics code is one of the few reforms of the 1970s that placed serious constraints on the new levels of independence House members had reached. Some members threatened to quit because of the limitations on outside income, and in several instances the ethics code contributed to the decision of members to retire. Since passage of the ethics code in 1977, financial misconduct and other wrongdoing have plagued the House. Recent scandals have touched Fernand St Germain, D-R.I.; Bill Boner, D-Tenn.; Mario Biaggi, D-N.Y.; Mary Rose Oakar, D-Ohio; and Charlie Rose, D-N.C.

The charges of wrongdoing are handled by the House Committee on Standards of Official Conduct. Except for headline-making probes, this committee functions largely out of the public eye. Composed of twelve members, it is the only House panel divided evenly between Democrats and Republicans. Critics charge that the House committee and its Senate counterpart, the Senate Select Committee on Ethics, are slow to act on various charges of misconduct, silent or secretive about others, and hesitant to recommend sanctions when they find violations of law in ethics codes. In other words, they too often serve as an ethical shield for members against the outside world rather than as a sword for the institution in ferreting out and ending ethical abuse.

Perhaps the committee's most sensitive action of recent years is the inquiry into Republican allegations against Speaker Jim Wright, D-Texas. These allegations, raised by Newt Gingrich, R-Ga., included charges of conflict of interest in Wright's behalf by two Texas oil companies, misuse of campaign funds and congressional staff, and abuse of political influence when Wright intervened with federal regulators in behalf of Texas savings and loan executives. To investigate these matters the ethics committee voted unanimously to hire an outside counsel, rather than to use someone on the congressional payroll. The investigation into Wright's activities, regarded by many as a Republican effort to deflect attention from the problems of Attorney General Edwin Meese, who resigned in July 1988, cast a cloud not only over the speakership but also over the 1988 Democratic presidential campaign. It highlighted the critical role that concern with ethics has in contemporary American politics.

## Trends in Reform

The changes in House rules and procedures in the 1970s and 1980s evidence two trends: the decentralization of power within committees and the centralization of authority in the party caucus, the Speaker, and a new budget committee. The move toward centralization continued, although in a less extensive fashion, during the 98th Congress. Frustrated by efforts of minority members to stir up controversy and obstruct House business, the Democratic leaders tightened House rules. The most controversial change was a restriction on appropriations bill riders. (Riders are amendments that are extraneous to the subject matter of a bill.) Conservative members often used riders to force roll call votes on controversial issues, such as school busing and abortion, while avoiding normal legislative procedures in such matters. The rules changes also increased the procedural authority of the Democratic leadership to avoid other types of nuisance votes. Other changes included efforts to strengthen limits on the number of subcommittees to which members can be assigned and the decision to elect the Democratic whip.

These various reforms demonstrate the significant changes that have occurred in the House during the postwar years. These formal reforms, however, have not been the only forces shaping the structure of committee politics or party leadership.

## Committees

The reforms of the 1970s sought to decentralize power in committees and to weaken the power of committee chairs. These reforms proved immediately successful and produced a period of subcommittee government and weak committee chairs, starting in the mid-1970s. By the late 1980s, however, a new sort of committee politics was emerging, a centralized committee oligarchy that reversed the decentralization of the 1970s. The rise of this new committee oligarchy resulted from the Reagan presidency, particularly the effect of large deficits and tight spending. In the area of committee politics, as will be shown in the area of party leadership, an environment of scarcity tends to produce centralized leadership, regardless of formal rules and procedures.

### Committee Decentralization

The effort to create committee decentralization grew out of the historic domination of the House by approximately twenty committee chairs. The era of committee government had begun in the 1920s and was characterized by brokerage politics: committee chairs, usually conservative, attempted, through bargaining and compromise, to aggregate the numerous competing policy interests within their committees' jurisdiction.[14] As liberals began to dominate the Democratic party in the House during the 1950s and 1960s, opposition to the existing structure of committee government escalated.

Aside from ideology, the opposition was fueled by other pressures. In particular, the increase in the number and complexity of federal concerns created the need for higher levels of legislative specialization, putting considerable pressure on the existing system and necessitating more meetings and investigations than could be handled by the standing committees. As reformers in the 1950s and 1960s looked for ways to deal with the workload, they strengthened the subcommittees. Their efforts resulted in the reforms of the 1970s, which had two major dimensions: the rise of subcommittee government and the decline of committee chairs.

Subcommittee government means that the basic responsibility for most legislative activity (hearings, debates, legislative mark-ups) occurs, not at a meeting of an entire standing committee, but at a meeting of a smaller subcommittee of the standing committee.[15] The decisions of the subcommittee are viewed as authoritative decisions, which are altered by the standing committee only when the subcommittee is seriously divided or when its decisions are considered unrepresentative of the full committee.

A measure of subcommittee influence is the growth in their number and staff. At the start of the 84th Congress (1955-1956), when the Democrats began their current streak as the majority party in the House, there were 83 standing subcommittees in the House; the 98th Congress had 135. Moreover, the chair and ranking minority members of each subcommittee were entitled to appoint at least one professional staff member. By comparison, in the 86th Congress, the first time the *Congressional Staff Directory* was published, only 57 of the 113 subcommittees had their own staffs.

With the rise of subcommittee government in the 1970s, basic responsibility shifted from approximately 20 standing committees to about 160 committees and subcommittees.[16] In the process, the *power of committee chairs* declined. Formal change in the power of committee chairs came in 1973 when the caucus passed rules that deprived them of their most potent weapon: their invulnerability to removal. The changes in the procedures and traditions surrounding the election of committee chairs, when combined with the other reforms of the early 1970s and the removal of three sitting chairmen in 1975, clearly altered their status and authority. The chairs lost the right to determine the number, size, and majority party membership of subcommittees. They lost the power to appoint subcommittee chairs, to control referral of legislation to subcommittees, or to prevent their committees from meeting. Finally, as a result of the growth of subcommittee activity, many were forced to defer to their subcommittee chairs in the management of legislation on the House floor.

The emergence of subcommittee government, together with the decline of committee chairs, altered considerably the character of House decision making.[17] It brought more members into the policy process, opened the possibility of policy innovation by a wider range of members, and probably increased legislative expertise in the House. But subcommittee government had its cost as well.

Most significantly, subcommittee government created a crisis of interest aggregation. It largely removed committees as arenas in which interests would be compromised, brokered, and mediated; and it led to increased dominance of committee decision making by clientele groups, to narrowly focused policy leadership, and to confusion in policy jurisdictions. These problems were not necessarily unmanageable; strong party leadership, for example, could have mitigated them. But by the early 1980s it was clear that the committee reforms of the 1970s had generated their own set of problems that would eventually need to be rectified.[18] Just as these problems were becoming clear, however, the structure of committee decision making again started to change, not as a result of conscious planning and rules reform by House members, but as a result of contextual change.

## The Rise of a New Committee Oligarchy

Committee decentralization and subcommittee government grew out of the vast expansion of governmental services that occurred in the 1950s and 1960s. An activist government required many specialized working groups to investigate, legislate, and oversee new and expanded programs. This need, together with career ambitions of junior legislators and the desire to break the power of conservative chairs, fueled the committee reforms of the 1970s. Just as subcommittee government was becoming firmly entrenched, the nation elected Ronald Reagan. The president pushed through giant tax cuts without a concomitant reduction in spending, and the country suddenly faced massive federal deficits, which blocked new programs and new spending. Seemingly overnight, the rationale for subcommittee government was gone: without money to spend, there was less need for a highly specialized system of subcommittees.

Instead of the extensive legislative agenda of the past, the House moved to what many members refer to as the "four bill" system.[19] In an average year there may be only four important domestic legislative vehicles—the budget resolution, continuing appropriations, supplemental appropriations, and the reconciliation package of spending cuts that the budget dictates. A fifth bill to raise the federal debt limit is sometimes needed. Members who can influence one of these "must pass" bills are important players in the House; the rest are largely spectators. The result is a new *committee oligarchy* different from committee government earlier in the century. In the earlier system, power was vested in seniority, and the chairs of the standing committees were the oligarchs. In the new system, power is concentrated not in the chairs of all committees, but in the membership of a few elite committees, primarily those dealing with money.

The elite committees certainly include Appropriations. Its power derives from its role in drafting the continuing resolution, the bill that funds all programs for which regular appropriations bills have not passed when the new fiscal year begins October 1. Because so few money bills clear Congress by the deadline, the continuing resolution is essentially a budget. It is all but certain of presidential approval and so massive that there is little chance to question any item placed on it by an Appropriations member. Members of less fortunate committees, even very senior members, must persuade Appropriations members of whatever rank to help them out. In this sense being a junior Appropriations Committee member can be more significant than being a subcommittee chair on an authorization committee.

Ways and Means is also an elite committee in the new oligarchy, partly because of its role in writing tax bills and partly because of its jurisdiction over "must pass" federal debt ceiling legislation—a vehicle for scores of legislative initiatives that might not pass on their own. Ways and Means also plays a significant role in the reconciliation process because of its jurisdiction over hundreds of billions of dollars in spending for health, Social Security, and other social need categories. This jurisdiction gives it leverage in the reconciliation process over reductions in these areas; in making the cuts, it can reshape the programs.

Aside from Appropriations and Ways and Means, several other committees deserve consideration as part of the oligarchy. One is House Energy and Commerce, the one authorization committee that continues to play a strong policy role in the 1980s. Its influence is a testament to its broad jurisdiction, which touches major regulatory agencies, nuclear energy, toxic waste, health research, Medicaid and Medicare, railroad retirement, telecommunications, tourism, and commerce. Another committee that is part of the new oligarchy is Budget, which oversees the preparation of the congressional budget resolutions and the reconciliation process. The power that membership on this committee bestows does not stem from a member's influence over the immediate content of legislation; rather it comes from potential influence on the debate over the nation's long-term policy agenda. The final member of the oligarchy is the Rules Committee, where every major bill must stop before going to the House floor. Its responsibility is to draft ground rules for floor debate on bills, which allows it to block legislation, set the parameters of debate, limit or bar amendments, and, therefore, to affect the ultimate content of legislation.[20]

Another influential committee, although not in the same league as the committee oligarchs, is Armed Services. This committee regulates the debate on the defense budget, which spends more than sixty cents of every discretionary federal dollar. The importance of Armed Services was demonstrated by the recent dispute over the selection of its chair, which included the 1985 removal of Melvin Price, D-Ill., from the chair and the strong challenge in 1987 to Les Aspin, D-Wis., the sitting chair, by Marvin Leath, D-Texas. This contentiousness would seem to reflect not just personal jockeying for power but the importance that members attach to Armed Services—concerns so strong that members were willing to take part in an extensive reconsideration of a sitting chair.[21]

Currently, no such importance attaches to the other authorizing committees. In principle, these committees—the vast number of standing committees that draft legislation to create programs or alter them—should be the heart of the policy process in Congress. Yet, according to a report by House Republicans, these committees "are rapidly approaching irrelevance—squeezed out by the budget and appropriations processes, and caught up in jurisdictional infighting and subcommittee strangulation." [22] The problems associated with committee decentralization and with budget limitations have crippled these committees: there is little discretionary money to fund new programs, and any authorization, particularly liberal ones, faced a Reagan veto threat. In addition, the committees are constrained by jurisdictional conflicts among their subcommittees and with other committees. The new oligarchy, ironically, addresses some of the problems of interest aggregation that arose with committee decentralization, providing fairly centralized consideration of a broad range of policy concerns. But, for the average member, the system is frustrating.

Part of members' frustration comes from the difficulty they find in explaining their powerlessness to their constituents. During the period of committee government most of them could argue that the seniority system and the power of committee chairs made it difficult for them to accomplish their goals. With the demise of committee government, that explanation no longer works. An honest explanation of their powerlessness would "involve parliamentary distinctions and power relationships so complex that few members want to attempt it." [23] Members are hard pressed to make constituents aware of the reality of their committee work and of their political limitations. Perhaps most frustrating is that there is so little members can do about this new committee oligarchy, as it arose not from new rules but from a new fiscal context.

## Consolidating Majority Party Leadership

The rise of a new oligarchy in the House means the consolidation of considerable power in the majority party leadership. Unlike the development of the committee oligarchy, the power of the leadership is grounded solidly in the rules reforms of the 1970s. Ironically, it took fiscal austerity and the Reagan presidency for the majority party leaders to use fully the powers given them by the reforms. While the Reagan revolution undercut the subcommittee reforms, it breathed life into the powers of the Speaker and party leadership. [24]

### The Party Caucus

The reform process of the early 1970s occurred largely through the efforts of the Democratic Caucus, the organization of all House

Democrats. During this period the Democrats expanded the powers of their caucus, particularly its power to approve the selection of committee chairs. Democrats also began to use the caucus to debate policy positions and to nurture personal careers. The activism of the caucus led to cries from some Republicans and conservative Democrats that "King Caucus" was running the House and overriding the wishes of its total membership. These dissidents called for opening meetings of the caucus in the hope that this would cripple its effectiveness.

The eventual opening of the caucus, together with the election of a Democratic president, did reduce its effectiveness in the mid- to late 1970s. The presidency of Jimmy Carter in particular defused the activism of the caucus by providing House Democrats with leadership and a program to support without extensive debate. The party caucus fell into disuse. Reagan's election confronted the Democrats with a Republican president and a conservative legislative program. In response, the caucus decided to meet again in closed session and to reclaim its position as the center of party debate. The caucus was successful enough for one of its chairmen, Richard Gephardt of Missouri, to use this post to launch his 1988 presidential race.

The long-term fate of the caucus is uncertain. So far it appears strong only when the opposite party controls the White House and when debates are held in private. Because of its size, the caucus may not be the best forum for handling strategic problems or making delicate party decisions. The caucus' Steering and Policy Committee may be the best arena for collective party leadership, and the Speaker remains the natural spokesperson for the party.

## The Speaker

Throughout most of the twentieth century, parties in the House have been unwilling to invest power in their party leaders.[25] This reticence stems from early in the century when Speaker "Uncle Joe" Cannon, R-Ill., used the considerable authority of the speakership to dominate the House. The 1910 insurgency against Cannon stripped the speakership of many of its major powers, including control over committee appointments, the Rules Committee, private and minor House business, the Special Calendar, and the party caucus. The rules changes also limited the Speaker's discretionary parliamentary prerogatives. After Cannon's downfall and a short flirtation with party caucus government, the House turned to committee government and reliance on the seniority rule.

Efforts to revitalize the speakership began in the early 1970s when the House majority party, the Democrats, needed strong leadership and a more coherent strategy to thwart the efforts by the Republican president, Richard Nixon, to dismantle the Democratic Great Society. The move toward a stronger speakership took several years, with major reform efforts occurring in 1973 and 1975. These reforms activated the long dormant Steering and Policy Committee, gave it the power of the Committee on Committees (that is, the power to nominate committee members and committee chairs), and made the Speaker its chair, with the authority to select a number of committee members. In addition, the Speaker was also given the power to nominate the chair and Democratic members of the House Rules Committee, thus bringing that committee more clearly into the control of the Speaker and the party. These developments meant that, for the first time in decades, a Democratic Speaker had a direct and significant role in committee nominations and the nominations of committee chairs, with total control of the Rules nominations. Members of the party seeking committee positions or leadership roles had far more reason to listen to and follow the Speaker than in the past because the office, perhaps more than any other, is critical to successful candidacies.[26]

Other reforms likewise strengthened the Speaker. First, increases in the financial and staff resources of the party whip office and in the number of whips appointed by the party leadership resulted in a stronger, more active whip system to assist the leadership in efforts to pass legislation.[27] Second, the Speaker regained some of the ground lost by Cannon concerning control over the referral of bills. Third, the creation of the new budget process provided mechanisms through which a skillful party leadership could control it and coordinate budget making by House committees.

One area in which the reforms of the 1970s did not seem to significantly redress the loss of ground after Cannon was the control of parliamentary procedures on the floor. Recorded votes on amendments and electronic voting (which has cut the time of roll call votes considerably and reduced leadership control over the pace of floor votes) have further reduced the Speaker's power as presiding officer and solidified the procedural protections of the rank and file. The Rules Committee has helped the Speaker gradually to overcome this problem of floor management. The sum of the changes thus constitutes a true resurgence of the speakership and, although a move constrained by the Subcommittee Bill of Rights and other rules changes that protect members' rights within committees and subcommittees, a move back toward the power enjoyed by Cannon.

## The Speakership from O'Neill to Wright

House Democrats adopted these various changes during Carl Albert's tenure, but it was Tip O'Neill who first had access to all of them as Speaker. O'Neill's success in passing a controversial energy program during the early years of the Carter administration suggested to some that an era of strong party leadership had arrived. Their optimism, however, proved premature. In fact, the leadership had to make extensive use of its limited resources to succeed with the energy package, and those resources once depleted were not easily replenished. Subsequent defeats during the Carter years, as in common *situs* picketing legislation, indicated that, even with strong leaders, increased substantive leadership powers, a president of the same party, and a two-to-one majority, the leadership could not overcome the independence of House members.

O'Neill's leadership problems increased substantially once Reagan took office. Although the more active party caucus provided him with a forum in which to seek support, he had a smaller majority to work with and faced a membership dispirited by the Reagan landslide in 1980. A voting alliance of southern Democratic Boll Weevils and House Republicans, who were almost perfectly cohesive, gave the Reagan administration the narrow majorities needed for passage of its budget resolution, reconciliation bill, and three-year tax cut program in 1981. The struggle over the Reagan economic program highlighted once again the limited resources of congressional leaders. O'Neill discovered at every turn that the president was able to outbid him for undecided House members. Only with the growing economic recession and the Democratic victories in the 1982 midterm elections was O'Neill able to fashion a reliable majority in the House.

The two Congresses following the 1982 election saw no landmark Democratic legislation, but O'Neill became a stronger, more effective Speaker. He was able to pack major committees with enough leadership loyalists to ensure predictable votes and to propose leadership budget resolutions that could win wide approval on the House floor. In addition, O'Neill—who had been savaged by Republican TV commercials treating him as the symbolic villain of the big spending Democratic House—was able to turn the tables and become the first media celebrity in the history of the speakership.[28]

Prior to O'Neill, Speakers shunned publicity and devoted their legislative strategy to coalition building within the halls of Congress. Partly because of the Republican commercials as well as televised House hearings and partly because the Republican president and Senate left O'Neill as the only symbol of Democratic power available to the media, he developed a speakership style that relied heavily on access to the media. He held well-attended news conferences, released a steady stream of news from his office, and sparred with the president constantly through television and the newspapers. This approach allowed O'Neill to influence House members not only through an *internal strategy*—buttonholing them in the cloakroom or House corridors for votes—but also through an *external strategy*—attempting to influence public opinion in members' districts as a way of getting their support on the House floor. In this sense O'Neill transformed the Speaker's job and the process of vote-gathering in the House, creating a new leadership politics for his successor, Jim Wright of Texas.

Wright came to the speakership from a background very different from O'Neill's. O'Neill, an Irish-American from Boston, had spent years on the Rules Committee; in the House he was concerned less with legislation than with "talking strategy with close friends over poker, golf, or dinner at a Washington restaurant." [29] Wright was a protégé of the most powerful Speaker of modern times, fellow Texan Sam Rayburn. Wright is a skilled legislator, having served most of his career on the Public Works Committee, and he is a policy activist by temperament. He is the consummate orator, especially when compared with other postwar Speakers. Wright knows legislation, knows how to relate to the media—at least as an orator—and, as Rayburn's protégé, knows how to wield power. If the 1970s prepared the speakership for a more forceful role, and O'Neill prepared it for media politics, Wright should be the person to put the power and media visibility of the Speaker behind a legislative agenda.

As Speaker, Wright acted quickly to establish himself as a hands-on leader who would be a "micromanager" of the legislative process.[30] Within days of his election, he announced an ambitious legislative agenda, including a clean water act, a highway bill, trade legislation, welfare reform, agricultural revitalization, and measures to reduce the federal deficit. The latter included a controversial proposal to consider a delay in scheduled income tax cuts for the wealthiest Americans. With his legislative agenda, Wright was announcing that he intended to use the speakership to be a policy leader in the nation. This approach received widespread support from his Democratic colleagues who had been looking for policy leadership and guidance that would help them overcome the policy inactivism generated by the Reagan deficits. And it came in part because Wright proposed, with the exception of the income tax delay, issues about which there was consensus among Democrats.

Wright also moved to take charge of the leadership machinery of the party, telling members of the Steering and Policy Committee that he wanted to use the panel to develop Democratic policy. Wright also differed from O'Neill in appointing members of Steering and Policy. O'Neill had allowed the freshman class, the Democratic members of the women's caucus, and the Congressional Black Caucus to choose the members from those groups to serve on the committee. Wright ensured that those groups were represented, but he made the choices. Wright has defended the legitimacy of his centralized leadership, arguing that "[t]he House should develop a program of action ... rather than leaving the making of policy to a fragmented group of 21 standing committees, without any cohesion. There has to be a sense of coordinated policy, a cohesive pattern to what the institution does." [31]

These actions put the party and the House on notice that Wright intended to be a strong, activist Speaker, using the office's power to the full to enact a legislative agenda. Subsequent events have borne out this intention. Wright has made aggressive use of the Rules Committee to restrict debate and to speed action on bills he considers top priority. Wright has proven much more concerned than O'Neill with the particulars of legislation, doing his homework so that he can discuss fine points of various bills with the subcommittee chairs who draft them. This close attention, moreover, spans a wide range of issues. Wright gave personal attention to legislation designed to protect Medicare beneficiaries against catastrophic health care costs, personally ensuring that the bill include coverage for prescription drugs. He lobbied the Banking Committee on legislation to bail out the federal agency that insures savings and loan deposits, seeking a bill more favorable to ailing thrift institutions, including those in Texas suffering from the state's oil depression. He has monitored budget resolutions, drawing on his knowledge of the budget process developed during a dozen years on the Budget Committee. Wright stood by his call for higher taxes to cut the deficit, a position that was vindicated when Reagan eventually signed a deficit reduction compromise that included a small tax increase.

Wright also has emerged as a powerful force in foreign policy, particularly on U.S. support for the Nicaraguan contras. Wright was drawn into the controversy in 1987 by the demand from several Central American presidents that the Sandinistas negotiate a cease-fire directly or indirectly with the contras. The Sandinistas wanted to talk with the United States, which sponsors the contras. Wright, who opposes contra aid, backed a policy of allowing the Central Americans to work out their problems among themselves. Although he could not completely control the American response to the Central American crisis, he was able to constrain Reagan's contra policy and to emerge, at least for a while, "as the single most influential U.S. politician on the issue." [32] In the process, Wright, not without criticism, has given the speakership a level of international significance it has previously lacked.

In short, the first two years of the Wright speakership saw the office transformed from consensus builder to agenda setter, from power broker to power wielder, and from congressional and national force into an international presence. The question is whether Wright will be able to sustain this performance. O'Neill's style kept fellow Democrats feeling involved and happy. Wright's efforts to determine and coordinate the legislative agenda, by contrast, rankles committee chairs, particularly Dan Rostenkowski of Illinois, who heads the powerful Ways and Means Committee. Conservative Democrats also strain against the aggressive and more liberal policy agenda Wright is pursuing, feeling that their voices are drowned out on budget, welfare, and other matters. And Republicans are likewise unhappy with Wright, saying that he is less straightforward and honest than O'Neill.

Much of Wright's future success as Speaker depends on the context in which he must work. He came to the office when a leadership void existed in Washington, with Reagan at the weakest point in his administration and Senate Majority Leader Robert Byrd, D-W.Va., still acting as a traditional congressional insider, not a national party spokesman. The House Democrats were frustrated by a budget that deprived them of the opportunity for policy activism. Moreover, public support for an activist government seemed to be growing. The scene was set for an activist Democratic Speaker to provide policy leadership. This is not to deny Wright credit for his accomplishments; rather, it is to point out that circumstances provided an opportunity that he skillfully exploited. It is less clear how effective Wright will be as these circumstances change. In particular, a more involved president might not leave a void for a Speaker to fill.

Even under these circumstances, the speakership will still be important. The various powers given it under Albert, the media visibility it attained under O'Neill, and the heightened policy role asserted by Wright may allow it to flourish. But much will depend on context, much on Wright's skillfulness and his willingness to become a team player, much on the outcome of his ethics investigation, and much on the quality of the support system the Speaker enjoys.

## The Majority Leader and Whip

The two other leadership positions within the majority party— and the Speaker's principal support team—are the majority leader and the whip. The majority leader is the party's point man on the floor of the House, ensuring that the party's daily legislative program flows smoothly while the Speaker presides over House deliberations. The majority leader also joins the Speaker in setting the legislative schedule and serving as party spokesperson. The majority whip is responsible for surveying party members on their policy positions and rounding up votes to pass party legislation.

The selection of Wright as Speaker coincided with the elevation of Tom Foley of Washington to majority leader from whip and the selection of Tony Coelho of California, previously the chair of the Democratic Congressional Campaign Committee (DCCC) as whip. The Wright-Foley-Coelho team is considered effective; Wright and Foley, from an older generation (they were sixty-five and fifty-eight, respectively, when elected to the leadership), have strengths and weaknesses that complement one another. Wright, the feisty, combative legislative partisan is balanced by Foley's cool temperament and more deliberative, inclusive, and noncombative approach.[33] Coelho (forty-four when elected) is a meticulous organizer who speaks for the younger generation in the House.

Coelho is the first whip elected by the party caucus. Previous Democratic whips were appointed, but for some years reformers had argued that the whip is so often a step to higher leadership positions— part of a leadership escalator as Robert Peabody argues—that members of the party felt they should have a say in who was selected for the position.[34] Proponents succeeded in January 1985, enacting the change by a vote of 133 to 36.

Coelho had five serious rivals for the post. The liveliness of the contest indicates not only that members see the whip position as a route to the speakership but also that House leadership races have become marathons, with steering committees, campaign managers, and well-funded political action committees (PACs). This modern whip system is larger than that of the earlier twentieth century. The office Coelho heads is a large intelligence-gathering operation, a four-tier system that includes a chief deputy whip, seven deputy whips, more than thirty at-large whips, and more than twenty assistant whips. The expansion reflects both the growing independence of House members and the pressure on House Democrats to find a vote-gathering device that could offset the early successes of the Reagan administration.

The legislative victories of Wright's first term as Speaker are due in part to the effective use of the whip's vote-gathering operation and in part to his listening to the information conveyed by the whip operatives. Yet to be seen is how effectively the expanded whip operation would mesh with the vote-gathering operation of the liaison team for a Democratic president—or how effectively members would cooperate with the whip system without the pressure of a conservative Republican president in the White House.

## Steering and Policy Committee

Another part of the Democratic leadership is the Steering and Policy Committee, a small "executive" committee composed of the

Speaker's appointees and members selected by regional caucuses. Ideally, the committee would be a representative body that provides an opportunity for healthy debate and innovative direction on matters of public policy, gives guidance to committees and subcommittees, and spurs the party leadership to an articulate, persuasive policy role that reflects the dominant sentiment of the party. Since its reactivation in 1973, the committee only occasionally has shown that it can perform such functions. More recently the primary role of the committee has been to make nominations to the standing committees. Wright's decision to name his own staff to the committee and to bring to it a greater policy focus may motivate it.

For the leadership to make the Steering and Policy Committee a more useful instrument and move the House closer to party government it must clean up the jurisdictional nightmare among House committees and subcommittees. The current structure of committees and sub-committees invites jurisdictional disputes from those who see their influence threatened and from those who realize that such disputes can be used to delay and defeat legislation. Such disputes led House Democrats in the 97th Congress to include on the Steering and Policy Committee the chairs of the Budget, Appropriations, Ways and Means, and Rules committees. The presence of these chairs may foster better coordination, but jurisdictional disputes are not likely to end without reform of the committee system. Not until the problem of overlapping committee jurisdictions is thoroughly addressed and resolved will the House leadership and the Steering and Policy Committee, no matter how skilled and well organized, be able to provide the institution with clear policy direction.

## The Future of Majority Party Leadership

Given their relative youth, the Wright-Foley-Coelho team could remain in office through the 1990s, perhaps even well into the twenty-first century, if the Democrats maintain control of the House. A challenge to one or another of them is not out of the question; rumors are already circulating that Coelho might someday challenge Foley. The most likely prospect, however, is for a long reign for these three westerners. The direction their leadership takes depends heavily on context.

Several contextual factors deserve attention when looking forward. The first is party control of Congress and the presidency —a double-edged sword for Jim Wright. Periods of Democratic control would give him the chance to enact a far more progressive body of legislation than otherwise, but would reduce his singular visibility on the national and international scene. Republican control of the Senate, the presidency, or both would give him a greater opportunity to play national party leader, but with less chance for solid legislative achievements.

A second concern is the size of the Democratic majority and the fear that Republicans may yet break the Democratic hold on the House. We find the latter unlikely in the near future, but fluctuation in majority party size, particularly with a weak Democratic or strong Republican national ticket, is a real possibility, one that should encourage the present Democratic leadership team to pay close attention to the DCCC and to congressional campaign politics. Wright and his team must realize that their exercise of power requires not only skill on the floor of the House and national and international visibility but also the electoral success of House Democrats.

A third factor is the cohesiveness of House Democrats. A great deal of frustration exists within today's party because most members have little policy-making power—not because of seniority or other formal arrangements of power, but because the national deficit leaves so little money for new or expanded programs, leaving power concentrated in the few committees that have important annual work. Wright's efforts to centralize power in his own hands and pursue a national policy agenda are in some ways acceptable to members because, in doing so, he is at least generating some significant legislation for them to consider in committee. But members are unlikely to accept Wright's dominance of the policy agenda indefinitely, and he will need to be sensitive to their concerns if he is to maintain party harmony and voting cohesiveness.

Fourth is the distribution of power among power brokers in the House. Wright's independence means that Foley and Coelho are not always consulted, a situation that could lead to dissension, although little has come to light. What has surfaced is criticism from committee chairs, particularly Rostenkowski, that Wright fails to consult the chairs or acknowledge their power. Wright has brought some committee chairs, such as Energy and Commerce chairman John Dingell of Michigan, into his inner circle. Rostenkowski has urged Wright to set up a "chairman's council," which would provide the leadership with advice from the people responsible for putting legislation together.[35] His proposal foreshadows the kind of pressure Wright may face.

The fifth factor is the fiscal and political climate. The austerity of the 1980s—and the consequent need for centralized leadership for House Democrats to find a national policy agenda—helped thrust the speakership into the national limelight. But the financial picture could improve; the growth of Social Security funds could loosen the spending constraints that currently exist in Washington. Recession or depression could increase demand for spending regardless of the national debt.

These and other developments could alter the majority party leadership in ways that are difficult to foresee, and that are probably only loosely related to the formal rules and procedures.

The point is that the future for Speaker Wright and the Democratic leadership is contingent on not only the skills and goals of the leadership but also electoral politics and organizational dynamics within the House and on the fiscal and political environment of the nation at large. Wright, Foley, and Coelho will need to be flexible and responsive as well as assertive and innovative.

## Conclusion

Since the early 1970s the House of Representatives has proven to be a remarkably fluid institution. Buoyed by an infusion of younger legislators dedicated to reform, the House overthrew a system of committee government that had dominated it for most of a century. In its place the members instituted a highly dispersed system of power in which subcommittees, assisted by the party leadership, were the emerging force. But in the 1980s, in response to the nation's altered fiscal and political environment, the role of subcommittees declined, and power became concentrated in a small number of committee oligarchs—particularly the money committees—and in a more assertive party leadership. By the late 1980s a number of senior, experienced legislators, many of whom had worked to pass the reforms of the 1970s, found little opportunity for political activism. As the 100th Congress drew to a close, power within the House was consolidated in a more centralized and concentrated manner than at any time since the days of Joseph Cannon.

Will the system of consolidated power last? The return to low membership turnover would suggest that the days of committee and party oligarchs are numbered: the increase in House careerists—all of whom want to exercise real policy-making power within their subcommittees and committees—should produce many frustrated legislators trying to reclaim their policy-making prerogatives. Pressure toward power dispersion is building up in the House, with the backing of House rules and procedures.

The power structure of the House, however, is not determined solely by its rules and procedures, the career interests of its members, or turnover patterns. The fiscal condition of the federal government, united versus divided party control of government, the character of the nation's policy agenda—these and related factors also determine the power arrangements within Congress. These factors are exceedingly difficult to predict. No one in the early to mid-1970s anticipated the Reagan tax cuts or massive federal deficits, but these developments probably had as much influence on power distribution in the 1980s as the new House organizational rules.

In the face of political and fiscal uncertainties, we can only suggest some alternative scenarios for the House. We expect the system of concentrated power to persist under conditions of continued fiscal scarcity and divided government. Even then, however, low turnover and high careerism could generate growing pressure for power distribution. Should fiscal pressures ease during a period of united government— and perhaps even in a period of divided government—the House could turn back toward subcommittee government and a significant but somewhat less powerful party leadership. United government and continued fiscal austerity—with the Democrats in power in the White House and Congress but with little new money to spend—would create an interesting new dilemma. Such a development would probably undercut the national visibility of the House party leadership, with a Democratic president replacing the Speaker as the party's visible policy agenda setter; it could also give renewed stimulus to subcommittee policy makers anxious to pursue a Democratic policy agenda. Yet, an aggressive Democratic party, constrained by deficits but committed to social spending, also might continue to work through the money committees to find the fiscal strategies to implement its domestic agenda, thereby continuing a degree of oligarchic control in the House.

Each of these scenarios is plausible, suggesting that the power arrangements of the modern House are subject to some very wide swings. Over the past decade, we have seen one of the most decentralized Houses of the twentieth century evolve into perhaps the most centralized power arrangement of the past seventy years. It seems possible that this centralized House might, before the next century, revert to a highly decentralized institution.

In sum, power in the House has been consolidated in a far more concentrated manner than would have seemed possible a decade ago, but there is no concomitant sense that power arrangements have become institutionalized—that a new governing system analogous to committee government has solidified. The failure of the contemporary House to develop an institutionalized power arrangement is an issue of considerable importance, one that students of Congress need to examine closely in the future.

# Notes

1. Charles S. Bullock III, "House Careerists: Changing Patterns of Longevity and Attrition," *American Political Science Review* 66 (1972): 1295-

1305. Bullock's operational definition of a House careerist is a member elected to ten or more terms.
2. Norman Ornstein, Thomas Mann, and Michael Malbin, *Vital Statistics on Congress, 1987-1988* (Washington, D.C.: Congressional Quarterly, 1987), 17-18.
3. For an analysis of retirements, see Joseph Cooper and William West, "The Congressional Career in the 1970s," in *Congress Reconsidered,* 2d ed., ed. Lawrence C. Dodd and Bruce I. Oppenheimer (Washington, D.C.: CQ Press, 1981).
4. Ornstein, Mann, and Malbin, *Vital Statistics,* 56.
5. Bruce I. Oppenheimer, James A. Stimson, and Richard W. Waterman, "Interpreting U.S. Congressional Elections: The Exposure Thesis," *Legislative Studies Quarterly* 11 (May 1986): 227-248.
6. Bruce I. Oppenheimer, "Split Party Control of Congress, 1981-1986: Exploring Electoral and Apportionment Explanations," unpublished manuscript.
7. See, for example, Lawrence C. Dodd and Bruce I. Oppenheimer, "The House in Transition," in *Congress Reconsidered,* 3d ed., ed. Lawrence C. Dodd and Bruce I. Oppenheimer (Washington, D.C.: CQ Press, 1985), 37-38.
8. *Congressional Quarterly Weekly Report,* Jan. 16, 1988, 110; and Ornstein, Mann, and Malbin, *Vital Statistics,* 210.
9. *Congressional Quarterly Weekly Report,* Jan. 16, 1988, 104-106.
10. See Herbert Asher, "The Learning of Legislative Norms," *American Political Science Review* 67 (1973): 499-513.
11. See Mark F. Feber, "The Formation of the Democratic Study Group," in *Congressional Behavior,* ed. Nelson W. Polsby (New York: Random House, 1971), 249-267; and Arthur G. Stevens, Jr., Arthur H. Miller, and Thomas E. Mann, "Mobilization of Liberal Strength in the House, 1955-1970: The Democratic Study Group," *American Political Science Review* 68 (1974): 667-681. For a discussion of the reform efforts in the House and the initial role of the DSG, see Norman J. Ornstein and David W. Rohde, "Congressional Reform and Political Parties in the U.S. House of Representatives," in *Parties and Elections in an Anti-Party Age,* ed. Jeff Fishel (Bloomington: Indiana University Press, 1976).
12. For a more extensive chronological discussion of the reform processes, see *Congress Reconsidered,* 1st ed., ed. Lawrence C. Dodd and Bruce I. Oppenheimer (New York: Praeger Publishers, 1977), 27-32; see also Norman J. Ornstein and David W. Rohde, "Congressional Reform and Political Parties in the U.S. House of Representatives," in *Congress Reconsidered,* 1st ed.; and Leroy N. Rieselbach, *Congressional Reform in the Seventies* (Morristown, N.J.: General Learning Press, 1977).
13. For an excellent discussion of the Bolling Committee, see Roger H. Davidson, "Two Avenues of Change: House and Senate Committee Reorganization," in *Congress Reconsidered,* 2d ed.; and Roger H. Davidson and Walter J. Oleszek, *Congress Against Itself* (Bloomington: Indiana University Press, 1977).

14. See George R. Brown, *The Leadership of Congress* (Indianapolis: Bobbs-Merrill Co., 1922); Richard Bolling, *Power in the House* (New York: Capricorn, 1968); Richard F. Fenno, *Congressmen in Committees* (Boston: Little, Brown, 1973); and the essays by Ralph Huitt in *Congress: Two Decades of Analysis,* ed. Ralph K. Huitt and Robert L. Peabody (New York: Harper and Row, 1965).

15. On the growing importance of subcommittees, see Steven S. Smith and Christopher J. Deering, *Committees in Congress* (Washington, D.C.: CQ Press, 1984), 194-198.

16. David W. Rohde, "Committee Reform in the House of Representatives and the Subcommittee Bill of Rights," *The Annals* 411 (January 1974): 39-47; Norman J. Ornstein, "Causes and Consequences of Congressional Change: Subcommittee Reforms in the House of Representatives, 1970-1973," in *Congress in Change,* ed. Norman J. Ornstein (New York: Praeger Publishers, 1975), 88-114; and Lawrence C. Dodd and George C. Shipley, "Patterns of Committee Surveillance in the House of Representatives" (Paper delivered at the annual meeting of the American Political Science Association, San Francisco, Sept. 2-5, 1975).

17. For case studies that demonstrate the legislative impact of committee change, see Norman J. Ornstein and David W. Rohde, "Shifting Forces, Changing Rules, and Political Outcomes: The Impact of Congressional Change on Four House Committees," in *New Perspectives on the House of Representatives,* ed. Robert L. Peabody and Nelson W. Polsby (Chicago: Rand McNally, 1977). For a discussion of the impact of committee change on legislative oversight, see Lawrence C. Dodd and Richard L. Schott, *Congress and the Administrative State* (New York: John Wiley & Sons, 1979).

18. For a more extensive discussion, see Dodd and Oppenheimer, "The House in Transition."

19. *Congressional Quarterly Weekly Report,* Sept. 13, 1986, 2136.

20. Ibid., Aug. 24, 1985, 672; Jan. 3, 1987, 22.

21. Ibid., Jan. 17, 1987, 103; Jan. 24, 1987, 139; Jan. 10, 1987, 83; Jan. 12, 1986, 1564.

22. Ibid., Jan. 3, 1987, 23.

23. Ibid., Sept. 13, 1986, 2136. For the impact of explanation in district politics, see Richard F. Fenno, Jr., *Home Style* (Boston: Little, Brown, 1978).

24. For a discussion of different leadership strategies in the postreform era, see Barbara Sinclair, "Party Leadership and Policy Change" in *Congress and Policy Change,* ed. Gerald C. Wright, Jr., Leroy N. Rieselbach and Lawrence C. Dodd (New York: Agathon Press, 1986).

25. See Joseph Cooper and David W. Brady, "Institutional Context and Leadership Style: The House from Cannon to Rayburn, *American Political Science Review* 75 (1981): 411-425.

26. On the Rules Committee in earlier eras, see James A. Robinson, *The House Rules Committee* (Indianapolis: Bobbs-Merrill, 1963); on the new Rules Committee, see Bruce I. Oppenheimer, "The Rules Committee:

New Arm of Leadership in a Decentralized House," *Congress Reconsid-ered*, 1st ed., 96-116.
27. On the whip system in an earlier era, see Randall B. Ripley, "The Party Whip Organizations in the U.S. House of Representatives," in *New Perspectives on the House of Representatives*, ed. Robert L. Peabody and Nelson W. Polsby (Chicago: Rand McNally, 1969); on the expanded whip system, see Lawrence C. Dodd, "The Expanding Roles of the House Democratic Whip System," *Congressional Studies* 6 (Winter 1979); and Barbara D. Sinclair, *Majority Leadership in the U.S. House of Representatives* (Baltimore: Johns Hopkins University Press, 1983).
28. *Congressional Quarterly Weekly Report*, Sept. 13, 1986, 2131.
29. Ibid., June 22, 1985, 1247.
30. Ibid., Dec. 13, 1986, 3067, 3070.
31. Ibid., July 11, 1987, 1487.
32. Ibid., March 12, 1988, 623.
33. Ibid., March 8, 1986, 551.
34. Robert L. Peabody, *Leadership in Congress* (Boston: Little, Brown, 1976).
35. *Congressional Quarterly Weekly Report*, July 11, 1987, 1427.

# 3. POLITICAL AMATEURISM IN THE UNITED STATES CONGRESS

## David T. Canon

The U.S. Congress is typically seen as an institution filled with career politicians who have been seasoned by experience in lower levels of political office. This view applies especially to the Senate. Certainly the 1986 Senate class is one of the most experienced ever elected.[1] In the House of Representatives, a growing proportion of new members— almost half since 1978—have served apprenticeships in state legislatures.

But, there is another side to the story. Most voters are familiar with celebrities who were elected to Congress without having served in lower office, including Representative Jack F. Kemp, R-N.Y., a former NFL quarterback; Senator John H. Glenn, D-Ohio, a former astronaut; and Senator Bill Bradley, D-N.J., who, after ten years in the Senate, is still trying to shake the prefix "former N.Y. Knicks great" from his name. In 1986 the House added several other notables: NBA player Tom McMillen, D-Md.; major league pitcher Jim Bunning, R-Ky.; Fred Grandy, R-Iowa, known for his role as "Gopher" on the television series "Love Boat"; and Joseph Kennedy, D-Mass.

The presence of amateurism in Congress, defined here as the lack of prior political experience, is more widespread than is suggested by these celebrities.[2] A prominent political journalist noted of the 98th Congress that 24 of the 100 incumbent United States senators were serving in their first elective office.[3] Political amateurism is even more common in the House, with an average of one-fourth of the members having no previous public office experience and in some years more than 50 percent with no elective experience.

This essay explores why the presence of amateurs is significant. First, some normative and theoretical questions concerning the place of

This research was supported by research fellowships from the University of Minnesota Graduate School and the Brookings Institution. I also would like to thank John Aldrich, Thomas Weko, and William T. Bianco for their helpful comments.

the amateur in the political system will be discussed. How have career paths changed? What are the implications of the presence of amateurs for understanding career structures and ambition theory? Finally, the essay discusses how amateurs get to office and how their presence affects the operation of the House and Senate.

## Amateurism in Politics: A Liability?

The term *amateur* has pejorative connotations. The *American Heritage Dictionary* defines an amateur as "a person who engages in any art, science, study, or athletic activity as a pastime rather than as a profession . . . one lacking in professional skill." The first part of the definition is not relevant here. Although politics was not the amateur's primary career, politics can no longer be a pastime, once the amateur is elected to Congress. The definition's second part is significant: the amateurs' untested political skills affect their chances of winning office and may influence their effectiveness in Congress.

Three aspects of amateurs' backgrounds hurt their chances of gaining office: the absence of prior campaign experience,[4] low name recognition (celebrities are the exception), and a general preference among voters for candidates who have prior experience.[5] These obstacles are not insurmountable. The successful campaigns of Senator Rudy Boschwitz, R-Minn., Senator Frank Lautenberg, D-N.J., and former representative Ed Zschau, R-Calif., among many others, indicate that large expenditures on consultants, staff, and advertising enable amateurs to overcome initial deficits. The impact of the last point—voters' preferences for experience—can also be overstated. The career structure in the United States is relatively open. Compared to nations with stronger party systems, the United States requires little in the way of party or office apprenticeship even for the highest offices.[6] Furthermore, all voters do not automatically prefer experience. The suspicions held by many Americans of career politicians and the longstanding tradition of "running against Washington" can be exploited by amateurs who can credibly claim that they are not "one of them."[7]

Although an amateur's deficiencies in electoral politics can be overcome with money and effective campaign strategy, nonpolitical backgrounds may be more of a liability in Congress. Robert Dahl says, "To suppose that one can run a complex political system without first learning the trade is, as Plato pointed out, as silly as to suppose that one can be a doctor or a carpenter without prior training."[8] After noting the wave of celebrities who entered politics from 1975 to 1985, Kevin Phillips concludes, "The sooner we spurn celebrity and revert to expertise, the better."[9] Others do not share this concern. Richard

Fenno speaks favorably of a "citizen-legislator" who, in the early 1970s, became interested in politics because of the Vietnam War. Once in Congress, he brought substantial skill and energy to bear on the issues that concerned him.[10]

Amateurism is not always a liability, but questions about the desirability of amateurs in Congress are not easily answered. Evaluating the effectiveness of amateurs is not the central aim of this essay; rather, the goal is to outline the distinctive nature of amateurs' careers and their theoretical significance.

## The Political Career Structure

To understand the place of the amateur in the political system one must begin with the career structure.[11] In its most basic sense, a career structure is the loose hierarchy of offices that begins with the least desirable and more numerous local offices and builds to the more attractive, less numerous federal offices. It is typically thought that the officeholders begin their careers at the base of the pyramid and that the lateral entry of amateurs high into the career structure is an anomaly. Further, it is usually assumed that career structures are stable. Neither assumption is consistent with the evidence presented here.

### Amateurs and the Career Structure

In a stable political system with strong parties, access to higher office can be limited mostly to those with prior experience. Hugh Bone wrote:

> It becomes essential in most communities for the citizen to be an active party member, a ward or district leader, or a committee member. From here the individual may work up through the ranks to obtain a nomination for a lesser local office, the state legislature, and so on possibly to Congress.[12]

The career structure described here, from the 1940s, would leave little room for amateurs in Congress. In reality, career paths in the United States have never been that rigid, even when parties exerted more control over nominations. Harold Lasswell makes a more realistic observation: "In American politics the escalator to the top is not a regimented, orderly lift, but a tangle of ladders, ropes, and runways that attract people from other activities at various stages of the process, and lead others to a dead end or a drop." [13]

Joseph Schlesinger was the first to give some order to the "tangle" of political careers and define the paths to higher office. Although there is regional variation in the paths by which politicians reach office, ambitious politicians recognize the local pattern of advancement, which generally involves some service in lower office. Individual ambitions fostered by the values derived from each office created a system of electoral advancement that encourages political experience for high office.[14]

Amateurs who were able to bypass the career ladder were seen as exceptions. In the period Schlesinger examines (1914-1958), only 8 percent of those elected to the Senate had no previous political experience. Amateurs became senators at approximately the same rate in the 1960s and early 1970s, but from 1972 to 1982 almost a third of the newly elected senators had no previous elective experience and 14 percent had no public experience at all. As can be seen in Figure 3-1, this trend was reversed in 1984 and 1986.

The proportion of amateurs in the House is considerably higher, but here the patterns are different. There was a consistent decrease in the proportion of amateurs elected to the House from 1966 to 1978 and a dramatic increase in 1980. Since then the proportion of amateurs has remained at slightly higher levels. Similar patterns are evident if only elective experience is considered (see Figure 3-2).

Perhaps more significant than the number of amateurs in recent years is the dramatically changed nature of their candidacies. In 1966 Schlesinger wrote:

> Men without office experience and lesser officials can win the office of senator and win early, *not because they have become conspicuous in the public eye* but because they have a close association with the party organization or the organized elements capable of helping them to office.[15]

He concludes that the "office of governor is by far the more likely outlet for those whom the French call 'notables,' the Senate the more likely outlet for the career politician." [16]

Clearly this distinction no longer exists. Amateurs elected to the Senate often run independent of party support and primarily on the basis of their conspicuousness. Celebrity candidates have name recognition that rivals that of their incumbent opponents, which contributes to their ability to run effective, well-financed campaigns. In Schlesinger's time, candidates were not required to be conspicuous because state party organizations were more able to secure the nomination for selected candidates. Schlesinger's argument concerned only the Senate, but many changes in the electoral system also affect the types of candidates who run for the House. Today's amateur congressional candidates use their celebrity status, business contacts, or personal wealth to acquire needed electoral resources through channels that are independent from party organizations.[17]

The absence of amateurs elected to the Senate in 1984 and 1986 may signal a backlash against inexperience in the "world's greatest legislative body." Several of the Republican amateurs elected in 1980 were defeated by experienced challengers in 1986. Other Republican amateurs conducted aggressive campaigns in 1984, but were defeated. Businessman Raymond Shamie spent $2.3 million in a decisive loss to Senator Edward M. Kennedy, D-Mass., astronaut Jack Lousma narrowly lost to Senator Carl Levin, D-Mich., and businessman John Raese barely lost to Senator John D. Rockefeller, D-W.Va., despite being outspent ten to one by Rockefeller's $12 million. In 1986 the Republican Senate primary in California saw a strong race from television commentator Bruce Herschenson and weak showing from economist Arthur Laffer; baseball commissioner Peter V. Ueberroth was rumored to be a serious candidate before the election. It remains to be seen whether the trend away from amateur candidacies in Senate elections will continue.

## The Dynamics of Career Structures

The previous section noted some changes in the career paths to the Senate and House: more amateurs were elected to the Senate in the late 1970s and early 1980s than before, and more representatives had prior elective experience. Yet, in the *aggregate,* stability stands out more than change. Throughout the period only about a quarter of all representatives and somewhat less than 10 percent of all senators had no public experience prior to their election. This is consistent with Schlesinger's observation that opportunity structures may change but shifts are slow and predictable. He said, "One might argue that the structure of political opportunities is one of the aspects of American life most resistant to change." [18]

The controlling words are "in the aggregate." When differences between parties are examined, significant patterns appear. During periods of increased political opportunity, such as the early 1930s for Democrats and 1980 for Republicans, more amateurs are elected to office and the overall levels of experience drop. In the realigning elections of 1930 to 1936 when the Democratic party became the nationally dominant party, 123 amateur Democrats were elected to the House compared with 30 Republicans for the same period (32.7 percent and 27.5 percent of the new members for each party in this period, respectively). Newly elected Democrats averaged 5.2 years of prior political experience from 1930 to 1936 while Republicans averaged 9.7 years. In 1934 more than a third of the Democrats elected were amateurs, and more than three-fourths had not previously held major elective office (compared with 15.2 percent and 48.5 percent,

Figure 3-1 Percentage of Incoming Senators Without Political Experience, 1913-1986

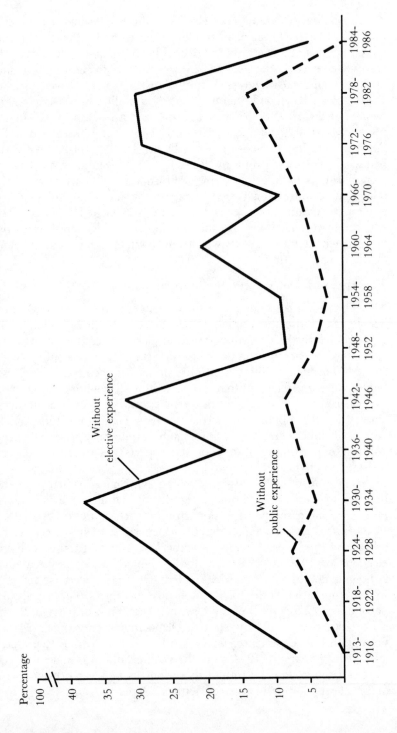

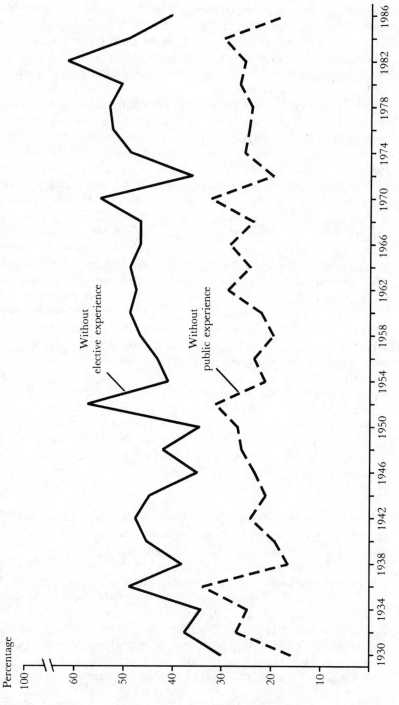

Figure 3-2    Percentage of Incoming House Members Without Political Experience, 1930-1986

Percentage

100

60

50

40

30

20

10

Without
elective experience

Without
public experience

1930    1934    1938    1942    1946    1950    1954    1958    1962    1966    1970    1974    1978    1982    1986

respectively, for the Republicans). The differences are even more dramatic when one controls for the South.[19] In 1938, when party fortunes turned and Republicans recouped some of their losses of the previous four elections, career patterns shifted as well; 29.3 percent of the Republicans elected that year were amateurs compared with only 15.3 percent of the Democrats.

This pattern is most dramatic in realigning years, but it holds in most high-opportunity elections. In fourteen of the seventeen elections from 1930 to 1984 in which one party won twice as many new seats as the other, the winning party had more newly elected amateurs. In 1980, when Republican congressional candidates enjoyed Ronald Reagan's landslide victory, 38.9 percent of them were amateurs, while less than a fourth of the Democrats were completely inexperienced.

In the Senate the patterns are similar. In 1932 and 1934 Democrats elected thirty senators while Republicans managed to win only one seat (four Democrats and one Republican also were appointed in this period). Eleven of the thirty had no prior elective experience (35.5 percent) and three had no public experience (10 percent). The comparable figures for Democrats elected in all other elections from 1913 to 1986 are 16.1 percent and 3.2 percent. High-opportunity years for Republicans reveal similar patterns. In 1946, when an unprecedented twenty Republicans gained seats, more than a third had no elective experience and three were complete amateurs, with no public experience. In 1980, when Republicans won control of the Senate by seating sixteen new members, Jeremiah Denton of Alabama, Frank H. Murkowski of Alaska, Mack Mattingly of Georgia, and John P. East of North Carolina all took office with no previous elective experience. In addition, Paula Hawkins of Florida, Alfonse M. D'Amato of New York, and Don Nickles of Oklahoma had less experience than is typical for Senate candidates.

## Explaining Change

Shifting career structures are caused by a change in the nature of opportunities facing politicians and potential candidates, which in turn are triggered by many factors. Opportunities are altered by the changing desirability of an office, changes in the rules of the game, the role played by parties, and the identification of a candidate with a new political agenda.[20] Although the first two factors are important in explaining changes in the career structure, neither can account for the disproportionate election of amateurs in periods of high electoral opportunity.[21] The role of parties and the importance of a new political agenda are more promising avenues for exploration.

Two aspects of the role played by political parties are central to an explanation of change: (1) the strength of the political party and (2) the control that parties have over nominations. Changes in a party's success at the polls is the surest way to alter the nature of political opportunity. Deviations in the partisan balance of power can be regional or national, and they can be gradual or sudden. The growing Republican strength in the South has created a new source of opportunity for amateurs because there are virtually no Republican politicians in many districts and states.[22] For example, Denton, who had never held public office, won as a Republican in Alabama, a strongly Democratic state. Opportunities open more suddenly along regional lines during partisan realignments, as already noted for the 1930s.

A more general understanding of how the changing strength of the parties can influence career paths can be seen in a supply and demand theory of careers that points to a depleted supply of political talent that cannot meet the electoral demands of the new majority party. The Democrats in the 1930s had not elected great numbers of candidates to any level of political office for more than thirty years; the same was true for the Republicans in the South in the first half of the twentieth century. When new opportunities opened up, amateurs were better able to compete than in normal political times.

The degree of control exercised by parties over nominations explains part of the shift in career paths to the Senate.[23] As discussed above, the changing electoral environment has created an independent base for the amateur candidate. Previously, elective office was the best way to achieve name recognition and to gain the support of the party organization, which was critical to success during the 1950s and 1960s. With the advent of sophisticated voter targeting and massive media campaigns, party support is no longer as important. Although this explanation has some validity for the late 1970s and early 1980s, it is not sufficient because it does not explain surges of amateurism in the House, nor for the Senate in other periods.

A final factor complements the supply and demand theory of candidate emergence. Periods of electoral upheaval often are accompanied by significant and rapid policy change. The young "new breed" of candidate in the emerging majority party often replaces the prior requirements of political experience with the simple qualification of being identified with the new trend, such as "I am an FDR man." The same phenomenon can be observed more recently, on a smaller scale, in the Republican party. In 1980 many amateurs were elected and then reelected by identifying themselves as part of the "Reagan team." They brought with them a new brand of politics, critical of the "old guard," which is willing to compromise with the Democrats. Increasingly frustrated with their party's seemingly permanent minority status in the House, the "Young Turks" advocate confrontation. By establishing themselves as a new type of politician (anti-Washington or even antipolitics), they make a virtue of their inexperience.

## Getting to Office

Little is known about the behavior of amateurs in the electoral environment. Are they pushed out of the electoral arena when experienced candidates choose to run? Are they recruited only for hopeless races, as Linda Fowler suggests? [24] Must ambitious amateurs challenge experienced candidates, who are preferred by the party in primaries, as in many Senate elections? Are amateurs as successful as experienced candidates in their attempts to gain office in similar electoral contexts? Answering these questions would provide a preliminary understanding of the differences between amateurs and experienced candidates in the electoral arena.

Predicting the career advancement of experienced politicians is a more certain enterprise than explaining the career decisions of amateurs. Current officeholders already have given some indication of their political ambitions and risk-taking propensities. They are sensitive to the opportunities facing them because of the central goal of perpetuating their political careers. Consequently, experienced politicians run for higher office when the chances for success are good.[25] Political neophytes have no such obvious set of incentives and patterns of observable behavior. They do not have as much at stake and therefore do not have to be as strategic in their thinking.

While this pattern is generally true, two puzzles must be considered. First, as demonstrated in the previous section, *more* amateurs are elected to office in periods of high electoral opportunity— a finding that is exactly the opposite of expectations derived from the strategic politicians hypothesis and current ambition theory. If experienced politicians seek higher office when their chances for success are favorable, one would expect more of them among the Democrats elected in the 1930s and the Republicans in 1980 rather than fewer. I suggest that office-seeking behavior must be examined in two distinct periods: when career structures are changing and when they are stable. When career structures change, the reason why a particular type of candidate is successful can be explained by the national partisan balance, the relationship of the "new breed" of politician to the changing issue agenda, and the shifting demand and supply of experienced candidates. In "normal" periods, when career structures are stable, district-level forces and economic conditions dominate.

The second puzzle involves the contradiction between the assumption that amateurs are pushed out of the electoral arena and the reality that many are elected to Congress. It is not likely that all amateurs are elected from the residual base, that is, only when experienced challengers choose not to run. Resolving this paradox is crucial in understanding how amateurs are elected to Congress. After examining and largely confirming the "push out" hypothesis, I will attempt to explain the exceptions.

## Pushing Out the Amateurs

The assumption that amateurs are pushed out of the electoral arena was stated by Robert Dahl in the context of races for governorships: "The pattern varies somewhat with region, time, and party system, but it is there; and the intrepid amateur without experience in public life . . . will probably fall flat on his face, as he deserves." [26] That amateurs are disadvantaged in the opportunity structure can be stated in two hypotheses: (1) when experienced candidates choose to run, amateurs generally will not enter the race, or they will drop out; and (2) when experienced candidates choose to run and an amateur contests the primary, the experienced candidate usually will win.

These two hypotheses can be thought of as "passive" and "active" removal of amateurs from the electoral process. The implication of these hypotheses, if they hold true, is that amateurs have a tough row to hoe in the path to Congress. They rarely have an uncontested path to the general election, especially in open seat races or other contests with a high probability of success. Experienced candidates get first choice, and the amateurs are given the leftovers or are faced with the alternative of challenging a strong candidate in the primary.

The results of this process are clear, but the mechanics are difficult to pin down. The "pushing-out" process derives from a combination of voter preference and the expectations of amateurs and experienced politicians. In other words, voters must generally prefer experienced candidates to amateurs, causing the active removal, and the resultant expectations of amateur candidates produce passive exclusion as they become reluctant to challenge experienced candidates. The hypothesis can be tested in three types of races: open seat primaries, opposition-party primaries to run against an incumbent in the general election, and challenges to an incumbent within a party's primary for both the House and the Senate.

**House Races.**   The confirming evidence for the House is strong in all three types of races (the data for the House and Senate races cover all elections from 1972 to 1984). In more than 91 percent of the races of the first type, amateurs were pushed out of the process (37.1 percent active and 54.3 percent passive pushing out). In open seat races amateurs were slightly more successful with 85.8 percent being pushed out when experienced candidates chose to run. These figures can be derived from the data in Table 3-1 by dividing the number of times an amateur defeated an experienced candidate by the sum of all the other races in which an experienced candidate ran.

Another type of race displayed in Table 3-1 suggests a reverse pushing out—when amateurs do not face experienced candidates. This situation occurred in almost three-fourths of the opposing party primaries and in 59 percent of the open seat primaries. That amateurs scare off experienced candidates is possible, but unlikely.[27] An assumption of the pushing-out hypothesis is that experienced candidates enter a primary when the probability of success is high. Therefore, when amateurs are unopposed, the race is not highly valued.

One way to test this point is to examine the proportion of amateurs and experienced candidates in competitive races, defined here as races in which the incumbent received less than 65 percent of the vote in the previous election. Approximately three-fourths of experienced candidates were in primaries to face a marginal incumbent, compared with less than half of the amateurs. The most highly valued races are those in which two experienced candidates run (89 percent were competitive), while the least valued are primaries in which an amateur was unopposed to face a Democratic incumbent; only a third of these were competitive. Thus, the "reverse pushing-out" hypothesis clearly is not valid.

The patterns are even stronger in primary challenges to incumbents. Experienced candidates generally are unwilling to challenge an incumbent in a primary because an unsuccessful attempt could alienate party leaders and activists and damage future plans to gain the seat. With the higher stakes, career politicians will be even more careful in choosing races with some chance of success. At the same time, it is not likely that many amateurs will enter a primary in which they would have to defeat both the incumbent and another experienced challenger. And if they do enter they are not likely to win, which is exactly what happens.[28] Amateurs were pushed out of 97.8 percent of the primary races! (Only 4 of 182 defeated an experienced candidate, 70 were defeated, and 108 were races in which an experienced candidate faced the incumbent alone.) [29]

The strategic behavior of experienced candidates is also evident in their strong showing against the incumbents. They received 11 percent more of the vote than amateurs and won proportionally six times as many of the races that they entered. Their success is partly explained by the tendency of experienced candidates to challenge incumbents who are "ripe for the plucking." Thirteen of the twenty-two races won by experienced candidates were against scandal-ridden incumbents, while

Table 3-1   Testing the "Push-Out" Hypothesis: Previous Experience of Primary Election Candidates, 1972-1984

| Previous experience of primary winner | To face Dem. incumbent | | To face Rep. incumbent | | Rep. open seats | | Dem. open seats | |
|---|---|---|---|---|---|---|---|---|
| | (%) | (N) | (%) | (N) | (%) | (N) | (%) | (N) |
| Experienced candidate defeated amateur | 8.6 | 116 | 16.2 | 153 | 25.6 | 81 | 23.2 | 76 |
| Experienced candidate defeated experienced | 1.9 | 26 | 6.0 | 57 | 20.0 | 63 | 36.7 | 120 |
| Experienced candidate unopposed | 12.5 | 168 | 15.1 | 143 | 15.8 | 50 | 11.9 | 39 |
| Amateur candidate defeated amateur | 23.5 | 315 | 27.5 | 260 | 16.1 | 51 | 10.4 | 34 |
| Amateur candidate defeated experienced | 2.2 | 29 | 3.6 | 34 | 9.8 | 31 | 12.2 | 40 |
| Amateur candidate unopposed | 51.3 | 689 | 31.5 | 298 | 12.7 | 40 | 5.5 | 18 |
| Total | 100.0 | 1,343 | 99.9 | 945 | 100.0 | 316 | 99.9 | 327 |

amateurs had this advantage in only two of their fourteen wins from 1972 to 1984

**Senate Races.**   Incumbent senators face more experienced, better financed, and more visible challengers than representatives. The implication for amateurs is that fewer make it to the general election. Those who do often use personal wealth or celebrity status outside politics to compensate for their deficiencies in campaign experience and name recognition. Do amateurs in Senate races get pushed out of the electoral arena like their House counterparts, or does the competitiveness of Senate elections make the amateurs' path even more difficult?

Table 3-2 shows the previous experience of candidates in Senate primaries. A greater proportion of Democratic primaries to run against Republican incumbents were contested by experienced candidates than were those to face a Democrat (88 percent compared with 75 percent). One-third of the former had two experienced challengers, while only 15 percent of the Republican challengers' primaries were so hotly contested. Furthermore, eight Democratic incumbent senators faced no general election opposition, 1972-1984, while no Republicans were so fortunate. Both parties' primaries exhibit the pushing out of amateurs, with amateurs losing or not contesting 92.8 percent of all races with an experienced candidate. Open primaries exhibited similar patterns, although an even greater proportion of candidates in these races had previous political experience.

Table 3-2　The "Push-Out" Hypothesis in Senate Primaries,
1972-1984

| Previous experience of primary winner | Primary to face an incumbent in the general election | | | | Open seat primary | | | |
|---|---|---|---|---|---|---|---|---|
| | Dem. Inc. | | Rep. Inc. | | Dem. | | Rep. | |
| | (%) | (N) | (%) | (N) | (%) | (N) | (%) | (N) |
| Experienced candidate defeated amateur | 31.7 | 33 | 31.2 | 24 | 20.9 | 9 | 28.6 | 12 |
| Experienced candidate defeated experienced | 15.4 | 16 | 33.8 | 26 | 51.2 | 22 | 38.1 | 16 |
| Experienced candidate unopposed | 13.5 | 14 | 19.5 | 15 | 14.0 | 6 | 9.5 | 4 |
| Amateur candidate defeated amateur | 13.5 | 14 | 7.8 | 6 | 7.0 | 3 | 2.4 | 1 |
| Amateur candidate defeated experienced | 6.7 | 7 | 3.9 | 3 | 7.0 | 3 | 11.9 | 5 |
| Amateur candidate unopposed | 11.5 | 12 | 3.9 | 3 | — | — | 9.5 | 4 |
| Incumbent unopposed | 7.7 | 8 | — | — | — | — | — | — |
| Total | 100.0 | 104 | 100.1 | 77 | 100.1 | 43 | 100.0 | 42 |

Primary challenges to incumbents occurred more often in Senate races than in House contests. Fewer than half of the Senate incumbents were unopposed in their primaries compared with almost 70 percent of the House incumbents. (Greater contestedness translates into more defeats; 6.7 percent of all senators and 2.0 percent of all House members were defeated in primaries from 1946 to 1984.) As in House races, experienced candidates are reluctant to challenge an incumbent unless they have a reasonable chance of success. This cautiousness is reflected in the election results: experienced candidates received at least 25 percent of the vote in twenty of the twenty-five races they entered and they won nine of those. Amateurs, on the other hand, won only two of the seventy-four primaries they entered and received at least 25 percent of the vote in only nine other races.

Some amateurs are elected by being in the right place at the right time. From 1972 to 1984, five candidates with little or no previous political experience won election after the incumbent was defeated in the opposing party's primary. Experienced candidates, who are not as willing to challenge incumbents, could not take advantage of the changed political stakes. In fact, no candidate with extensive political experience has been elected to the Senate in this manner since 1972.

## Explaining the Exceptions

Amateurs have a difficult path to both the House and the Senate, yet some are elected. Can one predict which amateurs are likely to survive the process? Ambition theory does not provide much assistance because it explains only current officeholders' decisions to run for higher office. To integrate amateurs into a theory of ambition, one must understand their motives for running. Some amateurs are primarily concerned with stimulating public debate on an issue, but would like to win. Others have no illusions about winning and are in the race for its intrinsic value or simply to advertise themselves in their professions.[30] But some are ambitious amateurs who did not want to waste time serving an apprenticeship in lower office. Ambitious amateurs' central goal is to establish a career in politics; therefore, they will be more strategic in their behavior. Gary Jacobson and Samuel Kernell's observation for career politicians that "running and losing ... not only interrupts a career, but may well end it" applies to these amateurs.[31] While ambitious amateurs do not have to *win* their initial attempt for office, they do need a strong showing to attract the attention of party leaders, activists, and national money for a future race. Their self-selection into more advantageous races makes this group of amateurs more likely to survive the winnowing process.

The way to predict which amateurs will be elected to Congress is to identify the ambitious amateurs. I suggest four means to distinguish between them and less serious amateurs: previous attempts at a congressional seat, celebrity status, age, and victories over experienced candidates in the primary election. An attempt at high political office involves the confluence of ability, desire, and resources. A previous campaign indicates both desire and ability (acquired campaign skills); celebrity status is a resource (name recognition and fund-raising capability); and age is strongly related to ambition.[32] Defeating an experienced candidate in the primary indicates in two ways that the nominee is probably not the typical sacrificial lamb. First, the race was valued highly enough to attract an experienced challenger, which means that the prospects for the November election were not completely dismal. Second, the amateur had enough political knowledge and support to defeat an experienced candidate.

The four factors account for 55 percent of the amateurs who win a House seat (71 of 129). Another way to examine the effectiveness of the theory is to examine the relative success of those the theory identifies as ambitious amateurs and those it does not. In contests against incumbents, 1.6 percent of those not identified as ambitious win (25 of 1,540). Ambitious amateurs win 30.3 percent of their contests (27 of 89). In open seat races the difference is less dramatic, but still significant: a fourth of nonambitious amateurs win open seat races, but 55 percent of ambitious amateurs win.

## Behavior in Congress

Although the effect of amateurs on career structures and the election of amateurs to Congress are important topics, most students of the institution are interested in understanding its behavior. Is there a link between lack of previous political experience and behavior? Anecdotal evidence abounds. Michael Barone noted that major league pitcher "Vinegar Bend" Mizell, R-N.C., decathlon champ Robert B. Mathias, R-Calif., and Jack Kemp, all elected between 1966 and 1970, were Richard Nixon's "team players," implying a connection between their sports-based loyalties and political behavior.[33] On the Democratic side, amateurs are not known for their party loyalty. Former Speaker Thomas P. "Tip" O'Neill, D-Mass., held amateurs partly responsible for legislative losses in the first year of the Reagan administration. Steven Roberts reports:

> Speaker O'Neill and other veterans refer caustically to some of these younger lawmakers as "bedwetters." Since they did not have to wait their turn to climb the party ladder, few had legislative experience before arriving in Washington, and thus had seldom been subjected to the kind of white-hot pressure applied by the Reagan administration. As a result, they melted quickly.[34]

Another common observation links previous experience and political temperament. The reelection of former talk-show host, Robert K. Dornan, R-Calif., in 1984 drew this reaction, "The interesting question is whether this politician who made his earlier political and media career literally sounding off is now prepared to be a constructive legislator, or will he again be more of a zealot or even zany." [35] To cite one of many other examples, Senator Denton, an amateur, had to convince many of his colleagues that he "was not a nut" after charging that a peace group founded by Betty Bumpers, wife of Senator Dale Bumpers, D-Ark., was guided by communists. More outrageous to many senators was his amendment to a criminal code revision in the 97th Congress to ensure immunity from prosecution for raping a spouse. In proposing the amendment he said, slapping his hand on the table, "Damn it, when you get married, you kind of expect you're going to get a little sex." [36]

Common wisdom holds that politicians who have been seasoned at lower levels of office are not as likely to be as extreme in their behavior. Augustus F. Hawkins, D-Calif., served for twenty-eight years in the state legislature before being elected to the House. "Such experience does not usually produce verbal militance," Barone notes.[37]

Differences between amateurs and experienced politicians are predicted by two theoretical arguments, which I have labeled recruitment and socialization. Recruitment theory sees inherent behavioral differences between amateurs and those who have chosen politics as their initial career; these differences are rooted in the absence or presence of the "political personality." Socialization theory holds that initial differences may be evident due to lack of shared experiences, but that once amateurs "learn the ropes" (are socialized) differences disappear. Advocates of the recruitment theory argue that differences persist because they are based in character and personality.

Both of these theories are overly simplistic in that they view amateurs as a single type. In the previous section I pointed out that amateurs run for office for a variety of reasons. Their motives and goals are reflected in a typology of amateurism that recognized differences among amateurs in their electoral and institutional behavior. I suggest three types of amateurs: policy, ambitious, and hopeless. Their goals and environmental constraints explain the differences among them rather than their personalities or shared experiences.

Policy amateurs seek office because they want to effect policy change. Politics is not a career for many of these people; they enter politics after establishing a career, usually in business or law. Typically they have a strong world view and concrete goals. After achieving those goals, or being frustrated in the process, some will retire from politics. Others undergo change after serving in Congress for several terms, losing their idealistic vigor.

Ambitious amateurs resemble their experienced counterparts. They are motivated primarily by their desire to establish a career in politics. The reelectoral goal is dominant early in their careers, but, as Lawrence Dodd argues, their goals are reflected in predictable "stages of mastery" (reelection, policy development, institutional influence, and organizational control).[38]

Hopeless amateurs are unexpectedly swept into office in landslide elections or in upset victories in nonlandslide years. Thirty-two candidates were identified in this category from 1972 to 1984, of whom only one had previous elective experience and twenty-five had none.[39] This finding is consistent with the push-out hypothesis and follows from my theory that experienced candidates are not likely to run when the chances for success are low. Consequently, hopeless amateurs are likely to be elected in districts that historically have favored the opposition party. Their relatively short careers will be consumed by the task of remaining in office.

I test the three theories of the behavior of amateurs in the House and Senate (recruitment, socialization, and my goal-based typology) with data on roll call behavior, committee assignments, floor activity, and careers within the institution. The simple dichotomy between amateurism and political experience generally cannot explain behavioral differences between amateurs and experienced members. With the exception of differences in tenure between amateurs and experienced members and the dominance of top legislative leadership positions by members with previous experience, the two groups are indistinguishable. Therefore, there is scant evidence for the claims of recruitment theory or socialization theory.

Stronger evidence supports the typology of amateurism. Policy amateurs' careers are short (3.78 years compared with 5.62 years for ambitious amateurs and 5.35 years for experienced candidates who served between 1972 and 1984); they are more likely to gain policy committee assignments; are more likely to submit amendments on the floor; are more ideologically extreme in their voting behavior;[40] and they do not pursue power goals through legislative leadership positions. Hopeless amateurs also have short careers (3.93 years), are more likely to serve on constituency committees, are less likely to be active on the floor, and generally do not gain leadership positions. Ambitious amateurs, on the other hand, resemble their experienced counterparts in every regard. Their career patterns are similar, and they are more ideologically moderate and pursue a variety of goals.

The patterns summarized here generally are more descriptive of the House than the Senate. The typology of amateurism cannot be as readily applied to the Senate because the numbers of each type are too small to allow inferences. Nonetheless, behavioral differences between amateurs and experienced senators on roll call voting and in the leadership system merit additional attention.

## Conclusion

The U.S. House and Senate are not exclusively the domain of the politically experienced. More than one-fourth of House members and more than 10 percent of senators who were elected between 1972 and 1984 had no previous public experience. The picture that emerges of the amateur in Congress shows that amateurs are disproportionately elected during partisan surges, especially in realigning elections. The amateur's path to office is distinctive. Without the advantage of name recognition and campaign experience that comes with holding office, amateurs often are at a disadvantage in the electoral arena. Experienced politicians generally choose to run in the most attractive races, while amateurs are left to contest incumbents or other seasoned politicians in open seat races. To overcome these handicaps, many amateurs rely on attack themes in incumbent races and on issue-based campaigns more generally. Amateurs who already have high name recognition (celebrities) or have already run for Congress or have defeated an experienced candidate in their party's primary election are more likely to succeed in the general election. Once elected to office, the different types of amateurs and experienced politicians exhibit significant behavioral differences—in roll call voting, committee assignments, careers in the institution, and activity on the floor.

Reaching normative conclusions about the place of amateurs in the political system is not easy, but one point is clear. Amateurs in Congress are not a "problem." Policy amateurs often bring with them an ideological fervor that is refreshingly untempered by previous experiences and frustrations in public office. Although the question remains open for systematic study, policy amateurs often appear to serve as an important component of policy change, as in the "Reagan Revolution" in 1981 or the early New Deal days under Franklin D. Roosevelt.[41] Hopeless amateurs are elected to Congress to the surprise of most. Without their gutsy campaigns (challenges that most experienced candidates are not willing to accept) incumbents would be even more entrenched than they are. The accountability that hopeless amateurs help impose by removing incumbents who are often tainted by scandals provides the electoral check that is central to the democratic process. Ambitious amateurs are not significantly different from their experienced counterparts. Initial adjustments and socialization may be hindered by the absence of a political apprenticeship, but most seem to learn quickly in the quest for a career in Congress. The presence of amateurs in Congress will continue to be felt, especially in periods of electoral and policy change.

# Notes

1. Eight House members, one governor, two former governors, a former secretary of the Transportation Department (and House member), and a state tax commissioner were elected to the Senate in 1986.
2. This definition is in contrast to the previous distinction between machine and "amateur" politicians used by James Q. Wilson in *The Amateur Democrat* (Chicago: University of Chicago Press, 1962).
3. "This Week With David Brinkley," transcript of show No. 155, Oct. 14, 1984, 13, George Will speaking.
4. See Sandy L. Maisel's *From Obscurity to Oblivion: Running in the Congressional Primary* (Knoxville: University of Tennessee Press, 1986),

chap. 2, for a good discussion of the bewildering array of issues confronted by first-time candidates.

5. David A. Leuthold, *Electioneering in a Democracy* (New York: John Wiley & Sons, 1968), 23-31.

6. The presidency may be the exception to this rule. In reaction to the perceived deficiencies of the Carter and Reagan presidencies, there was a significant focus on political experience in the 1988 presidential race. Robert Dole, George Bush, and Paul Simon all made the issue the center of their campaigns, with varying degrees of direct references to the pitfalls of inexperience in Washington. The candidacies of Pat Robertson and Jesse Jackson were met with skepticism, due in part to their lack of political experience. Dwight D. Eisenhower is the only true amateur to be elected president in this century.

7. Ronald Reagan's initial campaign for governor of California illustrates these points well. Reagan's consulting firm, Spencer-Roberts, was able to package their candidate perfectly. They turned Reagan's lack of experience to his advantage by labeling him a citizen-politician. By the end of the campaign his opponent, Governor Edmund Brown, was on the defensive for being a professional politician. See Jeff Greenfield, *Running to Win* (New York: Simon & Schuster, 1980), 256.

8. Foreword to Joseph A. Schlesinger, *How They Became Governor* (East Lansing, Mich.: Governmental Research Bureau, 1957), 3.

9. Kevin Phillips, "At Election Time, Celebrities Can Make Political Party's Day," *Minneapolis Star and Tribune,* June 18, 1985, A-11.

10. Richard F. Fenno, "What's He Like? What's She Like? What Are They Like?" in *The United States Congress,* ed. Dennis Hale (New Brunswick, N.J.: Transaction Books, 1983), 114-120.

11. The seminal work on career structures is *Ambition and Politics: Political Careers in the United States,* Joseph A. Schlesinger (Chicago: Rand McNally, 1966). Schlesinger uses the term "opportunity structure" rather than career structure to refer to the tiering of offices.

12. Hugh Bone, *American Politics and the Party System* (New York: McGraw Hill, 1949), 740.

13. Harold D. Lasswell, *Psychopathology and Politics* (New York: Viking Press, 1960), 303.

14. The value of an office is determined by the power of the office, the size of the constituency, its value as a stepping stone, the length of term, compensation, and electoral security.

15. Schlesinger, *Ambition and Politics,* 186-187. Emphasis added.

16. Ibid., 187.

17. The extent to which amateurs run independent of party organizations is difficult to determine. Parties generally do not become actively involved in primary battles but simply endorse the eventual nominee. This makes the experiences of several recently elected amateurs more significant. John Glenn, D-Ohio; Bill Bradley, D-N.J.; Orrin Hatch, R-Utah; Gordon Humphrey, R-N.H.; and Jeremiah Denton, R-Ala., all defeated hand-picked party candidates in their party's primary. While this evidence is

not conclusive, at minimum, modern campaign technology provides a potential base for running independent of party.

18. Schlesinger, *Ambition and Politics,* 20.
19. Because the Democratic party was already dominant in the South, no change in the career structure would be expected during the realignment. See David T. Canon and David J. Sousa, "Realigning Elections and Political Career Structures in the U.S. Congress" (Paper delivered at the annual meeting of the American Political Science Association, Chicago, Sept. 3-6, 1987). Career politicians also respond to changing opportunities by accelerating their decisions to run for high office and reentering politics after leaving public life for more than five years.
20. The importance of the changing desirability of an office is illustrated by the increased professionalization of state legislatures, which attract more able and experienced politicians. This change may account for the emergence of state legislatures as a clear stepping-stone to the House. The impact of the rules of the game may be seen in the adoption of the Seventeenth Amendment which provided for the direct election of senators. Although I do not test the proposition in this study, state legislators may have been more inclined than the general electorate to choose career politicians and party loyalists. Other less dramatic differences in nominating rules affect the types of candidates who run for office. When party activists play a greater role in the nomination process, fewer inexperienced candidates run for state legislatures than in states in which participation is broad based. Party endorsements have the same effect in congressional elections. For state-level evidence, see Richard J. Tobin, "The Influence of Nominating Systems on the Political Experience of State Legislators," *Western Political Quarterly* 28 (September 1975): 553-566.
21. The rules of the game have not dramatically changed in congressional elections since the early twentieth century; changes in state election laws are not systematic, nor are they parallel to observed changes in career structures; and the professionalization of Congress was largely complete by 1930. On the last point, see Nelson W. Polsby, "The Institutionalization of the U.S. House of Representatives," *American Political Science Review* 62 (March 1968): 144-169.
22. In Mississippi, for example, in 1987 Democrats held 122 of 129 state House seats. Other states are Texas with 150 of 156, Alabama with 105 of 121, Louisiana with 103 of 125, and Arkansas with 100 of 109. See Canon and Sousa, "Realigning Elections and Political Career Structures," 25.
23. This question is examined in more detail in David T. Canon, "Actors, Athletes, and Astronauts: Political Amateurism in the United States Congress" (Ph.D. diss., University of Minnesota, 1987). I also present a much more extended discussion of strategic behavior in primary elections and of behavior in the institution.
24. Linda Fowler, "The Cycle of Defeat: Recruitment of Congressional Challengers" (Ph.D. diss., University of Rochester, 1977), 132-137.
25. Previous versions of ambition theory consider only officeholders' decisions

to run for higher office. Although the existing literature does not examine the emergence of amateurs, it does provide a theoretical point of departure. For the initial formalization of ambition theory at the individual level, see David W. Rohde, "Risk Bearing and Progressive Ambition: The Case of Members of the United States House of Representatives," *American Journal of Political Science* 23 (February 1979): 1-26. See also Gary C. Jacobson and Samuel Kernell, *Strategy and Choice in Congressional Elections* (New Haven, Conn.: Yale University Press, 1983).

26. Schlesinger, *How they Became Governor,* 3.
27. One such case was Ed Zschau's, R-Calif., initial race for the House in 1982 in which he spent $250,000 in the Republican primary campaign even though he was unopposed. To my knowledge, there have been only a handful of cases in the last decade in which an amateur's financial and political backing was substantial enough to deter experienced challengers from running in an attractive race.
28. Indeed, from 1972-1984 only one amateur was able to win such a race. The race involved Richard Kelly, R-Fla., a central subject in the FBI Abscam investigation in the spring of 1980. Bill McCollum, a lawyer and political amateur, already had his campaign underway when the scandal broke. State senator Vince Fechtel entered the race in April, but McCollum narrowly won the initial primary, in which Kelly only received 18 percent of the vote, and then won the runoff with 54 percent.
29. In this analysis I exclude "frivolous" candidates who receive less than 5 percent of the vote.
30. The proportion of candidates who *realistically* have no chance of winning is quite high. Sandy Maisel says, "Politicians have an incredible ability to delude themselves about their own chances." *From Obscurity to Oblivion,* 23. Maisel discusses the various motivations that candidates have in running for office. See also Thomas A. Kazee, "The Decision to Run for the U.S. Congress: Challenger Attitudes in the 1970s," *Legislative Studies Quarterly* 5 (February 1980): 79-100.
31. Jacobson and Kernell, *Strategy and Choice,* 22.
32. See Schlesinger, *Ambition and Politics,* chap. 9, for a discussion of the relationship between age and ambition. In this analysis, age is not a sufficient condition in the coding scheme.
33. Michael Barone, Grant Ujifusa, and Douglas Matthews, *Almanac of American Politics* (Boston: Gambit, 1973), 750.
34. Steven V. Roberts, "Congressmen and Their Districts: Free Agents in Fear of the Future," in *The United States Congress,* 82.
35. Michael Barone and Grant Ujifusa, *Almanac of American Politics* (Washington, D.C.: National Journal, 1985), 190.
36. Alan Ehrenhalt, *Politics in America, 1984* (Washington, D.C.: CQ Press, 1983), 12.
37. Barone, Ujifusa, and Matthews, *Almanac of American Politics,* 1973, 101.
38. Lawrence C. Dodd, "Cycle of Legislative Change: Building a Dynamic Theory," in *Political Science: The Science of Politics,* ed. Herbert F. Weisberg (New York: Agathon Press, 1986), 87.

39. The hopeless amateurs are identified as the outliers in a multiple regressional analysis of a district's expected vote. See Canon, "Actors, Athletes, and Astronauts," for an extended discussion.
40. Democratic policy amateurs have Conservative Coalition scores that are 12.4 points lower than ambitious amateurs and experienced politicians, while the differences between these two groups for Republicans averages 11.6 points when controlling for party (including separating out Southern Democrats), seniority, and district ideology. Hopeless amateurs fall between these two groups.
41. As Canon and Sousa argue in "Realigning Elections and Political Career Structures," the impact of amateurs on the political system during realignments adds an important component to the discussion of the "governing side" of realignments. See Jerome M. Clubb, William H. Flanigan, and Nancy H. Zingale, *Partisan Realignment: Voters, Parties, and Government in American History* (Beverly Hills: Sage, 1980).

*Part II*

ELECTIONS AND CONSTITUENCIES

# 4. VOTERS, CANDIDATES, AND ISSUES IN CONGRESSIONAL ELECTIONS

*Robert S. Erikson and Gerald C. Wright*

Elections for the U.S. House of Representatives fascinate observers of American politics almost as much as presidential elections do. Unlike Senate elections with staggered six-year terms and gubernatorial elections with an irregular electoral cycle that varies from state to state, House elections provide a biennial measure of the national electoral pulse. Interest in House elections generally centers on the partisan balance of seats and the mood of the electorate that underlies this partisan verdict.

Still another source of fascination with House elections is that there are so many of them. Every two years, the composition of the new U.S. House is the result of 435 separate contests for 435 separate seats. In part, the results are determined by national electoral forces. But to a larger extent, they are determined by the candidates in these contests and the conduct of their individual campaigns.

In this essay, we examine first the national forces in House elections and their influence on the partisan divisions of the national vote and House seats. Next, we look at the role of candidates in individual House contests. Finally, we compare elections for the House with elections for the Senate.

## The National Verdict in House Elections

The national result of House elections can be represented either as the partisan division of seats won or as the partisan division of the national vote. Although the partisan seat division generally gets the most attention, it is largely determined by the partisan vote division in the 435 districts. Figure 4-1 shows the pattern of the two-party vote and

This research was partially supported by the National Science Foundation, grant SES 83-10443. The authors thank Kathleen Frankovic and Warren Mitofsky of CBS News for making available the CBS News/*New York Times* 1982 congressional candidates poll. We offer special thanks to Christine Barbour, Kathleen Knight, and James Stimson for their assistance.

the two-party seat division over thirty years. Between 1952 and 1982, the seat division varied from about an even split between Republicans and Democrats to a Democratic edge of more than two-thirds of the seats. This major movement is a response to far smaller vote variations, from about 50 percent to about 58 percent Democratic.

How many seats does a party gain for each percentage point gain in its vote? This quantity—often called the swing ratio—has been variously estimated at 1.90 and 2.14 over recent decades.[1] Conveniently, these estimates average out to about an even 2.0. Changes in the national two-party vote have an exaggerated impact on seat gains: a party wins an additional 2 percent of the seats for every 1 percent of the vote it gains. Each of the 435 individual House contests is won by the candidate who wins the most votes, or a plurality. In practice, the winner is almost always the major-party candidate with the majority of the two-party vote. A swing ratio of about 2.0 means that each party is generally one percentage point short of victory in about 2 percent of the districts. When the party gains an additional 1 percent of the national vote (and if this vote swing is reasonably uniform across districts), the party wins the additional 2 percent of the seats it would have lost.

Actually, the swing ratio varies considerably from one election to the next. A downward trend is noticeable since the mid-1960s, with the swing ratio in some years dipping even below 1.00.[2] The 1986 election provides the most extreme example. Between 1984 and 1986, the Democratic share of the House vote increased from 52.7 to 55.0 percent—a gain of 2.3 percentage points. But the Democrats increased their seat margin by only 1.1 percentage points, for a swing ratio of about .50! In other words, in 1986 it took an additional 2 percent of the national vote for a party to win an additional 1 percent of the seats.

The general decline in the swing ratio is readily explained. Since 1964 incumbents of both parties have held increasingly safe seats, insulated from the partisan tides. The reason for the slim number of Democratic seats gained in 1986 is that very few Republican-held seats were sufficiently marginal to tip to the Democrats with the addition of a few percentage points of Democratic votes.

## The Normal Vote

Figure 4-1 shows that the Democratic party does far better than the Republicans in House elections. This Democratic dominance at the congressional level—so unlike the recent dominance of the presidency by the Republican party—is one clear manifestation of the Democrats' numerical edge over the Republicans within the electorate. If most partisans were to vote for their party's candidate and the independent voters were to split about fifty-fifty, the outcome of a national election

Figure 4-1  House Seats and Vote over Time, 1952-1986

Percent

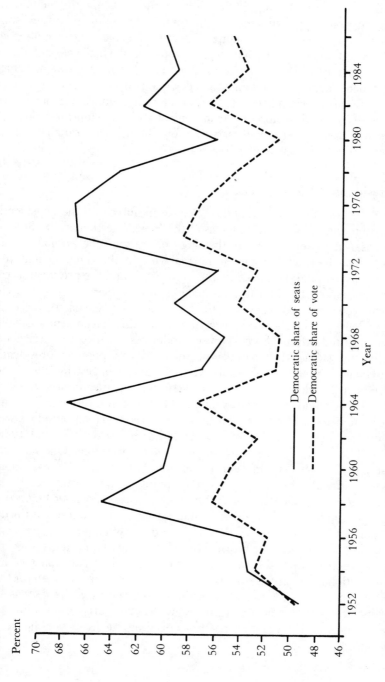

SOURCE: The data are from Norman J. Ornstein, Thomas E. Mann, and Michael J. Malbin, *Vital Statistics on Congress, 1987-1988* (Washington, D.C.: Congressional Quarterly, 1987), 47-48.

would be about 54 percent Democratic and 46 percent Republican. Such an outcome, in which the election is decided on a party vote, is called the "normal vote." [3] Observe in Figure 4-1 how the the national House vote approximates the normal vote, with relatively small oscillations around the baseline of about 54 percent Democratic.

Election outcomes that depart from the normal vote are due to short-term defections by partisans and to the temporary vote movement by independents. These temporary deviations from the normal vote are due to "short-term partisan forces" of the campaign. At a national level, short-term partisan forces intrude only lightly in House elections. As we have seen, even small perturbations in the vote can have major consequences in terms of party seats.

## Presidential Election Years

In presidential years, the short-term forces of the presidential election and the short-term forces of the House election are in the same partisan direction: the party that does better than the normal vote for president does better than the normal vote in the congressional vote. Whether this happens because the House vote and the presidential vote are influenced by the same national issues, or because people decide their congressional vote on the basis of their partisan choice for president, is not clear. Whatever the cause, this phenomenon is called the "coattail effect." Some House candidates seem to be carried into office by riding the coattails of their party's popular presidential candidate. Democratic coattails were at their strongest in 1964, when President Lyndon Johnson's landslide victory created an overwhelming 295-140 Democratic majority in the House of Representatives. Similarly, some of the best Republican years in recent House elections were with the strong Republican presidential victories in 1972 and 1980.

The size of the coattail effect is decidedly irregular. One statistical estimate for post-World War II elections puts it at .31 congressional votes nationally for every percentage point of the vote gained by the party at the presidential level.[4] Put another way, every added percent of the vote gained by a presidential candidate also adds almost one-third of a percent of the vote to the presidential candidate's congressional running mates. Prior to World War II, presidential coattails appeared to be stronger than they are today; the national presidential vote and the national congressional vote marched more in lock-step. One consequence of the weakening of the coattail effect is the increase in split-party control of government, with one party controlling the presidency and the other party controlling at least one house of Congress.

## Midterm Years

One regular pattern of House elections is that the party that wins the presidency suffers a net loss of votes and seats in the following midterm election. Of the twenty-two midterms of the twentieth century, for example, in only one (1934) did the president's party gain seats. And in only one midterm (1926) did the president's party increase its share of the House vote. What accounts for this regularity?

Among political scientists, the conventional explanation for midterm loss has been the withdrawal of presidential coattails. The argument goes as follows: in presidential years the congressional vote for the president's party is inflated by presidential coattails. At the next midterm, the congressional vote reverts to something close to normal. The result is a decline for the president's party.[5]

Although this is an appealing argument, it is wrong. The vote at midterm is not predictably normal. Instead, each party does worse at midterm when it controls the presidency and better at midterm when it does not. Moreover, the size of the midterm loss does not depend on the size of the presidential year victory as the coattail argument would predict. Under all conditions, at midterm the congressional vote for the presidential party is about four or five percentage points lower than two years before. Figure 4-2 illustrates this regularity for elections since 1946.[6]

It is as if the midterm electorate chooses to punish the president's party no matter what the circumstances. Why would the electorate do this? One explanation is that some portion of the midterm electorate engages in "negative voting"—a form of regular protest against the party in power. Another explanation might be the electorate's search for ideological balance between the president and Congress. Some segments of the midterm electorate may choose to vote for the opposition party as an ideological hedge. In this way, the relatively moderate electorate can balance the ideological excesses of the president by giving extra support to the opposition party at the congressional level.

## Electoral Change as a Search for Policy Direction

Every two years, the national vote for Congress produces a change in the party composition of Congress. When the electorate collectively creates a change in Congress's party composition, do voters intend a specific policy purpose? We have seen that the midterm electorate may possibly increase its support for the out party to balance presidential power. A similar process has been suggested for presidential years: that a moderate electorate chooses divided party control because it prefers

Figure 4-2   Democratic Congressional Vote by Election Year and
Presidential Outcome, 1944-1986

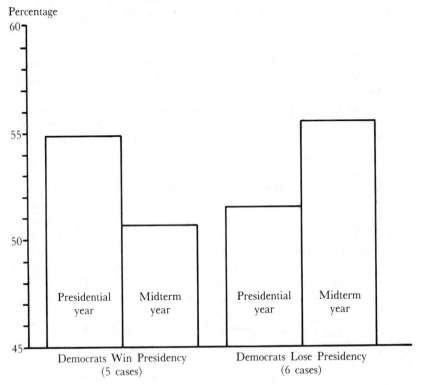

one party to control the presidency and the other Congress.[7] But apart
from the electorate's possible yearning for partisan balance, what do
congressional election results indicate about the electorate's policy
preferences?

The popular view, often promoted by pundits at election time, is
that Democratic congressional gains signify that the electorate wants
more liberalism and Republican gains signify that the electorate wants
more conservatism. Public opinion research, however, finds little
evidence to support this view. During the two years between congressional elections, public opinion rarely changes on specific issues of
public policy or in terms of general orientation to liberalism and
conservatism.[8]

If the electorate rarely moves ideologically, what are the actual
sources of electoral change? At the presidential level, the electorate's net
evaluations of the Republican and Democratic candidates are quite

important, if not always discernible in advance. The presidential electorate also responds to the national economy, rewarding the in party in proportion to the election-year degree of prosperity. Together, the electorate's reactions to the candidates and to the economy account for almost all of the short-term forces of presidential campaigns.[9] At midterm, short-term forces are more muted. Still, the midterm verdict often is viewed as a referendum on the president's performance, with the presidential party doing best when the president is popular and when the economy is healthy.[10] Even under the best of circumstances, however, the presidential party loses support at midterm.

Although presidential coattails influence congressional races, voters are not necessarily expressing policy preferences. Popular reports of how Ronald Reagan's 1980 victory (and the corollary Republican congressional gains) represented a strong public mandate for a move toward conservatism were exaggerated. Earlier Democratic victories, most notably the Johnson landslide of 1964, were also misinterpreted as signifying a public desire for change in the liberal direction.

The reason electoral shifts should not be taken as policy directives is that public opinion rarely takes abrupt liberal or conservative turns. The electoral system offers the public the means to give policy direction, if it wishes to. As we shall see, the two parties offer the electorate a policy choice, and individual constituencies respond to the menu of policy choices their candidates provide, with the candidates' party affiliations serving as a major cue.

## Policy Consequences of Electoral Change

Even if it is not the collective intent of the national electorate, the policy consequences of changes in the party composition of Congress can be substantial. When Republicans replace Democrats in the House, conservatives almost always replace liberals. When Democrats replace Republicans, liberals almost always replace conservatives.

We can illustrate these party differences using a poll of congressional candidates conducted by CBS/*New York Times* during the 1982 campaign. (No similar poll has been conducted since then.) The 1982 poll focused on the candidates' stands on ten issues that were thought important in the preceding Congress or that were likely to come before the new Congress.

Table 4-1 displays the patterns of responses for the pair of major-party candidates in each of the 371 district elections that were contested by both major parties. Column I shows, for each issue, the percentage of the districts in which the Republican took the liberal position and the Democrat took the conservative position. As the table makes clear, this pattern was rare. Columns II and III show patterns of agreement—ei-

Table 4-1    Candidates' Positions on Ten Issues, 1982 Contested House Elections (in percentages)

| | *Candidates' positions* | | | |
| | I | II | III | IV |
| *Republican:* | Liberal | Conservative | Liberal | Conservative |
| *Democrat:* | Conservative | Conservative | Liberal | Liberal |
|---|---|---|---|---|
| *Constitutional Amendments* | | | | |
| 1. States prohibit abortion | 6.3 | 15.8 | 33.2 | 44.6 |
| 2. Prayer in public schools | 4.5 | 13.2 | 28.2 | 54.1 |
| 3. For balanced budget | 1.1 | 22.2 | 9.5 | 67.3 |
| 4. Equal Rights Amendment | 1.8 | 7.9 | 40.6 | 49.6 |
| *Issues* | | | | |
| 5. Nuclear freeze with Soviets | 2.6 | 13.2 | 22.4 | 61.7 |
| 6. Domestic content, foreign cars sold in U.S. | 6.3 | 17.7 | 28.2 | 47.8 |
| 7. Cancel July 1983 tax cut | 1.8 | 18.7 | 7.1 | 72.3 |
| 8. Cut military spending increases | 3.2 | 7.7 | 54.9 | 34.3 |
| 9. Reduce domestic social programs | 2.4 | 15.3 | 20.1 | 62.3 |
| 10. Increase regulation of air pollution | 5.5 | 56.7 | 4.7 | 33.0 |

SOURCE: The data are from the CBS News/*New York Times* 1982 poll of congressional candidates.

ther both conservative or both liberal—on the ten issues. Levels of candidate agreement vary considerably. On some issues, such as a balanced budget amendment, agreement was quite low. On others, such as cutting military spending, the candidates generally agreed—in this case to slow down spending on arms. Column IV shows the extent to which the Democratic candidate held the liberal position and the Republican opponent held the conservative view. This expected pattern of liberal Democrats and conservative Republicans is most frequent, particularly for the balanced budget amendment, the nuclear freeze, tax cuts, and domestic spending cuts.

Generally, a congressional voter in 1982 had an easy way to cast a partisan ballot: to help elect the more conservative candidate, vote Republican; to help elect the more liberal candidate, vote Democratic. In fact, if we score each candidate from zero to ten on the basis of his or her number of conservative positions on the ten issues (extreme liberals score zero, extreme conservatives score ten), the Republican is the most

Figure 4-3    Distributions of Candidate Ideology, 1982 House
Elections

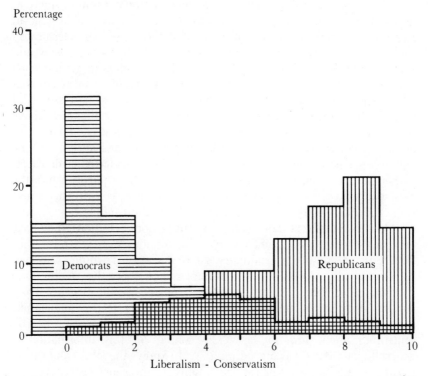

NOTE: Liberalism-conservatism is measured by an index constructed from the 1982
CBS News/*New York Times* poll of congressional candidates.

conservative candidate in 92.8 percent of the districts, the Democrat is
the most conservative in only 3.2 percent, and in 4.0 percent the two
candidates find themselves in a net tie on the ideological spectrum. This
result is not unique to the 1982 election. A similar pattern has been
found in studies of the 1966, 1974, and 1978 House elections.[11]

The overall differences between Republican and Democratic
candidates can be seen most readily if we cumulate their issue or
ideology scores on the zero-to-ten scale and compare all Republican
candidates with all Democratic candidates. The comparison is striking
(Figure 4-3). The vast majority of the Democrats are clumped well to
the left with only a few moderates and conservatives, and the
Republicans are markedly to the right. Clearly, the centers of gravity of
the two parties are quite different, and the election of Democrats leads
to a policy mix different from the election of Republicans.

## District-Level Outcomes in House Elections

So far we have discussed congressional candidates almost solely in terms of their party affiliation, as if all Democrats were alike and all Republicans were alike. Similarly, we have discussed the electorate's choice as if it were solely between the national Democratic party and the national Republican party. In actuality, candidates within each party differ considerably. Candidates often take positions on issues that depart from their party's norm, perhaps out of electoral necessity. And whether by posturing on issues or in other ways, candidates do have considerable effect on district election outcomes. Local candidates can do more than watch helplessly while constituency partisanship and the national partisan trend determine whether they are elected or defeated. Although constituencies tend to vote according to their partisanship (the local normal vote) and the national partisan trend, constituencies also vote according to the capabilities they see in the candidates.

When voters cast their ballots in congressional elections, they have two sets of cues: the candidates' party affiliations plus whatever they have learned about the candidates. At first glance it would seem that voters generally possess insufficient information about the candidates to vote on more than a partisan basis. Consider some evidence from surveys: only about one-half of the voting electorate can name their U.S. representative, and slightly less claim to have "read or heard" something about him or her. The content of this information is generally vague ("He is a good man." "He knows the job.") and rarely touches on policy issues or roll calls. Only by the generous criterion of *recognition* of the representative's name does the electorate perform well. More than 90 percent claim to recognize their representative's name when supplied with it. Candidates for open seats are even less visible than incumbent candidates. And challengers trying to defeat incumbent representatives are the least visible of all. Typically, only about 20 percent of the voting electorate can recall the challenger's name or recall anything about the challenger. Only about half will claim to recognize the challenger's name when supplied with it.[12]

Although voters are not well informed about their local House candidates, it does not follow that the candidates have little impact on election outcomes. Movements by relatively few voters in a constituency can create a major surge for or against a candidate. This movement, the "personal" vote, results from the constituency reaction to the specific candidates, as opposed to the "partisan" vote, which results from the constituency's partisanship.[13] The personal vote is about as important as the partisan vote in deciding elections.

One way of demonstrating the importance of the personal vote is

Figure 4-4    Vote in 1986 by Vote in 1984, for Districts with Different Candidates Running in the Two Elections

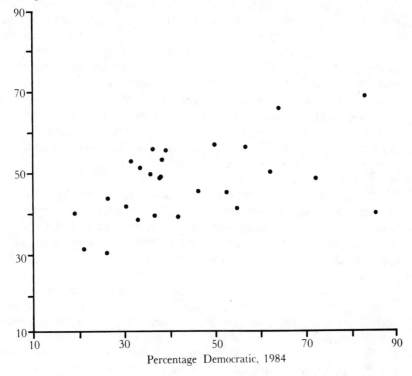

Percentage Democratic, 1986

Percentage Democratic, 1984

SOURCE: *America Votes, 17,* comp. and ed. Richard Scammon and Alice McGillivray (Washington, D.C.: Elections Research Center and Congressional Quarterly, 1987).

to show the relationship between the constituency vote in one election year and the same constituency's vote in the next election when the two major-party candidates change. For example, Figure 4-4 shows the relationship between the Democratic share of the two-party vote in 1984 and the Democratic share of the two-party vote in 1986 for the set of constituencies where both parties changed their candidates from one election to the next. The inertial effect of district partisanship allows some correlation across elections, but with new candidates the 1986 outcomes were not easy to forecast from 1984 results.

## The Value of Incumbency

House incumbents almost always win reelection. More than 90 percent of all House members seek reelection in a typical year, and of these more than 90 percent win. From one election to the next, therefore, more than 80 percent of the House membership will be the same.

There are three reasons why incumbents generally win. First, constituency partisanship is a strong influence on elections. To the extent that constituencies vote according to their partisan predisposition, incumbents enjoy a *partisan* advantage. Second, incumbents tend to enjoy a *personal* advantage. Apart from constituency partisanship and the national trend, elections are determined by whether the Democratic candidate or the Republican candidate has the stronger vote appeal. The stronger of the two candidates is more likely to achieve incumbency status. Incumbents win because they tend to have strong personal vote appeal. Third, and perhaps most important, incumbents win because incumbency status adds to a candidate's vote margin; this is the *incumbency* advantage.

How large is the incumbency advantage? The best way to measure it is to observe the size of the "sophomore surge," the percentage of the vote that candidates gain from their first victory to their first reelection attempt. Averaged across elections and adjusted for the national partisan trend, the sophomore surge is a simple but accurate measure of the vote share gained from incumbency.

Since about 1966 the sophomore surge has averaged about 6 percent of the vote.[14] This advantage helps protect incumbents from adverse electoral developments. For instance, suppose a newly elected House member wins with 51 percent of the vote, aided by a national vote trend that averages 4 percentage points in favor of the candidate's party. Without an incumbency advantage, our candidate would expect to lose when the partisan tide returns to normal:

$$51\% - 4\% = 47\% \text{ of the two-party vote.}$$

However, if we add the 6 percent incumbency bonus, our hypothetical House member would expect to win:

$$47\% + 6\% = 53\% \text{ of the vote.}$$

An adverse partisan tide, a popular challenger, or some decline in the candidate's own popularity could easily change a probable 53 percent win into a defeat. But even when the reason for a candidate's first election to Congress is some temporary benefit, such as an unpopular opponent or a favorable partisan tide, a 6 percent incumbency advantage may be sufficient to keep the new incumbent in Congress for a long time.

The size of the incumbency advantage has increased over time. In the 1950s and the early 1960s, the sophomore surge—and therefore the incumbency advantage—averaged less than two percentage points. The sudden increase to an advantage of six percentage points or so in the mid-1960s had the immediate impact of insulating the Democratic class of 1964. An unusually high number of freshman Democrats were elected in the Democratic tide of 1964 (on Lyndon Johnson's coattails), and the increased incumbency advantage helped keep a surprisingly high proportion of them in office for several years. Since then, the growth in the incumbency advantage has helped protect incumbents of both parties from adverse partisan swings. But why do incumbents have an electoral advantage, and why has this advantage grown? Three explanations seem plausible.

**Decline of Party.** Beginning in the mid-1960s when the electoral advantage of incumbency began to increase, the American electorate suddenly became less rigid in terms of its party identification. The proportion of voters who called themselves independents increased dramatically. Without partisan attachments, independents are likely to respond to the available cue of incumbency and select the candidate already in office. In this way the decline of partisanship may be responsible for the growth of the incumbency advantage.

**Perquisites of Office.** Congressional incumbents benefit from the perquisites of office such as the frank (or free mailing privilege), a generous travel allowance for visits home to the district, and money to maintain district offices. During the 1960s, at about the same time as the increase in the electoral advantage of incumbents, Congress bestowed upon its members many generous increases in its perks. These increased benefits may have generated sufficient positive publicity for incumbents to account for the increase in the incumbency advantage.

**Weak Challengers.** It might be possible to account for incumbency advantage in terms of weak challengers instead of strong incumbents. Recall that incumbents tend to be strong candidates in the sense that their personal vote appeal is what elected them. Strong incumbents tend to chase away strong challenges.[15]

Each of these explanations of the growing incumbency advantage has its weakness. Contrary to prediction, even partisan voters have become more attracted to incumbent candidates. The perquisites of office theory has its flaw: surveys do not show increased voter awareness of incumbents.[16] The strategic politicians explanation at best would seem to offer a reinforcement of an incumbency advantage generated from other sources. And it is not apparent how this explanation can account for a growth in the incumbency advantage. The incumbency advantage, therefore, remains a puzzle with no clear resolution.

## Candidates, Issues, and the Vote

Factors other than incumbency influence voters in House elections. Money is also important, particularly for challengers. Nonincumbent candidates gain the most from the money they spend because heavy spending is necessary to give them credibility and attention. Once elected, however, a member of Congress is about as well known as he or she will get, and additional campaign spending helps little.[17] The ceiling on the value of additional spending is ironic, given incumbents' ease at raising campaign contributions.

Some scholars see constituency service as a major source of candidate popularity. All things being equal, the House member who responds promptly to constituents' requests and stays in the local political spotlight probably makes a stronger candidate than a member who downplays constituency service.

Candidates' election chances also are influenced by their ideological position on major issues. As noted earlier, Republican candidates tend to be conservative and Democratic candidates liberal. Although the potential constituents hold a wide variety of views, the *average* constituent locates between the two candidates on the ideological spectrum. If voters are responsive at all to ideology and issues, candidates can gain votes by moving away from their party's norm toward the center of the spectrum. In principle, each candidate would maximize his or her votes by moving in the direction of the opponent. If both candidates do so, they meet in the center of the local ideological spectrum.[18]

In reality, candidates do not converge at the center. The countervailing forces of their own liberal or conservative beliefs and those of their strong supporters work against such a tendency. Still, within each party the candidates do vary in their ideological positions. And the degree to which they moderate their stands by moving toward the opponents influences the vote.[19]

The effect of candidate positions on the 1982 vote can be estimated by using the CBS News/*New York Times* candidate survey. Ideological positions are measured as the number of conservative positions (ranging from zero to ten) that the candidate supports on the ten issues listed in Table 4-1.

Electoral effects of candidate ideology are estimated using multiple regression analysis, with the results shown in Table 4-2. Separate regression equations were generated to predict the Republican congressional vote for districts with Democratic incumbent candidates, districts with Republican incumbent candidates, and open seats. Coefficients are shown for the estimated effects of three predictor variables, the Reagan

Table 4-2   Regression of the House Vote on Candidate and District
Ideology by Incumbency

|  | Type of district | | |
|---|---|---|---|
|  | Democratic incumbent | Republican incumbent | Open seat |
| Reagan vote | 0.556[a] | 0.760[a] | 1.223[a] |
| (standard error) | (.066) | (.099) | (.139) |
| Democratic ideology | −0.852[a] | −0.428 | −0.376 |
| (standard error) | (.296) | (.372) | (.541) |
| Republican ideology | −0.068 | −0.752[a] | −0.825 |
| (standard error) | (.304) | (.308) | (.660) |
| Constant | 7.962 | 24.340 | −10.659 |
| R | 0.568 | 0.540 | 0.800 |
| $\bar{R}^2$ | 0.310 | 0.277 | 0.620 |
| Number of districts | 163 | 152 | 56 |

[a] Statistically significant, regression coefficient is twice its standard error.

vote in the district (as a control), the Democratic candidate's ideology, and the Republican candidate's ideology.

Moderate candidates are the best vote getters; both conservative Democrats and conservative Republicans hurt the Republican vote. Therefore, we expect negative coefficients for both Democratic and Republican candidate ideology. All six coefficients for candidate ideology in Table 4-2 are negative, as expected. The strongest effects of candidate positions are for incumbents. For both Democratic and Republican incumbents, the coefficient for candidate ideology is about −.80 and statistically significant. A coefficient of this size means that, on the average, each digit moved toward the center on the ten-point scale is worth about .80 of a percent of the vote. For example, a Republican in the center of the scale at five should win about 4 percent more of the vote than an extreme conservative at ten.

The four coefficients for challengers and candidates for open seats are all in the appropriate negative direction but are not statistically significant. This corresponds to the findings of a similar study of the 1974 election.[20] Possibly, nonincumbent candidates' positions are insufficiently visible to have much impact, but take on electoral relevance when the candidate gains the notoriety of incumbency.

## Candidate Responsiveness to the Constituency

Constituencies reward and punish incumbents (and possibly challengers) on the basis of their policy positions. A second source of control is the candidates' expectations of these electoral sanctions. A candidate who fears electoral damage can move toward the center. The degree of adjustment depends on the electoral security of the district plus the district's mean position on the liberal-conservative spectrum. As a result, each party's most conservative candidates tend to be in the most conservative and Republican districts and the most liberal candidates in the most liberal and Democratic districts.

We can observe these tendencies among the candidates surveyed for the CBS News/*New York Times* poll. Figure 4-5, parts A, B, and C, show candidate positions as a function of the Reagan vote for each party when a Republican incumbent runs, when a Democratic incumbent runs, and for open seats. Each line represents the statistical regression of candidate conservativism on the Reagan vote. Note in particular the steep slopes for the two sets of incumbents. For them, ten percentage points difference in the Reagan vote appears to create a difference of about two points on the ideology scale.

Candidate responsiveness is less regular across the nonincumbent groups. Democratic challengers tended to be very liberal no matter how strong the Reagan vote. Democratic contenders for open seats were less liberal, but they too displayed the same ideological tendency for each level of the Reagan vote. Among nonincumbents, only Republican challengers and Republican contenders for open seats varied their position in response to the Reagan vote.[21]

For many elections, scholars have reported strong relationships between the positions of each party's incumbents (usually measured from roll call votes in Congress) and the presidential vote.[22] Actually, this relationship may not depend entirely on attempts by members to adjust their public positions for electoral considerations. For instance, the member may seem to follow the district because the member and the district share the same policy interests. Or, over time, the representative and the constituency may become more alike in their views because the representative educates the constituency rather than the reverse. Still, the tendency for each party's incumbents to take positions in ideological accord with the district's presidential voting certainly reflects that House members respond in advance to the threat of electoral sanctions.

## Congressional Elections and Representation

The political parties and the candidates provide the mechanisms by which constituencies can electorally determine the policy views of

Figure 4-5  Candidate Conservatism and Reagan Vote, 1982 Contests

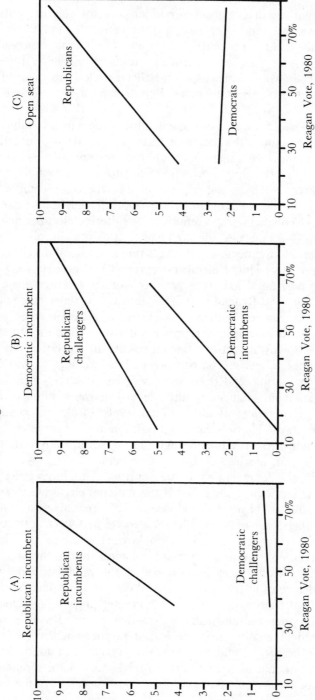

NOTE: Conservatism is measured by an index constructed from the 1982 CBS News/*New York Times* poll of congressional candidates. The vertical axis represents candidate conservatism, with ten the most conservative.

their representatives in Congress. First, consider the role of political parties. Democratic and Republican congressional candidates are sufficiently divergent from each other on the liberal-conservative spectrum to provide their constituencies with a clear choice. Liberal districts generally vote Democratic and thereby elect liberals, while conservative districts generally vote Republican and thereby elect conservatives.

Second, consider the role of the individual candidates. Candidates for Congress sometimes deviate from their party's ideological orthodoxy. By moving toward a more moderate position, one that is closer to the constituency's prevailing view, the candidate enhances his or her electoral chances and by doing so can enhance the representation of constituency views. The candidate who is more ideologically extreme runs the risk of enhancing representation by suffering electoral defeat.

As Figure 4-6 indicates, the net result is a clear pattern whereby the most liberal House members represent the most liberal districts and the most conservative House members represent the most conservative districts. The horizontal axis represents constituency conservatism as measured by the 1980 Reagan vote. The vertical axis represents policy conservatism as measured by the CBS News/*New York Times* ten-item scale. The upward moving line represents the regression for winning candidates; the downward moving line represents the regression line for losing candidates. Clearly, constituencies elect candidates who are ideologically compatible and reject those who are not.

But what about changes in the ideological composition of the House of Representatives at the national level? Ideological changes follow changes in the House's party composition, but, as we have seen, the forces behind these partisan changes do not involve any collective public desire for an ideological shift of direction.

Normally, the American electorate is rather static in its collective position on the ideological scale. But if the national electorate were to shift ideologically, could it get the House of Representatives to change with it? The likely answer is yes. The same forces that work at the constituency level to create representation would work at the national level to make the House responsive to a true ideological shift in the national mood. Because constituencies generally elect the candidate from the party most ideologically compatible with their views, an ideologically changed national electorate would elect a greater proportion of members from the more ideologically compatible party. Because local candidates tend to modify their ideological positions when the local constituency changes, candidates generally would tend to move in response to a national ideological drift. And because local candidates who are out of ideological step with their constituencies are the most

Figure 4-6   Candidate Conservatism and Reagan Vote, Winners and
Losers, 1982

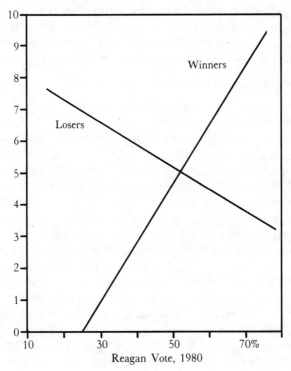

NOTE: Conservatism is measured by an index constructed from the 1982 CBS
News/*New York Times* poll of congressional candidates.

likely to lose, candidates who are out of step with a national ideological
movement would be more likely to lose. All these processes would
ensure that an ideologically changed electorate would get an ideologically changed Congress.

## House-Senate Differences
## in Electoral Representation

The Founding Fathers intended the Senate to be an elite chamber,
isolated from the democratic demands of the House. Regardless of how
well or poorly this intention has been realized, there are fundamental
constitutional differences between the two chambers. The Seventeenth
Amendment to the Constitution abolished the most remarkable difference by providing for direct election of senators. (Before 1918 state

legislatures selected each state's senators.) Still, each state elects two senators rather than a number based on population, as in the House. Senators have staggered six-year terms, freeing them from the never-ending campaigns of representatives with their two-year electoral cycles. And, for the most part, the constituencies senators represent are larger and much more diverse than those of representatives.

## Election Results and the Senate

In terms of national election results, the party composition of the Senate reflects the same forces that determine the party composition of the House. The division between Democrats and Republicans in the Senate is influenced by presidential coattails (in presidential years), presidential popularity (at midterm), and the electorate's reaction to economic conditions.[23] The Senate's partisan division responds more sluggishly to national trends, however, because only one-third of the senators are up for reelection in any election year.

As a general rule, Senate elections are more competitive than House elections. Nonincumbent Senate races are almost always sharply contested by both parties. And when an incumbent senator seeks reelection, the chance of defeat is considerably greater than that of the incumbent House member who seeks reelection. Senators are reelected at about a 78 percent rate, compared with 92 percent for House incumbents. One reason for closer Senate races is that the statewide Senate constituencies rarely are dominated by one political party as the smaller House districts are. Another major factor is the stronger challengers in Senate races. A senator is far more likely than a House member to face a politically seasoned and well-financed election opponent.

Although reelection to the Senate is more difficult, senators need to run only every six years, instead of the bienniel electoral hurdle of House members. The appropriate comparison of electoral security is a comparison of survival rates over the same period of time. Measured over six years, House members seeking reelection have a survival rate of approximately 78 percent—about the same as the reelection rate for senators.[24]

Thus, the six-year term for senators almost exactly offsets the greater incumbency advantage of the House. Senators run less often but at more risk. The long-run survival rates for the two houses would appear to be roughly equal.

## Representation: The House and Senate Compared

Is the Senate any less responsive to popular opinion than the House? Six-year terms would seem to provide senators with ample

Table 4-3   Regression of Incumbent Ideology (1982) on District/State Reagan Vote (1980) for the Senate and House

|  | *Constant* | *Party* | *Reagan vote* | $R^2$ | *N of cases*[a] |
|---|---|---|---|---|---|
| **Equation 1:** | | | | | |
| House | −4.1 | | .18 | .33 | 383 |
| | | | (.01) | | |
| Senate[a] | −5.1 | | .20 | .20 | 97 |
| | | | (.08) | | |
| **Equation 2:** | | | | | |
| House | −2.1 | 3.0 | .11 | .50 | 383 |
| | | (.3) | (.01) | | |
| Senate[a] | −4.8 | 3.0 | .16 | .40 | 97 |
| | | (.5) | (.04) | | |

NOTE: Coefficients represent unstandardized regression equations. Standard errors are in parentheses.

[a] 1982 retirees excluded.

freedom from electoral concerns, except for the final run up to election. And when senators decide to be attentive to their electorates, their diverse constituencies make full representation difficult.

Measured in terms of ideological responsiveness, representation in the two houses is remarkably similar. To show this, we returned to the 1982 CBS News/*New York Times* poll, which ascertained the policy positions of senators as well as House members. We used the 1980 district and states votes for Ronald Reagan as a surrogate measure for constituency ideological preferences. The results of regressing incumbent ideology on the Reagan vote and on the incumbents' party affiliations are shown in Table 4-3.

The coefficients show virtually identical responsiveness in incumbent issue conservatism to differences in both party and constituency ideology for the two chambers. Holding constant constituency voting, Democrats in each House are systematically more liberal (by about three points on our ten-point scale). Holding party affiliation constant, the responsiveness to constituency is also about the same in the two chambers, as measured by the .11 and .15 coefficients for the 1980 Reagan vote. At the most general level, then, the structure of representation is the same in the Senate and the House. In each chamber, the ideological tone of the members' policy positions are shaped by both their party affiliation and the ideological leanings of the constituencies they represent.

## State Populations and the Senate

Although states vary considerably in population, each has two senators. California's 25 million people get the same number of senators as Alaska's one-half million. To some extent, this constitutionally designed "malapportionment" favors political conservatism. Indeed, state population correlates rather strongly (+.34) with our measure of citizen liberalism, based on pooled CBS/*New York Times* surveys.[25] Small, politically conservative states enjoy an extra margin of representation.

During the Reagan years, when the Republicans enjoyed a six-year Senate majority, the Senate was clearly the more conservative chamber. One is tempted to attribute this senatorial conservatism to the Senate's overrepresentation of small states. But the movement of national political tides may be strong enough to overcome any conservative bias. In past decades, the Senate was often thought to be more liberal than the more provincial House of Representatives.

## The Six-Year Term

Because House members face election every two years, for them the election campaign, and hence the need to consider the electoral consequences of their behavior, are immediate. For senators, the six-year term can provide some leeway. Voters—so it sometimes seems—are electorally myopic, forgetting what senators do early in their terms and remembering only what they do closer to the election.

Whether this view of the electorate is valid, there is a good deal of evidence that senatorial roll call voting responds to the six-year cycle.[26] In the year or two before they must run again, incumbents move away from their party's extreme. Democrats inch in a conservative direction and Republicans edge over to the left. The purpose in each instance is to appeal to moderate voters.

Our ten-item measure of candidate liberalism-conservatism for 1982 can illustrate the nature of this dynamic. Here we regress candidate ideology on our survey-based measure of citizen ideology in the states. We do so for three different groups: those incumbents running for reelection, incumbent senators not up for reelection, and challengers/open seat candidates. The larger the coefficient for party affiliation, the more that Democrats and Republicans represent their parties' ideological extremes. Similarly, the larger the coefficient for citizen ideology in the state, the larger is our estimate of the group's responsiveness to public opinion at the time of the election.

Table 4-4 shows the results, which are completely consistent with the hypothesis that senators moderate their roll call voting toward the

Table 4-4 Regressions of Candidate Issue Conservatism on State Ideological Conservatism and Party Affiliation

|  | Constant | Party affiliation (Republican) | State ideological conservatism | $R^2$ | N |
|---|---|---|---|---|---|
| Incumbent running | 1.9 | 1.3 (.8) | 20.9 (4.9) | .44 | 32 |
| Incumbent not running | 1.3 | 3.8 (.6) | 18.9 (3.7) | .64 | 64 |
| Challengers/open seats | 1.5 | 6.0 (.6) | 9.0 (4.0) | .76 | 35 |

NOTE: Coefficients are unstandardized regression coefficients. Standard errors are in parentheses.

end of their terms. The party coefficient is much smaller for incumbents up for reelection in 1982 than for incumbents not under immediate electoral pressure. Meanwhile, the coefficient for state opinion is a bit larger for those facing reelection. These findings indicate that those facing reelection moderate their ideological positions.

Note also that the party coefficient is largest for challengers. Challengers appear not to moderate at all, instead running as party stalwarts unwilling to compromise party ideology to the needs of winning the election. We saw a similar pattern for House challengers. Challengers tend to be tied to the preferences of ideological supporters and party activists, while incumbents have the luxury of office and time to cultivate broader electoral coalitions in their states.

## Issues and Senate Elections

Because senators moderate their ideological positions as reelection approaches, they presumably have good reason to do so, and the reason must be that senators believe that moderation enhances their chance of electoral success. Earlier we saw evidence that House members are more electorally secure with moderate ideological positions. Is the same true for senators?

The policy positions that candidates take have an impact on their reelection chances. For the Senate, candidates do better if they avoid their party's ideological extremes. Gerald Wright and Michael Berkman estimated the impact of candidate issue positions by comparing different pairings of candidate ideological positions, while statistically controlling for the effects of several constituency characteristics and attitudes.[27] They estimated that whether a Senate candidate represents the party's moderate wing or more extremist wing creates a difference ranging from five to eight percentage points. This effect is similar to that observed for House elections.

## Conclusion

Along with presidential elections, congressional elections provide citizens with their main opportunity to influence the direction of national policy. When elections bring about significant changes in the party composition of Congress, we can be fairly confident of two things. One is that the new Congress will have a different ideological cast. Democratic and Republican candidates for House and Senate stand for quite different things. Therefore, electing more Democrats or more Republicans increases the likelihood of policy movement in the ideological direction of the advantaged party. Ironically, the second is that such changes are due less to the electorate's desire for new policy directions than to factors such as presidential coattails or the automatic slump for the presidential party at midterm.

Where we see the electorate's influence on policy direction is in the relationship between constituencies and their elected representatives. In terms of ideological direction, individual House and Senate members respond to their constituencies. In turn, ideological direction matters when constituencies decide which candidates they will elect and which they will not.

As individuals, voters know little about their representatives and only a bit more about their senators. House challengers are almost invisible, and only a portion of the electorate has even a modest amount of information about senatorial challengers. Nevertheless, this uninformed electorate manages to bring about very substantial levels of policy representation. The electorate is much more capable in the aggregate than as individual voters. It is as though all our individual ignorance and misinformed judgments cancel out, so that average perceptions and judgments are responsive to what the candidates say and do. The result is perhaps a more representative Congress than the electorate sometimes seems to deserve.

## Notes

1. Gary C. Jacobson and Samuel Kernell, "Strategy and Choice in the 1982 Congressional Elections," *PS* 15 (Summer 1982): 426; John A. Ferejohn and Randall L. Calvert, "Presidential Coattails in Historical Perspective," *American Journal of Political Science* 28 (February 1984): 131.

2. Stephen Ansolabehere, David Brady, and Morris Fiorina, "The Marginals Never Vanished?" Research paper No. 970, Graduate School of Business, Stanford University, December 1987.

3. Philip E. Converse, "The Concept of the Normal Vote," in *Elections and the Political Order,* ed. Angus Campbell, Philip E. Converse, Warren E. Miller, and Donald E. Stokes (New York: John Wiley & Sons, 1966), 9-39.

4. Ferejohn and Calvert, "Presidential Coattails."

5. Angus Campbell, "Surge and Decline: A Study of Electoral Change," in *Elections and the Political Order.*

6. See also Robert S. Erikson, "The Puzzle of Midterm Loss," *Journal of Politics* 50 (November 1988): 1011-1029.

7. Morris Fiorina, "The Reagan Years: Turning to the Right or Groping for the Middle?" in *The Resurgence of Conservatism in Anglo-American Democracies,* ed. Barry Cooper, Allan Kornberg, and William Mishler (Durham, N.C.: Duke University Press, 1988).

8. Robert S. Erikson, Norman R. Luttbeg, and Kent L. Tedin, *American Public Opinion: Its Origins, Content, and Impact,* 3d ed. (New York: Macmillan, 1988), chap. 3.

9. Robert S. Erikson, "Economic Conditions and the Presidential Vote," *American Political Science Review* 89 (June 1989, forthcoming).

10. See, for example, Edward R. Tufte, *Political Control of the Economy* (Princeton, N.J.: Princeton University Press, 1978).

11. John L. Sullivan and Robert E. O'Connor, "Electoral Choice and Popular Control of Public Policy: The Case of the 1966 House Elections," *American Political Science Review* 66 (December 1972): 1256-1268; Gerald C. Wright, "Elections and the Potential for Policy Change in Congress," in *Congress and Policy Change,* by Gerald C. Wright and Leroy Rieselbach (New York: Agathon Press, 1985).

12. On voter awareness of candidates, see Thomas E. Mann, *Unsafe at Any Margin: Interpreting Congressional Elections* (Washington, D.C.: American Enterprise Institute, 1978); Donald E. Stokes and Warren E. Miller, "Party Government and the Salience of Congress," *Public Opinion Quarterly* 26 (Winter 1962): 531-546; and Barbara Hinckley, *Congressional Elections* (Washington, D.C.: CQ Press, 1981), chap. 2.

13. Bruce Cain, John Ferejohn, and Morris Fiorina, *The Personal Vote: Constituency Service and Electoral Independence* (Cambridge, Mass.: Harvard University Press, 1987).

14. For various estimates, see Robert S. Erikson, "Malapportionment, Gerrymandering, and Party Fortunes in Congressional Elections," *American Political Science Review* 66 (December 1972): 1234-1245; David Mayhew, "Congressional Elections: The Case of the Vanishing Marginals," *Policy* 6 (Spring 1973): 295-318; and Albert D. Cover and David R. Mayhew, "Congressional Dynamics and the Decline of Competitive Congressional Elections," *Congress Reconsidered,* 2d ed., ed. Lawrence C. Dodd and Bruce I. Oppenheimer (Washington, D.C.: CQ Press, 1981), 62-82.

15. Jacobson and Kernell, "Strategy and Choice."
16. Cover and Mayhew, "Congressional Dynamics"; John A. Ferejohn, "On the Decline of Competition in Congressional Elections," *American Political Science Review* 71 (1977): 166-176.
17. Gary C. Jacobson, "The Effects of Campaign Spending in Congressional Elections," *American Political Science Review* 72 (June 1978): 469-491.
18. Anthony Downs, *An Economic Theory of Democracy* (New York: Harper & Row, 1957), chap. 8.
19. Robert S. Erikson, "The Electoral Impact of Congressional Roll Call Voting," *American Political Science Review* 65 (December 1971): 1018-1032; Gerald C. Wright, Jr., "Candidates' Policy Positions and Voting in U.S. House Elections, *Legislative Studies Quarterly* 3 (1978): 445-464; Robert S. Erikson and Gerald C. Wright, Jr., "Policy Representation of Constituency Interests," *Political Behavior* 1 (1980): 91-106.
20. Erikson and Wright, "Policy Representation."
21. Ibid. Very similar patterns were found for 1974.
22. John E. Schwarz and Barton Fenmore, "Congressional Election Results and Congressional Roll Call Behavior: The Case of 1964, 1968, and 1972," *Legislative Studies Quarterly* 2 (1977): 409-422; Erikson, "The Electoral Impact"; Erikson and Wright, "Policy Representation."
23. John R. Hibbing and John R. Alford, "Economic Conditions and the Forgotten Side of Congress: A Foray into U.S. Senate Elections," *British Journal of Political Science* 12 (1982): 505-513; Alan I. Abramowitz, "Comparison of Voting for U.S. Senator and Representative," *American Political Science Review* 74 (1980): 633-640; Alan I. Abramowitz and Jeffrey A. Segal, "Determinants of the Outcomes of U.S. Senate Elections," *Journal of Politics* 48 (1986): 433-439; Alan I. Abramowitz, "Explaining Senate Election Outcomes," *American Political Science Review* 82 (1988): 385-404; Gerald C. Wright, "Level-of-Analysis Effects on Explanations of Voting," *British Journal of Political Science* 19 (1989, forthcoming).
24. Amihai Glazer and Bernard Grofman, "Two Plus Two Plus Two Equals Six: Tenure of Office of Senators and Representatives, 1953-1983," *Legislative Studies Quarterly* 12 (November 1987): 555-563.
25. Gerald C. Wright, Robert S. Erikson, and John P. McIver, "Measuring State Partisanship and Ideology with Survey Data," *Journal of Politics* 47 (May 1985): 479-489.
26. Richard F. Fenno, *The United States Senate: A Bicameral Perspective* (Washington, D.C.: American Enterprise Institute, 1982); Martin Thomas, "Electoral Proximity and Senatorial Roll Call Voting," *American Journal of Political Science* 29 (1984): 96-111.
27. Gerald C. Wright and Michael Berkman, "Candidates and Policy in United States Elections," *American Political Science Review* 80 (1986): 253-283.

# 5. PARTIES AND PACS IN CONGRESSIONAL ELECTIONS

## Gary C. Jacobson

In the political market place, no less than in the economic market place, competition is the mother of invention. During the 1960s declining partisanship among voters, greater ease of travel and communication, augmented resources for serving constituents, and expanded government programs combined to offer new ways for members of Congress to please constituents and win votes. Among the consequences was a notable increase in the average incumbent's margin of victory, which appeared to make members less vulnerable to national trends and other electoral threats.[1] This turn of events naturally helped the Democrats, whose good fortune it was to be the majority party at the time.

Congressional incumbents were not left for long to enjoy the fruits of innovation. During the 1970s changes in the campaign finance laws produced two major new institutional forces in congressional elections: invigorated national party campaign committees and nonparty political action committees (PACs).[2] At first, both parties and PACs developed in ways that threatened to undermine the advantage of incumbents in general and of Democrats in particular. More recently, several of the major trends have been halted or reversed as Democrats (and incumbents) have responded with innovations of their own. Parties and PACs clearly have altered the electoral landscape, but the consequences for electoral competition remain in doubt. This essay attempts to explain what has happened and how new electoral institutions and practices have changed congressional politics.

## Origins

National party involvement in congressional campaigns is nothing new.[3] Political action committees, especially those run by organized labor, also have a notable history. Nor are corporations newcomers to campaign finance; the legal ban on direct corporate contributions enacted in 1907 was routinely circumvented.[4] But the new rules coming into force in the early 1970s with the Federal Election Campaign Act

(FECA) and its amendments drastically altered the legal environment of campaign financing, setting conditions that invited both national party committees and PACs to flourish. The result has been a qualitative as well as quantitative change in campaign roles.

The rules governing PACs evolved from a series of decisions by Congress, the Federal Election Commission (FEC), and the Supreme Court. In brief, these decisions clarified the ambiguous legal status of PACs and acknowledged their legal financial role in campaigns.[5] Organizations of all kinds may establish committees to solicit funds to contribute to candidates for federal office. If organized by a labor union or corporation, the parent organization may pay the overhead but may not contribute directly to the committee. To qualify as a multicandidate committee, a PAC must raise money from at least fifty people and contribute to at least five candidates. The maximum contribution is $5,000 per candidate per campaign, which means, in effect, $10,000— $5,000 each in the primary and general campaigns. PACs also may give up to $15,000 to a national party committee and $5,000 to any other political committee. There is no limit to the total amount a PAC may contribute to all candidates. The law gives PACs two significant advantages over private persons: individuals may give no more than $1,000 per candidate per campaign and may contribute no more than $25,000 in total to candidates or committees in any calendar year.

Most of the regulations governing PACs were worked out in Congress, sometimes in response to administrative and court decisions that had upset previous arrangements. Of necessity, Congress tried to balance the role of Democratic allies (organized labor) and Republican allies (business corporations). But one major decision was imposed by the Court quite against the desire of either party. The FECA had imposed a limit of $1,000 on how much people or groups could spend independently of candidates' official campaigns. The Court declared in *Buckley v. Valeo* that this limit was an infringement of First Amendment rights and hence void.[6] PACs and individuals, therefore, are free to spend as much as they can on independent campaigns for or against federal candidates.

Clear rules governing PACs eliminated the uncertainties inherent in their previously doubtful legal position and gave them a solid institutional role in financing campaigns. Their activities are thoroughly regulated, but compliance is not difficult, and the independent spending route is available to any group that feels overly constrained. Regulation, rather than discouraging entrepreneurial activity, has made it easier.

Incentives for building national party organizations also were greatly strengthened by the FECA. The experience of most members of

Congress was that parties were of little electoral help, financially or otherwise.[7] Hence the FECA Amendments of 1974 subjected party organizations to the same direct contribution limits as PACs. But the special character of parties could not be denied, and most members did not want campaign finance regulation to weaken what were already ailing institutions. State and national party organizations were, therefore, allowed to spend additional money on behalf of their candidates. The opportunity to spend money opened the way for national party committees to become major participants in congressional campaign finance for the first time.

Coordinated party spending, as it is called, also is limited, but the ceilings are higher than PACs' limits and, unlike contribution ceilings, rise with inflation. The original limit for a House campaign was $10,000; by 1988, inflation had pushed it up to $23,050. The ceiling for Senate campaigns varies with the population of the state ($.02 times the voting age population, adjusted for inflation since 1974, with a minimum of $20,000, also adjusted). The ceiling ranged from $46,100 (in the five least populous states) to $938,688 (in California) for the 1988 elections.[8]

State parties also may spend up to this ceiling for federal candidates, but almost no state party has the money to do it. Republican party officials have exploited this situation to double, in effect, the amount the national party may spend for its candidates. The national party committee simply contracts with each state party to act as its agent for raising and spending the money. The Democrats challenged the legality of this ploy but failed to persuade the Supreme Court.[9]

National party committees can thus make sizable contributions to congressional campaigns. In 1988, for example, a House candidate could receive as much as $76,100 in assistance directly or indirectly from national party sources (direct contributions of $5,000 in both the primary and general election from the party's national committee, the congressional campaign committee, and the state party committee, plus twice $23,050 in coordinated spending). For Senate candidates the ceiling varied from $119,700 in the least populous states to more than $1.9 million in California.

Before any money can be distributed, the national party committees must first raise it. Following the adoption of the FECA, Republican party committees assumed a wide lead over their Democratic counterparts in fund raising. The Republicans also were quicker to build organizations that were able to use party resources efficiently. Some reasons for the Republican advantage will be explored later. But it is hardly accidental that the minority party, facing a system of electoral politics highly favorable to incumbents, showed the greater knack for innovation.

Two other developments contributed to the flowering of parties and PACs. One is technological innovation: both the new national party committees and PACs are creatures of new technologies for raising and spending campaign money. The other is the expansion of the federal government's role in economic and social life.

The exponential growth in computer capabilities, combined with the continued development of electronic mass media, offered new ways of storing, retrieving, and exchanging information of all kinds. For example, computerized direct mail technology allows money to be raised efficiently through small donations from millions of individuals, tapping resources previously inaccessible to political organizers on a large scale. Republican party committees and conservative ideological PACs were quickest to take advantage of direct mail. Ideological entrepreneurs with a mission and, on occasion, an eye to profiting from selling services to the PAC, have been the most persistent direct mail innovators.[10] Direct mail is also used for campaigning because every solicitation contains a message and most messages include pleas for money.

Technological advances made polling much more sophisticated, allowed more careful targeting of campaign messages, and permitted greater efficiency through central coordination of campaign activities. But the new technologies are expensive to use; they raise the cost of campaigning and, therefore, the demand for the kinds of help PACs and parties deliver. Technological changes have contributed to both the supply of and demand for the services parties and PACs provide.

The federal government's expanded role in American life also has encouraged the growth of PACs. The greater the impact Congress has on the distribution of economic goods and social values, the greater the incentives for people and groups to engage in political action.[11] When government policy has a major influence on the balance sheet, it is simply good business to invest in politics. When Congress decides whose social values are to prevail, it is no surprise to find people passionately committed to a particular vision of the social good using whatever resources they can muster to influence elections and policies. The growth of political institutions in the private sector is a predictable consequence of an expanding public sector.

It is no small irony that the FECA's principal goals included putting a lid on campaign expenditures and reducing the financial role of "special interests." The first goal was stymied by the Court, which found spending limits unconstitutional. This ruling, along with the expensive new campaign technology, the increased incentives for putting money into politics, and a decade of inflation made it impossible to achieve the second goal. For as campaign spending has continued to grow, candidates have found it harder to ignore the superior efficiency of soliciting PACs, which can give as much as $10,000, rather than individuals, who are limited to $2,000. Rising costs also enhanced the position of party committees, whose coordinated spending limits are indexed against inflation. And, despite many instances of cooperation, parties and PACs remain, fundamentally, natural rivals. I will have more to say about this later.

## Growth

Party and PAC entrepreneurs wasted little time in responding to the new rules. The proliferation of PACs since 1974 is a familiar story to any observer of American politics, yet its meaning is obscure.[12] The category "political action committee" actually encompasses an enormously diverse set of organizations. The FEC's categories—labor, corporate, trade/membership/health, nonconnected, cooperative, and corporation without stock—only begin to suggest the variety. Even within each of these categories, PACs differ widely. Some are little more than lone entrepreneurs with mailing lists; others are adjuncts of large corporations or labor unions. In some, all contribution decisions are made centrally; others encourage extensive input from members. Some have immediate, narrow, self-interested goals; others pursue long-term objectives involving widely shared values or collective goods. Most PACs only give money; but a few of them also supply campaign workers, work to get out the vote, produce advertising, advise on campaign strategy, and recruit and train candidates. Some participate in coalitions of PACs or cooperate with one of the parties; others make independent decisions. Indeed, the variety is such that virtually everything said at one time or another about PACs is true of *some* PAC.[13] Caution is always advised when generalizing about them.

Between 1974 and 1988 the number of political action committees registered with the FEC grew from 608 to 4,527. Corporate and nonconnected PACs (PACs that are independent, self-sustaining organizations without any sponsoring body) multiplied the most rapidly over this period. PAC contributions to congressional candidates show a parallel increase, growing by 375 percent between 1974 and 1986 (adjusted for inflation).

These figures have been used, on occasion, to argue that PACs are swamping the electoral process. The data in Table 5-1 place them in context, showing that contributions from private individuals continue to be the most important source of direct contributions by a wide margin. The share of funds supplied by PACs has grown, but it still amounts to little more than one-third of House candidates' money and about one-fifth of Senate candidates' money. Party donations comprise only a small proportion of *direct* contributions to congressional candidates; most party assistance comes in the form of coordinated spending, which is not included in these data.

National party committee activities have grown as explosively as PAC activities—at least on the Republican side. Table 5-2 documents the growth of national party receipts between 1976 and 1986. The table actually understates Republican superiority because it does not include money officially credited to state and local parties that was actually raised by national party "agents." If state and local money is included, Republican party committees raised a total of $300 million in 1983-1984—more than was raised by all PACs combined during that election cycle. In 1985-1986, without the stimulus of the presidential campaign, total Republican receipts fell to $252 million, and PAC fund raising surged ahead to $353 million.

Not all party money goes to congressional candidates directly or as coordinated spending—PACs put a much larger share of their income into campaigns—but plenty of it does. Coordinated party spending has been concentrated disproportionately in Senate races, reflecting the much higher legal spending ceilings for these contests as well as intense party competition for majority control. In elections from 1980 through 1986, Republican House candidates got about 9 percent of their money directly or indirectly from the party, and Republican Senate candidates got about 12 percent. The equivalent figures for Democrats are 2 percent and 5 percent. Although Democratic committees have increased their coordinated spending in recent elections, Republicans retain a large advantage. In 1986 Republican party committees spent $4.2 million, and Democratic committees spent $1.8 million, on behalf of their House campaigns; Republican committees spent $10.1 million, Democratic committees, $4.1 million, for Senate candidates.

Republican committees are so much wealthier for several reasons. One is that they had a long head start in developing their direct mail fund-raising system; more than 75 percent of their funds come in small sums (less than $100) from regular contributors on their mailing lists. Democratic committees, in contrast, still rely heavily on large individual and PAC donations. Another is that Republicans perfected their direct mail fund raising during the late 1970s while they were the out party. It is easier to arouse people who oppose politicians and policies than those who support them. A third reason is that Republicans solicit a more affluent constituency than the Democrats. Finally, Republicans are more ideologically homogeneous; it matters little to contributors which one ultimately gets the money, so it makes sense to let the party

Table 5-1   Sources of Contributions to House and Senate Candidates, 1972-1986

|  | Average contributions | Percentage of contributions from | | | |
|---|---|---|---|---|---|
|  |  | Individuals[a] | PACs | Parties[b] | Unknown |
| *House* |  |  |  |  |  |
| 1972 | $ 51,752[c] | 60 | 14 | 17 | 9 |
| 1974 | 61,084 | 79 | 17 | 4 | — |
| 1976 | 79,421 | 70 | 25 | 8 | — |
| 1978 | 111,232 | 70 | 29 | 5 | — |
| 1980 | 148,268 | 67 | 29 | 4 | — |
| 1982 | 222,620 | 63 | 31 | 6 | — |
| 1984 | 240,722 | 60 | 37 | 3 | — |
| 1986 | 282,260 | 61 | 38 | 2 | — |
| *Senate* |  |  |  |  |  |
| 1972 | $ 353,933[c] | 67 | 12 | 14 | 8 |
| 1974 | 455,515 | 77 | 11 | 6 | 6 |
| 1976 | 624,094 | 81 | 15 | 4 | — |
| 1978 | 951,930 | 84 | 14 | 2 | — |
| 1980 | 1,079,346 | 78 | 21 | 2 | — |
| 1982 | 1,771,167 | 81 | 18 | 1 | — |
| 1984 | 2,273,635 | 80 | 19 | 1 | — |
| 1986 | 2,721,793 | 76 | 24 | 1 | — |

[a] Includes candidates' contributions and loans to their own campaigns.
[b] Does not include party expenditures on behalf of candidates.
[c] Some contributions made before April 7, 1972, may have gone unrecorded.

Table 5-2   National Party Receipts, 1976-1986 (in millions)

| Party | 1976 | 1978 | 1980 | 1982 | 1984 | 1986 |
|---|---|---|---|---|---|---|
| *Democrats* |  |  |  |  |  |  |
| DNC | $13.1 | $11.3 | $15.4 | $16.5 | $46.6 | $17.2 |
| DSCC | 1.0 | .3 | 1.7 | 5.7 | 8.9 | 13.4 |
| DCCC | .9 | 2.8 | 2.9 | 6.5 | 10.4 | 12.3 |
| Total | $15.0 | $14.4 | $20.0 | $28.7 | $65.9 | $42.9 |
| *Republicans* |  |  |  |  |  |  |
| RNC | $29.1 | $34.2 | $ 77.8 | $ 84.1 | $106.2 | $ 83.8 |
| NRSC | 1.8 | 10.9 | 22.3 | 48.9 | 81.7 | 86.1 |
| NRCC | 12.1 | 14.1 | 20.3 | 58.0 | 58.3 | 39.8 |
| Total | $43.0 | $59.2 | $120.4 | $191.0 | $246.2 | $209.7 |

SOURCE: Norman J. Ornstein, Thomas E. Mann, and Michael J. Malbin, *Vital Statistics on Congress, 1987-1988* (Washington, D.C.: Congressional Quarterly, 1987), 99-101.

decide. Contributors to the Democratic party have more reason to care about which Democrat gets the money (southern conservative or urban liberal?) and therefore to make that decision themselves.

Abundant money has allowed Republican party officials to build an extensive organization and to pursue an impressive range of party-building and electoral activities. The national party maintains a staff of more than 600 and keeps a flock of outside pollsters, media specialists, stationers, direct mail outfits, computer vendors, and advertising professionals on retainer.[14] It conducts registration drives, mounts national advertising campaigns, trains workers, teaches fund raising, and coordinates contribution strategies of cooperative PACs.[15] It has even employed caseworkers to help contributors deal with government agencies—a function members of Congress no doubt would prefer to monopolize themselves.[16] All of these functions are added to the primary task of helping candidates win elections.

> Its cash and resources equip the GOP to nurture candidates through the entire electoral process: initial ticket selection, preliminary organization, training, fundraising, polling, hiring of consultants, analysis of the opposition, manipulation of the media, computerized phone banks, advertising, direct mail and last-minute get-out-the-vote drives.[17]

Democrats offer many of the same services, though necessarily to fewer candidates and at lower levels. They lack the money to match the Republicans. Through 1980, while Republicans were surging ahead, the Democratic National Committee (DNC) was still trying to retire debts from the 1968 election.[18] Democratic party officials have subsequently improved their fund raising significantly, and the House and Senate campaign committees have grown at a rate that would be impressive if only they could avoid comparison with their Republican counterparts.

As Table 5-2 indicates, contributions to the Democratic Congressional Campaign Committee (DCCC) nearly doubled between 1982 and 1986, while contributions to the National Republican Congressional Committee (NRCC) fell by more than 30 percent, yet the NRCC still raised more than three times as much money as the DCCC. The Democratic Senatorial Campaign Committee (DSCC) made even greater gains but was even worse off with respect to the National Republican Senatorial Committee (NRSC). In 1986 Republicans retained a five-to-one advantage in party funds. So it is perhaps curious that through 1986 the Democrats retained a comfortable 258-177 majority in the House and had retaken the Senate, 55-45. This irony will be examined, if not fully explained, later.

## Parties Versus PACs

National party committees (especially on the Republican side) and PACs thrive in today's legal and technological environment. Sometimes they cooperate. Many Republican-oriented corporate PACs, for example, take cues from the NRCC and the NRSC when deciding where to contribute their funds, and labor PACs often look after the collective interests of congressional Democrats. But in a very basic sense, parties and PACs are natural rivals. They pursue conflicting goals and so follow conflicting electoral strategies.

Collectively, a party's main electoral goal is to win as many seats as possible.[19] In the abstract, it makes little difference to the party which individual candidates win, only that as many as possible do. The candidates, on the other hand, care very much who wins. Although one can imagine a situation in which winning is of little value unless one is part of a majority—a situation in which candidates would be willing to take considerable electoral risks to improve their party's chances—this is emphatically not true of congressional election politics. The fruits of victory by no means go exclusively to the majority. The primary interest of candidates, then, lies in maximizing their own likelihood of winning. The party's collective interests are decidedly secondary.

Parties and candidates therefore have different preferences about the distribution of campaign resources. The party would prefer to deploy resources in a way that maximizes the number of seats it wins. It would redirect resources from campaigns of its stronger candidates to the campaigns of weaker candidates up to the point where the expected marginal gains (in seats) among the weaker are matched by the expected marginal losses among the stronger. Individual candidates, on the other hand, would resist giving up resources if it means increasing the risk of defeat; losing candidates find little solace in a large aggregate victory for their party.

The outcome of this conflict depends on who controls resources. The greater the share controlled by the party and the freer its officials are to pursue collective ends, the more efficiently the party will deploy campaign resources and the more seats it should win. The more resources controlled by its stronger candidates, the less efficient and collectively successful it should be. In congressional elections, the central practical issues are the amount of money controlled by national party campaign committees and the extent to which these committees avoid domination by the party's incumbents.

With few exceptions, PACs pursue objectives that lead them to subvert collective party goals. Although all PACs mean to influence public policy, they differ in how broadly or narrowly policy objectives are conceived and in strategies for reaching them. To many business corporations, labor unions, and trade associations, the PAC is simply an aid to traditional lobbying for narrowly focused economic interests. Policy goals are specific and immediate: a tax break, regulatory relief, a higher price support subsidy, a loan guarantee. Money is given not so much to affect the outcome as to gain access and curry favor with those who wind up in a position to influence immediate economic interests. PACs of this sort contribute to sure winners who do not need the money, to members of both parties sitting on committees dealing with legislation they care about, and to newly elected members *after* the election. The popularity of this approach explains why PAC contributions as a whole strongly favor congressional incumbents (illustrative data are presented later in Tables 5-3 and 5-4). Money spent on sure winners or on candidates after they have won is, from the party's collective perspective, almost entirely wasted.

At the opposite end of the spectrum are PACs with broad ideological agendas. Like parties, they aim to maximize the number of seats held by people who share their views. Their idea is to change policies by changing members rather than by persuading members to change policies. They support promising nonincumbent candidates and concentrate their resources on close races. This practice makes conservative PACs the natural allies of Republicans and liberal PACs of Democrats, but it does not prevent an ideological PAC from subverting collective party interests when the PAC's objectives conflict with the party's simple goal of winning the seat. The 1984 election found the National Conservative Political Action Committee (NCPAC) endorsing liberal Democratic Senate candidate Paul Simon over Republican incumbent Charles Percy of Illinois. Percy, a moderate, was chairman of the Foreign Relations Committee; next in line was Jesse Helms, a favorite of the New Right. NCPAC's position was that "the prospects are far less of Paul Simon, as a freshman Democrat, doing damage to the Western World than Chuck Percy as chairman of the Foreign Relations Committee." [20]

Parties are more commonly troubled by passionate single-issue PACs that care only about an individual's position on their issue. Democrats have to contend with peace groups, feminists, gay rights activists, and radical environmentalists. Republicans have to put up with antiabortionists, school prayer enthusiasts, tax-cut activists, and the like. Although such groups often provide valuable support for the more congenial party, they also promote the nomination of more extreme, hence weaker, candidates and introduce campaign issues that their party's candidate would be better off ignoring.

Between the extremes are PACs that pursue both short- and long-term political goals. Many business-oriented PACs support incumbent Democrats when it seems certain that they will win reelection but switch to nonincumbent Republicans when their chances look unusually promising. Corporate PACs gave 39 percent of their funds to nonincumbent Republicans in 1980 but only 22 percent in 1982, reflecting different assessments of Republican prospects in the two elections. Their behavior contributes to the party's collective performance in good years but weakens it in other years. The common corporate preoccupation with short-term policy at the expense of the long-term political climate has frustrated Republican party officials for years.[21] But they have had only limited success in persuading business PACs that they would be better served by working to elect more right-thinking Republicans than by keeping their access to incumbent Democrats. Many business interests treat the situation as a variant of the familiar collective goods problem: Why risk the individual costs of offending Democratic officeholders to pursue the collective good of a more Republican Congress? Democratic leaders have, on occasion, forcefully reminded the business community of this logic.[22]

This thinking is fine for Democratic incumbents, but it does little to help the party collectively; it contributed to an inefficient distribution of Democratic campaign resources in 1982, when millions of PAC dollars went to Democratic incumbents who did not need money, while a number of promising challengers remained seriously underfunded.[23] The problem was compounded by the relative poverty of Democratic party committees; they spent a major portion of their funds on challengers and other candidates in close races, but the sums they had to spend were so small as to be nearly imperceptible. Since 1982 Democrats have done a better job of financing serious challengers, partly because of improved party finances, but mainly because the number of serious challengers has been small. Democrats have continued to raise about as much campaign money as Republicans overall, but because so much less of it flows through the party, it remains more difficult for them to apportion it efficiently.

## Democrats Versus Republicans

The initial expansion of party involvement in congressional elections favored Republicans over Democrats because Republican committees took such a wide lead in money and organization. Republican candidates could count on more help from the party, and party resources were concentrated where they were most likely to make a difference. By 1982 no Republican candidate with a reasonable chance of winning was inadequately funded.

Initial PAC development also favored Republicans. Democratic candidates continued to receive more PAC money, but their advantage eroded over time. In the early 1970s they routinely received about two-thirds of PAC money; by the early 1980s that proportion had decreased to a little more than half. They maintain an advantage only because of their solid House majority. The connection between Democrats and most corporate and trade association PACs, which now supply about two-thirds of PAC funds, is strictly a marriage of convenience and does not extend to nonincumbent Democrats, who have benefited little from the growth of these PACs.

In the most recent elections, however, several financial trends that had spelled trouble for Democrats have been halted or reversed. These and several other important features of PAC activity are illustrated in Table 5-3 and Table 5-4, which present selected data on trends in the distribution of PAC contributions in House and Senate elections from 1978 through 1986. (Data on PAC contributions from which the entries in these tables were taken are found in Table 5-7 and Table 5-8 at the end of this essay and in other sources.)

The entries for 1978 and 1980 represent the culmination of trends that threatened Democrats. Contributions from organized labor, almost all of which went to Democratic candidates, comprised a declining share of all PAC contributions, falling from one-half to one-fourth between 1974 and 1980. They were surpassed by corporate PACs in 1980 and by trade/membership/health PACs in 1982. This trend was particularly noteworthy because only labor PACs gave more than a trivial share of their funds to nonincumbent Democrats. Nonincumbent Republicans enjoyed much more generous support from corporate and trade association PACs. Furthermore, they were strongly favored by the growing contingent of ideological PACs in the nonconnected category, which were unique in their generosity to nonincumbents.

The Republicans' newly acquired financial and organizational resources were put to good advantage in the 1980 and 1982 elections. Both the national party committees and Republican-oriented PACs contributed to the Republican sweep in 1980. Among the Democratic victims were eight House members who had served more than nine terms, including five committee chairmen and the majority whip. Many of them had been shrewdly targeted by party officials in Washington, even though years of weak opposition had given them an air of invulnerability. Republicans also took nine Senate seats from incumbent Democrats—several by very narrow margins—to emerge with their first Senate majority in almost thirty years. Republican party committees and business-related and ideological PACs had concentrated their efforts in these races.[24]

Although aggregate election results make it less obvious, superior organization served Republicans at least as well in 1982. Republicans lost twenty-six House seats in 1982 while breaking even in the Senate. But given the state of the economy and the administration's low standing in the polls at the time of that election, the Republicans could have done much worse. Republican party officials used their centralized control over information and resources to adjust quickly to the deteriorating political environment, thereby rescuing a number of endangered incumbents. The Democrats' decentralized campaign finance system kept them from fully exploiting the opportunity handed them by the economy because they lacked the institutional means to redistribute resources from campaigns where they were no longer needed to campaigns where they might have put a competitive challenger over the top.[25]

The continuation of these trends would have meant serious long-term problems for Democrats. But the trends did not continue; congressional Democrats lost little ground despite Ronald Reagan's sweeping victory in 1984, and in 1986 they recaptured the Senate, defeating seven incumbent Republicans and losing none of their own (and gaining one net open seat) in the process.

Table 5-3 and Table 5-4 show the changes in PAC behavior that have accompanied the Democrats' strong showing in recent congressional elections. On the House side, resources of labor PACs, the Democrats' most loyal supporters, have grown in step with those of other PACs. Corporate and trade association PACs seem to have lost much of their enthusiasm for nonincumbent Republicans. More and more of their largess has been conferred on incumbents of both parties, with Democrats getting more because more incumbents are Democrats. The sharpest change, however, has occurred among nonconnected PACs. Once overwhelmingly Republican, this fastest-growing source of PAC funds now favors Democrats. At the same time, groups in this category have become less supportive of nonincumbents, although they continue to give a larger share of funds to nonincumbents than do PACs in any other category.

The change in the pattern of corporate and trade association PAC contributions reflects diminished opportunities. The main reason these groups have given smaller shares of their funds to nonincumbent Republican House candidates in recent elections is that they have found few with bright enough electoral prospects to justify an investment. Republicans fielded strong contingents of House challengers in 1980 and 1982. But their almost total failure in 1982—not surprising in light of double-digit unemployment and an unpopular administration—evidently discouraged potentially formidable Republican challengers in 1984; therefore, few were poised to exploit Reagan's

Table 5-3   Selected Trends in the Distribution of PAC Contributions to House Candidates, 1978-1986 (in percentages)

| Type of PAC | 1978 | 1980 | 1982 | 1984 | 1986 |
|---|---|---|---|---|---|
| *Labor* | | | | | |
| of PAC dollars | 30 | 25 | 25 | 26 | 26 |
| to Democrats | 96 | 95 | 96 | 94 | 94 |
| to nonincumbents | 36 | 26 | 43 | 23 | 35 |
| *Corporate* | | | | | |
| of PAC dollars | 25 | 32 | 31 | 31 | 31 |
| to incumbents | 63 | 68 | 77 | 82 | 85 |
| Democrats | (35) | (36) | (32) | (43) | (44) |
| Republicans | (28) | (32) | (45) | (39) | (41) |
| to nonincumbents | 37 | 31 | 22 | 19 | 15 |
| Democrats | ( 9) | ( 2) | ( 4) | ( 2) | ( 4) |
| Republicans | (28) | (29) | (18) | (17) | (11) |
| *Trade/membership/health* | | | | | |
| of PAC dollars | 34 | 31 | 27 | 27 | 27 |
| to incumbents | 63 | 71 | 76 | 83 | 83 |
| Democrats | (36) | (39) | (34) | (47) | (45) |
| Republicans | (27) | (32) | (42) | (36) | (38) |
| to nonincumbents | 37 | 30 | 24 | 17 | 18 |
| Democrats | (11) | ( 5) | ( 8) | ( 5) | ( 8) |
| Republicans | (26) | (25) | (16) | (12) | (10) |
| *Nonconnected* | | | | | |
| of PAC dollars | 8 | 8 | 12 | 12 | 13 |
| to Republicans | 77 | 68 | 47 | 48 | 41 |
| to nonincumbents | 74 | 62 | 52 | 45 | 46 |
| Democrats | (10) | ( 9) | (24) | (12) | (26) |
| Republicans | (64) | (53) | (28) | (33) | (20) |

SOURCE: Ornstein, Mann, and Malbin, *Vital Statistics*, 109-120.

triumphant reelection.[26] An even weaker group of Republican challengers emerged in 1986. Astute potential candidates were no doubt discouraged by the historical pattern of electoral disasters for a president's party in the sixth year of an administration, as well as by the sense that Democratic incumbents who had survived Reagan's victory in 1984 would be even tougher to defeat with Reagan no longer heading the ticket.

The major PACs take pains to ascertain which nonincumbents enjoy prospects attractive enough to be worth an investment, and, because they are better informed than ever before, it is unlikely that they inadvertently ignore many potential winners.[27] The dearth of

Table 5-4    Selected Trends in the Distribution of PAC Contributions to Senate Candidates, 1978-1986 (in percentages)

| Type of PAC | 1978 | 1980 | 1982 | 1984 | 1986 |
|---|---|---|---|---|---|
| *Labor* | | | | | |
| of PAC dollars | 28 | 22 | 22 | 16 | 16 |
| to Democrats | 91 | 90 | 92 | 94 | 93 |
| to nonincumbents | 55 | 27 | 37 | 66 | 70 |
| *Corporate* | | | | | |
| of PAC dollars | 36 | 41 | 38 | 41 | 41 |
| to incumbents | 52 | 39 | 67 | 77 | 61 |
| Democrats | (15) | (25) | (26) | (20) | (13) |
| Republicans | (37) | (14) | (41) | (57) | (48) |
| to nonincumbents | 48 | 61 | 33 | 22 | 39 |
| Democrats | (13) | ( 3) | ( 2) | ( 5) | (12) |
| Republicans | (35) | (58) | (31) | (17) | (27) |
| *Trade/membership/health* | | | | | |
| of PAC dollars | 27 | 24 | 22 | 22 | 21 |
| to incumbents | 50 | 54 | 76 | 75 | 60 |
| Democrats | (19) | (37) | (37) | (27) | (18) |
| Republicans | (31) | (17) | (39) | (48) | (42) |
| to nonincumbents | 49 | 47 | 24 | 25 | 40 |
| Democrats | (19) | ( 8) | ( 6) | (15) | (21) |
| Republicans | (30) | (39) | (18) | (10) | (19) |
| *Nonconnected* | | | | | |
| of PAC dollars | 7 | 11 | 14 | 18 | 17 |
| to Republicans | 74 | 73 | 50 | 44 | 45 |
| to nonincumbents | 70 | 71 | 51 | 53 | 59 |
| Democrats | (15) | ( 4) | (21) | (37) | (40) |
| Republicans | (55) | (67) | (30) | (16) | (19) |

SOURCE: Ornstein, Mann, and Malbin, *Vital Statistics,* 112-113.

plausible Republican challengers reinforced the Democrats' pointed reminders that corporate and trade association PACs would be wise to remember who it is they will be doing business with after the election—hence the increased share of contributions going to Democratic incumbents.

The shift among nonconnected groups from a strongly pro-Republican to a pro-Democratic bias reflects a change in the makeup of the groups in this category. Most of this money is raised by ideological groups through direct mail appeals. Such appeals are most effective when they invoke threats that make people fearful or angry enough to send a check, which is easier to do in opposition to current leaders and policies. Just as conservative PACs flourished in the late 1970s, when all bad things could be blamed on Jimmy Carter, Tip O'Neill, and Ted Kennedy, liberal PACs found gold in the Reagan administration, which, along with policies that threatened liberal values, offered serviceable villains such as James Watt and Edwin Meese. As a result, Democrats have more than redressed the financial imbalance among PACs of this type.

Liberal nonconnected PACs have been especially prominent in the successful Democratic effort to regain the Senate (see Table 5-4). In some ways, changes in the pattern of PAC contributions to Senate candidates have paralleled changes in House elections. But PAC activity in any year's Senate elections almost always differs substantially from PAC activity in that year's House elections.[28]

PACs of all kinds are more generous to Senate challengers than they are to House challengers, mainly because the former are more competitive. Corporate, trade association, and ideological PACs invested heavily in nonincumbent Republicans in 1978 and 1980, helping the Republicans take the Senate; labor and liberal PACs concentrated on nonincumbent Democratic challengers in 1984 and 1986 in hopes of returning it to Democratic control. Business-related PACs naturally moved to the defense of incumbent Republicans. But also note how little corporate PACs contributed to Senate Democrats in 1984 and 1986 compared to what they gave to House Democrats. This is evidence of the marriage of convenience I mentioned earlier.

If anything, then, changes in PAC activity since 1982 have favored Democrats over Republicans. Democrats have maintained a comfortable House majority, and in 1986 they recaptured the Senate. No simple causal connection is implied, if only because PACs respond strategically to expectations and so reflect, as well as enhance, electoral trends originating outside the campaign finance system. But certainly the pattern of PAC activity in recent elections has not damaged the prospects of congressional Democrats.

Other fortunate circumstances have helped Democrats to blunt the effect of the Republican advantage in party funds. In 1984 and 1986, in contrast to 1982, almost every serious Democratic congressional challenger was adequately financed. Part of the reason was the greater financial resources controlled by party committees and by the kind of PACs willing to support nonincumbent Democrats; but at least as important was the relatively small number of hotly contested House seats in these elections.[29] With fewer promising challengers and fewer incumbents seriously threatened by Republicans, House Democrats were able to deploy their more limited resources efficiently.[30] Democratic contributors could also devote more attention to the Senate elections. For the Republicans, money and organization could not compensate for a lack of high-quality candidates.

Giving up on the House, Republican contributors focused on retaining the Senate. But Republican money could not preserve the Republican majority. Six of the seven Republican incumbents who lost in 1986 outspent their victorious challengers, five by more than $1 million. The NRSC's six-to-one financial advantage over the DSCC (see Table 5-2) was of no avail. It was diminished, of course, by the FECA's ceiling on party spending for Senate candidates; if the party had spent every legal cent for its Senate candidates, the total would have come to only about $13 million of the $86 million the NRSC raised.

Several of these elections were very close; the transfer of about 55,000 votes, properly distributed, would have left the Senate in Republican hands. But with a similar redistribution of 42,000 votes in the other direction in 1980, Republicans would never have won a majority in the first place, and a shift of 35,000 votes in 1982 would have returned Senate control to the Democrats. In 1980 and 1982, when Republicans won most of the close ones, their financial advantage seemed a plausible explanation, but the 1986 election demonstrated that superior financing is not enough.

Observers attributed the Republican losses to two general causes. One is that a number of Republicans elected in 1980 turned out to be weak candidates who ran inferior campaigns, and they and other Republicans got little help from an uninspiring national campaign, which lacked a theme.[31] The other is that Democratic challengers, although outspent, raised *enough* money to get their message across to voters, and the message was persuasive. One Republican consultant put it succinctly, if hyperbolically: "Smart dimes can beat dumb dollars." [32]

The question of why Republicans were unable to use their resources more effectively cannot be answered fully here. Their failure to show much net electoral profit after nearly a decade of clear financial and organizational superiority—contrary, certainly, to my own expectations[33]—suggests that, at least up to now, the partisan impact of innovation in campaign finance has been surprisingly limited.

## Challengers Versus Incumbents

The expanded activities of PACs and national party committees raised new electoral difficulties for incumbents. Because PACs have always given much more to incumbents than to challengers, it is often argued that PACs' growing role in campaign finance must benefit officeholders,[34] which would be true only if campaign money were equally valuable to incumbents and challengers. It is not. The evidence is overwhelming that the marginal returns on campaign spending are much greater for challengers than for incumbents. Statistically, spending by incumbents is unrelated to their vote share, although it affects their probability of winning the election. The more challengers spend, on the other hand, the greater their share of the vote, and their level of spending has a substantially larger impact on their probability of winning elections than does the incumbents' level of spending.[35] This financial reality is why most contributions to incumbents are, from a party's collective perspective, a waste of money and why almost any increase in the amount of money available to help both challengers and incumbents will favor challengers—even if in absolute terms the incumbent enjoys the greater increase. A further corollary is that it matters less to incumbents what PACs and parties give to them than what they give to their opponents.

Beyond making more money available, parties and PACs are in a position to alter electoral politics in ways designed to frustrate incumbents' favorite reelection strategies. During the late 1960s and early 1970s, members of Congress exploited political and technological changes to strengthen their personal hold on constituencies. They gave themselves greater resources for travel, communication, and casework and used them to establish more independent, less partisan, political identities. A candidate-centered electoral politics also was encouraged by diminishing partisanship among voters and new communication technologies. Incumbents who took advantage of the new opportunities prospered.[36]

Their prosperity was contingent, however, on their ability to control the information going to the district, to define issues, and, most of all, to scare off vigorous opposition. Much depended on simple bluff. Members remained unbeatable by convincing potentially formidable opponents that they were unbeatable, thus avoiding strong opposition.[37]

Strong national parties and PACs threaten all of these conditions. They, like incumbents, have learned to play candidate-centered electoral politics. For example, national party officials (with Republicans, as usual, taking the lead) have recognized that winning depends on fielding strong candidates; the parties have invested heavily in recruiting and training promising challengers. Some PACs, notably of the New Right, have done the same thing. The skills they teach are the same as those mastered by incumbents.

Parties and PACs also have learned to make imaginative use of new communication technologies. Through centralized polling, Republicans are able to probe the real strength of any Democratic incumbent, to detect weaknesses not evident in vote margins achieved against feeble opposition. They also monitor individual campaigns, using tracking polls to tell them when and where the party's campaign resources can be used to best advantage. They are skilled at using direct mail; given enough money, a PAC or party can eliminate whatever advantage the franking privilege confers. They take advantage of centralized media production; the party provides highly professional, pretested television spots for Republican candidates. The list could go on. The point is that national party campaign committees and PACs have evolved into organizations as well suited to the present-day electoral environment as the most sophisticated incumbent.

This development has increased incumbents' sense of electoral insecurity. More resources are available to be mobilized against them, and, through coordination among PACs and parties, the resources can be mobilized quickly. Career-minded members, notoriously risk-averse, like to be prepared for the worst possible case. Their demand for campaign funds has increased dramatically, and they are spending ever-increasing amounts of money regardless of what their opponents are doing. In 1972 an incumbent would have spent, on average, about $86,000 (in constant dollars, 1986 = 1.00), if the challenger spent nothing; by 1986, the comparable figure had grown to more than $278,000.[38] Parties and, to an even greater extent, PACs are responsible because they increased the supply of and demand for campaign money among congressional incumbents.

Party and PAC activity also erodes the incumbents' ability to control the content of campaigns. Incumbents thrive on campaigns that center around personal performance, experience, and services. Few members are vulnerable if they can persuade voters that these matters are what the contest is about.[39] Trouble comes when campaign issues are framed in a way that makes them less relevant, which is what PACs and parties try to do. PACs with specific policy agendas naturally try to inject them into campaigns. Indeed, a basic aim of single-issue groups like antiabortionists or nuclear freeze proponents is to make sure that their issue enters the campaign. The idea is to give one or the other a weapon too useful to refuse. If both give in to the group's demands, so much the better. The greater the number of divisive and controversial issues introduced into the campaign, the more likely it is that an incumbent would face something like a Downsian coalition of minorities which, at least in theory, assures defeat.[40]

Conservative PACs in independent campaigns carried on the most extensive and best publicized work to weaken incumbents; their strategy was to raise new issues designed to make incumbents look bad. The distribution of independent expenditures in House and Senate campaigns, 1980-1986, is found in Table 5-5 and Table 5-6. Before 1986 the largest share of independent spending went for negative

Table 5-5   Independent Expenditures in Senate Campaigns,
           1980-1986

| Year | For candidate | Against candidate |
|------|---------------|-------------------|
| 1979-1980 | | |
| Democrats | $   127,381 | $1,282,613 |
| Republicans | 261,678 | 12,430 |
| Total | 389,059 | 1,295,043 |
| 1981-1982 | | |
| Democrats | 127,451 | 3,182,986 |
| Republicans | 298,410 | 483,750 |
| Total | 425,861 | 3,666,736 |
| 1983-1984 | | |
| Democrats | 326,031 | 410,428 |
| Republicans | 1,807,981 | 2,082,207 |
| Total | 2,134,012 | 2,492,635 |
| 1985-1986 | | |
| Democrats | 938,004 | 442,866 |
| Republicans | 2,751,139 | 305,123 |
| Total | $3,689,143 | $747,989 |

SOURCE: Ornstein, Mann, and Malbin, *Vital Statistics*, 120-121.
NOTE: Some of the money reported during any election cycle may reflect bills paid from the previous election cycle.

campaigns against Senate Democrats. Democratic leaders in the House also were targeted in 1982. Most of these negative campaigns were not intended to help any particular challenger—indeed, much of the money was spent long before anyone knew who the challenger would be. They were intended to soften up the incumbent for any eventual opponent.

The strategy looked effective; four of the six liberal Democratic targets of NCPAC and other conservative groups in 1980 lost their Senate seats (there are alternative explanations for all of these defeats). But by 1982 the independent campaigns themselves had become the issue. Terry Dolan, chairman of NCPAC, in a moment of candor, had acknowledged one advantage of independent campaigning: "A group like ours could lie through its teeth and the candidate it helps stays clear." [41] Democrats targeted in 1982 reminded voters of Dolan's admission and worked, with some success, to make NCPAC's activities rather than its charges the main issue.[42] Subsequently, several of the conservative PACs fell deeply into debt amid declining contributions and revelations that most of their income had gone to overhead rather than campaigns.[43]

Table 5-6    Independent Expenditures in House Campaigns, 1980-1986

| Year | For candidate | Against candidate |
|---|---|---|
| 1979-1980 | | |
| Democrats | $   190,615 | $  38,023 |
| Republicans | 410,478 | 45,132 |
| Total | 601,093 | 83,155 |
| 1981-1982 | | |
| Democrats | 241,442 | 862,654 |
| Republicans | 492,404 | 66,296 |
| Total | 733,846 | 928,950 |
| 1983-1984 | | |
| Democrats | 560,727 | 118,171 |
| Republicans | 633,646 | 26,847 |
| Total | 1,194,373 | 145,018 |
| 1985-1986 | | |
| Democrats | 2,335,484 | 212,380 |
| Republicans | 1,298,914 | 20,845 |
| Total | $3,634,398 | $233,225 |

SOURCE: Ornstein, Mann, and Malbin, *Vital Statistics,* 120-121.

NOTE: Some of the money reported during any election cycle may reflect bills paid from the previous election cycle.

The pattern of independent spending shifted in 1986. Relatively more money was spent independently in House campaigns, and more was spent to support rather than attack particular candidates. The American Medical Association's AMPAC, which spent more than $1.5 million on behalf of fourteen House and Senate candidates, the National Association of Realtors' PAC, which spent $1.6 million on behalf of six candidates, and the Auto Dealers for Free Trade PAC, which spent more than $1 million to help seven Senate incumbents, bear primary responsibility for these changes. In no case was independent spending clearly effective, and in several cases it failed conspicuously. AMPAC spent $570,000 on behalf of opponents of House Democrats Andrew Jacobs of Indiana and Fortney Stark of California, both of whom won reelection by the same margin they had won by in 1984. Nevertheless, all three PACs planned to do more of the same in 1988. The investment is justified by the claim that it enhances attention and respect in Congress for their political viewpoints.[44]

At present, independent spending still represents a small fraction of the money spent on campaigns; its significance comes from what it may portend. As PACs continue to raise greater amounts of money, the ceiling on contributions to candidates is bound to seem more limiting and the independent spending route more attractive. The richest PACs are capable of mounting full-scale campaigns of their own, and they have strong organizational incentives to do so, if only to justify their continued expansion. Independent spending discomforts incumbents in at least two ways: incumbents are its favorite targets, and, even when they are not targets, independent campaigns deprive them of control over the content of campaigns.

The growing institutional capabilities of PACs clearly make many members of Congress uneasy. They complain that PACs bring outside influences to bear on what should be purely local electoral decisions. National funding sources force national issues onto the local agenda, and candidates find it necessary to campaign on issues that may be of marginal interest to their constituents but of deep concern to groups outside the state or district.[45] A neutral observer might ask, so what? It is common in modern democracies for national issues to dominate campaigns for national legislatures. Because members of Congress make policy for the whole country, outsiders naturally try to influence elections.

Members are inclined to assume, on the contrary, that they should be beholden to no one but their own constituents, that representation should be strictly territorial. Although dated as political theory, it is easy to understand the appeal of this view to members whose political careers rest on diligent personal cultivation of constituencies.[46] A career strategy of this sort depends on maintaining *autonomy*, the freedom to maneuver as an independent political entrepreneur. PAC development threatens autonomy and so, fundamentally, the strategic basis of many congressional careers.

The development of vigorous national party organizations carries the same implications. Although sensitive to the need to tailor local campaigns to local conditions, national party officials inevitably inject a national component into local campaigns. Sometimes the nationalization is deliberate. The RNC spent $9 million in 1980 on a nationwide television campaign urging people to "vote Republican—for a change" and $14 million in 1982 urging them to "stay the course." The Democrats countered with ads ridiculing trickle-down economics and other "unfair" Republican policies, although they did not have enough money to broadcast them widely. National campaigns with common themes seem destined to become regular features of federal elections (the Republicans' themeless campaign of 1986 is now seen as a mistake). But national campaigns may disrupt incumbents' reelection strategies. Such campaigns make it harder for incumbents to separate themselves from an administration or party when this seems prudent. For example, "stay the course" reminded voters of the national economy in a year when Republican incumbents might have been better off ignoring it and running on their own performance.[47]

National party activities undermine members' autonomy in other ways. Coordinated campaign expenditures are, by law, controlled by the party, not the candidate. The party decides what to spend the money on, and candidates who want the party's help have to take what the party offers. On occasion, party officials have insisted that candidates hire specific campaign consultants as a condition of receiving the national party's full range of assistance.[48] In this way, the party influences campaign strategies and messages even if party officials do not consciously try to impose a uniform approach. Schools for candidates have a similar effect, as does the party's reliance on a common pool of outside campaign professionals.

More ominous for members who have learned to thrive on independence is the inherent possibility that party leaders will use control over campaign assets to impose party discipline. In September 1982 RNC officials and White House political operatives threatened to withhold party resources from Republican members of Congress who voted against the Reagan administration's "revenue enhancement" legislation.[49] This threat and a couple of others are inevitably mentioned whenever proposals are made to allow parties an even greater role in congressional campaign finance. Democrats are particularly prone to envision the imminent resurrection of Boss Tweed.[50] Much of this worry is disingenuous; Democrats are not about to unleash the parties while the Republicans are so much stronger. But it is not entirely insincere; parties, no less than PACs, may obligate members to interests outside the district, limiting the autonomy that is essential to their career strategies.[51]

If the expansion of party and PAC activity has favored challengers, congressional incumbents should be more vulnerable to defeat. Evidence suggests that while this observation may be true of the Senate, it is not yet true of the House. From 1960 through 1974, 83 percent of the Senate incumbents seeking reelection were successful; since then Senate reelection rates have fallen to an average of 73 percent. Senate seats have been the main targets of national party efforts and independent PAC campaigns during most of this period, so circumstantial evidence suggests that these new forces have altered the environment to the detriment of incumbent senators. Certainly some of the losers have thought themselves victims of a new kind of electoral politics.

House incumbents have continued to win reelection at about the same rate for three decades (approximately 92 percent, on average) with, if anything, some improvement in the 1984 and 1986 elections. On the other hand, travel to the district, franked mail, staff, district offices, and most of the other official perquisites members use to pursue reelection increased—in some cases steeply—from the early 1970s to the early 1980s without increasing incumbent security. Incumbents appear to be running harder just to stay in the same place. In this and other ways—notably the continuing increase in campaign spending beyond what seems justified by the challenge they face—members' behavior suggests that their feelings of electoral insecurity have grown. This insecurity naturally has consequences for what they do in office. How parties and PACs are changing congressional politics is the subject of the final section.

## Effects on Congress

David Mayhew showed that the workings of Congress are profoundly affected by how its members win and hold office.[52] It follows that changed electoral institutions and practices alter the internal politics of Congress. How have PACs and expanding national party organizations changed congressional life?

One change is undeniable: members now spend more time than formerly thinking about and pursuing campaign money.[53] PACs and parties have contributed to this change in at least three ways. By tapping new sources of contributions—and old sources more efficiently—they have increased the supply of campaign funds. By expanding the pool of resources that might be mobilized against incumbents, they have increased their demand for campaign funds (the demand among nonincumbents has always outstripped the supply). And by introducing expensive, sophisticated technology, they have raised the cost of campaigning.

PACs in particular have been singled out for their part in making campaigns more expensive. PAC critics have always included rising costs in their lists of "horribles," [54] and the public, convinced that too much money is spent on campaigns, concurs.[55] But in fact the great majority of congressional campaigns suffer from too little rather than too much money, as demonstrated by levels of popular knowledge of the candidates.[56] Candidate-centered electoral politics is unavoidably expensive. There is no real contest unless both candidates can reach voters with their messages, and reaching voters normally costs a great deal of money for most nonincumbents.

Accepting the value of well-financed campaigns does not, by itself, lay to rest the central question of how the concern with money might be influencing congressional decisions. For some observers, the answer is simple: PACs are corrupting the entire political process, turning fund raising into an obsession that exposes members of Congress to the pernicious influence of selfish special interests. Bluntly stated, the argument is that PACs buy votes and policy, period. The evidence offered for this claim is typically anecdotal and circumstantial. Common Cause or an enterprising reporter shows that members of Congress supporting legislation desired by some group—milk producers, used-car dealers, doctors, and the shipping industry have been cited—get more campaign money from PACs representing the group than do members who oppose the legislation.[57] Incidents have been reported of members being bullied by lobbyists whose PACs have contributed to their campaigns, and stories are told of unnamed members who admit to voting with a group because they received money from it.[58]

There is no reason to dismiss this kind of evidence, but it is hardly conclusive. Recipients of such PAC contributions inevitably argue, at least in public, that the PACs are merely helping out those members who have the wisdom to agree with their own quite defensible view of the public interest. Liberal Democrats do not support labor's interests because labor PACs have contributed to their campaigns; rather, labor contributes to their campaigns because the liberals share labor's notions of what constitutes good public policy. It would be bizarre to find *no* relationship between contributions and behavior; PACs do not distribute money randomly. Any simple cross-sectional comparison of contributions and roll call votes is necessarily inconclusive because the direction of causality is indeterminate.

A few studies have tried in various ways to untangle the complicated causal links between PAC contributions and roll call votes. Technical problems preclude definitive conclusions, but the pattern of findings suggests that PACs clearly do support members whose votes they like. Evidence that PAC contributions affect individual votes is much more limited and, on methodological grounds, open to question. Still, at least some members, on some issues (those drawing little public or district attention) seem to vote in a way that reflects prior PAC contributions independent of ideology, partisanship, or local interests.[59] The effects of prior contributions are usually dwarfed by other factors in these studies, but they remain statistically significant.

Roll call votes may also be influenced by the expectation of *future* contributions. And because the most effective reelection strategy is to avoid strong opposition, behavior also may be affected by members' reluctance to stir up groups that might finance their opponents. For example, a consultant who worked on campaigns sponsored by Environmental Action, a citizens' action group, to target the "Dirty

Dozen" members of Congress with the worst (by its standards) environmental records claimed that the tactic was "very effective at making congressmen think twice about certain votes. There were numerous examples of members or their staffs calling and saying, 'Is the congressman close to being on the list?' or 'Is this vote going to be used to determine the list?' " [60] An official with the American Medical Association's AMPAC, which spent $670,000 on futile independent campaigns to replace two particularly unsympathetic House Democrats in 1986, suggested that their main purpose was to put other unsympathetic Democrats on notice that they, too, could become targets if they did not become friendlier.[61] Needless to say, effects of this sort, involving influence by anticipated response, are extraordinarily difficult to measure systematically.

It would be surprising if research found that PAC contributions have no effect at all on congressional behavior; otherwise, why would interest groups be putting so much time, energy, and money into PAC activities? Irrationality on this scale would be difficult to explain. Officials of PACs that openly pursue narrow policy goals usually claim that they buy not votes but access, a necessary, if not sufficient, condition for successful lobbying. A contribution ensures a polite hearing when their lobbyist wants to make a pitch. To their most vehement critics, this alone makes PACs a corrupting influence, for it gives them an insider's edge.[62] Members of Congress freely admit to giving access to their contributors but quickly add that they also see people and groups who have given them nothing, particularly if they are connected to the member's state or district.[63]

Members have to handle the question of contributors' influence delicately. Those who contend that PAC money is corrupting imply that at least some of their colleagues have been corrupted. They are challenged to provide specifics: Have they themselves been corrupted? *Who* has been bought? Because members do not lightly attack one another's integrity (in public, anyway), the problem is redefined as the *appearance* of corruption and the loss of public approbation that follows. Proponents of the corruption thesis are at a serious rhetorical disadvantage because they can make their case only by impugning the honesty of fellow members of Congress.

Assuming that PAC contributions do, at least on occasion, influence congressional decisions, the question remains whether the influence represents any real change in congressional behavior. Congress has always practiced distributive politics, conferring narrow, particularized benefits that impose diffuse costs even when the costs plainly outweigh the benefits. Distributive politics involving groups is not new, nor is it inherently different from or more objectionable than distributive politics involving localities, the classic pork barrel. Therefore, much of what PACs do is little more than a continuation of familiar political practices. Indeed, Michael Malbin points out that only a small fraction of the money spent on lobbying takes the form of contributions to candidates. When it comes to lobbying, PACs are the tail, not the dog.[64]

Still, PACs (and parties) have visibly altered congressional politics. Consider lobbying. Raymond Bauer, Ithiel de Sola Pool, and Lewis Anthony Dexter's 1968 classic study of lobbying depicted a process dominated by insiders, of friends talking to friends. Lobbyists worked through friends and allies in Congress, encouraging them to take on projects they were already inclined to pursue by providing organizational backup. Lobbyists persuaded members to help them out by making members look good when they did so. Opponents were ignored; pressure tactics in the insulated social world of Congress were considered imprudent. Small wonder that members regarded lobbying as basically helpful and benign and lobbyists as a resource to be exploited.[65]

Few members would take such a sanguine view today. Insiders still lobby in the old way, although most now supplement their work with outside activities; many PACs have been created at the behest of Washington representatives who believe PACs make their inside work more effective.[66] But they have been joined by a host of activists and organizations working to influence Congress from the outside. Dozens of groups now follow and evaluate roll call votes, target opponents, stimulate mail and phone calls, and mobilize campaign volunteers—in addition to raising and distributing campaign funds. An effective outside strategy does not depend on maintaining friendly relations with incumbents, so outsiders are free to use pressure tactics. Single-issue and ideological PACs have no compunction about using threats to withdraw support from—or to support opponents of—members who oppose them. For many of them, this power is the whole point of having a PAC.

PACs have thus contributed to the shift in focus of congressional politics from the inside to the outside. More time and attention is devoted to politics outside the institution, and outside influences on internal politics have become stronger and more pervasive. PACs are by no means the only reason for this shift; they form but one part of a syndrome that includes changes in formal rules (creating a more decentralized, fragmented, and permeable legislative system far more exposed to public scrutiny) and in informal modes of behavior (aggressively independent entrepreneurial politics in and out of Congress). But they have pushed change by giving institutional form to activities designed to

Table 5-7   PAC Contributions to House Candidates, by Candidates' Status, 1979-1986 (in percentages)

| Committee type | Amount contributed | Incumbent | | Challenger | | Open seat | |
|---|---|---|---|---|---|---|---|
| | | Dem. | Rep. | Dem. | Rep. | Dem. | Rep. |
| **1979-1980** | | | | | | | |
| Distribution of candidates | (N = 738) | 34 | 19 | 13 | 23 | 6 | 5 |
| Labor | $ 8,883,834 | 69 | 4 | 16 | 0 | 10 | 0 |
| Corporate | 11,662,361 | 36 | 32 | 1 | 20 | 1 | 9 |
| Nonconnected | 2,831,209 | 21 | 15 | 5 | 41 | 4 | 12 |
| Trade/membership/health | 11,215,269 | 39 | 32 | 2 | 17 | 3 | 8 |
| Cooperative | 985,177 | 59 | 26 | 2 | 3 | 3 | 7 |
| Corporations w/o stock | 387,740 | 47 | 30 | 2 | 11 | 2 | 7 |
| Total | $35,965,590 | 45 | 24 | 5 | 15 | 4 | 7 |
| **1981-1982** | | | | | | | |
| Distribution of candidates | (N = 830) | 26 | 20 | 20 | 21 | 6 | 6 |
| Labor | $14,557,589 | 53 | 4 | 28 | 0 | 14 | 1 |
| Corporate | 18,136,407 | 32 | 45 | 1 | 9 | 3 | 9 |
| Nonconnected | 6,886,695 | 29 | 19 | 16 | 18 | 8 | 10 |
| Trade/membership/health | 15,901,781 | 34 | 42 | 4 | 8 | 4 | 8 |
| Cooperative | 1,650,239 | 52 | 33 | 4 | 1 | 6 | 3 |
| Corporations w/o stock | 771,847 | 51 | 32 | 5 | 3 | 5 | 4 |
| Total | $57,904,558 | 39 | 30 | 11 | 7 | 7 | 7 |
| **1983-1984** | | | | | | | |
| Distribution of candidates | (N = 816) | 32 | 19 | 19 | 25 | 3 | 3 |
| Labor | $18,686,078 | 71 | 5 | 17 | 0 | 6 | 0 |
| Corporate | 22,908,071 | 43 | 39 | 1 | 11 | 1 | 6 |
| Nonconnected | 8,641,416 | 41 | 15 | 8 | 24 | 4 | 9 |
| Trade/membership/health | 19,805,084 | 47 | 36 | 3 | 7 | 2 | 5 |
| Cooperative | 1,965,801 | 61 | 31 | 2 | 2 | 1 | 2 |
| Corporations w/o stock | 885,512 | 62 | 27 | 2 | 4 | 1 | 3 |
| Total | $72,891,962 | 52 | 26 | 6 | 8 | 3 | 4 |
| **1985-1986** | | | | | | | |
| Distribution of candidates | (N = 810) | 29 | 20 | 18 | 23 | 6 | 5 |
| Labor | $22,628,106 | 59 | 7 | 19 | 0 | 16 | 0 |
| Corporate | 26,807,069 | 44 | 41 | 1 | 3 | 3 | 8 |
| Nonconnected | 11,082,707 | 34 | 21 | 13 | 9 | 13 | 11 |
| Trade/membership/health | 23,364,783 | 45 | 38 | 3 | 3 | 5 | 7 |
| Cooperative | 1,898,110 | 53 | 36 | 1 | 1 | 5 | 3 |
| Corporations w/o stock | 1,393,586 | 52 | 32 | 2 | 4 | 4 | 7 |
| Total | $87,174,361 | 47 | 29 | 8 | 3 | 8 | 6 |

SOURCE: Ornstein, Mann, and Malbin, *Vital Statistics*, 109-111.

Table 5-8 PAC Contributions to Senate Candidates, by Candidates' Status, 1979-1986 (in percentages)

| Committee type | Amount contributed | Incumbent | | Challenger | | Open seat | |
|---|---|---|---|---|---|---|---|
| | | Dem. | Rep. | Dem. | Rep. | Dem. | Rep. |
| **1979-1980** | | | | | | | |
| Distribution of candidates | (N = 66) | 27 | 9 | 9 | 27 | 14 | 14 |
| Labor | $ 3,428,404 | 65 | 9 | 14 | 1 | 11 | 1 |
| Corporate | 6,445,566 | 25 | 14 | 1 | 47 | 2 | 11 |
| Nonconnected | 1,690,574 | 22 | 6 | 2 | 53 | 2 | 14 |
| Trade/membership/health | 3,816,424 | 37 | 17 | 3 | 32 | 5 | 7 |
| Cooperative | 325,050 | 65 | 11 | 1 | 11 | 6 | 6 |
| Corporations w/o stock | 214,853 | 40 | 18 | 3 | 27 | 5 | 7 |
| Total | $15,920,871 | 37 | 13 | 4 | 33 | 5 | 8 |
| **1981-1982** | | | | | | | |
| Distribution of candidates | (N = 66) | 29 | 17 | 17 | 29 | 5 | 5 |
| Labor | $ 4,830,051 | 56 | 7 | 27 | 0 | 9 | 1 |
| Corporate | 8,275,630 | 26 | 41 | 1 | 17 | 1 | 14 |
| Nonconnected | 3,150,309 | 28 | 20 | 15 | 23 | 6 | 7 |
| Trade/membership/health | 4,857,841 | 37 | 39 | 4 | 10 | 2 | 8 |
| Cooperative | 427,526 | 52 | 19 | 12 | 2 | 1 | 14 |
| Corporations w/o stock | 262,140 | 45 | 33 | 3 | 6 | 2 | 11 |
| Total | $21,803,497 | 36 | 29 | 10 | 12 | 4 | 9 |
| **1983-1984** | | | | | | | |
| Distribution of candidates | (N = 68) | 18 | 25 | 25 | 19 | 6 | 7 |
| Labor | $ 4,600,719 | 28 | 6 | 46 | 0 | 20 | 0 |
| Corporate | 11,398,143 | 20 | 57 | 2 | 6 | 3 | 11 |
| Nonconnected | 5,079,528 | 20 | 28 | 28 | 10 | 9 | 6 |
| Trade/membership/health | 6,003,397 | 27 | 48 | 9 | 4 | 6 | 6 |
| Cooperative | 450,942 | 31 | 49 | 10 | 1 | 8 | 1 |
| Corporations w/o stock | 368,185 | 33 | 39 | 11 | 4 | 7 | 5 |
| Total | $27,900,914 | 23 | 41 | 16 | 6 | 8 | 7 |
| **1985-1986** | | | | | | | |
| Distribution of candidates | (N = 68) | 13 | 26 | 26 | 13 | 10 | 10 |
| Labor | $ 7,214,361 | 23 | 8 | 43 | 0 | 26 | 1 |
| Corporate | 19,119,156 | 13 | 48 | 7 | 6 | 5 | 21 |
| Nonconnected | 7,623,401 | 15 | 26 | 25 | 7 | 15 | 12 |
| Trade/membership/health | 9,434,492 | 18 | 42 | 13 | 4 | 8 | 15 |
| Cooperative | 636,630 | 23 | 39 | 20 | 3 | 7 | 8 |
| Corporations w/o stock | 970,845 | 16 | 47 | 15 | 4 | 7 | 11 |
| Total | $44,998,885 | 16 | 36 | 18 | 5 | 11 | 14 |

SOURCE: Ornstein, Mann, and Malbin, *Vital Statistics,* 112-114.

exploit the new avenues of influence opened by changing patterns of congressional politics.

PACs and the proliferation of external demands on Congress they reflect and reinforce are therefore commonly blamed for Congress's inability to deal with tough, divisive national problems. A fragmented Congress that is too responsive to too many conflicting demands is susceptible to stalemate; it cannot make the hard choices that impose concentrated costs on organized groups to achieve widely shared general benefits. PACs also are responsible for forcing zero-sum redistributive issues onto the political agenda; moral issues, such as abortion, often are approached this way. Congress has particular difficulty dealing with such issues because normal politics—compromise, side payments, logrolling, and other common methods of coalition building—do not work. Internal congressional politics thrives on deals, on compromise; a focus on external politics promotes posturing and intransigence.

Structural fragmentation, the multitude of outside pressures, and aggressive individualism have raised new impediments to effective party leadership in Congress. Congressional leaders are the quintessential insiders, and their traditional methods of persuasion and coalition building are best suited to internal politicking. Effective presidential leadership also has traditionally depended on combining public activity with a skillful insider's game. But leaders have, of necessity, been learning to exploit outside approaches. During the Carter administration, House Speaker O'Neill occasionally worked through influential groups (primarily labor organizations) in the districts of members whose votes the party needed; he had local leaders calling on them to back the party's position.[67] The Reagan administration also recognized the possibilities of grass-roots lobbying and used it effectively in its battles to cut taxes and spending. Administration strategists mobilized groups around the country that had supported Reagan's presidential bid to rally in support of his programs. People and PACs that had given to both the Reagan campaign and to southern Democrats in 1980 were identified by computer and asked to lobby the so-called Boll Weevils to support the administration's bills.[68] The avalanche of letters and telephone calls that followed was instrumental in persuading some reluctant Democrats to cooperate.[69] "Going public" to bring grass-roots pressure on members of Congress to cooperate with the president has been a hallmark of the Reagan administration.[70]

Parties, however, remain the principal instruments of congressional leadership and coalition building. Observers who worry about the excessive fragmentation reinforced by PACs and other interest groups and see no legitimate way to suppress them often propose to strengthen the parties. If party committees were allowed to do more for congressional candidates, members would be less reliant on PACs for essential electoral resources and therefore less subject to PAC influence (or the appearance of it). The more money that passes through the parties' hands, the broader the interests represented by the campaign finance system.[71]

Republicans naturally think a greater financial role for parties is a terrific idea; with so much money coming in, their main problem is figuring out new ways to spend it legally for their candidates. The Democratic party is too poor to be bothered by the present ceiling. Still, even some Democratic leaders envision a day—to arrive after they have caught up—when parties are unleashed to counteract PACs.[72] Meanwhile, some Democratic incumbents with aspirations to leadership have taken to organizing personal PACs to help other Democratic candidates for Congress. They exploit their ability to raise PAC money beyond what they need for their own campaigns to enhance their internal influence in Congress. This helps nonincumbent Democrats who are usually slighted by most PACs and, in a small way, contributes to greater efficiency in the distribution of "Democratic" campaign money.[73]

While an enlarged financial role for parties and party leaders may appeal to congressional leaders, many members are not so sure. Remember that parties, no less than PACs, may diminish autonomy and so undermine the arrangements that keep members in office. The ghost of Boss Tweed invoked by Democrats every time the issue is raised is more than just partisan rhetoric. Moreover, members would not welcome an enlarged casework role for parties. Still, strengthening the parties is the only solution in sight to many of the problems raised by PACs.

Aside from political difficulties (Republicans are not about to give up the advantages they enjoy under the present law), legislation to restrict PAC contributions to candidates will only push PACs into more independent spending. The costs of organization have already been paid; the desires of PAC officials to maintain the organization and to keep their jobs would drive them to independent campaigning if other avenues of participation were closed off. As Malbin points out, the PACs whose overhead is covered by large parent organizations (corporations and unions) would do this most readily and so would gain an additional advantage.[74] If PACs cannot be curbed, the only option left is further development and expansion of countervailing institutions: the parties.

# Notes

1. For a summary of the extensive literature on this development, see Gary C. Jacobson, *The Politics of Congressional Elections,* 2d ed. (Boston: Little, Brown, 1987), 26-46.
2. The committees are the Republican National Committee (RNC), the National Republican Congressional Committee (NRCC), the National Republican Senatorial Committee (NRSC), the Democratic National Committee (DNC), the Democratic Congressional Campaign Committee (DCCC), and the Democratic Senatorial Campaign Committee (DSCC).
3. For a fascinating account of the party's role in congressional campaign finance in an earlier era, see Robert Caro, *The Years of Lyndon Johnson: The Path to Power* (New York: Alfred A. Knopf, 1982), chap. 31.
4. Joseph E. Cantor, *Political Action Committees: Their Evolution and Growth and Their Implications for the Political System,* U.S. Library of Congress, Congressional Research Service, Report No. 81-246, Nov. 6, 1981, 28-35.
5. See ibid., 35-44, for the details.
6. *Buckley v. Valeo,* 424 U.S. 1 (1976).
7. Charles L. Clapp, *The Congressman: His Work as He Sees It* (Washington, D.C.: Brookings Institution, 1963), 397; Richard F. Fenno, Jr., *Home Style: House Members in Their Districts* (Boston: Little, Brown, 1978), 113.
8. The Senate spending limit also applies to House candidates in those states with a single House seat.
9. *Federal Election Commission v. Democratic Senatorial Campaign Committee,* 343 U.S. 27 (1981).
10. Michael J. Malbin, "Looking Back at the Future of Campaign Finance Reform," in *Money and Politics in the United States,* ed. Michael J. Malbin (Washington, D.C.: American Enterprise Institute and Chatham House, 1984), 257.
11. The closer the relationship between an industry and the federal government, the more likely its firms are to have PACs. See Edwin M. Epstein, "Business and Labor Under the Federal Election Campaign Act of 1971," in *Parties, Interest Groups, and Campaign Finance Laws,* ed. Michael J. Malbin (Washington, D.C.: American Enterprise Institute, 1980), 133.
12. Frank J. Sorauf, *Money in American Elections* (Glenview: Ill.: Scott Foresman/Little, Brown, 1988), chap. 10; Malbin, "Future of Campaign Finance."
13. For a diverse collection of claims about PACs, see House of Representatives, Task Force on Elections, *Campaign Finance Reform,* hearings June 9, 16, 21, 23, July 8, Aug. 22, 23, and Oct. 12, 1983.
14. Thomas B. Edsall, "The GOP Money Machine," *Washington Post National Weekly Edition,* July 2, 1984.
15. Gary C. Jacobson, "Congressional Campaign Finance and the Revival of the Republican Party," in *The United States Congress,* ed. Dennis Hale (New Brunswick, N.J.: Transaction Books, 1983), 313-330; David

Adamany, "Political Parties in the 1980s," in *Money and Politics in the United States,* 70-121.

16. Thomas B. Edsall and Helen Dewar, "The GOP Aims to Please," *Washington Post National Weekly Edition,* June 4, 1984, 12.

17. Edsall, "GOP Money Machine," 7.

18. Adamany, "Parties in the 1980s," 77.

19. The idea that rational politicians would pursue a "minimum winning coalition" does not apply; see Gary C. Jacobson, "Party Organization and Campaign Resources in 1982," *Political Science Quarterly* 100 (Winter 1985-1986): 604.

20. Bill Peterson, "Strange Bedfellows in Illinois," *Washington Post National Weekly Edition,* June 11, 1984, 13.

21. Edward Handler and John R. Mulkern, *Business in Politics* (Lexington, Mass.: Lexington Books, 1982), 8-9.

22. Alan Ehrenhalt, "GOP Challengers Find PACs Wary This Year," *Congressional Quarterly Weekly Report,* Oct. 20, 1984, 2763.

23. Jacobson, "Campaign Resources in 1982," 613-622.

24. Gary C. Jacobson and Samuel Kernell, *Strategy and Choice in Congressional Elections,* 2d ed. (New Haven, Conn.: Yale University Press, 1983), 76-84.

25. Gary C. Jacobson, "Reagan, Reaganomics, and Strategic Politics in 1982: A Test of Alternative Theories of Midterm Congressional Elections" (Paper delivered at the annual meeting of the American Political Science Association, Chicago, Sept. 1-4, 1983); Jacobson, "Campaign Resources in 1982," 621-622.

26. Gary C. Jacobson, "Congress: Politics after a Landslide Without Coattails," in *The Elections of 1984,* ed. Michael Nelson (Washington, D.C.: CQ Press, 1985), 216-219.

27. Tom Watson, "PAC Pilgrimage Becomes Candidates' Ritual," *Congressional Quarterly Weekly Report,* March 22, 1986, 655-659.

28. All Senate patterns are more volatile, however, because the number of Senate candidates in each partisan and incumbency category is so much more variable from one election to the next; see Table 5-8.

29. Jacobson, "Coattails," 218-219; Alan Ehrenhalt, "Campaign '86: Few Real House Contests," *Congressional Quarterly Weekly Report,* Jan. 25, 1986, 171.

30. Paul S. Herrnson, "Party Strategies and Resource Distribution in the 1984 Congressional Elections," unpublished manuscript.

31. Alan Ehrenhalt, "Failed Campaign Cost Republicans the Senate," *Congressional Quarterly Weekly Report,* Nov. 6, 1986, 2803, 2871.

32. Steve Lilienthal and Stuart Rothenberg, "Did Republicans Get What They Paid For?" *Election Politics* 4 (Spring 1987): 19-21.

33. Gary C. Jacobson, "The Republican Advantage in Campaign Finance" in *The New Direction in American Politics,* ed. John E. Chubb and Paul E. Peterson (Washington, D.C.: Brookings Institution, 1985), 168-170.

34. See, for example, the testimony of Archibald Cox, chairman of Common Cause, in House, *Campaign Finance Reform,* 506.

35. Gary C. Jacobson, "Money and Votes Reconsidered: Congressional Elections, 1972-1982," *Public Choice* 47 (1985): 13-46; Gary C. Jacobson, "Enough Is Too Much: Money and Competition in House Elections," in *Elections in America*, ed. Kay Lehman Schlozman (Boston: Allen & Unwin, 1987), 173-195; for a contrary view, see Donald Philip Green and Jonathan S. Krasno, "Salvation for the Spendthrift Incumbent: Reestimating the Effects of Campaign Spending in House Elections," *American Journal of Political Science,* in press.

36. A summary of the literature on these changes can be found in Jacobson, *Congressional Elections*, 37-45.

37. Ibid., 45-58.

38. Ibid., 90. The equation for 1986 is incumbent's expenditures = \$278,455 + .73 (challenger's expenditures); $R^2$ = .27.

39. Jacobson, *Congressional Elections*, 134-138.

40. Anthony Downs, *An Economic Theory of Democracy* (New York: Harper & Row, 1957), 55-60.

41. *Dollar Politics*, 3d ed. (Washington, D.C.: Congressional Quarterly, 1982), 88, originally quoted in the *Washington Post,* Aug. 10, 1980.

42. Rhodes Cook, "Senate Elections: A Dull Affair Compared to 1980's Upheaval," *Congressional Quarterly Weekly Report,* Nov. 6, 1982, 2792.

43. Ronald Brownstein, "On Paper, Conservative PACs Were Tigers in 1984—But Look Again," *National Journal,* June 19, 1985, 1504.

44. Richard E. Cohen, "Spending Independently," *National Journal,* Dec. 6, 1986, 2932-2934.

45. See House, *Campaign Finance Reform*, 52, 143.

46. See Fenno, *Home Style,* for a detailed account of the various ways in which members cultivate their constituencies.

47. Jacobson, "Strategic Politics in 1982," 11-12.

48. Paul Herrnson, *Political Parties and Congressional Elections: Party Campaigning in the 1980s* (Cambridge, Mass.: Harvard University Press, forthcoming), chap. 3.

49. Dennis Farney, Leonard Apcar, and Rich Jaroslavsky, "How Reaganites Push Reluctant Republicans to Back Tax-Rise Bill," *Wall Street Journal,* Sept. 9, 1982, 1.

50. See comment by task force chairman Al Swift in House, *Campaign Finance Reform*, 658.

51. See comment by Representative Tony Coelho in ibid., 632-633.

52. David R. Mayhew, *Congress: The Electoral Connection* (New Haven, Conn.: Yale University Press, 1974), chap. 2.

53. Albert Hunt, "An Inside Look at Politicians Hustling PACs," *Wall Street Journal,* Oct. 1, 1982, 1; House, *Campaign Finance Reform*, 204, 610.

54. House, *Campaign Finance Reform*, 105-106, 139, 142.

55. Ibid., 164.

56. Jacobson, *Congressional Elections,* 111-114.

57. See, for example, the testimony of Joan Claybrook, president of Public Citizen (one of Ralph Nader's operations), in House, *Campaign Finance Reform,* 538-547; see also Elizabeth Drew, *Politics and Money: The New*

*Road to Corruption* (New York: Macmillan, 1983).
58. For examples, see Drew, *Politics and Money,* 44-45, 96; House, *Campaign Finance Reform,* 49, 533; Brooks Jackson and John J. Fialka, "New Congressmen Get Many Offers of Money to Cut Campaign Debt," *Wall Street Journal,* April 21, 1983, 1.
59. James Kau and Paul Rubin, *Congressmen, Constituents, and Contributors* (Boston: Martinus Nijhoff, 1982); Diana Evans Yiannakis, "PAC Contributions and House Voting on Conflictual and Consensual Issues: The Windfall Profits Tax and the Chrysler Loan Guarantee" (Paper delivered at the annual meeting of the American Political Science Association, Chicago, Sept. 1-4, 1983); John P. Frendreis and Richard W. Waterman, "PAC Contributions and Legislative Behavior: Senate Voting on Trucking Deregulation," *Social Science Quarterly* 66 (1985): 401-412; Candice J. Nelson, "Counting the Cash: PAC Contributions to Members of the House of Representatives" (Paper delivered at the annual meeting of the American Political Science Association, Denver, Colo., Sept. 2-5, 1982); Henry W. Chappell, Jr., "Campaign Contributions and Congressional Voting: A Simultaneous Probit-Tobit Model," *Review of Economics and Statistics* 64 (1982): 77-83; William P. Welch, "Campaign Contributions and Voting: Milk Money and Dairy Price Supports," *Western Political Quarterly* 25 (1982): 478-495; Kirk F. Brown, "Campaign Contributions and Congressional Voting" (Paper delivered at the annual meeting of the American Political Science Association, Chicago, Sept. 1-4, 1983); Janet M. Grenzke, "Shopping in the Congressional Supermarket: The Currency is Complex," *American Journal of Political Science,* in press; John Wright, "PACs, Contributions, and Roll Calls: An Organizational Perspective," *American Political Science Review* 75 (1985): 400-414.
60. "The Trail of the Dirty Dozen," *Congressional Quarterly Weekly Report,* March 21, 1981, 510.
61. Cohen, "Spending Independently," 2934.
62. *Dollar Politics,* 57.
63. See remarks of Representative Geraldine A. Ferraro, House, *Campaign Finance Reform,* 211-212.
64. Malbin, "Future of Campaign Finance Reform," 249-251.
65. Raymond A. Bauer, Ithiel de Sola Pool, and Lewis Anthony Dexter, *American Business and Public Policy* (New York: Atherton, 1968).
66. Theodore J. Eismeier and Philip K. Pollock III, "Political Action Committees: Varieties of Organization and Strategy," in *Money and Politics,* 124-126.
67. Lawrence Dodd and Terry Sullivan, "House Leadership Success in the Vote Gathering Process: A Comparative Analysis" (Paper delivered at the annual meeting of the Midwest Political Science Association, April 24-26, 1980).
68. Edsall, "GOP Money Machine," 7.
69. Elizabeth Wehr, "White House's Lobbying Apparatus Produces Impres-

sive Tax Victory," *Congressional Quarterly Weekly Report*, Aug. 1, 1981, 1372-1373.

70. See Samuel Kernell, *Going Public: New Strategies of Presidential Leadership* (Washington, D.C.: CQ Press, 1986), chap. 5.

71. Malbin, "Future of Campaign Finance Reform," 269-270.

72. House, *Campaign Finance Reform*, 171; Brooks Jackson, "The Problem with PACs," *Wall Street Journal*, Nov. 17, 1982, 30.

73. Bob Benenson, "In the Struggle for Influence, Members' PACs Gain Ground," *Congressional Quarterly Weekly Report*, Aug. 2, 1986, 1751-1754.

74. Malbin, "Future of Campaign Finance Reform," 255.

# 6. PERSONAL AND PARTISAN ADVANTAGE IN U.S. CONGRESSIONAL ELECTIONS, 1846-1986

## John R. Alford and David W. Brady

A great deal of scholarly thinking about the contemporary House of Representatives holds that the need to be reelected is the dominant influence on members of Congress. This need has a profound impact not only on their behavior but also on the structure of the House and, more broadly, on the nature of national politics and policy. Morris Fiorina argues that Congress funds and supports the Washington bureaucracy in part because the various departments' programs serve constituent interests or are sufficiently complex to require the members' intervention on behalf of the constituents, either of which makes members of Congress more necessary and hence more reelectable.[1] David Mayhew points out that, in their attempt to ensure reelection, House members have structured the organization to facilitate each member's ability to (1) claim credit for service and projects in the district; (2) take positions on public issues that appeal to their constituents without having to bear consequences; (3) advertise themselves to constituents to increase name recognition and electability.[2] The connecting thread in this argument is that their desire to be reelected causes House members to structure the institution and its policy outputs in ways that do no harm to their reelection chances. And, in fact, incumbent representatives do get reelected at an extremely high rate—more than 95 percent in the 1980s, and their average margin of victory has increased substantially since 1965.[3]

This portrait of the House of Representatives is not without its critics. One point of view is that House members have always tried to serve their constituents; in the 1890s members from agricultural districts got themselves appointed to the Agriculture Committee and voted to increase the size of the Department of Agriculture's budget. To counter this argument it is pointed out that the research on the decline of competitiveness (the success of incumbents) shows that incumbency as a dominant factor in House elections is a phenomenon of the mid-1960s and later.

If the incumbency phenomenon is post-1960s, the observation made by Fiorina and Mayhew about the House may well be correct; that is, Congress in the post-1960s period is more controlled than ever before by individual members' ability to ensure their reelection. For the Mayhew, Fiorina interpretation to be plausible, at least two conditions must obtain: (1) the incumbency factor must be a post-1960s phenomenon; and (2) individual members, not political parties, must exercise the greatest control over their electoral fate. We might call the second condition the "decline of party" condition. The weakening of political parties must be considered because the structure of the contemporary Congress and its policy outputs clearly would be different if the United States had strong parties competing at the national level for majority status. Strong parties imply definite stands on issues. One party, for example, would favor and implement budget constraints when elected, while the other would favor increased expenditures. Individual House members would be persuaded to act in the party's interest rather than their own. Under a stronger party system both the structure of the House and its policy outputs would be different.[4]

It seems clear that an important precondition for drawing reliable conclusions about the contemporary Congress entails determining when the incumbency factor arose in time as well as ascertaining the relative strength of partisan and individual electoral strength over time.

## The Literature

The first study specifically dealing with incumbency was Robert Erikson's 1971 article. He examined House elections from 1952 to 1960 and concluded that, although there was about a two percentage point advantage to running as an incumbent, most of the victory margin of incumbent candidates could be attributed to the safe party nature of their districts. In an update the following year, Erikson noted that his original findings might be time bound because in the 1966, 1968, and 1970 elections incumbency advantage had increased by about five percentage points. In 1974 Mayhew's often-cited article on the "vanishing marginals" argued that there had indeed been a sharp increase in incumbency advantage in the mid-1960s, and this increase accounted for the decline in close (marginal) elections.[5]

In the fifteen years that followed Erikson's discovery, a vast literature on incumbency advantage has appeared in the journals. Much of this literature has focused, inconclusively, on a search for the causes of the mid-1960s increase. The studies that focused on the degree of incumbency advantage have not changed the picture presented by Erikson and Mayhew, except to document the continuation of the trend into the 1980s. The focus has been almost exclusively on the post-World War II period, and thus, little is known about the long-term trend in incumbency advantage.

The only truly historical data on incumbency advantage in congressional elections are those provided in 1984 by James Garand and Donald Gross.[6] They present data on the competitiveness of House elections from 1824 to 1982, and the trend over time in this data proves quite interesting. They find, not unexpectedly, that there has always been some advantage to running as an incumbent (the smallest advantage was about three percentage points in the late 1800s). This finding is in keeping with what one would have assumed, based on the general election literature; that is, many of the factors thought to contribute to incumbent success, such as name recognition, visibility, sources of campaign funding, campaign experience, district service, and voter inertia, are perennial characteristics of congressional elections. The remainder of Garand and Gross's conclusions regarding the historical pattern of advantage are far less predictable and far more difficult to reconcile with the existing literature. Post-1965 levels of incumbency advantage are not uniquely high. Incumbency advantage was higher in the late 1920s than it was in the late 1970s. Even more surprising, the often-cited increased advantage of the mid-1960s is, according to Garand and Gross, actually a decline from the general trend of increasing advantage that dates from 1894.

Reconciling these findings with the congressional election literature is a daunting task. Virtually all of the past work, both empirical and theoretical, concerning incumbency advantage is incompatible with their observed mid-1960s decline. Even Garand and Gross are left with little to say regarding what might account for the trends they observe.

The difficulty of fitting the current literature to the historical trends provided by Garand and Gross may be the result of a problem fairly common in historical work, that of incommensurability; in other words, the comparison of two unlike sets of data. Garand and Gross have defined incumbency advantage as the margin by which incumbent winners outperform nonincumbent winners. It is not clear that this method translates in any direct fashion into what other studies of incumbency have measured, or even have meant by, incumbency advantage. Gross and Garand do not extend the current trend lines back into history; rather, they provide a largely novel series.[7] The task of placing the current incumbency data and literature in a historical perspective requires calculating measures of incumbency advantage for the pre-1946 period that are commensurable with the measures that are used in the existing literature to assess advantage, and changes in that advantage, in the post-1946 era.

## Data Collection

The scarcity of earlier historical series in this area is no doubt due to the volume of data involved (there are more than 9,000 individual House elections in the post-World War II series alone), combined with the fact that the available machine-readable election returns do not include information on incumbency. Relying on published sources, we compiled data on House elections from 1844 to 1986, including the vote margins of the major party candidates as well as whether there was an incumbent running in the election and, if so, of what party.[8]

The decisions we made concerning data coding bear mentioning. The vote results were coded as the percentage for the Democratic candidate, the percentage for the major opposition party candidate (which for the most part means the Republican or Whig, but occasionally refers to some other party, for example, Populist), and the percentage for the minor or third party candidates. Incumbency was coded in the same party categories as the vote. The election was coded as an open seat election unless there was a previously *elected* member of the House running for reelection in the same district that he or she had represented in the immediately prior Congress. This fairly conservative definition of incumbency should yield a clear, stable picture of incumbency advantage regardless of its source.

Two major exclusions from the data set were necessary. The first election following a reapportionment of the House (1852 for example) was excluded from each decade because of the difficulty involved in assigning and interpreting incumbency status where district lines have been shifted. Elections in which a candidate ran without major party opposition, although included in the original data set, were excluded from the computed trends. Whether a measure is based on average vote or interelection vote shift, the inclusion of unopposed election results will bias any arithmetic measure of central tendency. This sort of exclusion is common to most incumbency studies.[9]

## The Advantage of Incumbency

The simplest measure of incumbency advantage is the mean share of the two-party vote earned by incumbents seeking reelection. Because the average share of the two-party vote for major party candidates in open seats is always 50 percent (100% ÷ 2), the average vote share for incumbents can be compared implicitly or explicitly to 50 percent. If we found that the mean vote for incumbents in a given election was not significantly higher than 50 percent, we would conclude that incumbents had no particular advantage over nonincumbents.

Figure 6-1 presents the average incumbent share of the two-party

Figure 6-1  Average Incumbent Vote Share, All House Elections with Major Party Opposition, 1846-1986

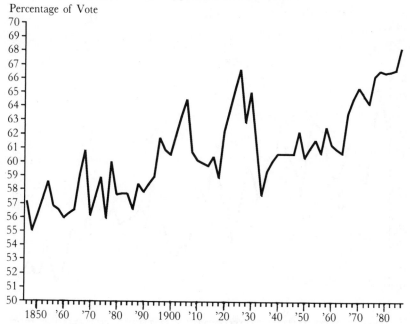

Percentage of Vote

SOURCE: Computed by the authors from *Congressional Quarterly's Guide to U.S. Elections* (Washington, D.C.: Congressional Quarterly, 1985).

NOTE: No data shown for first year following the decennial census.

vote, which is computed by election year from the major party means. The mean share of the vote for Democratic incumbents and the mean share for Republican incumbents are computed separately, and then the simple average of these two means is computed without regard to the number of observations on which each is based. This procedure yields a general measure of incumbent margin unbiased by the effects of a party tide in any given election.

The trend over time, presented graphically in Figure 6-1, is broadly consistent with the pattern reported by Garand and Gross. A general upward trend is evident throughout, with the series low coming in 1848 at 55.0 percent. This trend accelerates in the late 1800s with temporary abrupt surges upward in 1904 and 1906 and the 1920s. Indeed the 1926 high point of 66.7 percent is not exceeded until 1986, when the average incumbent vote rises to its all-time high of 68.2 percent. Unlike Garand and Gross,, however, we do find a sharp upward trend after 1964, and the sustained high levels of advantage in

Figure 6-2    Percentage of Incumbents with Marginal Vote Shares,
All House Elections with Major Party Opposition,
1846-1986

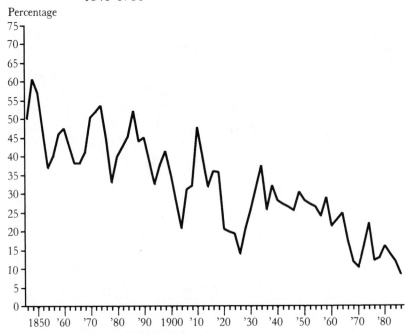

SOURCE: Computed by the authors from *Congressional Quarterly's Guide to U.S. Elections* (Washington, D.C.: Congressional Quarterly, 1985).
NOTE: Marginal vote shares equal 45 percent to 55 percent of the vote.

the 1970s and 1980s are unprecedented in the series. Therefore, the post-1950 portion of our data, while at odds with the findings of Gross and Garand, is fully consistent with the remainder of the existing incumbency literature.

## Incumbent Marginality

Another simple and widely used measure of incumbency advantage is the degree to which incumbent districts fall outside of some arbitrary marginal range. The issue of marginality has been closely intertwined with the incumbency literature beginning with Mayhew's investigation of the "Case of the Vanishing Marginals." [10] The figures for proportion of the districts in which the incumbent's share of the two-party vote fell in the marginal (45 percent-55 percent) range are presented in Figure 6-2.

The pattern here is consistent with that of incumbent vote share (Figure 6-1). The declining marginality of incumbents is clearly not a new phenomenon. Although somewhat erratic at times, the general trend has been one of declining marginality since the 1848 high point of 60.6 percent of incumbent districts in the marginal range. The low point is the 1986 election, in which for the first time the proportion of marginal incumbent districts dropped into single digits (8.5 percent). Beyond the overall trend, several other patterns are notable. The 1920s again are distinct, as they were in Figure 6-1, for the degree of incumbent advantage: the 1926 low of 14 percent marginal was not reached again until 1968, when the proportion marginal dropped to 11.7 percent, and as recently as 1980 the contemporary proportion marginal has been higher (16 percent) than it was in 1926 (14 percent).

Looking only at the pattern since World War II, the results presented in Figure 6-1 and Figure 6-2 are entirely consistent with the current incumbency literature. Average incumbent vote share, which had been stable in the 60-62 percent range from the early 1940s through 1964, jumped sharply upward in 1966, and by 1976 was stabilizing in the 66-68 percent range, an increase of about six percentage points. Marginality, stable in the 25-30 percent range in the 1946-1964 period, dropped sharply in 1966, and by the late 1970s was in the low teens. Both patterns clearly contradict the Garand and Gross findings regarding the post-World War II period.[11]

While the more recent data in Figure 6-1 fit well with the current literature, the historical trends are far less predictable and somewhat more troublesome to explain. Much of what is thought to explain the high contemporary levels of incumbency advantage, such as television, massive federal spending, rapidly expanded use of the frank, new home styles, and constituency service, is of little use in explaining the broader picture. The mid-1920s rise in advantage, for example, seems unlikely to be accounted for by any of these variables. Before we discredit any current explanations for their inability to explain similar past periods, we must, however, look a bit more closely at the possibility that the similarity of the 1920s to the 1970s is more apparent than real.

The problem in comparing the 1920s to the 1970s is that the measures we have used so far do not sort out personal incumbency advantage from party advantage. An example should make this point clear. Consider a midwestern congressional district in which the distribution of the vote is 58 percent Democrat and 42 percent Republican. The Democratic candidate wins elections with that exact vote share—58 percent. Imagine that a major automobile manufacturer buys up farm land in the district and builds a new factory that employs thousands of union auto workers who are predominantly Democratic.

Under these new conditions the average Democratic share of the vote reaches 65 percent. When we look at the incumbent House member's average vote, it will look as if the incumbent has increased his or her margin of victory when in fact it is the party that has increased its share of the distribution of the vote.

Contrast this case with one in which a Democrat wins a first election with 58 percent of the vote. Over the next three or four elections let us suppose that this representative works hard to be reelected—provides services to voters, claims credit for projects, advertises, and increases name recognition, thereby adding another 7 percent to his or her vote total; in other words, the representative wins with 65 percent of the vote. This 65 percent for the incumbent will look just like the party-controlled 65 percent in the previous example. Yet, a very important difference exists; namely, in the second case there is a *personal* incumbency advantage that is not present in the first case. The Fiorina, Mayhew assessment of the contemporary Congress rests on representatives having this sort of personal incumbency advantage, and the supposed impact of that advantage on the institution of Congress derives specifically from the contradistinction between personal and party advantage. To discover whether a personal incumbency advantage exists we will have to measure electoral results in a way that separates out the personal advantage factor.

## Personal Incumbency Advantage

Early studies of incumbency advantage developed two parallel measures to isolate personal advantage: sophomore surge and retirement slump. In each measure the personal advantage of incumbency is taken to be the difference between a party's vote share in an open seat contest (one in which no incumbent is running) and the vote margin of an incumbent of that party in an immediately adjacent election. For example, a Republican incumbent runs for reelection in 1948, wins 58 percent of the vote, and retires before the 1950 election, creating an open seat. In the 1950 election the Republican candidate wins with 56 percent of the vote, runs for reelection in 1952, and captures 59 percent of the vote. The 1948-1950 pair of elections produces a 1950 retirement slump estimate of minus two percentage points (the 1950 open seat margin of 56 percent minus the 1948 preretirement margin of 58 percent). The 1950-1952 pair of elections produces a 1952 sophomore surge estimate of plus three percentage points (the 1952 first incumbent reelection margin of 59 percent minus the 1950 open seat margin of 56 percent).

This approach to measuring incumbency advantage provides two benefits. By focusing on a single district and a set of adjacent elections,

Figure 6-3   Sophomore Surge and Retirement Slump, All House
Elections with Major Party Opposition, 1846-1986

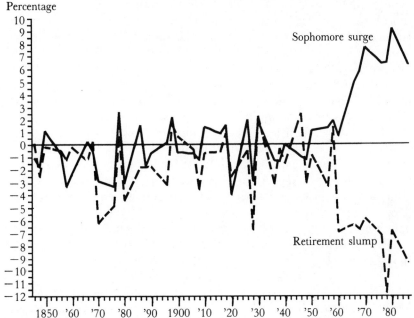

SOURCE: Computed by the authors from *Congressional Quarterly's Guide to U.S. Elections* (Washington, D.C.: Congressional Quarterly, 1985).

NOTE: No data shown for election years ending in "2" and "4."

it controls for district characteristics. By determining the difference between an incumbent performance and an open seat performance, the measurement removes from gross incumbency advantage that portion due to partisan advantage, as reflected by the party's performance in an open seat contest. The remainder is the net personal advantage enjoyed by the incumbent, above and beyond that which comes from the partisan or party organizational strength of the district itself. It is this concept of personal incumbency advantage that most of the incumbency literature, and the related work in the congressional literature, implicitly turns on.

The data in Figure 6-3 depict sophomore surge and retirement slump in the House from 1846 to 1986.[12] In each case the value for a given election year was derived by computing the mean slump or surge value separately for each party and then averaging together the two party surges or slumps, irrespective of their individual n's. As noted above, this procedure removes the biasing effect of a party tide.

Any doubt as to the historically unique nature of incumbency advantage in the post-World War II era should be put to rest by the data in Figure 6-3. Prior to 1945 there is little to indicate any, even short-term, personal advantage to incumbency. Were there such an advantage, we would expect at a minimum that sophomore surge would be positive and retirement slump would be negative. Prior to 1945 such a configuration occurs in only nine of thirty-one elections (28 percent of the time, compared to an expected 25 percent of the time due purely to chance), while after 1945 it occurs in ten of the twelve elections. Moreover, slump and surge prior to 1945 are never both in the expected direction for any adjacent pair of elections.

If we use a slightly more rigorous test for the existence of personal incumbency advantage—both slump and surge in the expected direction and both equaling or exceeding their respective standard errors, which is not a stringent test by usual statistical standards—the pattern is even more distinct. This standard is not met even once until 1966, and in every election since then both slump and surge have been more than twice their standard errors. Personal incumbency advantage, the fluctuations of which figure so prominently in the congressional literature since 1971, scarcely predates that literature.

In a strange way this discovery brings the literature on incumbency advantage full circle. In his original 1971 article, Erikson presented the first quantitative assessment of incumbency advantage and concluded that the conventional wisdom of a considerable incumbent advantage was incorrect. The importance of this finding was quickly eclipsed by Erikson's own finding that incumbency had suddenly risen to levels that were, albeit somewhat belatedly, in line with the conventional wisdom.[13] Our analysis suggests that Erikson's original conclusion was correct and remains significant. Moreover, even the modest levels of advantage that he found in the 1950s vanish when we move back just one decade. All of the numerous advantages that accompany incumbency yielded no *electoral* advantage to the incumbent until sometime after 1950.

On the basis of the data presented here it is clear that the Fiorina, Mayhew theory of Congress is plausible; that is, individual members seeking reelection may well have structured the House's organization and policy in a way that enhances their electoral success. Although our work does not prove their theory, it establishes the initial condition necessary for the theory to be true.

Another implication of this essay is that what Nelson Polsby called the institutionalization of the House was not the result of increased personal vote advantage. Polsby's seminal work showed that around the turn of the century (1890-1910) the House of Representatives became a career for its members.[14] Specifically, the average length of service in the House increased, leadership positions became routinized, meaning that longer service was needed before a member could advance, and housekeeping tasks, such as deciding contested elections, were done on a nonpartisan basis. In sum, the origins of the contemporary House are to be found in the House of the late nineteenth and early twentieth century. Given that personal incumbency does not occur until at least the 1950s, institutionalization cannot be the result of the rise in personal vote advantage.

## The Senate

To this point we have discussed Congress but presented data only on the House of Representatives, a pattern quite common among congressional scholars. But, as Barbara Hinckley has noted, "Congress is not unicameral and . . . 'House' is not a synonym for Congress," and she is right.[15] We turn now to a consideration of the patterns over time in Senate incumbency advantage.

In several 1980 studies of congressional elections, there is consensus that a greater electoral advantage to incumbency exists in the House than in the Senate.[16] Our concern here, however, is with the trend over time in the Senate rather than with differences between the chambers. With regard to Senate trends Warren Kostroski concludes that "the postwar trend has been toward even greater safety for senatorial incumbents." Joseph Cooper and William West, using data that are more recent than Kostroski's, disagree: "Whereas the advantage of incumbents in elections does appear to have increased for House members in the late 1960s and 1970s, the reverse appears to be true for Senate members." Others, including Albert Cover and David Mayhew, are not willing to conclude that any trend is definite.[17]

The relatively small number of Senate elections makes it more difficult to identify patterns with the same certainty as for the House. In a given year House elections are more than ten times as numerous as their Senate counterparts. This difference creates a particular difficulty for measures such as sophomore surge and retirement slump that depend on a small subset of all elections (those immediately preceding and following an open seat election). Any stable estimate of Senate patterns requires some aggregation of elections. We have chosen to aggregate by decade, a common choice, and the results are presented in Figure 6-4.[18] As was the case with the House data, each slump and surge is computed separately by party and averaged irrespective of their n's to remove the effects of party tides. Figure 6-4 begins with the 1920s because the election of 1920 was the first reelection opportunity for the directly elected class of 1914.

Figure 6-4   Sophomore Surge and Retirement Slump in the Senate, by Decade

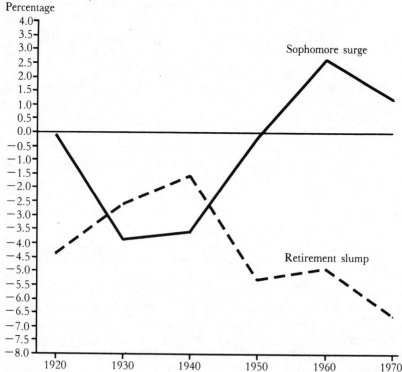

SOURCE: John R. Alford and John R. Hibbing, "Incumbency Advantage in Senate Elections" (Paper delivered at the annual meeting of the Midwest Political Science Association, Chicago, April 1983).

The patterns over time for the Senate are quite similar to those for the House over the same period. If we use the same standard we applied earlier of both surge and slump in their respective expected directions, only in the decades of the 1960s and 1970s is there evidence of personal incumbency advantage in Senate elections. The magnitude of this advantage is, however, much lower than that found in House elections where surge and slump are three or four points higher. Because senators generally have larger and more heterogeneous constituencies, both in population and geography, this smaller showing is not unexpected. Much of the explanation offered earlier for rising personal advantage in the House depends on a fairly close relationship between the member and his or her constituency.

## Causes and Some Implications

Four reasons have been cited for the rise of the personal incumbency factor in House elections: (1) congressional district lines have been drawn in the post-1960s period to favor incumbents; (2) incumbent members have increased resources to ensure reelection (franking privileges, campaign funding advantages, etc.); (3) congressional challengers are weaker; and (4) changes in the electorate weakened party identification.[19] Three of these explanations—redistricting, weaker challengers, and incumbent resources—are incumbent-related and essentially deal with the post-World War II period. The fourth explanation, changes in the electorate, postulates the decline of party identification in the electorate and dates the decline in competition around the turn of the century.

Among the incumbent-related explanations, only redistricting seems to be clearly incorrect. The Senate patterns are similar to those for the House, and no redistricting takes place in the Senate. The evidence for the incumbent resource and weaker challenger explanations is stronger yet inconclusive, and little has been done to explore its relevance for the Senate.[20] The decline in party identification may help account for the present situation because we know that incumbent representatives get a disproportionate share of split-ticket votes, and the decline would explain the bicameral pattern of growth in advantage.[21] However, if the decline of party identification began about 1900, it alone cannot account for the fact that the personal incumbency advantage begins in the post-World War II period. In short, there is no definitive answer to the question of what caused the rise in personal incumbency advantage. Careful time series analysis would be necessary to sort out the nature of the causal nexus.

Our own view is that during the 1950s and 1960s there emerged a new sort of congressional candidate and, inevitably, a new sort of incumbent member. For the first time large numbers of candidates took full advantage of the progressive era reforms of the local party and the nomination and election system. They ran vigorous campaigns, sometimes supplanting the old party organization, sometimes simply ignoring it.[22] Their goal was to win office, not just to carry the party banner, and they chose their races and ran them accordingly.

The impact of the new blood in campaigns was felt first in open seat races, which they made extremely competitive. Once in the incumbent ranks, the new members took steps to see that marginality would not stay with them for long. What the new member faced in the old House must have seemed as outmoded to them as the local party boss system in the district had. Rigid adherence to seniority, limited staff, and autocratic committee chairmen meant that old-timers held most of the power and enjoyed most of the perquisites in the House. In a discussion of the status of freshmen representatives, Herbert Asher quotes a Republican member:

> The old political machinery, both in cities and rural areas, that used to provide Congress with new members is breaking down. Both political parties are under increasing pressure to reject so-called party hacks for candidates and put up the best possible men in these competitive two-party districts. Thus a new breed of man is being elected to Congress—bright, young, combative, and in a hurry. The seniority structure of the House of Representatives works against the man in a hurry, and there is growing restlessness.[23]

Beginning in the 1950s with a variety of efforts aimed at procedural and structural reform, as well as the organization of the Democratic Study Group, and continuing through to the 1973 Sub-Committee Bill of Rights, the pattern of change in the postwar period has been one of distributing power more quickly and more broadly. Other changes, including increased personal staff, travel allowances, and use of the frank, assisted members in developing a personal district organization, further reducing their ties to the local party. While the old days of patronage and graft were mostly gone, there was a new sort of federal largesse to distribute. The revenues developed to fund the war effort were turned to domestic uses, and the advent of the New Society programs further accelerated the flow of federal dollars into the districts. The internal characteristics, combined with the rapid growth of the federal role, resulted in a situation highly conducive to the development of personal incumbency advantage.[24]

At present, personal incumbency advantage now rivals partisan advantage in its contribution to reelection margins, and the incumbent clearly has the upper hand. The local party no longer controls renomination or reelection; the value to the district of returning a member is high; the local benefits the member can claim credit for grow ever larger; and the opportunities for constituency service grow as well.

This thumbnail sketch of causes and consequences of the rise of personal incumbency advantage is largely speculative and broadly drawn. A great deal of work remains to be done in bringing available data to bear on various critical parts of the story. At this preliminary stage, the most that can be said is that it ties in with much of the existing congressional literature and that it is not contradicted by the data we have presented here.

# Notes

1. Morris P. Fiorina, "The Case of the Vanishing Marginals: The Bureaucracy Did It," *American Political Science Review* 71 (1977): 171-181.
2. David R. Mayhew, *Congress: The Electoral Connection* (New Haven, Conn.: Yale University Press, 1974).
3. See, for example, Robert S. Erikson, "A Reply to Tidmarch," *Polity* 4 (1972): 527-529; David R. Mayhew, "Congressional Elections: The Case of The Vanishing Marginals," *Polity* 6 (1974): 295-317; John A. Ferejohn, "On the Decline of Competition in Congressional Elections," *American Political Science Review* 71 (1977): 166-176; Albert D. Cover and David R. Mayhew, "Congressional Dynamics and the Decline of Competitive Congressional Elections," in *Congress Reconsidered*, 1st ed., ed. Lawrence C. Dodd and Bruce I. Oppenheimer (New York: Praeger, 1977); John R. Alford and John R. Hibbing, "Increased Incumbency Advantage in the House," *Journal of Politics* 43 (1981): 1042-1061; Melissa P. Collie, "Incumbency, Electoral Safety, and Turnover in the House of Representatives, 1952-1976," *American Political Science Review* 75 (1981): 119-131.
4. Joseph Cooper and David W. Brady, "Institutional Context and Leadership Style: The House from Cannon to Rayburn," *American Political Science Review* 75 (1981): 411-426.
5. Robert S. Erikson, "The Advantage of Incumbency in Congressional Elections," *Polity* 3 (1971): 395-405; Erikson, "A Reply to Tidmarch"; Mayhew, "Congressional Elections."
6. James C. Garand and Donald A. Gross, "Change in the Vote Margins for Congressional Elections: A Specification of Historical Trends," *American Political Science Review* 78 (1984): 17-30.
7. Gary C. Jacobson, "The Marginals Never Vanished: Incumbency and Competition in Elections to the U.S. House of Representatives, 1952-82," *American Journal of Political Science* 31 (1987): 126-141.
8. The election returns for 1852 to 1940 were compiled previously by Brady. The returns and incumbency data for 1946 to 1986 were compiled previously by Alford and John R. Hibbing. The election returns and incumbency data for the 1840s, as well as the incumbency data for 1854 to 1940, were compiled by Alford and Brady working together. In every case the source of the data was either Congressional Quarterly's *Guide to U.S. Elections* (Washington, D.C.: Congressional Quarterly, 1975, 1985) or the appropriate issue of the *CQ Almanac*.
9. See, for example, Erikson, "The Advantage of Incumbency"; and Cover and Mayhew, "Congressional Dynamics."
10. Mayhew, "Congressional Elections."
11. The differences between our findings and those of Gross and Garand are likely a function of the somewhat unusual measure of incumbent advantage they use. Incumbent winners' margins minus nonincumbent winners' margins is a troublesome and unstable way to assess advantage.

Incumbent winners' margins obviously exclude incumbents that lose and thereby often misrepresent short-term shifts. As marginal winners drop into the losing range, for example, the margins of winning incumbents may actually rise due to the weaker cases dropping out. Nonincumbents are made up of two distinct classes; open seat winners and challengers who defeat an incumbent. On average we would expect the margins of the latter group to be significantly lower than the former group. Therefore, changes in the proportion of open seats will affect the average margin of incumbent winners, independent of any change in the performance of either group of candidates.

12. These measures are based on vote shifts between two elections. As such, the exclusion of years following reapportionments, such as 1852, leads to the inability to compute surge and slump figures for the election immediately following. For this reason the surge and slump figures exclude both years such as 1852 and the following election of 1854, leaving us with the years ending in 6, 8, and 0 for each decade.

13. Erikson, "The Advantage of Incumbency"; Erikson, "A Reply to Tidmarch"; Robert S. Erikson, "Malapportionment, Gerrymandering, and Party Fortunes in Congressional Elections," *American Political Science Review* 66 (1972): 1234-1245.

14. Nelson W. Polsby, "The Institutionalization of the U.S. House of Representatives," *American Political Science Review* 62 (1968): 144-168.

15. Barbara Hinckley, "The American Voter in Congressional Elections," *American Political Science Review* 74 (1980): 641-650.

16. See, for example, Alan I. Abramowitz, "A Comparison of Voting for U.S. Senator and Representative in 1978," *American Political Science Review* 73 (1980): 633-640; Hinckley, "The American Voter"; Barbara Hinckley, "House Reelections and Senate Defeats: The Role of the Challenger," *British Journal of Political Science* 10 (1980): 441-460; Thomas E. Mann and Raymond E. Wolfinger, "Candidates and Parties in Congressional Elections," *American Political Science Review* 74 (1980): 617-632.

17. Warren Kostroski, "Party and Incumbency in Postwar Senate Elections" *American Political Science Review* 67 (1973): 1217-1218; Joseph Cooper and William West, "The Congressional Career in the 1970s," in *Congress Reconsidered,* 2d ed., ed. Lawrence C. Dodd and Bruce I. Oppenheimer (Washington, D.C.: CQ Press, 1981), 98; Cover and Mayhew, "Congressional Dynamics," 65.

18. The original data for this table are from John R. Alford and John R. Hibbing, "Incumbency Advantage in Senate Elections" (Paper delivered at the annual meeting of the Midwest Political Science Association, Chicago, April 1983).

19. For the redistricting argument, see Edward R. Tufte, "The Relationship Between Seats and Votes in Two-Party Systems," *American Political Science Review* 67 (1973): 540-554; for the resources argument, see Morris P. Fiorina, *Congress: Keystone of the Washington Establishment* (New Haven, Conn.: Yale University Press, 1977); for the weaker

challenger argument see Mann and Wolfinger, "Candidates and Parties"; or Barbara Hinckley, *Congressional Elections,* (Washington, D.C.: CQ Press, 1981); for the change in the electorate argument, see Walter Dean Burnham, "The Changing Shape of the American Political Universe," *American Political Science Review* 59 (1975): 1-28; and Ferejohn, "On the Decline of Competition."

20. For a recent discussion, see John C. McAdams and John R. Johannes, "Congressmen, Perquisites, and Elections," *Journal of Politics* 50 (1988): 412-439.
21. Mann and Wolfinger, "Candidates and Parties."
22. See David R. Mayhew, *Placing Parties in American Politics* (Princeton, N.J.: Princeton University Press, 1986): 329-332.
23. Herbert B. Asher, "The Changing Status of the Freshman Representative," in *Congress in Change,* ed. Norman J. Ornstein (New York: Praeger, 1975), 230-231.
24. Mayhew, *Congress: The Electoral Connection;* Fiorina, *Congress: Keystone of the Washington Establishment.*

# 7. MEMBERS OF CONGRESS AND THEIR CONSTITUENTS: THE HOME-STYLE CONNECTION

## *Glenn R. Parker*

Until the late 1970s most of our understanding of legislative politics was based solely on the Washington activities of senators and representatives. Indeed, legislators spend considerable time in Washington, participating in committee deliberations, floor debate and voting, and legislative bargaining, activities that fill the entire work week for many members. The weekends, however, are a different story: some legislators devote this time to leisure and family activities, but most spend it in their districts and states meeting and talking to constituents. On these weekends members perform a range of activities designed to cultivate and maintain the trust of their constituents. In short, while Washington-based activities occupy large amounts of time, they comprise only a partial and incomplete list of the demands on, and behavior of, members of Congress. Equally important, at least from the standpoint of the members, and as time-consuming, are the constituency activities they perform.

Members of Congress spend considerable time cultivating their districts and states and promoting the idea that they are personally attentive to the problems and interests of their constituents. The term *home style* refers to how members of Congress go about cultivating their constituencies.[1] Attentive home styles drive home the message that the member is *personally* (and heavily) involved in looking after the interests of constituents. Incumbents are constantly on the watch for ways to demonstrate such a personal concern, and the opportunities to do so are plentiful. Home styles exhibit remarkable stability over time; that is, once a member of Congress has established a home style that works—yields satisfactory reelection margins—he or she tends to follow the same pattern of behavior. Some of this consistency can be attributed to the uncertainty that accompanies electoral outcomes, and the interpretations of what these outcomes reveal about the electorate and the candidates. Since most members of Congress are "in the dark" about which aspects of their home style are responsible for what proportion of their electoral support, they continue existing patterns of behavior. There are, however, additional reasons for the stability of home styles which I describe later in this essay.

Home styles would not survive without the support of the institution: institutional arrangements, embodied in legislative procedure and practice, provide incentives for members to shower attention upon their constituents by minimizing the personal costs to the incumbent that stem from such attentiveness. These incentives complement each other, thereby reinforcing the motivation toward cultivating one's constituents. The fact that so many members exhibit attentive home styles is testimony to the significance of these reinforcing incentives. How these institutional arrangements function in this manner is described in the concluding section.

## Describing Home Styles

Most of what we know about home styles comes from Richard Fenno's extensive analysis of the constituency activities of eighteen members of the House of Representatives. Fenno suggests that home styles are an amalgam of three activities: the members' allocation of their personal resources and those of their staffs, their presentations to constituents, and their explanations of Washington activities.[2] Furthermore, Fenno notes that senators and representatives differ in how they approach constituents.[3]

### Allocation of Resources

How members allocate their time between Washington and their districts or states tells us a great deal about their priorities, because time is their scarcest and most valuable resource. In fact, if there is one perennial complaint among members, it is the lack of time. Incumbents jealously guard their own time, often creating barrier reefs of staff to protect them from claims on it. Members are very careful not to waste this scarce resource, and activities that squander a member's time are avoided, unless they involve constituents.

Personal staff, office space, allowances, expense accounts, and free mailings are just some of the resources provided each legislator for performing various constituency services. Although these resources help, they are no substitute for the personal time of the incumbent. Staff can perform many constituency-related functions, but their efforts only supplement those of their bosses. In the eyes of constituents, nothing can replace the personal attention of "their" senator or representative. Some situations require a "personal touch," like meeting with constituents and addressing large gatherings at home.

The personal time of the member of Congress is less easily divided than staff time. Staff can be distributed between the Washington and home offices without disrupting either law making or constituency service responsibilities of congressional offices. Not so with a member's time. The allocation of time to constituent affairs poses a dilemma because the time spent with constituents could also be spent in legislative activities that might enhance the realization of more personal goals. This potential "zero-sum" relationship (time spent with constituents cannot be spent on other things) creates a strain between the desire to attend to legislative business and the need to spend time on district and state matters. The strain is especially critical because most members of Congress would rather devote their time to legislative business, and many see constituency matters as interfering with the performance of these responsibilities. Yet, members willingly allocate large proportions of their personal time to constituent affairs.[4]

## Presentations and Explanations

The "centerpiece" of an incumbent's home style is the way he or she relates to constituents: the presentation of self. Incumbents believe that support at home is won by the kind of self they portray, and they are not reluctant to manipulate these presentations. "So members of Congress go home," according to Fenno, "to present themselves as a person and to win the accolade: 'he's a good man,' 'she's a good woman!' "[5] Incumbents emphasize three personal characteristics in these presentations: qualification, identification, and empathy. Every member of Congress creates the impression that he or she is qualified to hold office, can identify with the attitudes and beliefs of constituents, and can empathize with their problems. These personal characteristics are transmitted at each and every opportunity a member has to communicate with constituents: newsletters, mailings, meetings in the constituency, and personal visits. The more personal and pervasive the contact, the greater the probability that the message will be retained.

The third component of home styles is the way members of Congress explain their Washington activities to constituents. Explanations are the mechanisms through which incumbents describe, interpret, and justify legislative pursuits, especially their two major preoccupations, power and policy.[6] The pursuit of power, for example, can be justified by claiming that such influence is used to further district or state interests within Congress.

Incumbents make a point of explaining their votes and policy positions to their constituents when they are called upon to do so, even though they probably have little to fear from electoral reprisals for one or two unpopular votes. Because most constituents are unaware of their member's specific votes, and many perceive their representative as voting in line with constituent sentiment, explaining roll call votes creates few problems for incumbents.[7] A string of "wrong" votes could pose problems, but most members avoid creating such patterns in their votes by developing a good sense of the policy stands that are likely to produce adverse constituent reaction.[8] But there is always some uncertainty as to what votes a member may be called upon to explain, so members tend to "stockpile" more explanations than they need.[9]

Explanations can be used by members to gain some leeway in their pursuits in Washington. It is difficult for constituents to keep tabs on legislators, especially when they are in Washington; therefore, voters are largely uninformed about the behavior of their representatives and senators. This "invisibility" can be exploited by incumbents to pursue personal goals without worrying about constituent reaction. For example, some members seek independence from the policy preferences of their constituents to exercise their own judgment or to promote ideologically satisfying causes. The reservoir of trust built through diligent constituent attention enables members to exercise independence in their pursuit of personal goals. If constituents trust their representatives and senators, they are likely to grant them freedom from surveillance. This is not to say that constituents approve of their member's pursuits or would approve if they had knowledge of them. It seems more likely that constituents assume that their legislator is fulfilling constituency obligations and congressional responsibilities unless they hear otherwise, and rarely will they hear otherwise!

The home-style activities of members of Congress are not entirely self-serving because they meet legitimate representational responsibilities. Constituents expect to be kept informed about issues that are relevant to their concerns, and incumbents oblige by providing such information, while also taking the opportunity to further their own interests through these communications. Diana Yiannakis's study of the newsletters and press releases produced by a sample of members of Congress during the first six months of the 94th and 95th Congresses demonstrates exactly how adept incumbents are at fulfilling these dual objectives.[10] Yiannakis found that 42 percent of the paragraphs in these newsletters and press releases explained the incumbent's stands on national issues, and less than 10 percent was devoted to national or local information—an amount of space smaller than that allocated to claiming credit for particularized district benefits (11.6 percent).

## Stability

A major attribute of home styles is their permanence: once established, the patterns that mark home styles tend to persist. This is not to say that home styles are immutable. It would be more accurate to say that they are susceptible to change, but only when there are sufficient incentives. In most cases, the forces of stability preclude such changes. This stability can be explained by four factors: the strategies adopted by incumbents, the expectations of constituents, the natural course of constituency careers, and the absence of incentives for changing home styles.

Most incumbents want their constituents to see patterns in their home-style activities that reinforce the images they are constantly "polishing" and promulgating in their visits with constituents and in their communications to them. As well as engendering political support, home styles are designed to mesh with the personalities and goals of representatives and senators. A successful home style represents the fit between the electoral necessities that confront a member and his or her personal goals. This congruence tends to promote the maintenance of the existing pattern of behavior, especially because most incumbents probably have no clear idea of what aspects of their home-style behaviors are responsible for what proportion of their electoral support. Such uncertainty discourages changes in behavior. The simple strategy under these conditions would be to do the same things in the future that proved successful in the past.

By creating an image with constituents, an incumbent may be limiting his or her ability to change the home style in the future. Members mold constituent expectations as they establish their home styles. These expectations, in turn, constrain their home-style behavior because members feel that their constituents expect such behaviors and would react negatively to any attempt to alter them.

> If these House members failed to see ten people in Maple Grove or cancelled the open meetings or relinquished caucus leadership or left immediately after the clambake, they believe it would cost them dearly in electoral support. They might lose support they had "last time," because they believe that their present home style helped them to victory last time.[11]

Home styles, therefore, harden over the course of constituency careers. Fenno identifies two stages in the constituency careers of incumbents: an expansionist stage and a protectionist stage.[12] Incumbents in the expansionist stage of their congressional careers seek to enlarge their existing electoral coalition and to solidify a core of strong supporters. During the protectionist stage, in contrast, incumbents become less interested in building constituent support, and more concerned about maintaining the electoral support already attained. Home-style activities in the protectionist stage can be described as "preventive maintenance."

The expansionist stage during which the congressman cultivates first a primary constituency, then a reelection constituency and during which he works out a viable, comfortable home style, has a largely experimental impulse to it. Once in the protectionist stage, however, the dominant impulse is conservative.[13]

Finally, home styles may be resistant to change because there are too few incentives to change. Home styles represent the culmination of political experiences and experimentations. Changes in behavior, therefore, require strong incentives, but the pressures for stability seem to counter most incentives for altering home styles. Only incentives that can satisfy a variety of member needs, perhaps simultaneously, are capable of inducing widespread stylistic changes.

One example of the stability of the home-style behaviors of representatives and senators is the extent to which they spend about the same amount of time in their constituencies year after year—a pattern interrupted only by the expansion of the subsidies for constituency travel. The magnitude of the relationship (correlation) between the number of days legislators spent in their constituencies in successive Congresses within four seniority groupings (that is, members elected before 1958, between 1958 and 1963, between 1964 and 1969, and between 1970 and 1975) reveals considerable stability— large correlations—in over-time levels of constituency attention among both representatives and senators. Senators, however, exhibit higher correlations, and therefore somewhat greater stability, in their over-time allocations of personal time to the state than House members. The greater stability in the allocations of time to the state is even more remarkable when one considers the six-year term of senators. The longer term permits senators greater latitude than representatives in allocating their time to state affairs. With a six-year time span between elections, senators have greater flexibility in controlling the timing of their visits to the state. For example, senators appear to intensify their constituent contacts in the two years prior to the next election,[14] and there is evidence that they do not give voters the same level of personal attention throughout the term.[15]

In the House two patterns persist that are not as clearly evident in the Senate (see Figure 7-1). First, there is some evidence that the allocations of personal time to the district *gain* stability with time as illustrated by the upward trend in the correlations between time spent in the district during successive Congresses. While senators also exhibit some increased stability in their allocations of personal time to state voters, the pattern is not as clear as among representatives. Second, older House incumbents appear to exhibit even greater consistency in their attentiveness than younger cohorts: in most instances, the Con-

Figure 7-1   Correlations Between Number of Days Spent in the
District During Consecutive Congresses

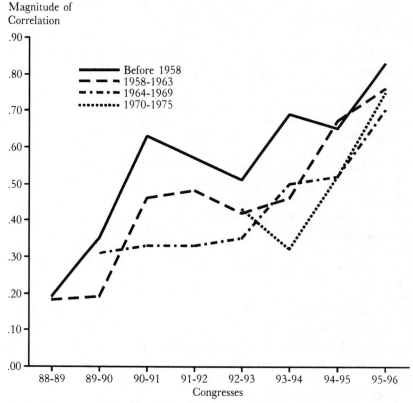

Magnitude of
Correlation

| | |
|---|---|
| ——— | Before 1958 |
| — — — | 1958-1963 |
| — · — · — | 1964-1969 |
| ·········· | 1970-1975 |

Congresses

SOURCE: Glenn R. Parker, *Homeward Bound: Explaining Changes in Congressional Behavior* (Pittsburgh: University of Pittsburgh Press, 1986), 47.

gress-by-Congress correlations are larger among the more senior congressional cohorts. The growing stability in attention, and the greater stability in the patterns of attention among older House incumbents, demonstrate how allocation patterns stabilize over time; these patterns are consistent with Fenno's contention that home styles tend to harden over time. Like presentations and explanations, allocations of time to the district and state also tend to gain in consistency and stability.

How members of Congress behave in their constituencies is only one side of the home-style connection; the other side is how constituents perceive them. It should be clear from the preceding discussion that incumbents place a heavy emphasis on transmitting images that appeal to constituents. They emphasize their service to constituents, their empathy and identification with the plight of constituents, and their best personal qualities. In addition, legislators justify their behavior in Washington in the hope that voters will approve and continue to trust them.

The success of these activities can be judged by the extent to which these home-style "messages" actually penetrate the consciousness of voters. In short, do constituents perceive their member of Congress as attentive, personally appealing, and trustworthy? Is there a coincidence between the home-style actions of members and constituent perceptions of them? This question serves as the focus for the next section.

## Popular Perceptions of Members of Congress

Because members of Congress work exceedingly hard to promote the image that they care about their districts and states, it may not be too surprising to find that constituents see them exactly that way. The personal qualities of members of Congress and their attention to district or state affairs are two criteria frequently cited by constituents in their evaluations of their representative.[16] Other "reasonable" criteria, such as political party identification, ideology, or positions on issues, are rarely mentioned.

Table 7-1 describes what voters in national opinion surveys conducted by the University of Michigan between 1978 and 1984 liked and disliked about their own representative. It is clear from this table that a member's attentiveness to the constituency, experience, and personal qualities dominate constituent evaluations. Constituent trust and leadership qualities also emerge in the evaluations, but they are less pervasive. Most of these attributes reflect well on incumbents, placing their overall performance in office in a very favorable light.[17] Perhaps more important, few constituents see their legislators in terms of policies or ideology, which probably adds to an incumbent's popularity because such factors are more likely to tarnish, rather than polish, a member's image.

In addition, constituents tend to view their legislators as successful manipulators and movers of governmental action. This image, and the reported success of incumbents in dealing with constituent problems, have created constituent expectations of service and successful bureaucratic interventions. More than 80 percent of the voters surveyed felt that their member of Congress could help them in some way (Figure 7-2). What is most remarkable about this expectation is that few constituents have actually contacted their representative (more than 85 percent of those interviewed in national surveys have *never* contacted

Table 7-1   Voter Likes and Dislikes of Their Representatives, 1978-1984

| *Respondent mentioned* | *Democratic incumbent* | | | | *Republican incumbent* | | | |
|---|---|---|---|---|---|---|---|---|
| | 1978 | 1980 | 1982 | 1984 | 1978 | 1980 | 1982 | 1984 |
| Experience | 21.0% | 14.6% | 14.3% | 15.7% | 22.1% | 18.3% | 15.3% | 17.6% |
| Trust | 14.2 | 13.1 | 11.2 | 12.3 | 12.9 | 11.0 | 12.6 | 12.9 |
| Leadership qualities | 3.1 | 2.4 | 3.6 | 3.4 | 2.3 | 2.0 | 3.3 | 3.7 |
| Constituency attention | 23.9 | 25.5 | 22.3 | 19.4 | 18.3 | 21.9 | 17.9 | 19.9 |
| Personal qualities | 16.0 | 16.4 | 17.6 | 21.2 | 16.7 | 17.3 | 18.4 | 15.2 |
| Party connections | 3.4 | 4.4 | 5.6 | 3.7 | 4.1 | 6.9 | 10.0 | 6.6 |
| Ideology | 3.5 | 4.7 | 4.1 | 3.7 | 7.4 | 5.7 | 4.0 | 6.0 |
| Domestic policy | 4.7 | 7.3 | 8.1 | 5.4 | 5.7 | 5.2 | 5.8 | 5.7 |
| Foreign policy | 1.0 | 1.4 | 0.7 | 1.6 | 0.7 | 1.2 | 1.5 | 1.8 |
| Group connections | 5.3 | 6.2 | 8.7 | 8.5 | 5.2 | 6.2 | 7.5 | 4.4 |
| Miscellaneous | 3.9 | 3.8 | 3.7 | 5.2 | 4.6 | 4.3 | 3.7 | 6.2 |
| Total responses | 1,088 | 834 | 749 | 1,203 | 754 | 562 | 602 | 564 |

SOURCE: University of Michigan, American National Election Studies, 1978-1984.

NOTE: Questions: Was there anything in particular that you liked about (name of candidate)? Was there anything in particular that you did not like about (name of candidate)?

their representative or senator). Constituents perceive their representative to be helpful even though they have no personal experience upon which to base such a judgment!

How can we explain these images held by constituents? There is no easy or simple answer. Perhaps constituents are sensitive to the performance of certain district or state-related responsibilities, and their perceptions of their member reflect the importance they attribute to those responsibilities. Incumbents, therefore, may emphasize constituency activities because they know that constituents value them. Alternatively, these images may persist because they form the focal point of most constituent-legislator interactions; constituents' perceptions echo what members of Congress say and do.

There is no way to tell whether the criteria used by constituents to evaluate their representative's performance is the result of the importance that constituents attach to attentive home styles,[18] or because incumbents emphasize these characteristics in their constituent contacts and communications. I suspect that it is a combination of both factors (value to constituents and behavior of members) that conspire to make a member's attentiveness to his or her constituency a salient feature of voter perceptions.

Figure 7-2   Perceived Helpfulness of Members of Congress

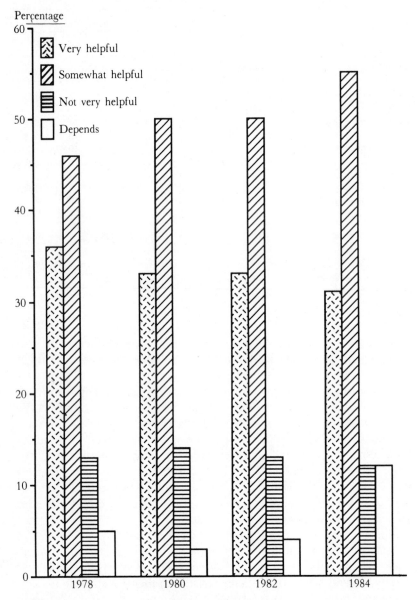

SOURCE: University of Michigan, American National Election Studies, 1978-1984.
NOTE: Question: If you had a problem that your representative could do something
about, do you think he or she would be helpful?

## Images of Senators

The major difference between the home styles of senators and representatives has little to do with the activities they pursue with respect to their constituencies because they generally do the same sorts of things.[19] They differ only in the emphasis they place on certain types of activities: senators do not feel that they can reach a large number of their constituents through personal contact, but representatives feel that such contact is worthwhile and effective. Hence, senators do not normally spend as much time in their states as representatives spend in their districts. Furthermore, Senate elections are different from House races because "Senate candidates talk about public policy questions more than House candidates do." [20] As a consequence, there is more evidence of ideological and policy voting in Senate elections than House contests.[21]

A basic cause of these differences in the home styles of representatives and senators is the size of the constituencies they represent. The smaller the size differential between a state and a congressional district, the greater similarity between the styles of the House and Senate incumbents representing these areas. Conversely, the larger the gap between the size of congressional and senatorial constituencies, the less the home styles of representatives and senators will come to resemble one another.[22]

As might be expected, therefore, the popular images of senators are not as colored by their attention to their constituencies. The differing responsibilities and representational arrangements of representatives and senators, such as length of term and constituency size, make constituency attention less relevant for evaluating the performance of senators. The smaller size of the Senate and the broader set of interests normally represented by senators suggest that the performance of senators is judged differently from the performance of representatives. Robert Swansborough's analysis of the constituent images of representatives and senators in four southern states illustrates the different emphasis that constituency behavior receives in voter images of representatives and senators.[23] Swansborough found that 34 percent of the constituents in these states cited the constituency behavior of their representative as "something they liked," but less than 20 percent of these respondents cited the constituency behavior of their senators as something liked.

This finding should not be construed to suggest that the constituency service provided by senators cannot rival the level or quality of district attention, since few constituents have anything negative to say about the constituency behavior of senators.[24] I expect constituency attention is less central to the images of senators because they gain the public's eye in so many other ways. Constituency attention, therefore, provides a positive component to the images of senators in the same way that such attention generates positive evaluations of representatives.

## Constituent Trust

According to Fenno, House incumbents are constantly attempting to project images that will engender political support and trust among their constituents.

> It is not an overnight or a one-time thing. It is hard to win; and it must be constantly renewed and rewon. "Trust," said one member, "is a cumulative thing, a totality thing. . . . You do a little here and a little there." So it takes an enormous amount of time to build and to maintain constituent trust. That is what House members believe. And that is why they spend so much of their working time at home. Much of what I have observed in my travels can be explained as a continuous and continuing effort to win (for new members) and to hold (for old members) the trust of supportive constituencies.[25]

Many of the communications between legislators and constituents reflect relentless efforts to reinforce constituent trust. For those members who are successful at this endeavor, electoral security and policy leeway are likely by-products.

The actions of incumbents (in Washington) may be virtually invisible to their constituents, but the incumbents themselves are not. Constituents find their legislators prepared and willing to explain their Washington activities, and their frequent appearances within their constituencies provide ample opportunities to question them about these activities. The fact that members make themselves available to constituents reinforces constituent trust.

> Qualification, identification, and empathy are all helpful in the building of constituent trust. To a large degree these three impressions are conveyed by the very fact of regular contact. That is, "I prove to you that I am qualified," or "I prove to you that I am one of you," or "I prove to you that I understand," by coming around frequently to let you see me, to see you and to meet with you. If, on the other hand, I failed to come home to see and be seen, to talk and be talked to, then you would have some reason to worry about trusting me.[26]

In fact, the home-style activities of legislators—allocation of resources, presentation of self, explanation of Washington activity—are all designed to generate constituent trust. Incumbents hope to develop home styles that will create sufficient trust to permit them to pursue personal goals within Congress without fear of adverse constituent reaction or interference. Constituents willingly invest trust in their legislators when they are convinced that their members are attentive to district or state interests and are likely to sustain that level of attention in the future.

One indication of the level of trust among constituents is the extent to which trust is mentioned in a positive or negative fashion by constituents in evaluating their member of Congress. Indications of constituent trust can be found in questions asking respondents to describe the things they *like* and *dislike* about their representative. Generally, distrusting responses refer to the incumbent's pursuit of self-interest, lack of integrity (principles), stupidity, untrustworthiness, dishonesty, or lack of independence (controlled by political bosses or parties). Constituent trust is reflected in responses that are the opposite of these, for example, honesty, trustworthiness, and integrity.

While the categorization of such open-ended responses is always somewhat subjective, the effort to identify trusting and distrusting comments is guided by the nature of the standard "trust-in-government" questions.[27] The useful properties of the scale that combines these questions, such as its validity and reliability, provide the rationale for using these items as a guide to classifying trusting and distrusting responses; it provides some assurance that the responses used as indicators of constituent trust reflect the same underlying concept—trust. For example, the responses categorized as reflecting constituent distrust capture the content of the items included as measurements of distrust in the standard "trust-in-government" scale: government officials are stupid, crooked, run by interests looking out for themselves, cannot be trusted to do what is right, and are undeniably self-interested.[28]

After eliminating respondents who fail to mention trust *either* positively or negatively in evaluating their representative, the remaining respondents can be assigned a score on the "trust index" by subtracting the number of distrusting responses from the number of trusting responses. This calculation results in an index of constituent trust that ranges from a high of $+3$ to a low of $-3$. The frequency of trust responses on this measure suggests that constituents maintain fairly high levels of confidence in their member of Congress: more than 70 percent of the respondents expressing a trusting *or* distrusting response gave more trusting evaluations than distrusting ones. This finding is consistent with Fenno's observation that members of Congress are concerned about levels of constituent trust and make concerted efforts to maintain it.[29] High levels of constituent trust suggest that the effort is successful.

Although constituent trust is mentioned less frequently than other home-style messages (Table 7-1), this may be the result of the differing media through which these messages are transmitted. The messages that inspire trust are most effectively conveyed and delivered in person. Other home-style messages can be effectively transmitted through newsletters, media coverage, and legislator-constituent correspondence, as well as through the member's appearances in the district. The greater the number of channels for disseminating the other home-style messages, the greater the saliency of these activities in voter perceptions of their member. However, the frequency of the member's message may be less important than its capacity to increase electoral support at home. If every constituent could recall a member's efforts to aid the district and its constituents, but that message had only a small effect on the subsequent vote, an incumbent would gain little. On the other hand, if a message were received rather infrequently because of the requirement that it be delivered personally, but it had a major impact on the voter's decision, the incumbent would benefit greatly despite the limited audience. Constituent trust qualifies as this latter type of message.

Constituent trust contributes to electoral support in at least two ways. First, constituent trust influences the popular standing of the member of Congress among constituents. Simply put, trusted members are quite popular with voters, and popularity translates into electoral support, although there is not a perfect relationship between popularity and trust. Second, constituent trust has a direct relationship to the vote: high levels of constituent trust tend to promote election victories. Moreover, constituent trust may be a unique component of candidate evaluation with respect to its effect on electoral support because it is a better predictor of electoral support than other components of candidate evaluation, such as personal characteristics, experience, and leadership qualities.[30] Thus, the direct and indirect effects of constituent trust enhance electoral support.

## Maintaining the Home-Style Connection

It should be clear from the preceding discussion that members behave in ways designed to cultivate a favorable image among their constituents and that these behaviors have the desired impact. It may seem rather odd, in light of the electoral relevance of these home-style activities, to ask why members undertake such time-consuming and demanding tasks. Certainly, the desire for reelection is a strong motivation, but spending time on constituent affairs leaves less time for the activity that members appear to value most, and that is legislating—formulating policies, debating issues, and mobilizing supporters. Attentive home styles, therefore, represent a real cost to members. With that understanding, we must look beyond the electoral imperative to see why members of Congress maintain attentive home styles. One of the basic reasons for the persistence of attentive home styles is that institutional arrangements within Congress provide reinforcing incentives for members to engage in activities associated with such home styles. These institutional arrangements have led members to emphasize their personal attention to the problems and needs of their constituents by minimizing the costs associated with this constituency emphasis. These arrangements evolved during the 1960s and 1970s and resulted in significant changes in how members relate to their constituents. One indicator of this change in home styles is the growth in the time that representatives and senators personally spend in their constituencies.

Although there is no way of directly calculating exactly how much time legislators in the early Congresses spent with their constituents, it seems likely that the time members spent in their districts and states was inversely related to the length of legislative sessions. Members were fairly anxious to leave Washington at the close of legislative sessions in the early Congresses. They stayed in Washington only as long as they needed to; time not spent in session was normally spent in the district or state (and traveling between the constituency and Washington). "Almost none of the members acquired homes in the capital or established year-round residence there. They merely wintered in Washington, spending more time each year with constituents than with each other." [31]

Old-time, part-time senators and representatives, then, spent considerable time in their constituencies, working at their trade or profession. Twentieth-century legislators found it considerably more difficult to devote similar levels of attention to their districts and states. One of the most obvious reasons for this state of affairs was the expanded scope, complexity, and volume of legislative business. By most measures of legislative activity—hours in session, number of committee or subcommittee meetings, volume of legislation, roll call votes—the legislative workload had grown to a staggering level. The leisurely atmosphere of legislative service was replaced by a far more hectic pace.

As the workload expanded, legislators found it necessary to spend more time in Washington and less time in their districts and states. Until the twentieth century, with the exception of the 1st Congress, rarely did the total length of a Congress exceed 400 days. Between the 2d Congress (1791-1792) and the 60th Congress (1907-1908), more than 400 days were spent in session in only five—the 27th, 40th, 50th, 53d, and 55th Congresses. During the next fourteen years, six of the seven Congresses remained in session for more than 400 days (61st-

Figure 7-3    Mean Number of Days Spent Each Month in the
District or State, 1964-1980

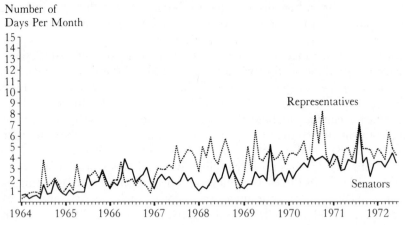

63d, 65th-67th). After the 73d Congress (1933-1934), no Congress lasted less than 400 days, and about one-half of them remained in session for more than 600 days!

Figure 7-3 displays the number of days that House and Senate incumbents have spent in their districts and states, respectively, between 1964 and 1980; these data were collected from the travel vouchers that incumbents filed with the clerk of the House of Representatives and the secretary of the Senate. It is clear from Figure 7-3 that the amount of time incumbents spend in their constituencies each month has grown since the mid-1960s. Today's legislators appear to have reversed a trend that has characterized the personal contact between constituents and their senators and representatives since the turn of the century: they are spending more rather than less time in their districts and states.

This change was facilitated by Congress to accommodate members' needs for electoral safety, services for constituents, and political leeway from constituency control.[32] These three member needs can be satisfied through diligent constituency attention. Although specific needs may vary in importance from member to member, the adoption of an attentive home style can simultaneously satisfy all of them, which made it attractive to House and Senate incumbents at every level of seniority. Moreover, the attraction of an attentive home style grew as its personal costs (to the member) were gradually minimized by measures such as increased office perquisites and adjustments in the legislative schedule that reduced conflicts between responsibilities in Washington and at home. In the process, strong incentives were established for

Number of
Days Per Month

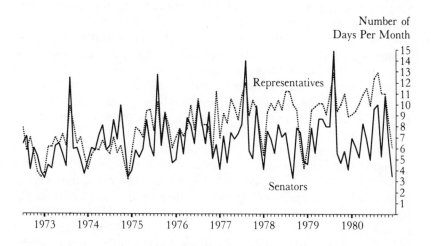

members to adopt or convert to more attentive home styles. These incentives persist today in the form of institutional arrangements that continue to influence the constituency behavior of members.

## Cost Subsidization and Shifting

Subsidies are the most direct way in which institutional arrangements for constituency attention are maintained. Many services, such as telephones and telegrams, postage and special delivery, and travel, are subsidized by legislatively authorized allowances. The franking privilege is just one example of a subsidy that is an incentive for increasing levels of constituency contact. American households are bombarded at regular intervals with an assortment of mail that bears the signature of a member of Congress in lieu of postage. The ease with which such mail can be addressed, the number of constituents that can be reached by these mailings, and the absence of direct costs to members for exercising this privilege make mass mailings useful mechanisms for maintaining contact with constituents. Further, there is an economy-of-scale-incentive for expanding this type of service if subsidies are increased: once established, the direct marginal cost to the member of expanding such a service is small. Mass mailings, for instance, can be distributed to a broader group without the member incurring any additional *personal* costs. Another example of direct subsidization is the provision of funds to defray the expense of traveling to (and within) the district or state. The expansion of subsidies for mailings and travel were critical in changing how members relate to their constituencies.

Increases in the subsidies for staff provide an example of cost shifting, which is a more indirect method of reducing the costs attached to constituency attention. As noted earlier, one of the inherent limitations on the member's ability to engage in constituency attention is that a member's time is finite. If there were some way of shifting the personal costs of constituency service to someone else, a member could increase the number of constituents served. The use of staff for constituency service activities enables members to shift the burden of such activities and expand the *range* of services without reducing the *level* of service to their constituents.

The growth in personal and committee staff has provided numerous opportunities for members to expand their contacts with constituents.[33] Senators and representatives have long recognized the value of staff in serving as their surrogates, and they have tried to increase the level of constituency travel by their staffs. Mark Hatfield, R-Ore., echoed the sentiment of most senators when he urged the passage of legislation that would reimburse staff for travel within the home state:

> What staff members are able to do in all states when they assist constituents in this manner is to help cut red tape facing everyone dealing with the government. In addition, better communication is achieved. Eyeball-to-eyeball contact is what should be encouraged. This bill will assist in enabling our staffs to better serve our constituents.[34]

## Legislative Scheduling

Another institutional arrangement that minimizes the costs attached to constituency attention is the structuring of the legislative schedule to allow members to spend time in their districts and states without detracting from their Washington responsibilities. By structuring the legislative schedule so that members can spend time with their constituents without jeopardizing legislative interests or responsibilities, Congress has reduced the costs of constituency attention. In the process, increased attention to constituency affairs on the part of representatives and senators has been encouraged.

The legislative schedules in the House and the Senate have been structured in several ways to facilitate the adoption of attentive home styles. Congress, especially the House, is infamous for its Tuesday-to-Thursday schedule of legislative business. This truncated schedule enables House members to spend long weekends in their districts without missing any legislative business. The House also has set aside blocks of time, called district work weeks, in the legislative schedule each year for incumbents to travel within their districts. Because most legislative business is scheduled to minimize conflicts with constituency travel, there is generally little relationship between voting participation in Washington and time spent at home in the district or state. Few members need to worry about their absenteeism becoming a campaign issue; they rarely miss a vote unless they want to avoid taking a position on an issue.

In the Senate, the scheduling of most business is, by definition, acceptable to all since it is conducted under unanimous consent agreements. These agreements are negotiated between the minority and majority party leaders and must receive the unanimous approval of the Senate; once approved, they serve as the schedule for Senate business. It is interesting to note that the use of unanimous consent agreements in the Senate increased at the same time that other institutional changes encouraging increased attention were occurring among senators. The use of unanimous consent agreements increased from twenty agreements in 1959 to sixty-seven in 1977.[35] Such accommodations encouraged attendance by senators by reducing the conflicts between legislative business in Washington and time spent at home.

Perhaps the most obvious way in which Congress structures the legislative schedule to reduce the costs of constituency attention is through the proliferation of recess periods (Figure 7-4). Congress normally conducts no legislative business during recess periods, so members need not worry about forsaking their legislative responsibilities while spending time with their constituents. Some recess and holiday periods are dictated by statute. For example, the Legislative Reorganization Act of 1970 specified that Congress was to adjourn from the thirtieth day before, to the second day following, Labor Day during the first session of each Congress. In essence, the legislation set aside the entire month of August for a congressional recess period. Although the establishment of the August recess significantly increased recess days, the trend toward more time away from Washington began even before the declaration of this special period. As Figure 7-4 reveals, the number of days that the House and Senate were in recess began to rise in the mid-1960s (after the 89th Congress).

In sum, by subsidizing constituency activities, increasing the size of staffs and permitting them a greater role in constituency affairs, and manipulating the legislative schedule to avoid conflicts between responsibilities in Washington and at home, Congress has established a structure of incentives that influences the constituency behavior of most legislators. This incentive structure takes the form of institutional arrangements that promote high levels of attention to constituency matters on the part of incumbents. Therefore, the pronounced change in home styles—increased attention to constituency affairs—brought

Figure 7-4    Total Number of Days House or Senate in Recess,
78th-98th Congresses

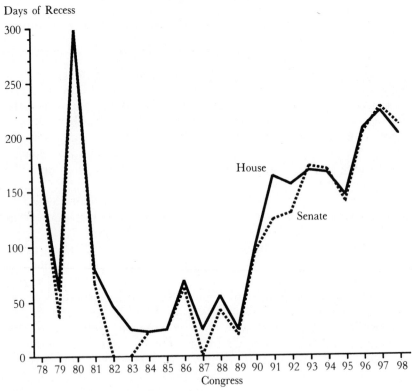

SOURCE: *Congressional Directory* (1985).

about by the evolution of this incentive structure during the 1960s and
1970s has become a permanent feature of the home styles of today's
senators and representatives.

## Summary

The home styles of members of Congress can be described in terms
of how they allocate their resources (and those of their staff) to
constituency affairs, present themselves to their constituents, and
explain their Washington activities to the voters. The images of
members of Congress held by constituents tend to reflect these
behaviors: incumbent senators and representatives are perceived in very
personal terms, and their attentiveness to the district or state, experi-

ence, and trust are their most positive qualities. The capacity of legislators to disseminate these images frequently and in subtle ways (for example, in mass mailings and during meetings with constituents) may explain some of the congruence between the actions of members of Congress and how constituents perceive their legislators. Equally important is the value that constituents attach to many of the features of an attentive home style.

More time is devoted to constituent affairs in the modern Congress. This change in home styles is sustained by institutional arrangements that have reduced the personal costs associated with maintaining an attentive home style. By allowing members to shift some of the costs of increased attention to others, while subsidizing a broad range of other constituency-related activities, and by structuring the legislative schedule to minimize conflicts between activities in Washington and at home, Congress has created a set of institutional arrangements that sustains high levels of attention to constituency matters.

# Notes

1. Richard F. Fenno, Jr., *Home Style: House Members in Their Districts* (Boston: Little, Brown, 1978).
2. Ibid.
3. Richard F. Fenno, Jr., *The United States Senate: A Bicameral Perspective* (Washington, D.C.: American Enterprise Institute, 1982).
4. Glenn R. Parker, *Homeward Bound: Explaining Changes in Congressional Behavior* (Pittsburgh: University of Pittsburgh Press, 1986).
5. Fenno, *Home Style*, 55.
6. For power, see Lawrence C. Dodd, "Congress and the Quest for Power," in *Studies of Congress*, edited by Glenn R. Parker (Washington, D.C.: CQ Press, 1985), 489-520. For policy, see Richard F. Fenno, Jr., *Congressmen in Committees* (Boston: Little, Brown, 1973).
7. Glenn R. Parker, "Incumbent Popularity and Electoral Success," in *Congressional Elections,* ed. Joseph Cooper and L. Sandy Maisel (Beverly Hills, Calif.: Sage Publications, 1981), 249-279.
8. John Kingdon, *Congressmen's Voting Decisions* (New York: Harper and Row, 1973).
9. Fenno, *Home Style*, 142.
10. Diana Evans Yiannakis, "House Members' Communication Styles: Newsletters and Press Releases," *Journal of Politics* 44 (November 1982): 1049-1071.
11. Fenno, *Home Style*, 191.
12. Ibid., 171-176.

13. Ibid., 189.
14. Fenno, *United States Senate.*
15. William A. Taggert and Robert F. Durant, "Home Style of a U.S. Senator: A Longitudinal Analysis," *Legislative Studies Quarterly* 10 (November 1985): 489-504.
16. Glenn R. Parker and Roger H. Davidson, "Why Do Americans Love Their Congressmen So Much More Than Their Congress?" *Legislative Studies Quarterly* 4 (February 1979): 52-61.
17. Ibid.
18. One reason why constituents may place such a high premium on constituency attention is that it distinguishes the incumbent from most members of Congress in the eyes of his or her constituents who frequently believe other legislators to be unresponsive to the voters. It may also be far more rational for constituents to vote for the candidate who has delivered district benefits in the past than one who espouses political issues to win favor with voters: constituent services can be delivered with high probability as a result of the personal efforts of the incumbent but incorporating district opinion into law faces a more perilous journey with a relatively low probability of success. Also see Parker, *Homeward Bound,* 121-123.
19. Fenno, *The United States Senate.*
20. Ibid., 170.
21. See, for instance, James H. Kuklinski and Darrell West, "Economic Expectations and Mass Voting in United States House and Senate Elections," *American Political Science Review* 75 (June 1981): 436-447; and Gerald C. Wright and Michael B. Berkman, "Candidates and Policy in United States Senate Elections," *American Political Science Review* 80 (June 1986): 567-588.
22. Fenno, *United States Senate.*
23. Robert H. Swansborough, "Southern Images of President Reagan, Congress, and Southern Congressmen" (Paper delivered at the annual meeting of the Southern Political Science Association, Atlanta, Oct. 28-30, 1982).
24. Ibid.
25. Fenno, *Home Style,* 56.
26. Ibid., 60.
27. The following questions are used to create the trust-in-government scale.
    (1) Do you think that people in government waste a lot of the money that we pay in taxes, waste some of it, or don't waste very much of it?
    (2) How much of the time do you think you can trust the government in Washington to do what is right—just about always, most of the time, or only some of the time?
    (3) Would you say the government is pretty much run by a few big interests looking out for themselves or that it is run for the benefit of all the people?
    (4) Do you feel that *almost* all of the people running the government are smart people who usually know what they are doing, or do you think

that quite a few of them don't seem to know what they are doing?

(5) Do you think that quite a few of the people running the government are a little crooked, not very many are, or do you think hardly any of them are crooked at all?

28. For a description of the content of the responses used as measurements of trust, see Glenn R. Parker, "The Role of Constituent Trust in Congressional Elections" (Paper delivered at the annual meeting of the American Political Science Association, Chicago, Sept. 3-6, 1987), appendix. Analysis of constituent trust is drawn from this paper.

29. Fenno, *Home Style,* 55-60.

30. See Parker, "The Role of Constituent Trust."

31. James S. Young, *The Washington Community: 1800-1828* (New York: Columbia University Press, 1966).

32. Parker, *Homeward Bound,* chap. 1.

33. See, for instance, *Studies Dealing with Budgetary, Staffing and Administrative Activities of the U.S. House of Representatives, 1946-1978,* committee print, 95th Cong., 2d sess., 1978, 24-43.

34. Senate, Committee on Rules and Administration, *Hearings Before Ad Hoc Subcommittee to Consider the Reimbursement of Actual Travel Expenses of Senators,* 92d Cong. 2d sess., June 20, 1972, 7.

35. Walter J. Oleszek, *Congressional Procedures and the Policy Process* (Washington, D.C.: CQ Press, 1978), 144.

*Part III*

COMMITTEE AND
SUBCOMMITTEE POLITICS

# 8. COMMITTEE DECISION MAKING IN THE POSTREFORM CONGRESS

## Richard L. Hall

If the commentaries of the past twenty years are correct, the U.S. Congress has become a highly decentralized institution. To century-old reflections on the importance of committees, we now can add comments about "rampant individualism," the "proliferation of workgroups," and the "fragmentation" of the institution. How one reads such accounts depends on one's historical method, but in some respects, they reflect not new departures but the continuation of old trends. With the growth of the American industrial (and now postindustrial) economy, the federal government also has grown. For instance, when Woodrow Wilson was writing his quotable aphorisms about committee government in the 1880s, federal outlays represented only a tiny fraction of the nation's total goods and services; today they account for almost 25 percent. The sphere of federal oversight and action has grown to cover almost every aspect of American society, directly expanding the range of constituents, industries, and groups that press their demands on Capitol Hill.[1] The workload of Congress has reflected that growth, has been related to it both as cause and effect.[2]

As others have noted, Congress has adapted to such changes with a more complex division of labor.[3] This has been the purpose of its committee and, more recently, its elaborate subcommittee system. But, as this essay attempts to show, committee jurisdictions and membership rolls provide only a rough sketch of the decision makers in a decentralized system. Unlike more bureaucratic organizations, the division of labor in Congress is not authoritatively imposed. It bubbles up, as it were, from individual members' day-to-day choices about which matters warrant their time, energy, and staff attention.

It is difficult to overestimate the importance of these decisions. Taken together, they determine which views and values matter on the particular issues Congress takes up. With occasional exceptions, a sustained effort by a member and her staff is a necessary if not sufficient condition for significant influence on an issue before her chamber. This point is neglected in the substantial literature that views decision making as a process of building voting majorities, either in committee or on the floor. The act of voting is only one—and probably not the most important—form of participation in the legislative process. Except in cases where the lines of disagreement are very closely drawn, parliamentary suffrage gives a member relatively little influence over the several decisions that shape a piece of legislation. Authoring or negotiating a legislative vehicle, drafting particular amendments, persuading colleagues to adopt one's point of view—all these activities weigh far more heavily in the decision-making calculus of most bills, especially in a legislature where committees play such an important role. David Mayhew states the general principle: "In small working units, formal voting tends to recede in importance as a determinant of outcomes, and what individuals do with their time and energy rises in importance." [4]

This essay examines decision making in congressional committees, taking Mayhew's principle as its point of departure. Who makes the laws in congressional committees, and how do the patterns of legislative involvement affect the health of Congress as a representative assembly? [5]

## Committee Assignments and the Accommodation of Interests

The analysis of committee decision making in Congress properly begins with the processes by which members seek and are selected for committees. Choices that members make about such assignments at the beginning of a session directly affect the patterns of participation and representation in the ensuing day-to-day decisions of their chamber. This is true for at least two reasons, the first related to the formal procedures governing participation at this stage, the second related to the fact that, once assigned, a member's position provides informal opportunities and resources that subsidize his legislative involvement at the committee level.

Unlike practices in most Western parliaments, much of the important legislative action in Congress occurs in standing committees and subcommittees or, more generally, in the network of formal and informal interactions that committee members and staff control.[6] This is where the original legislative vehicle normally gets formulated, the central issues debated, and most of the substantive and technical amendments reviewed and adopted. Members of Congress are allowed to attend the meetings of committees to which they do not belong, but they enjoy no formal right to participate; their presence cannot be counted toward establishing a quorum; they have no voting power;

they cannot call up legislation, raise points of order, or offer amendments.

These constraints are considerably more important in the House than in the Senate because there is no guarantee that House members will have full-blown opportunities to participate when a bill moves from committee to the floor. Important floor action in the House usually is governed by the Rules Committee, which decides the amount of time that will be allocated for floor debate, the members who will control that time, and the kinds of amendments that can be offered. House consideration of the 1977 Inland Waterways Act illustrates the potential importance of such constraints.[7]

Introduced by Berkley Bedell, D-Iowa, the bill proposed a new tax on the water freight industry to finance some of the government's costs of building and maintaining the nation's locks, dams, and waterways. In Bedell's view, the water freight industry had too long enjoyed a free ride at taxpayers' expense, while other freight carriers paid for their rights of way and thus suffered a competitive disadvantage. Because this bill involved a tax, it came under the jurisdiction of the House Ways and Means, a committee to which Bedell did not belong. When finally reported out of Ways and Means, the bill imposed only a modest tax on the industry and did not tie the tax rate to the government's cost of building waterway projects—a provision Bedell felt was essential. He went before the Rules Committee, seeking authority to offer amendments to the bill on the House floor. Instead, the Committee acceded to the request of the Ways and Means chairman, Al Ullman, D-Ore., that only amendments that *lowered* the tax be permitted, not those like Bedell's that raised it. Neither in committee nor on the floor, then, was the author of the original legislation able to offer and debate his proposals.

In the Senate, floor consideration is far more open, rendering access to the committee of jurisdiction less important. In addition, the potential of every senator to delay floor action through holds, nongermane amendments, and filibusters makes it more likely that nonmembers' views will be anticipated at the committee stage. Even so, in both chambers committee members have distinct advantages. They gradually develop political and substantive expertise in their committee's policy domains; they are more likely to enjoy ongoing interactions with interested actors both on and off the committee; and they have greater access to committee and subcommittee staff. Taken together, these are significant advantages that go a long way toward explaining why committee members individually and committees collectively exert disproportionate influence over matters within their jurisdiction.

As we will explore, every member endures tremendous demands

on her time and attention, making it impossible to stay informed on all issues that are before Congress at any given moment. On many matters outside the jurisdiction of her committees, a member and her staff learn of legislative action from the same sources available to almost any outsider: CQ's *Congressional Monitor,* the *Congressional Record,* the *Washington Post.* The legislative process on a particular matter can be well advanced before a member learns of decisions already made, deals already cut, timetables already arranged. In the Inland Waterways case, for instance, Bedell learned of an important compromise between House Speaker Tip O'Neill, D-Mass., and Ullman only after the fact.[8] Similarly, one former House staffer, now a legislative assistant for a Senate Democrat, observed:

> In the Senate, you don't *have* to be on the right committee like we did in the House, but it helps. We've been wanting to do some things in the tax area. For instance, we've had all these farmers calling and writing, complaining about the diesel fuel tax. . . . I can't even get the Finance committee staff to return my calls.

To be fully effective in a particular policy area, therefore, most members require assignment to the committee of jurisdiction, close to the important legislative action and the community of relevant actors. For this reason, the business of seeking committee assignments involves strategic calculation and substantial effort. The process begins even before the formal start of a new Congress, as new members explore committee vacancies and angle for particular slots. At the same time, sitting members reassess their current positions and weigh the benefits of adding another assignment or transferring to a new one.

Within certain important limits, the assignment process is largely self-selective.[9] As Kenneth Shepsle has observed, committee assignments are to the member what stocks are to an investor; both wish to acquire assets that will maximize the value of their portfolios.[10] In the legislative context, however, value is not economic profit but the advancement of the member's political goals or interests. Each member who seeks a change calculates the value of particular assignments, discounts them according to the likelihood that they can be acquired, and presents a rank-order list to the party's committee on committees. After a sometimes protracted process of lobbying and bargaining, these committees allocate the available slots, sometimes renegotiating a committee's size to accommodate the interests of as many members as possible.

This abstract account renders the committee assignment process somewhat more systematic than it is. (When asked how he got a coveted seat on Ways and Means in only his second House term, Wyche

Fowler, D-Ga., replied, "It beats the hell out of me.") [11] But it does convey the important point that committee assignments in Congress are interest-driven. What sorts of interests matter? One of the most common is serving one's constituents, which in turn enhances the member's ability to get reelected. Some committees are better suited to promote this goal than others, however. In his well-known study of committees in the 1960s, Richard Fenno found that members of both chambers sought positions on the Interior and Post Office committees for "political help," to promote "district interests," or to obtain specific projects for their states. [12] More recent studies have emphasized the attractiveness of the committees dealing with agriculture, armed services, appropriations, and public works to members concerned with getting reelected. [13]

Like most of us, however, individual members are not single-minded seekers of any one particular goal. [14] In requesting their assignments, members hope to put themselves in position to pursue other interests as well. Fenno identifies two additional goals that affect assignment requests—making good public policy and acquiring influence within Congress—and suggests that "all congressmen probably hold all three goals" in different mixes. [15] Any member can pursue several purposes through one of two committee-centered strategies. One is to diversify his portfolio by seeking positions on more than one committee, each of which is relevant to different interests. Many members do so, especially in the Senate where each member invariably receives more than one major assignment. For instance, when Paul Tsongas, D-Mass., came to the Senate in 1977, he requested a seat on Energy and Natural Resources because of his state's concern over energy supplies, and on Foreign Relations because of a long-standing personal interest in Africa that dated from his service in the Peace Corps. [16] In 1987 freshman senator Tom Daschle, D-S.D., sought assignment to Agriculture, whose jurisdiction was crucial to the economy of his state, and to Finance. One of his aides explained the latter choice.

> When Daschle came to the Senate, it was the first time in his political career that he didn't have to worry about reelection two years down the road. . . . [He] could go after a committee that he didn't feel he had to be on for political reasons. Finance gave him the chance to get involved in all the big issues he's interested in. Trade, tax, health—it's all right there.

A second, and perhaps more common, strategy is to seek assignment to a committee, the jurisdiction of which is suited to the pursuit of several purposes. In fact, most of the major committees in both chambers fit this description to some degree. The Finance Committee places members close to some of the most important national issues and may enhance a member's reputation for power within the Senate, but it also provides opportunities to secure preferential tax and trade provisions for constituent groups. Health and consumer issues within the purview of House Energy and Commerce evoke members' deep-seated policy concerns, while fights over energy pricing, toxic waste cleanup, and Amtrak reauthorizations turn more on local and regional interests. Even the agriculture committees, perhaps the most constituency-oriented in Congress, have jurisdiction over certain nutrition and environmental issues that strike strong ideological chords. In short, the committee assignment process is best understood as a set of institutional arrangements that channel member interests into positions of legislative advantage. But these arrangements are loose ones at best, and any notion of interest must be broad enough to encompass not only members' political self-interest but also their personal policy concerns and ideological commitments. Judgments about the desirability of a committee involve "on-average, best-guess" evaluations of the relevance of one's several interests to the various issues that might come before the committee over the coming two years. As a result, day-to-day participation in postassignment decision making is highly selective.

## Activity and Abdication in Congressional Committees

In the Congresses of the 1940s and 1950s, participation in committee activity was far more structured than it is today. Both informal norms and institutional barriers dictated who would participate, more or less, on the various issues the assembly considered. Members of a particular committee, for instance, were expected to concentrate on the thankless and not-so-thankless matters assigned to them—to practice an ethic of hard work and specialization. Autocratic committee chairs controlled legislative activity through their substantial powers to set the legislative agenda, appoint subcommittee chairs, and make subcommittee assignments. In contrast, junior members were admonished to "be seen and not heard" in the presence of their more experienced senior colleagues.[17]

In the postreform Congress the limits to legislative involvement on any given issue lie less in the institution's norms or traditions than in the time and staff resources a member is able to commit. Such resources are decidedly scarce. "I feel like I'm spread thin all the time," one freshman House member noted. "There's never any time to read or think an issue through or anything like that." The pressures of the congressional workload extend to senior members as well. Elizabeth

Drew quotes one representative who summarized the almost universal frustrations of the job:

> There are just too many votes, too many issues, too many meetings, too many attention-demanding situations. We're going to committee meetings, subcommittee meetings, caucuses—a caucus of the class with which you were elected here, the rural caucus, the steel caucus, you name it—and we're seeing constituents and returning phone calls and trying to rush back and forth to the district, and then we're supposed to understand what we're voting on when we get to the House floor.[18]

Such observations have been systematically confirmed in a survey administered by the House Commission on Administrative Review. Analyzing data drawn from that survey, Thomas O'Donnell concluded that House members' "ability to concentrate time on any single activity is severely constrained by the abundance and complexity of the demands that confront them." [19]

Contemporary senators face greater demands.[20] Elected from larger and more heterogeneous areas, senators must represent a wider range of interests; they receive greater media and interest group attention; and, given the relative size of the two chambers, individual senators face both greater obligations and greater opportunities for legislative involvement. The latter is reflected most clearly in their committee assignments. In 1988 the average number of committee and subcommittee positions for representatives was 6.6; for senators it was 11.1.[21] Multiple assignments produce scheduling conflicts that are a major source of frustration—members' avarice to expand their assignment portfolios at the beginning of a Congress comes back to haunt them during the everyday work of committee decision making. As one Senate staffer noted:

> [Scheduling conflicts] happen all the time, and it's a major pain. He's almost always got more than one hearing going on at the same time. Or he'll need to be on the floor, and there'll be a committee markup. The staffer has to monitor the thing, leave the room, and get on the phone and track him down. [The senator] just has to make on-the-spot decisions about where to be and how much to do. It really gets crazy sometimes.

The problems of time management and scheduling at the committee level became so serious during the mid-1980s that the Senate, with self-conscious appreciation of the irony involved, formed a select committee to study them. Named for Republican Dan Quayle, the junior senator from Indiana who chaired it, the committee received a litany of complaints that senators "have workloads which the hours of the day make it impossible to faithfully execute," are "burdened by a mass of obligations on [their] limited time," face multiple "responsibilities [that] are often directly in conflict." [22] Testifying before that committee, Daniel Evans, R-Wash., summarized the prevailing view:

> [W]e would all agree that there is member inconsistency regarding participation, disappointment regarding performance due to conflicting committee assignments, frustration with committees scheduled at similar or the same times, ineffectiveness due to the oversized membership of some committees, and sometimes member disincentives to participate ... at the maximum level.[23]

A clear indication of such constraints is the truancy rates at committee and subcommittee markups, which are often the most important meetings in the legislative process. Table 8-1 shows the incidence of nonattendance for a sample of approximately sixty bills in three House committees, where attendance is defined liberally by the committee clerk to reflect even momentary appearances during markup. The figures shown in column one are striking. The average absenteeism in Education and Labor, for instance, was 30 percent. In Energy and Commerce, one of the most powerful committees in the House, with jurisdiction over some of the most significant legislation, one committee member in four failed to appear at any point during the typical markup. Nonattendance in committee, however, does not necessarily mean that a member does not vote, since most committees permit voting by proxy. But in practice, proxy voting tends to augment the power of the active, not preserve the authority of the absent. Members often duck into a markup for a brief moment, leaving their proxy behind them with little knowledge of the way in which it will be used. Column two of the table shows the considerable frequency with which members abdicate their voting rights during committee markups.

Table 8-1   Attendance and Voting in House Committees

| Committee | Percentage absent | Percentage voting by proxy or not voting |
|---|---|---|
| Education and Labor | 30 | 45 |
| Energy and Commerce | 24 | 34 |
| Agriculture | 21 | 45 |

SOURCE: Minutes and transcripts of committee markup sessions.

NOTE: Entries are averages across a saturation sample of bills marked up in each committee during one Congress: the 97th Congress for Agriculture and Education and Labor, the 98th Congress for Energy and Commerce.

Table 8-2   Participation in Congressional Committees

| Policy area/bill | Percentage of committee members active during prefloor consideration | |
|---|---|---|
| | House | Senate |
| *Human Resources* | | |
| Job Training Partnership Act of 1982 | 59 | 75 |
| Older Americans Act Amendments of 1981 | 31 | 31 |
| Head Start Reauthorization of 1981 | 28 | 19 |
| *Commerce* | | |
| Universal Telephone Service | | |
|   Preservation Act of 1984 | 64 | 41 |
| 1984 Amtrak/Railroad Amendments | 24 | 18 |
| 1983 Textile Labeling Act | 21 | 12 |
| *Agriculture* | | |
| Farm Credit Act Amendments of 1987 | 65 | 68 |
| Wheat, Soybeans, and Feed Grains, | | |
|   1981 Farm Bill | 56 | 71 |
| Conservation Title, 1985 Farm Bill | 44 | 33 |
| Cotton Title, 1981 Farm Bill | 28 | 29 |

SOURCE: Staff interviews, secondary accounts, and committee records of the House committees on Education and Labor, Energy and Commerce, and Agriculture; the Senate committees on Labor and Human Resources; Commerce, Science, and Transportation; and Agriculture, Nutrition, and Forestry.

NOTE: Entries are the percentages of committee members who (1) offered at least one amendment during committee or subcommittee markup; (2) were major participants in markup debate; or (3) were cited in staff interviews, secondary accounts, or official records as having played a significant role behind the scenes.

Patterns of truancy in Senate committees are similar. Several senators who testified before the Quayle Committee noted the frequency with which committee or subcommittee chairs have trouble getting the 50 percent of the membership necessary for a quorum. At the commencement of its hearings, in fact, Chairman Quayle noted that "of the 12 members that are on this Select Committee, 9 of us have conflicts this morning with other committees and subcommittees in where we are supposed to be." An examination of the official record reveals that only three members of the Select Committee showed up for both days of its hearings, while five of the twelve did not appear even momentarily at either meeting.

A more general picture of committee participation is provided by Table 8-2. The statistics summarize the number of members actively involved in ten bills that went through House and Senate committees and reveal that, bill by bill, there is considerable variation. We will explore some of the factors that affect that variation in the next section. For now, two points are worth emphasizing. First, only in certain cases do we find a substantial proportion of a committee seriously involved in its deliberations. Based on staff interviews in the early 1960s, Charles Clapp estimated that "one-third to one-half of a committee's membership constitute the hard core that can be depended on in nearly every activity." [24] In the 1980s such estimates are clearly generous. For only half of the bills in Table 8-2 could even a third of the House or Senate committee be counted as full-fledged players in the decision-making process. Second, Table 8-2 confirms that the limits on participation are serious in both the Senate and the House. In almost every case, the proportion of Senate committee members participating is close to that of the House, suggesting that the greater time constraints and scheduling conflicts faced by the contemporary senator are at least partially offset by the greater staff support and range of legislative opportunities the position confers.

In sum, it is an organizational fact of life that individual members of Congress act in some areas, abdicate in others. They cannot do everything; they must choose. In making these choices at the committee level, members resolve themselves into the working subsets, issue by issue, that normally drive the legislative action. As we will explore in the final section, these patterns have important implications for the nature and health of representation in a decentralized Congress.

## Who Makes the Laws?
## Decision Making in Committee

Who makes the laws that emerge from the committee rooms of Congress? A general answer to this question is not easy to formulate. Even on a single committee or subcommittee, the particular individuals who make up the active subset change from one bill to the next. Members seldom have systematic strategies for allocating their time and staff among the various issues that come before their panels. Attempting to explain why her boss got so involved in one bill before the House subcommittee on Select Education, one staffer remarked: "One of [subcommittee chairman Austin] Murphy's staffers told me about the bill early on, and the congressman expressed an interest. So we just jumped in." Another staffer noted:

> I don't know that we really [budget our time]. . . . We just sort of react to things as they come up. ____ will say, "This is something we need to go after," and it's pointless to tell him that I've got sixteen other things going on. Some of them just fall by the wayside.

Senate staffers offer similar accounts. Asked how her boss sets his legislative priorities, an aide to one junior senator remarked:

> To ____, everything is a priority, which means that nothing is a priority. Last year he wrote a famous memo about what his priorities were going to be, where he wanted the staff to concentrate, and it basically included everything under the sun. Then he comes into the staff meetings and complains that he's not getting enough time to read and prepare.... Decisions about how we spend our time get made by default; it's not because we've got any kind of grand plan.

In short, member and staff are constantly pulled between the lure of legislative opportunities and the limits on what they can do. In resolving this strain, moreover, they seldom have sufficient time, information, or foresight to consider the range of all viable activities, weigh their relative costs and benefits, and rank them. Nonetheless, rough calculations do emerge on an issue-by-issue basis as the office makes sometimes quick decisions about whether a particular issue is, as one staffer put it, "worth our time."

## Participation and Interest

Several factors influence those determinations. Perhaps the most important is some general perception that an issue affects the member's interests; that is, the same concerns that preoccupy the member in her committee assignment requests carry over to her day-to-day decisions about committee involvement. The calculation of interest at this stage is simply more concrete and specific and hence has a more direct effect on committee outcomes. Serving one's constituents is a common theme in these calculations, even on committees that are not normally thought to be constituency-oriented. Historically, Senate Labor and Human Resources and its House counterpart, Education and Labor, have been among the most ideologically charged committees in Congress. Referring to his senator's activity on the Labor Committee, one staffer noted:

> There are certainly other committees that are better as far as our state is concerned. Appropriations would be better. But, then again, the education issues play well back home.... ____ was active in getting the elementary and secondary aid bill through last year, and it got us great press. He's probably given a dozen speeches on it back in the state.

Similarly, the legislative assistant to a senior member of House Education and Labor explained her boss's role in reauthorizing the Older Americans Act.

> [The] Older Americans [Act] is so important to the district for
> demographic reasons. The district is the tenth most senior district in
> the country, the other nine being in Florida. It's a very stable
> community of immigrants, and [the Older Americans] programs
> affect them directly.

More generally, however, members and their staffs cite a variety of
interests that affect their participation in committee work. As in the
committee assignment process, the member's personal policy views or
chamber reputation are important determinants. Although he may later
put it to good political use, Democrat John Dingell's House Commerce
Committee investigation of the Environmental Protection Agency
cannot be attributed wholly to its direct electoral benefits; Dingell is
virtually unbeatable in southeastern Michigan, giving him substantial
latitude to pursue his own agenda on Capitol Hill.[25] On Senate
Foreign Relations, Republican Jesse Helms' vigorous opposition to
economic sanctions against South Africa derived from his deep-seated
conservatism, not the issue's salience among his rural North Carolina
constituency. In pushing the 1986 Tax Reform Act through House
Ways and Means, Dan Rostenkowski, D-Ill., was concerned both with
helping the average taxpayer and enhancing his reputation as an
effective committee chairman.[26] Members seldom take the lead on
issues that will harm them politically, but concern with reelection is
only one of several interests that affect their committee participation.
One senior Republican member explained his participation on the
House Education and Labor Committee as follows:

> First, you look at how it affects your district. What legislation would
> be beneficial to your constituents. Second, there's personal interests.
> I'm a former school superintendent, so I'm going to be involved in
> education matters. Even within education, I have some real pets. If
> you're talking about the training of administrators, that's something
> I'd be interested in. If you're talking about recruiting teachers, that's
> something I'd be interested in. If you're talking about school lunch
> or child nutrition, the same. Because that's something I feel strongly
> about.

In general, then, legislation that deals with broad issues or affects
a wide range of states and districts is more likely to evoke the various
interests of a wide range of members. Another look at the bills listed in
Table 8-2 illustrates this point. The Job Training Partnership Act of
1982 was probably the most significant human resources initiative
during Ronald Reagan's first term. The act addressed major issues of
national employment policy, affecting displaced workers in almost
every state and district during a period of burgeoning unemployment.

Similarly, the Farm Credit Act of 1987 followed a deep depression in the agricultural economy, during which land values plummeted and thousands of farmers nationwide were pushed into bankruptcy. For both of these bills, committee participation was broad, with more than half of the committee members in both House and Senate actively involved in the decision-making process. In contrast, several of the other bills listed in Table 8-2 involved a much narrower range of interests and generated much less participation. The federal Head Start program was originally designed to address basic issues of equal education opportunity, but the 1981 Head Start bill was a simple reauthorization of existing law, with only minor policy changes. For the most part, the 1983 Textile Labeling Act involved a single regulatory issue and a single, regionally circumscribed industry; and the cotton title of the 1981 farm bill affected farmers in only a handful of states.

## Legislative Resources

Participation in committees tends to be interest-driven, but not all members are equally able to pursue their interests on more than a few bills with any efficacy. In both chambers, formal leaders enjoy a number of legislative advantages; committee and subcommittee chairs and, to a lesser degree, ranking minority members enjoy certain procedural prerogatives not available to the average backbencher.[27] They have considerable control over the committee's agenda, the scheduling of meetings, and the progress of legislation. If committee action is likely to conflict with other business the leader finds important or otherwise violates some strategic purpose, he is better able to adapt the nature and timing of committee events to suit his objectives.

Chairman Dingell of the House Energy and Commerce Committee provides an ongoing case study in how such prerogatives can be exploited to the leader's advantage. Consider, for instance, the 1984 Natural Gas Policy Act, a bill involving the deregulation of natural gas prices and hence the transfer of billions of dollars from one region to another and from consumers to natural gas corporations.[28] For almost a year during the 98th Congress, Dingell avoided bringing the bill to committee markup, fearing that proponents of deregulation had the votes to push through amendments that benefited the gas industry and hurt energy-consuming states like Dingell's Michigan. When Dingell finally convened a full committee markup, one member walked over to him and boasted, "John, we've got the votes," to which Dingell replied, "Yeah, but I've got the gavel." Dingell soon demonstrated the difference. When markup began, he first allowed consideration on two amendments that would reveal the strength of his coalition. When he lost both test votes, Dingell simply adjourned the markup, delaying consideration indefinitely.[29] He did not bring the bill up again until the following year, after he had managed to negotiate a substitute less favorable to industry. The committee then reported the substitute package over the vigorous objections of members from gas-producing states.

Beyond their procedural prerogatives, committee leaders of both parties have other resources that defray the costs of legislative involvement. Given their relative seniority and the repetitious nature of most committees' agendas, leaders are more likely to have greater experience in the politics and substance of legislation that comes before their panel. Many have dealt with the same programs, heard the same arguments, and even questioned the same witnesses in previous sessions. If leaders start with better backgrounds and more expertise, they also possess greater resources to purchase the marginal time and effort needed to research an issue, gather political intelligence, and develop legislative strategy.[30] Most important is their greater access to and control over professional staff. In both chambers, but especially in the Senate, the amount of staff time a member can allocate to an issue is a precondition for effective legislative involvement. One aide explained why his senator did so little to pursue his interests in the federal nutrition area during the 100th Congress.

> Well, it's not so much the political risks as it is the resources that we have to work with. Kennedy's been working on this for years. So has Panetta—his staffer is really sharp, really knowledgeable on the details. For my boss to take the lead on, say, something comprehensive in the hunger/nutrition area would take me years, given how little our office has to work with. . . . Notwithstanding the criticism of Hill resources, there is not a lot of staff around here.[31]

Finally, members with a formal institutional position occupy a central place in an information network that extends beyond the confines of the committee, but plays a crucial role in the legislative process. Given their control over the committee's agenda, committee leaders and their staffs become the focal points for outsiders wishing to press their ideas, analysis, and demands upon the government. A case in point is the Federal Insecticide, Fungicide, and Rodenticide Act (FIFRA), a bill to regulate the agricultural use of potentially harmful chemicals. While not likely to enthrall the average voter, FIFRA has far-reaching implications for the environmental quality of lakes, rivers, and groundwater; for farmers and fruitgrowers who use chemicals in raising their crops; for agricultural workers whose health might be affected by exposure to such products; and for private companies that manufacture and market them. The act has been up for reconsideration in every Congress since 1980, generating countless studies and endless controversies among the various interest groups and policy specialists. An aide to House subcommittee chairman George Brown, D-Calif., described the drafting of the bill in 1982:

> We spent weeks poring over all these reports and recommendations, and we finally put together a draft. But the environmentalists didn't like it, and there were fractures on the chemical industry's side—one side wanted some proposals relating to the release of health and safety data and the pesticide registration process. . . . So Brown said "You guys sit down with my staff and go through this thing, point by point, and figure out where you want to be." That was the beginning of four months of protracted negotiations with EPA, the industry, the environmentalists—sitting down, going back and forth, drafts and redrafts. Finally we got a negotiated settlement between the industry and the environmental groups and only then moved a bill, that comprehensive compromise, up to subcommittee markup.

If, as a group, formal leaders tend to be more active in their committee and the policy community that surrounds it, there are differences between the Senate and the House regarding the relative roles played by full and subcommittee leaders. Reforms passed in the early 1970s gave House subcommittee leaders greater advantages than their counterparts in the Senate. Under the rubric of the Subcommittee Bill of Rights, the House Democratic Caucus limited the ability of full committee chairs to determine the number, composition, and chairs of the subcommittees; constrained the authority of the committee chair to hold legislation at full committee; and guaranteed each subcommittee chair a staff and budget.[32]

In the Senate the changes have been more modest. Most legislative markups are held at full committee, and Senate committee leaders retain greater control over the hiring, firing, and allocation of professional staff.[33] Even so, subcommittee leaders and members exert disproportionate influence in the decision-making process of most Senate committees. In practice, subcommittee leaders usually have some additional staff assistance. Moreover, subcommittee leaders and members tend to be more interested in matters that come before their panels. We have already seen how the assignment process places members on committees whose jurisdiction interests them. The subcommittee assignment process permits a more refined matching of specific interests to legislative jurisdiction, and the considerable flexibility in setting subcommittee sizes permits the committee to accommodate most members' requests. Although this matching process is far more precise in the House, subcommittee members in both chambers are more willing than their nonmember colleagues to use their personal and staff time and forego opportunities for legislative influence elsewhere. One staffer described the involvement of Bill Bradley, D-N.J., on Senate Finance:

> Bradley's got certain interests. He's really got burning interests in trade, third world debt, and tax. He's on the trade subcommittee, he chairs the one on international debt, and all the tax stuff gets handled at full committee. He just doesn't get that involved in the rest of it. He doesn't have the time ... to go into other things.

Another staffer commented on the roles played by the chair and ranking minority member of the Senate Subcommittee on Health.

> There are really only a couple of senators who are really interested in Medicare—interested enough to understand it—and that's Mitchell and Durenberger. The others are intimidated and bored by it—intimidated because the discussion quickly progresses beyond their level of comprehension. It's such a technical program. I remember one day I was sitting alone in the ante room while Medicare hearings were going on. Senator ____ walks out and says to me, "You know, my eyes just glaze over when they start talking Medicare this and Medicare that, Part A this and Part B that. I don't understand any of it." Not ten minutes later, another senator walked out and said to me—he was clearly being sarcastic—"That Medicare is really interesting stuff, isn't it?" It's not that senators don't care—at one level they have to care. But they're really not interested. Mitchell and Durenberger, maybe Bentsen, are the only ones who have any real influence.[34]

Although ten bills from three committees is too small a sample from which to draw firm conclusions, the data in Table 8-3 bear out several of the general tendencies described here. The first two rows show that formal leaders were active in more than three-fourths of the observations. In the House, in fact, the subcommittee chair and ranking minority member were major players in every case, even though the bills spanned three committee and eight subcommittee jurisdictions. House subcommittee members, in turn, were more than twice as likely to participate as their full committee colleagues, reinforcing the general view that House decision making is highly decentralized. When one combines both the leader and rank-and-file categories, 72 percent of the reporting subcommittee members were active compared to only 29 percent of the nonmembers. In the House, at least, the combination of institutional resources and member interests is markedly apparent in the behavioral patterns of committee decision making.

Table 8-3 also illustrates important House-Senate differences in committee decision making. Specifically, the table confirms that sub-

Table 8-3   Institutional Position and Participation in Committee
Decisions: A House-Senate Comparison

| Institutional position | Percentage of members active during markup | |
|---|---|---|
| | House | Senate |
| *Formal leaders* | | |
| subcommittee | 100 | 75 |
| full committee | 80 | 70 |
| *Committee rank and file* | | |
| subcommittee members | 65 | 49 |
| subcommittee nonmembers | 24 | 24 |
| *All* | | |
| subcommittee members | 72 | 58 |
| subcommittee nonmembers | 29 | 32 |

SOURCE: Staff interviews and committee records for the ten bills listed in Table 8-2.

NOTE: Entries are the percentages of members in the row category who (1) offered at least one amendment during committee or subcommittee markup; (2) were major participants in markup debate; or (3) were cited in staff interviews, secondary accounts, or official records as having played a significant role behind the scenes.

committees are more important in the House than in the Senate. For the ten bills studied, 100 percent of the House subcommittee leaders counted as principal actors, compared to 75 percent in the Senate. Likewise, 65 percent of the House subcommittee rank and file were active, compared to 49 percent in the Senate. In general, the behavioral differences between full and subcommittee members were smaller in the Senate. At the same time, however, Table 8-3 clearly shows that it would be incorrect to impute insignificance to Senate subcommittees; the House-Senate differences regarding subcommittees are matters of degree, not of kind. Although most Senate markups take place at the full committee level, subcommittee members are much more likely to participate there than are nonmembers; and a subcommittee leader is more likely to participate than a full committee leader.

Table 8-4 provides additional evidence for each of the foregoing propositions and better illustrates the effect of members' interests and resources on their legislative influence. The table reports the extent to which members with and without institutional positions are successful in amending legislation during either full or subcommittee markup. In general, the patterns are strikingly similar to those of Table 8-3. Subcommittee leaders and members amend well beyond what their proportion of the total committee membership would suggest. House subcommittee members are normally outnumbered by nonmembers two

Table 8-4   Institutional Position and Amending in Committee
Markups: A House-Senate Comparison

| | Percentage of successful amendments | |
|---|---|---|
| *Institutional position* | House | Senate |
| *Formal leaders* | | |
| subcommittee | 39 | 31 |
| full committee | 5 | 15 |
| *Committee rank and file* | | |
| subcommittee members | 34 | 34 |
| subcommittee nonmembers | 23 | 20 |
| *All* | | |
| subcommittee members | 72 | 65 |
| subcommittee nonmembers | 28 | 35 |

SOURCE: Committee records for the ten bills listed in Table 8-2.

NOTE: Entries are the percentages of all successful, substantive amendments offered during committee or subcommittee markup in the respective chambers for which members of the row category were responsible. Not included are amendments affected by subsequent substitutes or by successful second-degree amendments that the author of the first-degree amendment formally opposed.

to one, but they are responsible for 72 percent of all successful amendments. This pattern holds, but to a lesser degree, in Senate committee decisions. For the committees studied here, subcommittee sizes averaged less than 40 percent of the committee membership, but subcommittee members were responsible for 65 percent of all successful amendments during markup action.

Table 8-4 likewise confirms the influential roles played by formal leaders in House and Senate committees. Again, the most important difference is between what subcommittee and full committee leaders do. I have already noted the crucial role played by subcommittee leaders in drafting legislation in the House. Table 8-4 shows that this domination of committee law making continues into the markup stage. By themselves, the subcommittee chair and ranking minority member of the subcommittee with jurisdiction over a bill are responsible for almost 40 percent of all subsequent amendments to it; in contrast, full committee chairs account for only 5 percent. In the Senate the full and subcommittee leaders are more nearly equal in amending legislation that reaches the markup stage, but the number of amendments by the latter is still greater than the former by a ratio of two to one.

In both chambers, the advantages of institutional resources and member interest are clearly important in determining who makes the laws at the committee stage, but they cannot by themselves form the basis for a full-blown theory of legislative influence. Their effects are contingent on political factors, the most important of which are party, ideology, and the relative position of the administration. Other things being equal, the leader or backbencher who enjoys majority status will more easily shape committee legislation. The chairs, far more than the ranking minority members, dominate the drafting of the original legislation, and majority member preferences are more likely to be accommodated in the drafting process. But even at the markup stage, the majority is more likely to make substantive changes. Of the several hundred successful amendments summarized in Table 8-4, approximately 68 percent in the House and 56 percent in the Senate were offered by majority party members. Similarly, the closeness of one's policy views to the committee majority and to the current administration tend to affect the degree to which interest and institutional position translate into legislative effect.[35]

## Representation in a Decentralized Congress

Institutional critics have long noted how the best democratic elections are undone in a legislative assembly that is itself oligarchic. Challenges to the uneven distribution of power within Congress have occurred repeatedly in this century and have brought about changes in the basic nature of the institution. In 1910 the House of Representatives revolted against the czar-like rule of Speaker Joseph Cannon. During the 1950s and 1960s liberal activists criticized the committee system, claiming that the power of southern conservative committee chairs prevented chamber majorities from working their will on major civil rights legislation. And the reforms of the mid-1970s significantly increased the number and autonomy of congressional subcommittees and diminished the automatic claim of senior members to positions of formal leadership.

More recently, the trend has been in a different direction. A number of changes have given the majority party leadership greater political leverage, especially in the House; and reform of the congressional budget process has concentrated control of each chamber's priorities in the budget committees and a few other principal budget actors. Still, neither chamber is organized with any sort of rigid authority structure; indeed, many critics suggest that the institution approximates anarchy more than oligarchy. Party discipline, institutional sanctions, and informal norms sometimes matter, sometimes not. They certainly impose far fewer constraints on members' day-to-day legislative behavior than in any previous era. This is not to say that decision making in Congress is egalitarian, however. As we have seen, legislative authority over a particular issue often is exercised by a small group of legislative players, and that group tends to be dominated by members with some formal institutional position. But as we have also seen, the size and composition of this group changes with the issue, and the distribution of influence is determined less by a formal bestowal of authority than by the distribution of members' interests and their ability to pay the time and information costs associated with effective involvement in the issue at hand.

The patterns of participation and influence described in this essay, therefore, have important implications for our evaluation of Congress. The focus of this final section is how these patterns affect Congress's representative character. The implications are not obvious; they become more clear when we first consider the traditional way the concept of representation has been used and the principal way it has been studied.

Perhaps the most influential work on representation in Congress is an essay by Warren Miller and Donald Stokes entitled "Constituency Influence In Congress." [36] The principal purpose of their study was to use available social science data to conduct a broad-based, empirical analysis of representation. Specifically, Miller and Stokes defined representation as the statistical relationship between members' roll call voting patterns and the general policy preferences of their constituents, a definition that squares well with ordinary language usage. Members who consistently vote in a way that contradicts district opinion, for instance, are normally said to be "unresponsive," "out of touch," or "unrepresentative" of their districts. Periodic elections ensure that such relationships remain reasonably strong, that the westerner who votes against water projects and the Texan who supports domestic oil taxes are replaced by individuals more likely to represent their constituents.[37]

Implied in the Miller-Stokes formulation, therefore, is a two-pronged premise: that representation is properly thought of as a relationship between member and constituency, and that the relationship is one in which the former purposively reflects the views of the latter. To use language loosely borrowed from Edmund Burke, the member is to act as a "delegate" of the electorate. This view has received considerable play in the empirical research on representation.[38] Less common are studies that consider how these 535 relationships add up to a full-blown assessment of Congress as a representative institution.[39] There are several organizational features of Congress that complicate this arithmetic. Our concern here is with its committee system or, more generally, the decentralized way in which Congress goes about making policy.

To be sure, members of Congress can and often do purposively reflect their constituents' views at the committee and subcommittee level. Mayhew goes so far as to suggest that, in the extreme, committees can be viewed as platforms contrived for the purpose of expressing and advancing district interests.[40] While I have suggested here that members have a diverse range of motivations, we have seen that constituency service is especially important. In selecting their committee and subcommittee assignments and in deciding how to allocate their time and energy in postassignment decision making, members regularly pursue opportunities to address district or state concerns. The point that needs to be emphasized, however, is that constituency-oriented behavior at the committee level tends to *undermine* representation in the legislative system, not promote it. Shepsle and other students of committee assignments have made this point, noting that committees are deep in "interesteds" and "unrepresentative of the regional, ideological, and seniority groupings" in the parent chamber.[41] The patterns of selective participation at the committee level, in turn, reinforce such biases. For any given issue, the membership of a committee is typically more diverse than the subset of self-selected members who dominate committee deliberations.

The paradox at work here is probably best illustrated through reference to a particular case. Consider, for instance, the 1987 Farm Credit Act, a sweeping reform of federal programs dealing with farm debt and the agricultural banking system. As it emerged from a protracted House-Senate conference, the farm credit bill provided up to $4 billion in financial assistance to keep the failing Farm Credit System afloat; it created a secondary market through which rural banks and system institutions could sell their farm real estate loans; and it required system institutions and the Farmers Home Administration to forgive portions of a farmer's debt in cases where the institution was unlikely to do better through foreclosure. The act's supporters promoted it as a major set of reforms, good for the depressed agricultural economy and good for the nation. Its detractors considered it a "bailout," especially objectionable when the size of the federal budget for agriculture had more than doubled in the previous five years and efforts at federal deficit reduction floundered.

In its particulars, the legislation was unusually complex, reflecting the nature of the institutions it was intended to reform. "The Farm Credit System is the most complicated and largest financial institution that has ever been bailed out in this country," one policy analyst observed.[42] The person who staffed the issue for David Boren, D-Okla., chair of the Senate subcommittee with jurisdiction, likewise noted: "It's probably the most complex issue we've dealt with at the Agriculture Committee, the most frustrating issue. In general, we've got a tremendous lack of understanding on the part of everybody." [43] As a result, legislative involvement in this area was labor-intensive, requiring a significant commitment of a member's personal and staff time. As we have seen, however, some members have greater incentives than others to make such commitments. In this case, the decision-making process was dominated by those who stood to gain politically by getting involved, farm state members whose constituencies were most affected by the agricultural debt crisis.

Table 8-5 illustrates this pattern, using data that reflect the levels of agricultural debt in states represented by various categories of members. The first two rows reveal the differences between states represented by agriculture committee members and nonmembers. As we noted, the self-selective nature of the assignment process produces panels of members that are unrepresentative of their parent chambers in ways that directly pertain to the committee's policy domain. On average, committee members in both the House and Senate represented states whose farm debt/asset ratios were half again as large as states represented by members not serving on the committees. Rows three and four show how this bias of interests is reinforced during committee decision making. The major players in both chambers tended to come from the states hardest hit by the failing farm economy: Iowa, Kansas, Minnesota, Nebraska, Oklahoma, and South Dakota. Finally, rows five and six reveal that, although the farm credit act received serious consideration on the floor of both chambers, the participants at that stage were biased toward farm state interests as well.

One can find cases of malrepresentation in Congress that are both more and less dramatic than the Farm Credit Act. In some respects, the interests of citizens not directly represented by the rural state activists were taken into account. The cost of the bail out to taxpayers was a visible concern throughout the process, leading committee activists in both chambers to anticipate how the legislative package would be received on the floor. Specifically referring to the cost of the House committee's package, ranking minority member Edward Madigan, R-Ill., commented: "I don't want to go to the floor with something that's going to be held up to ridicule." [44] In the Senate, likewise, the two leaders of the Budget Committee attached an amendment on the Senate floor that required the Farm Credit System to pay back its subsidies (without, however, any time limit). But generally, the political benefits and informational costs of active involvement inclined most nonfarm state representatives to remain passive. In the end, the major budget concerns were sidestepped through what was widely perceived as a budgetary sleight of hand. [45] And there was no serious attention given to the option of financing the bailout through gradual cuts in commodity price

Table 8-5    Representation in a Decentralized Congress: The Case of the 1987 Farm Credit Act

| States/districts represented by: | Agricultural debt/asset ratio (percent) | |
|---|---|---|
| | House | Senate |
| Committee nonmembers | 17.8 | 18.1 |
| Committee members | 25.1 | 27.1 |
| Committee nonactivists | 24.5 | 24.7 |
| Committee activists | 27.1 | 28.8 |
| Floor activists | | |
|   Committee nonmembers | 23.0 | 21.7 |
|   Committee members | 26.3 | 25.1 |

SOURCE: Calculated from *Economic Indicators of the Farm Sector: State Financial Summary, 1986,* United States Department of Agriculture.
NOTE: Entries are the median agricultural debt/asset ratios for states represented by members of the row category.

supports. "I advanced the idea to one of the Ag staffers early on," one Budget Committee economist commented, "and he looked at me first with a look of disbelief, then with the recognition that I was being mischievous. Which I was. It just wasn't something anybody there wanted to consider."

To be sure, the politics of representation are far more complex than a single case can convey, and this one is not intended to justify a general indictment of Congress. Democratic theorists have long debated whether the *intensity* as well as the direction of citizen preferences should matter in deliberations of a representative assembly; selective participation is one way in which intensities are registered, albeit in exaggerated form. In any case, the farm credit example suggests that the extent to which Congress meets some standard of representative government depends in part on the issue being considered. Not all issues that come before congressional committees are driven by state and district concerns. Not all members are equally attentive to such concerns when they arise. The principal actors in Senate Agriculture's consideration of the 1988 Emergency Hunger Relief Act represented the states of Iowa, Kansas, Minnesota, and Vermont—not states that benefit most from the food stamp program or other federal feeding efforts. The conservation title of the 1985 farm bill included provisions that imposed harsh penalties on farmers who drained waterfowl habitat for crop production or tilled highly erodible soil. Any close observer of Congress can cite countless other examples in which the policy views and ideological commitments of the principal legislative actors were crucial to the shape of the ultimate legislation, and it is a rare case where these factors are altogether absent.

Moreover, even where state and district concerns matter, many of the most important legislative battles in Congress involve broad issues with nationwide salience. Debates over Social Security policy, tax reform, and international trade fall into this category. On such issues, we normally find that participation is far less selective and that a wide range of members' ideas and interests enter the decision-making calculus. But the Farm Credit case does reveal the relatively common conditions under which electorally minded behavior undermines the representative character of the institution. Individual members, in allocating their legislative time and resources to constituency concerns, are in certain respects doing what we think representatives ought to do, what the electoral sanction—either through intimidation or natural selection—ensures that they do. But at the same time, such behavior generates cause for serious concern among critics of American democratic institutions. A division of legislative labor that tends to exclude a wide range of views and values from the deliberative process, one in which large numbers of legislators effectively abdicate their legislative responsibilities to more directly affected colleagues, should be troublesome to those of us who value representative government.

## Notes

All unattributed quotes come from interviews conducted by the author with members of Congress or congressional staff.

1. Jack L. Walker, "The Origins and Maintenance of Interest Groups in America," *American Political Science Review* 77 (June 1983): 390-406.
2. Roger Davidson, "Subcommittee Government: New Channels for Policymaking," in *The New Congress,* ed. Thomas E. Mann and Norman J. Ornstein (Washington, D.C.: American Enterprise Institute, 1981).
3. See especially Davidson, "Subcommittee Government."
4. David Mayhew, *Congress: The Electoral Connection* (New Haven, Conn.: Yale University Press, 1974), 95. Mayhew here is echoing the more general observation made in Bauer, Pool, and Dexter's well-known study of policy making on foreign trade. Bauer et al. note that the member's principal problem is "not how to vote but what to do with his time, how to allocate his resources, and where to put his energy." Raymond A. Bauer, Ithiel De Sola Pool, Lewis A. Dexter, *American Business and Public Policy* (New York: Atherton Press, 1963), 405.

5. For more extensive discussions of these questions, see David E. Price, *Who Makes the Laws? Creativity and Power in Senate Committees* (Cambridge, Mass.: Schenkman, 1972); Richard L. Hall, "Participation and Purpose in Committee Decision Making," *American Political Science Review* 81 (March 1987): 105-107. For more general treatments on committee decision making, see Steven S. Smith and Christopher Deering, *Committees in Congress* (Washington, D.C.: CQ Press, 1984); Richard F. Fenno, *Congressmen in Committees* (Boston: Little, Brown, 1973).

6. In the British House of Commons, for instance, committees act on legislation only after it has been introduced by the executive minister and approved in general form by the Commons as a whole. Even so, the importance of congressional committees can be overstated and often is. Committees are part of what is normally a sequential legislative process, in which actors at other stages have formal authority to preempt or review what particular committees have done. Woodrow Wilson's claim that Congress is a body that regularly meets to ratify the work of its committees is simply not true in the 1980s, if it were true in the 1880s when he was writing. In fact, it is increasingly common for committee bills to be amended on the chamber floor. Likewise, the congressional budget process has increased the importance of party leaders and the budget committees at the expense of the several authorizing committees. Neither of these developments undermines the general point that committee action is central to congressional decision making, however.

7. For an in-depth account of this bill's legislative history, see T. R. Reid's excellent case study, *Congressional Odyssey: The Saga of a Senate Bill* (New York: Freeman, 1980).

8. Reid, *Congressional Odyssey*, 77-79.

9. See Kenneth Shepsle, *The Giant Jigsaw Process: Democratic Committee Assignments in the Modern House* (Chicago: University of Chicago Press, 1978); David Rohde and Kenneth Shepsle, "Democratic Committee Assignments in the House of Representatives: Strategic Aspects of a Social Choice Process," *American Political Science Review* 67 (September 1973): 889-905; Irwin Gertzog, "The Routinization of Committee Assignments in the U.S. House of Representatives," *American Journal of Political Science* (November 1976): 693-713; Fenno, *Congressmen in Committees*, chap. 1.

10. Shepsle, *Giant Jigsaw*, chaps. 3-5.

11. Richard E. Cohen, "The Mysterious Ways Congress Makes Committee Assignments," *National Journal*, Feb. 3, 1979, 183.

12. Fenno, *Congressmen in Committees*, 5-8, 139-140.

13. See especially Smith and Deering, *Committees in Congress*, 105-110.

14. Although he is often cited as having done so, Mayhew makes no such empirical claim. See *Congress: The Electoral Connection*, especially 13-17.

15. Fenno, *Congressmen in Committees*, 1.

16. Cohen, "Mysterious Ways," 184.

17. Donald Matthews, *U.S. Senators and Their World* (Chapel Hill: Univer-

sity of North Carolina Press, 1960), 93-94; see also Charles L. Clapp, *The Congressman: His Work as He Sees It* (Garden City, N.Y.: Anchor, 1964).

18. Quoted by Thomas O'Donnell, "Managing Legislative Time," in *The House at Work*, ed. Joseph Cooper and G. Calvin Mackenzie (Austin: University of Texas Press, 1981), 128.
19. O'Donnell, "Managing Legislative Time," 138.
20. See C. Lawrence Evans, "Influence in Congressional Committees," in *Congressional Politics*, ed. Christopher Deering (Chicago: Dorsey, 1989), 155-175; Barbara Sinclair, *The Transformation of the U.S. Senate* (Baltimore: Johns Hopkins University Press, forthcoming); Barbara Sinclair, "Senate Norms, Senate Styles, and Senate Influence" (Paper prepared for delivery at the annual meeting of the American Political Science Association, Washington, D.C., 1986).
21. Norman J. Ornstein, Thomas E. Mann, and Michael J. Malbin, *Vital Statistics on Congress, 1987-1988* (Washington, D.C.: Congressional Quarterly, 1987), 130.
22. Hearing of the Temporary Select Committee to Study the Senate Committee System, 98th Cong., 2d sess., July 31 and March 4, 1984, Parts 1 and 2 (Washington, D.C.: U.S. Government Printing Office).
23. *Hearing of the Temporary Select Committee*, Part 1, 41. In late 1987 the Senate was again holding hearings on many of the topics taken up before the Quayle Committee. Freshman Democrats organized in 1988 to press the Senate leadership for reforms that would address the time constraints, scheduling conflicts, and general quality of life within the institution. Meanwhile, Senator Daniel Evans announced that he would retire at the end of the 1988 session, after only one term in office. See Martin Frazier, "Why Some Senators Feel Disenchanted, Burned Out," *Roll Call*, Dec. 20, 1987, 1, 19; Janet Hook, "Senators Look for Ways to Increase Efficiency," *Congressional Quarterly Weekly Report*, Dec. 5, 1987, 3001-3002.
24. Clapp, *The Congressman.*
25. Rochelle L. Stanfield, "Plotting Every Move," *National Journal*, March 26, 1988, 792-797.
26. Randall Strahan, "Committee Politics and Tax Reform" (Paper prepared for delivery at the annual meeting of the American Political Science Association, September 1987); Jeffrey H. Birnbaum and Alan S. Murray, *Showdown at Gucci Gulch: Lawmakers, Lobbyists, and the Unlikely Triumph of Tax Reform* (New York: Random House, 1987).
27. The advantages that a chairmanship confers are not what they were in the prereform Congress, however. See Smith and Deering, *Committees in Congress,* chap. 6.
28. See David Maraniss, "Power Play: Chairman's Gavel Crushes Gas Decontrol Vote," *Washington Post,* Nov. 20, 1983, A1.
29. Ibid.
30. See Richard L. Hall and C. Lawrence Evans, "The Role of the Subcommittee in Committee Decision Making" (Paper prepared for

delivery at the annual meeting of the American Political Science Association, September 1985); Evans, "Three Modes of Influence."

31. The references are to Senate Labor and Human Resources Chair Edward Kennedy, D-Mass., whose committee has jurisdiction over school nutrition programs, and Representative Leon Panetta, D-Calif., who chaired the House subcommittee with jurisdiction over food stamps and a number of other food assistance programs.

32. David Rohde, "Committee Reform in the House of Representatives and the Subcommittee Bill of Rights," *Annals of the American Academy of Political and Social Science* 411 (January 1974): 39-47.

33. See Smith and Deering's excellent discussion of House and Senate subcommittees in *Committees in Congress,* chap. 5.

34. The references are to the subcommittee chair George Mitchell, D-Maine; subcommittee ranking minority member David Durenberger, R-Minn.; and full committee chair Lloyd Bentsen, D-Texas.

35. For a more complete discussion of the conditions under which each of these relationships holds, see Richard L. Hall, "Explaining Legislative Influence" (Paper prepared for delivery at the annual meeting of the Southern Political Science Association, November 1986).

36. *American Political Science Review* 57 (1963): 45-56.

37. Hannah Pitkin strongly emphasizes the importance of legitimate elections in her discussion of the theory and practice of representation, but she does not suggest that individual legislators be strictly responsive to district opinion in their legislative decisions. See *The Concept of Representation* (Berkeley: University of California Press, 1967), chap. 10.

38. For instance, see Donald J. McCrone and James H. Kuklinski, "The Delegate Theory of Representation," *American Journal of Political Science* (1973): 278-300; Christopher Achen, "Measuring Representation," *American Journal of Political Science* (1978): 475-510; Morris P. Fiorina, *Representatives, Roll Calls, and Constituencies* (Lexington, Mass.: D. C. Heath, 1974). Richard Fenno's work on the subject pushes far beyond the delegate connection, although his focus remains at the member-constituency level. See *Home Style: House Members in Their Districts* (Boston: Little, Brown, 1978).

39. For an interesting exception, see Robert Weissberg, "Collective and Dyadic Representation in Congress," *American Political Science Review* 72 (1978): 535-547.

40. Mayhew, *Congress: The Electoral Connection,* 85-97.

41. Shepsle, *Giant Jigsaw Puzzle,* 259.

42. Jonathan Rauch, "The Farm Credit Fix," *National Journal,* June 13, 1987, 1517.

43. Ibid., 1513.

44. David Rapp, "House Panel Approves Farm Credit Shake-Up," *Congressional Quarterly Weekly Report,* Aug. 8, 1987, 1794-1795.

45. David Rapp, "Senate Approves $4 Billion Farm Credit Bill," *Congressional Quarterly Weekly Report,* Dec. 5, 1987, 2998.

# 9. FISCAL RESPONSIBILITY, FAIRNESS, AND THE REVENUE COMMITTEES

## Catherine E. Rudder

Despite congressional reforms of the early 1970s that shook the foundations of the House Committee on Ways and Means, it and its Senate counterpart, the Finance Committee, are the most powerful on Capitol Hill. Given their vast jurisdiction and their pivotal role in the preeminent policy debate of the nation—federal fiscal policy—it would be difficult to identify congressional committees more important. Their jurisdiction covers not only all federal taxation but also 40 percent of all direct federal spending.

## Shifts in Direction

The last fifteen years, however, have been a time of transition for the tax committees. The way they operate, the degree of autonomy they enjoy, their environment, and their chairmen have changed. As a result, the kind of policy these committees produce is quite different from that of the past. Tax policy has been unusually erratic during this period, the growth of revenues has slowed considerably, and large deficits in the range of $150-$200 billion annually have been experienced through the 1980s primarily as a result of tax policy decisions.[1]

The erratic shifts in policy are evidenced in the major tax bills enacted since 1976. The Tax Reform Act of 1976 had been hailed as a major tax reform measure because it broadened the income tax base by reducing tax expenditures—special tax breaks for groups of taxpayers—by $8 billion and maintained the mildly progressive structure of the personal income tax, which means that the higher one's income, the greater the proportion one pays in taxes. The Revenue Act of 1978 was an abrupt reversal. Tax expenditures were expanded in the interest of encouraging capital formation, and the tax structure was made less progressive.

By 1981 the concern for capital formation had been translated into "supply-side economics," which argued for reduced tax rates as a work incentive and for further reductions in taxation on capital to promote saving and investment. As the highest priority of Ronald Reagan's new administration, principles of supply-side economics were enacted into law in the Economic Recovery Tax Act (ERTA) of 1981. The act included major individual tax rate reductions over a three-year period and a number of other reductions, most notably in the number of years over which businesses and individuals could depreciate assets for tax purposes. Tax rates were indexed so that inflation would not artificially increase tax burdens, a provision which had a significant fiscal and revenue impact.

The staggering projected revenue loss from this legislation—$1.5 trillion through the end of the 1980s—resulted in structural deficits and a consequent fiscal crisis.[2] ERTA continued the reversal, begun with the Revenue Act of 1978, of the revenue-raising reforms of 1976.[3] Supply-side taxation lowered corporate taxes, reduced taxes on capital gains income, which is earned disproportionately by the wealthy, and increased the relative tax burden of the low-income taxpayer.[4]

Many mainstream economists predicted dire consequences of this legislation, which was not accompanied by comparable spending cuts. These predictions included higher interest rates, a slowdown in economic activity, a recession, substantial inflation, and great uncertainty in financial markets. Supply-side economists, on the other hand, saw the 1981 cuts as the beginning of an economic rejuvenation that would encourage Americans to work harder and American businesses to invest in plant and equipment. Neither set of predictions proved on the mark.

As economist Joseph Minarik reflected five years after the tax cut:

> At least in this country, people tend to work and save about the same amount regardless of the tax rate; reducing the tax rate elicits only a small, marginal increase in work and saving. Thus, this effect of the 1981 tax cut was muted.[5]

Although ERTA did not improve saving, investment, or work effort, it can be credited, in part, for the longest economic recovery the United States has experienced since World War II. After a severe recession in 1982, probably caused by the Federal Reserve Board's tight money policy, the economy took off with significant reductions in unemployment, healthy business growth, and, miraculously, low inflation.

Ironically, the role ERTA may have played in this outcome would not have been predicted by supply-side theory. By reducing revenues substantially, the 1981 tax bill contributed to the large annual budget deficits (not to increased savings and capital investment) that stimulated the economy. But the deficits also aroused concern among responsible politicians who realized that the bubble could burst; many said that the country was mortgaging its economic future.

Consequently, in another inconsistent but necessary move, the largest tax cut in U.S. history was followed by the largest peacetime tax increase. Many of ERTA's tax advantages were modified by the Tax Equity and Fiscal Responsibility Act (TEFRA) of 1982 in an effort to reduce anticipated deficits. The projected revenue gain of $99 billion over three years was accomplished by moderating some of the 1981 provisions benefiting business, increasing compliance, and accelerating corporate tax payments. Tax expenditures were reduced by thirteen provisions of the act, and the alternative minimum tax (to ensure that wealthy individuals pay some tax) was tripled. Still, the individual tax cuts of 1981 were maintained, a *sine qua non* for the president.

The approach of raising revenues by increasing the tax base was followed again in 1984, after a similar attempt to raise taxes failed in 1983. Conventional political wisdom was turned on its head when taxes were raised in an election year for the second time in a row. House Ways and Means and Senate Finance agreed on $50 billion worth of tax increases for fiscal years 1985, 1986, and 1987. To avoid a presidential veto, the Deficit Reduction Act of 1984, like the 1982 bill, did not raise tax rates directly, and the three-year tax cut of 1981 and the indexing of tax rates to inflation were not altered. Even though the 1984 act entailed substantial benefits to particular groups, the net effect was a considerable revenue gain.

Although deficits would continue to be a problem, by 1985 tax policy makers had shifted their focus yet again, this time from revenue raising to tax reform. Even with the 1982 and 1984 legislation, the tax system remained rife with tax preferences, which distorted spending and investment decisions by individuals and businesses. Moreover, those with similar incomes were paying different amounts of taxes, violating the basic tax principle of horizontal equity or equal tax burden within income groups.

With the impetus from Reagan, who declared tax reform the "number one legislative priority" of his second term, House and Senate conferees agreed on August 16, 1986, to the "most comprehensive restructuring of the federal income tax law since World War II." [6] Taxes were cut by $300 billion over a five-year period, and tax breaks were stemmed an equivalent amount. Taxes on business, in a partial reversal of the theory propelling the 1981 tax cut bill, were increased by $120 billion to pave the way for an equal cut for individuals. At the same time the top business rate was reduced from 46 percent to 34 percent. For individuals the fourteen existing tax brackets (fifteen for singles) were shrunk to two. The top tax rate for individuals was slashed by almost half from 50 percent to 28 percent (32 percent for a small group of taxpayers). Six million people at the lowest income levels would pay no income tax, making this legislation the most significant antipoverty measure in years. Most individuals would owe a flat 15 percent of their adjusted gross income to the federal government.

This fundamental restructuring of the tax code, which would "alter the finances of every American family and business," [7] was accomplished within the strictures of the president's nonnegotiable requirement: if the legislation were to receive his signature, the bill had to be revenue neutral in the aggregate. In other words, the projected revenues from federal income taxes would remain the same as before tax reform.

## Control of Tax Policy

What led to this erratic, unpredictable pattern of tax policy? The loss of Ways and Means as a control committee contributed. Before the congressional reforms of the early 1970s, Ways and Means was a small, elite body operating behind closed doors and without subcommittees. It brought bills to the floor under closed rules that permit no amendment, ensuring that compromises shaped in committee could not be torn apart on the House floor. The members were senior House members with safe seats, led by a knowledgeable, respected, and consensus-building chairman, Wilbur Mills, D-Ark., and they followed norms of restrained partisanship, "responsible" legislating, and apprenticeship. The committee was able to impose its will on the House—Mills rarely lost votes on the floor—and it had a substantial restraining influence on the Senate.

### Congressional Reforms

The reforms of the 1970s undermined the ability of Ways and Means to operate as a control committee. Expansion of the committee by almost 50 percent to thirty-seven members, the establishment of subcommittees, the requirement that meetings be held in public unless the committee chose in a roll call vote to close them, the loss by Democratic members of the committee of the role of assigning fellow Democrats to other House committees, the requirement that the chairman serve at the pleasure of the Democratic Caucus of the House, modification in the use of the closed rule for tax legislation on the House floor, and other changes all weakened the chairman's ability to lead. They also undermined the committee's ability to hold legislative packages intact on the House floor, to bargain effectively with Senate Finance in conference, and to withstand pressure from other members and interested groups. Autonomy was curtailed as members outside

Ways and Means not only challenged the committee's bills on the floor but also circumvented it by attaching legislative language affecting tax policy to appropriations bills.

Before the reforms it was much more difficult to hold individual members accountable for specific provisions of tax legislation. Instead, bills were collective, privately forged committee products that were presented to the House in a take-it-or-leave-it manner. Constituents had no way of knowing what members were doing in committee. Furthermore, because committee members had safe seats, they did not need to respond seriously to every person or group making a claim.

In the House, Democrats not serving on Ways and Means felt beholden to Democratic committee members for their committee assignments, and they realized that opposition to a Ways and Means bill could affect their chances to obtain a more desirable committee assignment. Therefore, bills crafted by Ways and Means met little meaningful opposition on the House floor.

With the congressional reforms the balance of power shifted. To retain their seats and to win House approval of committee bills, Ways and Means members had to be more responsive to requests from constituents, organized interests, and their House colleagues. These new pressures were intensified by the sunlight of open meetings. Ways and Means members could now be held accountable for their positions on every provision that made up a tax package. In short, the Ways and Means Committee was easier to penetrate, particularly by organized interests, and much less autonomous. In turn, the committee could no longer provide cover for House members.

Given this situation, one might expect tax policy that is unstable, unpredictable, and overly responsive to claimants. In 1981 especially the committee was vulnerable to almost every substantial economic interest group in Washington. The normal process of developing legislation broke down, turning into an "unprecedented bidding war" between the president and the Democrats, led by Ways and Means Committee chairman Dan Rostenkowski, D-Ill. Each was trying to attract floor votes for his version of the legislation, each upping the ante with new tax privileges.[8] There seemed to be little concern for the quality of the bill or the integrity of the tax code.

The reforms that led to the weakening of Ways and Means also explain some of the legislative outcomes of the 1980s. Rostenkowski, like his predecessor, Al Ullman, D-Ore., was at first not successful in controlling his committee and persuading the House to follow his lead. Even after the auction for votes that characterized the drafting of the 1981 Ways and Means bill and the Republican/Reagan administration alternative, Rostenkowski and the Democrats lost to the alternative, which was tendered by a junior Democratic member of the Ways and Means Committee, Kent Hance, D-Texas, and the ranking Republican on Ways and Means, Barber Conable, R-N.Y.[9]

## Changes in Approach to Tax Policy Making

Along with the reforms, two other factors have contributed to the difficulty of making tax policy in a consistent, restrained manner that preserves the integrity of the tax code. One of these factors is the prevalence of ad hoc policy making on tax matters: members often make decisions on the basis of ahistorical, prima facie arguments rather than well-reasoned arguments based on historical evidence. The confusion surrounding the application of economic theories has fostered ad hoc policy making. Stagflation of the 1970s left Keynesian economics in some disrepute and opened the way for supply-side economics, which in turn led to the highest deficits in history. Tax policy makers have little to lean on when making important decisions affecting fiscal policy other than the prevailing arguments of the moment.[10]

The second factor is the use of the tax code for nontax purposes. For example, to encourage preservation of historic buildings, a rehabilitation tax credit is offered rather than a direct subsidy. This practice gives the revenue committees almost unlimited jurisdiction and adds to the demands on the tax committees, which, in the postreform era, are unable to withstand effective lobbying.

The decentralizing reforms, the prevalence of ad hoc policy making, and the opening of the tax code for virtually any policy purpose all point in the same direction: a manipulable environment open to exploitation by effective lobbyists with facile arguments and strong grass-roots backing to pressure members, who are always running for reelection. Nevertheless, the 1982 and 1984 tax increases and the 1986 tax reform shifted tax policy back on an unexpected course: tax expenditures were reduced and revenues raised. The 1982 and 1984 feat is especially remarkable because Reagan opposed the tax increases and had to be persuaded to support the tax package. The 1986 reform hit some of the most powerful interest groups and radically changed the tax code, this time with presidential leadership but little public support. These bills demonstrate that the reforms affecting the Ways and Means Committee have not prevented Congress from enacting politically difficult and fiscally disciplined legislation.

Examining how Congress—the tax committees in particular—managed to pass such legislation is instructive for understanding the tax legislative process and its impact on policy outcomes and provides clues as to whether a pattern of more consistent, fiscally responsible policy making is emerging.

# The Deficit Crisis
# and the Emergence of Leadership

Rostenkowski and Senator Robert J. Dole, R-Kan., assumed the chairmanships of their respective committees after the 1980 elections but under very different circumstances. The Democrats had sustained a stunning blow in Reagan's landslide election and the loss of their Senate majority after twenty-six years of Democratic control. Dole took the helm of Senate Finance. As if to underscore the Democrats' loss, the Ways and Means chairmanship was open because Ullman was defeated in his reelection bid.[11]

The first year of Reagan's presidency saw the passage of his economic program, including his tax proposals. Rostenkowski and the Democrats could not muster a majority in the House to defeat them even though the Democrats nominally constituted the majority. When it became clear sometime later that the unprecedented tax cuts of 1981, coupled with other revenue-depressing factors such as the recession, would require large tax increases, Dole took the lead in addressing the problem.[12]

Congress passed the first concurrent resolution on the budget, a Republican measure, June 17, 1982, and set the parameters for a tax increase. Under the reconciliation instructions of the resolution, the tax committees were told to increase revenues by an estimated $98.3 billion and to cut health and welfare spending under their jurisdiction by $17 billion for fiscal years 1983-1985. In other words, Ways and Means and Senate Finance alone were responsible for producing half of the deficit reduction under the three-year budget agreement. Senate Finance was to report its reconciliation legislation by July 12, and Ways and Means by August 1.

The impending deficits and concern about their potentially devastating effect on the economy provided the impetus for action. Yet it was a touch-and-go matter from the start. Members were unenthusiastic about raising taxes in an election year, even if they worried about deficits as an election issue. This reluctance was especially evident among House Democrats who did not want to be saddled with the blame for a tax increase they believed the Republican-led tax cuts the previous year had made necessary. Moreover, no help came from the White House at first. Reagan was unwilling to sign any bill that reduced the personal tax cuts enacted by ERTA in 1981, and Secretary of the Treasury Donald Regan was unwilling to suggest ways to increase taxes enough to meet the reconciliation instructions. Initiative would have to come from Congress. Rostenkowski, however, refused to take the lead, although Ways and Means normally would have done so on behalf of the House as the originator of tax legislation under the Constitution.

Dole was willing to act. To compound the difficulty of reporting tax hikes, half of his committee—including six of its twelve Republicans—were up for reelection.[13] Nevertheless, Dole produced all the deficit reductions called for in the first budget resolution, and he did so ten days before the deadline. The reconciliation bill was reported out of committee on a straight partisan vote that reflected Dole's technique: the bill had been written in closed caucuses involving only the committee's Republicans and then, in effect, was ratified in committee. This reversal of the spirit of the open-meetings reform that extended to most congressional deliberations may have been indispensable in producing the legislation.

On the Senate floor Dole was aided by the Budget Act of 1974, which limits debate and amendments on reconciliation bills. When the Senate adopted an amendment to ease depreciation rules for real estate that lopped off $2.8 billion in revenues necessary to fulfill reconciliation instructions, Dole demonstrated legislative creativity by offering a successful alternative proposal—to restrict the rehabilitation tax credit enjoyed by the real estate industry—that recouped the loss. He threatened even greater tax increases if the Senate insisted on weakening the bill. He mustered a 50-47 majority, primarily Republicans.

In contrast, Rostenkowski was unable to unite the Democrats on his committee. In the absence of a presidential proposal, he offered his own tax package. It was rejected by Ways and Means Democrats, and the committee agreed instead to go to conference without a House bill. The House assented to this decision and in so doing broke the tradition of the House proposing tax bills. The constitutional problem was circumvented by attaching the Senate's bill to a minor House-passed tax measure unrelated to deficit reduction.

## Explaining Success

Despite predictions that no agreement would be reached, the conferees, particularly Dole, were committed to producing a report. By the time the conference was under way, the president was campaigning vigorously for this legislation. When the conference report reached the House, "the legislative machinery of both parties . . . was effective and essential" to its passage.[14]

In the face of opposition from the Business Roundtable, the U.S. Chamber of Commerce, and other influential business interests, and with the 1982 election only two months away, this major tax increase bill passed. The principal ingredients for enactment were: first, the use of the Budget Act, which structured the situation, set a timetable for action, and supplied strict germaneness rules on the Senate floor, where tax bills ordinarily are subject to numerous nongermane amendments; second, the sense of fiscal crisis stemming from projected budget deficits that led to the realization that doing nothing could be more damaging to reelection chances than voting for tax increases; third, Dole's leadership, including his techniques of using party caucuses and closing meetings; and, finally, the eventual team work of the administration, the revenue committees, and congressional party leaders in shaping successful legislation and securing final passage.

## Deficit Reduction Revisited

As projected deficits were again revised upward in 1983 and early 1984, Congress was faced once more with the prospect of raising revenues and reducing spending. By 1983 Rostenkowski had begun to exert leadership in deficit reduction. The jurisdiction of his committee had been strengthened by several changes in House rules. One rule made it more difficult to attach legislative riders to appropriations bills, and another allowed Ways and Means to raise a point of order to prevent bills with tax or trade restrictions from coming to the floor without the committee's approval.[15]

Even with these changes, however, Ways and Means was circumvented by the banking industry's successful effort to repeal a provision in the 1982 bill to establish withholding on dividends and interest, despite the vigorous opposition of Rostenkowski and Dole. Norman D'Amours, D-N.H., used a discharge petition to force House action on the bill, which Rostenkowski had bottled up in his committee. Robert Kasten, R-Wis., forced the Senate Finance Committee to act by threatening to attach the repeal amendment to a crucial bill to increase the debt limit. The repeal effort demonstrated the powerlessness of the tax committee chairman in the face of a strong, well-organized, grass-roots lobbying campaign.

Rostenkowski demonstrated leadership on the major Social Security financing bill enacted in 1983 and on a bill to limit the third-year tax cut that passed the House but not the Senate, but he faced a major defeat as the House turned down the rule permitting consideration of the Ways and Means deficit-reduction bill. This legislation conformed to the reconciliation instructions of the budget resolution, whose provisions to raise $12 billion for fiscal 1984 and $73 billion for fiscal 1984-1986 were not met before the close of Congress in 1983.

## New Tactics for Ways and Means

Rostenkowski devised methods of operating that were to characterize the more successful work of Ways and Means in 1984. First, he closed committee markups, even on uncontroversial bills. Second, he made frequent use of Democratic caucuses in the committee, just as Dole did with the Republicans on Senate Finance, to develop partisan majorities in the committee. Third, like Mills before him, he developed consensus "by molding legislation as much as possible to meet the major concerns of each member of the caucus." [16] Fourth, like Dole, he floated deficit-reduction packages to assess the strength of interest group opposition and the likelihood of passage. Fifth, like Dole, he worked for a package of tax increases that would be acceptable to the House and the president. Gaining acceptance entailed two related elements: considering legislation on the House floor under a closed rule so that legislative compromises could not be picked apart by forceful lobbying efforts and developing a package with enough "sweeteners"— benefits to particular interests that members care about—so that the total package could win a majority even though many specific provisions might not if voted on separately.

### Explaining Failure

In 1983 Dole had even less success than Rostenkowski. The sense of urgency had dissipated. Congress had just passed its largest peacetime tax bill in history, and, because the 1983 budget resolution provided for a three-year deficit reduction, Congress could always enact a reconciliation bill in 1984 to cover the relevant three fiscal years, 1984-1986. Also, in 1983 there was no cooperation, even late in the year, from the administration, which preferred a stand-by tax to be triggered in fiscal 1986, if necessary, to reduce deficits. In addition, certain interest groups, especially those working to protect the tax value of industrial development bonds, were strong enough to prevent action.

The failure to enact deficit-reduction legislation in 1983 suggests that the budget process, consensus-building leadership, in this case by both chairmen, and closed meetings are not enough. Missing were administration support, proposals that could withstand the onslaught of interest group opposition, and, most important, the will to act.

## Doing the Impossible

In many ways 1984 was a replay of 1982. Deficit projections were revised upward, and there was a general belief that Congress would be unable to reduce them. The administration not only failed to cooperate with initial efforts to raise taxes but also threatened vetoes if certain measures were passed, thereby reducing the options of the tax committees. Moreover, the administration's budget proposed costly new tax expenditures, including tax breaks for urban enterprise zones, individual retirement accounts for nonworking spouses, and tuition tax credits for parents who send their children to private schools, none of which was enacted.

As in 1982 much of the deficit reduction would have to emanate from the revenue committees. Once again Dole insisted from the beginning of the year that deficits had to be addressed even though short-term expediency might favor inaction. He took the lead by directing the Finance Committee staff to prepare a package of proposals that could be attached to the reconciliation bill that had not been enacted in 1983.

The primary differences in 1984, compared with 1982, were the leadership of Rostenkowski and the ability of his committee and the House to produce a deficit-reduction package. The techniques Rostenkowski had used in 1983, coupled with a sense of urgency and a desire to get credit for deficit reduction, propelled passage of a Democratic deficit-reduction bill in the House.

Ways and Means met behind closed doors to combine the previous year's unpassed reconciliation bill with provisions to close tax shelters and improve compliance. By a wide margin the House Rules Committee agreed to a closed rule and to allow the House to vote separately on almost $1 billion worth of cuts in Medicare, as opposition to the health spending cuts threatened defeat of the deficit-reduction package. On April 12, by a lopsided vote of 318 to 97, the House passed the deficit-reduction bill and on the following day defeated the Medicare cuts.

In the Senate Dole had rough going; the voting procedure used by the Finance Committee permits votes on individual provisions to remain open until work on the entire package is completed. "The lobbyists are changing votes faster than I can," Dole complained.[17] One proposal that was eliminated in committee, but reinstated on the Senate floor because of this procedure, was to limit the deduction allowed for the purchase of luxury automobiles for business use. Even with the open-ended procedure, Senate Finance managed to fend off a number of lobbying efforts to dilute the committee bill, including an all-out effort by the real estate industry to maintain a depreciation provision enacted in 1981 that encouraged investment in real estate. Although cutting the deficit was the overriding concern, the bill as passed by the Senate included $8 billion in new tax breaks, including the president's proposal for enterprise zones and an expansion of individual retirement accounts. Part of the Senate bill that dealt with major changes in taxation of the insurance industry had been forged by Ways and Means and then adopted by Senate Finance, thereby reviving the pre-1981 pattern of Ways and Means writing tax bills and Senate Finance amending them.

Deficit reduction was the overriding concern in both chambers, and the budget and tax committees were operating in tandem on this matter. Because by 1984 the Republican Senate and Democratic House were in a race to produce deficit-reduction legislation first and take credit for being the most fiscally responsible, tax legislation preceded House-Senate agreement on a budget resolution. However, the budget process provided the structure for action in 1984.

Rostenkowski and Dole were committed to producing a conference report under the imperative of reducing the deficit. Negotiations were held in secret, and Treasury Department officials and David Stockman, director of the Office of Management and Budget (OMB), were actively involved. The conference lasted for almost three weeks, capped by a marathon session beginning at 8:30 a.m. and ending a little more than twenty hours later at 5:15 a.m. The conference adjourned for hours while the participants from each house caucused in private, and messages were sent back and forth between the groups. The most difficult items were postponed until the end. The final legislation included $50 billion in new taxes and $13 billion in reduced spending, along with a number of new tax breaks.

## A Gestalt Shift

In his 1984 State of the Union message, Ronald Reagan announced that he would ask the Treasury Department to propose a reform of the tax system. Reagan said that Treasury was to report its recommendations by December 1, causing laughter throughout the bipartisan audience that understood that the proposal would, as a consequence, be irrelevant to the 1984 presidential campaign and probably never be taken seriously. An executive of one of the largest U.S. financial services companies remarked later, "The Wall Street consensus was that the president was really posturing for the elections," but by November "Wall Street [was] worried he really meant it." [18]

As Dole dryly observed, there was not "a groundswell of support out there for tax simplification." Survey after survey reported the public's indifference to the issue, which perhaps stemmed from skepticism that Congress and the president could enact meaningful tax reform as opposed to special interest legislation or tax increases masquerading as reform. Dole understood the enormity, if not impossibility, of the task. "We'll have twenty people shooting at us from every direction." [19] While tax reform in principle might be a worthy goal, "As soon as you get specific, support evaporates," William Armstrong, R-Colo., a frequent presidential ally, observed.[20]

To make matters worse, the Senate Finance Committee was to lose its strong, effective chairman. Dole became majority leader of the Senate, and Bob Packwood, R-Ore., an opponent of taxing fringe benefits and other "reform" measures, stepped in as chairman.

The elements for success simply were not in place. Neither party was enthusiastic. There was no public pressure for reform. Interest groups with special tax provisions to protect were stronger than ever as their political action committees contributed huge sums to the campaigns of members of the tax committees. The most pressing worry was high deficits, not tax distortions. And the majority leader of the House, Jim Wright, D-Texas, was opposed to tax reform as were many in the president's party. Few observers gave tax reform any chance of moving out of the Ways and Means Committee, much less out of Congress.

## Defining and Activating the Issue

The issue had been waiting in the wings since Jack Kemp, R-N.Y., and William Roth, R-Del., in the first such proposal, and Richard Gephardt, D-Mo., and Bill Bradley, D-N.J., in another in 1982, introduced variations on a flat tax scheme that would reduce the number of tax brackets and the tax rates in exchange for the elimination of most tax breaks. Although neither of these proposals caught the imagination of Congress and seemed unlikely to do so after the tax spending spree of 1981, the idea had been well publicized and was familiar to most on Capitol Hill.

The advantage to such an approach was that it took on tax expenditures as a whole rather than one at a time and, therefore, changed the balance of political forces and the arguments that could be used against reforms. For example, because the effective tax rates were so uneven among businesses, the proposal to reduce rates in exchange for certain tax breaks split the business community, even industries. Retailers and other service businesses were willing to see depreciation rules tightened—and tax rates lowered—because the liberal rules that came out of the 1981 act had not affected their profits, but heavy industry stood to lose considerably if the depreciation schedules were made less generous.

Proponents of wholesale change successfully appropriated the word *reform*—so much so that the single best journalistic account of the legislative battle never once questioned whether the act *was* a reform or why the content of the legislation changed as much as it did from the first Treasury proposal to the final version.[21] Because tax reform connotes the public interest, anyone opposing elements of the reform had to accept the onus of arguing against the public interest, even if the connotation was not entirely warranted. For example, cutting tax rates reduces the value of a charitable deduction to the taxpayer by whatever percentage the rate is cut. To the degree that donations to churches, colleges, and other institutions decline, it is proper, from at least one view of the public interest, to oppose large tax rate cuts. Or, by reducing tax incentives to construct low-income housing, shelter for the poor may become more scarce and rents may go up. One might argue that this situation is not in the public interest.[22]

Not only was the reform label commandeered but also *fairness,* which became the standard against which all arguments were measured, and fairness was defined in a legitimate, although particular, way. Perhaps most significant was that it put aside the principle of progressivity as a cornerstone of the U.S. tax system, in part because the existing system was so filled with inconsistencies that a modified flat tax was no less progressive than the status quo. Progressivity was, at least to some observers, sacrificed as a legitimate, positive, and morally compelling principle of taxation.

Not only had the flat tax seed been planted, certain—though not all—conditions were ripe to trigger action. First, there was the growing problem of tax avoidance through the underground (cash and barter) economy, so named because participants by-pass the tax system. Estimates of lost tax revenues vary, but at minimum the loss is in the tens of billions of dollars. Also, tax cheating seemed to be on the increase, a problem because the U.S. tax system depends on voluntary compliance.

In addition, concern was growing about the distortions in the economy created by tax incentives, which encourage people to engage in one activity rather than another or to use the tax code for nontax purposes. This practice leads to inefficiencies in investments such as new office buildings made profitable by the tax code even though they remain empty.

Finally, there were widely publicized reports that the tax system had become significantly less progressive between 1977 and 1984, that businesses were paying a much smaller share of the tax load than in the early 1970s, that many large, profitable companies not only paid no tax but actually made money on the tax system, that the taxes paid by the working poor were increasing, and that federal taxes were no longer seen as fair by the American public especially in comparison to state and local taxes—a reversal from the 1960s.

By themselves, however, these conditions could not overcome the serious obstacles confronting tax reform. The necessary additional elements were leadership, party competition, and procedures that encouraged discipline.

## The Mantle of Tax Reform

Lending credence to suspicion that President Reagan was not wholeheartedly committed to tax reform was his lukewarm reaction in late 1984 to Treasury's first proposal, dubbed "Treasury I." Even Secretary Regan distanced himself from the far-reaching, politically troublesome recommendations of Treasury I, which was seen by much of the Washington community as a creature of Treasury's technical staff, not a viable political document. Traditional economic allies of the president would have been hurt under Treasury I, and portions of it ran counter to aspects of supply-side theory, popularly referred to as Reaganism. Still, the president continued to press for tax reform and sent the Treasury staff back to modify its proposals.

By late November it was clear to Democrats that the president, who had just won the largest landslide in history, in part by promising never to increase taxes, had every intention of taking over the issue of tax reform, of demonstrating that the Republican party championed a fairer, simpler tax system, but without risking the political heat that comes with a concrete set of changes. Moreover, congressional Democrats, Rostenkowski in particular, felt that "tax simplification [was] too powerful an issue to simply be ceded to Ronald Reagan and the Republicans." In fact, strategists in both parties felt that "tax revision could be pivotal to a realignment of the national parties." [23]

Further stirring Rostenkowski's competitive instincts was his desire to build on his success as chairman and for his committee to regain the prominence it had enjoyed in the days of Wilbur Mills. As Rostenkowski had learned in 1982, he could ignore Reagan and the Senate Republicans only at his peril. Consequently, the chairman's strategy was to produce a tax reform bill, even if its prospects for eventual enactment were slender. "If I were a politician," he said in March 1985, "I would say, hell, let's give them a bill . . . and see what they can do with it." [24]

As Senator David Boren, D-Okla., later characterized the argument of the Democrats of the Ways and Means Committee, the attitude was "Let's don't kill it here." According to the *Washington Post,* he said, "That's how it got out of the Ways and Means Committee. That's how it got through the House." [25]

At the same time, Rostenkowski's strategy required the president's vigorous public support for tax revision so that Reagan could not blame the Democrats for unpalatable provisions as he had blamed them for tax increases. The president's representatives, newly appointed Secretary of the Treasury James Baker, the former chief of staff at the White House, and politically experienced Assistant Secretary Richard Darman, were in fact involved in the negotiations at every stage of the process.

In addition, had Reagan not intervened (upon the insistence of Rostenkowski and Speaker Tip O'Neill) by changing the votes of a crucial number of fellow Republicans, the bill would have died on the floor of the House. In the Senate, the president's forceful wishes were decisive as well. When asked why the Senate was considering tax reform legislation when there were more pressing problems like the budget deficit, John Heinz, R-Pa., replied, "The president wants it. Period." [26]

Still, moving the legislation was anything but easy. It had to be resuscitated time and again. As the *New York Times* reported, "Few pieces of legislation in recent years have had so many narrow escapes." [27] Each escape was orchestrated by leaders with personal and political stakes in not permitting the bill to die under their stewardship.

In Ways and Means and, later, in Senate Finance, the tax revision became so weighted with revenue-reducing provisions that the bill became untenable as tax reform. In both committees the chairman responded by proposing legislative solutions to seemingly intractable problems. Packwood had to confront the success of the House Democrats' strategy. On December 3, 1985, the House had produced a bill, and now it was the responsibility of the Republican Senate to respond.

Packwood, who had considerably less control of his committee than Rostenkowski had of Ways and Means, encountered the same revenue-draining pressures as the House chairman, but Packwood was not committed to tax revision. His first proposal, which safeguarded his state's interests, sent a clear message to fellow members of Finance: protect your own interests—not a philosophy designed to encourage sacrifice to produce reform in the public interest, no matter how defined.

However, the beating the Senate Finance Committee and Packwood, who was up for reelection in 1986, took in the press, coupled with the impossibility of handling his committee's special interest proposals, which totaled $100 billion, led Packwood to adjourn the committee and propose an entirely new plan. His surprising idea, taken from his Democratic colleague, Bill Bradley, would make tax rates even lower than the president had proposed and would eliminate many tax shelters and preferences, including a move to treat capital gains as ordinary income, which was not in line with supply-side economics.

Refinements were made by a small group of committee allies. The rest of the committee, convinced of the imprudence of voting against the bill, voted it out twenty to zero, sending the political hot potato to the Senate floor May 7. The bill was approved June 24 by an amazing ninety-seven to three, leaving lobbyists scrambling to influence the conference committee, which was made up of reformers of various degrees.

In conference deliberations broke down, once again requiring the intervention of the two chairmen who met alone day and night to arrive at a compromise acceptable to the conferees and their chambers. On August 16 the conferees approved the Packwood-Rostenkowski compromise, characterized by the *Wall Street Journal* as a "mindboggling turmoil of policy crosscurrents" [28] that would have unpredictable effects on the economy. Approved by lopsided, but not enthusiastic, majorities in the House and Senate in late September, the Tax Reform Act of 1986, which instituted the lowest personal income tax rate among advanced democracies and the lowest in the United States since 1931, was signed by the president in October.

### Techniques

Rostenkowski used techniques that had proved successful in 1984: Democratic task forces, lengthy closed meetings, and flexible, determined bargaining that he conducted. Although Packwood started out with open deliberations, he retreated into private negotiations and worked with a handful of committee allies from both parties. Neither chairman and neither committee wanted to be responsible for killing tax reform, and this fear was a powerful motivator at every stage of the process.

Further, under the leadership of Rostenkowski and Packwood, a disciplining rule developed that no proposal that reduced revenue would be in order unless it were coupled with a proposal to raise an equivalent amount, making revenue losers much harder to sell. This rule, self-imposed by the Senate, which by coincidence was in its first week of having its proceedings nationally televised, was the *sine qua non* for moving the legislation intact from the Senate to conference. Without it, tax reform would have collapsed on the Senate floor before the eyes of millions of Americans.

Perhaps the most important technique was that of sheer doggedness on the part of Rostenkowski and Packwood, as well as presidential representatives Baker and Darman. By the time the conferees met, the two chairmen had a great deal invested in the success of the legislation and were willing to go to extraordinary lengths to turn an impossibility into a reality.

## The Future

Conventional political wisdom has proved of little use in understanding the making of recent tax policy. Not only *can* taxes be raised in an election year, there can be more pressure to raise taxes to reduce deficits when elections are impending than when they are not. Tax policy can change radically and quickly. Moreover, Congress not only can initiate fiscally responsible legislation, but also it can do so in the face of presidential opposition and divided party government. Finally, Congress can make politically difficult decisions necessary for the long-term health of the economy.

While the decentralizing congressional reforms of the 1970s have left committees, particularly Ways and Means, more permeable, more susceptible to the influence of interest groups (especially those that can generate grass-roots activity), less autonomous, and harder to lead, the revenue committees have adapted to a new internal and external environment. Recent rules changes in the House have restored some Ways and Means control over the tax product. Tax committee chairmen Dole, Packwood, and Rostenkowski developed effective techniques—some of which negated the 1970s reforms—to produce successful legislation: using party caucuses within their committees, consulting widely on legislation, developing a salable product, using rules to keep packages intact on the floor, working with party leadership, closing meetings, and bargaining. Their leadership is especially notable when one considers that they have no formal coercive powers and that members of Congress, including members of tax committees, have great difficulty saying no to claimants.

The legislative successes of 1982 and 1984 can be attributed to the felicitous convergence of leadership (first Dole, then Rostenkowski and Dole), the mechanisms of the budget process, the desire of both parties and the administration to enact deficit reductions, and a fiscal crisis. The sense of an impending economic downturn, if not disaster, defined the legislative environment, just as the perceived need to improve economic performance through tax incentives defined it in 1978 and 1981.

In 1986 Ronald Reagan effected a gestalt shift from deficit control to tax reform. Just as the parties had vied not to be labeled deficit spender or tax increaser, Reagan set up a competition between the parties and the chambers not to be blamed for killing tax reform. He established the critical parameter that the bill must be revenue neutral, that it bring in no more or no less revenue than the tax system did before reform. As a consequence, most tax breaks that could have been removed have been. With the remaining revenue losses stemming from 1981, including the indexation of tax rates, and the 1986 broadening of the tax base, the avenues for reducing deficits are fewer, but the fiscal pressure is still on. As House member Leon Panetta, D-Calif., said prophetically, "Hidden in the closet during this whole debate on tax reform has been the deficit bogyman. That door will open." [29]

# Notes

1. There has also been a continued shift in the sources of revenue. While individual income taxes as a percentage of total revenues have ranged between 40 percent and 50 percent since 1960, payroll taxes, which fall most heavily on those with low incomes, have doubled from 16 percent of revenues in 1960 to 36 percent in 1984. By 1988 the effective social insurance rate exceeded the effective individual income tax rate for all but 10 percent of American taxpayers. Estate and gift taxes, which fall almost exclusively on upper income taxpayers, also have been substantially reduced, and corporate income taxes have declined from 23 percent in 1960 to 6 percent in 1983, but are expected to rise to 12 percent by 1990. See Congressional Budget Office, *The Changing Distribution of Federal Taxes: 1975-1990* (Washington, D.C.: U.S. Government Printing Office, 1987). For an overview of the U.S. income tax system, see John F. Witte, *The Politics and Development of the Federal Income Tax* (Madison: University of Wisconsin Press, 1985).

2. A deficit is the amount by which expenditures exceed revenues in a given fiscal year. A structural deficit is the projected amount by which expenditures would exceed revenues when the economy is operating at its full capacity. Sizable structural deficits are worrisome because they cannot be overcome even by excellent economic performance and are therefore "mortgaging the future."

3. Congress also enacted the Windfall Profits Tax Act of 1980, which raised taxes on oil companies but also included several new tax breaks.

4. Supply-side policies also contributed to the slowdown in the growth of federal revenues. Between 1980 and 1983, federal revenues grew at half the rate for the previous three-year period. At the same time, revenues declined as a percentage of the gross national product (GNP) from 20.1 percent in 1980 to 18.6 percent in 1983. See Congressional Budget Office, *Reducing the Deficit: Spending and Revenue Options* (Washington, D.C.: U.S. Government Printing Office, 1984), 184.

5. *Policy and Research Report* (Washington, D.C.: Urban Institute, August 1986), 3-4.

6. *New York Times,* Aug. 18, 1986, A1.

7. Ibid., Aug. 18, 1986, A1.

8. *Washington Post,* Aug. 2, 1981.

9. There are many reasons for the success of the 1981 bill, the most important of which was that President Reagan had an effective majority in the House and Senate although nominally the Democrats controlled the House. It also might be noted that the Democrats, led by Rostenkowski, were bidding for votes just as the Republicans were. Not only was the Ways and Means chairman unable to control the process, he was contributing to the raiding of the Treasury.

10. For further discussion of ad hoc policy making, see Catherine E. Rudder, "Tax Policy: Structure and Choice," in *Making Economic Policy in*

*Congress,* ed. Allen Schick (Washington, D.C.: American Enterprise Institute, 1983), 208-210.

11. Even though the power of the chairman had been diluted, Rostenkowski chose to become chairman rather than accept the position of House Democratic party whip, the third ranking Democrat in the House.

12. One might wonder why Dole took it upon himself to lead the tax increase battle and risk being known by his constituents as a tax increaser and face what then seemed to be probable defeat on the issue. He could have waited for public pressure to build until Reagan was forced to act and take the blame for increasing taxes. While it is difficult to attribute motives accurately, it is fair to say that by proposing to close tax loopholes, Dole was preempting the Democrats' position and was also transforming himself into a respected national political leader.

13. All were reelected in 1982, a fact that surely was not lost on members when faced with the prospect of raising taxes in the next election year.

14. *Congressional Quarterly Weekly Report,* Aug. 28, 1982, 2121.

15. Now Ways and Means can also raise a point of order if Senate amendments attached to a House-passed bill that are within the jurisdiction of Ways and Means, but have not been approved by Ways and Means, are brought to the House.

16. *Congressional Quarterly Weekly Report,* Jan. 29, 1983, 194.

17. Ibid., March 10, 1984, 536.

18. *Washington Post,* Nov. 20, 1984, 1.

19. *New York Times,* Nov. 18, 1984, D1.

20. *Wall Street Journal,* March 29, 1985, 1.

21. Jeffrey H. Birnbaum and Alan S. Murray, *Showdown at Gucci Gulch: Lawmakers, Lobbyists, and the Unlikely Triumph of Tax Reform* (New York: Random House, 1987).

22. For other examples, see Hemming Gutmann, "The Bad New Tax Law," *New York Review of Books,* Feb. 12, 1987, 26-28. Also see Congressional Budget Office, *The Effects of Tax Reform on Tax Expenditures* (Washington, D.C.: U.S. Government Printing Office, 1988).

23. *Wall Street Journal,* March 29, 1985, 1.

24. Ibid., March 29, 1985, 1.

25. *Washington Post,* Jan. 24, 1986, A14.

26. Ibid., Jan. 24, 1986, A14.

27. *New York Times,* Sept. 28, 1986, 34.

28. *Wall Street Journal,* Aug. 18, 1986, 9.

29. Ibid., Aug. 16, 1986, 2.

# 10. MULTIPLE REFERRAL AND THE 'NEW' COMMITTEE SYSTEM IN THE HOUSE OF REPRESENTATIVES

## Melissa P. Collie and Joseph Cooper

The reliance of Congress on a system of standing committees is one of the enduring institutional features of the national legislature. With the exception of the earliest Congresses,[1] the House and the Senate have used standing committees as their central means for organizing labor and formulating public policy. Accordingly, congressional scholars commonly acknowledge the preeminence of the standing committees in the legislative process even as they seek to explain the differences among committees and the changes that have taken place in the committee system over time.[2]

In light of their institutional endurance and the amount of attention they have attracted among congressional scholars, it is useful to step back for a moment and consider the basis for the standing committees' importance in the legislative process. Most scholars would agree that their importance rests centrally on their power to shape legislation in specific policy areas.[3] Committee power historically has derived from the confluence of two institutional rules. The first has been the establishment of fixed and specialized committee jurisdictions, which effectively define congressional policy in terms of discrete committee "domains." The second has been the longstanding rule of single referral, which permits each committee to be the sole arbiter of legislation within its jurisdiction. Together, these rules have enabled committee members to enjoy a disproportionate influence over policy within their committee's jurisdiction and committees to leave their imprimatur on virtually all legislation that is later (if at all) considered in the body as a whole.

This is not to say that the two rules enable any committee to control the final outcome on policy within its jurisdiction. As numerous

The authors thank Gary Cox, Mathew McCubbins, Michael Munger, Peter Ordeshook, Brian Roberts, and Thomas Schwartz for helpful comments during the preparation of this manuscript. A special thanks is due to Roger Davidson and Walter Oleszek for assistance in the data collection.

analyses indicate, such control is contingent on the nature of the rules under which committee bills are considered by the chamber[4] and is enhanced to the degree that internal norms include the development of expertise and specialization in committee work, deference and reciprocity among committees, and committee representation during the reconciliation of interchamber differences.[5] However, such considerations do not detract from the underlying significance of the two rules. Indeed, in their absence, committees' "gatekeeping" and "monopoly" powers over the agenda are rendered meaningless.[6]

While fixed and specialized committee jurisdictions are still synonymous with the operation of the standing committees, single referral is not. Both chambers now permit the referral of bills to more than one committee. In the Senate, though a formal rule defines the procedure for multiple referral, it invariably occurs through unanimous consent motions resulting from private negotiations among interested committees.[7] In the House, the rules of the chamber were amended in 1975 to provide for the multiple referral of legislation.

So far, the use of multiple referral has attracted relatively little comment from congressional scholars.[8] Yet it represents an abrupt departure from past practice and may well undermine one of the twin pillars of committee power. Multiple referral, therefore, would appear important not only on its own terms but because of the implications it has for our understanding of the committee system in the contemporary Congress. That the power of the standing committees traditionally has been linked with the institutional strength of Congress makes an assessment of multiple referral all the more compelling.

The major purpose of this analysis is to evaluate multiple referral in the House of Representatives. We first present results showing the importance of multiple referral in the House and within the network of its standing committees. With a focus on the individual interests of the membership, we next discuss why multiple referral has emerged in the contemporary House. Last, we consider the implications of multiple referral for the traditional link between the strength of the committee system and the strength of the House as an institution.

We contend that the adoption of multiple referral has transformed the operation of the committee system from one in which the standing committees acted as relatively autonomous actors to one in which they do not. Moreover, in evaluating this development from the perspective of both individual and institutional interests, we challenge the validity of a now prominent theme in the current congressional literature. In general, this theme presumes that an intractable tension, if not inherent incompatibility, exists between individual and institutional interests and that institutional developments in the contemporary House reflect the triumph of individualistic concerns over institutional ones. We argue that, as with most institutional developments that are lasting, multiple referral can be explained as a positive, albeit imperfect, response to both individual and institutional concerns.

## Bill Referral in the Modern House

In historical perspective, the adoption of multiple referral represents a turning point for the House that is potentially as significant as the development of the standing committees. Prior to its adoption, House committees had long enjoyed the opportunity to act as autonomous bodies within their jurisdictions. Only during the early Congresses, when committee decision making on bills was often guided or controlled by the floor,[9] and during the years of Thomas Reed's and Joseph Cannon's speakerships, when the leadership of important committees was under the thumb of the majority party leadership,[10] was the autonomy of committees highly constrained. To be sure, there were undoubtedly instances when committees conferred with one another on particular pieces of legislation, but such interaction was necessarily informal and voluntary because House rules precluded the referral of legislation to more than one committee even in the face of multiple committee claims.

As conceived by the 1973-1974 Select Committee on Committees, chaired by Richard Bolling, D-Mo., multiple referral was to accompany the clarification and consolidation of committee jurisdiction in the House. Despite the supplemental nature of multiple referral intended by the Bolling Committee, the House rejected comprehensive jurisdictional realignment but accepted the change in referral procedures.

The new rule generated three types of multiple referral: joint, sequential, and split. A joint referral involves the simultaneous referral of a measure to two or more committees for concurrent consideration. A sequential referral involves the successive referral of a measure to one or more committees in addition to the committee to which the measure was initially referred. A split referral occurs when all or some sections or titles of a particular measure are divided among and concurrently considered by two or more committees.

Since 1977 House rules have empowered the Speaker to impose and extend time limits on all three types of multiple referral. During the 97th (1981-1982) and 98th (1983-1984) Congresses, Speaker Thomas P. O'Neill, Jr., announced two additional clarifications of the way multiple referrals would be handled. In January 1981 the Speaker informed the House that henceforth he would multiply refer bills not only on the basis of the subject matter contained in the original text of the legislation but also on the basis of the subject matter contained in amendments proposed to the bill by the reporting committee. In January 1983 he explicitly asserted that he had authority under the referral rule to designate a primary committee on jointly referred bills and to impose time limits on other committees once the primary committee reported the bill.

Most multiple referrals have been joint referrals without time limits. However, since 1983 the party leadership often has designated primary committees and imposed time limits on bills in which it has a substantial interest. Sequential referrals have been used less frequently and always with time limits, which sometimes have been extended. Split referrals have been used least often because most bills are not easily divided by section or title.[11] In one form or another, however, multiple referral is now employed on a multitude of significant legislation and exists as a prominent feature of congressional operations. Among the legislation multiply referred during the 100th House (1987-1988) were bills concerning trade reform, drug control, welfare reform, budget reconciliation, Federal Trade Commission (FTC) reauthorization, aid to the homeless, catastrophic health care, campaign finance reform, South Africa sanctions, banking deregulation, amendments to the Clean Water Act, airport construction and airline safety, nuclear accident liability, amendments to the Clean Air Act, and extension of the GI bill.

Table 10-1 presents summary statistics on singly and multiply referred bills and resolutions during the 94th-99th (1975-1986) House. The results indicate that the percentage of multiply referred bills and resolutions in the House has fluctuated around 10 percent since the 94th (1975-1976) Congress, peaking at 14 percent in the 99th (1985-1986) Congress. Thus, while single referral has remained the norm, literally hundreds of measures have been referred to multiple committees in each of the past six Congresses.

As Table 10-1 also shows, many of these measures did not survive the committee stage, but neither did many of the bills and resolutions that were singly referred. The attrition rate is not surprising. As is commonly acknowledged, only a small proportion of the thousands of measures introduced in the House are reported out of committee. Still, the percentage of multiply referred legislation reported by committees has increased gradually and, in the three most recent Congresses, surpassed that of singly referred legislation.

On the floor, however, the proportion of singly referred measures passed has been consistently higher than that of multiply referred measures. We attribute the difference to two main factors. First, the body of singly referred legislation includes a large number of minor and even trivial items. For example, "commemorative" bills—measures

Table 10-1    Summary Statistics on Bills and Resolutions in the
94th-99th House of Representatives

| | *Multiple referrals* | | *Reported* | | *Passed* | |
|---|---|---|---|---|---|---|
| *Congress* | Percentage | (N) | Multiple | Single | Multiple | Single |
| 94th (1975-1976) | 6.0 | (1,161) | 3.3% | 8.0% | 2.2% | 8.8% |
| 95th (1977-1978) | 10.3 | (1,833) | 4.4 | 8.8 | 3.0 | 9.8 |
| 96th (1979-1980) | 11.7 | (1,241) | 11.8 | 12.2 | 6.0 | 15.1 |
| 97th (1981-1982) | 9.6 | ( 905) | 11.7 | 8.2 | 6.7 | 11.7 |
| 98th (1983-1984) | 11.6 | ( 965) | 14.1 | 11.5 | 9.9 | 17.3 |
| 99th (1985-1986) | 14.0 | (1,088) | 12.6 | 10.5 | 7.3 | 19.2 |

SOURCE: Walter J. Oleszek, Roger H. Davidson, and Thomas Kephart, "The Incidence and Impact of Multiple Referrals in the House of Representatives" (Washington, D.C.: Congressional Research Service, 1987).

honoring a certain food, product, ethnic group, or cause—typically are singly referred, and their numbers have increased substantially over the past several Congresses. In the 99th Congress, they accounted for roughly half of the bills passed, which helps to explain the sizeable difference shown in Table 10-1 between the success of singly and multiply referred legislation in that Congress.[12] Second, multiply referred bills, by definition, reflect the concerns of several committees and are thus far more likely to involve complex, controversial and important subject matter. Beyond the examples of multiply referred measures previously cited, further testimony to their complexity is provided by floor procedures. Multiply referred measures come to the House floor under rules or through suspension of the rules more than twice as often as singly referred bills.[13] In sum, the fact that multiply referred measures pass less frequently than singly referred measures reveals far more about the bills these two methods of referral typically involve than about the methods themselves.

Another aspect of multiple referral that is worth exploring is its impact at the committee level. For the last several Congresses, multiply referred measures have represented a substantial component of committee work. On the average, they accounted for 23.5, 19.7, 23.0, and 27.6 percent of committee workload during the 96th-99th Houses, respectively. Moreover, multiply referred legislation has represented an ever-increasing proportion of the total number of measures reported out of committee. For the 94th-99th Congresses, this proportion was 2.5, 5.4, 11.4, 13.2, 13.8, and 16.3 percent, respectively.[14] Therefore, the legislation considered by the chamber as a whole is more likely than ever to be legislation that has been shaped by multiple committees.

When combined with the results in Table 10-1, this increase suggests that multiple referral has become a significant aspect of the legislative process in the House even if single referral remains more prevalent. Nonetheless, it would be difficult to argue that multiple referral bears important implications for the committee system in the House if its use were restricted to only a few committees. This is far from the case, as the evidence presented in Table 10-2 and Table 10-3 indicates.

Table 10-2 presents the number of dyadic relationships per committee created under multiple referral during the 96th-98th Houses.[15] The results indicate that each committee has been compelled to share authority over legislation with other committees by virtue of multiple referral. The average number of dyadic relationships per committee was 202, 151, and 154 for the 96th through 98th Congresses, respectively. Quite clearly, the jurisdictions of some committees have lent themselves to multiple referral more readily than others. In each of the three Congresses, the Energy and Commerce Committee was most frequently intertwined with at least one other House committee. At the other end of the scale, several committees—Appropriations, District of Columbia, House Administration, Intelligence, Small Business, and Veterans' Affairs—have been less subject to the linkages engendered by multiple referral. Between these two extremes, however, lies the larger set of committees with jurisdiction in substantive areas of public policy, and they are all regularly engaged in partnerships with other committees through multiple referral.

The results in Tables 10-1 and 10-2 suggest that the use of multiple referral is associated with the development and growing importance of a network of intercommittee liaisons. Table 10-2 confirms that relatively few committees remain disconnected, at least from the network. However, the dyadic frequencies in Table 10-2 obscure the range or extent of intercommittee relationships. That is, they may reflect the frequency with which the same two committees share legislation or they may reflect a number of different committee dyads. While the former would not be unimportant, the latter would imply a far more complex and varied network of intercommittee relationships.

Accordingly, Table 10-3 presents results on the degree to which multiple referral linked each committee to other committees in the House. For each Congress, the first column indicates the percentage of standing committees with which each committee shared legislation under multiple referral. The percentages are striking. On average, each standing committee shared authority with roughly two-thirds to three-quarters of the other committees. Several committees—Armed Services,

Table 10-2 Multiple Referral and the Committee System in the House of Representatives During the 96th-98th Congresses

| | Frequency of shared jurisdiction | | |
|---|---|---|---|
| Committee | 96th | 97th | 98th |
| Agriculture | 183 | 167 | 189 |
| Appropriations | 15 | 19 | 21 |
| Armed Services | 132 | 135 | 138 |
| Banking | 243 | 200 | 199 |
| District of Columbia | 10 | 30 | 19 |
| Education and Labor | 174 | 168 | 214 |
| Energy and Commerce | 822 | 483 | 501 |
| Foreign Affairs | 174 | 166 | 187 |
| Government Operations | 237 | 104 | 117 |
| House Administration | 25 | 21 | 39 |
| Intelligence | 34 | 22 | 18 |
| Interior | 310 | 194 | 188 |
| Judiciary | 351 | 277 | 239 |
| Merchant Marine | 127 | 121 | 105 |
| Post Office | 109 | 133 | 150 |
| Public Works | 166 | 120 | 133 |
| Rules | 171 | 142 | 108 |
| Science and Technology | 226 | 96 | 104 |
| Small Business | 49 | 50 | 52 |
| Veterans' Affairs | 23 | 54 | 41 |
| Ways and Means | 667 | 470 | 462 |
| Average | 202 | 151 | 154 |

SOURCE: Compiled by the authors.

NOTES: The entries represent the number of times each committee shared jurisdiction over a bill or joint resolution with another committee. They are accordingly a reflection of the number of dyadic relationships (per committee) created under the process of multiple referral rather than a raw count of the number of multiply referred measures per committee.

Energy and Commerce, Judiciary, Post Office, and Ways and Means—shared jurisdiction with at least 90 percent of the standing committees during one or more of the three Congresses. While these were at the extreme, each committee was linked at one time or another to more than a quarter of the other standing committees.

The second column of percentages for each Congress indicates the degree to which committee partnerships created at the referral stage were sustained when legislation was reported from committee. The results indicate that with few exceptions committees report legislation with multiple partners. At this stage, the average proportion of

Table 10-3    Committee Interaction on Multiply Referred Bills and
Joint Resolutions in the U.S. House of Representatives
During the 96th-98th Congresses

| | Committee interaction | | | | | |
|---|---|---|---|---|---|---|
| | 96th | | 97th | | 98th | |
| | % Ref. | % Rep. | % Ref. | % Rep. | % Ref. | % Rep. |
| Agriculture | 66.7 | 42.9 | 81.0 | 38.1 | 76.2 | 33.3 |
| Appropriations | 28.0 | 23.8 | 42.9 | 23.8 | 47.6 | 19.0 |
| Armed Services | 85.7 | 42.9 | 95.2 | 70.0 | 90.5 | 33.3 |
| Banking | 76.2 | 33.3 | 85.7 | 38.1 | 85.7 | 42.9 |
| District of Columbia | 38.1 | 0.0 | 71.4 | 8.8 | 57.1 | 4.8 |
| Education and Labor | 76.2 | 28.6 | 76.2 | 33.3 | 85.7 | 47.6 |
| Energy and Commerce | 85.7 | 71.4 | 90.5 | 70.0 | 90.5 | 47.6 |
| Foreign Affairs | 81.0 | 57.1 | 85.7 | 70.0 | 81.0 | 47.6 |
| Government Operations | 81.0 | 33.3 | 71.4 | 19.0 | 81.0 | 33.3 |
| House Administration | 47.6 | 23.8 | 38.1 | 9.5 | 42.9 | 14.3 |
| Intelligence | 38.1 | 19.0 | 42.9 | 9.5 | 28.6 | 23.8 |
| Interior | 81.0 | 61.9 | 85.7 | 57.1 | 76.2 | 38.1 |
| Judiciary | 90.5 | 57.1 | 95.2 | 61.9 | 95.2 | 42.9 |
| Merchant Marine | 61.9 | 52.4 | 76.2 | 47.6 | 66.7 | 42.9 |
| Post Office | 85.7 | 47.6 | 95.2 | 28.6 | 90.5 | 28.6 |
| Public Works | 71.4 | 38.1 | 81.0 | 42.9 | 76.2 | 33.3 |
| Rules | 66.7 | 38.1 | 71.4 | 33.3 | 81.0 | 9.5 |
| Science and Technology | 71.4 | 33.3 | 85.7 | 47.6 | 76.2 | 42.9 |
| Small Business | 47.6 | 38.1 | 81.0 | 23.8 | 61.9 | 14.3 |
| Veterans' Affairs | 52.4 | 4.8 | 76.2 | 23.8 | 61.9 | 9.5 |
| Ways and Means | 95.2 | 76.2 | 90.5 | 47.6 | 90.5 | 52.4 |
| Average | 68.0 | 39.2 | 77.1 | 38.3 | 73.5 | 31.5 |

SOURCE: Compiled by the authors.

NOTE: The first column of percentages for each Congress reflects the percentage of standing committees with whom each committee shared legislation under multiple referral. The second column of percentages for each Congress reflects the percentage of standing committees with whom each committee reported legislation under multiple referral.

committee partners per committee was between 30 percent and 40 percent. In general, then, all committees reported legislation with fewer partners than were created under multiple referral, which is not surprising because some multiply referred legislation dies in committee. In any case, the multiplicity of partnerships created under the referral process, while subject to some erosion, remains quite evident when committees report legislation. As with referral, the proportion of standing committees reporting legislation with one or more other committees varied. Again, Energy and Commerce had the greatest number of partners with whom it reported legislation. Still, the results indicate that when the House is considering multiply referred legislation it is not continually encountering the products of a limited and enduring set of committee partnerships. Rather, it faces legislation that has been shaped by a variety of ad hoc intercommittee liaisons.

Overall, our results indicate that the referral of legislation to multiple committees is now a significant feature of the legislative process in the House. Roughly a thousand bills and resolutions are multiply referred each Congress, including a substantial portion of the most important business introduced for consideration. Few committees have been immune from the liaisons created under multiple referral, and several of the most important committees in the House find themselves with a variety of committee partners during the legislative session.

In light of this evidence, we maintain that the committee system in the House is now operationally quite different than before the adoption of multiple referral. The "new" committee system is characterized by an interdependence among committees that multiple referral now permits if not encourages. Interdependence, however, is but part of the story. Not only do committees now share authority with other committees, most of them share authority with a wide variety of other committees. Although some partnerships are undoubtedly more regular than others, the breadth or variety of these intercommittee unions implies that an equally important characteristic of the "new" committee system is its flexibility.

## Multiple Referral in Individual Perspective

Gauged by conventional wisdom, the adoption and persistence of multiple referral borders on the paradoxical. On the one hand, legislators and scholars acknowledge that committee jurisdictions are jealously guarded by committee members. Stories of jurisdictional infighting are legion, and turf protection so pronounced as to have frustrated all but the most minor changes in committee jurisdictions since 1945. On the other hand, multiple referral is now an important part of the legislative process. Thus, the same legislators who are characteristically engaged in the protection of committee "property rights" have created and supported a system where those property rights can be regularly violated and, given the precedents established by Speaker O'Neill, violated both during and subsequent to initial referral.

The paradox, then, is rooted in the uneasy coexistence of multiple referral and what almost everyone agrees is highly valuable committee turf. We are unwilling to conclude that for more than a decade House members have lived with a rule that is incompatible with their interests.

Rather, we interpret the arrival of multiple referral as a signal that committee turf is no longer what it has been cracked up to be. Our immediate concern is to identify the circumstances that would persuade members to share bills across committees.

Let us begin by exploring what was gained and what was lost by the adoption of multiple referral. Prior to its adoption, committee members could be certain of maintaining exclusive authority over the legislation referred to their committee, but they could not be certain of obtaining all legislation properly falling within their committee's jurisdiction. With the adoption of multiple referral, the situation is reversed: committee members can no longer be certain of maintaining exclusive authority over the legislation referred to their committee, but they can be virtually certain of obtaining all the legislation to which they have claims. In opting for multiple referral, therefore, legislators have reduced the uncertainties associated with committees' access to legislation, but increased the uncertainties associated with committees' autonomy over legislation. They have, in short, surrendered autonomy for access.

To explain the adoption and persistence of multiple referral, it is therefore necessary to explain why access has become more valuable to committee members—and thus to legislators in general—than autonomy. In the discussion that follows, we identify two primary conditions that are consistent with the maintenance of a system *prohibiting* multiple referral. These conditions deal with the relationship among member preferences, committee jurisdictions, and dimensions of public policy. Then we examine several institutional developments that suggest that these conditions no longer obtain.

The first condition concerns the correspondence between legislators' preferences and the jurisdictional arrangement associated with the existing committee system. Let us presume that a system of standing committees with fixed and relatively distinct jurisdictions assigns different dimensions of public policy to the jurisdictional domain of different committees. In other words, the jurisdictional arrangement associated with the standing committee system "bundles" the dimensions of the policy agenda into a set of *available* areas of specialization. Because legislators are usually prohibited from belonging to all committees, they must select from among the set of dimensional bundles established by committee jurisdictions those that best approximate the dimensions of public policy toward which they wish to devote a disproportionate amount of their time and effort.

Unfortunately, there is no guarantee that the available areas of specialization will be those in which legislators actually prefer to specialize. When there is a close correspondence between available and preferred areas of specialization, legislators have a strong incentive to maintain a system prohibiting multiple referral because such a system enables committee members to retain exclusive control of the legislation they presumably deem most important. In general, the greater the correspondence between available and preferred areas of specialization, the more unwilling legislators will be to surrender their exclusive control of committee bills. Therefore, the bundling condition establishes that the value of a system prohibiting multiple referral is contingent on the degree to which *available* and *preferred* areas of specialization coincide.

The second condition concerns the relationship between committee jurisdictions and dimensions of public policy. As noted, the rules of the House that define committee jurisdictions provide each committee with a fixed and specific set of policy questions over which it has authority. In a formal sense, then, committee jurisdictions in the House are separate or discrete. However, this does not mean that the policy dimensions associated with different committee jurisdictions are independent from one another. If dimensions of policy are *independent,* we may infer that changes along one dimension have no impact on any other. If dimensions of policy are *interdependent,* we may infer that changes along one dimension will have ramifications for at least one and possibly multiple dimensions of policy.

If dimensions of policy are independent, legislators have a strong incentive to maintain a system prohibiting multiple referral because all committee members can be certain that policy decisions made in other committees will not affect policy within their own committee's jurisdiction. Policy interdependence is not necessarily incompatible with the prohibition of multiple referral, as long as the interdependencies are captured *within* committee jurisdictions. Because, in such a case, the effects of the interdependencies may be managed and negotiated within committee, legislators retain an incentive to sustain a system prohibiting multiple referral. Problems occur when policy interdependencies cross-cut committee jurisdictions. In such cases, committee members have an incentive to surrender their exclusive control of committee bills precisely because they recognize that decisions made on policy outside jurisdictional boundaries have an impact on policy inside jurisdictional boundaries. Therefore, the "independence" condition establishes that the value of a system prohibiting multiple referral is contingent on the degree to which the policy dimensions associated with the jurisdictions of different committees are unrelated to one another.

Of the two conditions we have identified as compatible with the maintenance of a system that prohibits multiple referral, the independence condition is the more critical. One reason is that bundling problems can be alleviated by institutional remedies far less severe than the adoption of multiple referral. For example, if legislators become increasingly disenchanted with the available areas of specialization associated with the existing jurisdictional arrangement, then new committees and subcommittees may be created or committee and subcommittee memberships enlarged. In contrast, legislators who wish to avoid the ramifications of multiple referral for committee autonomy have one rather extreme alternative in the face of cross-jurisdictional policy interdependencies, which is to reorganize the jurisdictional arrangement so that policy interdependencies no longer crosscut committee jurisdictions. Even this solution will prove inadequate if cross-jurisdictional interdependencies are particularly widespread. As important or more important is the second reason. The existence of policy interdependencies that crosscut committee jurisdictions virtually ensures that legislators will be dissatisfied with existing jurisdictional arrangements. Therefore, when the independence condition does not obtain, chances are that the bundling condition does not obtain either.

Needless to say, neither the bundling nor the independence condition has ever been strictly inviolate. There has probably always been some level of disparity between available and preferred areas of specialization as well as some degree of cross-jurisdictional policy interdependence. Nonetheless, evidence suggests that both bundling problems and cross-jurisdictional policy interdependencies have been especially acute in the recent House.

First, let us consider developments in the House in light of the bundling condition. As already stated, one remedy for bundling problems is to enlarge the existing committee system, either by increasing the number of committees and subcommittees or by expanding their memberships. Such developments clearly preceded the adoption of multiple referral. While the number of committees increased marginally and gradually, the increase in the number and authority of subcommittees was almost explosive. These developments were accompanied by the expansion of committee and subcommittee assignments.[16] Thus, structural differentiation did not result in the concentration of member effort but in its dispersal, which in itself implies the inadequacy of "available" areas of specialization.

Despite these adjustments, House members increasingly delved into areas outside their committee work, and freshmen became, by most accounts, as likely to be heard as seen.[17] In addition, committee products were increasingly challenged on the floor.[18] One interpretation of this behavior is that House members no longer found specialization as appealing as they once did. Another, which is compatible with our perspective, is that House members increasingly found that the areas in which they could specialize were not the areas in which they wished to specialize.

Altogether, these developments provide a strong case that the disjuncture between available and preferred areas of specialization increased over the last few decades. But a bundling problem has not been the only, nor the most critical, stimulus to the adoption and maintenance of multiple referral. As we argued earlier, if bundling problems were the only problems legislators faced, the need for multiple referral would be far less compelling given the availability of less painful institutional remedies, of most of which House members have apparently already availed themselves.

Second, and more important, has been the development of a deep and pervasive web of policy interdependencies that crosscut committee jurisdictions. Figure 10-1 presents a map of the jurisdictional interdependencies based on shared and overlapping subject matter among nineteen of the twenty standing committees in the 96th (1979-1980) House. As Figure 10-1 shows, the interconnections among committees in the contemporary House are considerable. On the average, each committee considers policy that is related to the jurisdictional subject matter of almost eight other committees. The jurisdictions of six committees—Agriculture, Commerce, Interior, Judiciary, Merchant Marine, and Ways and Means—overlap those of at least ten other standing committees. Only the jurisdiction of Small Business is relatively self-contained.

Particularly worth noting is that there are no obvious clusters of overlap among committees. Rather, each committee's jurisdiction is connected with a variety of other committees. At the time, for example, energy policy involved the action of no less than fifteen of the standing committees; aspects of environmental policy, that of eleven; and natural resources policy, the efforts of six.[19] These numbers imply that jurisdictional realignment of any kind might reduce cross-jurisdictional interdependencies but would hardly eradicate them. In short, Figure 10-1 is testimony that the independence condition has been severely violated, if not vitiated, in the recent House.

This violation should not be surprising. The probability that such interdependencies will proliferate increases as the government becomes more active: the more the government does, the more likely the things it does will "bump" into one another, and the more likely the existing jurisdictional arrangement will fail to capture the interdependencies that exist. In view of the increasing scope of federal activity that has characterized policy making over the last several decades, it would be amazing indeed if existing jurisdictional arrangements in the House did not fall far short of capturing the interdependencies endemic to the

Figure 10-1    Jurisdictional Overlap Among Standing House Committees, 96th Congress

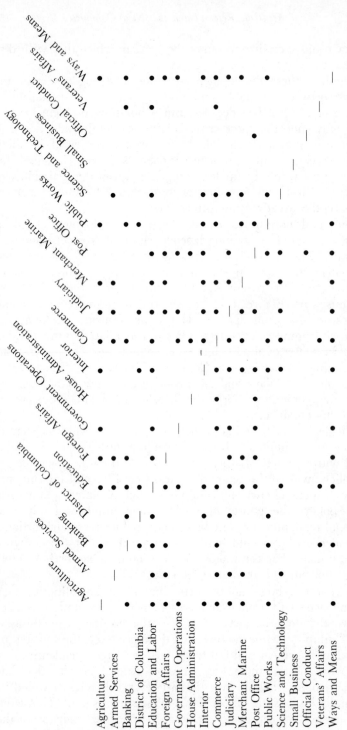

SOURCE: Compiled by the authors based on information in the *Final Report of the Select Committee on Committees*, H. Rept. 96-866, April 1, 1980, 404-416.

NOTE:    For each committee, a bullet represents jurisdictional overlap based on shared or similar subject matter pertaining to the jurisdiction of another committee.

current political agenda. It would be even more amazing if legislators were insensitive to the interdependencies. These days they have plenty of reminders. As Hugh Heclo[20] notes, President Dwight Eisenhower could propose a new interstate highway program in 1954 that was initiated, debated, and executed with minimal attention to nonhighway considerations. Today, such a program is likely to attract debates over the private car versus mass transportation, energy conservation, environmental impact, effects on urban development and neighborhoods, minority contracting, and regional development. Recent controversies over health care costs, energy, drug control, economic revitalization, trade, air and water pollution, welfare, and the banking system testify to policy considerations that inherently cut across jurisdictional boundaries. In sum, the value of an autonomy-for-access trade becomes likely if not necessary in the face of a political agenda that virtually defies well-defined and nonoverlapping compartmentalization within a system of standing committees.

If we are correct, the coincidence of multiple referral and the jurisdictional profile of the House is no accident, and the adoption of multiple referral far from paradoxical. On the contrary, it is a change that is understandable in light of the way policy, preferences, and jurisdictions now interrelate. This is not to deny that committee reorganization could trim the degree of jurisdictional overlap in the House and in so doing reduce its reliance on multiple referral. In the Senate, for example, multiple referral appears to have declined after committee reorganization in 1977.[21] Moreover, the House probably had little choice but to introduce multiple referral once it rejected the committee reorganization proposals of the Bolling Committee in 1974. In opting for multiple referral, however, members did more than simply choose the lesser of two evils. In this regard, the central and determining point to be borne in mind is that modern public policy involves such a high degree of interdependence across policy dimensions that no jurisdictional arrangement is likely to supply the incentives necessary to reestablish a system based exclusively on single referral. There is, in short, no way of resurrecting the political conditions of the nineteenth or even the mid-twentieth century no matter how much we may prize simplicity and neatness. From this perspective, legislators would have been irrational indeed had they not recognized the ways multiple referral advanced their personal interests just as they recognized the ways committee reorganization threatened them.

## Multiple Referral in Institutional Perspective

Given the historic nature of multiple referral, an equally important question is whether multiple referral is as valuable for the House as an institution as it would appear to be for its members. Such a query is by no means trivial. Indeed, a predominant theme in much of the current literature on Congress is that a deep and abiding conflict exists between individual and institutional interests and that institutional developments represent the triumph of individual concerns over institutional concerns. Typically, this theme is developed by identifying pivotal aspects of behavior and structure that can be attributed to member election and/or power goals but produce highly negative consequences for Congress as an institution. Well-known examples include Richard Fenno's analysis of members running for reelection by running "against" Congress, Lawrence Dodd and Richard Schott's analysis of the reasons behind institutional decentralization, and David Mayhew's and Morris Fiorina's analyses of member behavior and its institutional consequences.[22]

At first glance, the adoption of multiple referral seems only to confirm existing presumptions about the conflict between individual and institutional interests. Whatever its benefits for individual members, it appears highly detrimental to Congress's institutional strength and effectiveness. Underlying this assessment is a two-part logic that equates the strength and power of the standing committees with the strength and power of Congress.

The first part defines the important functions standing committees perform in satisfying the House's basic institutional needs. Now, as in the past, these functions are identified in terms of the role standing committees play in anchoring the division of labor in the House, with emphasis on their virtues as sifters and refiners of congressional policy.[23] Scholars also have acknowledged the contributions standing committees make to integration by facilitating the building of majorities and to motivation by inducing members to do substantive legislative work.[24]

With the functional contributions of the standing committee system identified, the second part of the logic establishes a direct and immediate tie between a powerful, effective standing committee system and institutional effectiveness. This equation, which lay at the heart of Woodrow Wilson's dissatisfaction with "congressional government," has been integral to four major reform efforts over the past fifty years, each of which identified strengthening the committee system as a primary objective.[25] Moreover, the linkage between committee power and institutional power has underlain a variety of less abrupt but even more critical institutional developments. For example, it is on this basis that the standing committees gained preeminence over the Committee of the Whole and select committees during the early nineteenth century, achieved automatic and exclusive power over referral and virtually unchallengeable discretion over reporting during the late nineteenth century, and assumed a dominant role in oversight as well as legislation during the twentieth century.[26] Thus, numerous historical examples support the conclusion that Congress has sought to strengthen itself institutionally by strengthening its system of standing committees.

In the context of this logic, multiple referral is a mechanism of dubious institutional benefit. The rationale that supports the power and prerogatives of a standing committee system identifies institutional effectiveness not with the ad hoc committee liaisons engendered by multiple referral but with the establishment of clear, comprehensive, permanent, and exclusive committee jurisdictions. At best, then, the traditional logic would accord multiple referral the status of an expedient, if not tortured, accommodation to political reality that provides no adequate substitute for what really needs to be done—jurisdictional realignment.

And yet it can be argued that the traditional view is outmoded, that it is based on assumptions about conditions that no longer exist. To develop a perspective that identifies and validates the institutional benefits of multiple referral, we shall draw selectively from a wide range of organizational analysis that deals with the relationship between an organization's environment and its structure and effectiveness.[27] Organization theorists now regard this relationship as contingent. That is, contemporary research indicates that no one form of organizational design is best; rather the value of particular designs varies in terms of the context or environment in which an organization exists. Two environmental variables are of primary importance: complexity and dynamism.[28]

Complexity refers to the character and configuration of an organization's environment at a fixed point in time. It varies according to the number and variety of environmental attributes that affect organizational operations and performance, the degree of interdependence among environmental attributes, and the state of knowledge concerning these attributes—in other words, the degree to which rational analysis can be applied to provide understanding of the relationships among attributes and their impacts. High degrees of complexity accordingly impair an organization's ability to order and regularize its relations with its environment.

Dynamism may be understood as movement or change over time in basic environmental attributes. Here too several determinants exist. Rapid, comprehensive change in an organization's environment disrupts established organizational routines and renders past organizational learning outmoded. Moreover, to the degree that change is not only rapid and comprehensive but also volatile and unpatterned, it resists analysis on the basis of existing knowledge. Thus, high degrees of dynamism also make events unpredictable and environmental relations difficult to order and regularize.

Contemporary organization theory therefore distinguishes between organizations that exist in simple and stable environments, complex and stable environments, simple and dynamic environments, and complex and dynamic environments.[29] And, as we have discussed, the idea is that different organizational designs are suitable to different organizational environments.

Research indicates that the key to successful organizational performance in complex and dynamic environments is to adopt more fluid and flexible forms of organizational structure.[30] A common strategy for accomplishing this result is to expand lateral relations within the organization, in other words, to create and multiply new patterns of interaction that crisscross existing vertical distributions of authority and tasks at various points in the organizational structure. Such expansions can take many forms, from the creation of temporary task forces or project teams to the establishment of high-level coordinators or coordinating teams to the introduction of formally structured matrices in which traditional functional lines of authority are permanently displaced.[31]

Designs that increase lateral relations enhance an organization's capacity for division of labor by permitting specialized expertise to be brought to bear more flexibly in relation to specific problems or tasks without the limits that rigid functional divisions entail. At the same time, they enhance integrative capability both by facilitating interaction among influential participants at earlier stages of decision making and by introducing new mechanisms of integration whose benefits cannot be matched by the traditional strategies of extending hierarchical authority, elaborating formal routines, or expanding information control.[32] In short, such designs involve organic forms of structure that enhance an organization's ability to deal with an environment in which increasing complexity and dynamism combine to threaten its viability.

In the context of organization theory, multiple referral may be viewed as a mechanism for enhancing lateral relations in a legislative institution, such as the House, where relations among members are collegial rather than hierarchical, where committees anchor the division of labor system, and parties the integrative system.[33] So viewed, multiple referral exists as an adaptive response to the House's needs as an institution rather than an expedient means of avoiding committee reorganization. However, to validate this claim it is necessary to establish that the environment of the House has become more complex and dynamic, that the result has been to strain the operational effectiveness of its committee and party systems, and that multiple referral has helped to relieve these strains.

As far as impacts on structure are concerned, the two most important elements in the House's proximate environment are the executive establishment and the electorate.[34] A variety of evidence testifies to increasing levels of complexity and dynamism in both, particularly during the 1970s when multiple referral was first introduced in the House.

Regarding the executive establishment, Herbert Kaufman has shown not only that the number of federal agencies increased over the period 1945-1973, but also that during the 1960s and 1970s their number grew at an accelerated rate.[35] The greatest change occurred between 1969 and 1972 when fifty-seven new federal organizations (an 18.2 percent increase over the previous four-year period) were created. In 1973 alone twenty-three new organizations were created. The expansion in the number of agencies went hand in hand with an expansion in bureaucratic discretion and in the variety or range of government activities.[36] Partial evidence (if any is needed) is provided by the *Federal Register,* the pages of which increased almost geometrically from the fifties through the seventies, with a particularly sharp rise during the early 1970s.[37] Moreover, as Heclo notes, the expansion in the number of federal activities brought with it an increase in the overlap and interrelatedness of issues and interests. Within two years after the creation of the Energy Department, for example, it was necessary to assemble twenty-two other federal departments and agencies to provide for the coordination of energy policy.[38] In sum, a number of trends concerning the executive establishment indicate that its structure has become more differentiated and more volatile and its tasks more extensive and more interrelated, all of which suggest increased complexity and dynamism.

To examine changes in complexity and dynamism within the electorate, we can look first at the status of the primary basis of regularity and predictability in the electoral process: party-in-the-electorate.[39] Here again, recent decades mark substantial change. Between 1960 and 1972 the percentage of split-ticket voting rose from 32 percent to 65 percent, increasing with each successive presidential election. Likewise, the percentage of independents rose from a low of 20 percent in 1958 to a high of 38 percent in 1974 and, after 1964, increased with each congressional election. These changes imply that what historically had been the most reliable and enduring basis of support for congressional candidates became increasingly unreliable and fragile. This change occurred alongside the mobilization of new, diverse, and intense groups, most of whom have a direct interest in various aspects of government activity and few of whom are inclined toward bargaining and compromise.[40] Since the mid-1970s the continuing disjunction between presidential and congressional voting patterns[41] as well as the rising costs of campaigns[42] have only exacerbated an electoral environment already fraught with crosscutting interests and issues as well as uncertainty and volatility.

When these factors are considered, it is no wonder that the modern House has exhibited signs of severe structural strain that are characteristic of institutions faced with highly complex and dynamic environments. Once again, these signs were particularly evident in the 1970s, a decade characterized by repeated attempts at party and committee reform.[43] In terms of division of labor the existence of strain was apparent in the high incidence of conflict in committee meetings, the proliferation of subcommittees, and the range and intensity of jurisdictional conflicts.[44] In terms of integration it was evidenced by the decline in party voting to historic lows, the decline of committee power on the floor as norms of deference and reciprocity eroded, and the rapid expansion of the whip system in the majority party.[45]

The introduction of multiple referral in the mid-1970s and its further growth and development in the 1980s have not eliminated strain in the operations of the House. Although altered in its precise manifestations by changing environmental circumstances, structural strain continues because it is too deeply rooted in the complexity and dynamism of the environment the House confronts to be cured by mechanistic innovations. Thus, for example, whereas party unity in the House has increased in large part because of changes in the electoral bases of southern Democrats, the budget process has been repeatedly threatened with breakdown because of the manner in which constituent program demands conflict with constituent support for taxation.[46]

With this caveat noted, what also should be recognized is that multiple referral has played a significant role in relieving the burdens the House's environment imposes on its party and committee systems. The growth and development of the device in the 1980s has in fact enhanced the House's capacity for both division of labor and integration.

As is the case generally of mechanisms that expand lateral relations, multiple referral enables the House to mobilize the expertise of its committees in far more flexible and efficient ways. Whether trade, health, or pollution programs are at issue, the House can now bring to bear all the forms of expertise needed to deal with the varied and wide-ranging problems these programs involve and do so at the stage in which policy is first examined and formulated. Even more important, given the fact that in the American political system legislatures are above all integrating institutions, multiple referral has enhanced the

House's capability for building majority coalitions and passing laws.

This is not to deny that by nature multiple referral increases the number of veto points and thus can produce delay or even obstruction. Such results, however, can be limited through the use of time limits, and, in any case, the same range of conflicting interests has to be faced and majority support assembled whether a bill is multiply or singly referred. Still, the primary reasons multiple referral enhances integrative capability are positive, not negative. The controlling point is that multiple referral restructures legislative decision making so that on balance the benefits for integration outweigh the costs.[47] The key to its power in this regard extends beyond its effects in institutionalizing the reconciliation of interests in a broader manner and at an earlier stage than single referral. As in the case of expansions in lateral relations generally, multiple referral has stimulated the creation of new integrating roles and techniques, and the resulting impact on integration has been substantial.

As might be expected in a legislative body, this expansion in integrating roles and techniques has taken the form of an expansion in the activities and leverage of the majority party leadership. On the one hand, multiple referral has made the committees more dependent on the assistance of the majority party leadership. The leadership has substantial discretion over the multiple referral of bills and the setting of time limits. It also controls the two principal mechanisms through which multiply referred bills gain access to the floor: the Rules Committee and the suspension calendar. Last but not least, committees anxious to pass legislation on matters such as homeless aid, catastrophic health care, South Africa sanctions, trade, or welfare need an honest broker, and the leadership exists as the main source for providing such services or superintending their provision by an influential committee leader.[48]

On the other hand, multiple referral has allowed the leadership to capitalize on existing sources of leverage and in so doing to extend its role and influence. Recent Congresses have witnessed an expansion in the number and variety of restrictive rules. This development, which increases the leadership's power to control the character and fate of legislation, has a close connection to multiple referral.[49] Not only are such rules applied more often to multiply referred bills, the need to protect committee bargains from unravelling on the floor provides a prime inducement to members to accept harsh limits on their ability to offer floor amendments. Finally, because several committees can now often claim jurisdiction over important bills, the number of conferees on such bills has multiplied.[50] This change also has added to leadership power and responsibility both in terms of expanded discretion over the choice of conferees and in terms of an expanded role in reconciling differences among conferees over the House position.

In sum, then, multiple referral need not be rejected on the basis of the traditional logic that links committee power and institutional effectiveness. This logic assumes an absolute tie between these variables when, in fact, the tie is contingent and far less governing than in the past. Policy questions and issue divisions are now too varied, interrelated, and volatile to be compartmentalized within rigid jurisdictional boxes, even if the contours of these boxes were to be redesigned. As in other organizational contexts where high levels of complexity and dynamism prevail, organizational effectiveness is enhanced when fixed and mechanistic structures are replaced by more fluid and organic ones. In the House, multiple referral represents exactly such a device. Although not without its warts and certainly not the only factor that has shaped the contemporary House, multiple referral constitutes a highly adaptive response to the aggregate of demanding circumstances the House now confronts. It is thus no accident that the story of important legislation in the House of the late 1980s is often a story of multiple referral, increased interaction among committees, and heightened leadership activity and influence. Indeed, this is a case in which it validly can be said that if multiple referral did not exist, it or some surrogate would have to be invented.

## Conclusion

In this analysis, we have had a number of purposes. The first was to highlight the fact that multiple referral has become an important feature of the legislative process in the House and has transformed its operations both in committee and on the floor. The second was to explain why members in the 1970s and 1980s would choose to institute and expand such a basic alteration in historic methods of doing business in the House. A final aim was to point out that multiple referral has positive consequences for institutional effectiveness as well, that it serves individual and institutional interests at one and the same time.

Many may find this last conclusion difficult to accept, given the emphasis much of the recent congressional literature has placed on individual self-interest. In closing, then, a few words on some very basic issues regarding institutional operation and performance are in order.

Conflicts between individual and institutional interests are endemic in all organizations. Still, organizations do not have to resolve this problem completely. What they have to accomplish is to master such conflict by reconciling individual and institutional interests in a manner that sustains the support of external constituencies and maintains the involvement of internal participants. This task is a continuing one. It is also one whose demands change as circumstances change. Nonetheless, to persist organizations must succeed in accommodating individual and institutional interests, and the higher the levels of accommodation they can achieve the higher their levels of performance are likely to be.

That multiple referral can serve both individual and institutional interests is therefore not surprising. The committee system as a whole accomplishes the same result. It serves the interests members have in reelection and personal power and defers to their policy commitments, while structuring their behavior so that it contributes to collective capacity for division of labor and integration. In a similar fashion, multiple referral protects the stakes members have in their formal positions in the organizational structure of the House and capitalizes on their desires for policy outputs, while rendering the application of expertise to problems more effective and enhancing the majority-building capability of party leaders.

Thus, the point is that the basic structures and processes of the House, just like those of any organization, must accomplish exactly what we have argued multiple referral does accomplish. To be sure, in the case of the House or any other organization, patterns of structure and process cannot eradicate conflict between individual and institutional interests; rather, benefits here as elsewhere are seldom achieved without costs. Nonetheless, such patterns must balance these interests; they must order the distribution of benefits and costs so that members remain engaged as individuals and organizations function and persist as collectivities, as systems of coordinated effort. It is time, therefore, for students of Congress to pay more attention to analyzing the conditions and modes of achieving such balances rather than focusing on the conflicts that exist or the manner in which members exploit institutional positions and resources for their own narrow advantage. In truth, if the story of organizations was nothing more than a story of conflict and exploitation, it is doubtful that organizations would be created and certain that they would not persist.

# Notes

1. Joseph Cooper, *The Origins of the Standing Committees and the Development of the Modern House* (Houston: Rice University Publications, 1970).
2. Richard F. Fenno, Jr., *Congressmen in Committees* (Boston: Little, Brown, 1973); Lawrence C. Dodd and Richard L. Schott, *Congress and*

*the Administrative State* (New York: John Wiley, 1979); Steven S. Smith and Christopher J. Deering, *Committees in Congress* (Washington, D.C.: CQ Press, 1984).

3. Leroy N. Rieselbach, *Congressional Politics* (New York: McGraw-Hill, 1973); Joseph Cooper, "Congress in Organizational Perspective," in *Congress Reconsidered*, 1st ed., ed. Lawrence C. Dodd and Bruce I. Oppenheimer (New York: Praeger, 1977); Barbara Hinckley, *Stability and Change in Congress*, 2d ed. (New York: Harper & Row, 1983).

4. Kenneth A. Shepsle, "Institutional Arrangements and Equilibrium in Multidimensional Voting Models," *American Journal of Political Science* 23 (1979): 27-59; Peter C. Ordeshook and Thomas Schwartz, "Agendas and the Control of Political Outcomes," *American Political Science Review* 81 (March 1987): 179-200; Barry R. Weingast, "Floor Behavior in Congress: Committee Power Under the Open Rule" (Working Paper P-88-2, Hoover Institution, Stanford University, 1988).

5. Richard F. Fenno, Jr., *The Power of the Purse* (Boston: Little, Brown, 1966); Kenneth A. Shepsle and Barry R. Weingast, "The Institutional Foundations of Committee Power," *American Political Science Review* 81 (March 1987): 85-104; Keith Krehbiel, Kenneth A. Shepsle, and Barry R. Weingast, "Why Are Congressional Committees Powerful?" *American Political Science Review* 81 (September 1987): 929-948.

6. Arthur T. Denzau and Robert J. Mackay, "Gatekeeping and Monopoly Power of Committees: An Analysis of Sincere and Sophisticated Behavior," *American Journal of Political Science* 27 (November 1983): 740-761.

7. Roger H. Davidson, "The Legislative Work of Congress" (Paper delivered at the annual meeting of the American Political Science Association, Washington, D.C., 1986). The Senate in 1977, as part of its reorganization of committee jurisdictions and assignments, instituted a new rule that provided for multiple referral upon the joint motion of the majority and minority leaders. However, the Senate continues to multiply refer by unanimous consent, and the leaders insist only on being consulted in advance. See Gregory B. Williams, "Multiple Referral: Its Uses and Implications from a Bicameral Perspective" (Unpublished senior honors thesis, Harvard University, 1985).

8. Walter J. Oleszek, "Multiple Referral of Legislation in the House" (Paper delivered at the annual meeting of the American Political Science Association, Washington, D.C., 1980); Walter J. Oleszek, Roger H. Davidson, and Thomas Kephart, "The Incidence and Impact of Multiple Referrals in the House of Representatives" (Washington, D.C.: Congressional Research Service, 1987); Joseph Cooper and Melissa P. Collie, "Structural Adaptation in the House: Multiple Reference and Interunit Committees in Organizational Perspective" (Paper presented at the annual meeting of the American Political Science Association, New York, 1981); Roger H. Davidson and Walter J. Oleszek, "From Monopoly to Interaction: Changing Patterns in Committee Management of Legislation in the House" (Paper delivered at the annual meeting of the Midwest Political Science Association, Chicago, Illinois, 1987); Roger H. David-

son, Walter J. Oleszek, and Thomas Kephart, "One Bill, Many Committees: Multiple Referrals in the U.S. House of Representatives," *Legislative Studies Quarterly* 15 (February 1988): 3-28.

9. Cooper, *Origins of the Standing Committees.*

10. Joseph Cooper and David W. Brady, "Institutional Context and Leadership Style: The House from Cannon to Rayburn," *American Political Science Review* 75 (June 1981): 411-426.

11. Davidson and Oleszek, "From Monopoly to Interaction," 6.

12. Lawrence J. Haas, "Commemoratives: Cheaper than Bacon," *National Journal,* May 7, 1988, 1198.

13. Davidson, Oleszek, and Kephart, "One Bill, Many Committees," 18.

14. Oleszek, Davidson, and Kephart, "The Incidence and Impact of Multiple Referrals."

15. The results reported in Table 10-2 and Table 10-3 exclude the Budget Committee. However, note that the reconciliation bill, the most important piece of legislation the Budget Committee manages, is by its nature multiply referred. For statistics on the Budget Committee and multiple referral, see Davidson, Oleszek, and Kephart, "One Bill, Many Committees."

16. Dodd and Schott, *Congress and the Administrative State;* Smith and Deering, *Committees in Congress;* and Michael C. Munger, "Allocation of Desirable Committee Assignments: Extended Queues versus Committee Expansion," *American Journal of Political Science* 32 (May 1988): 317-344.

17. Dodd and Schott, *Congress and the Administrative State;* Smith and Deering, *Committees in Congress;* Norman J. Ornstein, "The House and the Senate in a New Congress," in *The New Congress,* ed. Thomas E. Mann and Norman J. Ornstein (Washington, D.C.: American Enterprise Institute, 1981).

18. Steven S. Smith, "Why Don't We Do It on the Floor?" Brookings Institution Discussion Paper Series No. 5 (Washington, D.C.: Brookings Institution, 1986).

19. H. Rept. 96-866, 1980. In Figure 10-1 the Commerce Committee is the Interstate and Foreign Commerce Committee, renamed the Energy and Commerce Committee in 1981.

20. Hugh Heclo, "One Executive Branch or Many?" in *Both Ends of the Avenue,* ed. Anthony King (Washington, D.C.: American Enterprise Institute), 33.

21. Williams, "Multiple Referral." Multiple referral is less common in the Senate than the House. The percentage of bills multiply referred and the proportion of committee workload accounted for by multiply referred bills are only about half those of the House. These differences, however, are more attributable to the broader span of committee assignments held by individual senators, the greater ease of introducing amendments to committee bills on the floor, and the greater ease of combining committee bills into omnibus bills on the floor than to the neater system of committee jurisdictions that prevails in the Senate. In short, the smaller size and

greater informality of the Senate make the bundling condition easier to satisfy and the impacts of interdependence less severe. Nonetheless, multiple referral has become an important feature of Senate as well as House procedure. See Davidson, "The Legislative Work of Congress."

22. Richard F. Fenno, Jr., *Home Style: House Members in Their Districts* (Boston: Little, Brown, 1978), 164-68; Dodd and Schott, *Congress and the Administrative State;* David R. Mayhew, *Congress: The Electoral Connection* (New Haven, Conn.: Yale University Press, 1974); Morris P. Fiorina, *Congress: Keystone of the Washington Establishment* (New Haven, Conn.: Yale University Press, 1977).

23. Cooper, *Origins of the Standing Committees;* Charles O. Jones, *The United States Congress: People, Place and Policy* (Homewood, Ill.: Dorsey Press, 1982); Arthur Maass, *Congress and the Common Good* (New York: Basic Books, 1983); Roger H. Davidson and Walter Oleszek, *Congress and Its Members,* 2d ed. (Washington, D.C.: CQ Press, 1985).

24. Fenno, *Congressmen in Committees;* Mayhew, *Congress: The Electoral Connection;* Davidson and Oleszek, *Congress and Its Members;* Kenneth A. Shepsle, *The Giant Jigsaw Puzzle* (Chicago: University of Chicago Press, 1979); Peter Woll, *Congress* (Boston: Little, Brown, 1983); Barry R. Weingast and William J. Marshall, "The Industrial Organization of Congress; or, Why Legislatures, Like Firms, Are Not Organized as Markets," *Journal of Political Economy* 96 (1988): 132-163.

25. Woodrow Wilson, *Congressional Government* (Baltimore: Johns Hopkins University Press, 1981), originally published, 1885. See S. Rept. 79-1011 (Joint Committee on Organization of the Congress, 1946); S. Rept. 89-1414 (Joint Committee on Legislative Reorganization, 1966); H. Rept. 93-916 (Bolling Committee, 1974); H. Doc. 95-272 (Obey Commission, 1977); and H. Rept. 96-866 (Patterson Committee, 1980). For legislative histories of these reform efforts, see Roger H. Davidson and Walter Oleszek, *Congress Against Itself* (Bloomington: Indiana University Press, 1977); and Smith and Deering, *Committees in Congress.*

26. Joseph Cooper, *Congress and Its Committees* (Unpublished Ph.D. diss., Harvard, 1960).

27. T. Burns and G. M. Stalker, *The Management of Innovation* (London: Tavistock, 1961); J. D. Thompson, *Organizations in Action* (New York: McGraw-Hill, 1967); P. R. Lawrence and J. W. Lorsch, *Organization and Environment* (Boston: Harvard University Press, 1967); Pradip Khandwalla, *The Design of Organizations* (New York: Harcourt, Brace, Jovanovich, 1977); Jay R. Galbraith, *Organizational Design* (Reading, Mass.: Addison-Wesley, 1977); F. E. Kast and J. E. Rosenzweig, *Organization and Management* (New York: McGraw-Hill, 1979); Robert Miles, *Macro Organizational Behavior* (Santa Monica, Calif.: Goodyear Publishing, 1980).

28. Cooper and Collie, "Structural Adaptation in the House."

29. Miles, *Macro Organizational Behavior.*

30. Khandwalla, *The Design of Organizations.*

31. Lawrence and Lorsch, *Organization and Environment;* Galbraith, *Orga-*

*nizational Design.*

32. Galbraith, *Organizational Design.*
33. Cooper and Collie, "Structural Adaptation in the House."
34. Joseph Cooper, "Strengthening the Congress: An Organizational Analysis," *Harvard Journal on Legislation* 12 (1975): 307-368.
35. Herbert Kaufman, *Are Government Organizations Immortal?* (Washington, D.C.: Brookings Institution, 1976).
36. Theodore J. Lowi, *The End of Liberalism* (New York: Norton, 1979); Dodd and Schott, *Congress and the Administrative State.*
37. Norman J. Ornstein, Thomas E. Mann, and Michael J. Malbin, *Vital Statistics on Congress, 1987-1988* (Washington, D.C.: Congressional Quarterly, 1987), 170.
38. Heclo, "One Executive Branch or Many?" 33.
39. Frank J. Sorauf, *Party Politics in America* (Boston: Little, Brown, 1984).
40. Heclo, "One Executive Branch or Many?"
41. Randall L. Calvert and John A. Ferejohn, "Coattail Voting in Recent Presidential Elections," *American Political Science Review* 77 (June 1983): 407-419.
42. Gary C. Jacobson, *The Politics of Congressional Elections* (Boston: Little, Brown, 1987).
43. Smith and Deering, *Committees in Congress;* Davidson and Oleszek, *Congress Against Itself;* Joseph Cooper, "Strengthening the Congress."
44. Smith and Deering, *Committees in Congress;* Davidson and Oleszek, *Congress Against Itself;* H. Rept. 95-272 (Obey Commission): 641-644; H. Rept. 96-866 (Patterson Committee): 1-85.
45. Melissa P. Collie, "Universalism and the Parties in the U.S. House of Representatives, 1921-80," *American Journal of Political Science* 32 (November 1988); Lawrence C. Dodd and Bruce I. Oppenheimer, "The House in Transition: Change and Consolidation," in *Congress Reconsidered,* 2d ed., ed. Lawrence C. Dodd and Bruce I. Oppenheimer (Washington, D.C.: CQ Press, 1981); Dodd and Oppenheimer, "The House in Transition," in *Congress Reconsidered,* 1st ed.; Lawrence C. Dodd and Terry Sullivan, "Majority Party Leadership and Partisan Vote-Gathering: The House Democratic Whip System," in *Understanding Congressional Leadership,* ed. Frank Mackaman (Washington, D.C.: CQ Press, 1982); Barbara Sinclair, "Coping with Uncertainty: Building Coalitions in the House and Senate," in *The New Congress;* Thomas E. Cavanaugh, "Dispersion of Authority in the House of Representatives," *Political Science Quarterly* 97 (1982-1983): 623-638; Steven S. Smith, "Going to the Floor: Changing Patterns of Participation in the U.S. House of Representatives, 1955-1986," Brookings Discussion Paper No. 13 (Washington, D.C.: Brookings Institution, 1987).
46. David W. Rohde, " 'Something's Happening Here; What It Is Ain't Exactly Clear': Southern Democrats in the House of Representatives" (Paper delivered at the Conference in Honor of Richard Fenno, Washington, D.C., 1986).
47. Cooper and Collie, "Structural Adaptation in the House."

48. Note, for example, the role the leadership played in passing the catastrophic health bill in the first session of the 100th Congress (1987). See *Congressional Quarterly Weekly Report,* July 4, 1987, 1437-1438, and July 18, 1987, 1590-1591.
49. Steven S. Smith and Stanley Bach, "Craftsmanship on Capitol Hill: The Pattern of Diversity in Special Rules" (Paper delivered at the annual meeting of the Midwest Political Science Assoeiation, Chicago, Illinois, 1988).
50. The extreme case is the trade bill, passed in the 100th Congress (1987-1988), that had more than 200 House and Senate conferees from nine Senate and fourteen House committees. However, a more mundane bill, such as the homeless aid bill, had 40 House conferees from six House committees. See 100 *Congressional Record,* 2, H3582, May 24, 1988. It should also be noted that multiple committee involvement can occur and expand the number of conferees even when multiple referral is not formally present. This result can occur both as a consequence of giving House committees to whom bills are not officially referred a role in floor amendment because their jurisdictions are affected by committee action on singly referred bills or as a consequence of Senate amendments that affect the jurisdictions of House committees not formally involved in the referral or passage of an original House bill. The highway and mass transit bill, passed in the 100th Congress, provides an illustration.

*Part IV*

CONGRESSIONAL LEADERSHIP
AND PARTY POLITICS

# 11.  THE SENATE:
# IF EVERYONE LEADS, WHO FOLLOWS?

## *Roger H. Davidson*

*Father, relieve the weariness—the discouragement—the frustration—the feeling of disintegration and impotence.*

Rev. Richard C. Halverson
Chaplain of the Senate
December 15, 1987

The term *Senate leadership,* for many observers, is an oxymoron: a pure contradiction, like *military intelligence.* For one thing, nearly everyone in the Senate is a leader: in the 100th Congress (1987-1988), eighty-nine senators chaired or were ranking minority members of committees or subcommittees; indeed, they averaged 2.25 leadership posts apiece. The other eleven senators, all freshmen, soon bettered their lot. Party caucus posts are also generously spread around, with only five freshman Democrats and two Republicans left off the rolls of party committees.

The dispersion of Senate leadership extends far beyond formal party or committee posts, for the Senate is a collection of individuals, each of whom enjoys impressive prerogatives. Even scheduling of business is at the mercy of the whims of a handful of senators, sometimes a single member. With such rampant individualism, it is no wonder that the Senate is often paralyzed, unable to act coherently or decisively on legislation or other business. If everyone receives deference, what deference is left for the institution? If everyone leads, can anyone lead?

Senate party leaders—the subject of this essay—repeatedly voice frustration with their jobs. Majority Leader Robert C. Byrd, D-W.Va., once declared that if anyone asked his occupation he would put down "slave." [1] Robert Dole, R-Kan., lamented that a majority leader is "in some ways . . . the slave of all." [2] His predecessor, Howard H. Baker, Jr., R-Tenn., wondered aloud whether "the principal duty of the leadership is janitorial"—because the floor leader is the first to arrive in the Senate chamber and the last to leave, in the meantime cleaning up other people's messes.[3] Mike Mansfield, D-Mont., majority leader from 1961 to 1976, summed it up: "You don't organize chaos."

These expressions of self-pity may be exaggerated. Yet the underlying issue is whether Senate leaders are mere caretakers in an era of rampant individualism—one in which senators are preoccupied with tending their own careers and ministering to their constituencies. Are leaders' jobs merely glorified clerkships, to borrow political scientist Richard Neustadt's label for the presidency?[4] Given the pluralism and fragmentation of the political process, individual senators resist being led or managed. They expect leaders to run the Senate with minimum fuss and maximum deference to their differing goals and schedules. In such a setting, what sort of leadership is possible?

## Historical Evolution

The Senate has no lack of presiding officers, but these are not its leaders. The constitutional president of the Senate is the vice president of the United States. Early vice presidents, such as John Adams, took an active part in floor debates; modern vice presidents are prohibited from speaking unless granted permission by the body. Except for ceremonial occasions, they seldom preside over the Senate and vote only to break a tie. The Constitution also provides for a president pro tempore to preside in the vice president's absence. In modern practice, the president pro tem is the most senior majority party senator. Occupants of this post are apt to chair a major committee and be influential figures in their own right, but their influence does not flow from the post, which is mainly ceremonial. Usually junior majority members preside, serving brief stints in the chair each day. The Senate has no official comparable to the Speaker of the House, who combines political and parliamentary duties.

Formal party leadership came late to the Senate—in contrast to the House, where strong party and procedural leadership appeared in the early nineteenth century. Identifiable Senate leaders date from late in that century, and the modern floor leadership posts only from Woodrow Wilson's day.[5] The floor leader's job has not always been held in high esteem. "The office is one that requires no gifts of a higher order," proclaimed so astute an observer as Richard Rovere in 1953. "It has generally been held as a reward for enterprising mediocrity."[6] In the late 1940s and early 1950s, several floor leaders faced criticism, even rejection at the polls, as a result of their duties.

At the same time, a strong party leadership precedent was established, if not always followed. Democratic leaders such as John Worth Kern of Indiana (1913-1917), Joseph T. Robinson of Arkansas

(1933-1937), and Alben W. Barkley of Kentucky (1937-1947) were influential within the chamber and in working with activist Democratic presidents. And although Republican presidents of that period had more modest legislative agendas, upon occasion GOP Senate leaders also distinguished themselves.

The post surely came of age in 1953, when Robert A. Taft of Ohio, "Mr. Republican," took over as majority leader after nearly a decade of being GOP leader in everything but name. Across the aisle, the Democrats, temporarily in the minority, chose as their floor leader a senator who had been in the chamber only four years. Two years later that senator, Lyndon B. Johnson of Texas, became majority leader. In his brief tenure, Taft revitalized the floor leader's job; Johnson wholly remade it.

The Democrats have controlled the Senate for most of the modern period—from 1955 to 1981 and after 1986. Initially razor-thin, their majority swelled after 1959, peaking at sixty-eight in the 89th Congress (1965-1966). Republicans controlled the chamber from 1981 through 1986. Party majorities in the 1980s were modest. The parties' leaders and margins of seats are shown in Table 11-1.

Innovations in floor leadership have taken place more often, and more dramatically, under the Democrats, no doubt because they have been in the majority so often. However, changes tend to affect both parties' floor leadership.

## Lyndon Johnson's Senate

The pliability of the floor leadership was shown dramatically when Johnson took over as the Democrats' floor leader. As Americans soon learned, Johnson was not just another politician; he was a protean force. "He doesn't have the best mind on the Democratic side," conceded Richard B. Russell of Georgia, leader of the southern wing. "He isn't the best orator; he isn't the best parliamentarian. But he's the best combination of all those qualities." [7]

Johnson seized all the strands of power associated with the office and exploited them to the utmost. To these he added persuasive powers and attention to every detail of Senate business. As political scientist John G. Stewart summarized, "He set for himself no less an objective than *running* the Senate, in fact as well as in theory, by wielding decisive influence in generating majority support for the issues he permitted to come before the Senate for decision." [8]

Although Johnson mastered virtually all phases of the Senate's business—including strategy, tactics, and parliamentary procedure—he was most noted for one-on-one persuasion. No one subjected to the "Johnson treatment" ever forgot it. When reporter Stewart Alsop

Table 11-1  Senate Parties and Their Leaders

| Congress | Year | Democratic leaders | Party seats | | | Republican leaders |
| | | | D | R | Other | |
| --- | --- | --- | --- | --- | --- | --- |
| 83d | 1953-1954 | Lyndon B. Johnson (Texas) | 47 | 48 | 1 | Robert A. Taft (Ohio), 1953; William Knowland (Calif.), 1953-1954 |
| 84th | 1955-1956 | Johnson | 48 | 47 | 1 | Knowland |
| 85th | 1957-1958 | Johnson | 49 | 47 | — | Knowland |
| 86th | 1959-1960 | Johnson | 65 | 35 | — | Everett M. Dirksen (Ill.) |
| 87th | 1961-1962 | Mike Mansfield (Mont.) | 65 | 35 | — | Dirksen |
| 88th | 1963-1964 | Mansfield | 67 | 33 | — | Dirksen |
| 89th | 1965-1966 | Mansfield | 68 | 32 | — | Dirksen |
| 90th | 1967-1968 | Mansfield | 64 | 36 | — | Dirksen |
| 91st | 1969-1970 | Mansfield | 57 | 43 | — | Dirksen, 1969; Hugh Scott (Pa.), 1969-1970 |
| 92d | 1971-1972 | Mansfield | 54 | 44 | 2 | Scott |
| 93d | 1973-1974 | Mansfield | 56 | 42 | 2 | Scott |
| 94th | 1975-1976 | Mansfield | 60 | 37 | 2 | Scott |
| 95th | 1977-1978 | Robert C. Byrd (W.Va.) | 61 | 38 | 1 | Howard H. Baker, Jr. (Tenn.) |
| 96th | 1979-1980 | Byrd | 58 | 41 | 1 | Baker |
| 97th | 1981-1982 | Byrd | 46 | 53 | 1 | Baker |
| 98th | 1983-1984 | Byrd | 45 | 53 | — | Baker |
| 99th | 1985-1986 | Byrd | 47 | 53 | — | Robert Dole (Kan.) |
| 100th | 1987-1988 | Byrd | 54 | 46 | — | Dole |

published an article containing a couple of mildly critical sentences about LBJ's defense record, he was summoned that very day for a two-hour session with the majority leader.

> By gradual stages the relaxed, friendly, and reminiscent mood gave way to something rather like a human hurricane. Johnson was up, striding about his office, talking without pause, occasionally leaning over, his nose almost touching the mesmerized reporter's, to shake the reporter's shoulder or grab his knee. Secretaries were rung for. Memoranda appeared and then more memoranda, as well as letters, newspaper articles, and unidentifiable scraps of paper, which were proferred in quick succession and then snatched away. Appeals were made, to the Almighty, to the shades of the departed great, to the reporter's finer instincts and better nature, while the reporter, unable to get a word in edgewise, sat collapsed upon a leather sofa, eyes glazed, mouth half open.[9]

The "treatment" was the hallmark of Johnson's dominating *persona,* not only during his Senate years but in the White House and to the very end of his life.

Johnson's Senate was a joyless place to work for a senator or staff member outside the leader's circle. Rarely did he call all Democratic senators together: only five conferences of the chamber's Democrats were held during his first six years; under pressure from liberals, he held six meetings in his last two years. The Policy and Steering committees, which he chaired, usually ratified his decisions. In the Capitol, Johnson was omnipresent: he roamed the floor and cloak-rooms, talking to senators and staff members, listening, questioning, and cajoling.

Although Johnson brought extraordinary personal qualities to his duties, he also profited from two factors unique to the 1950s. First, Johnson's Senate majority was slender (until 1959, no more than two votes), while in the White House was Republican Dwight D. Eisenhower, a singularly popular president with a modest legislative agenda. Johnson's strategy was a holding action—"responsible opposition" and accommodation. (Johnson used to whip from his pocket newspaper clippings showing how much he had helped to pass Eisenhower's legislation.) To follow this strategy he had to expose his left flank; the small, frustrated band of liberal senators, who wanted to push farther, complained bitterly of the "Senate establishment."

Second, Johnson represented the center of gravity of the Senate Democratic party, if not the national party. The chamber was dominated by senators from the South and the Border States, who, in concert with conservative Republicans from the Midwest and West, kept the Senate on a conservative course. This conservative coalition, observers of the post-World War II Congress agree, set the tone and controlled the agenda on Capitol Hill. Their control was buttressed by a bipartisan "inner club" of influential senior senators and by a series of norms, or "folkways," that encouraged new senators to defer to the establishment.[10] It was the southerners' leader, Russell, who decided in 1953 that Johnson should be party leader. And it was Russell and his allies to whom Johnson turned repeatedly for advice.

Whatever Johnson's shortcomings, his tightly controlled leadership satisfied certain partisan and institutional needs. His leadership style, Stewart concludes,

> met the clear need of reducing the Democrats' penchant for factionalism and intraparty strife as they assumed responsibility for organizing the Congress in six of Eisenhower's eight years as president.[11]

Johnson provided his party with an identifiable spokesman and a rallying point during the Eisenhower years. (Each year, he issued his own "State of the Union" report.) In doing so, he was a faithful agent of the conservative coalition of Republicans and southern Democrats who dominated the congressional scene.

Pressures for a new leadership style eventually accelerated, however. For one thing, Johnson's centralized control of the senatorial program limited junior senators' chances to participate and reap the benefits of legislative activism. Gradually, the Johnson style exacted its toll in senators' patience, goodwill, and loyalty. "After eight years of Lyndon Johnson," one observer remarked, "a lot of senators were just worn out." [12]

Restlessness grew after the 1958 elections, which boosted the Democrats' margin from two to thirty seats and augmented the party's liberal wing. It was then that Johnson stepped up party conferences and invited three freshman senators to sit on the Policy Committee. As the Eisenhower years drew to a close, Democrats assumed a more aggressive stance, developing legislative alternatives and preparing for the 1960 campaign season.

## The Mansfield 'Revolution'

When the leadership shift occurred, it was sudden and sweeping. Following his election as vice president, Johnson resigned from the Senate to become its constitutional presiding officer. In 1961 Mike Mansfield, the party whip (a post of little note under Johnson), was chosen Democratic leader without opposition. A liberal, Mansfield was nonetheless respected by conservatives and universally praised for fairness and deference to his colleagues.

Mansfield had no taste for heavy-handed leadership. "We've had a dispersal of responsibility," he conceded. "I'm not the leader, really. They don't do what I tell them. I do what they tell me." [13] Nor did he hold to folkways that dictated, for example, that junior senators defer to senior colleagues and refrain from speaking out on issues. "Senators realize that they are treated as I'd like to be treated—as mature people. Their independence is not infringed upon. They know that everything is on the table. They know all about our moves ahead of time. There are no surprises." [14]

Mansfield deliberately abandoned many of the tools Johnson had used so vigorously. He shared leadership responsibilities, encouraged broad participation, and consulted widely before making assignments or appointments. Party conferences were held more frequently. Party bodies, most notably the Policy Committee, were more representative and met more often. The majority leader, though actively engaged, preferred to stay in the background, serving as arbitrator and executor of decisions. Mansfield's style, it seemed, was almost a photographic negative of Johnson's.

The Mansfield revolution did not occur without controversy. Some criticized his leadership as weak or aimless. The conservative hard-liners—old, increasingly outnumbered, and overcome by issues such as civil rights—suffered relative deprivation, because their seniority posts no longer protected them against younger senators. However, most senators flourished under Mansfield's regime, for its very looseness gave them the leeway they needed to pursue their increasingly diverse legislative and career goals. No longer outcasts, the liberals were naturally pleased. "The old times have changed," concluded Pennsylvania's Joseph S. Clark, one of the most vocal liberals. "The old Senate establishment is gone. Democracy is now pretty much the rule in the Senate." [15]

Just as Johnson enjoyed fortunate circumstances in the 1950s, Mansfield held enormous advantages in leading the Senate during the 1960s. First, John F. Kennedy and Lyndon Johnson were activist Democratic presidents with ambitious legislative programs. Second, in the hands of liberal Democrats, a wide range of legislative proposals had gained momentum since the late 1950s. Finally, the Democrats boasted a two-to-one Senate margin throughout this period.

The Democratic leadership strategy survived into the GOP era of Richard Nixon and Gerald R. Ford (1969-1976). With substantial majorities, Democrats continued to generate and enact lengthy legislative agendas. Despite the hostility between Nixon and the liberal wing, senators were free to negotiate with the administration to gain support for their proposals. Indeed, a huge body of major environmental, consumer, and welfare laws was enacted during this period, pushed by Senate liberals with bipartisan support.

Like his predecessor, Mansfield responded to political conditions inside and outside the Senate. The 1961 transition was sudden, to be sure, but long-term forces were rendering the Johnson leadership style obsolete. Johnson's reliance on the conservative coalition could not have survived as the party's center of gravity shifted leftward in the 1958-1978 period. Moreover, the increasingly independent careers pursued by senators (whether running for reelection or for the White House) demanded active participation and public exposure. Mansfield's permissive leadership allowed his colleagues to advance their career goals through activism within the chamber.

## Contemporary Leadership

Mansfield retired from the Senate in 1976, capping his distinguished career by serving as U.S. ambassador to Japan under Presidents Jimmy Carter and Ronald Reagan. Succeeding Senate leaders from both sides of the aisle faced conditions that were partly similar, partly different from those of Mansfield's day. The body's extreme individualism accelerated, manifesting itself in careerism, ever more demanding schedules, and dispersed influence. By the late 1970s, however, the liberal consensus favoring expanded government programs had collapsed, and by 1981 the Democrats' majority had disappeared. Policies were fiercely contested during the 1980s—accentuated by conflicts between the Reagan administration and Capitol Hill and by the federal government's shaky fiscal situation.

Taking over from Mansfield, Robert Byrd added another ingredient to Senate leadership: meticulous attention to the details of floor procedure. Byrd was the quintessential Senate insider; his climb to the leadership had been built on housekeeping chores—innumerable favors for colleagues and countless hours of presiding over the Senate. Neither Mansfield nor his whips enjoyed remaining on the floor for long stretches of time. So Byrd made himself available there, keeping a pocket notebook in which he jotted down requests from colleagues, informing them when matters of interest came up and scheduling debates at their convenience. When Byrd challenged Edward M. Kennedy, D-Mass., for the whip's post in January 1971, his record of service paid off and he won the conference vote, 31 to 24 (one of his votes was a proxy from the dying Richard Russell).

As whip and, after 1977, Democratic leader, Byrd continued to devote his time to floor proceedings and to stress procedural and scheduling matters. He instituted reforms to help the Senate conduct its business more efficiently. The legislative year was rearranged to permit scheduled recesses called "nonlegislative work periods." He perfected Mansfield's "track" system in which noncontroversial measures could be disposed of while controversial ones, even those being filibustered, were debated. Byrd also was involved in altering Senate rules, his interest in procedure remaining keen even while the Democrats were in the minority.

Byrd's leadership was even more service-oriented than Mansfield's. Senatorial independence had become so ingrained that forceful leadership would undoubtedly be resisted. Moreover, Democrats were becoming more fractious and less aggressive as the nation veered on a conservative course. Accordingly, Byrd built his leadership upon parliamentary adroitness and even-handed assistance to colleagues. Senators who differed with him on issues nonetheless respected his skills and dedication to the Senate.

When Byrd reassumed the majority leadership in 1987 he was, if anything, in a stronger position than before.[16] Although the Democrats no longer controlled the White House, the Reagan administration was nearing its close and waning in stature. Moreover, if Byrd had initially been too conservative for some of his Democratic colleagues, by the mid-1980s he was right in the mainstream. The changing policy agenda, not to mention an altered center of gravity among Democrats, brought about his political transformation. Still, criticisms of his style and media image persisted, even after a 1985 challenge was turned aside. By 1989 he was ready to relinquish the job, assuming the posts of president pro tem and chairman of the Appropriations Committee.

Senate GOP leadership followed a pattern roughly parallel to that of the Democrats. The similarity is in fact remarkable in view of partisan differences such as composition and ideological mix, relationships to the White House, and personalities and styles of individual leaders.

Centralized leadership prevailed over the first half of the period we are examining. When he became Republican floor leader in 1953, Robert Taft installed a strong, centralized structure. This activist style continued under successors William Knowland of California (1953-1958) and Everett M. Dirksen of Illinois (1959-1969). Both leaders dominated their party's policy-making bodies and played an active role in scheduling and floor strategy. Knowland's leadership drew controversial reviews because of his inability to rein in the reckless "Red-baiting" of Senator Joseph McCarthy, R-Wis., his foreign policy quarrels with the Eisenhower administration, and his humorless, unbending personal demeanor.

In contrast, Dirksen—one of the most colorful figures in Senate history—was regarded as singularly effective. Dubbed the "wizard of ooze," he was perhaps the last member of the Senate who could draw crowds to the galleries with his rhetorical skill. Beyond his theatrics, Dirksen was well placed to lead his party. An old-guard conservative Republican, Dirksen could be so flexible on issues that some called him the "great chameleon." [17] His dramatic last-minute support of the 1964 Civil Rights Act as "an idea whose time has come" and his support for Lyndon Johnson's Vietnam War policy angered Republican liberals.

When Dirksen died in 1969, Hugh Scott of Pennsylvania won the leadership by a narrow margin. Although regarded as a liberal, Scott was as flexible on the issues as Dirksen had been. He took pains to support the Nixon administration, even during the unfolding Watergate scandal. Within the Senate, Scott instituted an open leadership that looked very much like that of his counterpart, Mike Mansfield. His personal style of dealing with colleagues, quiet and gentle, was indeed like Mansfield's. He shared leadership tasks and, toward the end of his tenure, delegated many floor duties to his whip, Robert Griffin of Michigan.

Although personally more forceful, Howard Baker—Scott's successor—continued the low-key, collegial style. In January 1977 Baker decided at the last moment to challenge Griffin for the post, winning by a single vote. His colleagues apparently thought that his ability to articulate issues would serve the "loyal opposition" better than Griffin's acknowledged parliamentary skills.[18] Perhaps, too, they felt more comfortable with Baker's easy congeniality than with Griffin's hard-charging style.

Baker steered a middle course, aiding the Carter administration at crucial moments, most notably the Panama Canal treaties of 1978. As majority leader (1981-1984), Baker gained national stature as the pivotal figure of the first Reagan administration. However, his leadership fully respected the decentralized character of the Senate.

Chosen in 1985 to succeed Baker, Robert Dole adopted a more aggressive style, intervening to forge legislative solutions to problems. When Dole announced in 1985 that he would put together a Senate budget package, Reagan's White House staff realized they were dealing with an aggressive, independent operator. Dole's style also impelled his challenge to Vice President George Bush for the 1988 GOP presidential nomination.

In short, the collegial leadership instituted by Mansfield and imitated by Scott remains the order of the day. The wide distribution of power, a trend that began in the 1950s and came to full fruition in the 1960s and 1970s, remains intact. Today's floor leadership is a complex and frustrating enterprise that embraces a variety of formal and informal roles.

## The Leaders' Duties

Floor leadership is primarily a product of custom, not of the rules—although Senate rules give the leaders certain powers. For example, the majority and minority leaders jointly can waive the requirement that standing committees not meet while the Senate is in session (Rule XXVI); they can temporarily increase a standing committee's size to ensure that the majority party has a majority of seats (Rule XXV); move that a measure be referred to two or more committees (Rule XVII); and waive the rule requiring that reports be available for at least three calendar days before floor action (Rule XVII). Significantly, all these powers are conferred jointly on the leaders of the two parties.

But the Senate rules give little hint of the scope of leaders' duties in managing the chamber. The leaders, operating in tandem, represent their colleagues' interests in planning and conducting the work of the Senate. The floor leaders' jobs embrace the following responsibilities: (1) managing the affairs of their senatorial parties; (2) scheduling Senate floor business in accord with workload needs and individual senators' desires; (3) monitoring floor deliberations, which includes seeking unanimous consent agreements governing debates and votes; (4) serving as a conduit between the Senate, the White House, and the House; and (5) speaking for the Senate through the media. Not all leaders stress all of these duties; few leaders do all of them equally well. But they add up to responsibilities that far transcend the "tedious and unpleasant job" of the 1950s.

Although we speak of leaders, most leadership functions are collectively performed. The leadership includes not only the floor leaders and whips, but also the caucus chairmen and secretaries, as well as members of policy committees, campaign committees, and steering committees. All or most committee chairmen are likely to be included in leadership consultations. Senators respected for their expertise or acumen may also be brought in on specific questions. So while the leadership most often refers to the majority and minority floor leaders, the term is quite flexible.

Like all senators, leaders rely on staff aides to perform most routine duties. The majority and minority secretaries' offices are the nerve centers for Senate leadership. These staffs keep track of where senators are to be found and how they are likely to vote; they also receive individual senators' "holds" on legislation as well as requests for unanimous consent agreements. Procedural matters—including important questions of which committees receive disputed bills—are handled by the parliamentarian's office. (In 1981 and again in 1987, new

Senate majority leaders appointed new parliamentarians—presumably to punish the incumbent for adverse rulings rendered while the party was in the minority. This politicization of the parliamentarian's office is regrettable; but it indicates the extent to which party leaders regard the post as an arm of the leadership.) Most day-to-day leadership functions have been delegated to majority or minority staff who act on behalf of the leaders.

## Leader of the Party

Partisan leadership is the most obvious aspect of the leaders' jobs. Some leaders are, or become, national figures in their own right—Taft, Dirksen, Johnson, Baker, and Dole, for example. Others, such as Mansfield or Scott, are chosen because their ideological stance or personal qualities make them ideal bridges among party factions. Even if they come from one of the party's ideological tributaries, leaders are expected to swim in the party's mainstream, and most try to do so.

The two parties distribute their formal posts differently. Senate Democrats permit their floor leaders to chair the Policy Committee, the Steering Committee (which recommends committee assignments), and the Conference. Senate Republicans give these posts to different members.

Lyndon Johnson used his powers to advance allies and to exclude others. He and his chief staff aide, Bobby Baker, weighed senators' competing claims for assignments and made the initial designations, which were usually ratified by the Steering Committee. All factors were weighed, not the least of which was loyalty to the floor leader. Other perquisites—office space, campaign contributions, banquet speakers, added staff assistance, or overseas travel funding—were meted out with an eye to the degree of cooperation a senator had given or might be expected to give in the future. Stewart writes that

> scarcely any aspect of senatorial life, however routine and seemingly removed from the formulation of national policy, escaped Johnson's watchful eye or his uncanny talent for translating these activities into resources which could be used in running the Senate according to the Johnson formula.[19]

No one exploited perquisites quite as assiduously as Lyndon Johnson did, but other leaders of that era, most notably Taft and Dirksen, actively employed them.

In his first year as leader, Johnson decided to guarantee one major committee assignment to every party member regardless of seniority. The original purpose of this so-called "Johnson rule" was to expand the leader's bargaining chips, inasmuch as he retained tight control of the process.[20] But the long-term effect was to disperse desirable committee seats more widely. Later, rules were passed that spread out committee leadership posts as well. In the 100th Congress (1987-1988), for instance, two-thirds of all senators served on Appropriations, Finance, or Foreign Relations. Senators had, on average, three committee and seven subcommittee seats.

Today's Senate leaders do little more than oversee a selection process within the Steering Committee that is designed to be as accommodating as possible. The majority or minority secretary receives applications from all new senators and from returning senators who want to shift committees. When these are combined, the Steering Committee tries to satisfy as many requests as possible. Many senators get their first-choice committees; nearly all receive their second or third choices. That is not to say that the leader's word is not heeded, or that of other influential members; but there is less room than there once was to reward friends or punish enemies.

Leaders also influence their party by choosing other party leaders and appointing party committees. The range of discretion is not unlimited; various factions and interests must be included in the party's councils. In 1981 Byrd appointed nine task forces to develop party alternatives in fields such as industrial policy and tax reform. He also created the Democratic Leadership Council to "analyze what went wrong in the election and plan strategy and raise funds for the midterm elections of 1982." [21] These panels in fact helped rally Senate Democrats and, perhaps more important, helped unify the party in the chamber.

Party leaders sometimes need to resort to coaching psychology to foster team spirit. These efforts may go beyond the leaders' routine of weekly meetings and private consultations. In 1981 Senate Democrats were in disarray, reeling from a string of Reagan triumphs and still trying to adjust to minority status for the first time in a generation. Toward the session's end, Byrd held a private retreat for his colleagues at a West Virginia state park. There Senate Democrats decided to make a stand against what they saw as the unfairness of Reagan's programs. More significantly, the retreat permitted them to become better acquainted with one another. Surrounded by staffs and driven by their schedules, today's senators have few opportunities to get to know their colleagues really well.

## Chief Scheduler

Describing the leader's job, Byrd said: "He facilitates, he constructs, he programs, he schedules, he takes an active part in the development of legislation, he steps in at crucial moments on the floor, offers amendments, speaks on behalf of legislation and helps to shape the outcome of the legislation." [22] Of all of these various duties, scheduling probably consumes the most time and energy while the Senate is in session. It is undoubtedly the function that colleagues find most useful, but scheduling is frustrating because it depends on factors largely beyond the leader's control: the pace of committee deliberations and the vagaries of individual senators' schedules, as well as external events such as presidential requests or nominations and national crises.

Adjusting daily floor business to senators' peripatetic schedules, both in and out of Washington, is a longstanding challenge. By tradition, senators have the right to be informed when matters that concern them are taken up and to be present if at all possible. Their concerns are communicated through, and coordinated by, their respective floor leaders. In the Johnson-Dirksen days, such courtesies were selectively extended. William S. White wrote:

> I have seen one member, say a [Herbert] Lehman of New York, confined by niggling and almost brutal Senate action to the most liberal inhibitions of the least important of all rules. And again I have seen a vital Senate roll call held off by all sorts of openly dawdling time-killing for hours, in spite of the fact that supposedly it is not possible to interrupt a roll call once it is in motion, for the simple purpose of seeing that a delayed aircraft has opportunity to land at Washington Airport so that a motorcycle escort can bring, say a [Hubert] Humphrey of Minnesota in to be recorded. [23]

Since the Mansfield era, however, procedures have been applied more even-handedly.

At the same time, however, senators' schedules have become busier and more unmanageable. Part of the problem is that senators spend more time than formerly in their home states. In 1959-1960 senators spent an average of nine days a year in their states; by 1979-1980 this average had soared to nearly eighty days a year. [24] Like their counterparts in the House, senators were driven by rising constituent demands to stress constituent service and contact. Indeed, senators resemble representatives ever more closely in their "home styles." But senatorial schedules are crowded not only with trips back to their home states, but also with interviews and media appearances, speeches (often for a fee), and raising campaign funds. Aggressive self-promotion and nonstop campaigning vie for the senator's time with constituency service and legislative business.

Floor leaders in the 1980s all warred against their colleagues' schedules, with less than total success. When he became majority leader in 1981, Baker vowed to schedule floor activities in advance and to cut down on late-night sessions, Saturday sessions, and roll call votes. As a result, the average Senate day during Baker's regime was shorter than it had been previously.[25] Senators of both parties—not to mention their families and appointment secretaries—were grateful for shorter, more predictable Senate sessions. Baker's successor, Robert Dole, recalled that one of his greatest frustrations was

> trying to accommodate every senator and still get the work done because we were told, "We cannot vote on Monday," "I have to leave early on Friday," "I don't want to be here on Tuesday," "I would like to leave here Wednesday, but I will be here all day Thursday." That is one day. And then you have that 100 times or maybe 98 times.[26]

Dole favored wearing down his colleagues with lengthy sessions, hoping to force last-minute compromises. Dole's difficulty in controlling sessions was compounded by intensifying quarrels between the White House and Capitol Hill over legislative priorities.

In 1985 a quality-of-life group was launched by Senators David Pryor, D-Ark., John C. Danforth, R-Mo., and others to plead for more predictable, rational schedules. The quality of life they sought was for themselves—to enable them to plan home-state visits, keep longstanding speaking commitments, plan vacations, spend time with their families, and complete legislative work in daylight hours rather than late at night. There was even a wives' lobbying group, Ladies of the Senate Quality of Life Committee. Danforth's lament was typical:

> When will we adjourn? I don't know. What is the recess schedule for next year? I don't know. Will we be home for dinner? I don't know.[27]

One solution was to expand the Senate's workweek from three days to four days.[28] When Byrd became majority leader in 1987 he tried to enforce this schedule rigorously, scheduling no votes on Mondays but trying to keep the Senate going through Fridays, holding "bed-check" votes to keep members in town. Later it was decided to put the Senate on a five-day workweek—with every fourth week off for home-state duties.[29]

The main reason for the Senate's scheduling morass is the chamber's permissive rules, procedures, and precedents that give each and every senator the power to shape, delay, or even kill legislation. Among the prerogatives exercised by individual senators are: holds on legislation, strategic delays in floor consideration, repeated votes on budget or other items, and the privilege of offering amendments, relevant or not, to any section of a bill in any order before the bill's third reading. Underpinning these prerogatives is the Senate's most celebrated privilege, that of "speaking at great length," or filibustering, concerning a bill, any amendment thereto, and even the motion to take up the measure. These prerogatives loom larger today because more contested issues are handled on the floor and because senators are more apt to unsheath these procedural weapons on routine matters, not only on momentous issues.

Senators harboring substantive objections to measures, treaties, or nominations may place "holds" on them. The hold is an informal practice not mentioned in the rules and carried out through the two floor leaders. The effect is to delay Senate action on the pending matter. In his first two years as majority leader, Baker scrupulously observed holds for indefinite periods of time. In 1983, however, he and Byrd announced that they would no longer regard holds as sacrosanct orders preventing floor deliberation. Rather, senators would simply be notified when the bill would come up so they could come and object.[30]

Every senator's right to come to the floor and object is significant because of the Senate's habit of doing business through complex unanimous consent agreements, which set the guidelines for floor consideration of specific major bills. Usually proposed orally by the two leaders, such agreements often are worked out in advance through negotiations with influential senators. Once approved, unanimous consent agreements are transmitted in writing to all senators. "The fundamental objective of unanimous consent agreements," Walter J. Oleszek notes, "is to limit the time it takes to dispose of controversial issues in an institution noted for unlimited debate." [31] For this reason they are often called *time agreements.*

The leader's job is to forestall objections to such agreements by ensuring that everyone's interests are protected. "If the majority leader wants to take up a bill," observed Dan Quayle, R-Ind., "all 100 senators basically have to agree." [32] Because every issue potentially can be delayed by a single senator—a delay that can be prolonged if several senators are opposed—the Senate continually flirts with breakdowns in its schedule. And, although senators deplore the system, few are willing to yield their own rights under it. What keeps the Senate from recurring breakdown is the floor leaders' skill in negotiating with their colleagues, as well as the (usually unstated) premise that the institution's work must go on.

Two techniques for handling the Senate's unpredictable schedule are *quorum calls* and *vote stacking.* Quorum calls are used to buy time for behind-the-scenes bargaining, to wait for senators to get to the floor, or to stall between consideration of different pieces of legislation. Stacked votes are those that are grouped together for the convenience of senators, usually following long weekends. Leaders often voice exasperation at having to resort to such tactics. In his third year as majority leader, Baker not only clamped down on holds but announced he was no longer going to stack votes.

However impressive the leaders' skill, scheduling can collapse in the face of concerted opposition. Often nothing can be done but plunge ahead, allowing a filibuster to take place. As Walter Oleszek is fond of saying, the Senate operates under one of two rules: unanimous consent or exhaustion. If a compromise cannot be negotiated, then cloture can be invoked. The floor leaders usually support cloture as a courtesy to the bill's authors and as a means of getting Senate business back on track. However, the extent to which leaders lobby for the cloture motion varies with the individual leader and the issue involved. Several divisive measures, including abortion and school prayer amendments, were dropped after Senate filibusters against them could not be broken.

Historically, filibusters were mounted on major issues of conscience or public policy. Increasingly, however, they are invoked for lesser matters. "The trivialization of the Senate" is Quayle's phrase for the development. "The first time cloture was ever invoked was in 1919 on the Treaty of Versailles," he noted with irony in 1984. "The last time cloture was invoked was Monday, September 11, on a procedural motion to proceed on the banking deregulation bill." [33] In the last two weeks of the 1984 session, cloture was invoked five times, as often as during the 1919-1926 period, when the Senate voted on the League of Nations and the World Court, and more than during the civil rights debates of the 1960s.

An even more subtle leadership task is coordinating the activities of the Senate's scattered committees. Lyndon Johnson dealt with the committee barons of his day individually, one-on-one, encouraging them to deal through him, not with each other. Mansfield preferred to stay in the background and let the chairmen reach their own agreements. Baker took a collegial approach, meeting with the committee chairmen each Tuesday morning, just before the weekly lunch of all GOP senators. In his first year, Baker asked his staff to canvass all committee leaders to obtain their plans; a large chart was prepared outlining the proposed schedule for floor debates. Although the schedule could not be carried out to the letter, the most important elements were fulfilled by the end of the 1981 session. After that, scheduling became looser, lacking the impetus of a newly elected president with a focused plan of action.

Dole and Byrd preferred to give more latitude to their committee chairmen—stepping in vigorously, however, to hammer out agreements on critical measures. Byrd, for example, worked out a coordinated effort by three committees (Armed Services, Foreign Relations, and Select Intelligence) for considering the intermediate nuclear force (INF) treaty signed by President Reagan and Mikhail S. Gorbachev in December 1987.[34] A similar agreement was brokered for the omnibus trade bill in 1988.

Beyond these few high-priority measures, however, party leaders are exceedingly wary of treading on the toes of committee chairmen, who often are backed by their ranking minority members. Committee jurisdictions, for example, seem to be off-limits to leadership manipulation. Since 1977 the joint leadership has had the right, under Senate rules, to propose arrangements for consideration of measures by two or more committees (Rule XVII, 3a). The provision has never been invoked.

## Monitor of Floor Debate

The Senate has long styled itself as "the world's greatest deliberative body." If length of discourse is the standard, the label is merited. By most standards, however, the Senate is a very flawed deliberative body. As Nancy Landon Kassebaum, R-Kan. explained,

> Floor debate has deteriorated into a never-ending series of points of order, procedural motions, appeals and waiver votes, punctuated by endless hours of time-killing quorum calls. Serious policy deliberations are a rarity. "Great debate" is only a memory, replaced by a preoccupation with procedure that makes it exceedingly difficult to transact even routine business.[35]

As television viewers of Senate proceedings can attest, debate in the chamber typically is uninspiring and rarely deliberative in the sense that discussion is encouraged. Senators' speeches tend to be lengthy, read from staff-prepared manuscripts. Colloquies (exchanges) are sometimes staged to clarify legislative points, but true clashes of opinion are rare. Moreover, sessions are full of "dead time": according to Senator Pryor's compilations, 32 percent of the floor time in 1985 was consumed by roll call votes and 23 percent by quorum calls.[36]

Senate leaders, unlike those in the House, lack strong rules and procedures by which they can structure debate and limit the time devoted to specific measures. These strictures place a premium on the leaders' skill and patience. It is not surprising, therefore, that leaders take an active interest in what might be called "institutional maintenance"—reviewing or revising the chamber's rules and procedures. Mansfield, Byrd, and Baker all took on structural or procedural questions of consequence, such as filibusters, committee realignment, and televising the Senate.

In the case of extended debate, leaders' stakes in expediting floor deliberation have led them to devise innovations. The stakes are high. In the late 1940s, Majority Leader Scott W. Lucas, D-Ill., tried to change the rules to make it easier to end filibusters and pass pending civil rights bills. Caught in a crossfire between southern patriarchs angry at any assault on their prerogatives and liberals who charged he was not pressing hard enough, Lucas lost the fight and spent three weeks in the hospital recovering from exhaustion.[37] Nearly a decade passed before major civil rights legislation overcame the barrier of the filibuster.

The practice of extended debate continues to tax leaders' ability to produce timely votes on controversial measures. While he was majority whip in 1975, Robert Byrd helped liberalize the cloture rule to require three-fifths rather than two-thirds of the senators to shut off debate on all issues except proposed rules changes, where the old two-thirds requirement still applied. Senators such as James Allen, D-Ala., sidestepped cloture by perfecting the postcloture filibuster—dilatory amendments not subject to the 100-hour debate limit under cloture.

When the Senate convened in 1979, Byrd had a new plan to stop postcloture filibusters. The core of the plan (S. Res. 61, 95th Congress) was to make all Senate actions after cloture subject to the 100-hour limit. Many senators, including Minority Leader Baker, balked at limiting the minority's freedom of debate. Six weeks after Byrd unveiled his proposal, however, a scaled-down version passed the Senate by a 78-16 vote. Byrd gained his main objective, the 100-hour cap, by promising to jettison other aspects of his proposal.[38]

When he became majority leader in 1981, Baker proposed televising Senate debates (S. Res. 20, 96th Congress) as a way of stimulating changes. "Turning on the cameras to let the people see us as we really are," he told his colleagues, "can help bring a beginning of respect for public service and public servants again." He argued that TV coverage of selected debates was "an opportunity for the Senate to actually become the great deliberative body which it was thought to be when it was created, as it has sometimes been in the past, and that we would all like for it to be every day." [39]

The television cameras, in Baker's view, would do more than focus public attention on the body; they could also force major changes in the way the Senate conducted its business. Instituting "town meeting" sessions on major issues, he reasoned, could lead to other innovations, including greater regularity in floor sessions, streamlined procedures for disposing of routine business, briefer sessions over the calendar year, and perhaps even a thorough rewriting of the Senate's rules. Baker's intentions were not fulfilled. Although the Rules and Administration

Committee reported a TV coverage resolution, opponents staged a filibuster and a vote on cloture was unsuccessful.

In 1986 the Senate finally authorized televised sessions; the threat to the Senate's visibility posed by House TV coverage, which had begun in 1978, became too serious to ignore. A package of reforms that would have given Senate leaders greater control over floor proceedings was proposed to streamline Senate deliberations and make them more palatable to the viewers. The reforms were defeated by those who feared that expediting Senate business might curtail individual senators' prerogatives. The opposition was epitomized by an eloquent defense of minority rights by Senator Lowell P. Weicker, R-Conn.:

> From the day I arrived in the U.S. Senate . . . as the youngest and newest member of this body, the minute I walked through that door I had all the power, I have all the power of the majority leadership, minority leadership, or the Senate as a whole. I have all of that as one person. There are many ways I can exercise it. . . .
>
> [I]n this body where we have the opportunity to discuss and persuade each other, no automatic mechanisms, no diminishing of rights, no legislation to substitute for established practical experience—none of these things are going to work.[40]

With such widespread opposition, the expected tradeoff of TV coverage for streamlined floor procedures failed to materialize. The Senate's only concession to the cameras was to reduce its special order remarks from fifteen minutes to five minutes.

Thus, there persists criticism of what Pryor calls "procedural gridlock." He and other senators from the quality-of-life group proposed four changes in the Senate's rules to expedite debate: (1) curb nongermane sense of the Senate amendments by requiring that such amendments have at least twenty cosponsors; (2) limit to one hour all debate on any motion to proceed to consider any matter; (3) restrict roll call votes to fifteen minutes, as provided by Senate procedures; and (4) require amendments to be offered in order of the section of the bill being considered.[41] These proposals had enough support in 1988 to play a role in the campaigns of the three senators who wished to succeed Byrd as floor leader and to trigger a report on Senate rules by the Rules and Administration Committee.

An independent survey of twenty-six senators in late 1987 uncovered widespread support for reforms in scheduling and floor management. A majority of the respondents were surprised and dismayed by the inefficiency of the chamber.[42] Among the more frequent demands were: more advanced scheduling of legislative activity, stronger discipline for members, and more attention to the

Table 11-2   Twenty-six Senators' Views on Scheduling Reforms

| Proposal | Favor | Oppose | Don't know |
|---|---|---|---|
| Limit debate on issues already considered in a session | 80.7% | 15.4% | 7.7% |
| Limit filibusters on the motion "to proceed" | 76.9 | 23.0 | — |
| Five-day work week with one week per month of recess | 76.9 | 18.2 | 3.9 |
| Eliminate or curtail "holds to block or delay floor action" | 72.1 | 25.9 | — |
| Allow senators to decide all future floor amendments to a bill must be germane | 61.6 | 25.9 | 11.5 |
| Establish joint House-Senate leadership priority list annually, with departures subject to points of order from the floor | 50 | 42.3 | 7.7 |
| Restrict leaders' ability to schedule Monday or Friday votes | 26.9 | 61.5 | 11.6 |

SOURCE: Center for Responsive Politics, *Congressional Operation: Congress Speaks, A Survey of the 100th Congress* (Washington, D.C.: Center for Responsive Politics, 1988), 53-61.

partisan and congressional agenda. Support for change was especially strong among former House members, used to the tighter discipline of the larger chamber. Senators' views on specific scheduling innovations are listed in Table 11-2.

Participation in floor deliberation—framing strategies, coordinating the efforts of sponsors, taking part in debate, and soliciting votes—varies with the individual floor leader, and with the issue at hand. As usual, Lyndon Johnson stands at the activist end of the continuum. An observer summarized his impact:

> Since [Johnson] worked longer and harder than anyone else at the business of running the Senate, he became a legend in his time, a man who allegedly never made a move until he had the votes, a man who clearly established himself as the most crucial single factor in deciding what the Senate accomplished.[43]

Johnson actively participated in nearly every major issue that came to the Senate floor. Few measures got to the floor without his approval. Priding himself on legislative products, Johnson wanted to be sure a bill could be passed before taking it up; he compiled estimates of votes, consulted with pivotal senators, and, if needed, devised compromises that would attract sufficient votes. (Sometimes these deals hinged on assurances on other measures.) Once the bill was taken up, Johnson regulated the timing and pace of the floor debate. Then he would bargain for senators' votes, on the theory that every bill was a test of his leadership.

More recent leaders have assumed floor generalship selectively. Some do not specialize in floor procedure, preferring to delegate those chores to others or defer to committee leaders and bill sponsors. Issues simply have become too numerous and conflictual for leaders to invest in all of them. A first-year senator once came upon Majority Leader Baker sitting peacefully at his desk in the chamber while an intense debate was raging around him. When the newcomer wondered aloud why the majority leader was sitting out the debate, Baker replied with a homey epigram: "Ain't got no dog in this fight." [44]

Whatever their style, floor leaders jump in to handle emergencies. Some are recognized policy experts—for example, Johnson on the space program, Scott on legal issues, and Mansfield on the Far East. And all are active on issues important to their state or region, their party, or the incumbent president.

Senators do not relinquish local concerns when taking on leadership duties; indeed, they are better positioned to help their state or region. Byrd, for instance, once used his privilege of recognition to help West Virginia coal producers modify a strip-mining provision. Traditionally, floor leaders are recognized by the chair whenever they wish to speak. By controlling the floor, Byrd was able to prevent other senators from offering amendments, eventually forcing them to accept his own amendment. An opponent, Howard Metzenbaum, D-Ohio, complained: "I do feel very strongly that a member of this body should not be precluded by parliamentary procedures which favor the Majority Leader ... so far as gaining recognition is concerned." [45] But other leaders have done the same thing. Baker advanced projects for his home state, as did Robert Dole.

Partisan issues also engage leaders' skills. An early test of the Reagan-GOP Senate alliance was a 1981 vote raising the debt limit. Republican senators faced, many of them for the first time, the question of supporting their own president's call for raising the debt ceiling to fund government operations. Majority Leader Baker held a meeting of all GOP senators, calling upon Strom Thurmond of South Carolina, president pro tempore of the Senate, for an emotional appeal. When the bill reached the floor, Democratic leader Byrd engineered a steady stream of negative votes from his side of the aisle until the Republicans (many of whom had campaigned against debt-ceiling hikes) mustered enough votes to pass the proposal. Three years later, Democrats again withheld their votes—this time the deficit was indisputably Reagan's—forcing sixteen GOP senators who had departed for campaigning to scurry back (four of them aboard Air Force jets) to pass the debt-ceiling extension.

Not all measures engage the party leaders so directly, in view of the Senate's multiplicity of power centers and activist members. As Byrd explained, "The Senate usually works its will on legislation before [floor deliberation], and these chairmen, who are acting as managers of the bills, are able to work the things out themselves. It's better for a Majority Leader in that kind of a situation to stay in the background." [46]

In voting, most leaders are "middle people"; they stand near the center of their party and are acceptable to most factions.[47] They are products of a peer review process that starts as soon as they arrive in the Senate. Not only must they gain familiarity with chamber matters but—more important—they must win the confidence of their colleagues. Patience and fairness are the qualities most mentioned by senators in connection with successful leaders.

Despite personal and temporal variations, Senate leaders tend to be party loyalists in their voting. Figures 11-1 and 11-2 compare party unity scores of majority/minority leaders with average scores for the party. (Party unity votes are those in which a majority of Democrats are opposed to a majority of Republicans. A senator's party unity score is the proportion of times he or she goes with the party on such votes.) Only three times have Democratic leaders dipped below their party's norm: Lyndon Johnson in his first and fifth years as leader, and Robert Byrd in his first year. On only one of these occasions (Byrd in 1977) did the leader's party control the White House. GOP leaders' records are somewhat more variable, due mainly to Hugh Scott's straying from the party fold during the mid-1970s Watergate era. Dirksen fell below his party average in 1964, the first year his friend Johnson was in the White House. Baker, too, was below the party average in 1978-1979, when he drew criticism for supporting the administration on issues such as the Panama Canal treaties. Most of the time, however, leaders are paragons of party loyalty.

## Senate's Emissary to the White House

Maintaining a firm relationship with the incumbent president is an important facet of senatorial leadership. For one thing, leaders are expected to handle presidential requests and initiatives. This expectation is even stronger when the president and the leader are of the same party or when a crisis arises that threatens the nation's security. For another thing, the leader's access to the White House provides extra

Figure 11-1   Party Unity of Senate Democrats and Their Leaders, 1947-1987

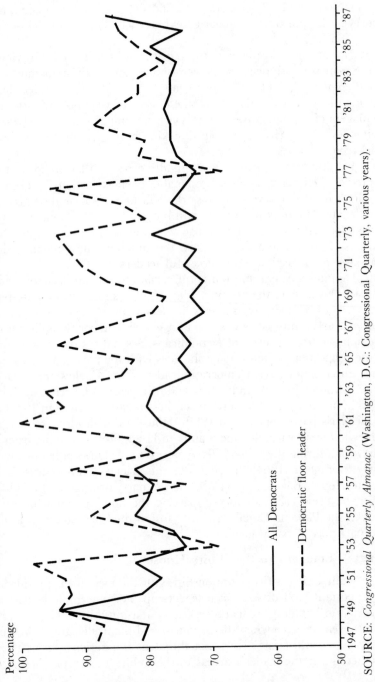

SOURCE: *Congressional Quarterly Almanac* (Washington, D.C.: Congressional Quarterly, various years).

NOTE: Scores recomputed to eliminate the effect of absences.

Figure 11-2  Party Unity of Senate Republicans and Their Leaders, 1947-1987

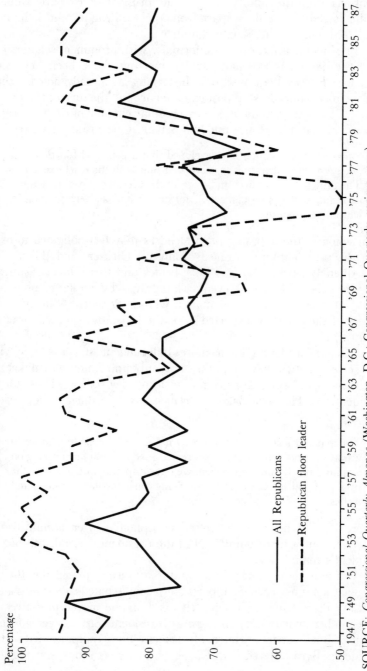

SOURCE: *Congressional Quarterly Almanac* (Washington, D.C.: Congressional Quarterly, various years).

NOTE: Scores recomputed to eliminate the effect of absences.

leverage for dealing with colleagues. Knowledge of the president's intentions and the ability to get the president's ear are valuable attributes that set leaders apart from their colleagues and help them build coalitions in the Senate chamber.

Presidents have consulted informally with prominent senators ever since the 1st Congress, and regular meetings have been held since Theodore Roosevelt's time. Some historians, as already noted, believe that the modern leadership post emerged around the turn of the present century in response to the need for a regular channel of communication between the White House and the Senate. One historian writes:

> Since 1900, a tradition has developed that a principal function of a
> Senate majority leader is to serve as a link with the chief executive.
> The growth of the power and scope of the presidency has created the
> expectation that presidents will formulate and actively promote a
> legislative program.[48]

Even when of the opposing party, leaders may feel obligated to assist with the president's program, as Johnson, Dirksen, and Baker often did. Alben Barkley, who was floor leader and then Harry Truman's vice president (1949-1953), even declared that "by and large, no matter what party is in power—no matter who is President—the Majority Leader of the Senate is expected to be the legislative spokesman of the administration." [49]

Modern leaders take a more independent stance. They view themselves as two-way conduits, not only informing lawmakers of executive plans, but also communicating legislative views to the president. As Howard Baker described his role during the Reagan administration,

> The majority leadership of this body has a special obligation to see to
> it that the president's initiatives are accorded full and fair hearing on
> Capitol Hill. By the same token, we have a special duty to advise the
> president and his counselors concerning parliamentary strategy and
> tactics.[50]

Robert Byrd, who struggled often to uphold Carter administration initiatives, put it more bluntly: "I'm the president's friend, I'm not the president's man." [51]

While leaders render advice and assistance to presidents, they do not owe them unswerving support. No recent Senate leader has gone as far as William Knowland, who left his desk and moved to the rear of the chamber when speaking against President Eisenhower's foreign policies. But sooner or later all leaders part company with their presidents. Byrd differed with Carter on many occasions, starting with the president's assault on water projects popular with western senators. Baker's role with the Reagan administration went through several phases. Initially, when Reagan's programs seemed invincible, Baker was a faithful lieutenant, commanding the GOP forces and keeping the troops in line. After 1981, however, he found himself more often informing and admonishing the White House, staking out a middle ground between the president and the Democratic House and quietly seeking alliances to seize the initiative when the president declined to take it.

Dole, as GOP leader during Reagan's second term, faced an even more delicate task: supporting the administration's cause in spite of the president's fading prestige and his own presidential ambitions. The GOP leader worked (unsuccessfully, as it turned out) to forge a compromise budget and hardly concealed his dismay at the Iran-contra fiasco.

Like all politicians, Senate floor leaders pay attention to presidential popularity in charting their course of action. Popular presidents, such as Eisenhower, Johnson in his heyday, and Reagan in 1981, are given wide berth, even by opposition leaders. When presidents falter or lose touch with public opinion, however, leaders display greater independence, as did Scott after Watergate and Baker and Dole after 1981. In short, leaders are expected to work with the president, but they retain their independence. Of equal importance, their colleagues expect them to represent the Senate as an institution in dealing with the White House.

When congressional control is divided, Senate leaders hold more leverage. In all three twentieth-century cases in which the Senate and House have been in opposite hands, one party has controlled the Senate and the White House. This enhances the Senate leader's role, because that chamber's support is essential for the president and provides leverage for dealing with the other body.

## Media Voice

Senate leaders are public figures and media personalities.[52] A mediating factor is that the leader's relationship with the White House is critical. A strong, activist president of the same party tends to reduce the visibility of the Senate leader. Although charged with managing the president's legislation in the Senate, leaders in this position take a back seat in initiating policy proposals. An exception of sorts was Baker, who early in the Reagan administration was credited with masterminding the strategy of concentrating on economic programs.

Senate leaders opposing the president usually have greater visibility; they are expected to challenge the president's initiatives and to propose alternatives. This "leader-of-the-loyal-opposition" role accounted for much of the media attention accorded Dirksen and Johnson. There is some evidence that Baker was chosen as minority leader in 1977 in part because he was deemed to have a smoother public style than his rival. By the same token, Byrd's indifferent media performance led to criticisms of his leadership during the Reagan years.

Some leaders gain great visibility through their press exposure. In the 1950s Johnson—who systematically cultivated the press—became the voice of moderate Democrats. He worked tirelessly to promote the notion that he was the only figure who could bind the party's warring factions together and get legislative results. Running for the presidential nomination in 1960, Johnson persisted in reciting his Senate victories while other candidates talked about broad issues. In the 1960s Dirksen was the voice of the loyal opposition, countering the Democrats' liberal thrusts but coming to their rescue at dramatic moments. The "Ev and Charlie Show"—press conferences featuring Dirksen and House minority leader Charles Halleck of Indiana—was amply publicized if often derided. In recent years only Howard Baker has commanded equivalent attention. As elsewhere, the leader's role rests largely on personal characteristics and skills.

## Summary

Beyond certain imperatives, Senate leadership is flexible and varied; it changes with the personality and priorities of the individual occupants. None of the recent leaders has been a carbon copy of his predecessor. Leadership positions shift in accord with personal skills, preferences, and styles; they are not yet wholly institutionalized in the sense that incumbents have to conform to rigorous models or sets of expectations. When Byrd was asked whether he modeled himself upon his predecessors, he denied it emphatically: "I haven't modeled myself. I'm the Robert C. Byrd model, and as Popeye used to say, 'I yam what I yam and that's all I yam.' I can't be someone else." [53]

This fluidity extends to other positions—the majority and minority whips and chairs of pivotal party committees. Some floor leaders, such as Mansfield and Dole, delegate floor work to their whips. Others ignore them and work independently. Flexibility also marks the operation of party committees. Republicans distribute these offices to different senators, and on occasion they operate quite independently.

Despite all this fluidity, the hard core of Senate leadership today is its stewardship—some would say subservience—to the scattered goals and schedules of the Senate's 100 members and to the Senate as an institution. Johnson, Taft, and Dirksen of the postwar generation could command loyalty and threaten reprisals, but today's leaders have far less firepower. The contemporary Senate, with its widely dispersed prerogatives, requires a more restrained leadership, one that relies not on forceful commandeering but on fairness, camaraderie, and accommodation.

In this respect the Senate responded quite differently from the House to the leading issues of the 1980s. In both chambers, the legacy of the past generation's reforms was greatly decentralized structure— affording expanded opportunities for individual members to take initiative and shape the course of legislation. This worked well in the 1960s and 1970s, when fiscal prosperity and demands for expanded government activity formed a favorable climate for new legislative programs. The fiscally bleak 1980s, in contrast, stressed difficult decisions about priorities among government programs. The House of Representatives succeeded in centralizing its processing of many tough questions through adroit scheduling and tight rules of debate, but the Senate found it harder to adapt. The Senate's extreme individualism and opportunities for delay stood out vividly in comparison to the House, bringing the Senate's basic principles under attack. Again the senators faced the question of whether preserving their individual prerogatives was worth jeopardizing the institution's ability to cope with the nation's policy agenda. "We are all-powerful or all-powerless," declared Daniel J. Evans, R-Wash., who retired in frustration after a single term. "I'm not sure which." [54]

## Notes

1. *Congressional Record,* 96th Cong., 2d sess., 1980, S3924.
2. Ibid., 99th Cong., 2d sess., 1986, S17294.
3. Ibid., 98th Cong., 2d sess., 1984, S4877.
4. Richard E. Neustadt, *Presidential Power: The Politics of Leadership from FDR to Carter* (New York: John Wiley & Sons, 1980), 7.
5. See David J. Rothman, *Politics and Power: The United States Senate 1869-1901* (Cambridge, Mass.: Harvard University Press, 1966); and Margaret Munk, "Origin and Development of the Party Floor Leadership in the United States Senate," *Capitol Studies* (Winter 1974): 23-41.
6. Richard Rovere, "What Course for the Powerful Mr. Taft?" *New York Times Magazine,* March 22, 1953, 34.
7. Robert L. Peabody, *Leadership in Congress* (Boston: Little, Brown, 1976), 323.
8. John G. Stewart, "Two Strategies of Leadership: Johnson and Mansfield," in *Congressional Behavior,* ed. Nelson W. Polsby (New York: Random House, 1971), 61-92.

9. Stewart Alsop, "Lyndon Johnson: How Does He Do It?" *Saturday Evening Post*, Jan. 24, 1955, 43.
10. See William S. White, *Citadel: The Story of the U.S. Senate* (New York: Harper and Brothers, 1967); and Donald R. Matthews, *The U.S. Senators and Their World* (Chapel Hill: University of North Carolina Press, 1960), chap. 5.
11. Stewart, "Two Strategies of Leadership," 70.
12. Ibid.
13. *New York Times*, July 17, 1961, 11.
14. Andrew J. Glass, "Mansfield Reforms Spark 'Quiet Revolution' in Senate," *National Journal*, March 6, 1971, 509.
15. Senate, *Congressional Record*, 89th Cong., 1st sess., 1965, 23495.
16. On Byrd's role in the minority see Richard E. Cohen, "Minority Status Seems to Have Enhanced Byrd's Position Among Fellow Democrats," *National Journal*, May 7, 1983, 958-960.
17. Edward S. Gilbreth, "Dirksen: The President's Chameleon," *Nation*, Feb. 5, 1968, 168.
18. Michael J. Malbin, "The Senate Republican Leaders—Life Without a President," *National Journal*, May 21, 1977, 776-780.
19. Stewart, "Two Strategies of Leadership," 66.
20. Ibid., 82.
21. Cohen, "Minority Status."
22. Richard E. Cohen, "Byrd of West Virginia: A New Job, A New Image," *National Journal*, Aug. 20, 1977, 1294.
23. White, *Citadel*, 83.
24. Glenn R. Parker, *Homeward Bound: Explaining Changes in Congressional Behavior* (Pittsburgh: University of Pittsburgh Press, 1986), 17-18.
25. Irwin B. Arieff, "Under Baker's Leadership Senate Republicans Maintain Unprecedented Voting Unity," *Congressional Quarterly Weekly Report*, Sept. 12, 1981, 1747.
26. *Congressional Record*, 100th Cong., 1st sess., 1987, S16.
27. Quoted by Janet Hook, "Senators Look for Ways to Increase Efficiency," *Congressional Quarterly Weekly Report*, Dec. 5, 1987, 3001.
28. See Senator Danforth's comments in *Congressional Record*, 99th Cong., 2d sess., 1987, S11605.
29. Helen Dewar, "Senate to Adopt New York Ethic—A Five-Day Week," *Washington Post*, Dec. 31, 1987, A17.
30. *Congressional Record*, 97th Cong., 2d sess., Dec. 6, 1982, S13901.
31. Walter J. Oleszek, *Congressional Procedures and the Policy Process*, 3d ed. (Washington, D.C.: CQ Press, 1988), 186.
32. *Congressional Record*, 98th Cong., 2d sess., 1984, S10957.
33. Ibid., 98th Cong., 2d sess., 1984, S10957-8.
34. See Senator Byrd's remarks in *Congressional Record*, 99th Cong., 2d sess., 1987, S17411.
35. Nancy Landon Kassebaum, "The Senate Is Not In Order," *Washington Post*, Jan. 27, 1988, A19.

36. Senator Pryor's remarks are found in Senate, *Congressional Record*, 99th Cong., 1st sess., 1985, 29990.

37. William S. White, "Rugged Days for the Majority Leader," *New York Times Magazine*, July 3, 1949, 14.

38. Ann Cooper, "Senate Limits Post-Cloture Filibusters," *Congressional Quarterly Weekly Report*, Feb. 24, 1979, 319-320.

39. Senate Committee on Rules and Administration, *Television and Coverage of Proceedings in the Senate Chamber*, 97th Cong., 1st sess., 1981, committee print, 5.

40. *Congressional Record*, 99th Cong., 2d sess., 1986, S1663-5.

41. Ibid., 100th Cong., 1st sess., Aug. 7, 1987, S11602.

42. Center for Responsive Politics, *Congressional Operation—Congress Speaks: A Survey of the 100th Congress* (Washington, D.C.: Center for Responsive Politics, 1988), 49, 70, 72.

43. Stewart, "Two Strategies of Leadership," 68.

44. Martin Tolchin, "Howard Baker: Trying to Tame an Unruly Senate," *New York Times Magazine*, March 28, 1982, 70.

45. Lance T. LeLoup, *The Fiscal Congress* (Westport, Conn.: Greenwood Press, 1980), 71.

46. Cohen, "Byrd of West Virginia," 1294.

47. Peabody, *Leadership in Congress,* 470.

48. Munk, "Party Floor Leadership," 41.

49. Simeon S. Wallis et al., *The Process of Government* (Lexington: University of Kentucky Bureau of Government Research, 1949), 46.

50. *Congressional Record*, 97th Cong., 2d sess., 1982, S16115.

51. Cohen, "Byrd of West Virginia," 1295.

52. See Stephen Hess, *The Ultimate Insiders: U.S. Senators in the National Media* (Washington, D.C.: Brookings Institution, 1986).

53. Cohen, "Byrd of West Virginia," 1294.

54. Quoted by Helen Dewar, "Frustration Without Achievement in the Senate," *Washington Post,* Jan. 4, 1988, A1.

# 12. HOUSE MAJORITY PARTY LEADERSHIP IN THE LATE 1980s

## Barbara Sinclair

Only hours after he was chosen Speaker of the House, Jim Wright, D-Texas, advocated increasing federal tax revenue by delaying the scheduled rate cut for the wealthy. Convinced of the urgency of reducing the huge budget deficit and of the impossibility of doing so through spending cuts alone, Wright, at a press conference, called for more taxes despite the opposition of the chairman of the Ways and Means Committee—the tax writing committee—and despite the belief among Democrats that advocacy of tax increases spells electoral disaster.

In accordance with the Speaker's suggestion to committee Democrats at the beginning of their deliberations, the budget resolution reported out of the Budget Committee stipulated reducing the deficit through equal amounts of spending cuts and tax increases. By passing this budget resolution, the House committed itself to raising taxes.

Aware of the potential electoral costs of their position, the Speaker and the rest of the top party leadership attempted to shape public perceptions on the issue with an aggressive media campaign. Through the Speaker's daily fifteen-minute press conference, formal speeches, informal chats with reporters in the halls, appearances on television news shows, and written statements, the Speaker, Majority Leader Tom Foley, D-Wash., and Majority Whip Tony Coelho, D-Calif., got their message out. The message was that the huge deficit was the inevitable consequence of Ronald Reagan's policy of cutting taxes while increasing defense spending, and the *only* feasible way of reducing the deficit was a balanced program of spending cuts and revenue increases. News analysis during 1987 pointed to Reagan's responsibility for the deficit more frequently than before, and public opinion polls showed that Democrats were seen as more capable than Republicans in economic policy. This changed climate of opinion made it easier for congressional Democrats to vote for a budget resolution that included taxes.

The budget resolution did not enact the tax legislation; to carry out the instructions in the resolution, the House Ways and Means Committee had to report out a bill. The Speaker, however, did not want just any tax bill. He felt strongly that the bill should be progressive, that those with higher income should pay higher rates. The president, who had said a tax bill would become law over his dead body, would certainly mount an all-out attack, and the Speaker wanted a bill he could defend.

A mixture of persuasion and pressure convinced Ways and Means to produce a bill that met the Speaker's requirements. Wright talked with the committee chairman and with the Democratic members, explained his rationale in numerous private meetings with House Democrats, and made numerous public statements. The bill was discussed frequently in the weekly whip meetings. A Democratic Caucus meeting showed the committee that most Democrats agreed with the Speaker—the tax bill had to be progressive, and the Speaker let the committee know that if the bill were not, he would allow liberals to offer a substitute on the floor. Ways and Means reported a bill that fully satisfied the Speaker's criteria.

Before the bill could be brought to the floor, however, the stock market fell 500 points. In response, the president finally expressed willingness to enter negotiations towards a deficit reduction package with Congress. These talks complicated the leadership's task. To enhance the Democrats' bargaining position, and because of deadlines set by the Gramm-Rudman-Hollings deficit reduction act, Wright believed it essential for the House to pass the reconciliation bill, which included the tax provisions and some but not all of the spending cuts specified by the budget resolution. The ongoing deficit reduction talks, however, gave those members still leery of voting for taxes an excuse to oppose the bill.

The leadership mounted a major vote-mobilization effort. Every Democratic member was contacted, many more than once. Even so, when the fifteen-minutes specified for a roll call ran out, the vote stood at 205-206. The majority leader, the whip, other Democrats involved in the effort, and senior floor staff scurried around looking for another vote while the Speaker, who was presiding, held the vote open. Finally a Democrat willing to change his vote was found, and the bill passed 206-205.

Despite the closeness of the vote, passage had the effect the Speaker envisioned. The deficit reduction package negotiated by Congress and the White House included $9 billion in taxes, less than in the House bill but much more than the president had wanted. Getting the president to agree to an increase in taxes meant that modest progress was made on the deficit, Democrat-supported domestic programs were spared further drastic cuts, and opposition to tax increases was blunted as a Republican election issue.

The story of how Congress came to pass tax legislation in 1987 nicely illustrates this essay's thesis: House majority party leadership in the late 1980s is stronger, more policy-oriented, and more media conscious than any of modern times.

## Leadership Functions, Leadership Strategies, and the Impact of Context

Building winning coalitions and performing party maintenance are the primary functions their members and prominent external actors expect party leaders to perform. Members, the president, if of the same party, and major interest groups allied with the party expect the leadership to engineer passage of legislation important to them. Party maintenance, or "keeping peace in the family," as the current leaders call it, involves promoting and maintaining intraparty harmony; it dictates that leaders help members satisfy their career expectations; it requires leaders to mitigate and foster cooperative patterns of behavior among party members. Just what leadership behavior is involved in building winning coalitions and keeping peace in the family has varied over time and depends upon the context or environment.

Many scholars argue that congressional leadership is best understood from a contextual perspective.[1] The broader political context and the internal House environment shape and constrain leadership styles and strategies. House and party rules distribute resources in the chamber, and the distribution of resources among party leaders, committee leaders, and rank-and-file members affects what leadership strategies are feasible. The size of the party contingent in the House is another major variable affecting strategy choices and the probability of success.

In the late nineteenth century, the speakership developed into an extremely powerful office. House rules gave the Speaker immense resources: he appointed the members and chairmen of all committees and chaired the Rules Committee, which controls the flow of legislation to the floor. In a period of strong parties, the Speaker, as leader of the majority party and holder of great institutional resources, could run the House. The leadership styles and strategies of Speakers such as Thomas B. Reed and Joseph Cannon were based on centralization and command.

The 1910-1911 revolt against Speaker Cannon stripped the office of much of its power: the Speaker was removed from the Rules Committee, and the power to appoint the members and chairmen of committees was taken away. The party system also weakened. By the 1920s seniority had become the sole criterion for appointment to chairmanships, and, as a result, chairmanships became independent positions of power over which the majority party had little control. This change in context dictated a change in leadership style. Sam Rayburn's style was based on persuasion. He made little use of formal leadership structures, relying instead on doing favors for members and building coalitions through negotiation with a few pivotal actors.

In the late 1950s and the 1960s, junior Democrats, predominantly liberal northerners, increasingly chafed under the rigid control of committee chairmen. Most of the chairmen were conservative southerners who ran their committees with an iron hand, denying junior members the opportunity for meaningful participation. In the late 1960s and early 1970s, a series of rules changes altered the distribution of influence. Rank-and-file members, subcommittee chairmen, and the party leadership all gained at the expense of committee chairmen. The chairmen's almost total control over the organization, staffing, and agenda of their committees was diluted, and subcommittee chairmen and rank-and-file members gained a real voice. The requirement that committee chairmen be approved by a secret ballot majority vote of the party membership made chairmen more responsive to both the rank and file and to party leaders. The Speaker was given greater control over committee assignments, new powers over the referral of bills to committee, and, most significant, the right to nominate all Democratic members of the Rules Committee subject only to ratification by the party caucus.

The desire of rank-and-file members to participate more fully in the legislative process was a major impetus for these changes. And much higher participation rates were the result. Therefore, while the party leadership gained new resources, it also confronted an environment made highly unpredictable by the larger number of actors.

These changes in the House made the Rayburn strategy obsolete. In an unstable environment, more formal and more systematic ways of gathering information are necessary, and a strategy based on personal negotiation with a few people cannot work when many are participating. In the late 1970s the newly elected leadership team of Speaker Thomas P. "Tip" O'Neill, Jr., D-Mass., and Majority Leader Wright developed a three-pronged strategy, which, with elaborations, is still used today. First, the leadership is service-oriented. In addition to doing favors for individual members, the postreform leadership also provides services, such as timely information on the legislative schedule, to the Democratic membership collectively. Because almost any member can cause problems for the leadership, rank-and-file satisfaction or dissatisfaction is taken more seriously than before. By providing services, the leaders contribute to party maintenance and develop a store of good will they can draw upon in their coalition-building efforts.

Second, the leadership uses its formal powers and its influence to structure choices so as to advantage the outcome it favors. Neither the leadership's limited resources nor current political norms make coercion of individual members a feasible basis for coalition building. Some of the powers leaders acquired in the 1970s, especially their control over the Rules Committee, augmented their ability to shape and therefore influence the choices members face on the floor. Such strategies require member acquiescence, overt or tacit, which limits their applicability. Members do not perceive their use as unreasonably coercive; consequently, the party maintenance function is not adversely affected.

The attempt to include as many members as possible in the coalition-building process—the strategy of inclusion—is the third prong. It consists of expanding and using formal leadership structures, such as the whip system, and of bringing other Democratic members into the process on an ad hoc basis. In the new House environment the core leadership is too small to undertake the task of successful coalition building alone; including other members provides the needed assistance. The strategy of inclusion is also a way for leaders to satisfy members' expectations that they play a significant part in the legislation process and thereby contributes to keeping peace in the family.

The 1980s brought major changes in the political context, which required further leadership adaptations. When Ronald Reagan won the presidency and Republicans took control of the Senate for the first time in a quarter-century, House Democrats faced a situation that threatened all their goals. Reagan's policy agenda was anathema to the core of the Democratic party, and Republican control of the Senate, combined with many members' perception of a Reagan electoral mandate, made passage of major elements of that agenda possible. Republican capture of the House and even an electoral realignment making the Republican party the majority party seemed possible, with the consequence that Democrats would be deprived of their institutional positions of power. During Reagan's first two years in office, the House Democratic leadership found itself on the defensive, devoting its efforts to limiting the damage of the Reagan assault as best it could. When the 1982 elections brought substantial Democratic gains in the House, a somewhat less defensive stance became possible. The 1986 elections in which Democrats retook the Senate, followed by the Iran-contra scandal, both of which weakened the president, further changed the context in which the leadership operates, expanding the opportunities open to newly elected Speaker Jim Wright.

## Coalition Building and Party Maintenance in the Late 1980s

The leadership strategies of the Wright-Foley-Coelho team show considerable continuity with those of its predecessor, but Speaker Wright's leadership style is different from O'Neill's. Wright is more policy-oriented than O'Neill; he is more interested and involved in the substance of policy. Wright also tends to lead with a stronger hand than O'Neill did. O'Neill was inclined to await the emergence of a consensus; Wright is likely to push and prod the relevant actors into making a decision and, on important matters, will lay out the shape he believes their decision should take. These style differences stem from the different personalities of the two men. As important, however, are the contextual factors that have made it possible for Wright to follow his proclivities.

### Choosing Priorities

Although there is consensus that the majority party leadership should build winning coalitions on legislation important to the party as a collectivity, there is less agreement on just what legislation fits that definition. Leaders have limited time and resources, so they must make choices. When the president is of the same party, House leaders are expected to make the president's top legislative priorities their own. The forces that led the president to make an issue a top priority are also likely to affect the party leaders, and the president's level of success reflects upon the party as a whole. O'Neill, therefore, used all his skill and a wide variety of resources to pass President Jimmy Carter's energy program in 1977.

For a majority party leadership that faces a president of the other party, the strategic situation is more complicated. The majority party can cooperate with the president to pass compromise policies; it can try to defeat the president's program; or it can try to pass its own program. In 1987 a set of conditions came together that made it possible for the new House majority party leadership to pursue the strategy of passing its own program more consistently and vigorously than any leadership in modern times. The 1986 Democratic recapture of the Senate, the Iran-contra scandal, and Reagan's lame-duck status weakened him and contributed to a growing consensus among Democrats that taking the policy initiative was the correct strategy. The passage of legislation stymied during the first six years of the Reagan presidency seemed a real possibility, and Democrats were eager to establish a reputation for effective governance to take into the 1988 elections.

Wright took advantage of this favorable set of circumstances to establish an agenda for the Democratic party and the House. Believing that "the Congress was meant to be and can be creative and dynamic," Wright, soon after his election as Speaker, announced an agenda that included a clean water bill, highway legislation, aid to the homeless, trade legislation, catastrophic health insurance, increased funding for education, and welfare reform. Deficit reduction partly funded by revenue increases also was a priority.

The agenda developed from Wright's own sense of what was needed and what was politically feasible as well as from discussions with Majority Leader Foley and the Steering and Policy Committee. Wright wanted a "limited agenda that could be achieved." At a weekend retreat for House Democrats in January, he announced a schedule for House action on these initiatives and on essential legislation such as the budget resolution and appropriations bills.

A modern Speaker proposing an agenda on this scale—and a schedule for its implementation—is unprecedented. Wright believes, however, that "someone is needed to give coherence to the efforts of the House; otherwise you have it going in twenty different directions." [2] In fact, so long as House Democrats believe that their party should follow the strategy of proposing and attempting to pass its own program, the Speaker is meeting their expectations.

Nevertheless, the course is risky. The Speaker is encroaching into the domain of the committees, and committee leaders might be expected to object. Three factors, which will be discussed in more detail later, have mitigated the potentially negative impact on party maintenance of the Speaker's aggressive policy leadership. First, Wright practices the strategy of inclusion; second, the committees and their leaders often need him to help pass their bills; and, third, his agenda generally has the support of a strong majority of the party membership. Clearly, a Speaker can set forth and enact an agenda only if most of the items included are those on which a reasonable level of intraparty consensus exists or can be created. A Speaker who pushed many highly divisive issues would be exacerbating rather than mitigating intraparty conflicts. Even Wright's advocacy of a tax increase, which many Democrats thought was politically risky, was considered substantively correct by most.

## Before Legislation Comes to the Floor

Current political and institutional conditions provide expanded opportunities for leadership involvement in legislation before it reaches the floor. As a consequence of the multiple referral rule instituted in the mid-1970s, many important bills are the product of more than one committee.[3] When a bill is referred to several committees, the Speaker has the power to set deadlines for the committees to report the legislation, and this gives him considerable leverage. An unenthusiastic committee cannot simply delay. How a multiply referred bill is to be handled on the floor, often a complex problem because there may be competing versions of the legislation, is decided by the Rules Committee, and the decisions it makes often have important substantive and strategic implications. The Rules Committee is now a reliable arm of the leadership, providing the Speaker with significant leverage. Finally, the leaders of the committees involved often believe that their chances of passing a bill depend upon their working out their disagreements before the bill reaches the floor. If they cannot do so on their own, they often turn to the party leadership, the only entity with integrative capability in a decentralized institution.

The catastrophic health insurance bill passed by the House in 1987 is a case in point. This bill was referred to Energy and Commerce and to Ways and Means, committees led by two of the strongest chairmen in the contemporary House, John Dingell, D-Mich., and Dan Rostenkowski, D-Ill., respectively. Speaker Wright, early in the process of bill development, had suggested adding a provision covering drug payments to put a Democratic stamp on the administration's bill. The notion was popular among Democratic-leaning elderly groups and was eagerly embraced by many committee Democrats, most particularly by California's Henry Waxman, liberal chairman of the Health and Environment Subcommittee of Energy and Commerce.

The bills the two committees produced, while similar in thrust, differed in a number of ways, with the Energy and Commerce bill being more generous. Because the administration had become increasingly hostile to the legislation, committee proponents believed that they had to work out their differences before the bill reached the floor. "A single bill with all the important players on board is necessary," a committee leader said. "And to get it, you, Mr. Speaker, need to be involved." "You need to take a major role," the Speaker was told. In this case, committee leaders, known as jealous guardians of their own turf, invited the Speaker's participation because without it they could not pass the bill. At a meeting of the committee and subcommittee chairmen, Wright brokered an agreement that resulted in one bill.

Another complication was the intention of Claude Pepper, D-Fla., chairman of the Rules Committee, to make in order his own amendment adding a long-term home care program to the bill. Committee leaders believed that if the Pepper amendment passed on the floor it would doom the bill to a presidential veto. Because most of the elderly groups supported the proposal, Democrats would find it difficult to vote against it. Younger constituents, on the other hand, might see the vote as an indication that Democrats still favored "tax and spend" policies; certainly Republicans would attempt to portray the vote that way. If the Pepper amendment were debated on the floor, Democrats would fight each other and the public would see dissension instead of legislative accomplishment and effective governance.

The committee leaders appealed to the Speaker to talk Pepper out of offering his amendment. Loath to lean too hard on the eighty-seven-year-old chairman of the Rules Committee, who had been advocating this program for forty years, Wright talked to Pepper over and over. When Pepper, a team player, had tentatively agreed in return for Wright's pledge of a floor vote on his program sometime later during the 100th Congress, Wright nailed down the agreement at a meeting of the task force assembled to pass the bill. By a show of hands from the twenty-five or so participants, he demonstrated to Pepper that the Democratic membership was overwhelmingly opposed to his offering the amendment. Wright also announced his commitment to Pepper and made it clear he intended to honor it.

The huge deficit that constrains legislative choices and the deep ideological divisions between congressional Democrats and the Reagan White House resulted in Congress doing much of its legislating through the passage of a few huge omnibus bills that are difficult for the president to veto. Congress's use of omnibus bills has made early leadership involvement more and more routine. Given the number of issues and the number of committees involved, as well as the stakes for the party, leadership coordination and strategic direction are inevitable.

Wright has taken advantage of this opening somewhat more aggressively than his predecessor did. Wright set the basic guidelines for the budget resolution, which in turn sets guidelines for House spending and taxing decisions. It was Wright's formula that deficit reduction be accomplished half by revenue increases and half by spending cuts that would be equally divided between domestic and defense cuts. The party leadership decides what new programs may be included in the reconciliation bill that carries out the budget resolution. Majority Leader Foley chaired the group from Congress and the administration that worked out a budget deficit reduction deal in the wake of the October 1987 stock market crash. When Congress carries out its essential business through a small number of broad measures, the majority leadership, the only entity that can speak for the party as a whole and with its command of that critical integrative mechanism, the Rules Committee, will of necessity play an important role.

Wright has also gotten involved in legislation on his priority list. "What I try to do is bring in the principal players most intimately involved and visit with them to have a somewhat collegial approach," the

Speaker explained. "Usually we find we're on the same wavelength, and they have a better feel for how I feel about the legislation." [4] Because, in fact, Ways and Means and the Speaker were not at first on the same wavelength on taxes, Wright engaged in a campaign of persuading members directly and pressuring them indirectly by cajoling other members and by making public statements. When the Agriculture Committee had not reported out an agricultural credit bill by late July, Wright called in the chairman and the subcommittee members. Many midwestern Democrats had won by promising to do something about the agricultural credit crisis, he pointed out. If the committee did not report a bill soon, there would be no time for the Senate to act and the year would end without a bill. Is that what they wanted? The committee reported a bill within a week.

Members acquiesce in leadership involvement at the committee stage because they need leadership help to put together a bill that will pass, because the leadership usually does so to further the legislative goals of a strong majority of Democrats, or because, without a strong leadership role, no legislation will result, and this will reflect badly on the party. They also acquiesce because of the mechanisms the leaders use: they do not dictate but rather they bring people in, they talk, they persuade, they coopt.

## Leadership Strategies

Wright's accession to the speakership has not created a major discontinuity in leadership strategies. The contextual factors that led to the development of the strategies described earlier still largely pertain. Those leadership strategies were refined during the 1980s under O'Neill and during Wright's first Congress as Speaker.

**Services and Favors.** The current leadership provides services to members collectively and favors to them individually. Because missing too many roll call votes is considered hazardous to members' reelection prospects, the leadership's floor scheduling intimately affects every member's life. Members want timely information on the schedule, they want predictability, and they want as much time to spend in the district as possible. They also want their own legislative priorities passed in a timely fashion. The leadership tries to be considerate of members' needs in scheduling, to inform them of the schedule as far in advance as possible, and to keep Mondays free of votes as often as possible. It tries to give members "something they can brag about" when they go home for a district work period. If a farm bill and the foreign aid bill are ready for floor consideration before a recess, the leadership will choose the farm bill. No one can brag about having passed a foreign aid bill.

Through the whip's office, the leadership disseminates a great deal of information to Democratic members: the schedule, whip advisories that explain each bill coming to the floor, and a variety of other materials—from fact sheets on issues to results of recent polls—that members might find useful.

Leaders perform a wide variety of favors for their members. A leader can intercede with a committee to stimulate action on a bill of importance to a member. Leaders can throw their considerable weight behind rank-and-file members' requests to executive departments or even foreign governments. The Speaker's signature on a letter requesting that the Soviets permit a family to emigrate may have expedited that request. At any rate, the Soviet ambassador personally brought Wright the news that the request had been granted. Members often ask the Speaker to make their amendments in order on the floor. They frequently make requests about the scheduling of bills. Members want the leaders' help in getting good committee assignments; they covet a slot on the Steering and Policy Committee or as a whip.

The leaders cannot satisfy every request. The supply of desirable committee assignments, for example, is limited, and the leaders must choose those who are reasonably loyal to party positions or risk their coalition-building efforts. The interests of party members as a collectivity must be the primary determinant of decisions about the structure of rules and the floor schedule. If a member requests the Speaker's help in bringing to the floor an issue that presents a politically unpalatable choice to many other Democrats, the results of acquiescence would be intraparty discord.

Leaders also are involved in fund raising for their members. The top leaders have established political action committees to solicit funds that they contribute to other Democrats. They attend Democratic Congressional Campaign Committee (DCCC) fund-raising events; during 1987 the Speaker traveled to twenty-five different cities to appear at DCCC events. They also go to the districts of individual members for fund raisers. Because they are good draws, the leaders increase the financial success of the events they attend.

Finally, there are a variety of small favors leaders can do for members. Important constituents can be impressed by a handshake and a photo—and by a few words of extravagant praise for their representative—from the Speaker. Roy Dyson, a Maryland Democrat, brought the Speaker not only two constituents but also a bushel basket of Chesapeake Bay crabs. Because oysters in the bay had become contaminated, Dyson and his constituents hoped that a picture with the Speaker in area newspapers would spread the word that crabs were safe to eat. Wright, a crab-lover, happily obliged.

These services contribute to party maintenance. The leaders help their members advance their individual goals of reelection, policy, and influence. A frequent by-product of these activities is information useful in the performance of leadership functions. For example, when a leader spends some time in a member's district, the leader gains a better understanding of that member's electoral circumstances, which can inform later persuasion efforts. Is the member safe enough to take a chance on a difficult vote? What are the truly dangerous issues for that particular member? Finally, the favors leaders do also contribute to coalition-building success. The House does not operate on a quid pro quo basis, but members who have benefited from leaders' favors usually feel obligated to return the favor when they can. Those who do not will find the leaders less receptive to their requests.

**Structuring Choices.**   Rules changes during the 1970s significantly enhanced the majority party leadership's tools for structuring the choices members face on the floor in ways that favor the leadership position. The Speaker strongly influences the character of rules for floor consideration of important legislation. A rule specifies the length of floor debate and whether amendments will be allowed. In addition to allowing all germane amendments (an open rule) or barring all amendments (a closed rule), a rule may make only certain amendments in order; it may specify the order in which amendments or substitutes are to be considered; it may waive points of order against the legislation, thereby allowing provisions that otherwise would be struck if one member objected; or, in still other ways, structure floor decisions.

The growth in rank-and-file participation in the 1970s manifested itself in a huge increase in amendments offered on the floor, the number more than doubling from 800 per Congress in the early 1970s to 1,700 in 1977-1978.[5] The Rules Committee responded by gradually increasing the proportion of rules that in some way restrict amendments. In 1977-1978, 88 percent of rules were open; this number decreased in each succeeding Congress to 64 percent during the 99th (1985-1986).[6]

To move his agenda according to schedule, Wright made frequent use of restrictive rules during 1987. Such rules contribute to "predictability of outcome and of timing," an aide explained. Through September 17, 43 percent of the rules contained some sort of restriction.[7] "The Speaker has correctly been trying to force the House to follow a schedule in the first year to show he means business," said Rules Committee member Martin Frost, D-Texas. "The Rules Committee has been a major factor in making that happen."[8]

How the character of the rule can affect the legislative outcome is illustrated by welfare reform legislation considered in late 1987. The

Ways and Means Committee, which had primary jurisdiction over the legislation, wanted a closed rule. A significant number of Democrats, however, thought the bill too expensive and wanted to amend it on the floor. The leadership determined that a closed rule would not pass. Tom Carper, D-Del., wanted to offer an amendment cutting the program's cost, but letting him do so, the leadership thought, would doom the bill because enough Democrats would join all the Republicans to pass the amendment. Adoption of the amendment would alienate most strong supporters of welfare reform, and they would join most Republicans to defeat the bill on final passage. The leadership decided to bar the Carper amendment but to allow an amendment by Mike Andrews, D-Texas, that also cut the program but not by enough to alienate the original bill's strong supporters. With this solution, those Democrats who wanted to demonstrate their fiscal responsibility were given a vote to trim the program. The rule, Andrews's amendment, and the bill all passed with relative ease.

In responding to complex legislative situations, the party leadership and the Rules Committee have grown more creative in crafting rules. The rule for consideration of the defense authorization bill in the spring of 1987 is a case in point. After the Armed Services Committee reported the bill, about 400 floor amendments were proposed. If the Rules Committee had granted a simple open rule allowing all germane amendments, floor consideration would have gone on for weeks, eating up time needed to consider essential money bills and other measures on the Speaker's agenda. The rule allowed about 200 amendments, set time limits for various amendments, and specified, or gave the committee chairman the discretion to specify, the order in which amendments were to be considered. The decisions on order provided important strategic opportunities to structure choices. "The House doesn't want to go on one tack for too long," committee chairman and bill manager Les Aspin, D-Wis., explained. "If it hits a couple of votes going left, the boys are then looking to tack back and go to the right. The rhythm of the place is important. You want to structure a debate so you catch the wave. It's like surfing." [9] The rule contained several "king-of-the-hill" provisions, a new procedure in the 1980s.[10] These provisions specified that a number of alternatives be voted on with the last alternative receiving a majority declared the winner. Clearly, the order in which alternatives come to a vote is critical here.

Debate on the defense bill lasted for two weeks, long for the House but almost certainly shorter than debate under an open unstructured rule would have been. Although 124 amendments were actually offered, the process was orderly and controlled, and the arms control amendments favored by the leadership were adopted.

Self-executing rules are another device used by the leadership. Such a rule stipulates that adoption of the rule simultaneously enacts another measure or amendment.[11] For example, those members who voted for the rule for consideration of the continuing (appropriations) resolution in November 1987 were also voting for making the resolution conform to the budget summit agreement and for denying a pay raise to members of Congress and other high government officials. The Appropriations Committee had reported the bill before the summit agreement. Going back into committee to make conforming changes would have delayed the bill and reduced the House's bargaining room in conference with the Senate. The pay provision was included to give Democrats some political cover and to bolster at least marginally the rule's chances of passage. Republicans and some of the press had attacked Democrats who voted for the reconciliation bill, claiming that they had thereby voted themselves a pay raise. Democrats thus were eager for a chance to vote against a salary increase. By making the provision self-executing, Democrats got their chance, and Republicans who opposed the rule could be portrayed as voting for a pay raise.

Restrictive rules by definition restrict members' discretion. By and large, Democrats go along with them because they believe they gain more than they lose. The leadership generally uses its powers to further policy goals favored by a strong majority of Democrats; it employs restrictive rules to protect Democrats from Republican attempts to confront them with no-win choices. Restrictive rules also shorten debate time and make the schedule more predictable—consequences that all members appreciate, even if most Republicans are unwilling to say so publicly.[12] Responding to Pennsylvania Republican gadfly Bob Walker's criticism of the defense bill rule, Armed Services Committee Republican Bob Badham of California said, "If . . . we did have an open rule . . . , we would never have a defense bill and this country would not have a defense because of the dilatory tactics, not of the Rules Committee, but of the membership of this body." [13]

Because a rule must be approved by a majority vote of the House, the membership can stymie the leadership's strategy by defeating the rule. In fall 1987 the first rule for consideration of the reconciliation bill was defeated. Ways and Means had asked the Speaker to include the welfare reform bill in the reconciliation bill because the latter contained new taxes to pay for the former. Providing new money to pay for new programs in the same bill was considered essential to passage; otherwise, supporters could be accused of increasing the deficit. Before the reconciliation bill came to the floor, the stock market crash further highlighted the deficit problem. A number of Democrats objected to voting for any new spending program, fearing it would send the wrong signal to the market and give future opponents electoral ammunition. Supporters of welfare reform, however, believing they had a commitment from the leadership, threatened to vote against the rule if their cause were removed from the package. Realizing that the chances of passing the rule were tenuous whatever he did, the Speaker chose to leave welfare reform in the bill. Enough Democrats joined the united Republican opposition to defeat the rule.

The need for member acquiescence in strategies based upon structuring choices through rules limits those strategies. Yet that requirement also acts as a safety device for the leadership. If it has misjudged what the membership will accept, the membership can let it know by defeating the rule. The leadership would rather lose any given coalition-building effort than create serious dissatisfaction among its members.

The reconciliation bill floor fight illustrates, in addition, the strategic use of the Speaker's procedural powers as presiding officer. When the rule went down to defeat, the Speaker asked the Rules Committee to report another rule excising the welfare reform proposal from the bill. House rules specify that a rule may be taken up the same day as reported only by two-thirds vote. The Republicans certainly would remain sufficiently united to block the rule because they opposed the bill, but the Speaker did not want to put off consideration until the next day, a Friday. Many members had previous commitments; they would be inconvenienced, and full attendance could not be assured. Employing an infrequently used parliamentary maneuver, the Speaker adjourned the House and then called it back into session for a new legislative day, thus making the rule in order. A majority of the House had to approve this maneuver; the leadership could not and did not force it on its membership. The new rule then passed with little difficulty. Most of the supporters of welfare reform voted for the rule, since the leadership had given them their chance.

Still final passage was difficult. If the Speaker had not used another resource at the command of the presiding officer, the vote would have been lost. The rules specify that members must be given at least fifteen minutes to vote, but how much longer is left to the Speaker's discretion. By holding open the vote for an extra ten minutes, the Speaker gave the rest of the leadership team time to find the crucial deciding vote.

**The Strategy of Inclusion.** The core party leadership—Speaker, majority leader, and whip—is too small to undertake the task of successful coalition building alone. House members are independent, active, and often unpredictable in their voting. Successful coalition building requires an extensive information-gathering and persuasion capability. To respond to this need, the party leadership has developed the strategy of inclusion; it attempts to include as many Democrats as possible in the coalition-building process. Over time the leadership has expanded and made more use of formal leadership structures, but it also brings other Democrats into the process on an ad hoc basis.

The whip system, which in the early 1970s consisted of the whip, an assistant whip, and eighteen or so regionally elected zone whips, expanded enormously during the 1970s and 1980s.[14] In the 100th Congress eighty-two Democrats—about 30 percent of the Democratic House membership—were part of the system. The system consists of the majority whip, the chief deputy whip David Bonier of Michigan, who has become a part of the core leadership, ten deputy whips, four task force chairmen, forty-four at-large whips and twenty-two zone whips.

During O'Neill's speakership, the zone whips conducted the initial count of Democratic voting intentions on important legislation. The other whips, all of whom are appointed by the leadership, were used in the effort to persuade Democrats to support the party position. On particularly critical legislation, the Speaker appointed a task force and charged it with engineering passage of the bill. The first task force was on President Carter's energy legislation; budget resolutions, difficult to pass, always received task force treatment. The chairmen and members of the task forces were not necessarily members of the whip system or of the committee of origin. A willingness to work on the bill at issue and the skill to do so were the criteria for inclusion.

Task forces now have become the standard way of handling legislation on which any significant leadership effort is deemed necessary. The leadership selects a chairman, or sometimes co-chairs with ties to different wings of the party. The choice of the chair carries a message and is considered carefully. To signal members that a bill providing aid to Central American refugees was not related to the contra aid issue, Peter Kostmayer of Pennsylvania, a contra aid opponent, and Larry Smith of Florida, a supporter, were made co-chairs. Ron Flippo, an Alabama Democrat, was asked to chair a task force on raising the debt limit because of his ties to southerners who would need to be persuaded and because his acceptance of the chair would tell southerners that this was a bill they could vote for. In most cases, all the whips and all the Democratic members of the committee of origin who support the legislation are invited to join the task force; other Democrats who are interested in working on the issue are also welcomed. Those who show up become the task force.

How long before the vote a task force begins work varies, and occasionally a "quick and dirty" effort is necessary. Around 11 a.m. on

May 26, 1988, Republicans, without warning, offered an amendment to the intelligence authorization bill to lift restrictions on CIA aid to the contras. Believing passage would scuttle the talks between the Nicaraguan government and the contras scheduled to begin the next day, the Democratic leadership went into its "fire drill": the deputy whips were told to work the doors; a computer list of members absent for the last roll call was printed out and those who supported the leadership were located and asked to vote; a whip call alerting all Democrats that an important vote was imminent was sent out over the automatic phone system.

The members of the Nicaragua task force were called to the floor; each was assigned some of the fifty-one members with no hard-and-fast position whose votes would make the difference. The task force mission was to inform and persuade. Meanwhile, the task force chair asked the most active Republican opponent of contra aid to make sure the small band of like-minded Republicans were on board. The chair also persuaded an influential moderate Democrat to lobby other moderates.

Because time was short, refining the whip count to ensure accuracy was not possible. As the vote approached, the leadership still lacked reliable information on sixteen members, and, because contra aid votes generally had been close, the task force was assigned to "baby-sit" the sixteen. Each task force member sat with an assignee and made sure that person was informed about the substantive and political effects of the vote. When the vote came at about 1:30 p.m., the Republican amendment was defeated 214-190.

More typically, sufficient time is available to allow the process to start with a count from the zone whips. The task force meets, discusses where it stands in terms of numbers and what arguments are most likely to be effective, and then parcels out the names of Democrats not committed to voting for the leadership position and any others the whip believes need to be rechecked. The likelihood of success in persuasion is the basis on which names are assigned, which means that task force members most frequently are assigned Democrats from their own state and region, or sometimes those who serve on the same committee, or those who were in the same entering class. After members have made their contacts, they meet again to assess their progress. Names may be reshuffled and the process repeated.

If the legislation is top priority and the outcome in any doubt, the core leadership becomes involved in the one-on-one persuasion effort. Those Democrats with whom task force members have not been successful will be divided among the Speaker, majority leader, and whip for a final attempt. During the three days preceding the vote on the reconciliation bill, the Speaker estimated he talked to thirty-five or forty members. Members find it more difficult—though certainly not impossible—to say no to the Speaker than to another colleague. In addition, the Speaker can sometimes alleviate their concerns. To a number of Democrats worried that a provision in the bill could be interpreted as approving a congressional pay raise, Wright promised a vote killing the raise later in the year. Another group of members upset by the Appropriations Committee's last-minute increase in defense spending by $3 billion more than they believed had been agreed were also guaranteed a later vote to reduce the figure.

Although the leaders become involved in one-on-one persuasion on the most difficult votes, task forces allow the leadership to husband its resources for the hardest cases. They also provide the leaders with the accurate information needed to plan legislative strategy most effectively. In the large and unpredictable House, no mechanism always works. The count on the first rule for the 1987 reconciliation bill was slightly inaccurate, and that was sufficient to defeat the rule. Yet this was the only vote of significance the leadership lost in 1987, and an altered rule was quickly approved.

Through the whip system and the task forces, the leadership has enlisted a large number and a broad variety of Democrats in its efforts. By August, more than half of the Democratic membership had served on at least one task force during 1987. The number involved in the typical task force makes one-on-one persuasion with a large proportion of the membership possible. The breadth ensures that the group has ties to all sections of the party. Clearly their contribution to coalition building success is substantial.

The strategy of inclusion also promotes party maintenance. By involving Democrats in leadership efforts through task forces, the expanded whip system, and the Steering and Policy Committee, the leadership satisfies members' expectations of meaningful participation in the legislative process. Task forces provide an especially useful way of channeling junior members' desires for participation into activities beneficial to the leadership and the party.

For many rank-and-file House members, the legislative process grew increasingly frustrating during the 1980s. The deficit reduced the scope for legislative entrepreneurship, and the move toward a small number of omnibus bills seems to freeze many members out of meaningful legislative activity. A frustrated membership bodes ill for the leadership, so its provision of opportunities for meaningful participation has become even more important.

**Influencing Opinion Through the Media.** During the 1980s the leadership became media conscious to the extent that systematic attempts to influence opinion through the media should now be considered a fourth leadership strategy. Democrats in Congress watched as President Reagan made skillful use of the media in pursuing a course that threatened their policy, reelection, and power goals. The leadership became convinced that without a media strategy of its own it had no hope of competing.

"There's infinite informal contact with the leadership," according to a Capitol Hill reporter. Indeed, the party leadership not only makes itself available to the press but also pursues a concerted strategy aimed at influencing opinion through the media. The Speaker holds a press conference every day before the House convenes; the majority leader, the whip, and the deputy whip usually attend and can be buttonholed by reporters after the Speaker leaves to open the House. On special occasions, the leaders hold a press conference in the TV-radio gallery on the third floor of the Capitol. In fall 1987, for example, Speaker Wright held a number of press conferences to discuss developments on the Central American peace plan. Wright also invites reporters to lunches, each usually devoted to some particular topic. All the leaders respond to requests for interviews from individual reporters. The halls of the Capitol are open to reporters, and they can often catch a leader emerging from a meeting. Top leadership staff also deal with the press on a daily basis.

The leaders, especially the Speaker and the majority leader, are often asked to appear on television. An appearance on one of the morning news shows provides an opportunity to influence the opinion of the general public; through appearing on the "McNeil-Lehrer News Hour" and the Sunday talk shows, the leaders reach the attentive public and the Washington policy community.

"Sometimes to pass a bill," Majority Leader Foley said, "you have to change the attitude of the country." [15] Before major votes, an effort is made to sell the party position. In addition to their regular contacts with the media, leaders may try to place op-ed pieces in the major national newspapers, hold a special press conference devoted to the legislation, or arrange a series of one-minute speeches by proponents on the House floor intended for pickup by local television.

During a coalition-building effort, evidence that elite or mass opinion favors the party position is considered good ammunition and is fully exploited. Favorable poll data will be reported at whip meetings and given to task force members to use in their persuasion efforts. Such data and supportive editorials may be enclosed with a "Dear Colleague" letter to all Democrats.

Influencing opinion is almost always a long-term process. And, despite the leaders' considerable access to the media, they lag far behind the president in their ability to get their message out. To be effective, leadership media strategies need to be designed for the long haul.

Permanent task forces charged with "managing" an issue, not just with winning a specific vote, are one response to the need for sustained, organized effort. The Nicaragua task force was the first and served as a model. Set up in early 1985, it is still in existence. Under Bonier's chairmanship it set out not just to round up votes against contra aid but also to get the aid opponents' message out, to assure that their views were covered by the press. To this purpose, a systematic long-range series of events was worked out for the press to cover. Hearings by the appropriate Foreign Affairs subcommittee, an allied group's report on human rights abuses, a trip to Central America by a congressional delegation, a protest of contra aid by church groups were some of the events. The task force was always prepared with an event on any day the president dealt publicly with Central America. Because the president's activities receive press attention and the media's professional fairness norms dictate coverage of opponents' activities, if any, such counterprogramming was an effective means of increasing the visibility of the opponents' point of view.

The leadership's attempt to influence opinion on budget policy and the deficit was also a long-range, concerted effort. All of the mechanisms discussed earlier—from op-ed pieces in the *New York Times* to appearances on "Good Morning, America"—have been used to convey the message. When the media's attention is focused on an issue, the leadership intensifies its efforts because the likely payoff in coverage is greater. In the last week of the budget negotiations, the Speaker or the majority leader and sometimes both appeared on television every day. A new tactic was tried in the summer of 1987. When Reagan traveled to several cities to give speeches blaming the congressional Democrats for the deficit, he was greeted with full-page newspaper ads saying, "It's your deficit, President Reagan." Sponsored by the DCCC, the ads through a simple graph showed how the deficit had ballooned during the Reagan years.

To the extent they are effective, these media strategies contribute to successful coalition building. Democratic members are more likely to support the leadership's position if they believe that is what their constituents want. Media strategies also can contribute to party maintenance. Democratic members expect their party leaders to project a favorable image and present the party's policies in a convincing way. The electoral losses Democrats suffered in the 1980s and the beating the party's image took at the hands of Ronald Reagan made Democrats more concerned about their party's image and more aware that it is malleable. Democrats increasingly believe the party's image affects their chances of attaining their policy and perhaps also their reelection goals. Poll figures showing that the Democratic party's image was improving during 1987 contributed to House Democrats' satisfaction with their new leadership team.

Because the leaders' ability to influence the party's public image is limited, their members' expectations could become a serious problem for the leadership. In its competition with the president for media attention, the leadership is seriously disadvantaged. The president no longer "has the only megaphone in town," but he certainly has the biggest. The leadership cannot ensure that all House Democrats "are singing from the same hymn book"; the clear message the leadership would like to convey may get garbled in a cacophony of disparate voices. Further experimentation with various media strategies and a further development of media-relevant capabilities are the leadership's likely responses to this situation.

## Leadership Styles, Strategies, and Success: An Assessment

The new leadership team of Wright, Foley, and Coelho was remarkably successful in 1987 and 1988. The House passed all the items on the Speaker's agenda, and, despite a frequently deadlocked Senate and a hostile president, most became law. Those not enacted by the end of the 100th Congress served as election issues for Democrats.

Jim Wright's stronger, more policy-oriented style was well suited to the context of a weakened president and a Democratic membership eager for legislative results and a record to carry into the 1988 elections. Democrats were more amenable to being led than they had been in a number of years, and the leadership's strategies were well designed to exploit the situation. The leadership aggressively employed its procedural powers to shape members' choices. Taking advantage of the media's interest in the leadership team because of its newness, the leadership made a more concerted, systematic effort to get its message out, both to influence the perception of issues and to ensure that its legislative success was credited to the party. By including large numbers of Democrats in the vote-mobilization process, the leadership not only increased the chances of winning the vote at issue but also gave those members an opportunity for meaningful participation. That and the wide consultation that usually precedes leadership policy and strategy decisions reduce the likelihood that many members will chafe under Speaker Wright's stronger leadership. The services leaders provide and the favors they do also contribute to member satisfaction.

If the stronger, more policy-oriented leadership were only a function of ephemeral political conditions, one would expect it to be short-lived. However, in addition to favorable political conditions, more permanent changes in House operations also invite that style. Given the prevalence of multiply referred major legislation, a coordinating integrating entity is now essential if the House is to function, and, given current structures, only the leadership has the institutional resources and the legitimacy to serve as that entity. The dependence of committee chairs on party leadership assistance to pass their bills results from the decline of committee autonomy, which is not likely to be reversed.

In a more speculative vein, I suggest several other reasons why strong party leadership may continue. With the increased importance of black support for Democrats in the South, the constituency-based cohesion of House Democrats has increased. To be sure, southern Democrats on the average are still more conservative than their northern party colleagues, and party cohesion depends upon which issues are salient at a particular time. Nevertheless, as Congressional Quarterly's voting studies show, House Democrats are more cohesive in their voting behavior than they have been in decades.

The experience of the Reagan years has encouraged a sense of shared fate among Democrats; it has convinced many that party success is critical to advancing their power and policy goals even if it does not directly affect their own reelection. That sense of shared fate may prove ephemeral, but it seems to have contributed to high voting cohesion.

The House majority party leadership of the late 1980s can exercise strong, policy-oriented leadership because it possesses valuable resources and the skills to use them effectively. Even more important, its membership wants such leadership. Changes in how the House operates have raised the costs of weak party leadership in terms of legislative opportunities missed, while changes in the electoral constituencies of southern Democrats have decreased the costs of strong leadership to those members. Consequently, rather than being a short-lived response to ephemeral political conditions, such leadership may characterize the Congress of the 1990s.

# Notes

1. See Joseph Cooper and David W. Brady, "Institutional Context and Leadership Style: The House from Cannon to Rayburn," Robert L. Peabody, "Senate Party Leadership; From the 1950s to the 1980s," and Charles O. Jones, "House Leadership in an Age of Reform" in *Understanding Congressional Leadership,* ed. Frank H. Mackaman (Washington, D.C.: CQ Press, 1981); and Barbara Sinclair, *Majority*

*Leadership in the U.S. House* (Baltimore: Johns Hopkins University Press, 1983).

2. All unattributed quotations are from interviews conducted by or meetings attended by the author.

3. Walter Oleszek, Roger Davidson, and Thomas Kephart, "The Incidence and Impact of Multiple Referrals in the House of Representatives" (Congressional Research Service, 1986). See also Bruce Oppenheimer, "Policy Effects of U.S. House Reform: Decentralization and the Capacity to Resolve Energy Issues," *Legislative Studies Quarterly* 5 (February 1980): 5-30.

4. Richard E. Cohen, "Quick-Starting Speaker," *National Journal*, May 30, 1987, 1412.

5. Janet Hook, "GOP Chafes Under Restrictive House Rules," *Congressional Quarterly Weekly Report*, Oct. 10, 1987, 2451.

6. Ibid., 2450.

7. Ibid.

8. Ibid.

9. Linda Greenhouse, "A Military Bill Like None Other," *New York Times*, May 13, 1987, 12.

10. Walter Oleszek, "Legislative Procedures and Congressional Policymaking: A Bicameral Perspective" (unpublished manuscript), 10.

11. Ibid., 9.

12. See Hook, "GOP Chafes," 2451.

13. *Congressional Record*, daily ed., 100th Cong., 1st sess., H3198.

14. See Randall B. Ripley, "The Party Whip Organization in the United States House of Representatives," *American Political Science Review* 58 (June 1964): 561-576; and Lawrence C. Dodd, "The Expanded Roles of the House Democratic Whip System: The 93rd and 94th Congresses," *Congressional Studies* 7 (Spring 1979): 27-56.

15. *Congressional Quarterly Weekly Report*, Sept. 23, 1986, 2134.

# 13. TAKING IT TO THE FLOOR

## Steven S. Smith

This essay concerns decision making on the House and Senate floors. The chamber floors deserve attention for several reasons. The floor is the one place where all members are equal, at least in theory. In committees and in conferences, participation is explicitly restricted. What happens on the floors provides a clue about the standing of the rank-and-file members in congressional policy making. Furthermore, the role of committees, parties, and leaders cannot be fully understood without knowing, in some detail, how the products of these legislative actors are handled on the floor. That nearly all measures taken up on the floor are passed, for example, tells us nothing about the meaning of floor amendments and other floor motions that shape committee decisions and policy outcomes. Finally, floor activity is a good barometer of more general patterns of decision making. All legislation must pass through the chamber floors, where voting alignments, amending activity, and patterns of participation reflect the preferences, resources, and environmental influences that shape congressional politics.

One theme explored in this essay is that the House and Senate floors are now far more active sites of policy making than they were in the 1950s. The second theme is that rules matter; rules within each chamber have shaped the roles of the floors in fundamental ways. The third theme is that, despite some remarkable similarities of changes on the House and Senate floors, the chambers differ in their responses to these changes; indeed the House and Senate differ in their capacity to respond.

## Floor Amending Activity

Congressional floor agendas were transformed in fundamental ways during the 1960s and 1970s. The number of separate measures passed by Congress declined, but the average length of measures and

The author thanks L. Earl Shaw for his comments and advice.

Figure 13-1    Public Bills in the Congressional Workload, 80th-99th
               Congresses, 1947-1986

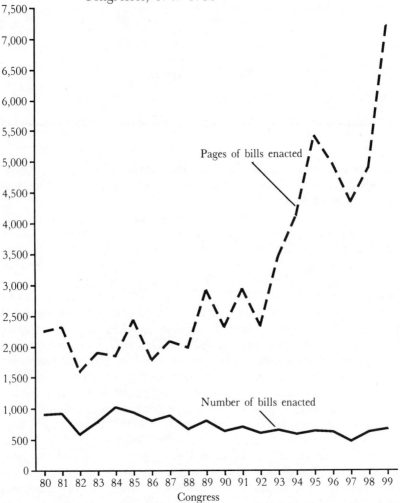

SOURCE: Norman J. Ornstein, Thomas E. Mann, and Michael J. Malbin, *Vital Statistics on Congress, 1987-1988* (Washington, D.C.: Congressional Quarterly, 1987), 170.

the total number of pages enacted into law increased dramatically, as Figure 13-1 indicates. These changes reflect a reduction in the number of small, routine bills, such as measures authorizing construction of individual bridges or post offices, coupled with expansion in the size and complexity of major legislation. One reason for this change is that federal programs have become far more complicated, and many of them must be periodically reauthorized. A typical measure now covers more distinctive policy subjects, sometimes in an attempt to integrate related policies but often as a matter of convenience for the authorizing committees.[1]

In the 1980s the trend toward longer, more complex legislation continued. Large budget deficits reshaped the congressional agenda, an agenda that created serious deadlocks between Congress and the president, House and Senate, and Republicans and Democrats. One consequence of political stalemate was that a small measure, such as the reauthorization of a health program, often could not make it through both chambers and the White House as a separate item. Budget politics created lengthy delays, with policy differences forcing protracted negotiations; and legislative gamesmanship led committees to incorporate more legislation into a few omnibus bills, such as continuing appropriations resolutions and reconciliation bills. By the 99th Congress (1985-1986), the average public bill enacted into law reached 10.8 pages, four to five times the size of the average measure in the mid-1950s.[2]

The changing formal agendas of the House and Senate floors reflected developments inside and outside of Congress. The political environment intensified demands on members of both chambers to champion the causes of outsiders. Members of both chambers faced larger, more heterogeneous constituencies at home. The tremendous growth of the federal bureaucracy, of constituency problems with the bureaucracy, and of organized interest group activity in Washington created more demands for members to take issues to the floor during the 1960s and early 1970s. The distinctive saliency and controversy of certain issues—civil rights, the Vietnam War, environmentalism, consumer protection, the energy crisis, drug abuse—affected both chambers. Such issues altered the incentives for participation among members of Congress, leading many members to carry policy disputes from committee rooms to the floor. Such a shift often produced dozens, sometimes hundreds, of floor amendments.

Inside Congress, committee chairmen were losing their grip over the activities of their committees. Chairmen often had been able to insulate their committees from the shifting winds of political events and public opinion by imposing, often quite autocratically, their own policy agendas. The decentralization of power within standing committees made agenda setting within them more responsive to the rank-and-file members and to the variety of political forces to which the rank and file respond. Decentralization helped to create less cohesive committees, increased the chances that committee disputes would spill onto the floor, and contributed to declining deference to committee recommendations.

Moreover, after the 1950s both chambers expanded the legislative staffs that make it possible for members to participate in committee and floor activity. Not only did personal, committee, and subcommittee staffs grow, but also new congressional support agencies—the Congressional Research Service, the Office of Technology Assessment, and the Congressional Budget Office—were created, and the functions of the General Accounting Office were expanded. The growth of the interest group community made available more policy experts to advise members and to draft legislation. Moreover, better educated individuals, including people with special policy expertise, were elected to Congress.

The effect of these changes can be seen in amending activity on the two chamber floors. Table 13-1 indicates that in both chambers the percentage of measures facing floor amendments nearly quadrupled between the mid-1950s and late 1970s.[3] By the late 1970s, between a quarter and a third of legislation reaching the chamber floors was subject to at least one floor amendment. The percentage of measures subject to ten or more amendments increased from less than one to more than five by the late 1970s in both chambers. In the 1980s fewer bills were the targets of amending activity, as much of the politically significant legislation was packaged into omnibus measures.

The volume of amending activity also mushroomed. Between the mid-1950s and the late 1970s, Senate amending activity more than tripled (Table 13-2). Other evidence suggests that the upward pattern was fairly smooth through the 1960s, but there was a jump of more

Table 13-1  Percentage of Measures Subject to Amending Activity

| Congress | | House | Senate |
|---|---|---|---|
| 84th | (1955-1956) | 6 | 8 |
| 86th | (1959-1960) | 6 | na |
| 88th | (1963-1964) | 11 | 10 |
| 90th | (1967-1968) | 18 | na |
| 92d | (1971-1972) | 22 | 18 |
| 94th | (1975-1976) | 25 | na |
| 96th | (1979-1980) | 23 | 31 |
| 99th | (1985-1986) | 14 | 19 |

SOURCE: Steven S. Smith, *Call to Order: Floor Politics in the House and Senate* (Washington, D.C.: Brookings Institution, forthcoming).
NOTE: na = not available.

Table 13-2   Senate Floor Amending Activity, 1955-1986

| Congress | Number of amendments | Percentage successful | Percentage contested [a] |
|---|---|---|---|
| 84th   (1955-1956) | 590 | 69 | 9 |
| 88th   (1963-1964) | 702 | 44 | 16 |
| 92d    (1971-1972) | 1,261 | 66 | 16 |
| 96th   (1979-1980) | 1,802 | 81 | 11 |
| 99th   (1985-1986) | 1,752 | 81 | 10 |

SOURCE: Smith, *Call to Order.*

[a] Contested amendments are subject to a recorded vote with a 60-40 or closer outcome.

than 300 amendments in the 92d Congress (1971-1972), after which the upward trend continued.[4] The success rate of amendments also grew, particularly during the 1970s. And yet the proportion of amendments resulting in close votes declined slightly at the same time. The tremendous growth in minor amendments during the 1970s, most of which were subject only to a voice vote, accounts for most of the increase in the success rates and for the decline in the percentage of contested amendments. However, the absolute number of contested amendments remains nearly as high in the 1980s as in the 1970s.

In the House, for which more complete data are available, more distinctive periods are apparent. As Table 13-3 indicates, the period from the mid-1950s to the early 1960s shows fairly steady growth in amending activity. Amending activity skyrockets in the 93d Congress (1973-1974) and the following two Congresses. The 93d Congress was the first in which the electronic voting system was used in the House. Two years earlier, the House had changed its rules to permit recorded voting in the Committee of the Whole, where most amending activity takes place. Previously, amendments were subject to voice votes, standing division votes, or teller votes in which members passed by appointed tellers to be counted for or against the amendment. The vote of the individual member was not recorded. Recorded voting appears to have increased the incentives to offer floor amendments. Committee chairmen could no longer exercise as much independent influence over members' voting decisions in the face of greater public scrutiny. Moreover, electronic voting reduced the practical difficulty of conducting a recorded vote by cutting the time required to conduct the vote by more than half. The success rate of House amendments also went up and, as in the Senate, is associated with a declining proportion of amendments subject to contested votes. The House success rate, however, has been and remains markedly lower than the Senate's.

Table 13-3   House Floor Amending Activity, 1955-1986

| Congress | | Number of amendments | Percentage successful | Percentage contested [a] |
|---|---|---|---|---|
| 84th | (1955-1956) | 405 | 52 | 19 |
| 86th | (1959-1960) | 446 | 38 | 16 |
| 88th | (1963-1964) | 614 | 43 | 19 |
| 90th | (1967-1968) | 847 | 50 | 20 |
| 91st | (1969-1970) | 877 | 46 | 14 |
| 92d | (1971-1972) | 792 | 47 | 19 |
| 93d | (1973-1974) | 1,425 | 52 | 16 |
| 94th | (1975-1976) | 1,366 | 55 | 17 |
| 95th | (1977-1978) | 1,695 | 61 | 17 |
| 96th | (1979-1980) | 1,380 | 69 | 13 |
| 99th | (1985-1986) | 1,074 | 77 | 11 |

SOURCE: Smith, *Call to Order.*

[a] Contested amendments are subject to a recorded vote with a 60-40 or closer outcome.

In the House, as in the Senate, floor amending activity receded during the 1980s. Budget politics, constraints on new policy initiatives, and omnibus legislation were instrumental in reducing the number of targets for amendments in both chambers, but the much sharper drop in House amending activity remains a puzzle. We will return to it shortly.

## The House Response to Chaos on the Floor

The surge in floor amending activity during the 1970s came as a surprise to many members of the House. When recorded voting in the Committee of the Whole was debated in 1970, no member predicted explicitly that the number of amendments would increase. The primary concern was that members would be called away from their offices and committee meetings to vote on amendments, distracting them from the "important" parts of their jobs. Thomas P. "Tip" O'Neill, D-Mass., the sponsor of the recorded voting proposal, predicted that only a few recorded votes would be held so that little would change in the way the House and individual members conducted their daily routines.[5] Two years later, when the electronic system was debated, the major argument of the proponents was that many hours of time would be saved with the speedier computerized voting system. No one foresaw that floor sessions actually might lengthen because of the stimulative effect the recorded electronic voting would have for amending activity.

Reformers did foresee that some amendment outcomes would change. Indeed, liberal reformers hoped to overturn several decisions on their amendments that had been made earlier. Recorded voting was credited for changing outcomes on a number of issues during the early 1970s, including action on the supersonic transport, the Vietnam War, and the antiballistic missile system.[6] As we have seen, success rates for amendments improved after the reforms of floor procedure were in place.

As experience with recorded voting in the Committee of the Whole accumulated, even some reformers' views of the procedural reforms were tempered by the deluge of Republican amendments. Minority party Republicans sponsored a disproportionately high number of the amendments from 1973 through 1979, after having sponsored no more than their proportionate share from 1967 through 1972. Moreover, Republicans were more likely than Democrats to push their amendments all the way to a recorded vote. Many Republicans relished the opportunity to force their majority party colleagues to cast recorded votes on politically difficult issues. A particular group of Republicans— John Ashbrook of Ohio, Robert Bauman of Maryland, and John Rousselot of California—deliberately badgered the Democrats with many amendments and requests for recorded votes. Bauman, the leader of the group, even entertained requests for amendments and recorded votes from Republican challengers to Democratic incumbents to get the most political value from his floor activity.[7]

House Democrats, including many who supported the reforms, became frustrated with their floor experiences as the 1970s wore on. Committee leaders did not appreciate the demise of the remnants of deference to their committees' recommendations. Even rank-and-file Democrats began to resent the dangers inherent in unpredictable floor amending activity. Repeated recorded votes on divisive issues posed special problems for incumbents looking for ways to explain their votes at home. And, if nothing else, extended floor sessions disrupted members' daily schedules, making it increasingly difficult to plan evening and weekend activities. The average daily session of the House expanded from 6.1 to 6.8 hours between 1967-1972 and 1973-1978.[8]

Democratic responses came in several forms. Within the first year of electronic voting, some Democrats demanded that the number of members required to call for a recorded vote be increased to forty-four from twenty, but no change was adopted until 1979 when the threshold was raised to twenty-five. A second avenue was to consider measures on the floor under a motion to suspend the rules. Such a motion simultaneously suspends the rules and brings a measure to the floor. No amendments are allowed, and debate is limited to forty minutes; the motion must be adopted by a two-thirds majority. Between 1973 and 1979, House Democrats succeeded in making several changes in the rule in order to permit suspension motions on more days. The effect was to increase the use of suspension motions to 453 in the 95th (1977-1978) from 255 in the 93d Congress (1973-1974).[9]

These responses to the dangers of floor amending activity produced only marginal results. The twenty-five-member threshold for recorded votes remained quite easy to meet on amendments of even modest importance. The expanded use of suspension motions, a procedure traditionally intended for noncontroversial measures, was a bit heavy handed, even for many Democrats. In fact, in 1979 the Democrats imposed on themselves a caucus rule that no measure authorizing or appropriating more than $100 million for a year could be considered by suspension of the rules without the special approval of the party's Steering and Policy Committee. The caucus rule also required that the Speaker give a three-day advance notice that a measure was scheduled for consideration under suspension of the rules. By the late 1970s, most major legislation remained vulnerable to unpredictable amending activity on the floor.

The Democrats' frustrations reached a boiling point late in 1979, when they suffered some major floor defeats and President Jimmy Carter's program was unraveling. More than forty Democrats wrote to Speaker O'Neill and the Rules Committee chairman to suggest a solution. They recommended increased use of "modified" special rules, which are resolutions from the Rules Committee that restrict in various ways the amendments that will be in order on the floor. For the most part, modified rules previously had been reserved for tax bills and a few others from the Ways and Means Committee. These Democrats insisted that a judicious use of modified rules, at least for major bills, would limit amending activity and yet provide an opportunity to vote on significant policy alternatives.[10]

There was more than just a little irony in the Democrats' demand for more restrictive special rules. They had sought to *limit* the use of restrictive rules in their attack on the Ways and Means Committee during the reform years in the early 1970s. By granting the Speaker the authority to nominate the Democratic members of the Rules Committee, they hoped to make Rules' decisions more responsive to the party's preferences. Committee chairmen were required to notify the House of their requests for protective rules and the Democratic Caucus assumed the authority to instruct Rules Committee Democrats to make certain amendments in order. The immediate effect of the reform era was a sharp cutback in closed and modified rules in the mid-1970s.[11]

By the late 1970s Democrats began to appreciate the nature of the problem they had created for themselves. On the one hand, individual Democrats benefited from the opportunity to offer floor amendments

Table 13-4    The Move to Restrictive Rules, 94th-99th Congresses (in percentages)

| Congress | Type of rule | | | Total |
|---|---|---|---|---|
| | Open | Restrictive | Closed | |
| 94th  (1975-1976) | 84.3 | 11.3 | 4.4 | 100.0 (248) [a] |
| 95th  (1977-1978) | 83.9 | 12.4 | 3.8 | 100.1 (186) |
| 96th  (1979-1980) | 68.9 | 20.0 | 11.1 | 100.0 (180) |
| 97th  (1981-1982) | 71.2 | 22.1 | 6.7 | 100.1 (104) |
| 98th  (1983-1984 | 64.0 | 22.4 | 13.6 | 100.0 (125) |
| 99th  (1985-1986) | 55.4 | 33.7 | 10.9 | 100.0 (101) |

SOURCE: Stanley Bach and Steven S. Smith, *Managing Uncertainty in the House of Representatives: Innovation and Adaptation in Special Rules* (Washington, D.C.: Brookings Institution, 1988), Table 3-3.

[a] Number of measures subject to a rule.

freely. Like their Republican colleagues, they found it useful to cater to special constituencies and to respond to constituent demands for amendment sponsorship. On the other hand, Democrats shared a collective party interest in reducing the policy and political damage of Republican amendments. The solution, made available by the ability of a House majority to approve a special rule, was to have Rules Democrats, under the guidance of the party's elected leader, the Speaker, write rules limiting amending activity on the floor.

The shift to more restrictive rules was swift. The Rules Committee's new chairman, Richard Bolling of Missouri, quickly assumed a leading role in designing restrictive rules, often in close consultation with Speaker O'Neill's top aides. Table 13-4 indicates that the proportion of rules with restrictive provisions increased a little in the 96th Congress (1979-1980), but shot upward in the Congresses of the 1980s. By the 99th Congress (1985-1986), only a slim majority of measures subject to a special rule—that is, most major bills—received a rule that did not limit floor amendments in some way.[12]

The data in Table 13-4 mask a remarkable variety of innovations in special rules during the 1980s.[13] As rules were written on a case-by-case basis, innovative provisions affected the ordering of amendments, the treatment of amendments to amendments, known as second-degree amendments, and special relations among amendments. Increasingly, restrictive rules specified which amendments would be in order, eliminating uncertainty about what amendments would be offered on the floor. Where rules did not explicitly limit permissible amendments, they often required advance notification, such as publication in the *Congressional Record*, so that majority party leaders and bill managers would know what to expect when the measures reached the floor.

It should not be assumed, however, that special rules restricting amendments are very restrictive. In many cases, restrictive rules put in order the amendments of nearly anyone appearing before the Rules Committee requesting a place in the rule. Restrictive rules would then prohibit additional amendments, including second-degree amendments, from being offered on the floor. In this way the Rules Committee can eliminate uncertainty about what will be offered and when it will be considered on the floor, without unduly limiting members' opportunity to participate in floor decision making. If the Rules Committee goes too far in limiting amendments, the House is free to reject the rule, as it has done often enough to make the Rules Committee sensitive to the reaction of the floor.

The move to more restrictive rules was reinforced by the budget-dominated politics of the 1980s. A few large budget-related measures dominated the first three Congresses of the 1980s. These measures were seen as vital to the policy interests of the majority party, but they were usually brought to the floor late in sessions when little time remained to get them enacted into law. And they usually were supported by fragile coalitions among House Democrats that were susceptible to erosion by well-crafted Republican amendments. Under such circumstances, Democrats were careful in designing restrictive special rules for the major budget measures—budget resolutions, continuing appropriations resolutions, and reconciliation bills. The combination of restrictive rules and budget politics reduced floor amending activity in the House during the 1980s.[14]

House Republicans objected strenuously to many of the restrictive rules. By requiring advance notification and restricting amendments, the Democrats eliminated much of the element of surprise that worked to Republicans' advantage in the 1970s. Republican amendments that might divide Democrats and endanger Democratic proposals could be avoided in some cases, and in other cases their effects could be mitigated by advance planning and compromise amendments put in order by special rules. Republican objections to restrictive rules produced much more partisan voting patterns on special rules, but, for the most part, large Democratic majorities have given Democrats the ability to pass rules without Republican support.

The House response to the surge in amending activity, then, took place in a majoritarian context. Changes in the standing rules could be accomplished by simple majority votes on the House floor, and restrictive special rules written by the Rules Committee could be adopted by simple majority votes. The assertion of majority party control over the Rules Committee, through the Speaker, made special rules a tool of the Democrats that had not always been available prior to the 1970s. Consequently, once the Democrats recognized a common interest in reducing the dangers of amending activity, they had the capacity to do so.

## The Senate Response
## to Chaos on the Floor

While majority party leaders in the House were groping their way toward more effective means for limiting floor amendments, their Senate counterparts continued to flounder under the effects of Senate Rule XXII. Rule XXII currently provides that cloture may be invoked—debate may be cut off—only if at least three-fifths of all senators, or sixty senators, agree to do so. The rule makes it possible for a sizable minority to block consideration of measures on the floor, or to block final action on amendments or measures, by conducting or threatening extended debate, or a filibuster.

In practice, invoking cloture is very cumbersome because it involves advance notice and lengthy debate after cloture is approved. The majority leader therefore depends on unanimous consent to bring up measures and limit debate, a procedure that permits the Senate to set aside its standing rules. Unanimous consent agreements may be quite complex: they may set limits for debate on individual amendments, specify certain times for votes, bar second-degree or nongermane amendments, amend a bill without a separate vote, and modify normal procedure in a number of other ways. But the necessity of gaining unanimous consent to limit or structure debate in these ways places substantial power to obstruct in the hands of individual senators.

The expansion of amending activity in the late 1960s and the early 1970s was accompanied by more frequent filibusters. The number of issues subject to cloture motions grew from two between 1951 and 1960 to sixteen between 1961 and 1970, to twenty-four between 1971 and mid-1975, when the current cloture rule was adopted, and then to thirty-eight between 1975 and 1980.[15] The focus on civil rights issues, the primary target of filibusters, had given way to a wide variety of issues by the late 1960s. More and more senators led filibusters; one count showed that twenty-seven different senators led filibusters between 1969 and 1985.[16] Far more threatened them.

The increase in filibusters was a part of the broader trend toward exploitation of floor opportunities and can be seen as a cousin of the growth in amending activity. Bruce Oppenheimer argues that severe time constraints, partly a function of expanding amending activity, improved the leverage gained by senators as a result of filibusters or threats of filibusters.[17] The usefulness of filibusters, Oppenheimer argues, encouraged their further use, made floor scheduling more difficult for the majority leader, and compounded the problems that expanding amending activity was creating for committee and party leaders.

Repeated efforts to change Rule XXII produced no results during the 1960s and early 1970s. In 1975 the Senate modified the 1959 rule that required that two-thirds of those present and voting support cloture. The new rule, as has been noted, requires that three-fifths of the entire Senate vote for cloture. The rule did not prevent obstruction-ist tactics in the form of dozens of procedural motions after cloture was invoked, so in 1979 the Senate included all floor activity in the 100-hour limit for postcloture debate. That provision was tightened to 30 hours in 1986.

Those modest but important changes in Rule XXII did not substantially weaken individual senators' ability to obstruct Senate proceedings by threatening to filibuster. The ability to invoke cloture was improved only a little; in most cases, floor leaders still were dependent on unanimous consent to limit debate and amendments. Efforts to reduce the damage of filibusters to the Senate schedule, such as Majority Leader Mike Mansfield's placement of the filibustered measure on one "track" while considering other legislation on another track, required unanimous consent. Indeed, such palliatives may have encouraged filibusters by reducing the interpersonal friction engendered by extended debate on a measure.

The leverage individual senators gain from threatened filibusters protects their floor amending opportunities. When floor leaders must take such threats seriously, and they must do so when they are facing legislative deadlines, rank-and-file senators' demands that time-limita-tion agreements not infringe on their ability to offer floor amendments must be accommodated. Therefore, it is probably not a coincidence that expanding floor amending activity in the late 1960s and early 1970s was associated with an increase in actual and threatened filibusters. Both developments represented efforts by rank-and-file senators to influence policy outcomes at the floor stage.

Rule XXII constrained Senate floor leaders' responses to expand-ing amending activity. Unlike their House counterparts, they could not impose amendment restrictions by simple majority vote, and they could not force limits through cloture motions without substantial support and cumbersome delays. Senate leaders had to turn to other ways to reduce the burden of amending marathons.

One way Senate leaders minimized the scheduling burden of floor amendments was to use tabling motions to defeat them. Because motions to table are not debatable and may be made at nearly any time, they speed the consideration of amendments. Amendment opponents, usually including the bill manager and the majority leader, find it easier to attract votes for a procedural tabling motion than votes against the substance of an amendment. Robert Byrd, D-W.Va., who became a majority whip in 1971 and assumed a leading role on the floor, understood these tactical advantages. In the 94th and 95th Congresses (1973-1976), amendments were subject to tabling motions more than 500 times, up from just two or three dozen times in a typical Congress in the 1960s.[18]

Handling floor amendments is complicated by the difficulty of predicting when amendments will be brought up and of getting senators to the floor to bring them up. Other business may keep senators away from the floor just at the time the majority leader would like to wade through proposed amendments. As a result, floor leaders spend hours in quorum calls waiting for amendment sponsors to get to the floor and imploring them to offer their amendments. Byrd, who became majority leader in 1977, and his Republican successors frequently called up amendments on behalf of absent colleagues, especially in late-night and weekend sessions. In the 99th Congress, there were more than 250 cases of "proxy sponsorship."

More important, majority leaders have been creative in their use of unanimous consent requests to limit debate and amendments. The use of complex unanimous consent agreements predates this century. Senators have long sought "gentlemen's agreements" to limit debate in the absence of a formal mechanism to do so.[19] Majority Leader Lyndon Johnson, D-Texas, is reputed to have transformed these agreements into a genuine tool of the floor leader during the 1950s.[20] Generally, Johnson's unanimous consent requests were fairly simple, including provisions to limit debate on the measure and amendments and to bar nongermane amendments. More complex agreements were employed from time to time to expand or limit amending activity.

Since the 1950s complex unanimous consent agreements have evolved to meet new circumstances and new leadership styles. Innovation has come about through ad hoc spontaneous adjustments to ever-changing circumstances, rather than intentional experimentation. Individual objections have produced alterations in the agreements, which in turn taught other senators how to protect their interests in the future.

Over time, some lessons were learned and others were forgotten but rediscovered as leaders and rank-and-file members sought ways to adjust to each others' political needs. Innovations often occurred at the initiative of rank-and-file senators, who have scheduling problems of their own and therefore usually want some kind of time-limitation agreement as much as the majority leader does.

A useful indicator of the changing complexity of unanimous consent agreements is the number of restrictive provisions in the agreements.[21] The mean number of restrictive provisions increased from 4.6 in the 84th Congress (1955-1956) when Johnson was majority leader and 3.7 under Mansfield in the 88th (1963-1964) to 5.5 in the 93d (1973-1974) and 5.3 in the 96th (1979-1980) when Byrd had responsibility for crafting most agreements. Provisions more common in the 1970s included special debate limitations for second-degree amendments and explicit authorization for particular amendments, such as nongermane amendments, that otherwise could not be offered. But many other types of provisions sometimes appeared to meet the particular political circumstances faced on the floor.

In the 1980s Republican leaders Howard Baker of Tennessee and Robert Dole of Kansas had more difficulty getting agreements accepted on the floor, often because of Byrd's objections on behalf of his Democratic colleagues. Their complex unanimous consent agreements tended to be approved on a more piecemeal basis and, as a result, were a bit shorter than Byrd's. In the 99th Congress (1985-1986), Dole's agreements averaged only 3.5 provisions, although his agreements varied more widely in length and content than Byrd's.[22] Compared with the agreements of the 1970s, Dole's agreements were more likely to provide for a final passage vote at a time certain, to explicitly prohibit certain amending activity, and to prevent recommittal and other motions that might intervene between debate and a vote. Most important, Dole was far more likely than his predecessors to specify the particular amendments that would be in order.

The struggle to manage floor amending activity, therefore, has taken Senate floor leaders in directions similar to the restrictive special rules in the House. The difference is that Senate leaders have been constrained by the need to receive unanimous consent. A brief example will demonstrate the combined effects of Rule XXII and the use of complex unanimous consent agreements.

One of the most convoluted unanimous consent agreements in Senate history was formulated in 1986, Dole's second year as majority leader. At issue were a contra aid package attached to a military construction bill, which liberals threatened to filibuster, and a bill to impose sanctions against South Africa, which conservatives threatened to filibuster.[23] After many hours of negotiation, Dole managed to break a two-week standoff by proposing an agreement providing for cloture votes on both issues, along with an automatic follow-up cloture vote if one of the first cloture votes failed, and requiring that cloture be successfully invoked for both measures before Rule XXII became effective for either measure. The agreement provided that 121 specified amendments on the two issues, insisted on by the various sponsors, would be in order. The agreement included one-and-a-half additional pages of single-spaced text explaining how the two measures were to be handled if cloture were successfully invoked in both cases; much of the agreement was devoted to closing procedural loopholes for extending debate.[24] Tying the cloture votes together worked; both measures eventually passed after being amended many times.

The agreement did not limit amending activity very much. Indeed, the necessity of finding an acceptable agreement to overcome the impasse on the two measures gave individual senators who wanted to offer amendments the leverage they needed to get them included in the agreement. Nevertheless, last-minute amendments were precluded by the agreement, so that a filibuster-by-amendment was prevented. And all senators were put on notice of the nature of the amendments they would face on the floor.

The budget politics of the 1980s consolidated the Senate's floor agenda, but, unlike in the House, did not reduce floor amending activity. In two areas, budget resolutions and reconciliation bills, debate is limited to twenty hours by the 1974 Budget Act. And yet, with only one exception, Senate budget resolutions, reconciliation bills, and year-long continuing appropriations resolutions faced many more floor amendments than the companion House measures. First budget resolutions averaged twenty-three amendments subject to a roll call vote in the Senate during the 1980s, but they averaged only three such amendments in the House.

Just as dependence on unanimous consent agreements grew out of the cloture rule, the practice of "holds" has sprouted from the dependence on unanimous consent. A hold is a notice, usually in writing, given to floor leaders, by a senator seeking to prevent floor consideration of a measure. Many hold notices indicate the nature of the senator's objection and under what conditions the senator would not object to a consideration of the measure. In effect, the practice institutionalizes the process of threatening to filibuster a measure. During the early 1970s, holds came to be viewed by many members as a right to exercise an individual veto, at least on measures that are not "must" bills. Holds can be used to reserve the right to offer amendments to measures that are considered under restrictive unanimous consent agreements. Efforts by floor leaders to overturn this practice have not worked, for the most part, because of credible threats by individual senators to conduct extended debate if their demands are not met.[25]

The Senate's parliamentary jungle of filibusters, cloture, unanimous consent, and holds has not yielded an effective mechanism for limiting floor amending activity. Efforts to do so, such as making it easier to impose germaneness requirements, have been stopped by the threat of filibuster. The Senate's response to chaos on the floor has been, more often than not, more chaos.

## House-Senate Differences in Perspective

In 1981 Norman Ornstein observed that the decade of the 1970s made "the House more like the Senate, and the Senate more like the House." [26] He was reacting to conventional views of Congress that originated in the 1950s and 1960s. He argued, quite convincingly, that during the 1970s the House became less formal and hierarchical and operated under more fluid rules and procedures. The House, he noted, became an "*ad hoc* institution, without firm control over its own schedule or priorities—much like the Senate." Ornstein provided less detail on the changes in the Senate, but cited the new uses of complex unanimous consent agreements, which, he said, represented a move toward more rigid floor rules. The implications he drew were that the House was no longer a specialized instrument for processing legislation, and the Senate, in the face of a larger workload and restrictive unanimous consent agreements, had become more preoccupied with legislative detail and had lost its character as a deliberative body. He concluded that "neither chamber is comfortable with its contemporary role."

Now, a few years later, it is obvious that Ornstein was right—neither chamber was comfortable with its role in the late 1970s. His perceptive interpretation of developments in Congress in the 1970s can be embellished, qualified, and extended, at least for what happens on the floor. The free-for-all on the House floor that stimulated Ornstein's observations was being reined in at the time he wrote. Since then, restrictive rules have been accepted, and even demanded, by many of the Democratic rank-and-file members who played major roles during the reform movement of the early 1970s. This is not to say that rank-and-file Democrats are now limited to the roles they played in the 1950s and 1960s. They are far more active in committee and party settings, including debates over the structure of special rules. And when the rule permits, they still vigorously pursue floor amendments. But there is now a widely accepted view among House Democrats that unfettered amending activity on the floor undermines efficient decision making and threatens the party's political well being.

Since the early 1980s very few major controversial bills have been considered on the floor without a special rule to structure debate. On the most controversial bills, the rules often have severely limited amending activity. Much of the uncertainty faced by committees and party leaders on the floor has been eliminated. In the 100th Congress, the new Speaker, Democrat Jim Wright of Texas, used restrictive rules even more aggressively than O'Neill to structure floor debate. Restrictive rules have not eliminated all the risks, however, because they are no substitute for having the votes necessary to win on substantive policy questions.

For the Senate, Ornstein correctly observed that floor leaders were seeking through complex unanimous consent agreements what could not be attained through the standing rules of the chamber. During the 1970s more measures were indeed considered under agreements that structured floor debate in some way. When complex agreements are used to specify the particular amendments that will be in order or even the order in which amendments will be considered, they have much of the same effect as restrictive rules in the House with respect to reducing uncertainty.

But, the Senate's complex unanimous consent agreements must not be viewed as rigid rules comparable to House special rules. The agreements are far less effective than special rules in reducing the volume of amending activity. The need to obtain unanimous consent, in the absence of cloture, forces leaders to make concessions prior to and during floor debate on a scale that would seem quite exotic in the House. The more creative and frequent use of complex unanimous consent agreements, therefore, should not deceive us about the chief underlying characteristic of Senate politics, which remains rampant individualism.

In retrospect, then, it appears that the similarities between the chambers that emerged during the 1970s faded during the 1980s. The House, acting as a majoritarian institution, found the tools to limit amendments and reduce uncertainty on the floor. But the House has not returned to its pre-1970 form, as the continuing need for restrictive rules indicates. Instead, the House has moved into a new era, a postreform era, that has its own special character. The Senate, bound to individualism and the protection of minority rights, has not yet found a general strategy for limiting amendments and reducing the dangers of floor decision making to committees and party leaders. In the view of many senators, the Senate's problems with floor activism are becoming more severe, with no relief in sight.

# Conclusion

It was indeed wise for Ornstein to conclude in 1981 that the two chambers had not reached comfortable equilibria in their decision-making processes. The question is whether they have done so since then.

The House, or the House Democrats, have moved a considerable distance toward establishing some stability in how floor activity is organized. While special rules are designed on a case-by-case basis, most members now expect and approve of rules that limit amending activity in some way. The stability of the new practices and expectations is contingent on Democratic control of the House, although Republicans probably would find these Democratic strategies fairly well suited to their needs.

Excessive individualism and chaos on the floor appear to be as much of an equilibrium as the Senate can achieve. Repeated efforts by floor leaders, ideological factions, informal bipartisan groups, and the Committee on Rules and Administration to modify Rule XXII or to mitigate its consequences have failed to achieve substantial improvement of floor procedure. Current efforts to make it easier to impose germaneness requirements on amendments or to order the amendment process are not likely to produce significant changes. The Senate muddles through with burdensome procedures, consuming hours of senators' time that could be spent on other matters, a dispiriting process interrupted by episodes of stalemate, frustration, and frayed interpersonal relations. Predicted breaking points for effective action have been passed and forgotten many times during the last three decades.

In their separate ways, then, the House and Senate floors are far more central to congressional policy making than they were in the late 1950s. The process of change was driven by developments in a common political environment and some parallel internal changes, but it also was molded by the institutional features and rules of each chamber. In the end, the chambers reacted very differently to the upheaval of the 1970s, producing quite distinctive chamber styles of floor decision making.

# Notes

1. On the complexity of the congressional agenda, see Allen Schick, "Complex Policymaking in the United States Senate," *Policy Analysis on Major Issues*, Commission on the Operation of the Senate, 94th Cong., 2d sess. (Washington, D.C.: Government Printing Office, 1977).

2. Norman J. Ornstein, Thomas E. Mann, and Michael J. Malbin, *Vital Statistics on Congress, 1987-1988* (Washington, D.C.: Congressional Quarterly, 1987), 170.
3. For details on amendment data, see Steven S. Smith, *Call to Order: Floor Politics in the House and Senate* (Washington, D.C.: Brookings Institution, forthcoming), appendix 1. All accounts of amending activity here exclude formally designated committee amendments.
4. Ibid., chap. 4; and Barbara Sinclair, "The Transformation of the U.S. Senate—Institutional Consequences of Behavioral Change" (Paper delivered at the Midwest Political Science Association meeting, April 9-11, 1987, Chicago, Illinois).
5. *Congressional Record,* July 27, 1970, 25796-25818.
6. For example, see *CQ Almanac, 1973* (Washington, D.C.: Congressional Quarterly, 1974), 782.
7. Interview with Robert Bauman, July 16, 1987.
8. Ornstein et al., *Vital Statistics,* 171.
9. See Stanley Bach, "Suspension of the Rules in the House of Representatives," Congressional Research Service, Rept. 86-103, May 12, 1986, mimeographed.
10. For the text of the letter, see Smith, *Call to Order,* chap. 2.
11. Stanley Bach, "Special Rules in the House of Representatives: Themes and Contemporary Variations," *Congressional Studies* (1981): 43, Table 1.
12. For more detail on the data on special rules, as well as more background on the design of special rules in the 1980s, see Stanley Bach and Steven S. Smith, *Managing Uncertainty in the House: Adaptation and Innovation in Special Rules* (Washington, D.C.: Brookings Institution, 1988).
13. Ibid., chap. 3.
14. For more details, see Smith, *Call to Order,* chap. 4.
15. These figures are taken from Bruce I. Oppenheimer, "Changing Time Constraints on Congress: Historical Perspectives on the Use of Cloture," in *Congress Reconsidered,* 3d ed., ed. Lawrence C. Dodd and Bruce I. Oppenheimer (Washington, D.C.: CQ Press, 1985), 393-413.
16. The count is Senator Thomas Eagleton's, as he reported on the Senate floor. See *Congressional Record,* Nov. 23, 1985, S16477.
17. Oppenheimer, "Changing Time Constraints."
18. See Smith, *Call to Order,* chap. 4.
19. For example, unlike the House, the Senate does not recognize motions to move the previous question. On the history of complex unanimous consent agreements, see Robert Keith, "The Use of Unanimous Consent in the Senate," *Committees and Senate Procedures,* Senate Commission on the Operation of the Senate, 94th Cong. (Washington, D.C.: Government Printing Office, 1977), 140-168.
20. Rowland Evans and Robert Novak, *Lyndon B. Johnson: The Exercise of Power* (New York: New American Library, 1966), chap. 6.
21. The content of complex unanimous consent agreements was coded for the

84th, 88th, 93d, 96th, and 99th Congresses. A list of the provisions included in this count is provided in Smith, *Call to Order,* appendix 2.

22. The standard deviation in the number of restrictive provisions was .89 in the 84th Congress, 1.63 in the 88th, 1.65 in the 93d, 1.89 in the 96th, and 2.72 in the 99th.
23. See *Congressional Record,* Aug. 9, 11, and 12, 1986.
24. See the Senate's *Calendar of Business,* Aug. 13, 1986, 2-5.
25. For more background on the use of holds, see Smith, *Call to Order,* chap. 4.
26. Norman J. Ornstein, "The House and the Senate in a New Congress," in *The New Congress,* ed. Thomas E. Mann and Norman J. Ornstein (Washington, D.C.: American Enterprise Institute, 1981), 363-383; quotes from pages 366, 367, 371.

# 14. CONGRESSIONAL CAUCUSES IN THE POLICY PROCESS

## Susan Webb Hammond

The contemporary Congress is characterized by member individualism. Changes in rules and procedures have given members the opportunity and resources to participate in policy making, and changing congressional norms have encouraged them. One of the consequences has been the establishment of congressional caucuses. Caucuses are voluntary associations of members of Congress, without formal recognition in chamber rules or line-item appropriations, that seek a role in the policy process. This essay examines these groups by first identifying different types of caucuses and then discussing why they are formed, how they operate, how they benefit members, and the effect they have on Congress.[1] Although no two caucuses are exactly alike, some features are common to all, and caucuses of each type share common characteristics.

The number of caucuses and the rate of establishment have increased rapidly. Prior to 1969 there were only 3 caucuses. Between 1970 and 1974, another 10 groups were established. By 1980, 57 new caucuses were formed. At the end of the first session of the 100th Congress (1987), there were 120 active caucuses; 40 others had become inactive. Participants cite two reasons for caucus formation: changes in the polity and deficiencies in congressional organization. Caucuses are a logical adaptive response by a structurally fluid organization to demand overload and to organizational inability to process those demands to meet member and institutional goals. When the formal structure failed members, informal structures were established.

Caucuses offer members of Congress a new way to take collective action. Members derive benefits—gaining information, being identified as a "leader"—from caucus activities. And caucus actions, such as agenda setting and coalition building, help members achieve individual goals. Caucuses also serve institutional purposes as adaptive mechanisms, and they serve representation purposes as expressive agents for a representative system undergoing change.[2]

# Types of Caucuses

Caucuses are not part of the formal structure of Congress, but they *are* formally organized. They are on-going, with stated purposes and an explicit, stable structure. All caucuses have a chair or cochairs; a senator and a representative often serve as cochairs of a bicameral caucus. Many caucuses select other officers such as vice chairs, a secretary, and a treasurer. Most of the larger House caucuses also appoint steering committees, which are geographically or ideologically representative of the caucus membership. Most caucuses are staffed by aides in the personal offices of caucus members. This pattern prevails for Senate caucuses and predominates in the House. During 1988 only fourteen House caucuses had separate staff and office space.[3]

All caucuses try to affect policy by exchanging information, influencing the issue agenda, developing legislation, or monitoring implementation. But caucuses also differ. If we group caucuses on a membership dimension—why senators and representatives join—six types can be distinguished. The caucuses in each group are alike because members share a common characteristic such as party and ideology or representation of constituency industries (Table 14-1).

Four types are constituency based. Members of the *national constituency* caucuses are perceived, and perceive themselves, as representing groups nationwide—blacks, women, Hispanics, Vietnam-era veterans—outside as well as within their congressional districts or states.

*Regional* caucuses bring together members in adjoining states or congressional districts to work on matters of particular interest to a geographic region: the Northeast and Midwest, New England, the western states, or the districts within a state.

*State/district* caucus members are from states or congressional districts with widely diffused characteristics such as rural or ethnic populations or family farms. The Rural Caucus, the Senior Citizens Caucus, and the two Irish caucuses are typical.

Members of *industry* caucuses are from districts or states with specific industries or businesses: coal, textiles, mushrooms, and tourism, for example.

A fifth group, *party* caucuses, are formed by intraparty groups whose members share a similar ideology. The Democratic Study Group (DSG) was established by liberal Democrats; the members of the Republican Wednesday Group, which takes its name from its weekly meeting day, are moderate and liberal members of the GOP. Class clubs established by newly elected freshmen of each Congress (100th New Members Caucus [Democrats], Republican Freshman Class of

Table 14-1   Congressional Caucuses, by Type

| Type | Number | Typical examples |
|---|---|---|
| Party concerns | 28 | Conservative Democratic Forum (Boll Weevils)<br>Conservative Opportunity Society<br>Democratic Study Group<br>Populist Caucus<br>Republican Study Committee<br>Wednesday Groups<br>Class clubs |
| Personal interest | 36 | Arms Control and Foreign Policy Caucus<br>Arts caucuses<br>Crime Caucus<br>Environmental and Energy Study Conference<br>Senate Caucus on the Family<br>Human rights caucuses<br>Military Reform Caucus<br>Population and Development Coalition<br>Ad Hoc Monitoring Group on Southern Africa |
| Constituency con-<br>cerns, national | 7 | Congressional Black Caucus<br>Congressional Hispanic Caucus<br>Congressional Caucus for Women's Issues<br>Vietnam Veterans Caucus |
| Constituency con-<br>cerns, regional | 22 | Border caucuses<br>Conference of Great Lakes Congressmen<br>Northeast-Midwest Congressional Coalition<br>Congressional Sunbelt Council<br>Tennessee Valley Authority Caucus<br>Western State Coalition |
| State/district | 28 | Export task forces<br>Family farm task forces<br>Task Force on Industrial Innovation & Productivity<br>Irish caucuses<br>Rural Caucus<br>Caucuses on Soviet Jewry<br>Suburban Caucus |
| State/district<br>industry | 39 | Automotive Caucus<br>Coal caucuses<br>Copper caucuses<br>Mushroom Caucus<br>Steel caucuses<br>Textile caucuses<br>Travel and tourism caucuses<br>Wine Caucus |

SOURCE: Author's data.

the 100th Congress) fall into this category. Party caucuses are partisan and chamber-specific.

In *personal interest* caucuses the shared characteristic is interest in an issue—the environment, foreign policy matters, or the arts, for example.

## Caucus Formation, Purposes, and Goals

Until about 1975 caucuses were generally House-based and partisan, with an interest in internal congressional organization or in a broad range of issues not tied to any particular concern. Since 1975 many caucuses have been created that are bipartisan, bicameral, and focus on a single issue or a single industry. Tables 14-2 and 14-3 display these data. Note the increasingly rapid rate of caucus formation, the later development of Senate caucuses, and in the most recent years a shift to bicameral or parallel House and Senate caucuses and a more narrow issue focus.

Caucuses are a response to changes external to Congress—events, economic shifts, and issue agendas—and to internal congressional changes that increased individual resources, weakened party leadership, and made organizational structure more fluid. The external catalysts to caucus formation vary by type of caucus. The primary motive in establishing national constituency caucuses was to represent groups distributed throughout the nation. Caucus members are contacted by these constituents who seek policy change on national problems of concern to them. Women turn to the Congressional Caucus for Women's Issues to address child care and economic equity matters, and Hispanic organizations work with the Hispanic Caucus. The emphasis on representation is typified by this group: "The main purpose of the Hispanic Caucus is really to represent the Hispanic constituency at the federal level of government. . . . [Members of the caucus] serve a broader constituency than their own district." [4]

Representation is the *raison d'etre* of all constituency caucuses, but specific events or changes in a constituency may serve as the catalyst for caucus formation. Fifty-nine percent of the regional caucuses were established to coordinate efforts on then-pending regional problems; 30 percent were a response to general economic decline in the region. The factors leading to formation of state/district caucuses are similar: 41 percent wanted to coordinate with other senators and representatives on an issue common to their constituencies; 31 percent wanted to address economic crisis or decline in specific areas such as family farms or rural communities. Economic crisis is the primary reason for establishing industry caucuses (77 percent). When several major steel plants closed with the loss of hundreds of jobs, members of Congress responded by

Table 14-2    Caucus Establishment, by Type and Time, 1959-1987

| Caucus type | 1959-1968 | 1969-1974 | 1975-1980 | 1981-1987 | (N) |
|---|---|---|---|---|---|
| Party | 2 | 5 | 7 | 14 | (28) |
| Personal interest | 1 | 1 | 7 | 27 | (36) |
| Constituency | | | | | |
| National | — | 1 | 5 | 1 | (7) |
| Regional | — | 2 | 10 | 10 | (22) |
| State/district | — | 1 | 9 | 18 | (28) |
| Industry | — | — | 19 | 20 | (39) |
| Total | 3 | 10 | 57 | 90 | (160) |

SOURCE: Author's data.

Table 14-3    Caucus Establishment in Each Chamber, 1959-1986

| Time | House | Senate | Bicameral | Total |
|---|---|---|---|---|
| 1959-1968 | 2 | — | 1 | 3 |
| 1969-1974 | 7 | 3 | — | 10 |
| 1975-1980 | 37 | 11 | 9 | 57 |
| 1981-1986 | 45 | 17 | 15 | 77 |
| Total | 91 | 31 | 25[a] | 147 |

SOURCE: Author's data.

[a] Eight caucuses in each chamber focus on the same industry: beef, coal, copper, footwear, mushroom, steel, textile, tourism, trucking. These parallel caucuses cooperate in bicameral operations.

establishing the House and Senate Steel caucuses. The Congressional Travel and Tourism Caucus and the Alcohol Fuels Caucus were founded in response to the gasoline shortage of 1977. The Automotive Caucus staff director described the representation purpose of industry caucuses: "The driving force in [caucus membership] is the auto industry presence in the districts. In that we're like the Steel Caucus— the presence in the district of a particular type of industry."

Party and personal interest caucuses are different: policy goals are emphasized when caucus formation is described. All but one of the party caucuses were explicitly established to achieve policy outcomes for an intraparty group. The Senate Steering Committee was started when "thirteen conservative senators decided they ought to meet on a regular basis and . . . develop the kind of full staff work which would enable them to be more effective on the floor." The Conservative Democratic Forum, whose members are known as the Boll Weevils because many are from the South, "are philosophically conservative; they felt like [*sic*] they were out of the mainstream of the direction that the Democratic Party was going and they wanted to get together and do something about it, especially on budget, economic and defense issues." Respondents emphasize their caucus' role as an ideological group within the congressional party. Conservative Coalition support scores for party caucuses bear out these perceptions: the mean score for members of the Democratic Study Group in the House is 36; for the United Democrats of Congress, 47; and for the (Republican) Wednesday Group, 64.[5]

Thirty-nine percent (eleven caucuses) of the personal interest caucuses were founded because members shared an interest in a particular issue (futures research, foreign policy) or wanted policy information on issues, the environment, for example. Twenty-one percent (six caucuses) resulted from an external event. The Ad Hoc Monitoring Group on South Africa was founded in response to the death of black activist Stephen Biko in a South African jail. Eighteen percent (five caucuses) were started because a problem such as crime or terrorism had become prominent on external issue agendas.

The internal structure of Congress has also encouraged caucus formation. Caucuses were established because members wanted to coordinate information, strategy, and voting clout on issues and felt that existing party leadership and committee structures were not doing this to their satisfaction. Representative Robert Edgar, D-Pa., chairman of the Northeast-Midwest Congressional Coalition in the 97th Congress, testified before a House Rules subcommittee, "Chief among the reasons [for caucus formation] were factors such as: failure of the parties and other congressional leadership structure to adjust to an era in which more educated, better informed members are requiring better leadership on increasingly complex public policy problems." [6] The Hispanic Caucus was formed to "overcome the inaccessibility of the House leadership." An aide describing the founding of the Industrial Innovation Caucus said, "There was a recognition that committee jurisdictions did not dovetail neatly with this issue. We needed another vehicle. So we turned to the idea of a caucus to try to mobilize congressional interest and opinion across committee jurisdictions."

Because caucuses operate outside the formal congressional structure, they are easier to establish than formal subunits and can operate across formal structural boundaries. Representatives formed the Populist Caucus rather than a Democratic party task force because a caucus does not require consensus in the House Democratic party conference before offering floor amendments. The establishment of the Senate Caucus on the Family reflects a similar theme. "A lot of issues that affect families are not in the jurisdiction of the Subcommittee on Family

Human Services [*sic*]: they fall under other committees' jurisdiction and nobody's got a handle on them. . . . [We formed a caucus because] creating a permanent committee takes a lot more time." The caucus wanted to focus on these cross-cutting issues without delay.

Different types of caucuses serve different goals. Members of the constituency-based caucuses view representation as their primary goal; policy change is pursued because of constituent representation goals. Members of party and personal interest caucuses emphasize policy goals. Generally, reelection goals are achieved as a consequence of representation or policy activities, but some caucuses serve directly (and only) reelection goals for entrepreneur founders or officers.

Party, personal interest, national constituency, and many regional caucuses are concerned with a broad range of issues. The DSG has worked on civil rights legislation, congressional reorganization, campaign finance, and foreign policy issues. During 1987 the caucus developed and won House approval of an amendment to require a ninety-day delay in the reflagging of Kuwaiti oil tankers in the Persian Gulf. The Clearing House on the Future, a personal interest caucus, in 1987 focused on diverse issues: aging, combating illiteracy, service credit banks, and "watershed political issues." The Hispanic Caucus was active on immigration, health, education, and small business issues.[7]

In contrast, state/district and industry caucuses have a narrower focus. Although they may bring together diverse groups—shippers, railroads, and passenger-users in the case of the Senate Rail Caucus, for example—these caucuses concentrate on *one* issue. The Travel and Tourism Caucus is typical. Its activities in 1987—planning National Tourism Week, arranging briefings on the federal government's tourism marketing programs, and working on National Tourism Week legislation— focused on a specific, narrowly bounded issue.

## Caucus Activities

If caucuses have been established because the formal committee and party structures of Congress are not functioning effectively, we would expect caucuses to fulfill some institutional functions, such as gathering and distributing information, influencing agendas, and building coalitions, traditionally carried out by the formal structure. Furthermore, we would expect to find systematic differences among the types of caucuses in the performance of their activities.

### Information Gathering and Exchange

All caucuses gather and exchange information. Caucuses prepare newsletters, briefing papers, and research reports and hold informal meetings to disseminate information on issues of interest, including the current status of proposed legislation and government action. The perspective on issues varies by caucus category, and the information they disseminate reflects that. Regional caucuses present a regional perspective; industry caucuses treat issues (trade, for example) from the perspective of a particular industry. Some caucuses focus *only* on information, explicitly choosing not to take a position on issues or to become involved in determining legislative strategy or building voting coalitions. The Environmental and Energy Study Conference chooses a nonadvocacy information role.

> We could be an advocacy group or we can be a bipartisan research and support, non-advocacy kind of group. If we're the former all we'll end up doing is talking to the believers and if we're the latter we reach out, educate, get the environmental point of view across. . . . Even though the founders of the group were themselves very strong environmentalists, they decided on the latter course. The group's goal is to inform the debate.

The moderate Republican Wednesday Group takes a similar position. "The caucus's purpose is information. . . . Members value the opportunity to exchange information, and perhaps get a different slant on an issue."

**Bringing Adversaries Together.**   By providing information, caucuses educate members and offer a different perspective, which can bring together adversaries with conflicting interests. The Senate Rail Caucus's operations are typical:

> There were a lot of us all over the country who weren't on the Commerce Committee but found that rail issues began to dominate our agendas because they were so important to our states. Different people came at it from different perspectives. . . . It occurred to all of us that if we were going to handle these issues properly, we had to acquire a much deeper knowledge of . . . rail operation. There were a lot of bankruptcies. On strong railroads, there are questions of service potential and how you maximize carrying capacity. . . . We try to create forums for exchanging views and learning as much about the operation of the industry and the issues confronting it as we can. . . . We usually have a panel presentation, bringing in people on both sides of the issues so you get a good clash. . . . When railroad matters come up now there is a tremendous network; we all call one another and hash out the issues. It has . . . produced a much more educated constituency here in the Senate, and it has made it easier to deal with . . . the issues.

**Research.**   Caucuses conduct systematic research on current and emerging issues. Because of the legislative schedule and the rapid pace of congressional life, this kind of research is rare on Capitol Hill.

Research on emerging issues is a major activity of the Republican House Wednesday Group, and its report on the volunteer army influenced the debate when the issue was before Congress in the 1970s. A 200-page "State of the Region" report prepared by the Northeast-Midwest Congressional Coalition included a number of different economic indicators by state and by region. Such background data can be used by members to identify emerging issues or for decisions about pending legislation. Lengthy issue-specific, comprehensive, analytical reports on programs that affect the region also serve to shape the perspective of debaters. The caucus takes an explicitly regional view (Which issues will affect the Northeast-Midwest? How will program changes affect the region?). A staff aide explained:

> The caucus has been especially important in compiling data to show the distribution of federal funds *throughout a region.* . . . [T]hat's the void that we filled by beginning to show there was a common interest, from New England across the mid-Atlantic states and into the midwest, that there were common forces at work, common problems, and in fact, common solutions.

Even when the research is long-range, reports may become unexpectedly timely: the Wednesday Group report in the early 1980s on U.S.-China trade became a best seller when a floor vote was scheduled on the issue.

Party and national constituency caucuses conduct research on a wide range of issues tied to ideological or constituent group concerns. Regional, state/district, and industry caucuses present data that inform a regional, state/district, or industry perspective. Research by personal interest caucuses offers an issue perspective that differs from that of formal committees or leadership groups; reports might draw together materials on a range of issues affecting families, or they might focus specifically on arts issues. Caucus research contributes to members' individual decisions and can affect congressional debate and outcomes.

**Information on Pending Legislation.** Most caucuses provide information on pending legislation of particular interest. The House Wednesday Group gathers to report on committee actions and to discuss bills scheduled for floor consideration. Each week the DSG prepares detailed information on legislation scheduled for floor debate, which supplements its issue briefs and research reports. The Environmental Study Conference issues analyses of pending legislation on environmental issues, including data on costs, expected effects, anticipated controversies, amendments, and possible votes. The Northeast-Midwest Congressional Coalition prepares analyses of the budget from a regional perspective. Although industry caucuses are less active on floor matters, they also monitor and prepare information on the occasional bill that affects their issue concerns.

The importance of caucuses as information sources is confirmed by a survey of information needs and sources conducted by the House Commission on Administrative Review. Thirty-six percent of the members surveyed and 66 percent of the legislative assistants cited the DSG as a source of information for votes on bills which had not been before the member's committee; 18 percent of the members and 41 percent of the staff used it as a source of information on bills from their committees. During 1987, 86 percent of House and 60 percent of Senate personal staff reported using information provided by congressional caucuses.[8]

### Influencing Agendas

Caucuses influence congressional and executive branch agendas and thereby affect the work of the formal governmental structure. Members' responsibilities as decision makers and their positions in the committee system facilitate placing caucus issues on governmental agendas.

Caucuses *set agendas* when they push an issue to consideration by a congressional committee, the full House or Senate, or an executive branch agency. The Congressional Caucus for Women's Issues has placed on governmental agendas issue such as day care, pension benefits, and the retraining of displaced homemakers. The DSG was instrumental in bringing campaign finance reform to the congressional agenda. The Military Reform Caucus has proposed new solutions—and therefore new agenda items—to recurring defense appropriations issues.

Groups *maintain agendas* when they keep the issues salient. The Environmental Study Conference tries to "keep environmental questions—the environmental implications of decisions—before the Congress at large." The caucus draws a distinction between keeping issues on the congressional agenda, and taking a position on those issues. It works on "keeping the air pollution issue before the Congress but not [on] keeping the clean air point of view. It's different." The Automotive Caucus, formed as an advocacy group to assist in obtaining a federal loan for the Chrysler Corporation, now seeks "to keep the problems of the domestic auto industry on the front burner in Congress."

Caucuses also carry on *negative agenda-setting*, keeping issues from consideration. The (Senate) Western Coalition takes credit for stopping the creation of a Department of Natural Resources, after Republican and Democratic senators in the coalition met at the White

House with the vice president, the secretary of the Interior Department, and White House staff.

> The Coalition demonstrated ... that [the proposal] wouldn't have the support of the western senators. ... They didn't see any real reason for it at the time, so why do it? And nobody could give us a good answer and that's pretty much where it died.

Party caucuses often keep legislation from a floor vote if it is unlikely to come to a vote in the other chamber.

All types of caucuses focus on the congressional agenda. Some also work outside Congress. National constituency caucuses follow a public agenda-setting model, seeking to place issues on public agendas so as to obtain subsequent placement on congressional agendas. The more narrow the focus of constituency caucuses, the more likely the caucuses are to turn attention to the executive branch's agenda: one-third of the industry caucuses seek primarily to influence this agenda, and another 44 percent emphasize executive and congressional agenda setting about equally. In contrast, 57 percent of party and of personal interest caucuses focus primarily on the congressional agenda.

Many party caucuses work with the top executive branch officials of their party to influence executive agendas. The Northeast-Midwest Republican Coalition (Gypsy Moths) are mostly moderate Republicans from the snowbelt. Energized in 1981 by President Ronald Reagan's first budget, they organized as a group to change it. They wanted to cut the proposed increase in defense, and they opposed some of the proposed domestic program cuts. Their attitude is typical of most party groups. "The first premise was they wanted to work with the president, they wanted to support his program ... but they kind of wanted to re-arrange the furniture, so to speak." The group met a number of times with David Stockman, a former Republican representative who was Reagan's first director of the Office of Management and Budget. The positions of both sides were flexible as negotiations proceeded, and consequently the caucus made no final proposal. "We didn't want to come out and propose some domestic cuts then that we'd have to live with later if we didn't need to propose them." But the group felt it made the point that the mix of cuts should be changed. Party caucuses also seek to affect the agendas of the national political parties by participating in drafting the party platform in a presidential election year or by influencing party rules changes.

## Building Coalitions

**Working Within the Party.** All party caucuses work within their congressional parties, where putting together a winning coalition is easier than on the floor. Party leaders who want to gain access to ideologically cohesive voting blocs and keep conflict within the party have incentives to respond to caucus demands.

For party caucuses an initial step in coalition building is success in obtaining party consideration of issues. The Conservative Opportunity Society (COS), founded in 1984, gained notoriety for confrontations with the Democrats on the House floor. Within the Republican party, however, it practiced the politics of accommodation by working with the Republican leadership, the Wednesday Group, and the '92 Group to plan congressional party conferences to discuss emerging issues and the role of House Republicans. According to one observer, the COS also "broke down the 'get along, go along' ethic" by succeeding in bringing the close election outcome in Indiana's Eighth District to the floor during the opening months of the 99th Congress for several bitterly contested votes.

**Developing Legislation.** Caucuses develop legislation and seek to gain support by framing issues in a broad way. The purposes of the Congressional Caucus for Women's Issues have remained the same since 1977, when the caucus was established: to work for legislation to improve the status of women and "to be a sort of member-at-large for all women." The caucus continues to focus on issues from the perspective of the impact on women, but caucus concerns have gradually shifted to issues which can be set in a broader context.[9] In 1985 the caucus formulated and introduced H.R. 2020, the Disability and Parental Leave Bill, which provides employees leave to care for newborns or seriously ill children, emphasizing that the legislation would strengthen families, rather than help only women.[10] The gender-neutral legislation was a response to a California state court decision striking down legislation that provided leave for women only. After consultation with outside groups, other congressional staff, and experts, the caucus drafted and introduced the bill in April. A hearing held jointly by four subcommittees was carefully structured: the bipartisan witnesses included labor union representatives, corporate executives, and child development experts, and both men and women testified to the importance of *parental* leave, for fathers *and* mothers, to strengthen families. Successor bills were approved by House and Senate committees in the 100th Congress. The Senate debated the legislation in September 1988 and approved floor amendments adding child care provisions and incorporating S. 2033, the Child Protection and Obscenity Enforcement Act. The expanded bill was filibustered and died when cloture could not be invoked. Supporters expected to reintroduce parental leave legislation in the 101st Congress.

Throughout the process of formulation and approval, the caucus sought to cast the issues as family issues. Within Congress the caucus built a bipartisan coalition that included women and men, liberals and conservatives, and members with strong labor and strong corporate ties. Agenda shifts in the polity assisted the caucus: the gender gap, increases in the number of working women and of two-worker families, and increased attention to issues affecting children. The caucus tapped into the shift in the national mood, helped shape the terms of debate, developed solutions acceptable to a broad range of groups, and served as coalition builder within Congress and coordinator between outside groups and Congress.

**Strategic Flexibility.** The activity of the House Textile Caucus in sponsoring the Textile Trade Bill of 1985 illustrates representation of constituency interests, integration of issue networks, and the willingness to be flexible to achieve goals. Generally, the Textile Caucus has worked to affect executive branch decisions. In 1985, however, Representative Ed Jenkins, D-Ga., the chair of the Textile Caucus, responded to industry concerns about increased textile imports by introducing H.R. 1562. Jenkins, a member of the Ways and Means Committee's Subcommittee on Trade, is an influential issue and regional leader and widely regarded as a "rising star." He used his positions in the formal and informal structures to build a winning coalition.[11] The party leadership supported the legislation, although the committees of jurisdiction opposed it. Other caucuses—the Competitiveness Caucus, the Export Caucus, and the Steel Caucus—worked with the Textile Caucus. During House debate the chairman of the Steel Caucus appealed to caucus members: "Quotas set on stainless steel bars and rod and tool steel . . . are clear examples of how quotas work, and the way they help American industry. Whether it is steel, specialty steel, or textiles . . . I hope every member of the House and the Steel Caucus will recognize the importance and value of this bill and vote for it." [12]

The policy arena was shifted from the executive branch to Congress by the introduction of the bill. The issue was set in a larger context: "Frustration with the administration's overall trade policy was a key factor in mobilizing support for the bill among members without significant textile interest in their districts." [13] And bipartisan coalitions mobilized by bipartisan caucuses were important.[14] Although a veto override vote did not succeed, the congressional process illustrates the flexible, and successful, tactics open to caucuses.

## Benefits to Members

Caucuses help members achieve their goals of representation, policy making, power, and reelection. These benefits accrue through individual actions as caucus members and through the activity of caucuses as collectivities.

Members receive representation benefits from caucus membership. Caucus concerns are often explicitly linked to constituencies: "The rail issue touches a large portion of a number of constituents' lives in a direct, immediate fashion"; "The presence in the district of a particular type of industry [auto] is the driving force for membership"; "Really, the thing all Footwear Caucus members have in common is that they have districts that have heavy footwear industry."

Members believe that constituents view caucus membership as a way to represent their concerns, and simply joining a caucus can yield symbolic benefits. One aide noted that caucus membership "shows constituents that the senator or representative really cares." Members report caucus memberships and activities in newsletters and radio-TV reports to constituents and through the national and specialized media. Symbolic activities can be important in building the trust that is crucial to long-term relationships between constituents and representatives.[15]

All caucuses help members respond to increased constituent expectations.

> Before about 1970, members were satisfied to become masters of a few areas and defer to their colleagues on other matters . . . and their constituents were satisfied. But now, members expect to be part of more things and their constituents expect that. . . . They are expected to be experts on just about every area . . . and the caucuses give them an opportunity to become involved in, and knowledgeable about, a lot of areas.

Members represent constituents through caucus agenda-setting and legislative activity. In 1980 the Northeast-Midwest Congressional Coalition achieved House approval of an amendment that helped some of its economically distressed industries compete for Defense Department contracts. The Congressional Caucus for Women's Issues placed child care legislation on the agenda of the 100th Congress, and worked to move the bills through committee and floor consideration.

Members may seek power in the institutions through caucus activity. They may become recognized issue experts and cue-givers. Freshman representative Barbara Boxer, D-Calif., dealt extensively with military procurement issues as a member of the 98th Freshman Budget Study Group; subsequently, she was appointed to the Armed Services and Budget Committees. Caucuses permit members to maintain legitimacy as continuing issue leaders. When one representative moved from the Public Works Committee to Ways and Means, his position as chair of the TVA Caucus helped him keep a profile on Tennessee Valley Authority issues, although he was no longer on the relevant committee. Caucuses also occasionally help members keep formal positions of power. The Port Caucus was started in 1977 as a "preemptive strike" to solidify the jurisdiction of the Merchant Marine Committee.

Caucuses serve as an alternate leadership structure, identifying and training future leaders. Caucus briefings, press conferences, and hearings give caucus officers visibility within their chamber and nationally. Caucus chairs are identified as national issue leaders. The media contact the head of the Export Caucus on export issues; the chair of the Agricultural Forum is viewed by constituent groups as a leader on agricultural issues. Through caucus activity a junior member can become identified as a leader. Caucuses also offer junior members opportunities to participate and to pursue their goals earlier in their congressional careers than is possible in the formal committee structure. The more senior a representative, the less likely he or she is to belong to a caucus ($r = -.18$). For some members, chairing one of the long-established caucuses (the Democratic Study Group, the Arms Control and Foreign Policy Caucus) gives leadership opportunities to members with middle-level seniority and may legitimate leadership within the broader environment of the House.

Members also gain policy benefits from caucus membership through in-depth information on issues, "early warning" of pending legislation, and information that supplements committee material. Caucuses are resource banks and informational network centers. A caucus aide reported, "We make a very conscious effort to direct the reports to the uses that the members have." One representative, commenting on the membership meetings of a caucus, said that the "information exchange is . . . often ahead of [personal] staff information, and it's especially useful because it gives members a chance to find out what is the likely position of a committee chairman on an issue." Caucus information systems save time: "It's the only place you can get a great sense of what's going on on an issue; otherwise, staff has to check with numerous subcommittees."

Caucuses give members an opportunity to pursue issues even if they do not serve on the relevant committee. Members use caucuses to discuss "broad policy matters with other members," to study cross-cutting issues like rail transportation "a little more deeply," or as a vehicle to focus institutional attention on an issue.

In addition, members use caucuses to build voting coalitions and to "coalesce political strength." Western Coalition senators believe that if they get agreement among themselves, their western concerns will be listened to more than if each had spoken out individually. For members of the minority party, there is "an advantage to be involved in this kind of bipartisan coalition." Some may seek support on issues through logrolling caucus membership, striking "you join my caucus and I'll join yours" bargains. A long-time congressional observer argued, "Things have to be done by groups of members working in concert. . . . Caucuses are clearly serving members' interests."

Reelection benefits can be considerable. An observer noted, "These days . . . you have to be on record and you have to do something about problems. . . . What better thing is there than to tell your constituents you are a member of the XYZ Caucus and you are seriously investigating the problem?" Another said, "It is politically attractive to members to say 'I'm doing something.'" The Balanced Budget Caucus was formed primarily for reelection purposes, according to a participant. "It was something people could organize around, give speeches about, and issue press releases on." Caucuses give members a "forum," enabling them to claim both participation and symbolic benefits.

Some caucuses prepare information that members can distribute to constituents. A pamphlet, "Guide to Solar Energy Conservation," was prepared by the Environment and Energy Study Conference staff for distribution by caucus members. Members have also used "Pocket Speech Cards" prepared by caucuses on legislative issues for meetings with constituents. Caucus members claim credit for caucus activities and successes. One staff aide refers all calls from local press to caucus members. Chairing a caucus offers further credit-claiming opportunities. "Caucuses are a couple of easy press releases a week," an observer stated. Another said, "It is a political gem to be the chairman of some of these [industry] groups. You get a lot of support and a lot of credit, and you really don't do a whole lot."

Members also receive solidary benefits from caucus membership. Wednesday Group members consider the weekly meeting to exchange information and meet with friends a major benefit of membership.[16] Friendships formed in class clubs last well beyond the lifetime of the club. These intangible benefits help members find a place in a decentralized and fragmented institution.

## Institutional Effect

If caucuses help members achieve their goals, how do they affect Congress as an institution? Although benefits to members are evident, the institutional consequences are less clear. Members have come to realize that the single-minded pursuit of individual goals may result in a Congress unable to carry out its collective functions or further members' goals. Caucuses contribute to the structural fragmentation of

Congress and reinforce the decentralizing trends of the 1970s, but the potentially negative effects are constrained in various ways. Caucuses supplement committee activity and seek to work within the formal system of committee and party leaders.

The structural decentralization that results from a larger number of subunits is balanced by caucus integration of issue networks and coordination across committee jurisdictions. Caucuses help manage conflict by bringing adversaries together, integrating issue networks, and working with party leaders. They enhance representation and bring to government agendas the concerns of district and national constituencies.

Congress's acceptance of caucuses as legitimate subunits is confirmed by responses to a survey. During the 100th Congress, more than 80 percent of the caucuses were contacted for information or strategy assistance. Of those, 56 percent were contacted by issue leaders in Congress. Committee leaders and executive branch agencies contacted nearly 50 percent, party leaders in Congress contacted 30 percent, and the White House called on 19 percent for assistance.

Caucuses are an efficient use of resources. They serve as central information resources and clearinghouses. "A caucus is much more efficient than 435 legislative assistants doing research on an issue," a senior staff aide said. They offer coalition-building opportunities on issues or perspectives that are neglected by the formal structure. Caucuses offer party leaders access to blocs of votes and opportunities for managing institutional conflict.

Caucuses serve a precommittee function by identifying problems, developing possible legislative solutions, and putting issues on committee agendas. Some serve a typical subcommittee function by cooperating with the executive branch in commenting on or assisting with the development of executive proposals. The Rural Caucus has helped write budget recommendations for the Farmers Home Administration; the Carter White House used as a "sounding board" the Northeast-Midwest Congressional Coalition, which also worked on Carter's urban policy proposal. The staff director of a caucus described working with the executive branch:

> The administration came to us and asked for our views and how do we think that [proposed] legislation might be improved a bit. It's clear that they're trying to use us to a large extent, and they want to push legislation that we might not normally want. In a situation where they know we'll be opposed, they don't bother, because they know that just gives us an opportunity to mobilize. . . . But if they think that [we might be persuaded], they will very often come over and say, "Can we deal on this?"

Caucuses also serve another function within each chamber; caucus activity coordinates issues and policy actors across committee jurisdictions. The family farm task forces dealt with agriculture, trade, and tax issues. The Senate Caucus on the Family was started by a senator who chaired a subcommittee with jurisdiction over some family issues after the senator realized that family issues cut across many committee jurisdictions and that "it was important to get a view, and a Senate group working on, the entire broad issue."

Regional caucuses coordinate across states. The TVA Caucus allows members, who come from the seven relevant states, to coordinate committee work on TVA-related issues. The Congressional Caucus on Human Rights coordinates Congress's activities on such cases to avoid duplication of effort by individual members. Caucuses coordinate legislative strategy. The ProLife Caucus was founded "because a lot of outside groups were using different legislative strategies. It was important to have a group *in Congress* which could decide on and coordinate a legislative strategy." And by offering a nonpartisan forum for members to get together (in contrast, often, to committees) caucuses serve a function in resolving differences and reaching consensus.

Caucus activity also integrates issue networks. As subunits outside the formal institutional structure, caucuses can operate informally. Caucuses offer a "vehicle for dialogue." The Agricultural Forum was established to "bring together some of those factions that simply refused in the past to discuss agricultural issues with each other." Other caucuses have brought together groups, traditionally adversaries, to develop solutions that all can support. Industry caucuses, for example, have worked with labor, management, and environmental groups. Regional caucuses have brought in state and local officials, including mayors and governors, as well as university experts, business, labor, and public interest groups. By integrating issue networks to achieve solutions supported by a broad coalition, caucuses serve as vehicles for moving beyond problem identification to interest aggregation and consensus building.

Some caucuses affect policy by focusing on specific issues within a larger agenda, such as railroads as a part of the transportation issue. Some take a different approach to an issue. The Military Reform Caucus focuses on programs, not dollar amounts: "Committees must necessarily be concerned with the budget and how best to fit available dollars to the programs. But a group like the caucus can start with the program and evaluate what kinds of programs are the best to keep this nation in a state of readiness." The result has been some reshaping of weapons policy by caucus members who prevailed in committee and on the floor.

Increasingly, regional and some industry caucuses are addressing particularistic interests as aspects of broader national needs. The Footwear Caucus "doesn't talk about import barriers but about trade issues in general, and adds the component of modernization and long-term growth of the industry." Issues of concern nationally as well as regionally—unemployment, worker retraining, and revitalizing urban areas—have been concerns of the Northeast-Midwest Coalition in recent years. This strategy has led to cooperation with other regional groups.[17]

Caucuses influence debate by keeping an issue on the congressional agenda, setting the parameters of debate through research, bringing adversaries together to discuss an issue, or affecting the voting decisions of individual senators and representatives through information. They mobilize votes through information and coalition building. They offer party leaders access to groups of members and, therefore, to potential voting blocs. In this way they facilitate leaders' work. And caucus strategy and coalition-building activities can affect vote outcomes.

Caucuses also affect representation. Some caucuses represent constituencies or work on issues that traditionally are less likely to have effective private sector organizations. And many serve as access points for outside groups.

## Conclusion

Caucuses can help the *individual* and the *institution* handle work and carry out responsibilities. They offer members an opportunity to address difficult, complex policy issues, to build coalitions within Congress, to integrate external issue networks, and to pursue individual policy, reelection, and institutional power goals. Caucuses reduce the costs to members of obtaining information for legislative decision making. And they do not require the same investment of energy or the procedural hurdles that establishing a subcommittee would. As adaptive mechanisms, caucuses serve institutional maintenance functions. They carry out policy and representational activities and coordinate policy actors and issue networks.

Caucuses reflect the pluralism of the polity and the lack of consensus on many issues. In a changing institution, caucuses offer benefits to individual members and supplement the formal structure by fulfilling institutional functions. In the contemporary Congress, caucuses are likely to persist.

# Notes

1. This chapter draws on research for a larger project to be published as *Informal Congressional Groups in National Policymaking*, with Daniel P. Mulhollan and Arthur G. Stevens, Jr. (Washington, D.C.: American Enterprise Institute, forthcoming). Data include semifocused interviews with caucus staff directors, a survey of caucus activities, and a computer file on caucus membership, which includes committee assignments and electoral and constituency data. I am grateful to the Everett McKinley Dirksen Congressional Leadership Research Center and American University for grants that assisted the research and to Carol de Frances and Scott Rudolf for research assistance. This article has benefited from comments by Chuck Jones, Tom Mann, Kathryn Mohrman, David Smith, and Joe White.
2. See Burdett A. Loomis, "Congressional Caucuses and the Politics of Representation," in *Congress Reconsidered*, 2d ed., ed. Lawrence C. Dodd and Bruce I. Oppenheimer (Washington, D.C.: CQ Press, 1981) for discussion of the latter point.
3. Members pay caucus dues and operating expenses from their personal office staff and expense allowances. Caucuses operating in the House may apply for Legislative Service Organization (LSO) status. LSOs maintain an account to receive contributions from members' office allowances and to pay caucus expenses. LSOs report income and expenditures quarterly.
4. Quotations are not attributed as all respondents were promised anonymity.
5. Conservative Coalition support scores are computed on a scale of 0-100 every congressional session for each member of Congress by Congressional Quarterly. Higher scores indicate greater support for conservative positions. The caucus score reported is the average of the individual scores of caucus members for the second session, 97th Congress. Eight Republicans who subscribed to DSG mailings are excluded from the computation.
6. House Committee on House Administration, Ad Hoc Subcommittee on Legislative Service Organizations, *Hearing,* Committee Print, 97th Cong., 2d sess., June 24, 1982, 57.
7. Legislative Service Organization Quarterly Reports to the Clerk of the U.S. House of Representatives, 1987.
8. House Commission on Administrative Review, *Final Report: Administrative Reorganization and Legislative Management,* H. Doc. 95-232, 95th Cong., 1st sess., 1977, 958, 959, 966, 1082, 1089; Center for Responsive Politics, *Congressional Operations: Congress Speaks—A Survey of the 100th Congress* (Washington, D.C.: Center for Responsive Politics, 1988).
9. Interviews; Congressional Caucus on Women's Issues, *Update,* 1981-1988; Irwin N. Gertzog, *Congressional Women: Their Recruitment, Treatment, and Behavior* (New York: Praeger, 1984), 200.
10. For a more complete discussion of strategy, see Joan Hulse Thompson,

"Caucuses, Women's Issues, and a Day on Capitol Hill" (December, 1985), mimeographed.

11. On the textile bill, see David M. Olson, "U.S. Trade Policy: The Conditions for Congressional Participation" (Paper delivered at the annual meeting of the American Political Science Association, Chicago, Illinois, 1987); on "rising stars" see *National Journal,* Jan. 24, 1987, 184.

12. *Congressional Record,* daily ed., 99th Cong., 2d sess., Oct. 10, 1985, H20798.

13. *Congressional Quarterly Almanac, 1985* (Washington, D.C.: Congressional Quarterly, 1986), 257.

14. See Olson, "U.S. Trade Policy."

15. See Richard F. Fenno, Jr., *Home Style: House Members in Their Districts* (Boston: Little, Brown, 1978).

16. Interviews; and see Sven Groennings, "The Clubs in Congress: The House Wednesday Group" in *To Be a Congressman,* ed. Sven Groennings and Jonathan P. Hawley (Washington, D.C.: Acropolis Books, 1973).

17. "Improbable Coalition Grows Wider," *New York Times,* July 29, 1985, A10.

# Part V

# CONGRESS, THE EXECUTIVE, AND PUBLIC POLICY

# 15. LEGISLATIVE-EXECUTIVE LESSONS FROM THE IRAN-CONTRA AFFAIR

## Michael J. Malbin

The summer of 1987 was a season of celebration for the bicentennial of the U.S. Constitution. It also was the season for the nationally televised hearings of the House and Senate select committees investigating the Iran-contra affair. By now the memory of those spectacular hearings has dimmed, the 690-page report[1] gathers dust, and perspectives have blurred. The purpose of this essay is to reawaken some of those memories and raise constitutional and practical issues that were not adequately explored in the public hearings or committee report.

Legislative-executive relations clearly broke down during the Iran-contra affair. What is most interesting for our purposes, however, is not the mere fact of a breakdown, but its character. The Reagan administration made a series of imprudent, impolitic, short-sighted decisions. In the course of pursuing those decisions, some steps taken by the National Security Council (NSC) staff may have skirted the edge of the law. The resulting conflict raised tough questions on a number of levels about the behavior and operating style of Congress and the executive branch. When Congress chose to investigate, however, it did so primarily to portray the administration's behavior as illegal. The legal judgments underlying the investigation almost all involved assertions, made with unswerving confidence, that serious lawyers can honestly debate. These legal disputes are fairly reflected in the majority and minority reports of the Iran-contra investigating committees. The majority's recommendations, and Congress's subsequent actions to change the laws about congressional oversight of covert action, flowed directly from the legalistic character of the committees' work.

An earlier version of this essay was presented at a conference, "The Embattled Executive," sponsored by the American Enterprise Institute, Washington, D.C., April 8-9, 1988.

The views presented are the author's alone, and not those of the Iran-contra committee's minority, the Republican Conference, or Representative Dick Cheney, who was the conference chairman and the ranking minority member of the House Iran-contra committee.

Missing so far has been an analysis of how and why the two branches let the situation reach such an impasse. Without such an analysis, Congress has limited its vision to "corrective" legislation that will only invite future conflict. No amount of good will can wish substantive disagreements away, but I shall argue there already are more than enough nonstatutory levers available for each branch to deter the other from letting disagreement degenerate into mutually harmful procedural warfare. Before we can reach this conclusion, however, it will be necessary to shift the grounds of the ongoing debate.

## Iran-Contra: Nicaraguan Issues

The argument of this essay does not require a detailed rehash of the Iran-contra affair, but a few points need to be made to set the stage for what follows. I shall begin with Nicaragua and then discuss Iran.

### Congressional Division

Perhaps the most striking changes in U.S. foreign policy during President Ronald Reagan's two terms of office were those that fit under the rubric of the "Reagan Doctrine." Simply stated, the idea behind the doctrine is that the United States will not automatically accept the permanence of communist successes in the Third World and is willing, where prudent, to give material or diplomatic support to anticommunist resistance forces to alter the status quo. Remarkably, this doctrine has *not* been controversial everywhere it has been applied. There was broad bipartisan support in Congress, for example, for both the Afghan and the Cambodian resistance.

There was nothing close to a consensus on Central America, however. At the heart of the Nicaraguan side of the Iran-contra affair was an intense dispute over the wisdom of Reagan's policy of providing U.S. support to the Nicaraguan resistance, known as the contras. That policy divided Congress almost evenly for most of the Reagan administration. The Senate consistently supported the president, sometimes by narrow margins. In the House the votes typically were close. About 190 to 200 members usually lined up on one side or the other. The pro-administration side included almost all the House Republicans and two to three dozen Democrats, mostly from the South. The anti-administration side included about three-quarters of the Democrats and a handful of Republicans. The remainder of the House—about twenty to thirty Democrats and ten Republicans—changed their votes with the context and therefore held the balance of political power.

The close division encouraged each side to look for procedural devices that would give it an advantage in gaining the votes of the swing members. In addition, because neither side could feel certain of winning a vote with enough of a margin to settle the issue once and for all, each had an incentive to avoid final decisions. The aim, particularly for the president's opponents, was to avoid giving the impression that any one vote would be the last. By portraying their decisions as being open to further review, swing members who voted against the president could protect themselves from blame if the situation in Central America worsened.

The intensity of the members' opinions was at least as important as the narrowness of the vote division. The president and his supporters believed that the Sandinista regime in Nicaragua was controlled by communists who were dedicated to a "revolution without borders" and who were giving substantial material assistance to the leftist guerrillas in El Salvador. A pluralistic, democratic Nicaragua would be less likely to pursue such policies. But because the Sandinistas were not about to give up their gains peacefully, the administration believed that the only way the Nicaraguan government would become pluralistic would be under military pressure from the resistance. Therefore, the administration maintained, the United States had to choose between helping the resistance now or waiting until U.S. national security interests compelled a future president to take forceful steps to restrain Sandinista behavior, perhaps even including the use of American troops.

On the other side, most congressional Democrats thought the Sandinista regime could be persuaded, through negotiations, to drop its support for revolution in neighboring countries, but only if the United States would first stop intervening in Nicaraguan affairs. Some Democrats also believed that an end to the war would be more likely than its continuation to lead to political reform. Whatever their views about the chances for democratization, however, the president's opponents generally felt that the contras inevitably would lose. The realistic choices for the United States were: (1) to accept Sandinista control inside Nicaragua and negotiate regional issues; (2) to back the contras until the Sandinistas won, without negotiating regional issues; or (3) to overthrow the regime by force.

Thus, each side saw the other's approach as a prescription for eventual war. Under the circumstances, neither was willing to go very far to accommodate the other. The result was a vacillating policy toward Nicaragua that changed almost every year for a decade, between 1979 and 1988. The shift that was most important for the Iran-contra affair was the now famous Boland Amendment of 1984.

## The Boland Amendment

The Boland Amendment, and its subsequent implementation, offers a good insight into how each side used the procedural levers at its disposal to pursue its policy objectives. In 1983 the House passed an amendment to the Intelligence Authorization Act that would have prohibited the U.S. intelligence community from spending funds directly or indirectly to help the resistance's military efforts. The Senate rejected the prohibition, and the result was a $24 million compromise that everyone understood would not be sufficient for a full fiscal year.

In 1984 the House again included the same prohibition in that year's Intelligence Authorization Act. This time, there was no separate vote in the House on Nicaraguan aid, a ploy that let swing members from conservative districts avoid the election year political risk of voting against contra aid. When the Senate refused to compromise, the House position was made part of the Defense Department appropriations bill, which in turn was made part of a more than 1,200-page year-end continuing resolution that packaged nine of the normal thirteen appropriations bills with an omnibus crime control measure. Once again, there was no separate vote on contra aid in the House.

The Senate continued to support contra aid, but the election was fast approaching. By October some pivotal senators on the conference committee were openly concerned about public works projects that were to be funded by the continuing resolution. Others just wanted to go home to campaign. When the House refused to give in, the Senate accepted a compromise that embraced the substance of the House position, but also set up expedited procedures for a vote the following February on a $14 million aid package. Some people urged the president to veto the continuing resolution and force a public debate during the election campaign, but the president signed the measure. It is not at all clear that a veto would have been sustained so close to the election, given the anxiety of members wanting to go home and the provision expediting a vote the following February.

The Boland Amendment, adopted in October 1984, read as follows:

> During fiscal year 1985, no funds available to the Central Intelligence Agency, Department of Defense, or any other agency or entity of the United States involved in intelligence activities may be obligated or expended for the purpose or which would have the effect of supporting, directly or indirectly, military or paramilitary operations in Nicaragua by any nation, group, organization, movement or individual.[2]

This wording was both convoluted and strange. One can appreciate just how strange by comparing Boland with the 1976 Clark Amendment:

> *Notwithstanding any other provision of law, no assistance of any kind* may be provided for the purpose, or which would have the

effect, of promoting or augmenting, directly or indirectly, the capacity of any nation, group, organization, movement or individual to conduct military or paramilitary operations in Angola.[3]

The clarity of the Clark Amendment stands in vivid contrast to the difficulties of Boland. The amendments differed in at least three ways. First, the Boland Amendment was a rider to an appropriations bill and prohibited only the expenditure of funds; the Clark Amendment prohibited assistance of any kind. Second, the Clark Amendment clearly and unequivocally applied to the entire U.S. government; the Boland Amendment only reached the CIA, Department of Defense, and other agencies or entities involved in intelligence activities. Finally, the Clark Amendment prohibited any assistance, anywhere, that would have augmented the capability of the Angolan resistance; the Boland Amendment only prohibited assistance that would have had the direct or indirect effect of supporting military or paramilitary operations inside Nicaragua. Based on these comparisons, it is easy to see why the legal debate during the Iran-contra investigation centered on two issues: who was covered and precisely which activities were prohibited.

## Administration Reaction

The administration reacted to the Boland Amendment by all but eliminating CIA support of the contras. The NSC staff, however, took a number of steps to help keep the contras alive.

—National Security Adviser Robert McFarlane and Lieutenant Colonel Oliver L. North, an NSC staff aide, met with third country representatives to encourage contributions to the resistance. About 90 percent of the funds the contras received during the period of the Boland Amendment came from these sources.

—North also met with potential contributors to private fundraising organizations to describe how private funds could help the contra cause.

—North encouraged retired general Richard Secord to set up a private air resupply operation for the contras, helped obtain secure communications equipment for the operation, sought the construction of an emergency air strip in a neighboring country, and engaged in detailed discussions with Secord about the contras' specific supply needs. The communications devices were supplied after Congress specifically changed the law in December 1985 to permit the U.S. government to give communications assistance to the contras. By this time, Vice Admiral John Poindexter had succeeded McFarlane as national security adviser.

—North also supplied the contras with intelligence information for the resupply effort, some of which was militarily useful for defensive purposes.

—Finally, North gave strategic advice to the resistance.

Many of North's actions probably were not illegal, taken individually. No one would maintain, however, that Congress knew about, much less approved of, the level of North's daily involvement. Every effort was made to make sure Congress did not know. The record of the NSC staff's efforts to keep Congress in the dark is well documented in the Iran-contra committees' majority report,[4] and there is no need to repeat the details here.

The majority and minority of the Iran-contra committees generally agreed on these points. However, the minority believed, and I share the belief, that the motive for deceiving Congress was not to cover up activities the NSC staff knew to be technically illegal, but to keep Congress from knowing about, and closing, legal loopholes the NSC staff was exploiting. The aim was to keep the contras alive while working to renew aid in Congress, not to take steps that would shut the aid down permanently.

In the short term, the strategy seemed to work. Opponents of contra aid in Congress tried to investigate North at the time of the next major vote, in 1985. Through various deceptions, the NSC staff kept Congress in the dark, and contra aid was gradually renewed. In 1986 Congress passed a $100 million package that included a significant amount of military support. Then, beginning in November 1986, the contra resupply effort and all of the NSC staff's deceptions became known, along with the administration's arms sales to Iran and the use of some proceeds from those sales to help the contras. The revelations and the subsequent congressional investigation changed the political climate within the United States, even as the contras were becoming more successful in the field. In late 1987 and early 1988, as a direct result of its weakened political position, the administration failed, after several close votes, to renew military aid for the resistance.

## Iran

The political background of the Iran arms sales was almost the opposite of the background of the NSC staff's efforts to help the contras. Instead of an intense political division, the Reagan administration had managed to fashion a broad, bipartisan consensus on a tough, publicly articulated antiterrorism policy.

The Carter administration November 14, 1979, had imposed an embargo on arms sales to Iran in response to the seizure of the U.S.

Embassy and its personnel in Tehran. President Reagan continued the embargo. On December 14, 1983, after three years of war between Iran and Iraq, the State Department began a vigorous program called Operation Staunch to persuade other countries to join the embargo. In addition, on January 20, 1984, the secretary of state declared Iran to be a sponsor of international terrorism. Four days later, the department announced in the *Federal Register* that this declaration would make Iran subject to the limit on the export of U.S. military equipment to "countries that have repeatedly provided support for acts of international terrorism." [5] The restrictions were tightened in September. In October 1984 the administration began articulating an increasingly tough public line toward terrorism and terrorists. On June 30, 1985, two weeks after Shi'ite terrorists hijacked a TWA airliner, the president said: "The United States gives terrorists no rewards and makes no guarantees. We make no concessions. We make no deals." [6]

About a month later, the United States agreed to a small Israeli shipment to Iran of arms Israel originally had bought from the United States. By November the United States became involved directly by helping to expedite an Israeli shipment that had run up against problems in a European country. In January the president signed a covert action "finding," as required by law, to authorize the United States to sell arms to Iran directly. The shipments were opposed by Secretary of State George Shultz and Secretary of Defense Caspar Weinberger. They were supported by CIA Director William Casey, Attorney General Edwin Meese, and National Security Adviser Poindexter. Between January and the end of October, three different arms sales took place—the first two using Manucher Ghorbanifar as an intermediary and the third using a so-called "second channel." The sales stopped when information about them was leaked by a disgruntled faction inside Iran to a Lebanese weekly news magazine.

The motivation for supporting the arms sales varied with different participants. For North, the idea of generating profits to divert to the contras appears to have been an important motivation beginning sometime in December or January. This motivation was not shared by others, however. Poindexter did not know about and authorize the diversion until after the president signed the finding of January 17. No one else involved in the finding—with the possible (although I believe unlikely) exception of Casey—even knew about the diversion until after the November revelations. In addition, the president was motivated strongly by a desire to see Iran persuade the Hizballah in Lebanon to release Americans being held hostage, as may be seen by his repeated references to the subject as months went by.

Finally, most of the participants also were motivated by a genuine desire to pursue relations with factions inside the Iranian government that were open to cooperation with the West. The United States had had no good intelligence information from inside Iran since the fall of the shah in 1979. Inaccurate rumors were rampant about Ayatollah Ruhollah Khomeini's health, combined with more accurate reports about factional divisions inside Iran and potential Soviet inroads among some of the factions. There was a legitimate policy reason, therefore, to be pursuing some kind of initiative to Iran at this time. That policy reason might not have justified the arms sales, but the combination of policy interests with hostages was enough to produce the covert operation.

Through the full ten months of the program, the U.S. government publicly reaffirmed its strong stand against terrorism, and the State Department continued to pressure other governments not to sell arms to Iran. During the same period, the president invoked his authority not to inform congressional leaders of the finding he had signed in January. After the information became public, the administration said that its decision not to notify Congress was based on a concern that leaks would be fatal for the hostages. There was legitimate reason to be concerned about leaks. Even under the most narrow statutory interpretation, notification would have included four congressional leaders plus the chairmen and ranking minority members of the House and Senate Select Committees on Intelligence. Unfortunately, experience has shown that even this group may not be immune from leaking.[7]

It is impossible to separate a concern about leaks from concerns about political controversy. The simple fact is that the more controversial a program is, the more likely it is to be leaked. In this case, the arms sales raised questions about their consistency with the administration's public positions about dealing with terrorists and selling arms to Iran. These questions fueled the public's reaction after the operation was disclosed. It is true that the administration distinguished between dealing with the Hizballah, who held the hostages, and dealing with a government that supported and influenced the Hizballah. But that distinction was difficult to make publicly, after the fact, and in any case it was a distinction that did not address the decision to sell arms.

Part of the administration's problem may have been with its rhetoric as well as with the arms sales. An administration sensitive to the foundations of democratic political power would have recognized that an inconsistency between action and rhetoric could undermine the credibility on which the administration's power depends. An administration that truly believed in not dealing with terrorists should have accepted the responsibility to explain that individuals who knowingly travel to dangerous places cannot expect to be bailed out by the government because negotiations would increase the risks for other Americans abroad. Alternatively, the administration might have taken an approach, similar to Israel's, of being open to negotiations, but also showing an ability and willingness to engage in effective, punitive retaliation. Either approach might have produced a more forgiving public reaction. The latter position, however, would have implied a subtler form of presidential rhetoric, quite different from the one that was the basis of Reagan's power and popularity.

"In Ronald Reagan, America found the rhetorical President," wrote Jeffrey Tulis.[8] The use of public rhetoric is an essentially modern (post-Woodrow Wilson) tool, according to Tulis, that carries with it the inevitable dilemma of maintaining a consistency between what is said in public and the subtler arguments appropriate for deliberation among knowledgeable policy experts. Too much of a disjunction, let alone inconsistency, is bound to come back to haunt a president. In this case, President Reagan's ability to control the future political debate was dealt a crippling blow from the public revelation of the Iran arms sales. As with the contra resupply program, the short-term benefits did not come close to matching the long-term political and policy costs.

## Congressional Narrowness

The congressional reaction to the Iran-contra affair was politically intense, but intellectually narrow. In contrast with the Tower Commission's decision to contract for a series of studies of past NSC operations,[9] the Iran-contra committees made no effort to examine other examples of tense or harmonious contemporary relationships between the legislative and executive branches. Such studies could have provided benchmarks for dissecting precisely what was different about these events and for making useful, broadly informed recommendations for the future.

Instead of taking a comparative approach, the congressional committees decided to hire criminal lawyers to run their investigations. Predictably, the lawyers made obedience to the law their central theme, to the exclusion of equally serious, less tractable questions about managing political and institutional conflict. This approach did make some sense from a short-term political point of view: whenever the committees moved beyond the "facts" and the "law" in public hearings, it became clear that the members' opinions were too diverse to have permitted a clear majority to emerge on broader issues. As long as the committees could concentrate on the law—defined not only to include statutes, but also those vague emanations known as the "intent" or the "will" of Congress—the committees could use *Federalist* No. 51 style institutional loyalties[10] to produce a *Federalist* No. 10 style multifactional coalition[11] that included some Democratic contra aid supporters and three Senate Republicans.

The following three examples give some sense of the legalistic tone of the committee's debate:

—The majority argued that all actions taken by NSC staff were covered by the Boland Amendment. The minority said that although the clear language of the 1976 Clark Amendment covered NSC staff actions toward Angola, the Boland Amendment used a phrase ("agency or entity of the United States involved in intelligence activities") that was originally crafted for the 1980 Intelligence Oversight Act, and repeated subsequently in intelligence law, specifically to exclude the NSC and its staff.

—The majority described all NSC staff efforts to encourage third country and private party contributions to the resistance as efforts to evade Congress's constitutional control over the purse. The minority said that the Constitution prohibits Congress from regulating the president's diplomatic communications or communications by any of the president's designated agents with foreign countries. These would include communications that lead to third country contributions for causes the president supports, as long as the contributions do not pass through, or under the control of, the United States. Similarly, the minority said that the president and his employees could not be prevented from encouraging private contributions, as long as the contributions were entirely private and not otherwise prohibited by U.S. law.

—The majority said that Israel's resale to Iran of arms it had originally bought from the United States violated the Arms Export Control Act (AECA). The AECA says that the president must approve, and Congress must be notified of, all such transfers from the original purchaser to a third country. The minority said that the AECA never was intended to apply to covert transactions governed by the National Security Act, that the attorney general had notified Congress of this legal interpretation in 1981, and that Congress had subsequently affirmed this interpretation.

In short, the general tenor of the majority's argument, following the style of a brief, was a series of legal conclusions asserted as if there were no room for doubt. The minority then replied to most of the majority's legal points in kind. The intense legal dispute, however, let the committees slip away from the harder questions. That point becomes obvious when one turns to the subject of remedies.

## Flawed Remedy

The major proposal to come out of the Iran-contra committees' work flowed directly from the legalism of its analysis. The underlying principle seemed to be this: if unacceptable behavior is legal, the solution is to make it illegal. In 1988 the Senate passed, and the House almost passed, legislation that was intended to prohibit the specific form President Reagan's uncooperative behavior took in the Iran arms sales. Almost all members of Congress believe the president abused the reporting discretion he was given under the 1980 Intelligence Oversight Act. The proposed "solution" was to tighten the statute in an ill-advised attempt to make it loophole-free.

Under present law, the heads of the CIA, the Department of Defense, and all other agencies and entities involved in intelligence activities are supposed to report in advance about all significant activities, other than pure information gathering, to the House and Senate Intelligence committees. Under unusual conditions, the president may choose to limit notification to the chairmen and ranking minority members of the two committees and the four leaders of the full House and Senate. The 1980 law also specifically notes, however, that there might be some conditions under which prior notice would not be given to anyone. In those situations, the law requires the president "to fully inform the intelligence committees *in a timely fashion.*"

The 1980 law does not claim to give Congress the right to approve covert operations in advance. Nevertheless, the reporting requirement gives the two intelligence committees the opportunity to play a significant role. They can and do try to persuade (or sometimes pressure) the administration to change its mind about particular activities, and they conduct an annual project-by-project budget review of all ongoing operations. On occasion, they move beyond persuasion to use the budget review to terminate operations with which they disagree.

Effective oversight and budget review rest on the important assumption that the executive branch tells Congress what it is doing. For eleven months after the Iran arms sale finding, President Reagan did not notify Congress. Even if some initial delay may have been justified, it stretches credulity to describe this notification as "timely." Once one acknowledges this much, however, what response is appropriate does not automatically follow.

Congress's immediate response was to "get back" at the president, or presidency, by trying to rewrite the Oversight Act. The objective was to eliminate the vague notion of timeliness and require the president to notify Congress of all covert operations, without exception, within forty-eight hours of their start. Unfortunately, the rigidity of this requirement raised constitutional difficulties that would have all but ensured future legislative-executive branch confrontations.

Presidents are sure to argue—I think correctly—that the Constitution gives them the authority (1) to initiate covert or overt actions, with the resources placed at their disposal, to protect American lives abroad and to serve other important foreign policy objectives, short of war and (2) to delay notification, if the president believes notification would be equivalent to making the action itself impossible.[12] For an example of a situation in which the ability to act and to withhold notification are inextricably bound together, consider the choice required when a foreign government makes withholding notification a condition of its willingness to help the United States. (The Canadians apparently did so when they protected six Americans inside the Canadian Embassy in Tehran during the 1979-1980 Iran hostage episode.[13]) In such a situation, a mandatory forty-eight hour notification rule would create a direct conflict between statute law and legitimate, discretionary constitutional authority.

If a mandatory notification bill passes, what would happen if a president nevertheless felt bound to withhold notice to live up to a constitutional obligation? Because courts prefer to avoid deciding these kinds of legislative-executive conflicts—and because, in any case, the legal point would become technically moot once members of Congress gain the information they would need to consider a lawsuit—Congress would need some extrastatutory enforcement mechanism to make the proposed statute stick. But if Congress has extrastatutory means available for pressuring presidents, the proposed statute would be redundant at best, and a potential new source of conflict at worst. If they approve of the president's decision, a delay in notification would be accepted, which is what happened in 1980. If they do not approve, as in 1986, extrastatutory sanctions would be brought into play. The attempt to use statute law to close all loopholes resolves little, therefore, and draws attention away from political mechanisms that would be more likely to produce results.

## Defending Institutions

To resolve conflict, it can be useful to get back to the source. Some commentators, in despair, have maintained that the real source of conflict is the constitutional separation of powers. Some constitutional reformers therefore would like to move the country toward a parliamentary system of government. However, as I have argued elsewhere,[14] such a "solution" would bring costs of its own. Parliamentary democracies with disciplined political parties either have two parties or more than two. Two-party systems normally do not show as many annual vacillations over specific policies as the United States, but they are more subject to polarized politics and to complete shifts in policy direction with an alternation of governments. Multiparty systems, in contrast, too often replace vacillation with paralysis and stagnation. A parliamentary model, in other words, would not necessarily improve foreign policy. In any case, there is little reason to believe the required constitutional amendments would ever pass Congress. Why should the members voluntarily amend the Constitution to make themselves less powerful?

Realistic analysis, therefore, should focus on making the separation of powers work better, not replacing it. Two obvious points have to be stressed at the outset. First, representatives, senators and the president have independent bases of political power. Second, courts are reluctant to adjudicate disputes over the allocation of legislative and executive powers over foreign policy. In John Locke's terminology, the two observations mean that in times of interbranch conflict, the two branches often must act as the judges of their own cases, with no common judge or authority above them. In such situations, Congress and the president have to work out their differences on their own.

It is important not to make things seem worse than they are. In general, the branches of government have a strong interest in containing conflict and working cooperatively. Legislative and executive power are not usually counterpoised on a zero-sum teeter-totter. Normally, each branch can gain power and achieve its policy objectives more effectively by sharing and cooperating than by trying to act unilaterally. For example, Congress began delegating more rule-making discretion to the executive branch during the late nineteenth century not because it was eager to give away legislative power, but because delegation let Congress increase the whole federal government's role and thus increase its own power. Congress took a smaller portion from a larger pie.

In addition, there often is a policy as well as a power basis for cooperation. That situation exists when both sides in a policy conflict believe that compromise, or even the other side's policy, would be better than no policy or an impasse. Legislative battles in this context often come to resemble what game theorists would describe as a game of chicken. Both sides may well have an incentive to appear intransigent and unwilling to cooperate. In the final analysis, however, neither side wants to be blamed for a stalemate. One side or the other backs off, and a compromise become law.

In other situations, one side or the other may prefer a stalemate. Perhaps one side prefers a clear-cut election issue or is willing to live indefinitely with the status quo. Even in these situations, however, the parties to a legislative disagreement normally are willing to contain their conflict within well-understood procedural boundaries. What distinguished the disagreement over Nicaragua policy was the intensity with which the participants held their opinions. Each side fervently believed the other's policy would be a disaster. As a result, each was willing to pull out all the procedural stops to achieve its objective. House Democrats used their control over the agenda to pass major limitations on presidential power without separate floor votes. They also used their control over the informal oversight levers available to committee and subcommittee chairmen to pressure for the strictest possible interpretations of ambiguous statutory language. In response, the president and his staff implemented the most permissive interpretations of the same language without telling Congress what it was doing.

Unfortunately, both branches end up damaging their long-term institutional interests with this kind of procedural gamesmanship. Congress suffers when it adopts major policy decisions without votes, over presidential opposition, as riders to massive "must pass" money bills. Such decisions lack legitimacy and therefore encourage presidents to seek ways around them. But presidents stand to lose even more from the destruction of interbranch comity. Relying on procedural levers does not work equally well for both sides of the legislative-executive divide. There are two basic reasons for the asymmetry. First, in the absence of either elite consensus or public support, the U.S. system of government gives the advantage to incremental or short-term decisions rather than overt decisions requiring long-term commitment and sacrifice. Second, the president's power ultimately depends on political support and public persuasion. Procedural end runs not only deny the president the ability to use a most important political tool; they also put a powerful political weapon into the hands of opponents who can use institutional arguments to undermine the president's support.

Because of this asymmetry, members of Congress who opposed the president's Nicaragua policies could engage in procedural warfare without endangering their underlying policy objectives. Assertions of congressional power that resulted in policy vacillation were perfectly consistent with preventing a sustained program of U.S. military support for the contras. In contrast, the president's objectives were to sustain and support action, not prevent it. His objectives left him with a more complicated position: the short-term steps needed to sustain specific program objectives one fiscal year at a time were not the best steps for maintaining the long-term political powers of his office.

Consider the choices with which the 1984 Boland Amendment presented the president. First, he could have vetoed the vehicle containing the amendment—the huge continuing appropriations bill—

three weeks before election day. A veto surely would have stimulated a public debate. The public was wary of contra aid, but the president was headed toward a near-certain landslide victory and forcing the issue could have helped him to claim a mandate. The risks of veto were that it might reduce his victory margin and that Congress might override it. Second, the president could have signed the bill under protest, announced his view that the NSC staff was not covered, and then proceeded openly with the policy he adopted covertly. Again, the public confrontation could have helped the president's long-term goals, but it could have provoked a tighter, loophole-free statute. Third was the course he and the NSC staff took. A fourth choice would have been to capitulate to those in Congress who were pushing the broadest interpretations of the Boland Amendment.

From the president's point of view, the fourth choice had nothing to recommend it. The first two would permit him to challenge Congress's use of appropriations riders directly. These choices probably would have been best, therefore, for preserving the institutional powers of the presidency. The danger was that either choice could have cut off the NSC's help for the contras and thus might have led quickly to the contras' defeat. The third option was the best for the contras, but hurt the presidential office.

What makes this kind of a choice particularly difficult is that presidents need a strong office to win support for and sustain controversial foreign policy objectives. President Reagan gave priority to Nicaragua because he foresaw a long-range danger of communist expansion in the Western Hemisphere. But a strong presidency—one that builds support for the exercise of discretionary power—may well be a prerequisite for defending against such foreign policy threats over the long term. Thus, the immediate policy that the president thought would leave the country in the best strategic position involved risking political support for the institutional powers he and his successors would also need to achieve the *same* long-term objective.

What should the president have done? Congressional opponents of any activist president can easily maintain a consistency between their policy goals and their desire to expand congressional power. They have no reason not to assert themselves, so they can be expected to do so. Therefore, I believe the president should let it be known, before the specifics of particular policy conflicts come into focus, that he (or she) intends to defend presidential power whenever it is challenged by Congress. The president needs to engage in what game theorists would think of as a strategy of "tit for tat." [15] In other words, the president needs to make clear, through action, that he or she will respond predictably and effectively to any congressional action that can be considered a usurpation of presidential power.

Most members of Congress understand tit for tat instinctively, although they would not articulate it in those terms. For example, Congress could have held a much more efficient, more informative, and less leaky set of Iran-contra hearings by conducting the hearings in executive session and then releasing the declassified transcripts. The decision to hold televised, public hearings—justified in the name of "public education"—essentially was a decision to raise the political penalty for the president. As a result of those hearings, the president lost control over the public agenda for a year. Similarly, it is not at all unusual to hear chairmen on other committees make Iran-contra-like statements about "the will of Congress" and then holding up an agency's budget to enforce conformity.

The problem is that neither Congress nor the president responds consistently. Procedural violations are overlooked when it is convenient to do so or when responding is too costly to the immediate policy at issue. If anything, the White House seems to have more problems responding consistently than does Congress. To some extent, the imbalance is systemic. Presidents may have more political cards to play than any one member of Congress, but it does not follow that the executive branch as a whole has as many as the whole Congress. A strategy of rewards and punishments can only be followed consistently for items near the top of a person's agenda. Because there are about 180 different committee and subcommittee chairmen in Congress, and only one president, the chairmen as a group inherently are better able to keep track of a larger number of priority items for their institution than the president is for his.

Consider, for example, President Reagan's procedural opposition to omnibus continuing resolutions. What may be the most remarkable thing about his threat, delivered in the 1988 State of the Union message, to veto any long-term, omnibus continuing resolution, regardless of content, is that it took him seven years to make such a statement. Continuing resolutions have the undeniable effect of weakening the president's veto power. Despite this direct threat to the powers of his office, Reagan, on this and many other matters, regularly sidestepped Congress's institutional challenges to obtain immediate policy objectives. The only way future presidents will be able to avoid this trap is to decide—as members of Congress routinely do—that preserving the power of the office is a top priority to be enforced *independently of the specific policy in dispute at the moment.*

The preceding is not meant to urge political leaders to stop fighting for deeply felt policy convictions. It is not too much to ask, however, that the two branches learn to limit the damage from such fighting. The interesting point here is that the best way to limit damage may not be to give in to the other side. Giving in only encourages the other side to be a bully. It turns out better for both sides if each stands up for itself. That is, it is best to arrive at an informal, mutual understanding of what constitutes procedural cooperation and then encourage each side to protect its own interest. If that pattern had been followed consistently, there is every reason to believe Congress would have clipped Oliver North's wings early and the president would have demanded an end to the procedural gimmicks Congress used on contra aid votes over the years.

Mutual cooperation is a necessary ingredient of a healthy foreign policy. Contrary to the Iran-contra majority, however, that cooperation does not have to rely either on trust[16] or the words of a statute. As a prominent game theorist noted, "the foundation of cooperation is not really trust, but the durability of the relationship," especially when durability is combined with a strategy that embraces reciprocity.[17] As rewards and benefits become predictable, and cooperative behavior is reinforced, Congress should not be so tempted to rely upon excessively rigid laws that weaken the presidency and invite future interbranch conflict. In addition, a system of mutually reinforced cooperation should reduce the temptation for both sides to use procedural sleights of hand and reduce the extent to which public debate is about wounded institutional pride instead of the substance of policy. In the long run, such a system should benefit both branches and therefore the country.

# Notes

1. U.S. House, Select Committee to Investigate Covert Arms Transactions with Iran and U.S. Senate, Select Committee On Secret Military Assistance to Iran and the Nicaraguan Opposition, 100th Cong., 1st sess., *Report of the Congressional Committees Investigating the Iran-Contra Affair, With Supplemental, Minority, and Additional Views,* H. Rept. 100-433, S. Rept. 100-216 (Washington, D.C., 1987). Hereafter cited as *Report, Majority Report,* or *Minority Report.*
2. P.L. 98-473; 98 Stat. 1837, 1937 (Oct. 12, 1984), Continuing Resolution, Department of Defense Appropriations Act, Sec. 8066 (a).
3. 22 U.S.C. 2293, emphasis added.
4. *Majority Report,* 117-153.
5. Ibid., citing 15 C.F.R. 385.4 (d).
6. Ibid., 161. The information in this paragraph all comes from the *Majority Report,* chap. 8.
7. See, for example, Pat Towell, "Leahy's Departure From Panel Followed

a Leak to Reporter," *Congressional Quarterly Weekly Report,* Aug. 1, 1987, 1741-1742; Helen Dewar, "Ethics Panel Criticizes Durenberger's Remarks," *Washington Post,* April 30, 1988, A7; John Felton, "Wright at Center of Nicaragua Policy Storm," *Congressional Quarterly Weekly Report,* Sept. 24, 1988, 2631-2633. See also *Minority Report,* 577. All of chap. 13 of the *Minority Report* is about leaks from Congress.

8. Jeffrey K. Tulis, *The Rhetorical Presidency* (Princeton, N.J.: Princeton University Press, 1987), 189.

9. The classified studies are referred to in the *Report of the President's Special Review Board,* John Tower, Chairman (Washington, D.C.: Government Printing Office, Feb. 26, 1987), appendix E.

10. "Ambition must be made to counteract ambition. The interest of man must be connected with the constitutional rights of the place." Alexander Hamilton, James Madison, and John Jay, *The Federalist,* Jacob E. Cooke, ed. (New York: World, 1961), 349.

11. "Extend the sphere and you will take in a greater variety of parties and interests; you will make it less likely that a majority of the whole will have a common motive to invade the rights of other citizens." Ibid., 64.

12. For the constitutional argument against mandatory forty-eight-hour notification, see Dick Cheney, "Clarifying Legislative and Executive Roles in Covert Operations" (Paper presented at a conference entitled "Separation of Powers in Foreign Policy: Do We Have an Imperial Congress?" sponsored by the American Bar Association Standing Committee on Law and National Security and the George Mason University School of Law, Student Bar Association, and International Law Society, March 30, 1988.) The paper was inserted over the course of three days into the *Congressional Record.* For the most relevant section, see *Cong. Rec.,* daily ed., April 21, 1988, Extension of Remarks, E1188-E1190.

13. U.S. House, Permanent Select Committee on Intelligence, Subcommittee on Legislation, 100th Cong., 1st sess., *Hearings on H.R. 1013, H.R. 1371, and Other Proposals Which Address the Issue of Affording Prior Notice of Covert Actions to the Congress,* April 1 and 8, June 10, 1987, 45, 46, 49, 58, 61, 158.

14. Michael J. Malbin, "Factions and Incentives in Congress," *Public Interest* 86 (1987): 107.

15. Robert Axelrod, *The Evolution of Cooperation* (New York: Basic Books, 1987), passim.

16. *Majority Report,* 20.

17. Axelrod, *Evolution,* 182.

# 16. CONGRESSIONAL INFLUENCE ON ADMINISTRATIVE AGENCIES: A CASE STUDY OF TELECOMMUNICATIONS POLICY

## John A. Ferejohn and Charles R. Shipan

Over the past twenty years—a period of major changes in telecommunications regulation—Congress has failed to enact any substantial change in the laws governing the industry. Repeated attempts to rewrite telecommunications law have foundered at various stages of legislative consideration. The substantial changes in regulatory law that have occurred during this period have come from the Federal Communications Commission (FCC), the courts, and the states, as well as from the industry itself. As a result, Congress is often regarded as unimportant in the telecommunications area.

Indeed, during this period members of Congress often have complained about the autonomy of the FCC and the courts as policy makers. To many members the FCC appears to be a classic "runaway" bureaucracy. Ernest Hollings, D-S.C., chairman of the Senate Commerce Committee, commenting about policy disputes with the FCC, said, "There is no question that we have a runaway animal in the FCC." [1] Representative Al Swift, D-Wash., discussing the Federal Communications Commission's broadcasting policy, put the matter just as sharply:

> Congress's policy intent was as clear as could be. . . . The FCC is taking full advantage of the fact that Congress is an extremely powerful, but muscle-bound, giant who sometimes has trouble getting up off its inertia to do anything. [2]

Congressional complaints about the independence of the courts in telecommunications policy are also common. Commenting on a 1987

We are indebted to David Austen-Smith, John Cogan, Terry Moe, Roger Noll, and Barry Weingast for helpful conversations and suggestions. Because these people disagree with each other on many of the topics discussed here, they cannot be held responsible for our conclusions. Partial support for this research was obtained from the Regulatory Studies Program at the Center for Economic Policy Research at Stanford University.

district court decision, House Commerce Committee chairman John Dingell, D-Mich., said:

> A single unelected, unaccountable federal judge has transformed himself into a regulator without portfolio, arrogating the power to determine whether and when the American people will be allowed to receive the advanced news services that are already available in countries with more enlightened telecommunications policies.[3]

In spite of these complaints, however, and in spite of the numerous bills that have been proposed and debated, the frequent hearings, and the occasional passage of bills by the House or Senate, no legislation has been enacted. Public policy has been made elsewhere, and such congressional action as has occurred seems to have had little effect on the industry.

There are two polar views that dominate recent studies of congressional policy making and that suggest alternative interpretations of this situation. The traditional theory, which we term the *deliberative* theory, expounded most recently by Arthur Maass, depicts Congress as a deliberative institution occupied with the formulation of public policy.[4]

According to Maass, people serve in Congress to try to implement their conceptions of the public interest. Congress is principally engaged in defining and adjudicating competing conceptions of the public interest, and most of the activities—the legislative proposals and debates and hearings—that take place there are directed toward these purposes. Congress is, in this sense, a legislative institution, and the central activity that members undertake is the enactment of laws regulating public and private conduct. In this theory, to the extent that legislative activity does not result in public law, such activity is seen as futile and as a failure of the policy process.

From the standpoint of the deliberative theory—a theory publicly endorsed by many members—telecommunications policy represents a failure of congressional action. When the major affected interests have widely divergent goals, it is extremely difficult to enact complex legislation. The legislative hurdles are so numerous and difficult to traverse that many groups can effectively veto attempted congressional action. In this view, Congress has been rendered inept by its own archaic institutional structure, and important policy making has taken place elsewhere.

The *electoral* theory, articulated most sharply by David Mayhew, views Congress as an institutional setting within which ambitious office holders seek to further their electoral interests.[5] To achieve their goals, they sometimes find that (collective) legislative activity is worthwhile, but, because Congress is a relatively large collectivity, pursuit of reelection goals by private means (targeted directly at the constituency) is usually more efficient than legislative action. Each member therefore spends most of his or her time and effort supporting issue positions popular with constituents, claiming credit for government projects in the district, and assisting constituents who are having difficulties with government agencies.

In the electoral view, deliberation and legislative activity are mere byproducts of the pursuit of reelection by ambitious and insecure members. Congressional actions that seem to be directed to the formulation of legislation are best interpreted as posturing before audiences of constituents rather than as attempts to make laws. In the electoral theory, failure to pass legislation is quite normal because members are not centrally concerned with their collective product.

By this account, members' complaints and grumblings are simply the reflections of constituent concerns and interests rather than expressions of legislative intentions.[6] As legislative proposals are merely attempts to identify with popular issue positions, congressional sponsors neither believe nor hope that the proposals become law. From this point of view, we do not see congressional failure; rather we see a pattern of posturing and insincerity that may be even more troubling to students of democratic institutions than the portrait of ineptness and immobility found in the deliberative account.

While each of these perspectives is valuable as a way to view congressional institutions and practices, we think they fail to illuminate an important range of congressional activity that *is* aimed at shaping public policy. Specifically, we argue that some important congressional activity is directed neither at the production of legislation nor to the service of constituents. Rather, it is aimed at influencing public policy by convincing other policy makers—federal or state bureaucrats, judges, private companies, or foreign nations—to alter their behavior or face legislative intervention.

Attempts to persuade other policy makers take many forms: threatening speeches, legislative proposals, hearings, committee reports, and enactment of legislation by one chamber. Sometimes these actions are aimed at producing legislation, but if such actions were a *sure* sign that legislation was forthcoming, agencies could simply adjust their actions to reflect congressional interests without any formal action. In reality, however, agency personnel are not certain that legislation will be enacted or even reported from committee. Because agency leaders believe that committee members are relatively sympathetic to the agency's actions,[7] leaders may doubt that the committee will take legislative proposals to the floor, where the committee would have to persuade skeptical or indifferent congressional peers. Agency personnel, therefore, may believe they can safely discount committee criticism and pursue their own preferred policies. To counteract these beliefs, committee members have an incentive to act as if they will sometimes resort to legislation: they may try to establish a reputation for having preferences that are sufficiently different from those of the agency that they would pursue legislative action if the agency is intransigent. A committee, therefore, may act as if it prefers the position of its chamber to the position of the agency, even if its actual preferences are the reverse.

The *signaling,* or *reputational,* theory is positioned between the deliberative and electoral theories. As in the deliberative theory, we assume that members are concerned with shaping public policy. Congressional institutions are structured to mitigate the conflict between private electoral incentives and public policy goals. For example, the delegation of the authority for overseeing administrative policy activities to small subcommittees makes it more likely that individual members of Congress will find the pursuit of public policy goals a useful way to ensure reelection. But, as in the electoral theory, legislative activity is not taken at face value. In the signaling theory, members are posturing before external audiences, but these audiences include other policy makers as well as constituents.

In this essay we present a case study that exemplifies signaling by congressional committees in the policy process.[8] As noted, despite the great changes in telecommunications policy since the late 1960s, Congress has not passed any major legislation. But the lack of new legislation does *not* mean that Congress has been inefficient or that members were simply posturing for their constituents. In fact, in many cases Congress had a marked impact on the policy outcome.

An example of this impact occurred in the mid-1980s, after the Bell telephone system had been dismantled. Due to several changes brought about by divestiture, the FCC proposed in 1982 to charge all telephone customers a monthly access charge, or fee, for connection to the phone system.[9] These fees did not represent new costs—they had previously been embodied in cross-subsidizations between various parts of AT&T, mainly the long distance and the local operating companies—and the FCC argued that this new method of recovering costs would be more economically efficient. Members of Congress, however, were less concerned about the economic than the political implications of the change. What mattered to them was that their constituents might think their rates had gone up because of the new method. As a result, several bills and amendments were proposed in both chambers. In the end, despite the surge in activity, no legislation was passed.

The signaling theory provides a useful interpretation of these events. We argue that, although no legislation was passed, Congress exerted a strong influence on the agency and that agency actions reflected concern about possible legislation. Congress did not fail to act because powerful minorities blocked legislation, as the deliberative theory might argue, and its members were not simply posturing before constituents, as the electoral model might surmise. Rather, Congress affected policy by signaling to an agency both the nature of its intent and the strength of its opinions, and the agency responded by changing its course of action.

## Theoretical Considerations

When Congress delegates authority to an agency, it allows the agency to make the first move in a policy formation game, either by implementing previously legislated policy or by proposing a new policy. Once the agency has taken the policy position, the congressional committees may either accept it, by not reporting corrective legislation, or reject it, by reporting such legislation.[10] If the committees report legislation, the agency has an opportunity to change its policy position, and, if it does so, each committee may either withdraw its legislation (perhaps by not getting it scheduled for floor debate) or go forward with its proposals to the floor of its parent chamber. For the present we assume that floor consideration occurs under an open rule and that the outcome in the event of congressional action is at M, midway between the median positions of the parent chambers.[11]

Some of the implications of the model can be seen most simply if the preferences of the actors are known and can be placed along a single dimension as follows. We assume that each actor has a most preferred point along the line and that he or she prefers outcomes closer to that point to those farther away. In this case, we can represent the preferred position of a chamber or a committee as the median position of that body.[12]

By way of illustration, in Figure 16-1 we denote the agency's preferred position as A, the most preferred points of the median members of the House and Senate are designated as H and S, respectively, and the outcome of the congressional process is assumed to be midway between these positions at M. The most preferred points of the median members of the House and Senate committees are written as $H^c$ and $S^c$, respectively.[13] Finally, we let M* stand for the point at which the committee closest to the agency is just indifferent between M (the outcome if the committee reports legislation to its chamber and thereby permits legislative action) and M*. In other words, M* and M are equidistant from the committee's preferred point.

Figure 16-1   Distribution of Ideal Points of Congressional Actors

If the legislative rules allow either the House or Senate committee to keep legislation off the congressional agenda, and if the committees are closer to Congress's preferred point than to the agency (that is, $H^c$ and $S^c$ are closer to M than to A), the agency will anticipate congressional action if it locates anywhere to the left of M*, and it will set its policy position at that point. Thus, in this case, agency behavior is constrained by committee preferences.[14] This situation does not guarantee that the committee gets what it wants; it means that the agency picks a policy such that the committee is indifferent between passing legislation and accepting the agency's actions. Note that if the committee positions were nearer to A than to M, the agency would be unconstrained and the policy outcome would be at A.

Agency actions, therefore, will be constrained by committee preferences if, and only if, the committees are not too sympathetic with agency goals. If the committees become too close to the agency, they become its "captives"; M* would be located to the left of A, and the committee's threats will be ignored by the agency. This fact—that captive committees are powerless to alter agency actions—gives committees an incentive to claim (or signal) that their preferences are closer to those of their parent chamber than to those of the agency.[15]

The absence of uncertainty in this simple model permits the agency to anticipate congressional preferences correctly and to choose a policy that provokes no actual legislation. But in most real situations, such as the access charge case, the agency does *not* know the committees' preferences and may not be able to choose a policy that will avoid potentially detrimental legislation. When there is uncertainty as to congressional preferences, legislation may be enacted.

To examine a situation with imperfect information, consider a unicameral legislature in which the preferred positions of both the agency (A) and the House (H) are known. The location of the committee, however, is uncertain; only the committee knows its true position. The agency does not know whether the committee is closer to the agency or to the House floor, and the earlier argument shows that the agency needs this information if it is to avoid costly legislation.

The agency now has to determine, in the face of uncertainty, what it can get away with or what it can propose and implement while still avoiding legislation. If it faces a "tough" committee—a committee located much closer to the House's position, such as $C^t$ in Figure 16-2, it must take a position to the right of H* or the committee may report a bill to the floor.

Figure 16-2   Preferences with Incomplete Information

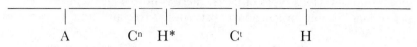

On the other hand, a "nice" committee ($C^n$ in Figure 16-2) would be one that is more sympathetic to the position of the agency than to the position of the House floor. If the agency believes the committee is nice, it can implement its preferred position, A, without fear of legislation, because the committee prefers A to H.

Now consider the committee's perspective on this situation. The committee wants to induce the agency to locate as close as possible to the committee's position, but the agency gets to make the first proposal. If the committee is nice and lets this fact be known, the agency will take advantage of this knowledge and propose A, which is acceptable but not optimal for the committee. The committee therefore has an incentive to act tougher than it actually is.[16] By acting tougher than it actually is, a committee might induce an agency to modify its proposal, thereby producing an outcome, such as H*, that the committee prefers (and that the agency also prefers to a legislative outcome from the floor).

By scheduling hearings or reporting legislation, the committee may try to signal that it is tough and thereby convince the agency to change its policy and forestall legislative correction. Legislation will be enacted only if the committee is truly tough, but the agency, making a calculated gamble, incorrectly believes that the committee is nice. Thus, while legislation is rare, legislative activity, which sends a message about committee type to the agency, is not. Unless an agency adopts a position the committee likes, the committee may initiate legislation.

## Changes in the Structure of the Telecommunications Industry

The access charge case provides an excellent illustration of the signaling theory of congressional activity. As a prelude to the discussion of our case, it may be helpful to describe briefly the relevant events in telecommunications during the 1960s and 1970s. We restrict attention to two main areas: the admission of competition into long distance services and the procedures by which costs are allocated across regulatory jurisdictions.[17]

A central principle of telephone regulation until the 1960s was the requirement of "universal service"—to ensure high rates of penetration of telephone service, telephone rates were "averaged" over broad classes of customers in such a way that high-cost users were subsidized by low-cost users. Although there was a great deal of uncertainty as to the costs of service for various types of users, there is little doubt that this policy priced long distance usage above costs so that (certain) local rates were kept low.[18]

Beginning with a 1959 decision (the *Above 890* decision), the FCC inaugurated a sequence of actions that had the effect of undermining this policy of cross-subsidization. The commission began by allowing competition in the provision of private lines for long distance service, thereby permitting the development of a fledgling market for specialized long distance services. Over the next two decades, a series of court cases and agency decisions continued this trend. Competition in the provision of long distance services forced AT&T to begin pricing these services competitively and removed a source of funds for cross-subsidy.

While the FCC and the courts were removing regulatory barriers to competition in long distance service, the share of the fixed or network costs of telephone service allocated to long distance users was steadily increasing.[19] State regulation of local telephone companies proceeds by specifying an allowed rate of return on capital, then placing a usage-based charge or "tax" on long distance service, and then recovering the residual or remaining funds through local rates. Under a series of federal-state agreements, the recovered funds from long distance steadily increased, reaching an average of more than 25 percent by the early 1980s.[20]

The increase in the tax on long distance usage was on a collision course with the FCC's policy of permitting entry into the long distance market. On one hand, the tax increase would cause long distance rates to rise. On the other hand, however, deregulatory decisions at the FCC forced AT&T to price its services competitively, creating inexorable pressures to reduce long distance charges, thereby lowering the subsidization of high-cost users.

Because AT&T continued to retain a dominant share in most of its markets even after the introduction of competition, the Justice Department (DOJ) in 1974 filed an antitrust suit, arguing that AT&T had both the incentive and opportunity to engage in anticompetitive practices and that it had done so repeatedly in the past.[21] The DOJ argued that the only effective method of preventing these practices was structural: the separation of regulated (local exchange) services from unregulated services. Thus, the DOJ advocated the complete legal separation (or divestiture) of local exchanges, which were seen as natural monopolies, from the long distance and equipment manufacturing operations.

In January 1982, after eight years of legal maneuvering and several months of litigation, AT&T and the Justice Department settled the antitrust suit essentially on the department's terms. This agreement is embodied in the Modification of Final Judgment (MFJ), which is technically a revision of a 1956 consent decree.[22] In the MFJ, AT&T agreed to divest itself of the local exchange services and to place them in seven regional holding companies. These companies would be regulated in the traditional fashion while AT&T, after a transition period, would be permitted to provide competitive services in unregulated markets.

It is important for future discussion to see that if the transfer of revenues from federal to state jurisdictions were to continue after divestiture, the proceeds of the implicit tax on long distance services that provided these funds would now have to flow between separate legal entities and not simply among units within AT&T. In other words, if the existing policy of rate setting were continued after divestiture, it would require a mechanism for imposing the tax on long distance services operated by various long distance companies. It was clear to both Harold H. Greene, the trial judge in the antitrust suit and the arbiter of the MFJ, and to the Department of Justice that such a mechanism—an interexchange access charge—was consistent with the consent decree but, as we shall see, the FCC was unenthusiastic about this alternative and preferred to impose access charges directly on the end users.

## Congressional Reactions to the FCC's Access Charge Decisions

Following a 1978 decision (the *Execunet* decision), AT&T and its long distance competitors came to an agreement (called the ENFIA—exchange network facilities for interstate access—agreement) as to the access charges that long distance companies had to pay for connecting to local exchanges. This agreement allowed competitive carriers to pay significantly less than AT&T for interconnection on the grounds that the quality of the connections was inferior to those provided to AT&T. These agreements were recognized as an interim solution to the interconnection problem, and the FCC inaugurated proceedings (Docket 78-72) aimed at producing a permanent system of charges for access to local exchanges.

There was no doubt (outside of AT&T, at any rate) that, sooner or later, competitive long distance companies would have to be able to obtain equivalent quality interconnection at the same prices, but there was considerable dispute as to what these prices should be. The pricing problem results from the fact that a significant portion of the cost of telephone service is fixed or independent of usage.[23] Indeed, except for peak periods the variable costs of telephone service are very low.

Traditionally, fixed costs have been recovered through usage charges, and an increasing portion of these costs have fallen on long distance users. As a result of these practices, high-volume long distance users found themselves paying telephone rates that were sufficiently above the variable costs of service that they had an incentive to "bypass" the system by building or leasing private lines. As the costs of bypass technology fell, phone companies faced the prospect of growing numbers of large users leaving the system and having to allocate more and more of the fixed costs of telephone service to the remaining customers.

To recover fixed costs in an economically efficient manner, the FCC resolved (in Docket 78-72) to move to a pricing scheme that removed the incentive for bypass by aligning prices with costs of service. The FCC's solution was a two-part tariff: a fixed monthly fee, called a customer access line charge or CALC, that covered the fixed costs of connection to the system, plus a usage-based charge. Once in place, this system would have the effect of reducing the possibilities of cross-subsidization among classes of users.

The imposition of this new system was complicated by a number of transitional issues. Foremost among these was that AT&T's competitors did not yet have access to equal quality interconnection; the new pricing scheme would remove most of their cost advantages under ENFIA and allow AT&T to offer substantially higher quality service at a similar price. Moreover, to the extent that the introduction of the new scheme would lead to shifting charges among user groups, these groups could be expected to complain.

But the most important complicating issue arose with the divestiture. The Justice Department and Judge Greene were at pains to point out that the divestiture did not have any necessary connection with how fixed costs were recovered. If the FCC decided to do so, the traditional cost recovery scheme could be continued, but the flows of funds would now occur among separate legal entities and be visible to politicians and their constituents. And, if the issue were to get to Congress, the arbitrariness of the traditional arrangements would surely become a matter of contention.

In its original access charge proposal, announced in December 1982, the FCC recognized some of these difficulties and attempted to resolve them. First, the access charges were set uniformly and did not reflect the actual interconnection costs of particular users; high-cost users would continue to receive a subsidy through what was called the

Universal Service Fund. Second, the access charges were phased in gradually over a six-year period so that shifts in rates would be less wrenching. Third, long distance competitors were not required to pay as much for interconnection as AT&T, although their charges would be greater than under ENFIA.

Predictably, the FCC's announcement of the access charge scheme led to a political uproar. While AT&T and the new regional holding companies supported the changes in pricing—as did many leading economists—consumer groups, state regulators, and smaller long distance companies opposed them. During 1982 telephone companies had begun requesting massive rate increases from state public utility commissions (PUCs). While these requests reflected inflationary cost increases and regulatorily imposed changes in depreciation practices, many state commissions claimed that they also reflected the anticipated effects of the new access charge scheme. Virtually all of the PUCs opposed the FCC's plan in comments before the commission, and many appeared before congressional committees to voice their complaints. Moreover, although the new long distance companies supported the FCC's general pricing concept, they opposed the actual plan because it offered them less favorable rates than did the continuation of the existing system of interexchange access charges.

Within the first few months of 1983, several bills were introduced in Congress aimed at stalling or modifying the commission's proposals. The proceedings reflected considerable confusion over the causes of local rate increases, and members of Congress saw that constituents might hold them responsible. Members were motivated to try to keep rates down if they could. One way they could accomplish this was to try to influence the FCC's access charge plan.

In midsummer the Commerce committees of the two chambers held hearings on a variety of legislative proposals. The two plans that took center stage were the bills proposed by Senate committee chairman Robert Packwood, R-Ore., (S. 1660), and a plan by Representatives Timothy Wirth, D-Colo., and John Dingell, D-Mich., (H.R. 3621, later embodied in H.R. 4102). Each of these proposals aimed to stop the FCC from imposing its access charge scheme and to continue to recover fixed costs from usage charges. Both dealt with the threat of bypass by regulatory means: the Senate bill simply prohibited various forms of bypass, and the House legislation directly taxed bypassers to pay for the costs of the local loop. House committee chairman Dingell succinctly stated the central purpose of both proposals. "As I see the situation, we are preserving the status quo," he said. "The shifts of money around the country stemming from allocations of costs between long distance and local service, between different regions, would remain

... substantially the same as they are today." [24]

The intensity of congressional interest in access charges was demonstrated by the holding of joint committee hearings, a rare occurrence. Just as these hearings got underway, the FCC issued a revision of its original access charge plan, which diminished the magnitude of the charges and made the phase-in more gradual. The tone taken by the representatives and senators in the hearings suggests that the agency had not gone nearly far enough. The following exchange between Packwood and FCC chairman Mark Fowler illustrates congressional impatience with agency actions:

> Chairman Packwood: Now, in your statement you indicate the Federal Communications Commission acts under a congressional mandate, and you read the directive, "to provide service so far as possible to all the people of the United States," and "it should be a rapid, efficient, nationwide service with adequate facilities at reasonable charges," correct?
>
> Mr. Fowler: Yes, sir.
>
> Chairman Packwood: And, indeed, you are a creature of Congress and you attempt to administer in this case the telephone laws in accordance with what you think Congress has intended.
>
> Mr. Fowler: With true fidelity, yes sir.
>
> Chairman Packwood: Is it also true that the consent decree between AT&T and the Justice Department has nothing to do with your long-distance charges?
>
> Mr. Fowler: You mean with the access charge decision?
>
> Chairman Packwood: You can put the access charge in if you want. But the consent decree in no way limits your ability to decide what you are going to charge for long distance?
>
> Mr. Fowler: Yes, sir.

The hearings continued:

> Chairman Packwood: Now for years you have followed this policy of subsidizing rural and residential rates with long-distance charges, acting on what you thought was Congress [*sic*] mandate, and Congress never said anything. . . .
>
> What has given you the impression that Congress has changed its mind as to what we want you to do? [25]

As the hearings proceeded, it became increasingly clear that congressional action was likely. Wirth, Dingell, and Packwood all indicated in the tenor of their questions to witnesses that they expected to get bills to the floors of both chambers by late fall. However, major obstacles stood in the way of enacting legislation.

The hearings revealed significant congressional concern as to the distributional impact of the bills. Senator Frank Lautenberg, D-N.J., emphasized these concerns: "I guess what we are trying to do is to re-make by legislation the AT&T system as it existed before, because we are trying to get the parts of the system that were subsidizing local residential service to pay a share of that subsidy again." [26] Members from low cost-of-service states, such as New York, New Jersey, and Michigan, wondered why their states should be subsidizing those with higher costs, primarily sunbelt states such as Florida, Nevada, and Arizona.[27] Indeed, the only successful amendment offered in committee was proposed by James Florio, D-N.J. The amendment encouraged the FCC to "de-average" rates so that urban states would no longer subsidize rural states through their phone bills.

Following a contentious markup session, the House subcommittee reported H.R. 4102 on a 10-5 party line vote, and in late October, after a long partisan dispute in which a number of Republican amendments were defeated, the Commerce committee finally reported the bill to the floor for consideration. While the committee deliberations were proceeding, the FCC tried to diminish the sense of haste by delaying the imposition of the access charges for another four months. In spite of these disagreements and after defeating two partisan attempts to weaken the legislation, the House November 10 passed H.R. 4102 by voice vote.

The going was just as tough in the Senate. After initially accepting an amendment by Lautenberg that removed the prohibition on end-user charges and imposed a one-year moratorium on the FCC rules instead, the committee reached a compromise that contained a two-year moratorium and reported the bill in late October. It was clear, however, that the lack of committee agreement on a legislative vehicle made Senate prospects for successful legislation dim, and the leadership kept S. 1660 off the Senate floor until 1984, giving Senate leaders time to work on the FCC.

When the Senate postponed floor action, the agency was given a "window" within which it could (again) issue a revised access charge plan in the hope of forestalling legislative correction. On January 16, 1984, it issued a new decision that reduced the charges still further and delayed their implementation until the middle of 1985. Given the divisions within the Senate, the agency was not forced to capitulate completely: it had only to concede some ground and to delay the impact of its decision so that the urgency of congressional consideration was lost and the matter deferred until after the 1984 congressional elections.

Ten days later, one day after the FCC reaffirmed its decision to delay the charges, the Senate voted 44-40 not to take up S. 1660, effectively killing it. Chairman Packwood said the bill was defeated not because of AT&T's massive lobbying effort, but because the FCC had deferred the imposition of the access charges. According to Lautenberg, who proposed substituting the moratorium for Packwood's prohibition on access charges, "I thought our goal all along was to change the commission's course and change it we have."[28]

## Conclusions

The access charge decisions represent an almost perfect case of congressional influence on agency decisions. The agency made or revised its access charge order four separate times: in December 1982; in July 1983, just before the joint committee hearings; again in December 1983, during the House committee markups; and finally in January 1984, just prior to the scheduled Senate vote on S. 1660. Each time, the agency scaled back the access charges and delayed their implementation, but, until its 1984 decision, Congress continued to signal its unhappiness with the agency's position and continued to threaten new legislation. In the end, the agency was permitted to go forward with access charges but only on terms that Congress—in this case the Senate floor—would accept.

If we interpret the dimension of competition as the proportion of telephone charges to be recovered through usage-based charges, congressional and agency preferences in this case would seem to fit our illustration in Figure 16-1. But, in this case, the House and Senate committees would probably be relatively close to their parent chambers, and the parent chambers were probably not far apart. Although there was significant congressional disagreement as to where subsidies should go, most members preferred usage charges to access charges as a way of recovering fixed costs of telephone service. The threat of legislation, therefore, was quite credible, and the conditions for congressional influence were maximized. As a result, even though the agency made the final decisions, the policy reflected congressional preferences.

While the access charge case seems a clear instance of successful congressional influence in regulatory policy, our theory suggests that in other circumstances there may be very little influence. If, for example, the preferred positions of the committee are (or are believed to be) close to the agency's preferred policy outcome, or if, for whatever reason, the committee must bear significant costs by going to the floor, the agency may be able to ignore congressional threats. We also have not focused any attention at all on the informational advantages that agencies might have relative to congressional committees. Such phenomena will mitigate congressional influence. In addition, to the extent that the president is willing to use the power to veto to forestall congressional action, congressional intervention will become less credible.

Finally, the importance of heterogeneity of preferences should be emphasized. If Congress is sending signals to an agency, Congress wants those signals to be as strong as possible. If preferences within Congress are mixed, the signals received by the agency will likewise be mixed; the threat of legislation may seem less credible; and the agency will be less likely to modify its stance. We therefore caution the reader not to assume that the access charge case is, in some sense, typical.

Nevertheless, the dynamics of the case may throw light on previously observed congressional phenomena associated with the committee system. For example, in our model, Congress is more powerful insofar as it can keep its committees from becoming captured. Clarence Cannon's practice of keeping agency sympathizers off appropriations subcommittees might be interpreted as enhancing congressional influence rather than just keeping budgets small.[29] Indeed, congressional influence is maximized when committees are random samples of the whole chamber. Insofar as legislative committees are prone to agency capture, the institution of the "dual" set of appropriations committees might be seen as providing an alternative source of congressional influence. Allowing members to choose subcommittees based on seniority on the full committee rather than on subcommittee seniority would provide another check on committee capture.

The signaling, or reputational, theory emphasizes the ambiguous role of committees in achieving congressional influence over agencies. Traditionally, the committee system was seen as a way in which members of Congress specialized their activities so that the inherent informational advantages of administrative agencies were reduced. To achieve the advantages of specialization, members are permitted to serve on committees that supervise programs of special interest to them and, therefore, are likely to be sympathetic with agency goals. But, we have seen that if committees are too sympathetic, Congress loses some of its control over the agency. This phenomenon may be mitigated by the formation of the committee's reputation, but it is an inherent limitation in the use of committees to control agencies.

Finally, we turn to the evaluation or interpretation of congressional action. In our theory, Congress was efficacious in influencing access charges. Moreover, the reputational theory provides conditions under which we should expect successful congressional influence without legislative intervention. Thus, unlike the deliberative theory, which holds Congress to too strict a test, and the electoral theory, which holds it to no test at all, the reputational theory provides a plausible basis for assessing congressional influence on external actors.

# Notes

1. Paul Starobin, "FCC and Congress Clash Over Proper Roles," *Congressional Quarterly Weekly Report,* Feb. 27, 1988, 479.
2. Ibid., 480.
3. *Public Utilities Fortnightly,* Oct. 15, 1987, 32.
4. Arthur Maass, *Congress and the Common Good* (New York: Basic Books, 1983).
5. David Mayhew, *Congress: The Electoral Connection* (New Haven, Conn.: Yale University Press, 1974). See also Morris P. Fiorina, *Congress—Keystone of the Washington Establishment* (New Haven, Conn.: Yale University Press, 1977).
6. Mayhew refers to this as *position taking.* Members of Congress can stake out and visibly promote positions favored by their constituents, thereby improving their standing with those constituents at little cost.
7. Members of Congress often *self-select* onto committees. They choose a specific committee because of their own interests or the interests of their constituents and tend to be sympathetic toward relevant agencies. For example, representatives from tobacco growing regions are disproportionately found on the Agriculture Committee, which has often enjoyed a close relationship with the Department of Agriculture. On the assignment of committee seats, see Kenneth A. Shepsle, *The Giant Jigsaw Puzzle: Democratic Committee Assignments in the Modern House* (Chicago: University of Chicago Press, 1978); and Irwin N. Gertzog, "The Routinization of Committee Assignments in the U.S. House of Representatives," *American Political Science Review* (November 1976): 693-712.
8. In one sense, the case we cite represents a partial failure of signaling in that the agency was initially unpersuaded that the committee would take legislative action and continued to pursue a congressionally unpopular course. In the end, however, the agency altered its policies after it became convinced that Congress would intervene.
9. It should be noted that the FCC supported user access charges, but rejected other cost recovery schemes, such as interexchange access charges, on the grounds of economic inefficiency.
10. The assumptions about congressional and agency preferences are related to those in Kenneth Shepsle and Barry Weingast's paper on committee power and in Brian Marks's work on the relations between the courts and Congress, while the structure of Congress-agency interaction is similar to that proposed by William Niskanen. See Kenneth A. Shepsle and Barry R. Weingast, "The Institutional Foundations of Committee Power," *American Political Science Review* (March 1987): 85-104; Brian A. Marks, "A Model of Judicial Influence on Congressional Policymaking: *Grove City College v. Bell,*" working paper, Washington University, 1987; and William Niskanen, *Bureaucracy and Representative Government* (Chicago: Aldine Press, 1971).
11. The assumption of open rule consideration of committee proposals gives

the committees an incentive to accommodate agency requests rather than resorting to the relatively less controllable floor. The desire to settle policy disputes away from the floor is an example of E. E. Schattschneider's well-known "mobilization of bias." *The Semi-Sovereign People* (New York: Holt, Rinehart, & Winston, 1960).

12. Note that if we were to give explicit consideration to presidential veto powers, the critical parameter for a chamber would not be its median but a point at which it could successfully override a veto. When the legislative veto is permitted, a more subtle analysis is required. We leave this to another occasion.

13. The president plays a role in assigning members to the agency, thus determining the agency's position. During the access charge debates, the House was Democratic, and the executive branch and the Senate were Republican. This division contributed to a situation in which the agency and the House held policy positions that were far apart and in which the Senate was more sympathetic to the agency than the House. Now that the Senate has fallen back under Democratic control, it is less likely to be as sympathetic to an agency, and one might expect to find stronger congressional influence as a result. It should be stressed that the signaling theory is not meant to be descriptive of all policy debates; rather it holds true only when certain conditions are met. These conditions are discussed throughout the essay.

14. See Barry R. Weingast and Mark J. Moran, "Bureaucratic Discretion or Congressional Control? Regulatory Policy-making by the Federal Trade Commission," *Journal of Political Economy* 91 (1983): 765-800. For a discussion of the theory behind such constraints, see Terry M. Moe, "An Assessment of the Positive Theory of Congressional Dominance," *Legislative Studies Quarterly* 12 (November 1987): 475-520.

15. We note that if agency preferences (A) are influenced by presidential appointments, internal organizational processes, or external ideological shifts, the model allows ample scope for presidential influence, bureaucratic autonomy, or ideological influence. The point is this: even though congressional actors may override agency policy choice, if agency preferences shift sufficiently, policy changes can occur anywhere within the congressionally constrained region. On presidential influence, see Terry M. Moe, "Interests, Institutions and Positive Theory: The Politics of the NLRB," *Studies in American Political Development* 2 (1988): 236-299; for internal shifts, see James Q. Wilson, *The Politics of Regulation* (New York: Basic Books, 1980); and on external shifts, see Martha Derthick and Paul J. Quirk, *The Politics of Deregulation* (Washington, D.C.: Brookings Institution, 1985).

16. The agency anticipates the committee's incentives to act tough but will not be able to take them completely into account.

17. We do not discuss a variety of important issues that may turn out to be useful for a broader understanding of policy formation in this area: computers and telecommunications, international issues, technological change, and telecommunications. To be sure, these issues are just beneath

the surface of the developments discussed here. Considerations of space, time, and unity of argument prohibit their explicit treatment.

18. Exactly which residential rates were priced below cost remains in some dispute. Most analysts agree that people living in low population density areas are more costly to serve than others, so that rural and small town rates were subsidized.

19. The allocation of costs between local and federal jurisdiction was known as the Separations and Settlements process. Our discussion relies on Roger Noll, "State Regulatory Responses to Competition and Divestiture in the Telecommunications Industry," *Antitrust and Regulation,* ed. Ronald E. Grieson, forthcoming.

20. Again, this was done to keep local rates low. The Separations and Settlements procedures in effect during this time were known as the Ozark Plan.

21. For excellent discussions and analyses of the years leading up to the divestiture, see Steve Coll, *The Deal of the Century* (New York: Atheneum Books, 1986); Fred W. Henck and Bernard Strassburg, *A Slippery Slope: The Long Road to the Breakup of AT&T* (New York: Greenwood Press, 1988); and Peter Temin and Louis Galambos, *The Fall of the Bell System* (Cambridge: Cambridge University Press, 1987).

22. This earlier consent decree settled an antitrust suit brought by the government against AT&T in 1949 to divest Western Electric from the rest of the Bell system.

23. Included in these fixed costs are the costs of terminal equipment (which would no longer be embodied in telephone rates), wiring on the customer's premises, and the costs of maintaining the local loop (the exchange plus the wiring from the exchange to the customer's location).

24. U.S. Congress, Joint Hearings, "The Universal Telephone Service Preservation Act of 1983," Serials 98-30, 98-39, 98th Cong., 1st sess., July 28, 1983, 155.

25. Ibid., 67.

26. Ibid., 149.

27. The redistributional aspects of telephone pricing had been quite well understood by most members of Congress all along. What made it controversial in 1983 was that the transfers of funds were published in agency documents and committee hearings and members of Congress could henceforward be held accountable for supporting or opposing them.

28. *Congressional Quarterly Almanac, 1984* (Washington, D.C.: Congressional Quarterly, 1985), 282.

29. Clarence Cannon was the powerful Democratic chairman of the Appropriations Committee in the 1950s and 1960s. See Richard Fenno, *Power of the Purse* (Boston: Little, Brown, 1966).

# Part VI

# CONGRESS AT WORK

# 17.  THE HOUSE OF REPRESENTATIVES: A REPORT FROM THE FIELD

## *David E. Price*

On November 4, 1986, I was elected to the U.S. House of Representatives from the Fourth District of North Carolina, a five-county area that includes the cities of Raleigh, Chapel Hill, and Asheboro. On January 6, 1987, I took the oath as a new member of the 100th Congress. My previous political experience included service as a U.S. Senate aide, the staff directorship of the Democratic National Committee's Commission on Presidential Nomination, and various campaign and party posts, including the chairmanship of the North Carolina Democratic party. My principal career, however, had been teaching and research. I had studied and written about Congress for some twenty years—including an article on congressional committees published in earlier editions of *Congress Reconsidered.* It is perhaps in light of this dual background as a political practitioner and analyst that I have been asked to offer, for the present edition, some reflections on my first term as a member of the House. The essay deals with a number of topics: the obstacles I faced in running against an incumbent, the different kind of politics I encountered in moving from the campaign to the early weeks of the 100th Congress, my main legislative project on the Banking Committee, the budget crisis that overshadows the work of the Congress, and the various ways I relate to my district.

## Getting Elected

In the community meetings I hold around the district, I am often asked about various proposals for reforming congressional elections. Several times I have responded that I, too, have questioned the two-year House term, high-spending campaigns, and thirty-second campaign commercials. But then I must add that it was precisely those factors that let me shake loose a House incumbent in 1986!

I wish to thank Gene Conti, Don DeArmon, Paul Feldman, Mac McCorkle, John Maron, and Sally Maddison for their assistance with this essay.

My race was one of a handful nationwide—two in primaries and six in the general election—in which a challenger defeated a sitting member of the House. Nationally, the general election success rate for incumbents seeking reelection has not fallen below 94 percent since 1976. North Carolina has been an exception to that pattern: close contests have been the rule in those western districts where both parties historically have had strong bases and in those Piedmont and urban-suburban districts where split-ticket voting has become more common and GOP candidates often have benefited from national trends. The state has become notorious for expensive, contentious campaigns, with the tone often set by Senator Jesse Helms and his organization, the National Congressional Club.

My district, the Fourth, has displayed considerable volatility—voting for Governor Jim Hunt by 14,282 votes when he unsuccessfully challenged Helms in 1984, for example, while giving President Ronald Reagan a 46,552-vote margin in his victory over Walter Mondale. That same year, six-term Democratic representative Ike Andrews was narrowly defeated by Bill Cobey, a Republican challenger with close ties to the Congressional Club. I was serving as state Democratic chairman and was deeply stung by these defeats. At the same time, I recognized the volatility of the district and the vulnerability of the new incumbent, whose political beliefs placed him considerably to the right of modal opinion in the district. By early 1985 I had decided to challenge him for the seat. I announced my candidacy at the time of the county Democratic conventions in April.

The primary field eventually expanded to four. The front-runner was a state senator from the largest county in the district. I maintained my full teaching schedule through the end of 1985, but managed to campaign extensively. Much of this effort was directed at prominent political and community leaders. Major breakthroughs came, for example, when the preeminent Democratic fund-raiser in my district and a respected black city council member in Raleigh agreed to help me. I also attended countless community functions where a local supporter would make certain I was introduced to as many people as possible. Despite a year of campaigning, however, our first poll in February 1986—when we finally could afford one—showed my name recognition among Democrats to be only 11 percent and confirmed that I was destined for a second-place primary finish.

What changed all that was television. The kind of campaigning one does in small towns and rural areas is not sufficient to reach many people in a growing district like the Fourth—people who may be new to the area, whose community roots do not go deep and whose political contacts are few, and most of whose political information comes through television. Fortunately, four of the district's five counties are in a single media market. But the market was the second most expensive in the state, and my campaign was struggling financially.

By April 1986 we had raised $155,000, a sum that is quite respectable for a challenger running in a contested primary, but not enough to permit an extensive television campaign. I had some fund-raising advantages. I had more contacts and more credibility in Washington circles than would have been true for most challengers, and I cultivated potential donors, calling on them personally and sending them a steady flow of information about the campaign— particularly any coverage that suggested I might win. But these efforts did not pay off with many groups until I had proved myself in the primary. I received early endorsements and contributions from a number of labor organizations that had reasons to oppose both the incumbent and my major primary opponent. An endorsement by Raleigh's major black political organization was critical organizationally, but less so financially. Other groups, like doctors and teachers, gave to my primary opponent, to whom they felt obligated because of help she had given them in the state legislature. Mainly, the organized groups and political action committees (PACs) simply stayed out of the primary. Their general rule of thumb is to support an incumbent if he or she has been reasonably receptive to their concerns. Playing the percentages, it is reasonable for PACs to expect that the incumbent will survive and that they will need to deal with that member in the future. But even those issue-oriented, Democratic-leaning PACs who had good reason to like me and to oppose the incumbent were usually unwilling to help me until I had survived the primary and could show that I had a good chance to win in November.

I have undertaken few ventures as difficult and discouraging as raising money for the primary campaign. The campaign's trademark became "low-dollar" fund-raisers to which a host or group of sponsors would invite their circle of friends and associates. These events were profitable politically as well as financially, but with net receipts per event of $500 to $2,500, the dollars added up only slowly. (I seldom had the heart to tell sponsors of such events that their labors would underwrite the purchase of *one* prime-time thirty-second television spot.) We sent mail appeals to party activists and to lists of donors from the 1984 Senate campaign and then periodically resolicited all who had given. I spent a great deal of time approaching potential large contributors, with mixed success. My wife and I shed our inhibitions and contacted our Christmas card lists from years past, our professional colleagues at home and across the country, and far-flung family members. Finally, we did what we had said we would never do; we took out a $45,000 second mortgage on our home.

With all this, the campaign was able to buy $75,000 worth of television time during the three weeks before the May primary and went some $80,000 in debt. We also spent $20,000 on radio spots—an often underestimated medium that is useful for boosting name familiarity. With limited resources and a need to make a forceful impression in a fluid primary situation, we decided to produce three low-budget television ads. One featured quotes from an endorsement by a prominent newspaper. The two that we ran most often showed me talking straight into the camera about a single theme: the need to reject the politics of distortion and personal attack in North Carolina and to campaign positively on the real issues. We knew from polling and from campaign experience that this was a powerful theme, drawing on people's negative memories of the 1984 Senate race and their reactions to the nasty Senate Republican primary then underway. But it was not until the primary results came in that we realized just how right we had been. I received 48 percent of the vote, and my main opponent, who polled 32 percent, elected not to call for a runoff.

Fund raising for the general election was a continuing struggle, but one that paid richer dividends. We spent $550,000 in the fall campaign, including $300,000 for television air time. This budget permitted a more diversified ad campaign—"soft" biographical spots in September and more forceful issue-oriented spots in October. Some of the latter dealt with the incumbent's record. I knew that I had to take him on directly to give voters sufficient grounds for distinguishing between us, but I also knew that I had to be careful not to violate my own injunction to put North Carolina politics on a more positive, issue-oriented footing. The ads focused on three areas, Social Security, African famine relief, and farm credit, that showed how far the incumbent's roll call votes were from mainstream opinion in both parties. In the ads I looked into the camera and simply said I would have voted differently.

The campaign could afford more polling after the primary. What we learned from the polls was that the incumbent was vulnerable; although he enjoyed considerable personal popularity, there was a sizable gap between the number of voters who recognized his name and those who gave him a high job performance rating or who were committed to vote for him. The early "horse race" numbers were inconclusive, measuring mainly the gap between him and me in name familiarity, but they did document a narrowing of that gap over the months of the campaign. The incumbent's lead went from twenty-one percentage points in July, to ten points on October 4, to one point on October 26. But the only poll that showed me ahead was the election itself, in which I received 56 percent of the vote, the highest percentage by which a challenger defeated an incumbent nationally in 1986.

Television was no doubt the major factor producing this result, but other campaign efforts played a part as well: organizing and personal campaigning in small towns and rural areas, voter-contact and turnout operations undertaken in conjunction with party and other organizations, canvassing and literature-drops that involved hundreds of volunteers and helped raise the campaign's visibility. My opponent was damaged when the press headlined a "Dear Christian Friend" letter he had sent to a religious-right mailing list, encouraging the faithful to support him lest he be replaced by "someone who is not willing to take a strong stand for the principles outlined in the Word of God." Although our polling could not measure precisely the impact of the letter, my guess is that it helped both by raising the visibility of the race and by framing a major issue for some groups, white-collar suburbanites, for example, that I very much needed to reach. Finally, we were helped by the year's electoral trends—the absence of presidential coattails and a return to the fold of enough Democrats to produce senatorial victories in North Carolina and across the South.

After raising $854,616 for the 1986 primary and general election campaigns and setting out to raise a like amount for my first reelection effort as soon as the 1986 debt was retired, I naturally have misgivings about how much money a serious race for Congress requires, the good people it eliminates, and the constant preoccupation with fund raising it requires. I do not, however, have an easy solution to suggest. Spending limits per se are not the answer: I *needed* to spend $850,000 to reach the voters of my district because of the dominance of political communication by television and the incumbent's many advantages. But if spending limits must be high enough to permit full, effective campaigns, there is much that might be done to relieve fund-raising pressures and to encourage a healthy diversity of funding sources. Solutions might include the provision of a "floor" of matching public funds financed by an expansion of the tax checkoff system, tax incentives for small contributors, incentives or requirements for the provision of free or reduced-rate television time, and the encouragement of an expanded role for the parties in political finance.[1]

I will also never forget how difficult it was to raise the first dollars. I understand quite well why many potentially strong challengers and potentially able representatives simply cannot or will not do what it takes to establish financial "viability" and why so many who do reach that point can do so only on the basis of personal wealth. The modus operandi of most large contributors, PACs, and even party committees often makes their calculations of an incumbent's "safety" a self-fulfilling prophecy. Only six challengers defeated incumbent House members in the general election in 1986, and only fifteen did so in 1984. These successful challengers spent an average of $517,000, and only two spent less than $300,000. Yet few challengers', campaigns can raise that amount: only fifty-two challengers spent $300,000 or more in 1984, and only forty-seven in 1986. Many of these challengers did rather well, all things considered. In 1985, twenty-nine of the fifty-two won at least 45 percent of the vote, as did twenty-three of the forty-seven challengers two years later. With more money earlier in the campaign, the balance in many of the cases might have been tipped. In several dozen other potentially promising districts, challenger races never reached a viable financing threshold, or strong candidates could not be recruited because of the daunting financial prospect.

There are many reasons for the advantages congressional incumbents enjoy, but the status quo orientation of political finance surely ranks high on the list. The parties have considerable potential to serve as a counterweight. Gary Jacobson credits the GOP with undertaking recruitment and financing efforts that enabled them to take full advantage of favorable national trends in 1980 (picking up thirty-three House seats) and to avoid disaster (losing only twenty-six seats) when the political tides turned in 1982.[2] In contrast, the Democrats did not recruit and finance the field of candidates they needed to capitalize fully on the opportunities of 1982. This pattern held in 1984; forty-one of the fifty-two challengers spending $300,000 or more were Republicans. But in 1986 the balance shifted considerably; twenty-seven of the forty-seven well-financed challengers were Democrats, which suggests that the efforts of the Democratic Congressional Campaign Committee (DCCC) to improve its performance were bearing some fruit. In any event, the obstacles challengers face are at once a major challenge to the political parties and a major reason for strengthening their role in the recruitment and support of candidates.

## Getting Started

"The orientation process has emotional ups and downs that compare fully with the campaign," I wrote in a journal I kept during the early weeks of the 100th Congress. "Most new members seem to come in with euphoria from election night still lingering, full of campaign stories. But a sense of relief and satisfaction at simply being here quickly becomes mixed with anxiety about all there is to be done and about one's own status in the unfolding order of things." Indeed, the new member comes from the electoral arena into one that is equally political and equally challenging, though not identical in the skills it requires or the behavior it rewards—the arena of House politics.

New members have several opportunities to get oriented to House operations and to the issues they will be addressing. Briefings are offered by the party organizations in conjunction with the sessions held in December, before the new Congress convenes, to elect party leaders and to adopt rules for the party caucuses. Most freshman members from both parties then adjourn to the Kennedy School of Government at Harvard University for a valuable week of lectures and discussion. Many in my class also took advantage of a supplementary orientation in Williamsburg in January offered by the Brookings Institution, the American Enterprise Institute, and the Congressional Research Service of the Library of Congress.

Most members find these sessions rewarding, not only in furnishing a common background on various issues but also in providing an introduction to the workings of Congress—far preferable to just "sinking or swimming" after the formal session begins. The orientation weeks also help establish a strong bond among the entering legislative class, an identity that stays with the cohort throughout their legislative careers. The class of 1986 was small (twenty-six Democrats, twenty-three Republicans). It primarily comprised members elected to open seats (that is, without incumbents) on the basis of factors peculiar to their districts, rather than swept in by virtue of some national trend. We were reminded often of how different our situation was from that of some classes, especially the large post-Watergate class of 1974, in which the incoming members were critically important in reforming the House—changing party and chamber rules, deposing unpopular committee chairmen, and so forth. Our relative conventionality probably said less about us than about the circumstances of our election and the political temper of the times. Still, an effective bonding took place during these early weeks, and an easy accessibility and familiarity was established among class members that would be replicated more slowly and more irregularly as we took our place among our seniors in the House.

## Electing Leaders

The 100th Congress represented a changing of the guard in House leadership, but not one attended by a great deal of conflict or controversy. Majority Leader Jim Wright of Texas was unchallenged in his race for the speakership, as was Tom Foley, D-Wash., in his move from majority whip to majority leader. The only contested leadership race found Tony Coelho, D-Calif., to whom many members felt indebted for his energetic chairmanship of the DCCC, defeating two other contenders for the post of majority whip. Coelho was beginning his fifth term; his selection, like the reelection of sixth-termer

Dick Gephardt to head the Democratic Caucus, showed how accessible the leadership ranks had become to aggressive young members. It also reflected the fact that, despite the high reelection rate for incumbents, increased rates of voluntary retirement had produced a younger, more junior House membership. A majority of the Democratic members seated in the 100th Congress had first been elected within the last decade.

Voting procedures in the Democratic Caucus for committee chairs are designed to favor incumbent chairmen. The caucus votes yes or no on this name and does not consider other names unless the sitting chairman is voted down. Only one chairman was rejected in this fashion at the beginning of the 100th Congress, although some received enough negative votes to alert them to brewing discontent. Armed Services chair Les Aspin, D-Wis., was on the short end of a 124-130 vote on January 7, 1987. The vote meant that the caucus would have to choose between Aspin and his main challenger, Marvin Leath, D-Texas, who was backed by an incongruous (and probably unstable) coalition of some of the committee's and the House's most liberal and most conservative members, united only by their dissatisfaction with Aspin's leadership. Also in the running were Nicholas Mavroules, D-Mass., and Charles Bennett, D-Fla., the Armed Services Committee's second-ranking member, who had been passed over two years earlier when Aspin had defied seniority to unseat the aging and infirm committee chairman, Melvin Price, D-Ill.

We new members encountering the Armed Services battle, I noted at the time, felt like we "had walked into a blood feud," the background of which we only partially understood. I, like most freshmen, was sought out for lengthy conversations by Aspin, Leath, Mavroules, and Bennett and was subjected to repeated pleas and pressures by their various allies. One Steering and Policy Committee member went so far as to tie his willingness to help me with my preferred committee assignments to a vote for Leath. Such heavy-handedness was exceptional, but the closeness of the race put the incoming freshmen in a critical position. I chose to keep my own counsel on the race, seeing little to be gained by declaring for one candidate or the other. In the end, Aspin narrowly retained his chairmanship; although a majority of the caucus had been willing to vote against him, that majority was not available to any one of the challengers. Moreover, some members, having delivered a reprimand to Aspin on the first vote, were willing to let it go at that.

## Staffing

I was preoccupied in these early weeks with two matters I knew would have a major impact on the rest of my term: choosing a staff and lobbying for favorable committee assignments. I had decided to ask my campaign manager to come to Washington as my administrative assistant. She and I were given a tiny cubicle to interview prospective aides and to handle calls and letters until permanent office space could be assigned. We were immediately confronted with thousands of pieces of mail that had accumulated since the election, with no possible way of responding until mid-January. Two items had arrived in such volume—requests for me to back American Airlines's application for a London "gateway" from Raleigh-Durham Airport and letters opposing the startup of a nuclear power plant in my district—that we decided to use an outside mail house to send the responses before we set up our office. Unfortunately, the mail house confused the two lists, sending several hundred power plant responses to people who had written about the airport! So we were more than ready to get our house in order when the day to move into my assigned office finally came.

I deployed my staff in a fashion that has become common in the House, setting up several district offices and locating most constituent-service functions there. The main district office in Raleigh we staffed with a district manager, two field representatives, two casework specialists, and two people who alternated between receptionist and clerical duties. We also established one-person constituent service offices in Asheboro and Chapel Hill. In Washington I hired a legislative director who combined that position with the job of administrative assistant after my original administrative assistant left to attend law school. We also had an office manager, who oversaw everything from computer operations to my personal schedule; an assistant legislative director, who helped me handle committee work; a press secretary; a computer operator; a receptionist; and three legislative assistants, who covered specific projects but mainly helped us cope with the flood of mail on pending issues.

My allowance for staff salaries was just over $400,000, which sounds like more than it is. I was well aware of the need to hire relatively senior people with Washington experience for the top positions. Then, like most members, I hired younger people, who were hoping to gain in experience and exposure what I could not pay them in dollars, for most other staff jobs. Some came to the congressional staff from the campaign staff, and most had helped with the campaign. Although I did not make it an absolute condition, every staff member, as it happened, had some past or present North Carolina connection.

## Committee Assignments

I began the committee assignment process with both a strong first preference and an awareness of how hard it would be to get it. The Energy and Commerce Committee has become one of the most sought after in the House. Its jurisdiction ranges across health, communications, energy, the environment, consumer protection, transportation, and securities and exchanges. Many of these areas are important to North Carolina and to my district in particular, but the state has no member on the committee and has not had a majority member since 1980. Energy and Commerce also interested me on a more personal level. My earliest Washington experience, as an aide during the 1960s to Senator E. L. Bartlett, D-Alaska, involved extensive work with the Senate Commerce Committee, of which he was a senior member. My academic work also had this focus, including a study of the House and Senate Commerce Committees and an examination of the House committee's oversight role.[3]

Several powerful House committees—Appropriations, Ways and Means, and Rules—are virtually off-limits to first-term members both because of the intense competition for seats and because the party and committee leadership wish to take the measure of a member before placing him or her in such a critical position. Energy and Commerce has become almost as desirable by virtue of the increasing salience of its jurisdiction and the success of its chairman, John Dingell, D-Mich., in carving out an assertive and expansive role for the committee. When I began to talk with party leaders about my committee assignments, I was advised to push—at least up to a point—for Energy and Commerce, for which my state's needs and my own credentials were unusually strong. Even if I did not make it, I could leave a strong impression for possible future reference. But I was also advised that many second- and third-term members would be putting in strong bids and that I should be prepared to indicate a back-up choice. If I held out too long, I might end up without any desirable alternative.

One of the critical House reforms of the 1970s was to take the committee-assignment function for Democrats from the Democratic members of the Ways and Means Committee, where it had resided since 1911, and to place it in the party's Steering and Policy Committee. The Steering and Policy Committee has thirty-one members, including the Speaker and other top party leaders, twelve representatives elected by the regional party caucuses, and eight at-large members appointed by the Speaker. This arrangement obviously enhances the leadership's role in committee assignments. But that control is not absolute, and on many assignments the leadership has no overriding preference. So new members like myself were well-advised to seek out all or most of the Steering and Policy members, to get acquainted, and to make as strong a case as possible for a suitable assignment. In my case that also meant stressing that I would consider the Banking Committee as a back-up choice, particularly if it were combined with an appointment to Science, Space, and Technology as my second or "minor" committee. It was becoming clear that no freshman was apt to get Energy and Commerce, as unsubstantiated but plausible rumors circulated that that was Speaker Wright's preference and that Chairman Dingell, who was also a Steering and Policy Committee member, was prepared to endorse three members, none of whom was a freshman, for the slots.

In the end, I got both the Banking and Science assignments, although by a rather circuitous route. The balloting for Banking slots was complicated by the late entry of members who had missed out on other assignments, and I failed to obtain a seat by one vote. I then was the first member chosen for the available seats on Science, no doubt as a consolation prize. But two additional Banking slots were later added as part of a interparty agreement, and I was able to obtain one of them. Some weeks later, after all assignments had been made, I was offered a temporary assignment on a second "minor" committee, Small Business, presumably because the leadership saw this committee as relevant to my district and felt that this assignment might enhance my reelection prospects. I accepted the assignment eagerly, for Small Business was a possibility to which I had been drawn from the beginning.

These three assignments—Banking, Science, and Small Business—were as strong a combination as I could have hoped for, and I have been able to make good use of each of them. The Banking Committee has presented the greatest challenge in several respects—the difficulty of its subject matter, the number of major policy questions on the agenda, and the complexity of committee politics, both internally and in relation to outside groups. To my surprise, however, it is the Banking Committee that has proven most amenable to my own legislative projects, one of which I will describe in the next section.

The Science and Small Business committees are less torn by conflicting interests than is Banking. Their history is one of promotion and advocacy for American scientific leadership and the well-being of small businesses, respectively; these missions often have attracted like-minded members to the committees and helped mute partisan conflict. On the Science Committee, however, this tradition of advocacy is running up against the painful choices necessitated by an era of budget constraint. The space station, the superconducting supercollider, healthy National Science Foundation budgets: the Science Committee historically, and often effectively, has said "We want it all." The trade-offs are indeed difficult to make, and, as the committee faces the necessity of setting priorities, it may find its bipartisan promotional consensus coming under increasing strains.

On both Science and Small Business, I concentrated at first on securing compatible subcommittee assignments, preferably under young, aggressive chairs who would pursue an expansive agenda and would welcome my participation. Such criteria are often more important than the subcommittee's precise jurisdiction, because the subject matter lines are rather ill-defined, and an aggressive chairman generally has wide latitude in exploring policy questions of interest. Thus, I was able to secure the cooperation of Chairman Doug Walgren, D-Pa., in bringing our Science, Research, and Technology Subcommittee to my district for a day of hearings on "workplace literacy," which examined the knowledge and skills that will be required in the workplace of tomorrow. Similarly, the Small Business Committee held hearings on government and military procurement in the district, asking how small businesses could participate in that process more effectively. The Antitrust Subcommittee, chaired by Dennis Eckart, D-Ohio, came to North Carolina to explore the availability and affordability of liability insurance for small businesses. My early experience has left no doubt of the compatibility of my committee assignments with my own policy interests and with the needs and concerns of my district. But that compatibility does not necessarily manifest itself automatically; considerable effort and initiative are required to ensure that the "fit" is a good one and that it results in productive activity.

## Entrepreneurship

My staff work in the Senate, undertaken when I was casting about for a doctoral dissertation topic, led me to question one piece of conventional wisdom in the political science literature of the time: "The President is now the motor in the system; the Congress applies the brakes." [4] My staff work also put me in a good position to build on the studies of congressional committees then being pioneered by Richard Fenno, Ralph Huitt, and others. [5] I wrote a dissertation, later published as *Who Makes the Laws?*, which delineated congressional and executive roles on thirteen major pieces of domestic legislation during the 89th Congress (1965-1966) and focused on the three committees handling the bills in the Senate. [6] I found the congressional role in legislation to be significant even for major administration initiatives at the height of President Johnson's Great Society program. But I also found that the congressional role varied a good deal at different stages of the legislative process and that it depended significantly on the incentives, opportunities, and resources present in various committee settings. [7]

In searching for the sources and conditions of congressional policy initiatives, I soon came to focus on the emerging phenomenon of "entrepreneurship" among senators and their aides. The 1960s were a time when public opinion seemed to underwrite an expansive government role, when the Senate "folkways" that had discouraged and inhibited legislative activity down through the ranks were beginning to erode, and when a new breed of activist senators exemplified by Hubert Humphrey, Joseph Clark, Philip Hart, Edmund Muskie, and Jacob Javits were beginning to make their mark. I particularly emphasized the importance of entrepreneurship within congressional staffs—a continual search for policy "gaps" and opportunities, a job orientation that stressed the generation and promotion of policy initiatives, designed to heighten the public visibility of the senator and his or her leadership role within the chamber. Senate committees like Commerce and Labor and Public Welfare (later renamed Labor and Human Resources) became hotbeds of legislative innovation, and the development of an entrepreneurial orientation on the part of members and aides was a critical element in the productivity of these committees in the 1960s and beyond.[8]

Policy entrepreneurship was slower to emerge in the House, where the size of the body placed greater restrictions on the independence and impact of most members and where members' electoral fortunes depended more on district services and relations and less on media exposure than was true for most senators. But House members also faced a changing political environment, one that increasingly left them "on their own" electorally. An important element in this change was the decline of political parties—members faced voters less inclined to support them on partisan grounds alone, and party organizations were becoming less effective in communicating with and mobilizing the electorate. Party decline, together with the rise of television as the dominant news and campaign medium, gave members incentives to seek a higher public profile. For many representatives, especially those from districts where public awareness of and concern for national policy questions were high, policy entrepreneurship was a promising means to that end. The desire for a more prominent policy role was, therefore, a powerful motivation behind the House reforms of the 1970s—reforms that, for the most part, parceled out authority and resources to subcommittees and individual members. These changes, in turn, encouraged policy initiatives down through the congressional ranks—although the fragmentation of power, ironically, also made it more difficult for the House to handle conflict and to bring many legislative initiatives to fruition.

The 1980s have seen some waning of entrepreneurial activity. The 97th Congress, during the first two years of the Reagan administration, saw the number of public laws enacted drop to 473, the lowest since World War II. The volume of committee hearings tapered off somewhat after the peak years of the 1970s and reached a postwar low in 1986.[9] A number of factors have contributed to this decline: shifts in the political climate that seemed to reduce public support for legislative activism, the advent of an administration hostile to much policy innovation, and, most important, the constraints imposed by the budget crisis on any new departures in policy, especially those that cost money. Still, authority and resources are distributed in both houses of the U.S. Congress in ways that give large numbers of members opportunities for legislative entrepreneurship, and many members still find it advantageous, as they consider both their electoral prospects and their standing within the legislature, to carve out a policy-making niche for themselves.

I thus came to the House with some entrepreneurial experience (I had handled the Radiation Protection Act of 1967 for Senator Bartlett, who was its chief Senate sponsor), some awareness of the conditions of successful activism, and strong personal and political motivations to develop such a role for myself. At the same time, as a new member, I realized that on most major bills I would need to follow the lead of like-minded senior members. As for my own legislative ventures, I felt that they should be limited in number and chosen with care. Some of the bills I introduced were prompted by district needs or campaign pledges. One such proposal was to repeal the Nuclear Waste Policy Act's requirement for a second (and probably eastern) repository for high-level waste; another was a bill to restore tax deductibility for interest on student loans. But the project that best fit the traditional entrepreneurial pattern was a bill I managed to steer through the Banking Committee and on to final passage, the Home Equity Loan Consumer Protection Act of 1988.

Home equity loans were a hot new financial product in 1987. The Tax Reform Act of 1986 had phased out income tax deductibility for interest on most consumer loans and credit card accounts, but had left deductibility in place for loans secured by one's home. Thus, home equity loans, second mortgages that ordinarily had a variable interest rate and an open line of credit up to a substantial portion of the value of the house, were vigorously marketed, and many consumers (including me) found them attractive and advantageous. This aggressive marketing and the possibility that, with a rise in interest rates, borrowers might find themselves in "over their heads," with their homes at risk, made certain basic consumer protections desirable. Yet these loans were subject to little advertising regulation, and under the Truth-in-Lending Act they were treated as an open-end product, like a credit card, rather than as a closed-end product, like an adjustable-rate or fixed-rate mortgage. Consumers could be given considerably less information than would be required in the case of other loans secured against their homes, and even this information might be provided only after they had paid nonrefundable fees or closing costs. It seemed obvious that home equity loans should be subject to disclosure requirements at least as stringent as those that applied to other mortgages.

Having discovered a promising policy "gap" and feeling anxious lest other members might be getting similar ideas, I hurried to draft a bill and to circulate a "Dear Colleague" letter inviting other members to join me as cosponsors. My staff and I solicited suggestions from several consumer and banking groups and, most important, from the staff of the Federal Reserve Board, which was already working on new regulations for the timing and content of disclosures for adjustable-rate mortgages. One critical early decision was to make this primarily a disclosure bill, which, while it went beyond what most industry associations preferred, still fell short of the "wish lists" of the consumer groups. I made this decision on the merits; I did not want to place regulations on home equity loans that went far beyond what was required of comparable products or to see these loans increased in price or made less available. But I also wanted the bill to attract a broad base of political support. An alternate approach would have been to introduce a much stronger bill with the idea of compromising later if necessary. In fact, Charles Schumer, D-N.Y., later introduced such a home equity loan bill, to the applause of the consumer groups. But I chose to draft a bill that I thought could pass and that came close to what I thought Congress finally should produce. This approach paid off: no potential opponents got *too* upset, and the bill attracted a bipartisan group of twenty-three original cosponsors, including the chairman and ranking Republican member of the House Banking Committee.

Frank Annunzio, D-Ill., chairman of the Banking Committee's Subcommittee on Consumer Affairs and Coinage, scheduled hearings on the bill for October 6, 1987, and his top subcommittee aide, Curt Prins, worked with my banking aide, Paul Feldman, to get a consensus bill reported. These negotiations were not easy. Annunzio had a well-deserved reputation as a consumer champion, and Prins had no desire to see him attacked by the consumer groups, which had begun rather noisily to object to my initial draft. At the same time it was clear that the industry groups, which, like the consumer groups, had formed an informal coalition for purposes of negotiation and lobbying, would resist adding substantive restrictions on home equity loans to the disclosure and advertising regulations contained in my bill. It was not difficult to imagine the lenders deciding to oppose the bill; their success in defeating interest rate caps on a related credit card bill suggested that they might be able to do the same if the home equity bill were amended to contain such restrictions. Moreover, they could assume that if Congress was unable to act, the Federal Reserve Board would promulgate regulations they could live with. Therefore, I was eager to keep both groups at the table because I knew that the disaffection of either would break up the coalition of members who had joined in sponsoring the bill and would make its passage far less likely.

At the House subcommittee hearings I identified several areas where I thought the bill could be strengthened and substantive restrictions ought to be considered: limiting the ability of a lender arbitrarily to manipulate the interest rate, for example, and tightly restricting the lender's right to call in a loan or to change its terms. Fortunately, the consumer groups also chose to focus on such potential areas of abuse rather than to push hard for the kind of broad limits on the terms of home equity loans contained in the Schumer bill. But it was on these questions that our negotiations became most contentious and came close to breaking down. We got a revised bill reported out of subcommittee only by promising all concerned that they would get another crack at it before full committee markup.

In the meantime, the Senate Banking Committee took up the home equity issue, using my bill and Schumer's as the basis for a day of hearings November 18, 1987. The committee leadership later decided to append a home equity loan disclosure provision to their bank powers bill, Senate Banking's most ambitious legislative project in the 100th Congress, which passed on March 30, 1988. Home equity legislation had not originated in the Senate, and the home equity title that the Senate approved was a hastily drawn proposal. Yet this temporary shift to the Senate of the negotiations among industry and consumer groups served us well on the House side, for the prospect of immediate floor action forced everyone to reveal their "bottom line" in short order, and we were able to use the Senate language to resolve several difficult issues that were slowing our progress toward full committee markup in the House.

The House Banking Committee approved the Home Equity Loan Consumer Protection Act by a unanimous vote on May 19, and the House passed the bill by voice vote on June 20. Although I had been happy to see the bill pass the Senate expeditiously as part of the bank powers legislation, I wanted to pass it as a separate bill in the House, where the prognosis for the bank powers bill was far less hopeful and home equity's prospects could be harmed if it became entwined in the conflicts surrounding the broader measure. This strategy preserved both options—taking home equity to conference as part of the larger bill or passing it as a free-standing measure if the bank powers bill failed.

This strategy proved to be a wise one, for the bank powers bill ran into major obstacles in the House. But Senator William Proxmire, D-Wis., and Senator Jake Garn of Utah—chairman and ranking Republican, respectively, of the Banking Committee and the chief sponsors of the legislation—were reluctant to pass home equity separately because they believed it enhanced the broader bill and increased their leverage to get it approved. It was only after the prospects for bank powers were seen as completely hopeless that separate passage of home equity could even be discussed. By then, time was so short that the only feasible approach was for the Senate to pass the House's free-standing home equity bill and send it directly to the president, thus making further House action or a House-Senate conference on the bill unnecessary.

I spent many hours during the closing days of the session working with allies that included several House members and aides as well as industry and consumer lobbyists, trying to secure Senate passage. The task was complicated by the fact that the Senate was conducting its business in the waning hours essentially by unanimous consent. Any one member, therefore, could block approval, and several placed "holds" on the home equity bill, hoping to use it as a vehicle or a bargaining chip for proposals of their own. The Senate committee staff worked all day on October 21 to accommodate as many of these members as possible and finally, at 2:00 a.m., got home equity to the floor as part of a package of three bills. With one hour remaining before final adjournment of the 100th Congress, the Home Equity Loan Consumer Protection Act passed the Senate by voice vote and was on its way to the White House.

The home equity case suggests several conditions facilitating and shaping policy entrepreneurship in the House. First, the committee environment was relatively favorable. The full committee and subcommittee chairmen both wanted the committee to be active and productive in consumer protection, and they adopted a permissive, accommodating leadership style with respect to member initiatives in this area. These committee leaders handled certain other areas of their jurisdiction quite differently, encouraging initiatives and sharing power much less readily. But in the consumer protection area, leadership style and the effective decentralization of the committee fostered entrepreneurship and gave it a fair chance of success. The committee's mode of partisanship also had a positive effect. While House Banking Committee members often experienced serious conflict, these divisions shifted from issue to issue and often cut across party lines. There was a tradition of cross-party collaboration on discrete measures upon which I could draw in introducing and refining the home equity bill.

Second, the political conditions surrounding the home equity issue were also favorable.[10] The bill spoke to a problem of growing public salience, one that promised some recognition and reward to legislators who addressed it. In addition, the issue was not saddled with the kind of debilitating conflict that would have discouraged legislative involvement. Members could see it as a consumer protection measure with considerable potential public appeal, but at the same time they could be relatively certain that support of the bill would not draw them into serious conflicts with outside groups or with their colleagues.

The relevant "interested outsiders"[11] had good reasons for adopting a constructive, cooperative posture, although it was by no means always certain that they would do so. The Federal Reserve Board, having acknowledged the need for home equity loan regulation and having begun its own rule making, needed to ensure congruence between its action and Congress's. Industry groups recognized that the price of noncooperation might be a more punitive and less workable bill; this realization led to a rather grudging decision by the American Bankers Association not to oppose the bill actively and to much more positive collaboration by other industry groups. Some of the consumer lobbyists were inclined to push for "their bill or none," to test the limits of the developing consensus. But others, most notably the American Association of Retired Persons (AARP), needed to deliver a bill to their constituents, and committee allies of the consumer groups like Annunzio and Schumer let them know that they would not back an absolutist stance.

Although these conditions facilitated a successful initiative, they by no means guaranteed it. Successful entrepreneurship requires members and their aides to *push,* to push continually and to push hard. And one must *shape* such an initiative to make the most of favorable conditions. In the home equity case, this approach meant taking full account of the Federal Reserve's preferences as the bill was drafted and refined. It meant consulting with and deferring to the committee leadership. It meant drafting the bill to attract bipartisan support, seeking that support, and insisting that all the major players be brought along at each successive stage. It meant working hard to keep the intergroup negotiations on track.

Policy entrepreneurship is irreducibly personal. It does not lend itself to easy predictions or hard-and-fast explanations. We can identify the conditions that encourage or facilitate entrepreneurial ventures, but the shape and the success of such initiatives still depend on the motivation, style, and skill of members and their aides—the kind of job they wish to do and the strategies they adopt in pursuing their goals.

## The Budget Crisis

I am sometimes asked what alarmed me most during my first term in the House and what has changed most since I first worked in Congress and began studying it twenty-five years ago. The answer to both questions is the same: the continuing and deepening fiscal crisis in our national government. The crisis is not just one of economic profligacy and mismanagement, but also of political irresponsibility and intragovernmental gridlock.

Congressional operations have been decisively altered by the budget process instituted by the Budget and Impoundment Control Act of 1974. The act was a response to President Richard Nixon's frequent impoundments of appropriated funds and his accusations that Congress was fiscally irresponsible, but it also reflected long-term congressional concern about failures of budgetary coordination and control. New House and Senate budget committees were authorized to bring to the floor early in each congressional session a resolution setting overall limits, binding other committees as they passed individual authorization, appropriations, and tax bills. The budget committees have continued to operate in a context of fragmented power; they lack specific spending and taxing authority, and the House especially has limited its Budget Committee's independence and continuity of membership. The targets and limits set by the budget resolutions have sometimes provoked defiance by one committee or another. Still, "for every confrontation there have been dozens of legislative decisions routinely made with fidelity to the budget process." [12]

During the first year of Ronald Reagan's presidency, the concentration of budgetary power reached new heights, albeit under conditions that enhanced presidential rather than congressional control and with results that mocked the ideal of fiscal responsibility. In 1980 Congress had experimented with early implementation of the budget act's "reconciliation" procedure, originally designed to bring congressional spending decisions into line with the final, end-of-session version of the budget resolution. This procedure was brought to the beginning of the congressional budget cycle in 1981 under a plan promoted by David Stockman, Reagan's budget director. The first budget resolution that year included a set of authoritative instructions to Congress that increased the constraints the budget process placed not only on appropriations but also on the authorizing committees and on entitlement programs.

The Reagan administration exploited the reconciliation process—and political momentum from the 1980 elections—to push through a series of omnibus bills that reduced revenues over the next five years by some $750 billion, reduced domestic spending by some $100 billion over three years, and paved the way for substantial increases in defense spending. The numbers, obviously, added up to massive annual deficits and eventually to a tripling of the national debt. As a repentant Stockman observed after the president's successful 1984 reelection campaign, "The White House proclaimed a roaring economic success ... when, in fact, [its policies] had produced fiscal excesses that had never before been imagined." [13]

That feat was not matched by the administration in subsequent years. Shifts in the political climate induced by the recession of 1982-1983 soon weakened the president's hand, and Congress found his budget proposals less and less palatable. But consensus within Congress was difficult to achieve as well; the budget committees in the Republican Senate and Democratic House often produced widely disparate budget resolutions, and both committees were challenged by restive appropriations and legislative committees. Just how much the process had deteriorated—and how difficult it was going to be to secure the cooperation between the parties and between the branches of government necessary to make the machinery work well—became clear soon after the 100th Congress began.

The president's proposed fiscal 1988 budget, which he acknowledged would be $108 billion in deficit (and other analysts expected to produce as much as a $135 billion shortfall), was not accepted even by members of his own party: it received only twenty-seven votes on the House floor and eleven votes in the Senate. "This is the only democracy in the world," quipped Majority Leader Foley, "where the members of the executive's own party will consider it a dirty trick if you ask them to vote on his budget." Most Republican House members in fact chose to vote for no budget resolution whatsoever. Minority Budget Committee members withheld cooperation as the committee formulated its budget resolution, and when that resolution passed the House on April 9, 1987, it was with Democratic votes alone. Many seemed to take to heart the counsel of GOP whip Trent Lott, R-Miss.: "You do not ever get into trouble for those budgets which you vote against." To which Foley retorted, " 'Don't vote and you won't get into trouble.' What a motto for statesmanship." [14]

During most of this century, the budget process has been presidentially driven and has relied for passage on executive-congressional cooperation. For all of its jealous guardianship of the power of the purse, the House has depended on the executive to propose a viable budget and has generally altered that document only marginally. The process, instituted in the 1920s, assumed that Congress was ill-suited to undertake budgeting on its own and that executive leadership was required. The budget reforms of the 1970s did not alter that fundamental reality, although they left Congress somewhat better equipped to develop its own budget in the event of serious intergovernmental conflict or executive default. That is basically the test that the 100th Congress faced, and it is not surprising that the results fell short of the ideal.

The Democratic budget resolution anticipated a deficit of about $1 billion less than the president's budget did; it directed House committees to match $18 billion in new revenues with $18 billion in reductions from projected spending, equally divided between military and nonmilitary accounts. While subsequent House action remained largely within these guidelines, there were some departures from the budget committee's formula—partly because of the necessity of compromise with the Senate, whose budget resolution was less stringent because it anticipated revenue from the sale of government assets; partly because of the ambiguity of the "section 302" process (named for the relevant portion of the Budget Act) that assigned spending ceilings to individual appropriations subcommittees and the desires of the subcommittees to stretch these limits; partly because the Ways and Means Committee came up with not only the requisite revenue measures but also an ambitious scheme for welfare reform.

I thus had a difficult decision to make when confronted with the postappropriations reconciliation bill on October 29. Democratic leaders, in touting the earlier budget resolution, had pledged that any revenue increases would be at least matched by spending cuts and that all revenue increases would be earmarked for deficit reduction. But neither of these criteria was met by the reconciliation bill and the accompanying spending measures. I therefore did something I was reluctant to do, voting against the leadership on an important budget measure. I have never doubted that my vote was correct—both in maintaining my own credibility and consistency and in holding the party to its own professions—but it was nonetheless a tough one, made more so by the narrow margin of its 206-205 passage.

In the meantime, the budget landscape had shifted in ways that created intensified pressure on Congress and the president to reach a settlement. Although the House had passed most of its appropriations bills on time, it became clear over the spring and summer that the closely divided Senate was going to have difficulty acting on them and that, in any event, the president was likely to veto anything that was sent him. As the prospect of deadlock loomed, a number of members, some of whom had opposed the original Gramm-Rudman-Hollings law of 1985, came to see in the reinstatement of this measure, minus the constitutionally questionable provisions that had led to its rejection by the courts, a way to force all parties to the table and to guarantee that significant deficit reduction would take place.

The basic concept of G-R-H was to impose increasingly stringent deficit-reduction targets on the budget process over five years, so that at the end of the period the budget would be in balance. If the target were not met in a given year, uniform percentage cuts would be imposed across all accounts, except Social Security and some other mandatory programs, to bring the budget into line. Presumably, the threat of such an indiscriminate "sequestration" would give all parties the incentive to reach a settlement. The administration, which had paid lip-service to Gramm-Rudman-Hollings originally, was notably unenthusiastic about its revival, perceiving that it might force President Reagan to modify his rigid stances on new revenues and/or defense spending, which were making substantial deficit reduction impossible. Proponents therefore chose for the proposal the one legislative vehicle they knew the administration had to request: an increase in the debt ceiling. After protracted negotiations, during which the administration was able to get the deficit reduction target for 1988 reduced to $23 billion from the $37 billion contained in the congressional budget resolution, the debt ceiling increase with Gramm-Rudman attached was cleared in September 1987.

It was not apparent, however, that even the threat of sequestration would bring the administration to the table. Congressional leaders speculated that the president might be willing to see the indiscriminate cuts occur, assuming that Congress would receive the blame for the ensuing damage. What changed all that was the stock market crash of October 19, which made the adverse impact of the budget crisis on the national interest plain for all to see and created political perils for anyone who appeared to be stalling the process.

By this time the fiscal year had ended, and Congress was forced to resort to a series of continuing resolutions to keep the government running. Negotiations between congressional and administration leaders dragged on. It was in this context that the reconciliation vote of October 29 occurred, but, because of the closeness of that vote, it largely failed in its intended purpose, which was to strengthen the House leadership's hand in negotiations. The negotiators finally reached agreement on a package that included domestic spending cuts of about $8 billion for 1988, defense cuts of some $5 billion, and $5 billion in federal asset sales. Additional revenues would total $9 billion in 1988, produced through tightening some loopholes and continuing some taxes that were to expire, but including neither excise tax increases nor any general increases in personal or corporate income taxes. This package produced $30 billion in deficit reduction for 1988, and its second-year provisions were to net a reduction of $46 billion for 1989. These figures were well within the Gramm-Rudman targets, although considerably short of what many had hoped for as the negotiations began. The fiscal 1988 agreement was packaged in two omnibus bills—a full year continuing resolution and a reconciliation bill—which cleared the House and Senate in the early morning hours of December 22.

This agreement resulted in reduced budget conflict during the second session of the 100th Congress, with both House and Senate producing their fiscal 1989 appropriations bills on schedule. The lull, however, was deceptive. The budget crisis has not gone away, and the Gramm-Rudman-Hollings targets for 1990 and succeeding years are going to be far more difficult to meet than those for 1988 and 1989. Yet the demands for spending are nearly limitless: to maintain an adequate defense posture, to support investments in education, infrastructure, and research, to sustain a "safety net" for the elderly and infirm, to fund major projects in science and space, and to ensure adequate and affordable health care and housing for all Americans.

In this fiscal environment, the new president and the new Congress need to develop a good working relationship and a common understanding, not about every budget detail, but about the responsible exercise of each branch's statutory and constitutional responsibilities for budgeting. The president should submit a fiscally sound and politically realistic budget. Congress should revise and refine this document in line with its own priorities, but it should neither expect to construct a new fiscal blueprint nor be expected to construct one. On both sides the primary need is not for new machinery, although proposals for new gimmicks like the line-item veto abound, but for the political resolve to make the existing machinery work as it was intended. It may be that a grand compromise of the sort that resolved the Social Security crisis in 1983 is an appropriate model for the new president and the 101st Congress. Heightened levels of bipartisan cooperation and public understanding will be required to make it succeed.

Nothing should be higher on the presidential and congressional agendas than getting our budgetary house in order. Beyond its critical impact on the country's economy and its role in the international marketplace, the budget crisis has compromised and constrained the workings of Congress itself—preempting the kinds of innovations and investments that need to be made, devaluing the work of the standing committees, and shifting policy debate away from substance and into primarily fiscal terms. If the political will—and goodwill—can be mustered to make the budget process work, then what Allen Schick has termed the "fiscalization" [15] of congressional policy making may turn out to be a product of the 1980s and not a permanent institutional state.

## Serving the District

My concentration in this essay on congressional politics and policy could be somewhat misleading if taken as an indication of the balance most members strike between the Washington and home district aspects of their job. Like many others, I keep my main residence in the district and return there every weekend. The House typically works on a Tuesday-Thursday schedule, so most weeks I am at home more than in Washington, working in and around the three district offices where half of my staff is based. Much of what we do in Washington is district-centered as well—most of my work on appropriations, for example, and the work of my legislative assistants, most of whose time is spent dealing with the policy concerns of local groups and correspondents.

### Appropriations, Grants, and 'Casework'

Richard Fenno, studying the Appropriations Committee in the 1960s, identified its first "strategic premise" as "to reduce executive budget requests." [16] The House's need for a more effective mechanism for achieving fiscal control was one reason for instituting the new budget process and establishing the Congressional Budget Office and the budget committees in 1974. The Appropriations Committee, therefore, has been largely displaced in its role of fiscal control, and its first strategic premise no longer seems dominant. But the committee's second strategic premise, "to provide adequate funding for executive programs," [17] is as viable as ever. This second premise was potentially at odds with the first and reflected the ambivalence of House members about how they wanted this powerful committee to perform.

Today, the second premise frequently puts the Appropriations Committee at odds with the Budget Committee, as we have already seen. But Appropriations still controls the purse strings, determining the amounts to be spent for specific agencies and programs, and Appropriations seats are still anxiously sought after. And members like me, who are attempting to ensure that, within overall budget allocations, worthwhile projects receive the support they need, have many occasions to approach our Appropriations colleagues and ask for their assistance.

The thirteen Appropriations subcommittees enjoy a great deal of autonomy, so the critical contact is the relevant subcommittee chairman. My approach has been to talk to the chairman, to follow up with a letter making the case more systematically, and to make certain that the contacts are replicated at the staff level. It is also important to let the full committee chairman and his staff know of the request, to secure the assistance of any Appropriations Committee member from one's state delegation (in my case, Bill Hefner, D-N.C.), and to enlist the help of any other Appropriations members who might have special knowledge of or interest in the case. In this fashion, I took several Fourth District projects to the Appropriations Committee and was able in most instances to secure favorable action: $5 million for the permanent installation of an experimental radar system to increase the capacity of Raleigh-Durham Airport; a $1.2 million planning grant to prepare for construction of a laboratory on the University of North Carolina campus that will be leased by the Environmental Protection Agency; committee report language directing that priority be given to construction of new National Institute of Environmental Health Sciences facilities in the Research Triangle Park; and a $550,000 federal share for the restoration of a historic building on a predominantly black college campus. These are all worthwhile projects, but few of them would have been funded had not I and those working with me made the effort to place and keep them on the agenda.

It is more difficult to pinpoint responsibility for another group of projects—those that are funded at the discretion of an executive agency—but that does not prevent members from claiming credit when such awards come through! I have had to make many decisions about where my intervention with an executive agency would be appropriate and helpful. Sometimes I have become involved with the applications of local governments and organizations, such as requests for funds to construct rental housing for the elderly or applications for Federal Aviation Agency assistance for general aviation airport construction or expansion. Sometimes I have intervened when trouble developed in what should have been a routine review and award process, for instance, when a local university's grant from the National Science Foundation got held up in an interagency dispute. Such applications from local groups, institutions, and governments are far more numerous than requests for direct appropriations, and the procedures for handling them, located in the executive branch of government, are far more routinized. But a member of Congress does well to follow them closely, and can sometimes intervene with good effect.

The staff members in my three district offices spend most of their time on what is called casework—assisting individuals, and sometimes companies or organizations, in their dealings with the federal government. The most common areas of concern are Social Security, Medicare, veterans' benefits, tax problems, immigration and naturalization, and passports. Some of these services are routine, as when we expedite the issuance of passports, while others involve convoluted disputes over benefits or entitlements that have been years in the making. Often, upon determining that we can and should do nothing to change a situation, we try to ensure that a case is given fair consideration and that the person understands the reasons for the decision. Sometimes, however, our intervention brings about the correction of an agency error or the rectification of an injustice.

In one such case, the wife of a serviceman had spent six months trying to get a claim processed for their daughter under CHAMPUS, the armed forces health care program for dependents. My office contacted the agency office holding up the claim, and within two months, my constituents received payment on the claim amounting to $1,659. Another woman, the wife of a veteran, had applied numerous times for Veterans Administration (VA) survivor benefits for her daughter, but because of various bureaucratic snafus the claim had never been processed. Four days after my staff contacted the VA regional office, the benefits were started and retroactive payments totaling $2,632 were sent. A third case involved a small business with considerable experience in doing specialized electronics work for the military. The company was unable to bid on a particular job because military procurement officials had decided not to open the project to competitive bidding. My inquiries revealed that the military had no defensible reason for this decision; the bidding process was opened, and the local business was able to pursue the contract.

Congressional offices thus operate a kind of appeals process for bureaucratic decisions, a function that sometimes has been likened to that of the ombudsman in Scandinavian countries. It is not an ideal mechanism, and constituents vary considerably in their ability and inclination to use it. But House members have a strong incentive not only to deal with those constituents who present themselves but also to advertise the availability of their services and then to handle the cases in ways that will inspire favorable comment. A reputation for good constituent service is an important political asset, but helping people in these ways, where the results are often more tangible than in legislative work, is also inherently satisfying. A member daily confronts the fact that he or she is only 1 of 435 attempting to shape national policy in Washington. But constituent requests and needs are a healthy reminder that that member is the *only* 1 of the 435 with the responsibility for assisting individuals and organizations in his or her particular district in their dealings with the federal government. It is a responsibility that should be taken seriously.

### Covering the District

Much of my time at home is spent traveling the district and maintaining an extensive schedule of public appearances. During my first twenty months in office I addressed twenty-one civic clubs or Chamber of Commerce meetings, spoke to twenty-three school classes or assemblies and at three commencements, held fifty "community meetings" across the five counties, visited some twenty-one churches and synagogues, sometimes delivering the Sunday sermon, and toured twenty-seven district plants and research facilities. Most of these were "congressional" rather than campaign functions. Members of Congress develop a good sense of what is and is not appropriate on such occasions, most of which they approach not as partisans but as representatives of all their constituents. Still, these events are a valuable opportunity for outreach, a chance to become known and to establish relationships beyond one's present circle of friends and supporters. Richard Fenno has found members' "careers" in relating to their constituencies typically proceed from "expansionist" to "protectionist" stages.[18] I doubt that either my own temperament or the nature of my district—fast growing, politically volatile—will ever permit me to move completely beyond the expansionist stage. In any event, that is where I am now, and a heavy schedule of public appearances has been invaluable in widening my circle of engaged constituents.

The community meetings have been especially important. After some initial experimentation, we settled on a format that seems to work well: franked postcards announcing the session are sent to every boxholder in a given area, and then I hold an open meeting on the date announced, giving a brief report on congressional activities and taking any and all questions from the floor. In rural areas we may schedule several such meetings in a single day, stopping at one country store or community building after the other. The meetings in the larger towns and at the county courthouses last longer, are scheduled for the evening hours, and usually draw 75 to 125 people. Most of my presentation is about policy matters, but I always have staff members along to assist constituents with individual problems. These meetings find a receptive audience in my district—with its high levels of education and issue-awareness and its large numbers of retirees and persons involved in government, teaching, and research—and they have proved an invaluable means of outreach during my first term.

I also communicate with the district through regular newsletters, which go to every boxholder, and more specialized mailings, which go to people I know are interested in particular issues. In addition, I try to maintain effective contact with the news media in the district. The media, especially television, are often attracted to campaign fireworks, but it takes considerably more effort to interest them in Congress's day-to-day work. We send weekly radio feeds and, less frequently, satellite television feeds to stations in the district, offering news and commentary. A quite different strategy is required to meet the needs of smaller radio stations and weekly newspapers, who usually cover a member only when he or she visits the community or announces something that pertains to that locality.

All this adds up to a constant attentiveness to the district, in proposing legislation and securing appropriations, in interpreting and explaining what Congress is doing and how I have represented the district, in deploying staff and budgeting my own time and attention. This focus on the district may be particularly intense for a first-term member from a contested district, but it is built into every member's job description. Life in Congress is by definition a divided existence—living in Washington and in the district, serving at once as a national legislator and a local representative. These multiple roles create strains and tensions with which members must learn to deal. But the mix can also be enormously challenging and stimulating. At least that is the way I feel about it. I know of no other job like the one I have, and I feel extraordinarily fortunate to be where I am.

## Notes

1. For a more complete discussion of possible campaign finance reforms, with a particular concern for strengthening political parties, see David E. Price, *Bringing Back the Parties* (Washington, D.C.: CQ Press, 1984), 254-260.
2. See Gary Jacobson, "Running Scared: Elections and Congressional Politics in the 1980s," in *Congress: Structure and Policy,* ed. Matthew McCubbins and Terry Sullivan (New York: Cambridge University Press, 1987), especially 61-65.
3. David E. Price et al., *The Commerce Committees* (New York: Grossman Publishers, 1975); and Price, "The Impact of Reform: The House Commerce Subcommittee on Oversight and Investigations," in *Legislative Reform,* ed. Leroy N. Rieselbach (Lexington, Mass.: Lexington Books, 1978).
4. Robert A. Dahl, *Pluralist Democracy in the United States: Conflict and Consent* (Chicago: Rand McNally, 1967), 136. Dahl qualified this view considerably in later editions. See, for example, *Democracy in the United States: Promise and Performance,* 4th ed. (Boston: Houghton Mifflin, 1981), 135-138.
5. See especially Richard Fenno, *The Power of the Purse: Appropriations Politics in Congress* (Boston: Little, Brown, 1966); and the essays collected in *Congress: Two Decades of Analysis,* ed. Ralph Huitt and Robert L. Peabody (New York: Harper & Row, 1969).
6. David E. Price, *Who Makes the Laws?* (Cambridge, Mass.: Schenkman, 1972).

7. For a summary and update of these findings, see David E. Price, "Congressional Committees in the Policy Process" in *Congress Reconsidered,* 3d ed., ed. Lawrence C. Dodd and Bruce I. Oppenheimer (Washington, D.C.: CQ Press, 1985), chap. 7.

8. See David E. Price, "Professionals and 'Entrepreneurs': Staff Orientations and Policy Making on Three Senate Committees," *Journal of Politics* 31 (May 1971): 316-336.

9. Roger H. Davidson and Carol Hardy, "Indicators of House of Representatives Workload and Activity," Congressional Research Service Report 87-4925, June 8, 1987, 13, 32, 63; and Ilona B. Nickels, "The Legislative Workload of the Congress: Numbers are Misleading," *CRS Review,* July/August 1988, 23-24. These articles also point up a number of difficulties in using such data as a precise indicator of the fall off in legislative initiative. Data on numbers of bills introduced are especially problematic because of changes in the rules of cosponsorship in the House.

10. On the incentives to policy entrepreneurship provided by "environmental factors," especially perceived levels of public salience and conflict, see David E. Price, *Policymaking in Congressional Committees: The Impact of "Environmental" Factors* (Tucson: University of Arizona Press, 1979).

11. See Richard Fenno, *Congressmen in Committees* (Boston: Little, Brown, 1973), 15 and passim.

12. Allen Schick, *Congress and Money* (Washington, D.C.: Urban Institute, 1980), 361.

13. David A. Stockman, *The Triumph of Politics* (New York: Avon Books, 1987), 409.

14. *Congressional Quarterly Weekly Report,* April 11, 1987, 659.

15. See Allen Schick, *Reconciliation and the Congressional Budget Process* (Washington, D.C.: American Enterprise Institute, 1981), 35.

16. Fenno, *Congressmen in Committees,* 48.

17. Ibid., 49.

18. Richard Fenno, *Home Style: House Members in Their Districts* (Boston: Little, Brown, 1978), 172.

# 18. THE NEW CONGRESS: FLUIDITY AND OSCILLATION

## Lawrence C. Dodd and Bruce I. Oppenheimer

One benefit we have derived from preparing four editions of *Congress Reconsidered* is an increased sensitivity to institutional change. Today's House and Senate are different in meaningful ways not only when compared to the institutions of the early twentieth century, but also since the first edition of this book in 1977. These changes have been documented across the four editions.

Change is most apparent in the House. The first edition described the extensive reforms that took place in the House in the early and mid-1970s. These reforms weakened the historic power of committees and committee chairs, thereby undercutting committee government that had ruled since the 1920s. In its place the new rules instituted bifurcated government, with some power decentralized in a strengthened subcommittee system and some power centralized in the party leadership and a new budget process. By the second and third editions of *Congress Reconsidered*—in 1981 and 1985—the various contributors were reporting the rise of subcommittee government, the weakening of party leaders, and problems in the budget process. In the present edition we witness a reversal in these patterns, noting the emergence of a new House oligarchy in which the party leaders and a few money committees dominate House decision making, with subcommittee power on the wane.

In truth, we did not foresee the fluidity of the modern House, particularly the possibility of a new House oligarchy, nor do we know of anyone who did. In 1977 the signs pointed to the spread of power among a diverse range of actors, particularly the subcommittee chairs. If anyone was likely to suffer a further diminution in power, it was the party leaders and budget committee.

The failure to anticipate the current swing to greater centralization, a stronger speakership, and more cohesive parties in the House of Representatives presents us with several questions. First, why was the potential for centralization so badly underestimated by numerous scholars and observers in Congress? Second, is there something about the Senate that makes it immune to such major fluctuations, or does the potential for major change exist there as well? And third, what are the consequent implications for how we understand Congress today and how we assess its future performance?

## Why Did We Err?

The failure to foresee the potential for greater centralization occurred, we suspect, for three primary reasons. First, changes were taking place in congressional elections, which profoundly affected the cohesiveness of congressional parties and did so in ways not fully apparent in the mid-1970s. In part, the greater cohesiveness resulted from the Federal Elections Campaign Act, which expanded the role of congressional party organizations in financing House and Senate candidates, perhaps making the candidates more beholden to the party leaders. In addition, the legislation resulted in more active involvement by the national parties in the recruitment, training, and molding of House and Senate candidates. While they continued to appeal to diverse constituencies, they did so with similar messages prepared by the national parties, which promoted policy cohesion. But more important was the Voting Rights Act of 1965.

By ensuring that blacks in the South could register and vote, the Voting Rights Act altered the nature of southern representation in Congress. To win Democratic House and Senate primaries in the South, most candidates needed to attract the support of black voters. Thus, as conservative southern Democrats retired from Congress, their replacements began to look less like regional Democrats and more like national Democrats. Once in office, these new members frequently voted more like their northern Democratic colleagues than their southern predecessors. In some southern constituencies, Republicans appealed to disaffected conservative Democrats and won traditionally Democratic seats. These southern Republicans voted in the more conservative manner of national Republicans. As a result, the conservative coalition of Republicans and southern Democrats began to decline, with the decline halted only momentarily by the Reagan landslide of 1980 and consequent southern Democratic support for his economic proposals in 1981. The rise in the number of national southern Democrats necessarily meant that a skillful party leadership could develop a more cohesive and unified party under supportive conditions.

The second factor in the rise of a centralized leadership was the passage of reforms designed to strengthen the party leaders. In the 1970s most reforms emphasized the democratization of the House and the move from committee to subcommittee government. Yet one group of congressional reformers of the late 1960s and early 1970s clearly viewed democratization as secondary to building cohesive party organizations headed by strong party leadership.

Representative Richard Bolling, D-Mo., was the major long-term player in this group, although there were a number of other important participants. Their strategy was to create as many vehicles as possible for a more centralized party operation of the House and a strong party leadership. The hope was that although some of the mechanisms might never work properly, others might be effective. Included in this array were committee reorganization, movement of committee assignment powers to the Steering and Policy Committee, the budget process, multiple referral powers for the Speaker, the Speaker's power to nominate Rules Committee Democratic members, the development of complex rules, the use of ad hoc committees, the work of the Obey Commission, and the strengthening of the policy role of the Steering and Policy Committee.

Some of these efforts proved unsuccessful, and others, such as the budget process, required modification. The full impact or potential of these centralizing reforms awaited the right circumstances. Having been adopted during the speakership of Carl Albert, D-Okla., and then institutionalized by Thomas P. "Tip" O'Neill, D-Mass., they came to be most fully exercised by Jim Wright, D-Texas.

The third factor in the rise of the centralizing forces in the 1980s (and in the missed prognosis of the 1970s) is the sensitivity of the reformed House to the influence of environmental context. It is normally assumed that political institutions such as Congress change very slowly and with great difficulty. They are seen as stable or stagnant, held in place by their own inertia and by complex rules that reinforce inertia. Certainly that was the image of Congress that scholars held during the era of committee government, when the seniority system seemed to make congressional change impossible.

In creating a bifurcated governing system—with power spread between subcommittees and congressional leaders—the new order created two contending centers of power. Ideally, these contending centers would be integrated in a unified governing arrangement. But in reality they exist in considerable tension, each seeking to dominate the other and each with some considerable formal authority to use in the struggle. In the immediate aftermath of the reforms of the 1970s, it looked as if the subcommittees would become the locus of power, but by the late 1980s the party leaders and committee oligarchs had emerged as prevailing powers. Given the strong, cohesive parties and the rules reforms of the 1970s, the tilt from subcommittee government to oligarchy, and perhaps back again at some point, is tied to the fact that the dominance of each depends on very different environmental conditions. The subcommittees, as we argue in chapter 2, require extensive spending power and the opportunity for innovative program development to be viable decision-making actors. Centralized leadership flourishes during periods of divided government and under conditions of fiscal austerity that require coordinated budget making.

Power in today's House, therefore, can be seen as resting on a delicate balance of contending forces. No single locus of power dominates, as in the era of committee government, and no single rule determines power, as with the norm of congressional and committee seniority. Power is divided between committees and centralized leadership in such a way that relatively short-term forces—the move from united to divided government or the variation in available revenues and spending authority—can have a sizable impact on the distribution of internal congressional power and thus on its decision-making processes. Rather than being impervious to change, the modern House may be a very permeable institution acutely responsive to the forces of change. In fact, short-term environmental changes may tip the delicate internal balance in ways that magnify and exaggerate their significance far beyond the degree of change actually occurring in the external world. The result is a fluid House of Representatives capable of extensive reversals in its governing processes and in the distribution of internal power.

## Whither the Senate?

The picture presented here is of a modern House far more susceptible to dramatic institutional swings and to periods of central party government than seemed possible in the 1970s. How well does this description apply to the Senate? We suggest three points for consideration.

First, the possibility of stronger centralized power in the House rests on increasing cohesion in the House parties. The Senate is subject to some of the same forces—the nationalization of the southern party, in particular. But the Senate differs from the House in the sense that, whatever the nature of electoral politics, senators tend toward greater autonomy and individualism. Their six-year terms make them somewhat less open to electoral pressure and give them more leeway for pursuing individual policy positions. Their greater national visibility and potential for a presidential or vice-presidential nomination give them an incentive to develop distinctive identities. And because the Senate is a small chamber of only 100 members, the institution can better tolerate the personal idiosyncrasies of its members; it can function in a collegial and orderly manner without strong leaders, a situation less likely in the House. These factors militate against strong party control of the Senate; even when senators vote with the party on a regular basis, their votes reflect personal circumstance rather than the power of the party.

Second, formal rules play very different roles in the House and Senate. The power of party leaders in the House ultimately depends on their formal authority, although personality and skill also matter. But in the Senate interpersonal relations and skill are the primary tools of the leaders. There is no mechanism analogous to the House Rules Committee that Senate leaders can use to dictate the character of Senate debates. Unanimous consent agreements providing for Senate floor consideration of bills often are reached only through extensive bargaining. Nor is there an elaborate whip system for contacting and cajoling members on crucial Senate votes. The reforms of the 1970s did not greatly affect the power of Senate leaders in any direct manner, although developments such as the modification of the filibuster were designed in part to ease the majority leader's task in passing major legislation. Party government in the Senate, therefore, is not as formalized as in the House, and it depends, much more than in the House, on the emergence of skilled legislative leaders, such as Lyndon Johnson in the 1950s. It is possible that the change of Democratic leadership at the start of the 101st Congress may have such an effect.

The third point is that the oscillations of the House, in response to shifting environmental conditions, are less likely to be evident in the Senate in the same extreme form. Clearly, fiscal austerity and divided government together may inhibit subcommittee activism in the Senate, just as they do in the House. But the resulting vacuum does not necessarily serve party leaders and central committees, at least not as decisively as in the House. The members of the Senate, as individuals, retain far more personal visibility and influence, even in periods of congressional inactivism, than do House members. They are not as tied to subcommittees or to party for personal career success and power as House members. Therefore, the vacuum left by inactive subcommittees may be filled by aggressive career entrepreneurship on the part of senators, rather than a turn to central leaders. For centralized leadership to develop probably would require a very skilled, persuasive senator to capture the majority leadership in a period in which widespread consensus existed on the desirability of a more cohesive majority party in the Senate.

The modern Senate, therefore, does not match the House in its current sensitivity to contextual change. Yet neither is it impervious to change. The very existence of swings between decentralization and centralization in the House may have an impact on the Senate, with the strengthening of the Speaker, in particular, producing pressure for a more effective and skilled Senate spokesman who can represent its majority. This development may well have been why Majority Leader Robert Byrd, D-W.Va., chose to step aside at the end of the 100th Congress, setting the stage for the selection of a new Democratic leader. Moreover, precisely because rules are less controlling in the Senate than in the House, the Senate can effect change through a diverse range of strategies that may be less viable in the House at any particular point in time.

## Conclusion

The four editions of *Congress Reconsidered,* stretched across twelve years, document the rich complexity and changing character of the contemporary Congress. They portray a Congress that has experienced a type of change quite distinct from that documented in the literature on the Congress of earlier decades. Congress today looks in many ways like a different institution from that of the earlier twentieth century, different not only in its structure but in its susceptibility to extensive short-term change.

The reforms of the early 1970s seem to have altered Congress, particularly the House, in some very fundamental ways. The combination of subcommittee government and strong central leaders created the potential for extensive fluidity and oscillation in the power arrangements of the House. Far more so than in the past, power now can swing back and forth between subcommittee decentralization and centralized leadership. Such swings can occur in response to external factors such as united or divided government and fiscal austerity, as well as in response to the skillfulness of internal leaders and the career aspirations of House members. Whereas in the past we thought of power as located in one place—in committee chairs during most of this century, or in the Speakers in the late nineteenth century—we seem now to be in a period of bifurcated government in which the formal rules establish two potential power centers, with external influences largely determining which power center, if either, dominates at any one point. Such swings probably are most evident in the House, with the Senate better insulated from outside forces but following the House pattern to some extent.

Yet to be determined are the consequences that such fluidity will have for the long-term power of Congress. Scholars have long believed that the decline of congressional power during the twentieth century resulted in significant degree from its insulation from external forces and from its domination by archaic and unchangeable institutional arrangements. These criticisms seem less applicable to the new and more fluid Congress. Today's institution, in its oscillation between decentralization and centralization, may respond so strongly to external forces as to magnify and distort their importance. Does this response mean a resurgence in congressional power, as its organizational arrangements become more attuned to external developments? Or does it mean a destabilized Congress so dominated by the impact of outside forces that it is unable to develop and sustain an orderly and predictable decision-making process? These are among the most pressing questions facing Congress as it moves into its third century.

# CONTRIBUTORS

**John R. Alford** is associate professor of political science at Rice University. He received his Ph.D. from the University of Iowa in 1981 and is the author of numerous articles on congressional elections.

**David W. Brady** is the Bowen H. and Janice Arthur McCoy Professor of Political Science, Business, and Environment in the Graduate School of Business and professor of political science, School of Humanities and Sciences, Stanford University. He received his Ph.D. from the University of Iowa in 1970. His publications include *Congressional Voting in a Partisan Era: A Study of the McKinley Houses* (1973), *Public Policy and Politics in America,* 2d ed. (1984), *Public Policy in the Eighties* (1983), and numerous articles in professional journals. His most recent book is *Congressional Elections and Congressional Policy Making* (1988).

**David T. Canon** is assistant professor of political science at Duke University. He received his Ph.D. from the University of Minnesota in 1987 and was a Brookings Fellow (1985-1986). He has written on political amateurism, partisan realignments and political careers, congressional elections, and political leadership in Congress.

**Melissa P. Collie** is an assistant professor at the University of Texas at Austin. She received her Ph.D. from Rice University in 1984. Her articles in professional journals have focused on congressional elections, legislative voting coalitions, and distributive policy making.

**Joseph Cooper** is John M. Olin Visiting Professor of Political Science at the Stanford Graduate School of Business and Herbert S. Autrey

Professor of Social Sciences at Rice University. He has served as staff director of the U.S. House Commission on Administrative Review and as the program chair for the 1985 American Political Science Association meeting. He is the author of a monograph on the development of the committee system and of numerous articles on congressional structures, processes, and politics.

**Roger H. Davidson** is professor of government and politics at the University of Maryland. He has been a White House consultant, worked for House and Senate committees, and served as senior specialist at the Congressional Research Service of the U.S. Library of Congress. He is the author of more than one hundred articles and books about national policy making, including *The Role of the Congressman* (1969), and coauthor of *Congress Against Itself* (1977), *Congress and Its Members,* 3d ed. (1989), and *A More Perfect Union,* 4th ed. (1989).

**Lawrence C. Dodd** is professor of political science and director of the Center for the Study of American Politics at the University of Colorado, Boulder. He is the author of *Coalitions in Parliamentary Government* (1976), the coauthor of *Congress and the Administrative State* (1979), and coeditor of *Congress and Policy Change* (1986). He has served as president of the Southwestern Political Science Association (1979-1980), as a Congressional Fellow (1974-1975), and as a Hoover National Fellow (1984-1985).

**Robert S. Erikson** is professor of political science at the University of Houston. He received his Ph.D. from the University of Illinois. He is the coauthor of *American Public Opinion: Its Origins, Content, and Impact,* 3d ed. (1988), and the author of numerous articles on congressional elections.

**John A. Ferejohn** is William Bennett Munro Professor of Political Science and senior fellow at the Hoover Institution at Stanford University, where he also received his Ph.D. His research interests include Congress and public policy, congressional elections, and theories of legislative behavior. He is the author of *Pork Barrel Politics* (1974) and the coauthor of *The Personal Vote* (1987), a study of legislators and constituencies in the United States and Great Britain.

**Richard L. Hall** is assistant professor of political science at the University of Michigan, where he also teaches in the Institute of

Public Policy Studies. He received his Ph.D. from the University of North Carolina at Chapel Hill in 1986 and served as a Congressional Fellow (1987-1988). He is currently completing a book on decision making and congressional committees.

**Susan Webb Hammond**, professor of political science and director of the University Honors Program at American University, received her Ph.D. from Johns Hopkins University. She has written on congressional organizations and reform and is coauthor of *Congressional Staff: The Invisible Force in American Lawmaking* (1977). She is currently working on a study of informal caucuses in the U.S. Congress.

**Gary C. Jacobson** is professor of political science at the University of California, San Diego. He received his Ph.D. from Yale University in 1972. He is the author of *Money in Congressional Elections* (1980) and *The Politics of Congressional Elections*, 2d ed. (1987) and the coauthor of *Strategy and Choice in Congressional Elections*, 2d ed. (1983).

**Michael J. Malbin** is associate director of the House Republican Conference. He served on the minority staff of the House Select Committee to Investigate Covert Arms Transactions with Iran, held a grant at the University of Maryland to study legislative-executive relations, and was a resident fellow at the American Enterprise Institute. He received his Ph.D. from Cornell University. He is the author of *Unelected Representatives* (1980), editor and coauthor of *Money and Politics in the United States* (1984), and coauthor of *Vital Statistics on Congress, 1987-1988* (1987).

**Bruce I. Oppenheimer** is professor of political science at the University of Houston. He received his Ph.D. from the University of Wisconsin and was a Brookings Fellow (1970-1971) and a Congressional Fellow (1974-1975). His publications include *Oil and the Congressional Process* (1974) and articles on energy policy, House and Senate rules, and congressional elections. He is the primary author of *A History of the Committee on Rules* (1983).

**Norman J. Ornstein** is resident scholar at the American Enterprise Institute for Public Policy Research and codirector of the *Times Mirror*/Gallup study of the American electorate. His books include *Groups, Lobbying and Policymaking* (1978), *The New Congress* (1981), and *Vital Statistics on Congress, 1987-1988* (1987).

**Glenn R. Parker** is professor of political science and a member of the Policy Sciences Program at Florida State University. He received his Ph.D. from the University of California, Santa Barbara, and has served as a Congressional Fellow (1972-1973). He is the author of *Characteristics of Congress* (1989) and *Homeward Bound: Explaining Changes in Congressional Behavior* (1986), coauthor of *Factions in House Committees* (1985), and editor of *Studies of Congress* (1985).

**Robert L. Peabody** is professor of political science at Johns Hopkins University. He served as associate director of the American Political Science Association's Study of Congress project and as staff assistant to former House Speaker Carl Albert. He is the author of numerous books on Congress, including *Leadership in Congress* (1976). He is coauthor of *To Enact a Law: Congress and Campaign Finance* (1972) and *Congress: Two Decades of Analysis* (1969), editor of *Education of a Congressman* (1972), and coeditor of *New Perspectives on the House of Representatives,* 3d ed. (1977).

**David E. Price** was elected in 1988 to his second term in the U.S. House of Representatives from North Carolina's Fourth District. Formerly a professor of political science and public policy at Duke University, he is the author of *Who Makes the Laws?* (1972), *The Commerce Committees* (1975), *Policy-Making in Congressional Committees* (1979), and *Bringing Back the Parties* (1984). He has chaired North Carolina's Democratic party and served as staff director of the Democratic National Committee's Commission on Presidential Nomination (Hunt Commission).

**David W. Rohde** is professor of political science at Michigan State University. He is a former Congressional Fellow. He received his Ph.D. at the University of Rochester and is the author of numerous articles on congressional reform and congressional elections. He is a coauthor of *Change and Continuity in the 1984 Elections,* rev. ed. (1987). He is currently editor of the *American Journal of Political Science.*

**Catherine E. Rudder**, executive director of the American Political Science Association, received her Ph.D. at Ohio State University. She has worked for two members of the House Committee on Ways and Means and has written about tax policy since serving as a Congressional Fellow (1974-1975).

**Charles R. Shipan** is a Ph.D. candidate in political science at Stanford University. His research interests include the politics of regulation and the relationship between Congress and the bureaucracy.

**Barbara Sinclair** is professor of political science at the University of California, Riverside. She received her Ph.D. from the University of Rochester and has served as a Congressional Fellow (1978-1979). Her writings on Congress include *Congressional Realignment* (1982) and *Majority Leadership in the U.S. House* (1983). She spent 1987-1988 in the Office of the Speaker researching party leadership.

**Steven S. Smith** is associate professor of political science at the University of Minnesota and staff associate at the Brookings Institution. He served as a Congressional Fellow (1980-1981). He is the author of *Call to Order: Floor Politics in the House and Senate* (forthcoming), from which his essay is drawn, and numerous articles on congressional politics. He is coauthor of *Committees in Congress* (1984) and *Managing Uncertainty in the House of Representatives* (1988).

**Gerald C. Wright** is professor of political science at Indiana University and was formerly the political science program director at the National Science Foundation. He received his Ph.D. at the University of North Carolina at Chapel Hill. His publications include *Electoral Choice in America* (1974) and numerous articles in professional journals. He coedited *Congress and Policy Change* (1986).

# SUGGESTED READINGS

Aberbach, Joel D. "Changes in Congressional Oversight." *American Behavioral Scientist* 22 (1979): 493-515.

Abramowitz, Alan I. "A Comparison of Voting for U.S. Senators and Representatives in 1978." *American Political Science Review* 74 (1980): 637-640.

_____ . "Explaining Senate Election Outcomes." *American Political Science Review* 82 (1988): 385-404.

Abramson, Paul, John H. Aldrich, and David W. Rohde. "Progressive Ambition among United States Senators: 1972-1988." *Journal of Politics* 49 (1987): 3-35.

Arnold, R. Douglas. *Congress and the Bureaucracy.* New Haven, Conn.: Yale University Press, 1979.

Asher, Herbert B. "The Learning of Legislative Norms." *American Political Science Review* 67 (1973): 499-513.

Asher, Herbert B., and Herbert F. Weisberg. "Voting Change in Congress: Some Dynamic Perspectives on an Evolutionary Process." *American Journal of Political Science* 22 (1978): 391-425.

Bach, Stanley, and Steven S. Smith. *Managing Uncertainty in the House: Adaptation and Innovation in Special Rules.* Washington, D.C.: Brookings Institution, 1988.

Bacheller, J. M. "Lobbyists and the Legislative Process: The Impact of Environmental Constraints." *American Political Science Review* 71 (1977): 252-263.

Bauer, Raymond A., Ithiel de Sola Pool, and Lewis A. Dexter. *American Business and Public Policy.* New York: Atherton, 1963.

Bibby, John F., and Roger H. Davidson. *On Capitol Hill.* 2d ed. Hinsdale, Ill.: Dryden, 1972.

Bolling, Richard. *House Out of Order.* New York: E. P. Dutton, 1965.

_____ . *Power in the House.* New York: E. P. Dutton, 1965.

Bond, Jon R., Cary Covington, and Richard Fleisher. "Explaining Challenger Quality in Congressional Elections." *Journal of Politics* 47 (1985): 510-529.

Born, Richard. "Changes in the Competitiveness of House Primary Elections, 1956-1976." *American Politics Quarterly* 8 (1980): 495-506.

Brady, David W. *Congressional Voting in a Partisan Era: A Study of the McKinley Houses.* Lawrence: University of Kansas Press, 1973.

Brady, David W., Joseph Cooper, and Patricia A. Hurley. "The Decline of Party in the U.S. House of Representatives, 1887-1968." *Legislative Studies Quarterly* 4 (1979): 381-407.

Bullock, Charles S., III. "House Careerists: Changing Patterns of Longevity and Attrition." *American Political Science Review* 66 (1972): 1295-1305.

____ . "Redistricting and Congressional Stability, 1962-1972." *Journal of Politics* 37 (1975): 569-575.

____ . "House Committee Assignments." In *The Congressional System: Notes and Readings.* 2d ed. Edited by Leroy N. Rieselbach. North Scituate, Mass.: Duxbury Press, 1979.

Cain, Bruce, John Ferejohn, and Morris Fiorina. *The Personal Vote: Constituency Service and Electoral Independence.* Cambridge, Mass.: Harvard University Press, 1967.

Clausen, Aage R. *How Congressmen Decide.* New York: St. Martin's Press, 1973.

Clem, Alan L., ed. *The Making of Congressmen: Seven Campaigns of 1974.* North Scituate, Mass.: Duxbury Press, 1976.

Collie, Melissa. "Incumbency, Electoral Safety and Turnover in the House of Representatives, 1952-1976." *American Political Science Review* 75 (1981).

Cooper, Joseph. *The Origins of the Standing Committees and the Development of the Modern House.* Houston, Texas: Rice University Studies, 1971.

____ . "Strengthening the Congress: An Organizational Analysis." *Harvard Journal on Legislation* 2 (1975): 301-368.

Cooper, Joseph, and David W. Brady. "Institutional Context and Leadership Style: The House from Cannon to Rayburn." *American Political Science Review* 75 (1981).

____ . "Toward a Diachronic Analysis of Congress." *American Political Science Review* 75 (1981).

Cooper, Joseph, and G. Calvin Mackenzie. *The House at Work.* Austin: University of Texas Press, 1981.

Cover, Albert D. "One Good Term Deserves Another: The Advantage of Incumbency in Congressional Elections." *American Journal of Political Science* 21 (1977): 523-541.

____ . "Contacting Congressional Constituents: Some Patterns of Perquisite Use." *American Journal of Political Science* 24 (1980): 125-134.

Cover, Albert D., and David R. Mayhew. "Congressional Dynamics and the Decline of Competitive Congressional Elections." In *Congress Reconsidered.* 2d ed. Edited by Lawrence C. Dodd and Bruce I. Oppenheimer. Washington, D.C.: CQ Press, 1981.

Davidson, Roger H., David M. Kovenock, and Michael K. O'Leary. *Congress in Crisis: Politics and Congressional Reform.* Belmont, Calif.: Wadsworth, 1966.

Davidson, Roger H., and Walter J. Oleszek. *Congress Against Itself.*

Bloomington: Indiana University Press, 1977.

_____ . *Congress and Its Members*. 2d ed. Washington D.C.: CQ Press, 1985.

Davidson, Roger H., Walter J. Oleszek, and Thomas Kephart. "One Bill, Many Referrals: Multiple Referrals in the U.S. House of Representatives." *Legislative Studies Quarterly* 13 (1988): 3-28.

Deering, Chistopher J. *Congressional Politics*. Chicago: Dorsey Press, 1989.

Dexter, Lewis A. *How Organizations Are Represented in Washington*. Indianapolis: Bobbs-Merrill, 1969.

_____ . *The Sociology and Politics of Congress*. Chicago: Rand McNally, 1969.

Dodd, Lawrence C. "Congress and the Quest for Power." In *Congress Reconsidered*. 1st ed. Edited by Lawrence C. Dodd and Bruce I. Oppenheimer. New York: Praeger, 1977.

_____ . "The Expanded Roles of the House Democratic Whip System." *Congressional Studies* 6 (1979).

Dodd, Lawrence C., and Richard L. Schott. *Congress and the Administrative State*. New York: John Wiley & Sons, 1979.

Eckhardt, Bob, and Charles L. Black, Jr. *The Titles of Power: Conversations on the American Constitution*. New Haven, Conn.: Yale University Press, 1976.

Edwards, George C., III. *Presidential Influence in Congress*. San Francisco: W. H. Freeman, 1980.

Erikson, Robert S. "The Advantage of Incumbency in Congressional Elections." *Polity* 3 (1971).

_____ . "Is There Such a Thing as a Safe Seat?" *Polity* 8 (1976): 623-632.

_____ . "The Puzzle of Midterm Loss." *Journal of Politics* 50 (1988): 1011-1029.

Eulau, Heinz, and Paul Karps. "The Puzzle of Representation." *Legislative Studies Quarterly* 2 (1977): 233-254.

Fenno, Richard F., Jr. *The Power of the Purse*. Boston: Little, Brown, 1966.

_____ . *Congressmen in Committees*. Boston: Little, Brown, 1973.

_____ . "If, as Ralph Nader Says, Congress Is 'the Broken Branch,' How Come We Love Our Congressmen So Much?" In *Congress in Change*. Edited by Norman J. Ornstein. New York: Praeger, 1975.

_____ . *Home Style*. Boston: Little, Brown, 1978.

_____ . *The United States Senate: A Bicameral Perspective*. Washington, D.C.: American Enterprise Institute, 1982.

Ferejohn, John A. *Pork Barrel Politics*. Stanford, Calif.: Stanford University Press, 1974.

Fiorina, Morris P. *Representatives, Roll Calls and Constituencies*. Lexington, Mass.: Lexington Books, 1974.

_____ . *Congress: Keystone of the Washington Establishment*. New Haven, Conn.: Yale University Press, 1977.

Fiorina, Morris P., David W. Rohde, and Peter Wissel. "Historical Change in House Turnover." In *Congress in Change*. Edited by Norman J. Ornstein. New York: Praeger, 1975.

Fishel, Jeff. *Party and Opposition*. New York: David McKay, 1973.

Fisher, Louis. *President and Congress: Power and Policy*. New York: Free Press, 1972.

_____ . *The Constitution Between Friends: Congress, the President and the Law.* New York: St. Martin's Press, 1978.

Fowler, Linda. "Candidates' Perceptions of Electoral Coalitions." *American Politics Quarterly* 8 (1980): 483-494.

Fox, Harrison W., Jr., and Susan Webb Hammond. *Congressional Staffs: The Invisible Force in American Lawmaking.* New York: Free Press, 1977.

Frantzich, Stephen E. "Computerized Information Technology in the U.S. House of Representatives." *Legislative Studies Quarterly* 4 (1979): 255-280.

Freeman, J. Leiper. *The Political Process.* New York: Random House, 1955.

Froman, Lewis A., Jr. *The Congressional Process: Strategies, Rules and Procedures.* Boston: Little, Brown, 1967.

Glazer, Amihai, and Bernard Grofman. "Two Plus Two Plus Two Equals Six: Tenure of Office of Senators and Representatives, 1953-1983." *Legislative Studies Quarterly* 12 (1987): 555-563.

Goehlert, Robert U., and John R. Sayre. *The United States Congress: A Bibliography.* New York: Free Press, 1982.

Goldenberg, Edie N., and Michael W. Traugott. *Campaigning for Congress.* Washington, D.C.: CQ Press, 1984.

Goodwin, George, Jr. *The Little Legislatures.* Amherst: University of Massachusetts Press, 1970.

Hall, Richard L. "Participation and Purpose in Committee Decision Making." *American Political Science Review* 81 (1987): 105-127.

Harris, Joseph. *Congressional Control of Administration.* Washington, D.C.: Brookings Institution, 1964.

Hayes, Michael I. "Interest Groups and Congress: Toward a Transactional Theory." In *The Congressional System: Notes and Readings.* 2d ed. Edited by Leroy N. Rieselbach. North Scituate, Mass.: Duxbury Press, 1979.

Henry, Charles P. "Legitimizing Race in Congressional Politics." *American Politics Quarterly* 5 (1977): 149-176.

Herrnson, Paul S. *Party Campaigning in the 1980s.* Cambridge, Mass.: Harvard University Press, 1988.

Hershey, Marjorie R. *The Making of Campaign Strategy.* Lexington, Mass.: Lexington Books, 1974.

Hibbing, John R. "Ambition in the House: Behavioral Consequences of Higher Office Goals among U.S. Representatives." *American Journal of Political Science* 30 (1986): 651-665.

Hibbing, John R., and John R. Alford. "Economic Conditions and the Forgotten Side of Congress: A Foray into U.S. Senate Elections." *British Journal of Political Science* 12 (1982): 505-513.

Hinckley, Barbara. *Stability and Change in Congress.* New York: Harper & Row, 1971.

_____ . *The Seniority System in Congress.* Bloomington: Indiana University Press, 1971.

_____ . "The American Voter in Congressional Elections." *American Political Science Review* 74 (1980): 641-650.

Hoadly, John F. "The Emergence of Political Parties in Congress, 1789-1803." *American Political Science Review* 74 (1980): 757-779.

Holtzman, Abraham. *Legislative Liaison.* Chicago: Rand McNally, 1970.

Huitt, Ralph K., and Robert L. Peabody. *Congress: Two Decades of Analysis.* New York: Harper & Row, 1969.

Huntington, Samuel P. "Congressional Responses to the Twentieth Century." In *The Congress and America's Future.* 2d ed. Edited by David B. Truman. Englewood Cliffs, N.J.: Prentice-Hall, 1973.

Hurley, Patricia, and Kim Quarle Hill. "The Prospects for Issue-Voting in Contemporary Congressional Elections." *American Politics Quarterly* 8 (1980): 425-448.

Jackson, John. *Constituencies and Leaders in Congress.* Cambridge, Mass: Harvard University Press, 1974.

Jacobson, Gary C. *Money in Congressional Elections.* New Haven, Conn.: Yale University Press, 1980.

____ . "The Marginals Never Vanished: Incumbency and Competition in Elections to the U.S. House of Representatives, 1952-81." *American Journal of Political Science* 31 (1987): 126-141.

____ . *The Politics of Congressional Elections.* 2d ed. Boston: Little Brown, 1987.

Jacobson, Gary C., and Samuel Kernell. *Strategy and Choice in Congressional Elections.* New Haven, Conn.: Yale University Press, 1983.

Jewell, Malcolm E. *Senatorial Politics and Foreign Policy.* Lexington: University of Kentucky Press, 1962.

Jewell, Malcolm E., and Samuel C. Patterson. *The Legislative Process in the United States.* 3d ed. New York: Random House, 1977.

Johannes, John R. *Policy Innovation in Congress.* Morristown, N.J.: General Learning Press, 1972.

Jones, Charles O. "Representation in Congress: The Case of the House Agricultural Committee." *American Political Science Review* 55 (1961): 358-367.

____ . "The Role of the Congressional Subcommittee." *Midwest Journal of Political Science* 6 (1962): 327-344.

____ . *The Minority Party in Congress.* Boston: Little, Brown, 1970.

____ . "Will Reform Change Congress?" In *Congress Reconsidered.* 1st ed. Edited by Lawrence C. Dodd and Bruce I. Oppenheimer. New York: Praeger, 1977.

Kazee, Thomas. "The Decision to Run for the U.S. Congress: Challenger Attitudes in the 1970s." *Legislative Studies Quarterly* 5 (1980): 79-100.

Keefe, William J. *Congress and the American People.* Englewood Cliffs, N.J.: Prentice-Hall, 1980.

Keefe, William J., and Morris S. Ogul. *The American Legislative Process.* 4th ed. Englewood Cliffs, N.J.: Prentice-Hall, 1977.

Kingdon, John W. *Candidates for Office.* New York: Random House, 1968.

____ . *Congressmen's Voting Decisions.* New York: Harper & Row, 1973.

Krehbiel, Keith, Kenneth A. Shepsle, and Barry R. Weingast. "Why Are Congressional Committees Powerful?" *American Political Science Review* 81 (1987): 929-948.

Kuklinski, James H. "District Competitiveness and Legislative Roll Call Behavior: A Reassessment of the Marginality Hypothesis." *American Journal of Political Science* 21 (1977): 627-638.

LeLoup, Lance T. *Budgetary Politics*. Brunswick, Ohio: Kings Court Press, 1977.

LeLoup, Lance T., and Steven Shull. "Congress Versus the Executive: The 'Two Presidencies' Reconsidered." *Social Science Quarterly* 59 (1979): 704-719.

Loewenberg, Gerhard, and Samuel Patterson. *Comparing Legislatures*. Boston: Little, Brown, 1979.

Lowi, Theodore J. *The End of Liberalism*. New York: W. W. Norton & Co., 1969, 1979.

Maass, Arthur. *Congress and the Common Good*. New York: Basic Books, 1983.

Maisel, Louis S. *From Obscurity to Oblivion: Running in the Congressional Primary*. Knoxville: University of Tennessee Press, 1982.

Manley, John F. *The Politics of Finance*. Boston: Little, Brown, 1970.

Mann, Thomas E. *Unsafe at Any Margin: Interpreting Congressional Elections*. Washington, D.C.: American Enterprise Institute, 1978.

Mann, Thomas E., and Norman J. Ornstein. *The New Congress*. Washington, D.C.: American Enterprise Institute, 1981.

Mann, Thomas E., and Raymond E. Wolfinger. "Candidates and Parties in Congressional Elections." *American Political Science Review* 74 (1980): 617-632.

Matthews, Donald R. *U.S. Senators and Their World*. New York: Vintage Books, 1960.

Mayhew, David R. *Party Loyalty Among Congressmen*. Cambridge, Mass.: Harvard University Press, 1966.

_____ . *Congress: The Electoral Connection*. New Haven, Conn.: Yale University Press, 1974.

McAdams, John C., and John R. Johannes. "Congressmen, Perquisites, and Elections." *Journal of Politics* 50 (1988): 412-439.

Moe, Terry M. "An Assessment of the Positive Theory of Congressional Dominance." *Legislative Studies Quarterly* 12 (1987): 475-520.

Nelson, Garrison. "Partisan Patterns of House Leadership Change, 1789-1977." *American Political Science Review* 71 (1977): 918-939.

Norpoth, Helmut. "Explaining Party Cohesion in Congress: The Case of Shared Party Attributes." *American Political Science Review* 70 (1976): 1157-1171.

Ogul, Morris S. *Congress Oversees the Bureaucracy*. Pittsburgh: University of Pittsburgh Press, 1976.

Oleszek, Walter J. *Congressional Procedures and the Policy Process*. 3d ed. Washington, D.C.: CQ Press, 1988.

Oppenheimer, Bruce I. *Oil and the Congressional Process: The Limits of Symbolic Politics*. Lexington, Mass.: Lexington Books, 1974.

_____ . "The Rules Committee: New Arm of Leadership in a Decentralized House." In *Congress Reconsidered*. 1st ed. Edited by Lawrence C. Dodd and Bruce I. Oppenheimer. New York: Praeger, 1977.

——— . "Policy Effects of U.S. House Reform: Decentralization and the Capacity to Resolve Energy Issues." *Legislative Studies Quarterly* 5 (1980): 5-30.

——— . "Changing Time Constraints on Congress: Historical Perspectives on the Use of Cloture." In *Congress Reconsidered*. 3d ed. Edited by Lawrence C. Dodd and Bruce I. Oppenheimer. Washington, D.C.: CQ Press, 1985.

Orfield, Gary. *Congressional Power: Congress and Social Change*. New York: Harcourt Brace Jovanovich, 1975.

Ornstein, Norman J. *Congress in Change: Evolution and Reform*. New York: Praeger, 1975.

Ornstein, Norman J., and Shirley Elder. *Interest Groups, Lobbying and Policymaking*. Washington, D.C.: CQ Press, 1978.

Ornstein, Norman J., Thomas E. Mann, and Michael J. Malbin. *Vital Statistics on Congress, 1987-1988*. Washington, D.C.: Congressional Quarterly, 1987.

Ornstein, Norman J., and David W. Rohde. "Shifting Forces, Changing Rules, and Political Outcomes: The Impact of Congressional Change on Four House Committees." In *New Perspectives on the House of Representatives*. Edited by Robert L. Peabody and Nelson W. Polsby. Chicago: Rand McNally, 1977.

Parker, Glenn R. "Some Themes in Congressional Unpopularity." *American Journal of Political Science* 21 (1977): 93-110.

——— . "The Advantage of Incumbency in House Elections." *American Politics Quarterly* 8 (1980): 449-464.

——— . *Studies of Congress*. Washington, D.C.: CQ Press, 1984.

——— . *Homeward Bound: Explaining Changes in Congressional Behavior*. Pittsburgh: University of Pittsburgh Press, 1986.

Parker, Glenn R., and S. L. Parker. "Factions in Committees: The U.S. House of Representatives." *American Political Science Review* 73 (1979): 85-102.

Payne, James L. "The Personal Electoral Advantage of House Incumbents, 1936-1976." *American Politics Quarterly* 8 (1980): 465-482.

Peabody, Robert L. *Leadership in Congress: Stability, Succession and Change*. Boston: Little, Brown, 1976.

Peabody, Robert L., and Nelson W. Polsby, eds. *New Perspectives on the House of Representatives*. 3d ed. Chicago: Rand McNally, 1977.

Peters, John G., and Susan Welch. "The Effects of Charges of Corruption on Voting Behavior in Congressional Elections." *American Political Science Review* 74 (1980): 697-708.

Pierce, John C., and John L. Sullivan. *The Electorate Reconsidered*. Beverly Hills, Calif.: Sage Publications, 1980.

Polsby, Nelson W. "Institutionalization in the U.S. House of Representatives." *American Political Science Review* 62 (1968): 144-168.

——— . *Congress and the Presidency*. 3d ed. Englewood Cliffs, N.J.: Prentice-Hall, 1976.

Polsby, Nelson W., Miriam Gallagher, and Barry Rundquist. "The Growth of the Seniority System in the House of Representatives." *American Political Science Review* 63 (1969): 787-807.

Powell, Lynda W. "Issue Representation in Congress." *Journal of Politics* (1982).

Price, David E. *Who Makes the Laws?* Cambridge, Mass.: Schenkman, 1972.

Price, H. Douglas. "Congress and the Evolution of Legislative Professionalism." In *Congress in Change*. Edited by Norman J. Ornstein. New York: Praeger, 1975.

Ragsdale, Lyn. "The Fiction of Congressional Elections as Presidential Events." *American Politics Quarterly* 8 (1980): 395-398.

Ragsdale, Lyn, and Timothy E. Cook. "Representatives' Actions and Challengers' Reactions: Limits to Candidate Connections in the House." *American Journal of Political Science* 31 (1987): 45-81.

Reid, T. R. *Congressional Odyssey: The Saga of a Senate Bill.* San Francisco: W. H. Freeman, 1980.

Rieselbach, Leroy N. *The Roots of Isolationism.* Indianapolis: Bobbs-Merrill, 1966.

——— . *Congressional Politics.* New York: McGraw-Hill, 1973.

——— . *Congressional Reform in the Seventies.* Morristown, N.J.: General Learning Press, 1977.

——— . ed. *Legislative Reform: The Policy Impact.* Lexington, Mass.: Lexington Books, 1978.

Ripley, Randall B. *Party Leaders in the House of Representatives.* Washington, D.C.: Brookings Institution, 1967.

——— . *Majority Party Leadership in Congress.* Boston: Little, Brown, 1969.

——— . *Power in the Senate.* New York: St. Martin's Press, 1969.

Ripley, Randell B., and Grace N. Franklin. *Congress, the Bureaucracy and Public Policy.* Homewood, Ill.: Dorsey Press, 1980.

Rohde, David W., and Kenneth A. Shepsle. "Democratic Committee Assignments in the U.S. House of Representatives." *American Political Science Review* 67 (1973): 889-905.

Rothman, David J. *Politics and Power.* New York: Atheneum, 1969.

Rudder, Catherine E. "Committee Reform and the Revenue Process." In *Congress Reconsidered.* 1st ed. Edited by Lawrence C. Dodd and Bruce I. Oppenheimer. New York: Praeger, 1977.

Saloma, John S., III. *Congress and the New Politics.* Boston: Little, Brown, 1969.

Schick, Allen. *Making Economic Policy in Congress.* Washington, D.C.: American Enterprise Institute, 1983.

Schneider, Jerrold E. *Ideological Coalitions in Congress.* Greenwood, Conn.: Greenwood Press, 1979.

Schwarz, John E., and L. Earl Shaw. *The United States Congress in Comparative Perspective.* Hinsdale, Ill.: Dryden Press, 1976.

Seidman, Harold. *Politics, Position, and Power.* 2d ed. London: Oxford University Press, 1975.

Shepsle, Kenneth A. *The Giant Jigsaw Puzzle.* Chicago: University of Chicago Press, 1978.

Sinclair, Barbara Deckard. "Determinants of Aggregate Party Cohesion in the U.S. House of Representatives." *Legislative Studies Quarterly* 2 (1977): 155-175.

——. *Majority Leadership in the U.S. House.* Baltimore: Johns Hopkins University Press, 1983.

Smith, Steven S., and Christopher J. Deering. *Committees in Congress.* Washington, D.C.: CQ Press, 1984.

Stone, Walter J. "The Dynamics of Constituency: Electoral Control in the House." *American Politics Quarterly* 8 (1980): 399-424.

Sundquist, James L. *Politics and Policy.* Washington, D.C.: Brookings Institution, 1968.

——. *The Decline and Resurgence of Congress.* Washington, D.C.: Brookings Institution, 1981.

Truman, David B. *The Governmental Process.* New York: Alfred A. Knopf, 1951.

Turner, Julius. *Party and Constituency: Pressures on Congress.* Rev. ed. Edited by Edward V. Schneier, Jr. Baltimore: Johns Hopkins University Press, 1970.

Unekis, Joseph, and Leroy N. Rieselbach. *Congressional Committee Politics: Continuity and Change.* New York: Praeger, 1984.

Uslaner, Eric M. "Policy Entrepreneurs and Amateur Democrats in the House of Representatives." In *Legislative Reform: The Policy Impact.* Edited by Leroy N. Rieselbach. Lexington, Mass.: Lexington Books, 1978.

Vogler, David J. *The Third House.* Evanston, Ill.: Northwestern University Press, 1971.

——. *The Politics of Congress.* Boston: Allyn & Bacon, 1974.

Wahlke, John C., Heinz H. Eulau, W. Buchanan, and L. C. Ferguson. *The Legislative System: Explorations in Legislative Behavior.* New York: John Wiley & Sons, 1962.

Wayne, S. J. *The Legislative Presidency.* New York: Harper & Row, 1978.

Weisberg, Herbert F. "Evaluating Theories of Congressional Roll Call Voting." *American Journal of Political Science* 22 (1978): 554-577.

Westefield, L. P. "Majority Party Leadership and the Committee System in the House of Representatives." *American Political Science Review* 68 (1974): 1593-1604.

Wildavsky, Aaron. *The Politics of the Budgetary Process.* Boston: Little, Brown, 1964.

Wilson, Rick. "Forward and Backward Agenda Procedures: Committee Experience and Structurally Induced Equilibrium." *Journal of Politics* 48 (1986): 390-409.

Wilson, Woodrow. *Congressional Government.* Gloucester, Mass.: Peter Smith, 1885, 1973.

Wolfinger, Raymond E., and Joan Heifetz Hollinger. "Safe Seats, Seniority, and Power in Congress." *American Political Science Review* 59 (1965): 337-349.

Wright, Gerald C., and Michael B. Berkman. "Candidates and Policy in

United States Senate Elections." *American Political Science Review* 80 (1986): 567-588.

Wright, John. "PACs, Contributions and Roll Calls: An Organizational Perspective." *American Political Science Review* 75 (1985): 400-414.

Young, James S. *The Washington Community, 1880-1828.* New York: Columbia University Press, 1966.

# INDEX